Human Factors in Aviation

Academic Press
Series in Cognition and Perception

Series Editors:
Edward C. Carterette
Morton P. Friedman
Department of Psychology
University of California, Los Angeles
Los Angeles, California

Recent titles in this series are listed at the end of
the volume.

HUMAN FACTORS IN AVIATION

Edited by

Earl L. Wiener
Department of Management Science
University of Miami
Coral Gables, Florida

David C. Nagel
Aerospace Human Factors Research Division
NASA-Ames Research Center
Moffett Field, California

With a foreword by Jerome Lederer

ACADEMIC PRESS, INC.
Harcourt Brace Jovanovich, Publishers
San Diego New York Berkeley Boston
London Sydney Tokyo Toronto

ACADEMIC PRESS, INC.
1250 Sixth Avenue
San Diego, California 92101

United Kingdom Edition published by
ACADEMIC PRESS INC. (LONDON) LTD.
24-28 Oval Road, London NW1 7DX

Library of Congress Cataloging-in-Publication Data

Human factors in aviation.

(Academic Press series in cognition and perception)
Includes index.
1. Aeronautics—Human factors.   I. Wiener, Earl L.
II. Nagel, David C.   III. Series.
TL553.6.H86   1988   629.13   87-31829
ISBN   0-12-750030-8   (alk. paper)

PRINTED IN THE UNITED STATES OF AMERICA
88 89 90 91   9 8 7 6 5 4 3 2 1

CONTENTS

ONE   Introduction

1   Introductory Overview
Elwyn Edwards

2   The System Perspective
Thomas B. Sheridan

3   System Safety
C. O. Miller

TWO   Pilot Performance

4   The Human Senses in Flight
Herschel W. Leibowitz

5   Information Processing
Christopher D. Wickens and
John M. Flach

6   Human Workload in Aviation

**Barry H. Kantowitz and
Patricia A. Casper**

7   Group Interaction and Flight Crew Performance

**H. Clayton Foushee and
Robert L. Helmreich**

8 Flight Training and Simulation
Paul W. Caro

9 Human Error in Aviation Operations
David C. Nagel

10 Aircrew Fatigue and Circadian Rhythmicity
R. Curtis Graeber

THREE   Human Factors in Aircraft Design

11   Pilot Control
Sheldon Baron

12   Aviation Displays
Alan F. Stokes and
Christopher D. Wickens

FOUR   Vehicles and Systems

CONTRIBUTORS

Numbers in parentheses indicate the pages on which the authors'
contributions begin.

Gary L. Babcock (529), Air Line
Pilots Association, 1625 Massachusetts
Avenue, N.W., Washington, D.C. 20036

Sheldon Baron (347), Bolt Beranek
and Newman, Inc., Cambridge,
Massachusetts 02283

Paul W. Caro (229), Seville Training
Systems, Inc., Irving, Texas 75038

Patricia A. Casper (157),
Department of Psychology, Purdue
University, West Lafayette, Indiana
47907

Elwyn Edwards (3), Human
Technology, Meadow House,
Alderminster, Stratford-upon-Avon
CV37 8PA, England

Robert G. Fainter (463), Department
of Computer Science, Arizona State
University, Tempe, Arizona 85287

John M. Flach (111), Department of
Psychology, University of Illinois,
Champaign, Illinois 61820

H. Clayton Foushee (189), NASA-
Ames Research Center, Moffett Field,
California 94035

R. Curtis Graeber (305), NASA-
Ames Research Center, Moffett Field,
California 94035

Sandra G. Hart (591), NASA-Ames
Research Center, Moffett Field,
California 94035

Robert L. Helmreich (189),
Department of Psychology, University
of Texas, Austin, Texas 78712

V. David Hopkin (639), RAF
Institute for Aviation Medicine,
Farnborough, Hampshire GU14 6SZ,
England

Barry H. Kantowitz (157), Battelle
Laboratories, Seattle, Washington
98105-5428

Herschel W. Leibowitz (83),
Department of Psychology,
Pennsylvania State University,
University Park, Pennsylvania 16801

C. O. Miller (53), System Safety, Inc.,
McLean, Virginia 22102

David C. Nagel (263), NASA-Ames
Research Center, Moffett Field,
California 94035

Malcolm L. Ritchie (561), Ritchie,
Inc., 630 Brubaker Drive, Dayton, Ohio
45429

George A. Sexton (495), Lockheed-
Georgia Company, Marietta, Georgia
30063

Thomas B. Sheridan (27),
Department of Mechanical
Engineering, Massachusetts Institute
of Technology, Cambridge,
Massachusetts 02139

Alan F. Stokes (387), Institute of
Aviation, University of Illinois,
Willard Airport, Savoy, Illinois 61874

Richard B. Stone (529), Air Line
Pilots Association, 1625 Massachusetts
Avenue, N.W., Washington, D.C. 20036

Christopher D. Wickens (111,
387), Department of Psychology,
University of Illinois, Champaign,
Illinois 61820

Earl L. Wiener (433), Department of
Management Science, University of
Miami, Coral Gables, Florida 33124

Beverly H. Williges (463),
Department of Industrial Engineering
and Operations Research, Virginia
Polytechnic Institute and State
University, Blacksburg, Virginia 24061

Robert C. Williges (463),
Department of Industrial Engineering
and Operations Research, Virginia
Polytechnic Institute and State
University, Blacksburg, Virginia 24061

FOREWORD

ATTENTION! Aircraft Designers, Operators, Airmen, Managers. Anxiety never disappears in a human being in an airplane—it merely remains dormant when there is no cause to arouse it. Our challenge is to keep it forever dormant.

Harold Harris, Vice President,
Pan American World Airways, circa 1950

At the beginning of jet operations in 1958, the rate of fatal accidents was one accident in only 100,000 hours of flying. Transport operations of U.S. air carriers are now approaching two million hours per fatal accident. This astounding safety accomplishment resulted largely from advances in technology, procedures, and training, plus an improved infrastructure and the exchange of intelligence on accident prevention under an umbrella of safety regulation. If public safety is measured by the chance of becoming involved in a fatal accident, airline operations are safe. But a negative public perception of airline safety habitually dominates the favorable statistics. Aircraft operations could and should be made safer. This also applies to general aviation.

The same dedication to the reduction of losses that industry has applied to technical and procedural problems has the potential, when applied to human factors, of doubling safety performance. This calls for further recognition of the comprehensive role of human factors to expand aviation safety.

Human factors research includes human engineering (fitting the machine to human limitations). The aviation industry has adapted human engineering technology to cockpit and cabin design. It is now turning its attention to other, more subtle human factors such as cockpit organization, crew interaction, fitness for duty (fatigue, health), judgment, sensory illusions, distraction, and complacency induced by reliability of equipment. It is comforting to know that timely attention to air traffic control is also included in the book, for this activity is often overlooked by aviation authors.

For many years human factors specialists encountered lethargy among engineers and designers in accepting improvements derived from human factors research. Fortunately, military organizations and other government agencies appreciated the improved efficiency and loss-prevention potential of this relatively new discipline and supplied the resources to support human factors research. The National Transportation Safety Board and the Federal Aviation Administration have enlarged their staff of human factors specialists, assuring that these factors are included in investigations to uncover root causes of accidents. The future for reducing design-induced and operationally induced crew error looks promising.

Human factors have not been entirely disregarded in the past. The Aeromedical Laboratory of the U.S. Air Force at Wright Field pioneered the classification of design-induced pilot errors such as substitution errors (confusing flap, gear, power plant controls), adjustment errors (turning fuel selectors to the wrong tank), forgetting errors (take-off with locked flight controls or incorrect trim settings), reversal errors (pushing instead of pulling a control), and inability to reach controls or to find a control. The accident literature is replete with instances of these errors, especially in the era of piston–propeller power plants.

May I be permitted a personal experience? When invited to observe the in-flight operation to touchdown of a newly developed automatic pilot, I noticed that the cuff of the pilot's jacket accidentally operated the toggle switch that disconnected the automatic pilot. I did not advise the pilot when he appeared surprised to discover the plane's unexpected departure from the programmed flight path. When I pointed out the problem later, he promised that the design staff would be notified. Surely human factor corrections to such design problems will not be overlooked as lessons are learned.

The very comprehensive texts *Human Factors in Air Transport Design* (1946) and *Human Factors in Air Transportation* (1953) by the late maestro of human factors Ross McFarland, supplemented by the contributions of Alphonse Chapanis, Julian Christensen, Paul Fitts, David Meister, and their colleagues, filled a gap in human factors until the growth of further specialization resulting from technological and research advances.* The special advantage of this volume is that it deals with the current state of the art in human factors. The authors are recognized authorities in their respective disciplines, fully capable of interlocking theory with good practice.

---

*McFarland, R. A. *Human factors in air transport design* (New York: McGraw-Hill, 1946); *Human factors in air transportation* (New York: McGraw Hill, 1953).

Former FAA Administrator Admiral Don Engen was quoted in the February 1, 1986 issue of the *Monitor*, the monthly newsletter of the American Psychological Association, as saying "We spent over fifty years on the hardware, which is now pretty reliable. Now it's time to work with the people."

Jerome Lederer
Director of Safety, NASA, Retired
Adjunct Professor, University of Southern California
Institute of Safety and System Management
President Emeritus, Flight Safety Foundation.

PREFACE

By the standards of most areas of scientific endeavor, the field of human factors is still an infant. Most of the pioneers are alive today. The field was born during World War II, out of the frustration that the machines of war were becoming so complex and demanding that they were outstripping the abilities of the military personnel to safely and effectively manage them. Most of the early work took place in aviation systems—aircrew equipment, training devices, instrument and cockpit design, and later radar. Aviation has remained the dominant area in military application of human factors, although virtually all military equipment purchased today requires that human factors be taken into account from inception through design, field testing, training considerations, and even "consumer" acceptance.

Today, human factors scientists are at work in an ever-widening variety of endeavors: consumer products, industrial design and safety, computer hardware and software, health care systems, law enforcement, architecture, and even toys, to name just a few. Yet in human factors, as in many fields, other areas look to aviation for technological leadership.

After World War II, the late Ross McFarland of Harvard University wrote his two classic works, *Human Factors in Air Transport Design* and *Human Factors in Air Transportation*. Since that time, a number of specialized books dealing with human factors have been published but few have dealt with aviation per se, with the exception of Stan Roscoe's *Aviation Psychology*, published in 1980, which chronicles the excellent work of his laboratory at the University of Illinois. Still, no comprehensive books on the subject have appeared since McFarland's. We felt that, given the vast amount of published literature and the great acceptance of human factors in today's aviation world, it was time for an update.

We conceived of a book written not for fellow human factors specialists but for the widespread aviation community—a book that could be helpful and interesting to engineers, scientists, pilots, managers, government personnel, and others. In selecting our contributors, we chose authors who were not only experts in their fields but persons who could write for a wider audience than they customarily address. We described our prospective reader to them as knowledgeable in aviation and interested in human factors but not trained in the field. The authors who have written this book rose to the challenge.

In the early years, human factors scientists were not always warmly received by traditional scientists and engineers. The field was seen as fuzzy, the data suspect, the jargon arcane, and the answers often not concrete enough to aid designers. Today the situation seems to have swung to the opposite extreme; human factors practitioners are not only accepted, we are all too often seen as wizards, expected to give answers to questions far beyond the current state of knowledge. The accident at Three Mile Island, the ground collision of two 747s at Tenerife, the President's Task Force on Crew Complement, and the 1986 Challenger disaster have almost made human factors, or its European equivalent, "ergonomics," a household word. The current debate over the safety of visual display terminals in the workplace will bring even more visibility to this new profession. We hope that this volume will also be of interest to persons in nonaviation fields.

The organization of the book takes the reader from the general to the specific. In the first part, Edwards's introduction, Sheridan's system overview, and Miller's chapter on system safety paint a broad picture. The second, third, and fourth parts cover pilot performance, human factors in aircraft design, and vehicles and systems, respectively. We have limited the book to the behavioral interpretation of human factors. The physiological and medical aspects are well documented in other places. The closest we come to physiology is Graeber's chapter on fatigue and desynchronization.

Although we did not plan it this way, we are pleased that our contributors are about evenly distributed among the academic world, government laboratories, and private enterprise. This gives balance to the book. We are most happy that Jerry Lederer, the towering figure in aviation safety of this century, consented to write the foreword. At an age when most persons should be allowed to enjoy retirement, his talents and knowledge are continually in demand. We and our contributors are indebted to our many colleagues at the NASA-Ames Research Center for their encouragement and technical support. We also appreciate the support of staff persons at Ames and at the University of Miami, and we appreciate as well the assistance and patience of the staff at Academic Press.

Finally, we acknowledge the forbearance of our wives, Sally Wiener and Joan Schreiner. They may never understand where all the Saturdays and Sundays went.

E. L. W.
Coral Gables, Florida

D. C. N.
Los Gatos, California

PART ONE

INTRODUCTION

Introductory Overview

1

Elwyn Edwards

The Emergence of Aviation Ergonomics

The Aerospace Achievement

Human endeavor to attain the capability of flight engaged both the imagination and the ingenuity of men for centuries before the epic achievement of Orville and Wilbur Wright in 1903. Earlier attempts to emulate bird flight had failed, partly as a consequence of inadequacies in the understanding of aerodynamics and partly due to the lack of a power unit having an appropriate power-to-weight ratio.

By the turn of the century, the relevant technologies made possible the commencement of an evolutionary program which has led to supersonic civil transport, to spaceflight, and to awesome military capabilities. Huge resources continue to be devoted to the development of aircraft design and to the enabling technologies in such fields as materials, structures, propulsion, and electronics. As a result of these efforts, aircraft have become faster, larger, and more economical; moreover, they cause less environmental pollution and

Human Factors in Aviation
Copyright © 1988 by Academic Press, Inc.
All rights of reproduction in any form reserved.

demonstrate increasing operational capabilities. Indeed, it is difficult to imagine a more impressive tribute to the applied physical sciences than a review of twentieth century progress in aeronautics and astronautics.

The description of aerospace achievements in purely engineering terms is, however, incomplete. With but a few exceptions, vehicles are crewed by people who, along with many ground support personnel, play no small part in the safety and effectiveness of the operation. An understanding of the human role in aircraft operations is therefore an essential ingredient of the total story. During the present century, considerable advances have been made in the disciplines concerned with fitting the person to the job, and the job to the person. Flight crews and other personnel involved in the complex operations of the aviation industry must be carefully selected and trained, their equipment must match the capabilities and limitations of human performance, and they must be protected from the hazards of the environment in which they work. These matters demand the attention of the applied human sciences.

Engineering, then, provides only part of the story; people and the jobs they do figure prominently in the wider scene. Nowhere is this made more clear than in the study of aviation disasters, where, in more than two cases out of every three, accident investigators are driven to conclude that human error plays a major role. These errors are not normally due to sudden illness, to suicidal tendencies, to willful neglect, or to the lack of basic abilities. More typically they arise from temporary breakdowns in skilled performance because, in many instances, system designers and managers have paid insufficient attention to human characteristics and skills. The discipline of human factors (HF) attempts to address this issue systematically, in order to attain both the well-being of everyone involved—whether as a contributor or as a user—and the maximum effectiveness of the planned operation.

The Formal Discipline

As an independent discipline, HF has emerged relatively recently, although its origins may be traced far back in history, intermingled with such other subjects as production engineering, design, education, psychology, medicine, work study, and the law. It was in the late 1940s in the United Kingdom that an interdisciplinary group of scientists who had been engaged upon a variety of human problems associated with the war effort took the decision to form a society concerned with the human aspects of the working environment. Thus in 1950, the Ergonomics Research Society (now the Ergonomics Society) was born. The word *ergonomics,* coined by the late Professor K. F. H. Murrell, derives from the Greek meaning "the science of work." In the United States, analogous developments took place leading, in 1957, to the formation of the Human Factors Society, which now has a membership in excess of 4,000. More recently, numerous national societies have been founded worldwide and are linked via the International Ergonomics Association, an organization which held its first congress in 1961.

Emphases have varied in different parts of the world. In the United States much of the earlier work was centered around the defense and aerospace industries and, being principally concerned with human information processing and control, relied almost exclusively upon the techniques and data of applied experimental psychology. In Europe comparatively more attention has been paid to physical performance, drawing upon the techniques of biodynamics and work physiology. For the present purposes, however, the terms *ergonomics* and *human factors* may be regarded as synonymous.

As a formal, named discipline, HF appeared some 50 years later than the first manned flight, but just as the Wright brothers' success followed many earlier groping attempts, so too HF can be seen as the culmination of countless previous attempts to address the diverse issues surrounding the practical utilization of human skills. Indeed, much of the work carried out prior to the 1950s was HF or ergonomics in all but name.

The Early Pioneers

At the stage of development when many basic engineering problems have yet to be solved, it is inevitable that careful tailoring of equipment to the needs of its operator is given fairly low priority. So it was in the early days of flying, when such human resources as ingenuity, tenacity, versatility, and adaptability were strained to the utmost in order for progress to be made. Flying was uncomfortable, difficult, and hazardous. Experience indicated, however, that certain basic aids were essential in order to achieve an acceptable level of control. Early amongst these was the famous piece of string tied either to the trailing edge of an elevator or to a lateral frame member so that the pilot could avoid skid or slip during a turn by keeping the fluttering string parallel to the fore-and-aft axis of the aircraft.

Without this aid, turns could easily lead to a spin from which there might be no recovery.

The unreliability of engines probably caused the majority of inadvertent terminations of flight, and so the revolution counter soon became an essential piece of equipment. In itself, of course, this did nothing to enhance the probability that the propeller continued to receive power, but it reduced considerably the number of sudden descents which caught the pilot by surprise.

Airspeed indicators based upon manometric principles or upon gravity-balanced mechanisms helped to reduce stalling accidents. The Wrights themselves developed an incidence meter, and instruments based upon the spirit level were used to indicate attitude in both the pitch and roll axes. Magnetic compasses were introduced and the barometric altimeter came into use, this latter being the one instrument which had benefited from the earlier endeavor of ballooning.

The use of aircraft during World War I brought about huge increases in the demand for instruments together with the attendant production problems. About this time, the question of standardization of instrument layout on "boards" also attracted some attention—a matter which later necessitated extensive programs of study and which remains an important facet of the HF of flight-deck design.

Between the wars, passenger travel as we know it today was born, although standards of comfort and safety of passengers—to say nothing of the speed of progress—were very different. A contentious point in relation to piloting skill was whether flight instruments should be regarded as mere aids to the interpretation of more basic sensory information, or whether they could be treated as primary sources of data. Prior to 1930, most experienced pilots tended to relegate instruments to a subsidiary role, and little or no mention was made of their use in programs of flight training. The epic demonstration of Lt. James Doolittle in the United States in 1929 provided the turning point. Doolittle was able to take off, maneuver, and land back on the field without any outside vision. In the United Kingdom, W. E. P. Johnson demonstrated the impossibility of maintaining control for more than a few minutes in a hooded cockpit without instruments, and he was able to recommend the type of instruments and the programs of training which were necessary for blind flying.

During the 1930s the first automatic pilots appeared, thereby introducing automation on to the flight deck such that the control task became shared between human and machine. No aspect of aviation ergonomics remains more topical than that of designing the optimal relationship between the human and automatic controllers of contemporary and future aircraft.

The War Years

Skilled Performance

A massive impetus to the development of aviation was provided by World War II, and here the human problems loomed large. Personnel had to be selected and trained in large numbers. The performance of aircraft used in combat was pressed to the limit, and the success of missions depended wholly upon the skills of the crew members involved, who were required to perform their tasks in extremely hostile environments. Large gaps in the understanding of the acquisition and maintenance of skills appeared, and numerous research programs were put in hand to deal with the problems.

At Cambridge University, the head of the Psychological Laboratory, Professor Sir Frederic Bartlett, was requested in 1939 by the Medical Research Council to direct his attention to some of the problems associated with military aviation. Leading a team whose members were destined to dominate academic psychology in the United Kingdom for the next generation, Bartlett planned and executed a program of research directed towards an understanding of the fundamental nature of human skills.

The practical outcomes of the Cambridge program included contributions in the areas of aircrew selection and training, the effects of sleep loss and fatigue, and various aspects of visual perception and display design.

One interesting piece of experimental equipment used in these studies was built around a Spitfire cockpit into which was fitted a panel with instruments driven such that they responded in a realistic manner in relation to the movements of the controls. This apparatus, due in large measure to the ingenuity of K. J. W. Craik, became known as the "Cambridge cockpit" and was extensively employed in the studies described by Drew (1940) and Davis (1948).

When fatigued, pilots exhibited the characteristic disintegration of skilled performance which leads to a loss in the overall management of a complex task. Peripheral activities, such as checking fuel contents, were overlooked, and there was a tendency to pay undue attention to one or two instruments with the penalty of neglecting others. Using more recent computer terminology, this decrement in performance may be described as being the result of a failure in the principal supervisory program while retaining adequate levels in the execution of individual subroutines. The hallmark of the expert is his ability to "get his act together". This involves anticipation, planning, and timing. Items must be attended to in the proper sequence and must be handled in a manner appropriate to the prevailing circumstances. Less-skilled performers may well demonstrate equal prowess in the execution of such individual subroutines as tracking particular instruments, but they lack the ability to integrate these partial skills into a total coherent performance. During the learning phase it is first necessary to acquire the abilities at the subroutine level. Later, the supervisory skills are acquired and honed by practice. The Cambridge cockpit studies demonstrated that the breakdown of a skill occurs in the reverse order.

Stress

Very early in World War II the effects of stress upon RAF bomber crews became apparent. At the worst periods in 1942, the chances of surviving a tour of 30 operations could be as low as 10%. Inevitably, neurotic symptoms appeared not only toward the end of extended duty tours but, in some individual cases, along with the earliest experience of operational flying.

In the judgment of examining physicians, neurotic symptoms were brought about as a result of (1) flying stress, that is, experience of unusual levels of danger; (2) nonflying stress, including marital and domestic problems; and (3) most especially by an individual's "predisposition", that is, a relatively low resistance to stress (Symonds & Williams, 1943). Considerable emphasis was therefore placed upon methods of selection by psychiatric interviews and psychological tests in order to detect those individuals who were vulnerable. Those unfortunate individuals judged not to display neurotic symptoms but who nevertheless avoided flying duties were said to exhibit "lack of moral fiber" and were hurried away from the company of flying colleagues in order to avoid contamination.

Further attempts were made to limit the duration of duty tours and to keep close medical supervision of crews in order to detect signs of breakdown (Reid, 1979). For a variety of reasons, not all of which are clear, far less neurosis was in evidence during the later years of the war.

Some Classic Studies

Several American studies published shortly after the end of the war concentrated upon the design of instruments and other display devices. Fitts and Jones (1947) described a study of errors made in the interpretation of instrument indications, and they were able to classify these into nine major categories which included misinterpretation of multipointer instruments, legibility problems, scale interpretation errors, illusions, and accepting data from inoperative or faulty sources. The same authors carried out an analogous study of errors in the operation of controls, and they described six major categories including substituting one control for another, reversing the direction of operation, and inadvertently operating a control.

Published in the same year, a report by A. C. Williams (1947) contained a systematic analysis of the pilot's task based upon a division into the four subgoals described as directional, attitudinal, temporal, and mechanical. Attention is then directed towards the optimal format of display necessary to achieve the appropriate manipulation of the aircraft controls.

Numerous publications of the 1950s have become classics in the literature. These include Mackworth's (1950) studies of vigilance, human engineering summaries edited by Fitts (1951), Chapanis (1951) on the analysis of errors, and the work on control performance by Birmingham and Taylor (1954).

A Definition of Human Factors

Various definitions have been employed in attempts to describe the subject matter of HF. One such definition reads:

> Human factors (or ergonomics) may be defined as the technology concerned to optimize the relationships between people and their activities by the systematic application of the human sciences, integrated within the framework of system engineering.

A few points within such a definition require further elaboration.

1. The differences in emphasis have been referred to above, but the words *human factors* and *ergonomics* are regarded here as being interchangeable.

2. In describing HF as a technology, emphasis is placed upon its practical nature; it is problem oriented rather than discipline centered. The relationship between HF and the human sciences might

be compared with that between engineering and the physical sciences.

3. Early definitions of ergonomics frequently employed such phrases as "man and his work." This has been modified to "people and their activities" for several reasons. First, the revised form includes both genders. Second, the plural form indicates an interest in communication between individuals and in the behavior of groups of people. Third, ergonomics has extended beyond the workplace to include the home, the public building, the hospital or school, and even leisure activities.

4. The human sciences comprise all those studies of the structure and nature of human beings, their capabilities and limitations, and their behavior both singly and in groups. In common with all technologies, HF is concerned with seeking and using concepts and data selected upon the criterion of their relevance to a practical problem, not of their location within a formal classification of knowledge.

5. In order to make an effective input into the design and operation of systems, it is necessary for ergonomists to integrate their contributions with those of other people. They must therefore have a grasp of the goals and methods of their partners and some understanding of the difficulties and constraints under which those partners must make decisions. It may be necessary for ergonomists to translate their own concepts and information into a form that allows them to be absorbed within a broader framework. Ergonomists must pay careful attention to the timing of their contributions. Experience has shown that offering advice from the sidelines in the language of the "pure" human sciences will most often be quite ineffective and may even be counterproductive.

6. The optimization of relationships comprises two sets of criteria. The former is concerned with human well-being, and the latter with the effectiveness of system performance. Well-being is achieved not merely by the avoidance of traumatic injury and long-term deleterious effects, but by inducing satisfaction and fulfillment as a result of the activity. Effectiveness is measured by the extent to which the system goals are achieved, taking into account the cost of such achievement. The relative weightings afforded to these two criteria will vary in different contexts. In military conflict, for example, risks to human life and limb may well be set at levels wholly unacceptable in the context of competitive recreations, whereas considerable emphasis will be placed upon the effectiveness of human performance in achieving specific military targets. Again, in many industri-

al situations, optimization of effectiveness might be achieved through the simplification of tasks by means of equipment redesign or procedural modification without disturbing the well-being of personnel, whereas an analogous proposal to improve performance at golf by increasing the diameter of the holes and decreasing their separation would be unlikely to attract wide support!

The SHEL Model

System Resources

The translation of the above definition of HF into a stage nearer the implementation of a program of work might be assisted with the aid of a conceptual model (Edwards, 1972). System designers (whether or not making claim to so grandiose a title) typically have at their disposal three types of resource. The first consists of physical property—buildings, vehicles, equipment, materials, and so forth. This might be termed *hardware*. The second resource is much less visible, comprising the rules, regulations, laws, orders, standard operating procedures, customs, practices, and habits which govern the manner in which the system operates and in which the information within it is organized. This is the *software*, much—but not all—of which will be set down in a collection of documents. Finally, human beings, or *"liveware,"* make up the third resource.

No arrangement of hardware, software, and liveware exists *in vacuo*. In reality, these resources will operate in the context of an environment made up of physical, economic, political, and social factors. It is a matter of convenience to regard all those factors over which the system designers have no control as being *environmental* rather than classifying them in the same terms as system resources. This is simply a convention to distinguish between "our" system and the rest of the universe, with parts of which the system will be interfacing. The relationships between these four components, represented by their initial letters (SHEL), are shown in Figure 1.1.

The L–H Interface

The lines joining the system components in the figure represent the interfaces through which energy and information are interchanged. It is at these boundaries that many of the problems occur under operational conditions. It is certainly true that mismatches at

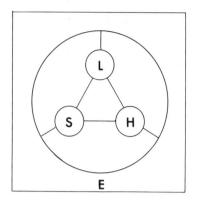

Figure 1.1.   The SHEL model illustrating the interrelationships between the three types of system resource and their environment.

the interfaces, rather than catastrophic failures of single components, typify aviation disasters.

In considering a given interface, such as that between H and L, knowledge of both component types is obviously necessary. The ergonomist's role is to provide the expertise concerning the liveware component. An example of engine power setting, a task requiring L–H interaction, might illustrate some of the features of the interface design. The aircraft engines will be required to operate over a range of settings; these will be determined by the pilot during different phases of flight. Some hardware devices on the flight deck will therefore be necessary to facilitate communication. Engineers will provide data concerning the forces and the amount of movement required to achieve engine control. On the basis of such data, the ergonomist will consider which type of control element is most suitable. If it is decided to maintain the traditional power levers moving fore and aft, then numerous detailed issues require attention. Are the levers situated such that they can be operated by all the appropriate crew members? Are the required forces excessive? Is the degree of sensitivity of the control devices suitably matched to human capabilities? Can the levers be operated simultaneously without difficulty? Is it possible to relate a particular lever to the engine it controls in multiengined aircraft? Such questions can only be answered by reference to information describing the capabilities and limitations of human performance.

Each system component may, to some extent, be tailored to suit the characteristics of the other. The nature and degree of tailoring, however, is highly variable. On the human side, selection, initial and recurrent training, together with all the techniques of personnel management, are available to fit the individual to the job. Liveware, nonetheless, cannot be fundamentally redesigned to suit a particular application; its properties are variable only within relatively narrow limits. Other system resources, conversely, may be contrived for the sole purpose of fulfilling their roles as system resources; design decisions are bounded only by the laws of nature, by the constraints imposed by the environment, and by the limits of the designer's ingenuity. For these reasons, the most fruitful approach to system design comprises an initial acceptance of liveware characteristics followed by the choice or design of other resources to match these human properties which must be accepted as "given". Such an approach is frequently inhibited by an inherent human tendency to design for individuals as they "should" be, or as they are mistakenly believed to be.

The L–S Interface

The design of the L–H interface is probably the best-known and the earliest part of aviation ergonomics, dating back to the "knobs-and-dials" studies of the 1940s and early 1950s. Later experience has drawn attention to the importance of other interfaces within the system, not least of which is that between L and S. The aircraft pilot is required to conform with several sets of rules, regulations, conventions, and operating procedures. Some of these are incorporated within international agreements for the regulation of air traffic; some will be determined by the legislation of the nation in whose airspace the pilot is flying; some will be dictated by the authorities responsible for the certification of the aircraft; some will be determined by the operating policy of the aircraft company.

In order to achieve safe and effective operations, the interface between S and L requires very careful engineering. The software must not be in conflict with human characteristics; it is futile to formulate rules with which conformity cannot be attained and unwise to formulate them such that undue difficulty is generated. During the investigation of violations of a particular type, it is profitable to enquire whether the rules, rather than the violators, are basically at fault.

During their basic training, flight crews will have incorporated into their repertoire of knowledge and skills much of the relevant software associated with flying. During the transition training on to a particular aircraft type they will have committed to memory such additional details as the procedures associated with a variety of emergency conditions. Much more information, however, needs to be employed, and this is obtained, if and when required, by way of manuals, checklists, maps, charts, tables, and graphs. In so far as such documents are physical objects, they can be regarded as pieces of hardware, and certain matters, for example, the recommendations for the size and shape of alphameric characters, will remain much the same whether these characters are to appear on a printed page or upon an instrument dial. In a well-designed document, however, proper attention will have been paid to numerous other aspects of interfacing S with L. What, for example, should be the principle of subdivision and of indexing in order to achieve swift and error-free retrieval of information? To what extent should abbreviations, symbolic codes, or other language devices be employed? Should numerical data be presented in the form of a graph, a look-up table, or a formula? How should three-dimensional constructs be represented upon a two-dimensional page? What are the relative merits of diagrams and prose sentences for conveying instructions? The solutions adopted to such questions of information design will play a crucial role in the effective functioning of the L–S interface.

The L–E Interface

Encompassed within E are all those factors over which designers of aviation systems have no control. Due to the wide range of variability of these factors, the L–E interface must be examined in many different ways. The most immediate properties to consider are those of the hostile physical environment—temperature, radiation, air pressure, weather, and so forth—in which aircraft operate. With respect to these, L–E interfacing is largely a matter of devising ways to protect crews and passengers from discomfort and damage by using pressurized cabins, thermal insulation, and the like. In contemporary transport aircraft, satisfactory solutions have been achieved in most respects, although the problem of low relative humidity remains, as does the risk of injury resulting from atmospheric turbulence.

Many additional aspects of the environment will interact with the system resources S, H, and L, since an aviation system operates within the context of broad political and economic constraints. The system must be constructed such that it can survive and prosper within this environment, and it must have the ability to adapt to changing circumstances. A few examples might clarify the nature of some L–E interfaces. During the 1960s, low oil prices brought about substantial increases in air travel. In Europe, holiday traffic escalated, particu-

larly in and out of the Mediterranean resorts. Crews were thus introduced to new routes, new airports, more intensive work schedules,
and changes in the type of clientele. Conversely, at other times the
supply of qualified flying personnel has exceeded the economic demand, resulting in furloughing; that is, L components have been temporarily removed from the aviation system due to changes in E. A
more recent example would be the economic policy of deregulation,
initiated in 1978 by the United States, allowing operators more freedom in some respects but leading to fierce commercial competition
and new motives for additional economies. Obviously, such an environmental disturbance brings about substantial realignments, not
least of which are those relating to the L–E interface.

A Third Dimension

Four Areas of HF Concern

It may be helpful to add an additional dimension to the SHEL
model in order to emphasize that systems typically comprise several
units of each type of resource. The modified diagram is shown in
Figure 1.2.

Engineers and other hardware specialists will be very familiar with
H–H interfacing. In this area lie such considerations as plug and
socket design, standardization of power supplies and of signal data
formats, and impedance matching. Closely analogous considerations
occur within the S–S interface. Here it is necessary to ensure, for example, that company operating procedures are consistent with na-

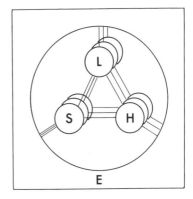

Figure 1.2.   The three-dimensional SHEL
model.

tional and international air traffic rules and with the accepted procedures which form part of the process of aircraft certification.

It is, of course, with the L–L interface that HF is principally concerned. On the aircraft flight deck, interest centers primarily around the interrelations among the members of the two- or three-person flight crew, but also encompasses members of the cabin staff, air traffic controllers, ground crew, and other personnel with whom communications are conducted.

In sectors of high traffic density, the workload involved in radio communications is high. Inevitably errors occur, including confusion about call signs, misunderstanding of information and instructions, setting wrong radio frequencies, and failure to follow the prescribed communication procedures (see Ruffell Smith, 1979). Since the earliest days of airborne radio, steps have been taken to combat the problems associated with communication in the presence of noise. The use of the well-known phonetic alphabets and the highly restricted vocabularies serve as examples. In spite of the efforts made to achieve compliance with agreed international standard procedures, violations are commonplace. It is probably the case that the gap between theory and practice is wider in radio communication procedures than in any other facet of aviation.

Command and Authority

The communication of factual information is but one aspect of the L–L interface. The small team on the flight deck comprises highly trained personnel whose efforts must be coordinated smoothly in order to achieve the safe and efficient operation of flight. This team is led by the aircraft commander, who is given considerable powers to discharge his or her duties effectively. In doing so, the commander must achieve satisfactory working relationships with the crew; neither an overbearing, dictatorial approach nor one in which the command function is obscured will be satisfactory. Problems have arisen, and have been reflected in the accident record, when the captain's role has been overemphasized and when it has been underemphasized. The variable to be optimized has been named *trans-cockpit authority gradient*, or TAG (Edwards, 1975). With some groups, the appropriate TAG might be established quite naturally as a function of the personalities involved, but to ensure a uniformly high standard of flight-deck management and interpersonal relationships, training schemes in social skills and related management techniques have been developed and used in several organizations.

The captain's responsibilities extend beyond the flight deck and include the performance of the cabin crew and the well-being of the passengers. The captain must liaise with air traffic controllers, with maintenance engineers, and with operations personnel. Should an emergency or any other unforeseen event occur, it is the captain's responsibility to use all possible means to achieve a safe conclusion to the flight. Fortunately, several command development programs have adopted the model of the aircraft captain as the manager of a set of system resources within an operational environment and take due regard of the L–L interfaces within such a model.

System Stability

A well-designed system exists in a state of equilibrium which is dependent upon highly interactive links between its component parts. Any changes within a SHEL system may have far-reaching repercussions. A minor equipment modification (change in H), for example, needs examination in relation to its interfaces with operators and maintenance personnel (readjust L–H); it may necessitate procedural changes (readjustment of S) and hence some further training programs (to optimize L–S). Unless all such potential effects of change are properly pursued, it is possible for a comparatively small modification in a system component to lead to highly undesirable and dangerous consequences.

Even in the absence of modifications to the resource components, continuous review of a dynamic system is necessary in order to adjust for changes beyond the control of the system designers and managers (E). Each of the three types of system resource are susceptible to these influences.

Using the SHEL model, HF may thus be seen as a discipline based upon the study of the L component and concerned with the design and management of those system interfaces which include L; namely, L–E, L–H, L–S, and L–L.

Skill and Error

To Err Is Human

The value of human beings as components within the aviation system derives from their capacity to acquire and employ skills. In aviation's early years the primary requirement lay in the area of manual control, that is to say, the ability to apply the appropriate movements to the aircraft controls in order to achieve the required flight path. This aspect of pilotage has, perhaps, tended to receive excessive weighting in the selection and training of crew members at the expense of such other skills as communication, team management, risk assessment, and stress control. In the design and management of system interfaces, the capabilities and limitations of all such skills need to be given due emphasis.

The notion of skill is inseparable from that of error. Since classical times, the tendency to err has been regarded as an essential attribute of human nature. This can lead to pessimism concerning the prospects of achieving acceptable standards of safety without the elimination of human performance from system operation. An alternative philosophy, that which forms the basis of HF, is to study the nature of error, and having done so, to take the necessary steps to control it.

Errors do not appear in a random, unpatterned fashion independently of their surrounding circumstances. Errors may be classified into types having different etiologies and different treatments. Their frequency of appearance will be dependent upon a wide range of variables, some of which are properties of the individual—such as age or state of fatigue—and others of which are related to the interfaces between the individual and the components with which he or she interacts. One goal of HF is, then, to minimize the occurrence of human error.

Error reduction, however, is not the only approach to the problem of error. The second line of attack is directed towards the elimination of disastrous consequences of error. Two processes are involved here. First the error must be detected, and then corrections must be introduced to eliminate any deleterious effects.

A Program for Error Control

An example may help to clarify the HF approach to error control. In a study of errors encountered in reading aircraft instruments, Fitts and Jones (1947) found that the greatest single source of error was the multipointer altimeter, which led to a discrepancy of 1,000 feet or sometimes 10,000 feet in the reading. The dangers associated with such faults in altitude interpretation are readily apparent and have led to many aircraft accidents. The first step in the rectification program was made when the multipointer instrument was thus identified as an error source at the L–H interface. Later designs of altimeter using a single pointer together with a drum or counter are well known. This redesign of the hardware leads to a huge reduction in the probability of an instrument misreading. The ideal instrument results from studies of the effect upon performance of such details as the design of the pointer, of the numerals, and of the graduation marks, the size and location of the instrument, the colors used, and the lighting provided.

A small number of errors may still occur following the hardware modification, and so it is necessary to consider methods of error detection and correction. Detection may be carried out automatically or by using human monitoring. Both methods are in frequent use upon the flight deck. The altitude-alerting equipment will provide auditory and visual indications of approach toward or departure from a selected altitude (or flight level), and at critical times a second crew member will have the task of monitoring the handling pilot to ensure that any errors are detected and reported. Sufficient time must be available and adequate flexibility must be present to allow corrections to be made so that no harmful effects result from the initial error.

The same general approach may be applied to all cases in which a skill breaks down and errors occur. Accident investigators have moved away from the position of regarding the phrase "pilot error" as an appropriate explanatory cause. It is necessary to ask why the error was made and why it was not detected and corrected.

The L-Centered Approaches to Error

Some analyses may indicate that the most fruitful component to modify is L, that is, by way of training. Certain types of error might suggest that human operators lack some specific skill, that they have failed to appreciate the relationship between two physical variables, or that they are too slow in the performance of a particular task. In such cases as these, a training program may bring about the reduction of errors to an acceptable standard. Obviously, care must be taken to ensure that the demands made upon a person are not such that undue levels of stress are generated to the detriment of the individual and, ultimately, to the system of which he or she is a part.

Frequently, it is possible to achieve a measure of error control by any one of several routes, according to which system resource is to be reengineered. There may, for example, be trade-offs to consider between the choice of training (L), of equipment modification (H), or of procedural changes (S). The right decision should be made on the basis of cost—in the widest sense of that term.

A second human-centered approach to error is to determine the point in the sequential chain of human information processing at which a breakdown occurred. Information is received at the sense organs, which convert physical stimuli into neural signals. Here, information may be masked by noise or may suffer distortion. The next stage, that of perception and identification, involves the integration of a mass of sense data into an interpretable, structured whole. The elaborate mosaic on the retina, for example, might be structured into a view of a solid world containing a number of discrete objects against a background. Once again, there is scope for deception by illusion, for the disregard of certain detail, for the addition of expected but missing items, and for the substitution of one item for another. Short-term memory, that notoriously unreliable capacity, plays a part here in that it is frequently necessary to store separate parts of a message until sufficient intelligence is available for the creation of a gestalt. Following the perceptual processes come activities involving data manipulation such as arithmetic and logical operations, withdrawals from long-term memory store, the weighing of evidence, and the consideration of tentative hypotheses. These lead to decisions concerning the appropriate action which should be taken under the prevailing circumstances as these are interpreted. Finally, muscular activity is necessary in order to implement a course of action, such activity comprising speech, limb movements, or locomotion, as appropriate. Some examples of errors classified in this way are set out in Table 1.1.

Table 1.1.　Examples of Errors Classified in Terms of the Part of the Human Information Processing System at Which the Faults Occur

Type of error	Possible causal factors
Failure to detect signal	Input overload Adverse environment
Incorrect identification of signal	Lack of differential cues Inappropriate expectation
Incorrect signal recalled	Confusion in short-term memory Distraction before task completed
Incorrect assessment of priority	Values inadequately defined Complex evaluation required
Wrong action selected	Consequences of action misjudged Correct action inhibited
Incorrect execution of action	Clumsiness due to excessive haste Selection of wrong control device

The result of such an analysis should suggest ways in which the probability of error may be diminished and appropriate means of detection and correction can be applied.

Management skills are equally susceptible to this approach. Problems may arise due to failures in communication between crew members or to inadequacies in the form of leadership provided. Analysis indicates the precise nature of the failure and leads to the devising of solutions which may involve new selection techniques, additional training schedules, changes in operating procedures, or even the removal of unsuitable personnel from positions of command.

The Contemporary Scene

In its best-known application to the human–machine (L–H) interface, HF has the task of keeping abreast of new developments in hardware technology. The color cathode ray tube is now established on the flight deck, and several flat panel devices are under development. The keyboard has also become a familiar data input device, and work has long been in progress upon other devices such as small side-arm controllers. Direct voice input to hardware devices may well become a viable alternative for certain forms of communication.

Much of the current activity in aviation centers around the introduction of sophisticated automatic systems concerned with the control of the aircraft. As a result, the flight deck of the future may have a very different appearance from that in contemporary aircraft. One proposal for a future "pilot's desk flight station" has been developed by the Lockheed–Georgia Company in collaboration with NASA. Less obvious, but of more significance than the hardware changes, are the repercussions upon the skills required of the crew members as a consequence of automation (Edwards, 1976; Wiener & Curry, 1980).

Numerous aspects of these issues have been discussed over the last decade; each of the interfaces involving the L component is profoundly influenced. Pilots' tasks are now little concerned with the direct control of the vehicle during normal operation but rather with providing strategic decision making and supervisory management of the automatic systems. They remain, however, standby controllers and may be called upon suddenly to perform a task at which they have had little recent—or even total—practice. They must retain spatial and temporal orientation during the flight in spite of their lack of immediate involvement in the control functions. The pilot becomes single-handed in the event of the incapacitation of a colleague. These and many related issues need to be addressed with some energy if the benefits of the new technologies are to be enjoyed without unfortunate penalties in safety.

It is a wholly mistaken notion that automation has taken over in the air and that aviation ergonomics is consequently a vestigial technology. Since the earliest days of flying, the various "aids" provided for pilots have been concerned not with making their task easier but with increasing the operational capability of the S–H–L resource package. The flight instruments advocated by Doolittle and by Johnson made possible effective flight without visual contact with the real world. In so doing, these instruments created a veil between humans and the world as they knew it from ordinary day-to-day contact. From the artificial horizon they learned to read the attitude of the aircraft; from the altimeter, its height. Later instrumentation allowed them to deduce their horizontal position. All this information can be assembled into a three-dimensional mental picture of the present situation which in turn provides a basis for deciding the appropriate control actions to bring the aircraft to its destination.

Perception through the veil is not, as the accident record shows, without its problems. Altimeters and maps have been misread, leading to disastrous impacts with the ground in a manner which would be virtually unknown in conditions of visual contact. Similarly, errors of horizontal position have occurred in conditions where a brief glimpse of the real world would have rectified the blunder. As more elaborate aids appear, so the opacity of the veil increases, and both the inputs to the pilot and the outputs required from him or her become less directly related to the familiar mental representation of the real world. One part of the answer to this dilemma derives from the deployment of interfacing devices superior to conventional instrumentation in their semantic power. The widespread popularity of the map mode available on recent electronic navigation displays serves as an example.

It is necessary to keep the crew informed about the state of the onboard systems in respect to both normal operation and malfunction. Such devices as fire warning bells and gear horns have been commonplace for decades. More complex aircraft, however, give rise to a requirement for elaborate alerting systems, the design of which raises numerous HF issues (Edwards, 1979). As many as 17 aural and over 800 visual alerting devices have been used aboard some aircraft (Veitengruber, 1978).

The pace of technological change has, quite properly, been the subject of considerable debate. Reductions in the size, weight, and cost of electronic devices coupled with corresponding increases in computing power and reliability have made possible a rate of change in H which might well exceed the pace at which processes of evaluation and readjustment involving S and L can keep abreast. Some caution is required to prevent the hardware developments being counterproductive in the short term. This caution was in evidence when the initial designs of primary instrument formats were implemented on cathode ray tubes. Airspeed and altitude displays, for example, remained circular in shape and retained their conventional positions. After a short period, alternative designs were developed incorporating vertical scales for these parameters. At a later stage of development it may well be feasible to question whether some of the traditional parameters should be displayed at all. Airspeed and magnetic heading are obvious candidates for review, since both require several stages of arithmetic to bridge the gap between the displayed value and a usable parameter. Alternative indications may therefore supplant them.

The question about the future role of pilots is frequently asked. Are they to be automated out of the system? Arguments about their unique abilities frequently refer to their very large associative memory store and their ability to recognize patterns and to draw upon wisdom and past experience in order to deal with novelty. Such functions as these are characteristic of the expert systems currently being investigated with the aid of large and fast computers. New techniques, involving the utilization of artificial intelligence will, no doubt, find applications in aviation. This is not to say, of course, that the flight crew will swiftly disappear. Even the most sophisticated form of artificial intelligence is unlikely to be allowed to function without human supervision for a very long time ahead. The issue to be addressed in the future is unlikely to be "pilot versus no pilot", but rather "ground-based managers supervising several flights in one geographical sector versus airborne supervisors for individual flights". There will be many arguments to favor the latter solution.

Ironically, one of the most pressing human problems in long-haul flying is a very old one, dating back to such epic flights as Lindbergh's Atlantic crossing in 1927. Sleep disturbance and deprivation associated with desynchronization of diurnal body rhythms are still a major problem for some individuals. HF research is actively involved in attempts to reduce the debilitating effects of the schedules which make such severe demands upon human performance.

Summary

System design is the art of procuring and deploying appropriate resources to achieve system goals. System management is concerned with maintaining or improving system performance in the face of internal or external change. Both these tasks require detailed understanding of the nature of the system resources—software, hardware, and liveware—in order that their mutual interactions, together with the effects of the uncontrollable environment, lead to no undesirable consequences.

A considerable amount is known about human beings and their behavior, although much more remains to be discovered. There is a pressing need for existing knowledge to be applied to the full, and for further research and development work to attract an appropriate level of support. We tend, as a society, to neglect the study of ourselves in our attempts to achieve our various goals. Nowhere is this policy more counterproductive than in the field of aviation, in which so much dependence is placed upon human performance for the safe and efficient achievement of our enterprises.

References

Birmingham, H. P., & Taylor, F. V. (1954). A design philosophy for man–machine control systems. *Proceedings of the Institution of Radio Engineers, 42*, 1748–1758.

Chapanis, A. (1951). Theory and methods for analyzing errors in man–machine systems. *Annals of the New York Academy of Sciences, 51*, 1179–1203.

Chorley, R. A. (1976, February). *Seventy years of flight instruments and displays.* The Third H. P. Folland Memorial Lecture presented to the Royal Aeronautical Society, Gloucester, UK.

Davis, D. R. (1948). *Pilot error: Some laboratory experiments.* London: His Majesty's Stationery Office.

Drew, G. C. (1940). *An experimental study of mental fatigue* (FPRC Report 227). London: Medical Research Council.

Edwards, E. (1972). Man and machine: Systems for safety. In *Proceedings of British Airline Pilots Association Technical Symposium* (pp. 21–36). London: British Airline Pilots Association.

Edwards, E. (1975, October). *Stress and the airline pilot.* Paper presented at British Airline Pilots Association Medical Symposium, London.

Edwards, E. (1976). Some aspects of automation in civil transport aircraft. In T. B. Sheridan & G. Johannsen (Eds.), *Monitoring behavior and supervisory control* (pp. 2–11). New York: Plenum.

Edwards, E. (1979). Flight-deck alarm systems. *Aircraft Engineering, 51* (2), 11–14.

Fitts, P. M. (Ed.). (1951). *Human engineering for an effective air-navigation and traffic-control system.* Washington, DC: National Research Council.

Fitts, P. M., & Jones, R. E. (1947, October). *Analysis of 270 "pilot error" experiences in reading and interpreting aircraft instruments* (Report TSEAA-694-12A). Wright-Patterson Air Force Base, OH: Aeromedical Laboratory.

Mackworth, N. H. (1950). *Researches on the measurement of human performance* (Medical Research Council Special Report Series 268). London: His Majesty's Stationery Office.

Reid, D. D. (1979). The historical background to wartime research in psychology in the Royal Air Force. In E. J. Dearnaley & P. B. Warr (Eds.), *Aircrew stress in wartime operations* (pp. 1–8). London: Academic Press.

Ruffell Smith, H. P. (1979). *A simulation study of the interactions of pilot workload with errors, vigilance, and decisions* (Technical Memorandum 78482). Moffett Field, CA: NASA-Ames Research Center.

Symonds, C. P., & Williams, D. J. (1943, August). *Clinical and statistical study of neurosis precipitated by flying duties* (FPRC Report 547). London: Medical Research Council.

Veitengruber, J. E. (1978). Design criteria for aircraft warning, caution, and advisory alerting systems. *Journal of Aircraft, 15* (9), 574–581.

Wiener, E. L., & Curry, R. E. (1980). Flight-deck automation: Promises and problems. *Ergonomics, 23,* 955–1011.

Williams, A. C. (1947). Preliminary analysis of information required by pilots for instrument flight. In S. N. Roscoe (Ed.), *Aviation Research Monographs, 1*(1). Urbana: University of Illinois, Aviation Research Laboratory.

The System Perspective

2

Thomas B. Sheridan

Introduction

In essence the system approach is merely a way of breaking some selected slice of the real world into identifiable pieces and looking at how those pieces interact. It sounds like a pretty obvious way of dealing with any problem, and in one sense it is quite obvious. But as one pursues this approach, gets more specific, more objective, more quantitative (and this is the point—one must eventually get specific and quantitative to make it work in a useful way), one finds that many insights emerge which were not otherwise understandable or communicable. The system approach is a discipline, proven useful over many years in a myriad of applications, ranging from electronics and other forms of engineering to transportation, economics, and health care.

Bounding and Scoping the Problem

In doing system analysis one is free to bound a problem by as large or as small a slice of reality (both in terms of physical size and in

Human Factors in Aviation

terms of number of interacting factors) as one wishes. Intense system analysis of how the pilot detects a signal from a given warning light and sets a given switch could lead to new understanding about how response times add up or about differences in location of the light and switch in relation to one another, and thus to redesigns which might save many lives. On the other hand, if this particular light signal and switch were not so time-critical, focusing so much system analytic effort on the problem could be unwarranted.

Yet insistence on a holistic approach and compulsion to qualitatively consider everything in relation to everything else—that is, refusal to bound the problem or to analyze it into specific component pieces—can merit the charge of vagueness and ambiguity. Quite clearly a system analysis which considers as component elements the physical stimuli, cognitive activities, and responses of pilots and ground controllers, as well as the electrical and mechanical interactions of many physical variables within the aircraft and the ground-based equipment, cannot at the same time be enlarged in scope to consider the whole national airspace system. That is too many pieces to keep track of; the number of interactions is intractable. One must be selective, choosing a level of bounding the problem and breaking it up into a tractable number of pieces, which might vary from five to five hundred, depending of course upon the size of one's computer and one's budget.

The criterion of success in applying the system perspective to modeling, analyzing interactions among system components, designing, evaluating, and managing systems is in the end one of subjective judgment, a trade-off made by responsible persons among factors of performance, dollar cost, and safety. Does this ultimate subjectivity of success negate the objective nature of system analysis? Not at all, as will be explained below.

Examples at the One-Pilot–One Aircraft Level

So let us then consider some examples, starting with a one-person–one-airplane system, Figure 2.1. The pilot is one organism that can be broken into component functions for purposes of system modeling and analysis. He or she has various senses that pick up signals from the instrument panel and from the view out the window. We may choose to call the different senses components; certainly we know a lot about the specific characteristics of these different senses. We may also posit some specific cognitive functions of the pilot's brain to account for decisions and memory. These are harder to

ALL STIMULI:

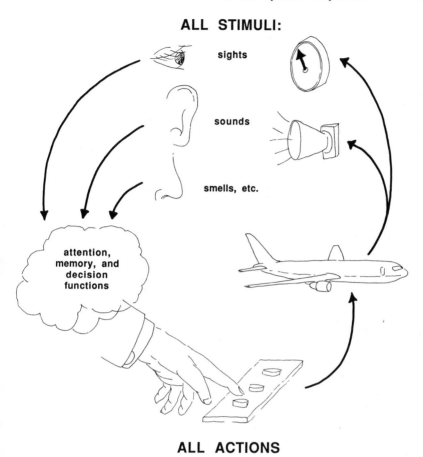

sights

sounds

smells, etc.

ALL ACTIONS

Figure 2.1.   General pilot–aircraft system.

break out as separate physical components, but we may try. The pilot's arm and hand may be lumped as another component.

   In considering the aircraft, we see immediately that there are
many, many mechanical and electronic components. In no way
would it make sense to name all of these as components in our system model; we must consider aggregates of these which may serve
different functions of energy storage, energy conversion, signal processing, signal display, control actuation, and so forth.

   Very quickly we come to the realization that even at the level of a
pilot–aircraft system, the proper breakdown into components depends upon our purpose. For example, we might be interested in the

reliability with which a particular type of engine failure will be detected and a proper response taken. In that case, many aircraft systems would be deemed irrelevant, including many controls and displays in the cockpit. Depending upon the possible cues that might result from the failure, most or all of the pilot's senses may be relevant, and certainly memory and decision will be. On the other hand, the neuromuscular reaction characteristics or the ability to reach various points on the panel may not be considered so important because the proper responses for this particular failure may not be time-critical.

Our system representation, then, might consist (Figure 2.2) of (1) various salient signals at various magnitudes at or near the source of the failure, (2) the filtering effects of electromechanical components which carry those signals (in altered form necessarily) to the attention of the pilot's various senses, (3) the pilot's memory for various systems and what they mean, and (4) his or her criteria and learned habits of failure detection and decision. The variables would be (1) probabilities of various signal magnitudes, (2) correlations of these signals with the failure of interest, (3) filtering effects (including reductions and distortions in signal level, the addition of noise in carrying the signals to various displays, and whether the threshold levels of various preset alarms are exceeded), and (4) the probabilities of the pilot's attention to various cues, memory for various symptoms, and decision to take proper actions.

Given our motives for doing the system analysis, the modeling representation and the form of analysis go hand in hand, and improvements in both are likely to suggest themselves as we start collecting and analyzing data. There are many system techniques which might be used in such an analysis; some will be described below. Any of these may be used to predict the performance of a given system or to study the sensitivity of overall performance to changes in the performance characteristics of some one component.

Now suppose our purpose, still at the level of one-pilot–one-aircraft, was quite different. Suppose we wished to examine whether the pilot can reach certain controls and still see what is needed to carry out the proper actions. Then we are not concerned about aircraft components except for a few control and display components in the cockpit, the seating configuration, and possibly some items of personal clothing or other equipment which could constrain pilot body motions or impede the view. In this case we would be obliged to consider the shortest female and the tallest male pilot, and possibly pilots of various shapes in between. Our system analysis would

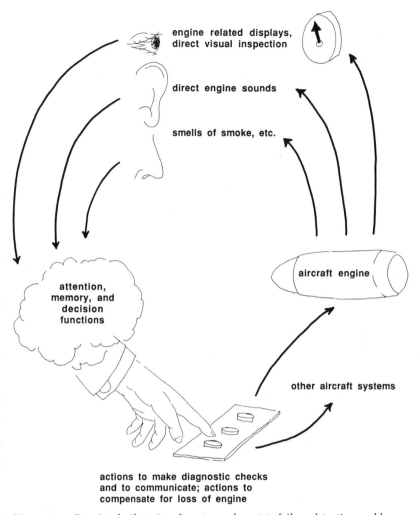

engine related displays,
direct visual inspection

direct engine sounds

smells of smoke, etc.

attention,
memory, and
decision
functions

aircraft engine

other aircraft systems

actions to make diagnostic checks
and to communicate; actions to
compensate for loss of engine

Figure 2.2.   Restricted pilot–aircraft system relevant to failure detection problem.

also be concerned with adding geometric distances and triangulating.
A number of ergonomic modeling techniques, most of them computer-based, have emerged in recent years for handling such problems.

Suppose, finally, our one-pilot–one-aircraft problem is to study
how quickly our pilot might activate a control and confirm the correct response. The same controls and displays mentioned above
might be involved, but our system analysis would now be based

upon the reaction times of reaching and observing. We might even start by assuming that the static reach and viewing were completely satisfactory. Now, however, the major problems are those of activating and observing. Activating includes time to reach and, by vision or touch, find the right control and muster the proper level of force. It also includes type of hand motion required to activate and position sensitivity of both control and hand motion, which if insufficient may result in the control not being set accurately. Observing includes time to visually find and accommodate, time to wait for the aircraft system to respond, and time to recognize proper response. Some representation of all these factors must be made in the system model, clearly not as separate physical components, but as component contributors to the measure of interest, completion time.

Examples at the Level of the National Airspace System

Now let us jump to the consideration of system analysis at a much more aggregate level, including all the pilots, all the ground controllers, and all the other personnel along with all the aircraft, radar, communications, and computer and display equipment required to provide air traffic control and air navigation for the nation. In the present configuration we are dealing with a multilayered system of navigation aids, communication sites, and surveillance facilities, involving a variety of differently equipped airports (both in terms of capability and type of equipment). This system is now being modernized, partly in order to improve performance capability (to meet increasing traffic demands and to reduce human error and equipment failure), partly in order to standardize hardware, software, and procedures, and partly to reduce staffing and costs of operation and maintenance.

The job of system modeling and analysis, therefore, is to predict demands for service on facilities at all levels and to get a much better idea than is now available of what worst-case transient conditions might occur. The systems analysis should help decide on criteria by which the pilot requests are honored or refused, criteria for aircraft separation under different weather and facilities considerations, and what weather information should be sent by data link to pilots. Major government and private capital expenditures must be scaled and justified to taxpayer and corporate shareholders; system analytic investigations are a primary way to do this. Major decisions must be made in implementing new systems such as TCAS (Traffic Alert and Collision Avoidance System), Mode S transponders, and ILS/MLS.

Again, the system perspective must be used selectively as to level of bounding and complexity of analysis within that aggregation level. And further, one must be aware that, just because the term *system* is stuck on every complex assemblage of equipment and protocol, it is not necessarily the case that one therefore is doing "system analysis" or making good use of the system perspective.

The new configuration of the national airspace system has four clusters of equipment appropriate to four quite different functions (but certainly with some necessary overlap in hardware for computing and communications): (1) navigation, involving VORTAC, VOR/DME, and 4D and satellite area navigation; (2) communication, involving VHF, Mode S, data link, and satellite communication; (3) separation, involving ATCRBS (radio beacon), Mode S, and TCAS; and (4) landing, involving ILS/MLS, area navigation (RNAV), and head-up display (HUD).

Systems analyses will necessarily have to be done for each of these separately, certainly for each at the level of a single aircraft as well as for the interaction between aircraft. It probably makes little sense to scale any single system analysis to include more than a relatively small number of aircraft, since the effects of interaction between small numbers of aircraft can be extrapolated to those between large numbers of aircraft fairly easily by statistical methods.

Some kinds of system modeling and analyses should be done at larger aggregate levels. Maintenance of separation and traffic density generally will necessarily involve facilities interacting at many locations. Analyses which have aggregate economic implications (e.g., how does the cost vary as a function of the size or extent of the implementation?) surely involve consideration of large aggregates.

The point is that the amount of physical reality that is considered in any one system model and the degree to which that is broken into component pieces and the interactions among the pieces studied (on paper or by computer simulation) is very dependent on the purpose one has in mind.

Aircraft Production as a System

The process of aircraft production, like production of anything, might initially be considered a simple control loop (Figure 2.3), much as the previous example of piloting the airplane. The first box in the top row represents management's decision to produce some number of a particular aircraft in response to an order (there being no inventory initially), followed by the manufacturing process itself,

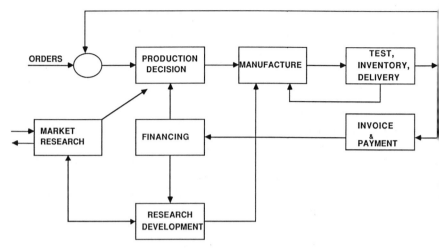

Figure 2.3.   System model of aircraft production.

followed by test, certification, inventory, and delivery, here combined. Each of these processes creates some time lag. As aircraft are delivered, they satisfy and therefore have a negative effect on the initial demand. Such a representation is too simple, however, and one might then consider that the production decision is driven, not only by firm orders, but also by market research, which has many inputs (including for example, the success of the aircraft in service). No production can go on without financing, which has external inputs (borrowing as well as payment for aircraft delivered). The output of financing goes two ways: to affect (and pay for) decisions to produce and to finance research and development. The output of research and development is an important input to market research (it provides one basis for predicting new orders), and it affects substantively how the aircraft is to be manufactured. Some fraction of the manufactured aircraft will fail certain tests and have to be sent back for rework. And so on. The system model of production can be elaborated almost indefinitely.

Abstract Definition and Representation of Systems

The elements taken to represent system components must be specified in terms of their independent or input variables, their dependent or output variables, and the formal logic or mathematical relationships between the two. The system is then defined by the configuration of interconnection between these elements, wherein certain outputs from some elements become inputs to other elements (Figure 2.4). Any variable which is not an input to the system from outside the system boundary (i.e., an output from an element within the system) can be regarded as a system output. Normally one seeks to predict the values of one or more output variables, given certain elements (each having specified input–output relations), and given a particular configuration of connections between elements.

Once the system analyst has selected variables and determined the component input–output relations (e.g., the mathematical rules that describe and predict precisely how inputs get converted to outputs), he or she generally has no further interest in the elements themselves. That is, for the analyst's immediate purposes, all that is important about a given person or agglomeration of physical or biological matter is the value of certain input and output variables and how the inputs affect the outputs. While such an attitude may be considered by some to be callous or unrefined, it is a discipline without which the system analyst could not function. Of course as a human being the analyst is interested in the nature and culture of

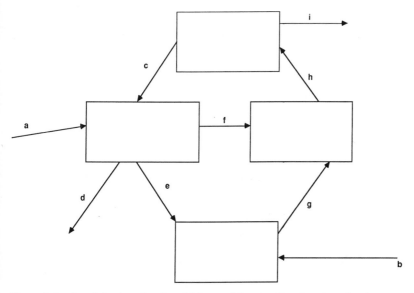

Figure 2.4. An abstract system in which *a* and *b* are system inputs and *c–i* are system outputs. All but *d* and *i* are both inputs to and outputs from individual elements.

the human elements or groups. As a scientist he or she is interested in how and why the physical elements are as they are, and there may be good reasons for interest in what is inside the elements. However, as a system analyst he or she is happy to abstract these components into blocks, variables, and equations.

System inputs are of two types: (1) those which can be manipulated (with the help of engineers, psychologists, managers, or bankers, i.e., with the help of physical mechanism, human communication, administration, or money); and (2) those which cannot be manipulated, even though they may be observed and measured. Examples of the latter are weather, fuel prices, environmental effects of corrosion, and so forth. Typically there are many input variables which influence real systems, but if in a particular model these are known to have little or no influence on the output variables of interest, the system analyst will neglect them.

In solving mathematical equations, the explicit dependent variables are sometimes called unknowns. We may then define a class of never-made-explicit variables called "unknown unknowns." Analysts try to avoid unknown unknowns which have any significance with respect to the system behavioral criteria that are important to themselves or their clients.

System analysis would be cleanest if (1) all the variables were quantitative, either in discrete categories or continuous, (2) all the variables were perfectly measurable and had unambiguous meanings, and (3) all the relations between the variables were deterministic and linear. Then everything could be described in terms of linear algebra or, at the most, linear differential equations. Unfortunately, life is more complex, and some important variables are very difficult to quantify except on an ordinal scale, for example, passenger acceptance. Of those variables that are quantifiable, some seem best defined as continuous and some as discrete, so that both must be considered in the same system.

Many variables are not known with even close to 100% surety, and they must be treated as random variables, specified in the system analysis with some margins of uncertainty or probability density. Even if the variables are cardinal numbers and easily measured, the relations between them may be nonlinear, time-varying, or stochastic (and often the distinction between these is difficult to make). One naturally hopes for approximate linearity, at least for "small" changes in the input variables. Figure 2.5 gives examples of various types of input–output relations which become the basis for mathe-

ALGEBRAIC EQUATION

    continuous linear $y = Ax + 3$

    nonlinear $y = Bx^2 - 4$

    piecewise linear   for $x \leq 2$, $y = Cx$; for $x > 2$, $y = Dx$

    discrete   for $x=1$, $y=5$; for $x=2$, $y=7$;
                                           for $x=3$, $y=10$

DIFFERENTIAL EQUATION

    continuous linear $dy/dt = Ax + By + 7$

    nonlinear $dy/dt = Cx^3 + Dy - 1$

    piecewise linear   for $x \leq 3$, $dy/dt=Ex$; for $x>3$, $dy/dt=Fx$

STOCHASTIC (PROBABILISTIC) EQUATION

    continuous $p(y) = Ae^{-x^2}$

    discrete contingent   for $x = 1$, $p(y=1)=0.2$, $p(y=2) = 0.8$
                                         for $x=2$, $p(y=1)=0.4$, $p(y=2) = 0.6$

Figure 2.5. Some examples of input–output relations.

matical models of systems. From such relational elements the system analyst seeks to build up larger structures, the input–output behavior of which mimics (simulates or models) the behavior of that part of the real world which is of interest.

What Is Gained by the System Perspective?

The system perspective has proven useful in a number of ways. It is more than a way of drawing diagrams or of doing mathematics. Most of all it is an intellectual discipline—a way of thinking intensively and comprehensively about problems.

In considering the advantages to be gained by the system perspective, perhaps the first is its use in helping *formulate the problem.* It demands that the scope of the system (the problem) be bounded—at least for formal analysis. It demands that independent variables (inputs) be identified—both the kind that can be manipulated (by the computer, the muscles, the decision of pilot or air traffic controller, the aircraft designer, the airline manager, the regulator, or the public) and the kind that may be measured but cannot be changed. Then it requires that the key dependent variables be identified (which are internal to the system and affect one another through various relationships which demand to be identified). There is generally no point in breaking a system model into pieces so small that the outputs cannot be measured or do not matter. It is better to keep the representation in chunks whose input and output variables are those one can work with.

A second advantage is that the system model, once formulated, can be run on a computer to *simulate* the system behavior under various hypothetical inputs, parameter changes, and so on. This yields to the system analyst a kind of *qualitative understanding* or gestalt which cannot otherwise be obtained (except after the fact by experience and hindsight, which often is too late for important design, management, and operational decisions). The emergence of fast computers and high-quality computer graphics has meant that such simulations may be run quickly, in real time or even faster time than the counterpart reality being modeled. This has the advantage that the analyst can get a good intuitive sense of the relative dynamic time constants.

A third advantage, following directly from the second, is the ability to make *quantitative prediction* of information to be used directly by the planner, researcher, designer, pilot, or computer. Formally this is the most obvious function of system analysis—to predict the behavior of the whole from the behavior of the parts.

A fourth advantage of the system perspective is that it serves as an *accounting framework* to check that variables or relationships have been considered when planning, designing, training, operating, testing, repairing, cost accounting, and so forth. One principle for designing training aids is to define training goals or functional objectives in a hierarchy, and within any low level, to organize these as blocks according to the time sequence of steps in the process to be trained. The same is true for writing procedures or system checkout, and so on. The system perspective helps to provide assurance that the various interfaces have been connected or properly attended to.

A fifth advantage of the system perspective is related to all the others—*archival description*. The systems model is an orderly and unambiguous way to codify information about design and operation so that others may find and understand it. It is amenable both to the printed page and to recording within a computer.

History and Practice of System Analysis

History

In a sense system analysis is as old as formal mathematics. However, the application that probably was critical in the formal development of systems theory was commercial telephony. In the 1920s and 1930s, long copper wires were strung around the country, elaborate switching systems were set up, and Bell Laboratories was already at work on theoretical analyses of both engineering and economic considerations about telephone communication systems.

During the 1930s both radio and industrial electronics were growing in popularity. The first glimmerings of feedback control were evident, and new control devices appeared in the form of synchros and servos. In the 1940s the Second World War placed accelerated emphasis on technological development of all kinds, including radar theory and development, servo theory and development, and analog computers, the first of which was the Bush differential analyzer. The electronics for all of these devices involved large vacuum tubes which consumed much energy and were not very reliable. The MIT Radiation Laboratory series published in the late 1940s was among the first set of widely available books on system theory and application. At about the same time the community of theoretical physicists turned to practical analysis of military operations and called it "operations research." The first widely accepted volume on this subject was *Methods of Operations Research* by Morse and Kimball (1951).

Shortly after the war ended, digital computers began to emerge, and along with them the systems theory appropriate to them. In 1948 Norbert Wiener wrote his widely acclaimed *Cybernetics*, pointing to the close relationship between electronic systems and animal physiology. In 1949 C. E. Shannon published *Communication in the Presence of Noise* (summarized in more readable form in Shannon & Weaver, 1963), outlining his theory of information, and not too long afterwards many psychologists were trying to measure how many bits per second could be transmitted to or from humans by various means. By 1950 a number of texts on linear control theory had emerged, and it could be said that by then system theory was alive and well, at least in the world of electrical engineering. The early work of Birmingham and Taylor (1954) and others led to consideration of the human operator as a control system element.

Current Practice

By far the largest current group of practitioners of system theory are the engineers—representing electronics (including computers, communication, and control), aeronautics and astronautics, and mechanical design. The Institute of Electrical and Electronics Engineers (IEEE) is the largest professional society and most of its members are involved in "systems" in one way or another. Both human–machine systems and biomedical systems have their own professional groups within IEEE. Software system engineering has gradually emerged as something rather different from the traditional domain of the engineer, which is hardware.

The next largest group of practitioners of system theory are the operations researchers, trained these days in either industrial and production engineering or management. The Operations Research Society of America (ORSA) and The Institute of Management Science (TIMS) are their professional societies in the USA. As might be expected, operations researchers approach problems with an economics and policy orientation much more than do engineers. Operations research (OR) is concerned more with people and institutions, less with physics, and is inclined to be much more probabilistic in its analyses than, for example, servo system control theory.

On the periphery of engineering is the relatively new but much-in-vogue group that identify with artificial intelligence. Without a doubt they are bringing new models and insights to system theory and may in time come to be the principal agents of software system theory. Another new group are the cognitive scientists, who combine the insights of cognitive psychology with those of computer science. A smaller group, which has been contributing heavily, are the experimental decision psychologists, who put to test the theories developed by others. Finally there are "general systems" theorists, who try to combine mathematics, technology, social science, and philosophy through the medium of system theory.

While urging the "system approach" upon the unconverted is no longer as appropriate as it once may have been, it is clear that the technologist is not sufficiently educated unless he or she has some appreciation of the system perspective.

Goals, Decision, and Control

In what follows, three critical steps in the modeling, analysis, and design of systems are discussed. The first has to do with formalizing

the *goals* or *objectives* of the system in quantitative form so that
there is some basis for knowing which performances (what values of
output) are better and which are worse. One may then engage systems *decision* analysis in order to choose specific design alternatives.
Insofar as possible, one tries to build "continuous design" into the
system by making the system continuously and automatically adjust
its parameters to meet changing inputs; we call this *adaptive control*.

Goals

   System analysts practice their art (some of it may be science) for a
purpose—to eventually make the system perform better. In more rigorous terms, that means to make some output or dependent variable
conform more closely to some goal or norm. It is important to consider how this goal should be, could be, and is, in practice, specified.
   Ideally the goal can be specified as a scalar "objective function" of
system input and output variables. That is, a single variable which
defines ultimate goodness or badness is written in terms of time, accuracy, energy used, errors, and costs.
   When this "ultimate trade-off" function can be defined in numbers, theoretically the optimum or very best trade-off can be found. If
this objective function *and* the equations representing the system to
be optimized are well behaved (i.e., continuously differentiable and
unimodal), then the optimum trade-off can be determined with relative ease. Formally this amounts to minimizing or maximizing this
objective function (depending upon whether it is defined in terms of
cost or reward) *together with* solving the set of system equations
(sometimes called the system constraints, meaning nature's constraints on the trade-off of desirable performance variables apart from
what any individual intends).
   If one only had to optimize the objective function, one simply
would choose the highest speed, greatest accuracy, least energy, least
error, and least cost, with no constraints. We all know of politicians
who blissfully assert demands for "the greatest performance at least
cost, with 100% safety" and seem not to understand that such statements make no sense.
   When there are reasonable quantitative specifications of system
constraints and objective function, even if the equations are not well
behaved or if probabilities must be assigned to many conditions, a
computer can be set to searching for the optimum.
   Unfortunately even the determination of the optimum trade-off sel-

dom makes sense. In fact, usually the interaction of all the key variables in the system is not well understood and, furthermore, there is little consensus on what is the trade-off between the system variables in terms of relative goodness or badness. For example, what are the equally good combinations of speed, safety, and comfort for an air trip? Clearly it depends on both the person and the situation. This is especially true when people are part of the system, for we know less about human behavior and what is good and bad with respect to people than we do about physical systems. Thus to talk of the "optimum human–machine system" is usually either a gross misuse of words or a revelation of naïveté.

This change in appreciation of the difficulty of specifying the system objective function is exemplified by recent trends in the way decision theorists have begun to abandon the concept of global goodness or multiattribute utility in favor of local utility or "satisficing." *Utility*, with its roots going back to the English philosophers of the last century, primarily Jeremy Bentham and John Stuart Mill, presupposes a fixed individual and hedonistic (private) objective function which every person carries in his head. John Von Neumann (Von Neumann & Morganstern, 1944) set the foundations for modern utility theory by his axiom that utility of an event multiplied by its probability of occurrence equals the effective (subjectively expected) utility, and thus the utility of any event (or object) can be established in terms of a lottery on other events for which the utility has already been established. Consider, for example, the utility U:

$$U(\text{cloudy day}) = p[U(\text{sunny day})] + (1-p)[U(\text{rainy day})],$$

where probability p might be adjusted until an experimental subject was indifferent between the cloudy day for sure and the lottery of either sun or rain. Alternatively we might find an indifference sum x such that the subject would be indifferent between accepting x with certainty and a 50–50 chance of getting \$1,000 or nothing; that is,

$$U(\$x) = 0.5\, U(\$1,000) + 0.5\, U(\$0).$$

Only rarely would $x = \$500$. Usually the subject would be "risk averse" and settle for U closer to \$300 or \$400. This same idea can be extended (in theory) to many attributes (Keeney & Raiffa, 1976), for example, utility of cars in terms of attributes (variables) like length, power, fuel economy, and so on.

Though utility theorists have applied their methods to a number of complex and real decision problems, the empiricists have run into serious problems getting people to render judgments in terms of objects or events which correspond to nonfamiliar situations. What now appears much more tractable is to let individuals initially specify "aspiration" points in "attribute space," that is, say what they would like. Point 1 in Figure 2.6 might be such a point in a two-attribute space, where A is, for example, the ride quality or comfort of a trip and B is the speed. Then, by successive interactions with a computer, all neighboring points (combinations of the attributes) might be considered to find a point that is satisfactory in all respects. A computer, properly programmed with constraint equations, can return a judgment of feasibility or infeasibility of an initial aspiration, as for example in Figure 2.6, by letting the person know that a closest allowable point is 2, assuming a rough equivalent weight on the two attributes. Then the subject might decide that if this is the case more of attribute A and less of B would be preferable, as represented say by Point 3. The computer can then point out that the subject can do even better, for example, Point 4—and so on in iterative exchange until the individual is satisfied with the trade-off. This procedure has come to be called *satisficing* (March & Simon, 1958; Wierzbicki, 1982).

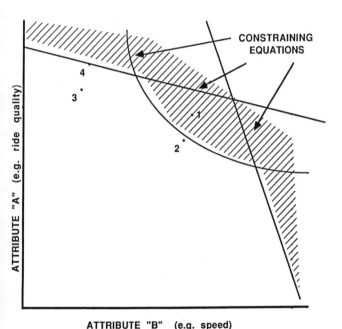

Figure 2.6.   The process of satisficing.

Thus what is more tractable than seeking optimums is to undertake to make a system *satisfactorily better* in terms of the trade-offs between the various performance and cost variables. One may think of betterment as a discrete change in the system; that is, it goes from one static configuration to another. Alternatively one may think of betterment in terms of control—changes in hardware or policy which continuously act to make the system conform to the goal in spite of spurious disturbances or changing conditions.

Decision

System analysis aimed at producing discrete improvements in a system is usually performed by ignoring the ultimate combined trade-off between goods and bads and assuming some relatively simple criterion, such as dollar cost, to be minimized. Then other criteria, such as some minimum level of performance, some maximum available time, and the like, can be specified as constraints. The procedure then is to minimize cost in view of the system constraints (the equations characterizing the physical process) plus the constraints imposed as additional performance criteria. This is easy to do by computer, using a technique called linear programming, which graphically is somewhat like what the computer did in Figure 2.6, except in this case the constraint boundary is searched for that point yielding the minimum cost.

Various other mathematical techniques are employed by system analysts to make the best discrete decisions, given system characteristics plus some combination of added criteria constraints and some simple objective function. Examples are (1) dynamic programming, where events at later stages in time depend upon events at earlier stages, as in most aircraft scheduling; (2) queuing theory, wherein objects or events line up to be serviced like aircraft awaiting takeoff or maintenance; and (3) game theory, where for each "move" the outcomes for each of two or more "players" are dependent upon the joint actions of all players, as in marketing competition between airlines.

Common to all decision theories is the element of risk and what to do about it. Risk means circumstantial events are uncertain, and consequently the payoffs (benefits and costs) are uncertain. What the system analyst usually does is to estimate the probabilities of events, construct a probabilistic payoff matrix, adopt a criterion, and decide

circumstances

	x	y	expected value	min	max
A	6	4	5.4	4	6
B	5	5	5.0	5	5
C	7	0	4.9	0	7

actions

Figure 2.7.   A payoff matrix. For x, $p = .7$ and for y, $p = .3$.

accordingly. For example, Figure 2.7 shows a payoff for the joint occurrence of each of two circumstances x and y for each of three decisions, A, B, and C. Probabilities for the occurrences of x and y are
given in the figure caption. The most conservative decision maker
would select action B, using the "minimax loss" or "maximin gain"
(minimize the maximum loss or maximize the minimum gain) criterion, since with B the worst outcome would be that y would occur
and the payoff would be 5, while with A or C worse outcomes (4 or
0) could occur. "Expected value" decision makers who could afford
to take some risks would select A, and if they repeatedly played
such games (as do insurance companies) they would be quite sure to
win the most with this strategy in the long run. Gamblers might select C in hopes that y would not occur and they then would earn the
greatest possible amount.

Control

In contrast to making one-at-a-time, off-line decisions, control involves setting up a decision process to respond more or less continuously to maintain or improve performance in spite of disturbances.
The idea of control can be simply explained by an example. Let us

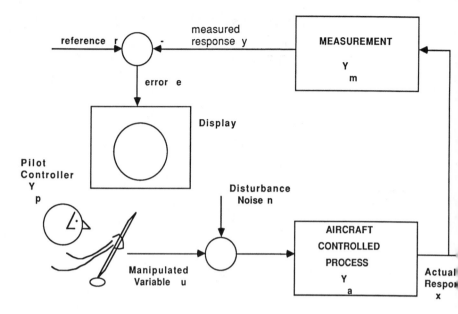

Figure 2.8. Simple aircraft control system.

consider a pilot flying an aircraft (Figure 2.8). Suppose the pilot seeks to maintain a commanded course r by observing the discrepancy e from the measured position of the aircraft y. In the simplest "error nulling" control, he continually observes and corrects the error. However, wind gusts or other disturbance noises counteract the intention signal r and tend to drive the aircraft off course.

Note that the idea of control can be applied at any level to any system. All that is required is that certain output variables be made to follow certain reference or intention variables in spite of other noise or disturbance variables. Our air transport system intends to operate on schedule in spite of unpredictable delays, intends to maintain safety in spite of hazards, and intends to make money in spite of rising costs. Automatic control systems are intended in all of these cases!

The reader interested in communication, decision, and control models of human–machine systems may consult Sheridan and Ferrell (1974) or Rouse (1980) for surveys.

Supervisory Control: A New Approach to Systems

A current trend in aviation is an increasing release of pilots from direct control of their aircraft. Computers are entering more and more as intermediaries in a *supervisory control* relation (Sheridan, 1986). The pilot is becoming a "flight manager" supervising not one, but many computers. These computers are becoming intelligent subordinates to which the pilot gives high-level (macro) commands and specifies goals, constraints, and context information. These subordinate computers then perform the direct control, executing the tasks as requested and reporting back to the pilot as to whether the goal has been achieved or whether there has been trouble along the way.

Often the low-level computers are very limited microcomputers. In this case, interposed between the pilot and the low-level computers, as seen in Figure 2.9, is a "human interactive" computer, the func-

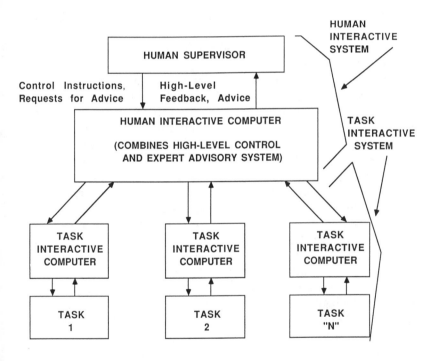

Figure 2.9. Supervisory control.

tions of which are (1) to interpret and provide integrated packaging of information coming in from myriad sensors scattered around the aircraft (the integrated display function); (2) to provide advice (through "expert systems") and planning capability (through off-line "what-would-happen-if" models); (3) to incorporate a user-friendly, high-level command language enabling the pilot or flight engineer to query the system, change set points, or specify subgoals. One or many low-level microcomputers (task-interactive computers) receive these commands and implement control with the mechanical systems.

In assuming this new supervisory role, the pilot undertakes five functions: (1) planning what to ask the computer to do; (2) teaching (commanding, programming) the computer; (3) monitoring its performance and detecting and diagnosing failures if they occur; (4) intervening to take over control directly if and when necessary and maintaining and repairing the semiautomatic systems; and (5) learning from experience.

The supervisory control paradigm is hierarchical. At the highest level it involves human planning and learning with respect to goals and constraints and computer representation of knowledge. At an intermediate level it may involve either person or computer recognizing patterns of input and response variables and commanding of preset computer algorithms to respond to those patterns. At the lowest level it involves computer control and analog servo mechanisms to perform continuous control functions. The national airspace system tends to be organized just this way.

The trend toward hierarchical or supervisory control bears close analogy to what we know of the animal nervous system. Certain low-level autonomic control functions operate continuously and occur virtually without any consciousness: postural reflexes, heart and lung function, eye blinks, and smooth muscle response, for example.

Intermediate-level behavior patterns appear to include first, recognition of certain sensory patterns, then triggering or relatively open-loop response patterns. Recognition of a predator triggers patterns of attention, pursuit, and evasion. Recognition of food triggers a pattern of eating. Recognition of a child may trigger a pattern of nursing, and so forth. The human exhibits similar sensory-triggered algorithmic or open-loop response patterns. In work situations they may be well learned.

At the highest level the organism (human or other higher form) encounters new circumstances which cause it to "stop and think," to consider goals and constraints more generally, to explicitly design the problem for itself, and to weigh alternative strategies.

Rasmussen (1986) has coined the terms *skill-based, rule-based,* and *knowledge-based* to describe these three levels of information processing. He represents the interaction of these three levels qualitatively in a hierarchical control scheme (Figure 2.10), and uses the terms *signals, signs* and *symbols* to represent the variables which trigger each kind of behavior. Presumably the response at each level is turned over to the next lower level for implementation.

Hierarchies or "loops within loops" of this sort have long been implicit in system analysis. Intentions and decisions taken within the higher or outer loop clearly determine decisions in the lower or inner loop, but so too feedback of success or failure at the lower or inner loop may affect decisions of what to do at the higher- or outer-loop level. In driving a car on a trip, the decision of what cities to visit and where to stop for the night affects what highway routes to take, which in turn affects where to stop for gas, which affects when

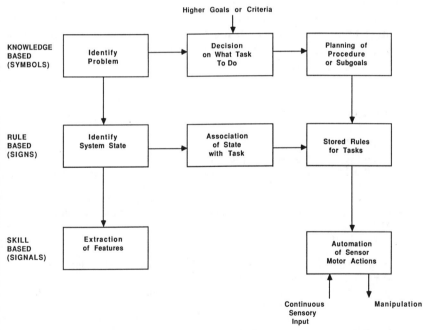

Figure 2.10.   Rasmussen paradigm for structure of human operator. (From Rasmussen, 1986.)

to change lanes or pass, which in turn affects how to steer and brake. Higher-level control drives lower-level control. But difficulty at any of the lower functions clearly affects the higher-level decisions. Those functions can be represented as nested decision-control loops.

In the air transport context, flight planning, navigation, enroute communications, and continuous flight control can similarly be seen as more or less nested loops. Wiener and Curry (1980) discuss this idea further.

Conclusions

The systems perspective has been used successfully for 40 years to model, analyze, design, evaluate, and manage air transport and other systems. It is a set of techniques which imposes a discipline on the analyst to (1) bound the problem and divide it into specific elements, each having observable and measurable inputs and outputs and quantitative relations between them, then (2) test the interaction of these elements. Prediction of system performance is the nominal aim, but the discipline of doing (or trying to do) this bounding and quantification itself usually leads to a better understanding of the nature of the problem, and this may be as beneficial as the quantitative prediction of performance.

References

Birmingham, , H. P., & Taylor, F. V. (1954). A design philosophy for man–machine control systems, *Proceedings of the IRE, 42:* 1748–1758.

Keeney, R. L., & Raiffa, H. (1976). *Decisions with multiple objectives, preferences and value tradeoffs.* New York: Wiley.

March, J. G., & Simon, H. A. (1958). *Organizations.* New York: Wiley.

Morse, P. M., & Kimball, D. (1951). *Methods of operations research.* Cambridge, MA: MIT Press.

Rasmussen, J. (1986). *Information processing and human–machine interaction.* Amsterdam: Elsevier North-Holland.

Rouse, W. B. (1980). *System engineering models of human–machine interaction.* Amsterdam: Elsevier North-Holland.

Shannon, C. E., & Weaver, W. (1963). *The mathematical theory of communication.* Urbana, IL: University of Illinois Press.

Sheridan, T. B. (1987). Supervisory control. In G. Salvendy (Ed.), *Handbook of human factors/ergonomics.* New York: Wiley.

Sheridan, T. B., & Ferrell, W. R. (1974). *Man–machine systems: Information, control and decision models of human performance.* Cambridge, MA: MIT Press.

Von Neumann, J., & Morgenstern, O. (1944). *Theory of games and economic behavior.* Princeton, NJ: Princeton University Press.

Wiener, E. L., & Curry, R. E. (1980). Flight-deck automation: Promises and problems. *Ergonomics, 23,* 995–1011.

Wiener, N. (1948). *Cybernetics.* New York: Wiley.

Wierzbicki, A. P. (1982). A mathematical basis for satisficing decision-making. *Mathematical Modeling, 3,* 391–405.

System Safety

3

C. O. Miller

System Safety and Semantics

As with *human factors, system safety* has had many meanings. Agreement is not complete even among experienced practitioners in the field, although the varying interpretations can most often be traced to the particular part of a system's life cycle in which the commentator is engaged. (More will be presented on "life cycle" later.) Accordingly, explaining system safety can be approached best by first dissecting the term in the semantic sense. Thereafter, generally accepted views can be presented, especially in comparison to how safety has been seen in the past.

The common dictionary definition of safety is "freedom from harm" (Barnhart, 1963). As with most abstract concepts, no such absolute application exists. There is no absolute freedom from harm. The real world has hazards we accept, live with, or otherwise integrate into our daily lives. Indeed, we should think realistically of safety in relative terms. Recall the old vaudevillian exchange in which the straight man asks, "How's your wife?" to which the comic responds, "Compared to what?" Keep that in mind when someone asks, "Is flying safe?"

The definition of safety has often been changed by edict. For example, the U.S. Supreme Court has supported practicality and decreed, "safe is not the equivalent of 'risk free' " (*Industrial Union Dep't. AFL-CIO v. American Petroleum* et al., 1972). For several decades, the Department of Defense (DOD) has defined safety, as portrayed currently in its System Safety Program Requirements document, MIL-STD-882B: "the conservation of human life and its effectiveness, and the prevention of damage to items, consistent with mission requirements" (Department of Defense, 1984). Similar interpretations can be found in Federal Aviation Administration (FAA) and National Aeronautics and Space Administration (NASA) policy documents (Department of Transportation, 1973; FAA, 1973; NASA, 1970, 1983).

Likewise, *system* has matured from meaning simply a set of things or parts constituting a whole. The Gestalt theorist points out that the whole may be something greater than the sum of its parts. Others identify "system" with "systematic," meaning some organized approach to examining relationships between parts, components, or subsystems. The term may even refer to relationships between managerial actions, as depicted in Figure 3.1, which illustrates such ac-

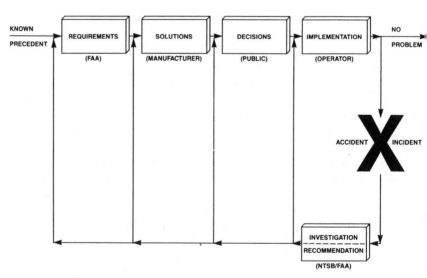

Figure 3.1.   The civil aviation accident prevention system. The principal parties in each are shown in parentheses.

tions as applied to aviation safety. The figure displays the requirements–solutions–decisions–implementation sequence originating from known precedent. Given perfect performance of all the participants along the way, no problem arises. Accidents do occur, however, and following effective investigations, they provide informational input to upgrade the system. Obviously, the diagram is grossly simplified. Many more participants and information loops could be cited, using very little imagination.

Modern systems theory, at least with regard to safety, emphasizes the need to examine *all* elements which may have a bearing on the task at hand. Indeed, a critical first step in any safety analysis is to carefully define the system under consideration, taking care to identify other systems with which the original one interfaces. More often than not, the safety problem is at the interface between systems, as distinguished from within a system or area under the exclusive control or primary interest of the particular investigator.

All too often, one person's system is another's subsystem, or vice versa. Indeed, it was just this rationale which prompted the System Safety Society (the professional association of system safety specialists) to avoid using "systems" in its title, preferring to emphasize the generic nature of the term *system*.

The System Safety Program Requirements document, MIL-STD-882B, defines "system" as:

> A composite, at any level of complexity, of personnel, procedures, materials, tools, equipment, facilities, and software. The elements of this composite are used together in the intended operational or support environment to perform a given task or achieve a specific production, support, or mission requirement. (DOD, 1984)

Elements of the aviation system would include at least the aircraft, personnel (crew and support), maintenance equipment, training equipment, training and procedures manuals, computer programs, and facilities.

When the above interpretations of system and safety are combined to become "system safety," the contemporary meaning evolves. As early as 1965, this author defined system safety as "the integration of skills and resources, specifically organized to achieve accident prevention over the life cycle of an air vehicle system" (Miller, 1965).

This definition seemed to reflect the predominant view of the early practitioners in the field without being constrained by jargon implicit in DOD specifications.

The most current definition of system safety by DOD, again from MIL-STD-882B, is, "the application of engineering and management principles, criteria, and techniques to optimize safety within the constraints of operational effectiveness, time and cost throughout all phases of a system's life cycle."

This differs from previous military standard definitions only by emphasizing application of effort vis-a-vis a condition of an optimum degree of safety acquired in a manner as shown above.

In broader language, system safety was described in a 1984 study for the Office of the Secretary of Defense as

> a highly technical discipline employing a variety of safety engineering and management tasks . . . which addresses all aspects of safety, having its greatest impact when applied during the early design and development stages of a new system . . . the process by which hazards are identified and controlled throughout the life cycle of a system. (Frola & Miller, 1984, p. 1-1)

Thus system safety has become a method of modern accident prevention. More concerning its evolution will be described in the next section. For now, however, realize that system safety has added to the original concepts of safety by

1. The recognition of *relative* freedom from danger or a conservation of resources approach rather than absolute safety
2. Broadening of hazard prevention to physical entities besides people
3. Inclusion of the mission (including economics thereof) as a reason for needed safety emphasis in addition to the moral consideration implicit with personal injury or death
4. Inclusion of systems engineering and management thinking in accident prevention efforts
5. Application of specific accident prevention requirements and tasks over the entire life cycle of a system
6. Identification of specialized personnel, organizations, and funds to accomplish system safety programs in addition to safety being part of everybody's job.

Evolution of System Safety

Most scholars identify the motivation for specialized attention to safety as early as the Industrial Revolution in the nineteenth century, during which time machinery and employment conditions became particularly hazardous to the workers. However, the period just before World War I saw the first organized safety effort, as evidenced by the virtually concurrent formation of the National Safety Council and the American Society of Safety Engineers.

Explosives handled haphazardly in the immediate post-World War I era and catastrophic fires in that same general period gave rise to federal attention to much needed safety measures in these fields. The "white scarf" age of aviation in the 1920s and 1930s, punctuated eventually by loss of prominent people in air transportation crashes, resulted in a civil aviation investigation and regulatory structure which remains little changed in principle to this day (Miller, 1981a).

Actually, until World War II, accidents were basically thought of as people oriented, and accident prevention concentrated on motivating people to "be safe." Safety related only to injury or death. Luck was against those who were hurt or killed. Especially in "those durn fool airplanes," it was a matter of "if your number is up, that's the way it goes."

This is not meant to denigrate the design improvements of the 1920s and 1930s which contributed to air safety immeasurably—for example, instruments for "blind" flying, deicing equipment, and radio navigation. Indeed, the first full-scale crash fire research, performed by ramming aircraft into barriers, occurred at McCook Field in 1924 (J. Lederer, personal communication, August 6, 1985). Nevertheless, air safety per se was hardly a recognized technology in those days.

During World War II, however, new dimensions of safety gave rise to the birth of modern safety thinking. For example, it became tragically apparent that more aircraft and pilots were being lost in stateside operations than in combat. In 1943, approximately 5,000 aircraft were lost stateside compared to about 3,800 in combat. Similar ratios held for crewpersons (Stewart, 1965). Statisticians were quick to point out that in terms of accident rates per flying hours, the data were understandable. But the top generals, examining the war pragmatically, saw their combat mission being degraded severely by losses which were just pure accidents. Thus conservation of equipment and safety as a contributor to the mission became added factors to the scope of safety. Consequently, military aviation safety centers were formed at San Bernardino, California, Norfolk, Virginia, and Ft. Rucker, Alabama for the Air Force, Navy, and Army, respectively, during the early 1950s (Miller, 1965).

During the immediate post-World War II era and early 1950s, the basic precepts of system safety appeared in the literature. The landmark paper in this regard, entitled "The Organization and Utilization of an Aircraft Manufacturer's Air Safety Program," was given by Amos L. Wood of the Boeing Company in January 1946. Wood (1946) emphasized "continuous focus of safety in design," "advance analysis and post accident analysis," "safety work . . . most effective when it is not fettered by administrative pitfalls," "importance of incident or near-accident reporting," "safety education programs," "*accident preventive design to minimize personnel errors,*" "statistical control of post-accident analysis," and many more principles and techniques used in accident prevention today. Note the plea (in italics for emphasis) for what later became identified with human factors–human engineering.

The late William I. Stieglitz of the Republic Aircraft Corporation referenced Wood's ideas in a 1948 paper and added his own magnificent contributions (Stieglitz, 1948). Consider the following extracts from that text:

> Safety must be designed and built into airplanes, just as are performance, stability and structural integrity. A safety group must be just as important a part of a manufacturer's organization as a stress, aerodynamics, or a weights group.

> A safety program can be organized in numerous ways and there is probably no one best way.

> Safety is a specialized subject just as are aerodynamics and structures. Every engineer cannot be expected to be thoroughly familiar with all the developments in the field of safety any more than he can be expected to be an expert aerodynamicist.

> The evaluation of safety work in positive terms is extremely difficult. When an accident does not occur, it is impossible to prove that some particular design feature prevented it.

These precepts, voiced nearly four decades ago, are as valid now as they were then.

The first known use of the term *systems safety* was in 1954 at a Flight Safety Foundation (FSF) seminar (Miller, 1954). FSF was also spawned in the wake of World War II, with its original purpose being to improve aircraft cockpits through better human engineering (Jerome Lederer, FSF's original managing director, personal communication, September, 1984.)

As supersonic aircraft made their operational appearance in the 1950s with, among other complexities, their new, powered flight control systems, flight safety engineering at aircraft companies took on the role envisioned by Wood and Stieglitz (Miller, 1983). In a concurrent activity, the Air Force conducted over 50 conferences during the 10 years beginning in 1954, each treating some specific subsystem as it might be classed today (electrical, power plants, maintenance, etc). This was a gathering of the flight safety engineering clan, so to speak, in an atmosphere of unbridled exchange of safety information probably unmatched since that time because of the growing litigious nature of our society in recent years. (Lawsuits inhibit open communication in safety matters).

In 1953, the University of Southern California (USC) began its aviation (and later aerospace) safety efforts, first emphasizing accident investigation but rapidly expanding to other prevention topics. Begun in the mid-1960s, the first system safety courses were associated with the advanced safety management programs and the missile safety officers' course. Human factors subjects were included heavily from the very beginning of all USC's safety courses.

The 1960s brought forth the first formal requirements for system safety, driven in large part by a new order of magnitude of hazards associated with ballistic missiles and other space vehicles with their high-energy and toxic rocket propulsion system fuels. The Air Force Ballistic Systems Division released BSD Exhibit 62-41, "System Safety Engineering: Military Specification for the Development of Air Force Missiles," in June of 1962, the first time the term *system safety* appeared in a requirements document (thanks to the diligent efforts of the late Col. George Ruff, USAF). This was followed on September 30, 1963 by MIL-S-38130 (USAF), "General Requirements for Safety Engineering of Systems and Equipment," covering aircraft and missiles, and by the Army's MIL-S-58077 (MO), "Safety Engineering of Aircraft Systems, Associated Subsystems, and Equipment; General Requirements for" on June 30, 1964. Whereas the Navy had system safety philosophy in one of its air-launched guided missile specifications—MIL-S-23069 (WEP)—as early as October 31, 1961, it never really climbed aboard the system safety requirements bandwagon until MIL-S-38130A became a tri-service specification in 1966.

MIL-STD-882, "System Safety Program for Systems and Associated Subsystems and Equipment," first appeared July 15, 1969. It differed from the previous documents cited by being program oriented and clearly extending beyond just the engineering phase. It was something the program manager was generally obligated to apply but with the caveat that more detailed specifications could be (and usually were) used to define a particular system safety program. MIL-STD-882 has undergone only two significant revisions; the first in 1977, reflecting lessons from early application of the standard and finally

in 1984, where the substance of the standard was left essentially un-
changed, but a task format was used to simplify application contrac-
tually.

The evolution from BSD Exhibit 62-41 to the current MIL-STD-
882B illustrates one facet of system safety that has often been misunderstood. The early requirements were concentrated in vehicle development, simply because a safety engineering void existed there,
compared to operational safety efforts. Accordingly, some people erroneously thought of system safety as only an engineering function.
The fallacy of that reasoning is apparent in the basic definition of
system safety in life-cycle terms and from the necessity to appreciate
feedback loops in any systems-oriented process. As is shown in the
next section, system safety tasks have their application during system development, test, operation, and, indeed, for some systems, disposal.

Beginning in the 1960s, and certainly by the 1970s, system safety
principles and practices began to appear in industries beyond aviation and aerospace. For example, officials in the surface transportation modes of the National Transportation Safety Board (NTSB) were
instrumental in getting system safety requirements into rapid rail
transit. Hazard analysis techniques in particular were picked up by
the oil industry among others. Interestingly enough, civil aviation, as
represented by the FAA and especially the general aviation manufacturers, has not adopted system safety as a doctrine in the terms described above. The civil aviation regulatory structure inhibits this
adoption to a large degree. Nevertheless, many of the techniques of
system safety are applied by the progressive manufacturers and operators, tasks which are just not identified with system safety as such
(Miller, 1983, 1985).

System Safety and Human Factors: The Interface

Certain accident prevention fundamentals must be understood
prior to examining the relationship between the doctrines of system
safety and human factors. First is the matter of "known precedent,"
which was briefly mentioned earlier in connection with Figure 3.1.
(The phrase was first heard during the early USC accident investigation courses taught by David H. Holladay.) Known precedent used in
a safety sense simply means that it is rare, if ever, that new accident
causal factors appear. The bitter lessons of the past are available in
accident reports, conference minutes, a handbook, or elsewhere. All

too often, those lessons are unattainable in a timely or economical manner or no analytical process is used to apply the information. Reasonable remedial actions are known, albeit controversies abound over which party should take what action. For example, should a cockpit control be redesigned by the manufacturer, or should the operator simply train the pilots better. Known precedent is the data base from which new programs can become improvements over the old ones. Its development and application is essential to the system safety process.

The second fundamental is that accidents are always a sequence of events when considered from a professional safety point of view. The object is to identify the causal chain so as to be able to break one of the links in any potential recurrence. Take the Chicago DC-10 crash of 1979, for example (National Transportation Safety Board [NTSB], 1979). An engine fell off during takeoff rotation, ostensibly due to failure of the pylon attach fitting. Before the case was concluded, however, the adequacy of the procedures given to (and followed by) the crew, the pylon attachment's basic design, the aircraft's hydraulic system, the airline's maintenance procedure, and the FAA's surveillance and malfunction reporting system all came under criticism and presumably became subject to corrective action.

An important corollary to this idea of a sequence of events is to realize the severe limitations inherent in analyzing aviation accidents statistically, particularly in air carrier aviation. Only 1 fatal and 11 nonfatal accidents occurred in 1984 involving scheduled Part 121 (airline) operations, killing just four people. Part 135 (air taxi) operators had just 29 accidents, involving only 96 fatalities. Even general aviation (those operations which do not fall under Parts 121 and 135 of the Federal Aviation Regulations) kept the total accidents to about 3,000, 529 of them being fatal, with the loss of 998 lives (NTSB, 1985a).

Obviously, even several years of air carrier experience may not produce data from which reasonable statistical inferences can be drawn. Also, general aviation investigation results can be meaningless and, indeed, misleading, unless extreme care is used in establishing appropriate cause–effect relationships. This introduces the third fundamental, probable cause. The NTSB defines this as follows:

> Probable Cause(s) . . . condition(s) and/or event(s), or the collective sequence of condition(s) and/or event(s) that most probably caused the accident to occur. Had the condition(s) or event(s) been prevented or had one or more condition(s) and/or event(s) been omitted from the sequence the accident would not have occurred. (NTSB, 1973)

Note the acknowledgment of the principle of a sequence of events and its relation to prevention. However, note also the option given to an accident analyst to use a single factor if desired. In fact, it was not until around 1970 that the safety board's definition was expanded to include the (s). The tendency over the years, not only with the board but also with the public, has been to highlight the (singular) probable cause. This goes back to the legal heritage of accident investigation (Miller, 1981a). Legal cause is described as follows: "*Proximate Cause* . . . that which, in a natural and continuous sequence, unbroken by any efficient, intervening cause, produces the injury and without which, the result would not have occurred" (Black, 1976, p. 1391).

Observe the "but for" similarities between the board's alleged safety-oriented cause and legal cause. "But for" this or that, the accident would not have happened. This gives rise to two very significant problems at the system safety–human factors interface. First is the depth of an investigation. If an investigation is not carried through sufficiently to identify all cause–effect relationships amenable to reasonable practical remedy, the result is oversimplified blame, more often than not on the pilot, who is at the end of the sequence chronologically. This is not to imply that individuals should not be accountable for their own performance. On the contrary, it simply means the total accident sequence and all reasons for nonpreventive action should be explored to see if more practical ways exist to break the chain than merely crying "pilot error." These include, but should not be limited to, behavioral modification techniques that clearly should be applied to the individual as appropriate.

The other major problem with blame-oriented oversimplification of causation is its impact on people faced with possible social stigmatization or disciplinary action through the legal system or in the workplace. Even psychological stress through the person's conscience can be severe. Thus a safety-oriented system of accident cause identification, and communication thereof, is critical to improving human performance in aviation, which is what both system safety and human factors personnel try to do.

It has long been this author's view that the emphasis should not only be shifted to multiple causation, but that aircraft accident investigations should always conclude with recommendations for corrective action. Indeed, except to support the cognitive process during an investigation, "cause" is more trouble than it is worth. In the final analysis, it will probably stay around because the public (especially the media) demands simple answers. Recognizing this fact of life, a safety definition of probable cause has been offered: "a description of the physical nature of the event producing injury or damage, amplified by those cause–effect relationships about which viable and timely preventive action can be taken in furtherance of air safety" (Miller, 1981a; unpublished communications with the NTSB, circa 1970). Given this understanding of accident causation, which will be illustrated in more detail shortly, appreciate that the concept can be used in a predictive or analytical sense before the (accident) fact as well as in accident investigations.

Then comes the necessity to organize system safety factors so that any complex safety problem under consideration can be attacked in an effective manner. Figure 3.2 illustrates one such conceptual approach of proven value to the author for over two decades (Miller 1966, 1983).

Figure 3.2 identifies the traditional man–machine–medium (environment) factors for either accident causation or prevention in a framework of system safety principles identified in the very definition of the term, namely, the influence of the mission and the overall role of management in system safety. It shows not only the significance of a given factor, for example, man, but also that factor's mu-

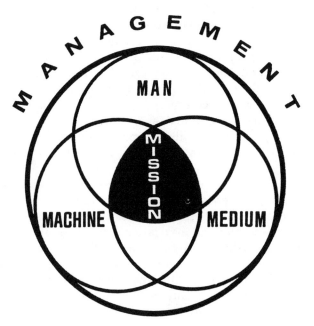

Figure 3.2. System safety factors.

tual subset relationship to other factors. In practical terms, it suggests a problem has not been analyzed completely until the investigator or analyst asks whether the case has really been examined from all key points on the diagram.

For example, take the infamous 14th Street Bridge air carrier accident near Washington National Airport, January 13, 1982 (NTSB, 1982). The accident occurred under icing conditions. The aircraft struck the bridge less than two miles from start of takeoff roll. The machine came into question because of the aircraft's aerodynamic characteristics with ice-contaminated wings. The captain had quite limited experience in winter flying weather—the man factor. The weather was very snowy with severe visibility restrictions, and another part of the medium (environment) was the airport's relatively short runway.

The man and machine came together at the cockpit instruments where, indeed, the influence of the medium was felt because of ice formation on critical engine thrust-sensing probes, which resulted in false engine pressure ratio gauge readings (used to set takeoff thrust). The mission came into the equation based upon recent airline deregulation, placing economic pressures on the airline and the crew. Management of the situation by the airline in terms of crew assignment, dissemination of icing-effects information, coordination of ground servicing, and the like, was involved throughout the case. So was cockpit management, including the interpersonal relationships between the captain and first officer. The first officer seemed to sense something was wrong during the takeoff roll but never did challenge the judgment of the captain. Even FAA management involvement in the situation was a factor meriting close attention. Their oversight of the airline was minimal, and even the air traffic control procedures the night of the accident came into question. Most, but not all, of these factors were addressed by the NTSB in its study of the accident.

Using Figure 3.2 in a preventive sense of avoiding such a takeoff accident on a short runway under icy conditions, would it not be reasonable for qualified people to (1) identify, ahead of time, case-critical man–machine safety information requirements; (2) assure that such information is available in a timely manner through management to flight and ground crew and between flight crew members· and (3) make sure the pilots have requisite experience under proper supervision before being thrust into positions in which paying passengers are along on a winter familiarization flight? The only point to be made, again perhaps, is the need to apply known precedent in some effective manner. Figure 3.2 shows just one approach among many devoted to this purpose that exists through the efforts of system safety and human factors professionals (Miller, 1980, 1982).

Similarly, the role of human factors in system safety can be approached in many ways as well, for example, by identifying areas of human factors activity throughout the life cycle. These would include

1. Personnel planning, selection, assignment, and performance assessment
2. Safety-related interface considerations (e.g., materials compatibility, electromagnetic interference)
3. Design and test of the aircraft in terms of human engineering of controls and displays
4. System biomedical considerations
5. Procedures and training
6. Operational personnel situational awareness and motivation.

The next section provides a system safety framework to which these activities can be related.

System Safety Tasks

MIL-STD-882B

As noted earlier, MIL-STD-882B, the DOD System Safety Program Requirements document, now uses a task format. This is shown in Table 3.1.

Observe two broad categories, "Program Management and Control" and "Design and Evaluation." Within these categories in the document, are pages explaining what the military wants done under each particular task. At the proposal stage for a new aircraft, the contractor obviously can and does use ingenuity to submit specifics on how the tasks are to be accomplished. Eventually, agreement is reached on the scope and direction of the program, which then becomes monitored as time progresses.

From just a review of the short titles of the tasks, one can see where human factors efforts need to be integrated with the system safety work. For example, under Task 104, "System Safety Group/ Working Group Support," it would be highly desirable to have human factors specialists present at these meetings, which basically ascertain and correct, or otherwise track, hazards throughout the aircraft's life cycle as they become known. Human factors personnel

Table 3.1.   System Safety Tasks: MIL-STD-882B

Task	Short title
	Program management and control
100	System Safety Program
101	System Safety Program Plan
102	Integration Management of Prime Contractors, Associate Contractors, and Architect and Engineering Firms
103	System Safety Program Reviews
104	System Safety Group/Working Group Support
105	Hazard Tracking and Risk Resolution
106	Test and Evaluation Safety
107	System Safety Progress Summary
108	Qualifications of System Safety Personnel
	Design and evaluation
201	Preliminary Hazard List
202	Preliminary Hazard Analysis
203	Subsystem Hazard Analysis
204	System Hazard Analysis
205	Operating and Support Hazard Analysis
206	Occupational Health Hazard Assessment
207	Safety Verification
208	Training
209	Safety Assessment
210	Safety Compliance Assessment
211	Software Hazard Analysis
212	Safety Review of Engineering Change Deviation/Waiver
213	GFE/GFP System Safety Analysis

need to lend their expertise to evaluating those hazards which have human performance significance. Task 208, "Training," is even more self-evident as being of interest to human factors personnel.

Hazard Analysis as a Principal Task

By far the largest area of system safety effort in military aircraft development encompasses the hazard analysis process, Tasks 105, 201 through 207, 211, and 213. To understand this further, consider first what hazard analyses do. They enforce a logic in searching for hazards—basically a "what happens if" exercise. They improve communications between areas of design and program management that otherwise might not occur. They reveal critical areas for development of procedures and training and for priority inspections. They provide a framework for feedback as to the efficacy of assumptions made during design about the hardware or the in-place operational procedures. In short, they try to predict hazards, help eliminate or control them, and provide a baseline for management decisions regarding safety during the entire program.

Figures 3.3 and 3.4 illustrate the system safety–human factors relationship further. Both illustrate nominal phases of an aircraft program in DOD terminology, from concept determination through deployment. Depending upon the particular system, relative duration of each phase may vary considerably. For example, a subsonic transport's development and deployment schedule would undoubtedly differ from that of a supersonic bomber. The full scale development phase is where the bulk of the engineering and test work is accomplished.

Figure 3.3 displays an approximate time history for application of the different kinds of hazard analyses called out in MIL-STD-882B. As the name implies, preliminary hazard analysis is a first cut at identifying and controlling hazards inherent in the design, ensuring

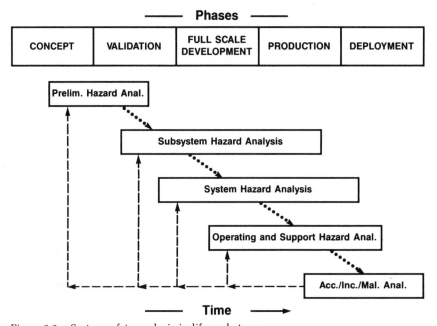

Figure 3.3.   System safety analysis in life-cycle terms.

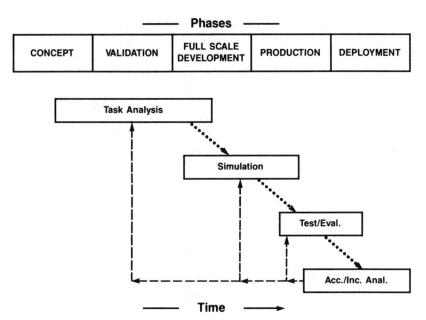

Figure 3.4.   Human factors analysis in life-cycle terms.

that mishap data and other known precedent has been utilized in the ever-present trade-off decisions which will inevitably be made. The scope of this analysis is broad and includes

1. Hazardous components (e.g., fuels, explosives, pressure systems)
2. Safety-related interface considerations (e.g., materials compatibility, electromagnetic interference)
3. Environmental constraints (e.g., noise, vibration, lightning, radiation)
4. Operating, test, maintenance, and emergency procedures (including training and certification for safety operations)
5. Safety-related equipment (e.g., fire suppression).

Appreciate that the preliminary hazard analysis will define and structure the system to be considered; hence, it can have far-reaching effects downstream.

The subsystem hazard analysis identifies hazards associated with the subsystem design, including component failure modes, critical human error inputs, and functional relationships between subsystems. It builds upon what was done earlier, but then follows the design, including changes thereto, well into production.

System hazard analysis continues to be a predominantly two-dimensional paper exercise, but at a higher level of system configuration. Typically, a subsystem might be a hydraulic pump; the system might be the landing-gear system. The system hazard analysis should also extend to three-dimensional hardware typified by the early test and production models of the entire airplane. This is necessary to examine such problems as possible control rod interference with adjacent structure or proximity of fuel leak paths to ignition sources, which are next to impossible to determine just from drawings.

The final hazard analysis technique identified in MIL-STD-882B is the operating and support hazard analysis. This reflects a realization that what the designer assumes personnel performance will be may not be the case, especially if the mission of the aircraft changes with passage of time. Accordingly, operations input must be considered in design and evaluated during test and deployment. The results must then be fed back to the basic process, as are all analysis outputs shown in Figure 3.3. Simulators can be used effectively in operating and support analyses.

Not found in MIL-STD-882B, but shown in Figure 3.3 and considered by this author as essential in the overall hazard analysis spectrum, are the accident/incident/malfunction analyses, performed based on operational experiences. There is no substitute for accurate investigations of reasonable depth into such occurrences during aircraft use, since the development and test process is never perfect despite well-meaning safety efforts of all concerned.

Numerous techniques are used in these hazard analysis efforts, one of the most common being the *fault tree*. This technique assumes something catastrophic as a top-level undesired event, for example, explosive disintegration of the aircraft in flight. It then examines what things could happen, singly or in combination, to produce that result (structural overload, fuel-induced explosion, collision with other objects, etc.). The logic process is then extended to more detailed levels such that the graphic representation resembles a "tree," narrow at the top and broad at the bottom. The results can be qualitative or quantitative, with the validity of the latter being dependent upon the adequacy of appropriate hazard data.

Reliability versus Hazard Analyses

It is important to recognize the difference between hazard analyses and reliability analyses which, in the end, are complementary to one another. Reliability analyses are failure oriented: to be unreliable, something must not function in the manner in which it was supposed to function. Hazards can and do exist even when everything is functioning as designed, as for example, an aircraft exceeding a structural limit because the wrong gain was designed into the autopilot for a particular sequence of use. Also, reliability analyses rarely account for human error. An adequate data base simply does not exist to allow much quantitative performance prediction for the complex human actions implicit in aircraft operations. Reliability engineering tends to be highly probability (numbers) oriented. On the other hand, failure modes and effects analyses, another mainstay of the reliability field, are very important to safety. They are accomplished in the opposite direction from fault trees—from the bottom up, that is, from a malfunction towards the critical result. Thus they develop information of considerable value to the safety engineer, information that can be fed into the broader-based hazard analyses.

Human Factors Analysis in System Safety Terms

Figure 3.4 is presented to show analyses comparable to those done in system safety but performed under the banner of human factors. The task analysis (mainly on paper), followed by simulation, test–evaluation, and accident–incident analysis parallels in theory the analyses done in the name of system safety. The only real difference is the perspective of the human factors specialist, which will include objectives such as efficient workload allocation, personnel manning tables, and the like, which are not safety per se. The important thing is to ensure coordination between these two analysis programs to assure the best possible effort in minimizing human error.

Another Approach to System Safety Tasks

The preceding discussion has emphasized the DOD approach to system safety, mainly because they have done more in adopting the field than any other entity. Other approaches and models explaining the field can be found. This author, for example, has used the following 14-item system safety tasks list for over 20 years of teaching, investigating, and consulting in aviation and other aspects of safety:

1. Develop and coordinate implementation of safety plans; for example, accident prevention program, system safety engineering, accident/incident investigation, disaster control, and security.
2. Assist in establishment of specific accident prevention requirements.
3. Conduct or participate in hazard analyses, including the resolution control process related thereto.

4. Determine and/or review emergency procedures.
5. Participate in program reviews and similar milestone events during product development and use.
6. Maintain an accident/safety known precedent center.
7. Effect liaison with other safety organizations.
8. Provide recommendations for and/or conduct safety research, study, and testing.
9. Implement safety education, training, indoctrination, and motivation programs.
10. Conduct or otherwise coordinate safety surveys, audits, and inspections.
11. Participate in group safety efforts such as councils and standardization boards.
12. Direct or otherwise participate in accident/incident investigations.
13. Develop and follow up recommendations resulting from investigations.
14. Provide objective response to safety inquiry as a staff advisor, in a confidential sense when appropriate.

The rationale has been that when approaching management for resources, one must be quite specific in what will be done and what results can be expected if the go-ahead is provided. Experience has shown that the tasks listed have accident prevention value anywhere in the life cycle. They can be communicated readily, although some are not amenable to procurement or regulatory language. Many are simply borrowed from management technology and just require safety-qualified people to complete effectively tasks like safety surveys or inspections.

System Safety Precedence

One final thought on the system safety–human factors interface involves the principle of "system safety precedence," documented most currently in MIL-STD-882B, Paragraph 4.4. *System safety precedence* means one should follow an "order of precedence for satisfying system safety requirements and resolving identified hazards." That priority is as follows:

1. *Design for minimum risk.* Eliminate the hazard if possible through selection of a suitable design alternative. For example, avoid an aircraft spin accident by limiting longitudinal pitch control authority so as to preclude the wing from being able to reach aerodynamic stall angle of attack. If the wing cannot stall, the aircraft cannot spin.

2. *Incorporate safety devices.* Include in the design something that, if possible, automatically prevents the hazard from becoming an accident. For example, a stick "pusher" that senses an approaching stall angle of attack and physically moves the stick forward would thus avoid the stall.

3. *Provide warning devices.* Include devices to alert personnel to the hazard, presumably in time for them to take remedial action. For example, a stall warning-horn system set to a low enough angle of attack would allow time for the pilot to move the stick forward before the stall.

4. *Develop procedures and training.* Provide instructions and understanding thereof such that the pilot will use cues otherwise available to him to control the hazard. For example, teach a thorough knowledge of airspeed minimums for different aircraft configurations, effects of bank angle, sounds, or aerodynamic buffet indicative of impending stall.

The human factors practitioner, the system safety specialist, and especially any program manager should be alert to at least an ethical responsibility to approach hazard resolution as described above. No suggestion is ever made that the aircraft can or should be designed or operated without risk. It is a matter of reasonable judgment combined with use of available techniques for ascertaining and controlling hazards.

The Future and Its Challenges

Earlier in this chapter, factors influencing the development of safety system were described. World War II was the influence of the 1940s, flight safety engineering in the 1950s, and missile and space activities in the 1960s. The 1970s were cited as witnessing the application of system safety principles to areas beyond aviation. (Actually, this can be ascribed to the consumer activism that was prevalent during that decade, as much as to the maturing of system safety itself.) But what about the remainder of the 1980s, and what about the 1990s or beyond?

Refining the Meaning of System Safety

Some of the old problems remain; for example, the need for a more uniform understanding of just what constitutes system safety, even as viewed by its practitioners. After all, if the presumed experts in the field cannot agree, how can the derivative ideas be communicated to others. To this end this author has come to use a new working definition of system safety for purposes of making a particular point (Miller, 1985). The 1965 definition cited earlier was modified to read, "the *application of engineering, operations, and management tasks*, specifically organized to achieve accident prevention over the life cycle of the air vehicle." (The italicized words indicate the changes.) The purpose of the change was not only to voice agreement with the task approach of MIL-STD-882B but also to further emphasize operations. Recent studies indicated that, even in the military, operating personnel were not involved in the system safety process as much as they should be (Frola & Miller, 1984). Consequently, basic understanding of the system safety doctrine continues to be one of the challenges of the future.

Forcing-Functions toward More System Safety Thinking

Like the previous decades, the 1980s have applied forcing-functions to system safety. Four can be postulated here: economic trends, deregulation, litigation, and human performance considerations. Which one will assume the major historical impact or become system safety's largest challenge or benefactor remains to be seen.

The economic and deregulation impacts are intertwined, with both being associated with the current Federal Administration's conservative fiscal policies, which seem to wield a double-edged sword regarding safety. On one hand, the Administration professes to want long-term economies which, by any logic, would mean conservation of resources with effective mission payoff—the essence of system safety. Still, government personnel policies and willingness to "let industry do it" tend to work against formalized safety programs. Manufacturers and operators need urging (if that is the correct word) to expend resources for preventive measures, especially in the highly competitive atmosphere that characterizes aviation today.

The fact is, no overall federal safety policy exists in terms of fundamental safety precepts (Miller, 1981b). This encourages those few system safety policies on paper within individual departments of the government to become just so much window dressing. Similarly, industry has been shown to mirror government's organizational structure and policies, especially when contracting with them. This means if the government's safety posture is weak, the motivation for industry to do better is also weak.

The third forcing-function, the current propensity of our society to litigate everything, also is a double-edged sword. It cuts deeply into free exchange of safety information. On the other hand, and especially in aviation, only the legal process is ensuring accident investigation to some measure of reasonableness, given the existent personnel shortages in both quantity and quality at the NTSB and the FAA. Unfortunately, no effective feedback mechanism for accident knowledge exists between the legal system and the safety system, although this has been recommended on more than one occasion (Miller, 1981c).

Human factors personnel should be pleased to know they have been discovered by all segments of the legal profession. "Human factors" is part of a major reference text used by attorneys (Lawyers Cooperative Publishing Co., 1979), and human factors articles have begun to appear in defense bar publications as well as journals aimed at plaintiff's representatives (Wallace & Kay, 1984).

The human performance impact on system safety in the 1980s is a tribute to all those human factors personnel who have been beating their discipline's drum over the years. There is a long way yet to go, particularly in civil aviation, but progress has been made. For example, the Aviation Safety Reporting System, sponsored financially by the FAA and administered by NASA and Battelle personnel at the NASA-Ames Research Center, is a magnificent example of human performance-oriented incident investigation and analysis (FAA, 1985). This program has been so successful that it has been used as the basis for a similar human performance reporting system underway in the nuclear power industry (Pate, 1985).

The NTSB, as a matter of policy and organization in recent years, has lent identity to human performance investigation. Although a human factors branch was formed as early as 1969, it remained concentrated on crash survivability factors throughout the 1970s. Needed emphasis on human performance investigation has now occurred, as suggested by Figure 3.5, which illustrates NTSB's approach to fact determination in this area (NTSB, 1983).

Unfortunately, the FAA has generally failed to adopt modern approaches in their operating policies and regulations concerning either human factors or system safety (Miller, 1983, 1985). For example, their regulations and a currently proposed advisory circular concerning aircraft system design analysis do not address human error analysis (Aerospace Industries Association, 1985). The FAA uses a very narrow definition of the term *system*. Also, FAA task analysis requirements are workload oriented, not necessarily aimed at what hazards can occur and how best can they be handled. FAA human engineering regulations are so broad as to be virtually meaningless.

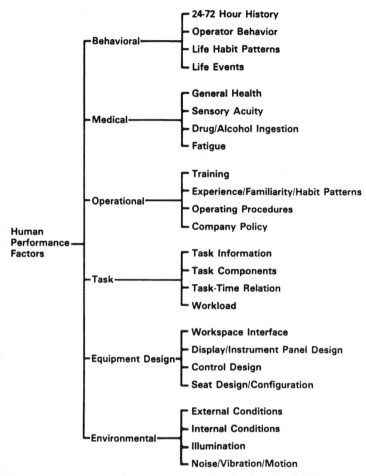

Figure 3.5.   Human performance investigation factors. (From NTSB, 1983.)

Much of this situation can be traced to FAA's organizational inertia regarding human factors and system safety; however, even more of the problem can be traced to the unbelievably complex nature of Federal Aviation Regulation development, modification, and interpretation.

The minimal effectiveness of NTSB in human factors areas is both technical and managerial. It is very difficult to establish and follow practical limits in human performance investigations. Not only does the question of available time arise, given current scarce resources, but also numerous investigation protocol questions provide serious challenge. For example, how far does the investigator invade the privacy of parties to the accident? How does one evaluate "proof" of adequate human performance (or lack thereof) compared to fact determination concerning inanimate objects (for example, personnel fatigue as an accident cause factor compared to structural fatigue failure of a metallic part)? How does one communicate human performance findings to those unschooled in the human factors field (board members, Congressmen, media representatives, and others), especially when many of them make value judgments based only upon their personal experiences?

The intent is there among the staff at NTSB to do more in the human factors field and within a system safety context, but they have been severely inhibited by inadequate resources and de-emphasis on aviation over the past decade or more (Miller, 1984). Also, effectiveness of the board overall has been degraded in recent years by questionable qualifications of several appointees, if and when they are even made. Multiple vacancies on the five-person board have been allowed to exist for years. Given the deficient aviation accident investigations from NTSB now in virtually all but the major catastrophes, the accident lesson feedback loop to the civil aviation system is in serious trouble.

Looking to the 1990s

One trend is clearly apparent: the integration of the various forms of safety. As mentioned earlier, system safety has been accepted in fields well beyond aviation and aerospace. This has put it in juxtaposition to, and sometimes in competition bordering on conflict with, other established modes of safety, for example, fire, explosive, occupational, and the like. Resolution of this challenge seems to rest with recognition of system safety as a more programmatic activity, whereas, the other safety modes are more functional.

To draw an analogy with a large corporation's engineering organization, system safety is similar to a project office. A project office coordinates and sometimes directs the overall team efforts of functional areas such as propulsion, structures, electrical design, and the like, towards a particular objective. All of these areas have their own fields of expertise. Similarly, the trend seems to be that system safety organizations are assuming an umbrella, program-oriented role in relation to the other safety modes. The optimum result is obtained by application of all skills towards a common goal using the best management format available. For programs or organizational entities of any significant size, that management technique seems to involve the project-functional mode of operation. Evidence of this form of management's perception of system safety has already made its appearance in some military organizations and with some contractors.

On the technology side, and especially with respect to application of advanced computer-based system developments (e.g., artificial intelligence), one can expect system safety to be impacted heavily in the hazard analysis area. Especially with accident investigations, protocols and models have been described which need only to become understood and perhaps refined somewhat before they are applied widely (Benner, 1985).

Concluding Remarks

It has been reported that during recent times, the DOD loses from accidents about 210 aircraft and a like number of highly trained aviators each year. The annual cost of aircraft accidents and safety modifications directly related thereto is about $1 billion! The annual Air Force loss of aircraft due to accidents, despite an excellent record compared to past years, equals the loss of an entire tactical fighter wing (Frola & Miller, 1984). No wonder the military is serious about system safety and continually trying to improve it.

In the civil aviation field, the motivations for safety are theoretically the same and, indeed, may be a bit greater than for military aviation. Following the loss of a Boeing 747 with a large passenger load, for example, probably well over $100 million would change hands among various parties. However, in addition to the moral, economic, and mission factors, the civil world seems to react to self-preservation and public pressures more than does the military. In terms of fatalities, civil aviation experiences a small proportion of total transportation losses, on the order of 4% (NTSB, 1985b). Hence, some comments heard privately question the need for continuing aggressive air safety efforts. Fortunately, other commentators are keeping things in better perspective. Congressman Norman Y. Mineta of San Jose, California, Aviation Subcommittee Chairman in the House of Representatives, responding to the question "How safe is safe?" said recently:

> [It] varies widely by mode of transportation. . . . Feelings [of safety concern] are what determines how safe is safe.

For aviation our society basically has a two-part answer: Safer than for other modes of transportation, and by a large margin; and safer with each passing year. (Mineta, 1984)

At the same meeting, John H. Enders, president of the respected Flight Safety Foundation answered the same "How safe is safe" question by saying: "It is as safe as our societal capabilities and determination allow it to be."

In a later commentary, FAA Administrator Donald D. Engen also put matters succinctly: "You're never happy with any safety record. You're always striving to do better" (Engen, 1984).

In a more pragmatic vein, this author believes that as long as it is possible to have high fatality-density accidents (those which can kill from about ten to several hundred people at one place within a matter of seconds), we are not safe enough. The public react emotionally, if not always rationally. They will not let us forget what we should have been doing all along, especially when known precedent is identified during the investigation—and it usually is. To do what we can, when we can in the interests of air safety: that is the ever-present challenge of the future. In the immediate situation, that means doing all we can to assure the disciplines of human factors and system safety integrate their efforts to the greatest extent possible. Pilots, other crew, maintenance personnel, and air traffic controllers are not only parts of the causation sequence from time to time, but they are also the principal accident preventers. We need to help them all we can.

References

Aerospace Industries Association. (1985). *Proposed advisory circular 25.1309: Airplane system design analysis.* Memorandum of March 8. Washington, DC: Author.

American jurisprudence, proof of facts 2d (Sections 7–16). (1979). Rochester, NY: Lawyers Cooperative Publishing Co.

Barnhart, C. L. (Ed.). (1963). *The world book encyclopedia dictionary.* Chicago: Doubleday.

Benner, L. (1985). Rating accident models and investigative methodologies. *Journal of Safety Research, 16,* 105–126.

Black, H. C. (1976). *Black's law dictionary.* St. Paul: West.

Department of Defense. (1984). *System safety program requirements* (MIL-STD-882B). Washington, DC: Author.

Department of Transportation. (1972). *Safety policy* (DOT Order 5800.2). Washington, DC: Author.

Engen, D. D. (1984). Statement during television program, *Meet the Press.* December 15.

Federal Aviation Administration. (1973). *DOT safety policy* (FAA order 1000.29). Washington, DC: Author.

Federal Aviation Administration. (1985). *Aviation safety reporting system* (Advisory circular 00–46). Washington, DC: Author.

Frola, F. R., & Miller, C. O. (1984). *System safety in aircraft acquisition.* Bethesda, MD: Logistics Management Institute.

Industrial Union Department, AFL-CIO v. American Petroleum et al., 448 U.S. 607 (1980).

Miller, C. O. (1954, November). *Applying lessons learned from accident investigations to design through a systems safety concept.* Paper presented at the Flight Safety Foundation seminar, Sante Fe, NM.

Miller, C. O. (winter, 1965). Safety and semantics. *Alumni Review.* Los Angeles: University of Southern California, Aerospace Safety Division.

Miller, C. O. (1966). *The role of system safety in aerospace management.* Los Angeles, CA: Author.

Miller, C. O. (1980, spring). Human factors in aircraft investigation. *International Society of Air Safety Investigators Forum.*

Miller, C. O. (1981a). Aircraft accident investigations: Functions and legal perspectives. *Southern Methodist University Journal of Air Law and Commerce, 46-2.*

Miller, C. O. (1981b). Comparative analysis of federal legislative mandates for public safety. In *Proceedings of the 5th System Safety Society Conference,* Denver, CO.

Miller, C. O. (1981c, December). *Past recommendations to the NTSB and others for improved aviation accident investigations.* Paper presented at the Air Line Pilots Association symposium, Washington, DC.

Miller, C. O. (1982, November). *Recent trends in human factors analysis in aviation accidents.* Paper presented at the Florida Bar Association 6th Annual Aviation Law Symposium, Tampa, FL.

Miller, C. O. (1983, December). *A comparison of military and civil aviation system safety.* Paper presented at the Air Line Pilots Association symposium, Washington, DC.

Miller, C. O. (1984, May). *NTSB investigation of civil aviation accidents: a current overview.* Paper presented at American Bar Association's Third National Institute sponsored by the Aviation and Space Law Committee, Washington, DC.

Miller, C. O. (1985). U.S. civil aviation and system safety. In *Proceedings of the 7th International System Safety Conference,* San Jose, CA.

Mineta, N. Y. (1984, May). *Address at the annual meeting of the American Institute of Aeronautics and Astronautics.* Washington, DC.

National Aeronautics and Space Administration. (1970). *System safety* (NHB 1700.1 V3). Washington, DC: Author.

National Aeronautics and Space Administration. (1983). *Basic safety manual* (NHB 1700.1 VI-A). Washington, DC: Author.

National Transportation Safety Board. (1973). *Bureau of Aviation Safety, analysts handbook.* Part II. Washington, DC: Author.

National Transportation Safety Board. (1979). *Aircraft accident report, American Airlines Inc. DC-10 . . . Chicago, Illinois, May 25, 1979* (NTSB AAR-79-17). Washington, DC: Author.

National Transportation Safety Board (1982). *Aircraft accident report, Air Florida Inc. Boeing 737-222 . . . near Washington National Airport. Jan. 13, 1982* (NTSB AAR-82-8). Washington, DC: Author.

National Transportation Safety Board Human Performance Group. (1983). *Accident investigation of human performance factors.* Unpublished manuscript. Washington, DC: Author.

National Transportation Safety Board (1985a). *U.S. airlines achieve low 1984 accident rates* (SB-85-01). Washington, DC: Author.

National Transportation Safety Board (1985b). *U.S. Highway; Transport Fatalities Up in 1984, Reversing a 3-Year Decline* (SB-85-25). Washington, DC: Author.

Pate, Z. T. (1985, June). Announcing lifted leads. *Lifted Leads.* Atlanta, GA: Institute of Nuclear Power Operations.

Stewart, C. B. (1965, December). *Address before the graduating class.* University of Southern California, Aerospace Safety Division, Los Angeles.

Stieglitz, W. I. (1948, February). Engineering for safety. *Aeronautical Engineering Review.*

Stieglitz, W. I. (1965). *Letter to the Aerospace Systems Safety Society.* Oct. 18.

Wallace, W. H., & Kay, J. A. (1984). Human factors experts: their use and admissibility in modern litigation. *For the Defense.* Dec.

Wood, A. L. (1946, January). *The organization and utilization of an aircraft manufacturer's air safety program.* Paper presented at the Institute of Aeronautical Sciences, New York.

PART TWO

PILOT PERFORMANCE

The Human Senses in Flight

4

Herschel W. Leibowitz

Some History

Human factors engineering is based on knowledge of the fundamentals of our sensory, perceptual, memory, and motor systems. This information is used to optimize human performance and to design more efficient human–machine systems. Because we obtain most of the information about the external world from our eyes, the capabilities and limitations of the visual system have been a major interest of human factors engineers. Even before the founding of experimental psychology in the late nineteenth century and the formal introduction of human factors engineering in the 1940s, astronomers studied the role of human visual capabilities in limiting the resolving power of telescopes. Later problems have been concerned with, but by no means limited to, the role of vision in transportation systems, medical diagnosis, aviation and space flight, night lookouts in the military, viewing video display terminals (VDTs), and athletics.

Human Factors in Aviation
Copyright © 1988 by Academic Press, Inc.
All rights of reproduction in any form reserved.

Sources of Information

Many of the examples presented in this chapter derive from the military. Although human factors engineering considerations are potentially important whenever humans are required to engage in tasks which are near or at the limits of performance capabilities, until this century, machines and tools were relatively uncomplicated. If a "human factor" limited performance, it was usually related to the strength or endurance of the human. However, as technology progressed, the role of the human had less and less to do with strength and endurance and progressively more with sensory, perceptual, memory, and motor skill factors. Although these considerations were manifesting themselves throughout our society, particularly in automobile and air transportation and in industry, the urgency and magnitude of problems in aviation and in the military provided the impetus for systematic consideration of human factors engineering problems. It is generally agreed that the remarkable safety record of commercial aviation, the spectacular achievements of the manned space program, and the efficiency of our armed forces would not be possible without human engineering contributions. There is every indication that these trends will continue in the future. As technology progresses, the role of the human in interacting with equipment will become more complex. While machines will be expected to take over more and more of the routine and predictable tasks, greater emphasis will be placed on the unique abilities of humans to solve unanticipated and nonroutine problems. Future systems will require increasingly great efforts from the human factors engineer.

The information on which a human factors engineer relies comes from a variety of sources. The behavioral sciences, particularly psychology, provide data describing our ability to see, hear, perceive, remember, make decisions, react, and interact with other individuals. This information must frequently be supplemented by contributions from other disciplines. Because humans are frequently required to perform under adverse conditions involving high and low temperatures, high altitudes, and altered gravitational fields, information from the basic medical sciences is often indispensable. Human factors engineering is typically multidisciplinary, combining information from engineering, medical, and behavioral sciences.

A valuable source of information is the previous experience of human factors engineers in dealing with human–machine interactions. Although each situation is unique, there are some similarities among the demands on human capabilities whether one is driving an automobile, train, or airplane. For this reason, some of the principles important in aviation will be introduced utilizing tasks other than aviation, particularly automobile driving. The goal of this chapter is to familiarize the reader with principles which will assist in understanding human capabilities and limitations and also provide the basis for solving future problems.

Some Limitations of Vision: The See-and-Avoid Principle

A question frequently encountered in human factors engineering is whether the role assigned to the human being is within his or her capabilities. In some cases, the task assigned to the human is so difficult that it can not be performed reliably. Consider, for example, two jet aircraft on a head-on collision course. At normal cruising speeds, they will be approaching each other at 1,100 miles per hour or 18 miles per minute. Estimates of the time required to recognize an approaching aircraft and take evasive action range from 5.0 to 12.5 seconds, which corresponds to recognition distances from 1.5 to 3.8 miles. Even when the weather is clear and there is no interfering glare from the sun, the task of detecting other aircraft at these ranges is difficult for a number of reasons:

1. At distances of 1.5 to 3.8 miles even a large airplane will appear to be quite small; the smaller the object the more difficult it will be to detect. This ability is systematically degraded as the image is viewed in the more peripheral regions of the visual field. Objects in the periphery are not only difficult to see, but their contours tend to become obscure. The small image of a distant aircraft, if it is seen at all, may appear similar to an imperfection in the windshield, particularly if the pilot is not looking directly at it. Even under optimum conditions, detection of other aircraft in three-dimensional space can be difficult; even when pilots are informed of aircraft in their vicinity and given the approximate location, they are often not seen.

2. As a result of collision geometry, two objects moving at a constant velocity and approaching each other in a straight line will appear to be stationary. Thus, airplanes on a collision course will remain in the same position in the windscreen of the approaching aircraft. This lack of movement is not a serious problem for recognition if the pilot is looking directly at the other aircraft, but it can be a serious obstacle if the aircraft is viewed indirectly. We know from personal experience that our ability to detect objects in the peripheral visual field is normally aided by movement. If we hold our eyes

still, small objects in the periphery will disappear. For this reason, we wave when we want to attract someone's attention, and advertising signs frequently make use of movement to attract attention. The lack of apparent movement of an approaching aircraft on a collision course, and the small image size, can make it very difficult to detect visually.

3. The task of recognizing approaching aircraft is also hampered because under most flying conditions adequate clearance among aircraft is maintained reliably by the air traffic control system. Particularly in the vicinity of an airport, information about aircraft in the vicinity is provided by the ground controllers. Although pilots are aware that errors do occur in the system and that they are responsible for seeing and avoiding other aircraft, the high reliability of the air traffic control system and the low probability that aircraft will be on a collision course reduces the expectation of a collision. This reduced expectation is important for two reasons. In order to scan the sky for other aircraft, pilots must shift their attention away from the instrument panel. Since the information from the instruments is critical especially during takeoff and landing, it is natural to place a higher priority on the instruments than on the rare possibility of a midair collision. In addition, the time it takes to recognize unexpected objects may be several seconds longer than when they are expected. In aviation, even a few seconds can be crucial. An ironic implication of the fact that the air traffic control system works so well under most conditions is that pilots are not as well prepared for the rare cases in which the system fails.

Although the final responsibility for avoiding collisions in clear weather rests with the pilots under the "see-and-avoid principle," consideration of the capabilities and limitations of humans suggests that timely visual recognition of approaching aircraft is not always reliable. Consideration of the see-and-avoid principle is relevant to an analysis of visual factors in aviation because it illustrates an important example of how knowledge of the capabilities and limitations of human vision are essential in aviation safety.

Dual Approaches to Vision: Anatomical and Functional

One of the most valuable assets of the human factors engineer is knowledge of how the human sensory systems function. As an aid to achieving this understanding, analysis of the role of the visual system in human performance may conveniently be formulated in terms of the fact that there is more than one kind of vision. The dual nature of vision was first recognized in terms of the light-sensitive receptors in the retina of the eye. The optical imaging system in the front part of the eye, the cornea and lens, focuses an image on the retina in a manner analogous to the lens of a camera. This image then stimulates the light-sensitive receptors in the retina, located in the back part of the eye, which in turn send a message to the brain where the process of perception takes place. In the retina, there are two different types of light-sensitive receptors, the rods and the cones, with significantly different properties (Figure 4.1). This duali-

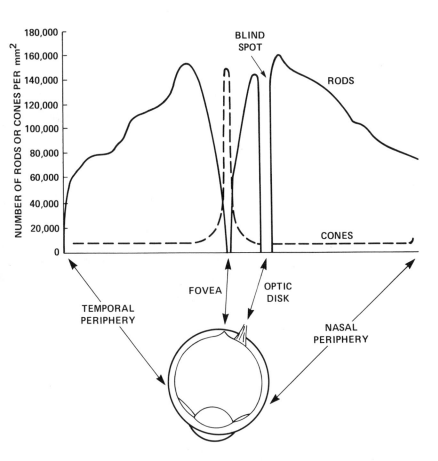

Figure 4.1.   Distribution of rods and cones for the right eye as seen from above. The complete absence of cones in the fovea and the high density of rods in the near periphery should be noted. (After Sekuler & Blake, 1985.)

ty of anatomical function, referred to as the *duplex,* or *duplicity, theory of vision,* has important implications for seeing, especially in aviation.

A second "dual" approach to vision is concerned with the mode or function of vision. The characteristics of the visual system which deal with recognition (e.g., reading or recognizing objects) are different in many important respects from those that deal with orientation (e.g., walking or steering a vehicle). This distinction is referred to as the "two modes of processing visual information."

Duplicity Theory of Vision: Rods and Cones

A convenient way to introduce the implications of the differences between rods and cones is in terms of an example often encountered during nighttime observations.[1] When the level of light falls below approximately that supplied by the full moon and there are no artificial light sources present, a situation often encountered in aviation, it is often not possible to see a small object by looking directly at it. The reason is related to the fact that the cones and the rods have different functional and anatomical properties. With respect to function, the cones provide superior detail, color, and motion perception but require relatively high illumination levels. Under lower light levels, the cones do not respond but, fortunately, vision is then mediated by the rod receptors, which require much less light for activation. The rods, however, provide a much poorer quality of vision than the cones, as they are completely insensitive to color and are less sensitive to fine detail and to movement. Because under high illumination levels normally encountered in the majority of everyday activities, superior detail, color, and motion perception is achieved with cone vision, we habitually move our eyes so that the images of objects fall on a region in the center of the retina, the fovea, which contains the highest density of cones, but no rods. In effect, to "look at" an object means to align the object with the cone-rich foveal region of the retina. The foveal region is relatively small, subtending a visual angle about the width of viewing our thumb when our arm is extended, but it transmits almost all of the visual information about objects.

---

[1]Numerous texts on vision, perception, human factors, and psychology include a description of the anatomical and functional differences between rods and cones. Two particularly useful references, which also describe sensory and perceptual functions and mechanisms, are *Eye and Brain* (Gregory, 1978) and *Perception* (Sekuler & Blake, 1985).

The problem arises under low light levels because the fovea contains only cones, and central vision becomes functionally "blind." Fortunately, outside of the fovea the retina has a plentiful supply of rods (approximately 120 million) so that under low light levels, it is still possible to see small, dim objects by pointing the eyes so as to image objects on a region of the retina containing rods. This can be accomplished by looking to the side of rather than directly at an object. Because virtually all observations normally take place under light levels high enough to activate the foveal cones, we have developed a strong tendency to position our eyes to ensure foveal vision by looking directly at objects. However, in order to see small objects at night, we must at times temporarily disregard this well-practiced habit and purposely look to the side of small objects. Although this seems unnatural at first, it can be learned and is an effective technique. The reader can demonstrate this by looking at dim stars on a clear night. Some of them will be invisible with direct viewing but will be discernible with indirect vision. Since the maximum density of rods is found about 10° from the fovea, the visibility of dim objects is maximized by looking approximately one hand width (held at arm's length) away from them.

Implications for Aviation. In aviation, a common task is the visual detection of other aircraft at night. This is usually not a problem in clear weather because aircraft are equipped with lights. However, in bad weather the intensity of these lights may be reduced so that they are no longer visible by direct observation. In this case, detection will be enhanced by looking to the side of areas of interest. This same technique is also effective when searching for marginally visible objects on the ground. The important principle to remember is that under low illumination the central field of vision becomes functionally blind, so that we must adopt an unnatural mode of looking to the side of objects. This enhances their visibility by imaging them on a portion of the retina containing rods.

It should be noted that this technique will not improve the visibility of red objects or red lights. The reason is that, although for white or nonred objects the rods are more sensitive than the cones, for red, the rods and cones have the same sensitivity. For blue lights, the rods will be activated by energy levels 1000 times less than the cones! Because the rods do not mediate color, only shades of gray, the enhanced visibility of nonred objects with the rods is achieved at the expense of a loss of color perception.

The reader may ask why red is utilized so frequently in warning lights in view of the fact that we are relatively insensitive to red. Part of the answer is that red has been traditionally associated with danger, so that red lights carry an important implicit message. This is an example of "color coding," the use of color to convey important information. If a red light is seen at all, some red color, depending upon the relative mixture of rods and cones, will be perceived. However, nonred lights, even though they can be detected at lower intensity levels, may be perceived as colorless. To be effective, some warning lights must not only be visible but also convey information by means of color. The use of red and green lights on planes and ships to regulate passing patterns would be compromised in the absence of color. The tradition of using red lights for danger is probably also related to the fact that there are very few situations outside of the aviation and marine environments in which warning lights are marginally visible. In any event, in order to maximize the effectiveness of our visual system it is helpful to be aware of its basic characteristics. Such information can be invaluable during demanding or marginal visibility situations.

Two Modes of Processing Visual Information

A second duality is related to the function or mode of vision, specifically whether the visual task involves object recognition or visual guidance (Leibowitz & Post, 1982). This distinction was suggested by studies of brain function in animals. In the early 1960s, Gerald Schneider of the Massachusetts Institute of Technology discovered that the effect on vision of destroying brain tissue in the hamster depends on the function being tested. The hamsters in Schneider's study were required to first position themselves in a certain location and then to visually differentiate between two patterns. When he removed the outer layer of the brain (or cortex), the animals were no longer able to distinguish between the different patterns. This result was to be expected from previous studies of animals as well as brain-injured humans. However, in spite of the hamsters' inability to recognize patterns, they were still able to position themselves or orient normally. Furthermore, if he removed a different part of the brain in other animals, these hamsters were no longer able to orient but, if positioned at the appropriate location, were able to recognize the different patterns!

These results, along with other studies, suggest that there are two different kinds of visual functions that depend on which part of the brain is involved. For the purposes of this chapter, we will not be concerned with brain anatomy but rather with the implications of the two modes of processing for performance. One mode is concerned with pattern recognition, the other with visual guidance. This distinction is illustrated by an experience familiar to us, that is, walking and reading at the same time. Although our attention is dominated, if not completely absorbed, by the reading material, we are nevertheless able to walk normally and to avoid obstacles even in unfamiliar surroundings. For the purpose of analyzing human performance, there are in effect two independent kinds of vision concerned with either recognition or visual guidance.

Some Implications of the Two Modes of Processing

One of the problems encountered in modern technology arises from the fact that in the twentieth century humans are now required to perform tasks which we never faced during the entire previous history of humankind. Until the advent of automobiles and airplanes, we moved by walking or running at relatively slow speeds, compared to those encountered in vehicular transportation. During self-locomotion, our sensory capacities are quite adequate to permit us to avoid obstacles and to recognize hazards. When our ancestors were transported on land, it was on horseback or by horse-drawn carriages, which extended the range over which they could travel without imposing unusual demands on their sensory capacities. However, with the advent of the automobile and the airplane, transportation speeds have been suddenly increased to many times those encountered in walking, running, or on horseback. At these higher speeds, the mechanisms which were highly adaptive for self-locomotion or travel on horseback become the basis for major human factors problems in transportation safety. A convenient way to introduce this topic is to analyze the problem of automobile accidents, before considering the implications for aviation.

A challenging problem for human factors engineers is to understand the basis of automobile accidents, which result in more than 50,000 deaths annually. If we understand the basis of accidents, or any other behavior, we are in a much better position to propose corrective measures. The two modes of processing visual information may provide an answer. As suggested by the reading and walking example mentioned in the previous section, recognition requires attention, while visual guidance can be carried out with little if any awareness. The low attention requirement for visually guided behavior is very convenient. It permits us to engage in routine activities "automatically" while we devote our limited attentive capacities to unpredictable and irregular events in our environment which require conscious recognition. Clearly, the ability to move automatically has many advantages when the mode of transportation is walking or running. However, the lack of awareness during visually guided behavior can have serious consequences while driving a vehicle. If our attention lapses while we are walking, we may fail to recognize a person or object. Although this may be potentially embarassing or inconvenient, the consequences are minor compared to lapses of attention while driving a car or piloting an airplane. Human factors analysis of automobile accidents reveals that the most frequent cause of accidents is "looking without seeing" (Shinar, 1978). At night, of course, many hazards such as pedestrians, trucks, railway cars, animals, objects on the roadbed, or potholes are simply not visible. However, "looking without seeing" occurs frequently during daylight even when the hazards are clearly visible.

The basis for these accidents follows from the dual nature of vision and the fact that we can guide or steer our vehicles with very little attentional effort. If, due to inattentiveness we fail to recognize a hazard, we nevertheless maintain the same vehicle speed, all too often with disastrous consequences. In effect, the ability to carry out two activities simultaneously, which is so valuable in everyday activities such as walking, eating, typing, and the like, can be the basis for accidents when the activity involves vehicle guidance. Many of us have suddenly realized while driving that we were not paying attention to the roadway. In most cases, there were no adverse consequences because the only requirement was to maintain the vehicle within the prescribed highway limits, but if a hazard had been present, we could have failed to recognize it in time.

The ability to steer without awareness is particularly applicable to the problem of night driving which, on a mileage basis, is almost four times more hazardous than driving during daylight. As with most accidents, it is unlikely that the high nighttime rate could be attributed to any single factor. Driving at night often interferes with sleep habits, and drinking alcohol is more common at night than during daylight. However, there is evidence that the ability to see can play a significant role, as indicated by the reduction in accidents over highways which have been illuminated artificially. The reduced accident rate following the introduction of overhead lights suggests that visual capabilities play a role. Another indication of the importance of illumination is given by the accident rates in northern European cities which, because of their short day lengths in winter and their long day lengths in summer, provide a "natural" experimental situation. In these cities, more accidents occur during darkness than during comparable daylight hours, further supporting the assumption that the reduced illumination level contributes to nighttime accidents (Boyce, 1981).

We know from numerous experimental studies as well as everyday experience that nighttime vision is poorer than vision during daylight. Even when there is adequate illumination to see with direct vision, the ability to appreciate detail is degraded. For example, when the lights are turned down, it is more difficult to read or to find an object which has fallen on the floor. However, in spite of this common knowledge, most drivers do not slow down at night. This practice is undoubtedly responsible for many nighttime accidents. Analysis of nighttime pedestrian accidents reveals that inability to see in time to take evasive action is a major factor in most accidents. In approximately 25% of nighttime pedestrian accidents, the sound of the impact was heard before the pedestrian was seen! In effect, most motorists "overdrive" their headlights by maintaining nighttime highway speeds which do not permit them to see hazards in time to take evasive action (Shinar, 1978).

The distressingly high nighttime accident rate may have a logical explanation in terms of the dual nature of vision (Leibowitz & Owens, 1986). Driving is a dual task in which we perform a sequence of motor responses automatically while simultaneously directing our attention to the immediate environment. The speed at which we drive is determined in part by the posted limits as well as by our own estimate of the safe speed. The key to understanding the particular hazards of night driving may be the introduction of a novel factor, the selective degradation of visual abilities at night. Everyone "knows" that we do not see as well under low illumination. Visual scientists have systematically documented the degradation in vision under various illumination levels, as illustrated by the curve labeled "recognition" in Figure 4.2 (Leibowitz & Shupert, 1984). This curve represents the relative visual efficiency of recognition vision, that is, the ability to appreciate fine detail or depth, as a function of the available illumination. As illumination is increased, these visual abilities improve until they reach a stable value at higher illumination levels. (The two branches of the curve are related to whether rods or cones are involved.) There is a wealth of information in this curve. One aspect is particularly critical for night driving. Note that although the light levels typically encountered during night driving involve the cones, there is a precipitous loss in efficiency. As a con-

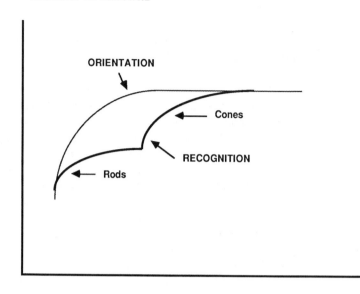

LOG LUMINANCE

Figure 4.2.   The relative efficiency of recognition and orientation vision as a function of luminance. The maximum has been arbitrarily equated for the two functions. (After Leibowitz & Shupert, 1984.)

sequence of this loss it is much more difficult, if not impossible, to see unlit low contrast objects such as pedestrians, objects on the road, potholes, trucks, or trains.

Perhaps because appreciation of detail is so important in many visual tasks, such as reading, most of the studies in the vision literature are concerned with visual acuity or resolving power. However, vision also plays a critical role in everyday adjustment because it contributes to our ability to locomote. Consider the example discussed above in which we read and walk simultaneously. This would be impossible without the outer portions or periphery of the visual field. In fact, normal locomotion is extremely difficult in the absence of peripheral vision, as is evident if you try walking around while looking through a tube or opening provided by your cupped hands. Clearly, vision plays a dual role, as it is involved with recognition as well as visual guidance. Recently it was discovered that illumination is not as critical for visual guidance as it is for recognition. Referring again to Figure 4.2, note that the curve marked "orientation" remains flat for illuminance levels at which the recognition curve is dropping sharply. In fact, the efficiency of visual guidance is unaffected until illuminance levels are extremely low, in the vicinity of the absolute threshold for rod vision.

Selective degradation is also illustrated by the familiar task of reading and walking. This dual task can be readily accomplished during the day, but at night, even though it is no longer possible to read, one can still locomote without difficulty!

Selective degradation is thought to be a major factor contributing to the high nighttime accident rate. Under daylight conditions, both the ability to guide the vehicle, or steer, and the ability to recognize hazards are maximally efficient. However, as night approaches, the ability to recognize hazards is systematically impaired, while the ability to steer is unaffected. Unfortunately, there is no indication to drivers that their recognition vision has been degraded. In fact, because the ability to steer has not changed, drivers' confidence in their driving ability is not altered. Studies have demonstrated that drivers do not typically slow down at night, an observation which is consistent with this analysis. The net result is that many motorists overdrive their headlights and are not able to recognize unlit hazards in time to avoid accidents (Leibowitz & Owens, 1986).

Another way to consider the implications of selective degradation is in terms of self-confidence. Rational motorists will choose speeds at which they feel self-confident regarding their ability to take evasive action if an emergency should arise. We drive more slowly in the vicinity of a school or playground than on an interstate, and faster in clear, dry weather than during a snowstorm. When we are aware of it. In effect, selective degradation results in unjustified self-confidence, with the result that we assume dangerous risks by driving too fast during twilight and at night. Because we can steer efficiently, we are simply unprepared for the infrequent demands on our degraded visual recognition system. This is a good example of the dictum that "it is not the devil we know but the one we do not know that will cause difficulty." In order to take precautions against a threat, we must first be aware of it. For this reason, selective degradation and the associated unjustified self-confidence should be considered as one of a class of "silent killers" which pose a threat to safety unless special steps are taken to make us aware of them.
sidered as one of a class of "silent killers" which pose a threat to safety unless special steps are taken to make us aware of them.

Unjustified self-confidence may result from factors in addition to the selective degradation of vision. Even small amounts of alcohol artificially enhance our feelings of well-being and promote self-confidence. Alcohol is particularly dangerous in aviation because its effects are exacerbated with altitude. It is not surprising that so many accidents of all types are alcohol related. Paradoxically, self-confidence may also be enhanced by experience. As we drive a car or pilot an airplane successfully, the possibility of a mishap seems progressively more remote. This in turn leads to a lowered "perceived risk" and reduced vigilance. The fact that up to a certain point the accident rate for novice pilots *increases* with experience is probably related to this phenomenon. Unjustified self-confidence can arise from sensory as well as nonsensory factors, all of which are encountered in aviation. Since we are not normally aware of them, the best countermeasure is knowledge of their origins and implications.

Implications for Aviation: Nighttime Landing Accidents

The hazardous implications of the dual modes of vision are particularly relevant to aviation. Both driving an automobile and flying an airplane are dual-mode tasks, one mode of which is carried out automatically with little or no conscious awareness. Although this has advantages during self-locomotion, it can pose difficulties when the pilot is unaware that there is a change in the accuracy requirement of the automatic task.

When the Boeing 727 aircraft was first introduced into commercial service in the late 1960s it was involved in a large number of landing accidents. Investigation of these accidents revealed that there was no reason to suspect mechanical or structural failure. Conrad Kraft, a human factors engineer with the Boeing Company, noted that there were striking similarities among the circumstances of these accidents. They all involved landing short of the runway at night under clear visibility conditions. Furthermore, the area under the aircraft during the approach was dark, either water or unilluminated terrain (a "dark hole" approach). Based on these observations, Kraft initiated a series of experiments to determine whether some previously unsuspected visual factor may have been involved. It is not feasible to carry out such studies with real aircraft. Rather, he utilized a flight simulator from which the pilot viewed a scene similar to that which would be encountered during a nighttime visual landing (see Figure 4.3; Kraft, 1978).

Based on the pattern of circumstances of the accidents, Kraft suspected that the pilots may have assumed that their altitude during the approach to the runway was higher than was actually the case. He tested this possibility by eliminating the altimeter from the simulator and asking the pilots to visually estimate their altitude during

Figure 4.3.   Night visual approach simulator and typical nighttime scene. (After Kraft, 1978.)

the approach to a simulated nighttime landing. The results indicated that even the most experienced pilots thought they were higher than was actually the case. He then asked them to fly a typical approach without reference to an altimeter. Typical results are given in Figure 4.4, which presents the flown altitude as a function of distance from the runway. The upper curve is the altitude at which they should have been during a normal landing. The bottom curve represents the estimated altitude. These data clearly indicate that under these special conditions (nighttime, clear weather, and landing approach over dark terrain), pilots may visually overestimate their altitude. As a consequence, they tend to fly too low, and if not aware of the error in time, they may land short of the runway. In addition to data obtained from the simulator, Kraft documented a number of reports from pilots of "near misses" under these same conditions, in which pilots discovered that they were flying too low in time to take correc-

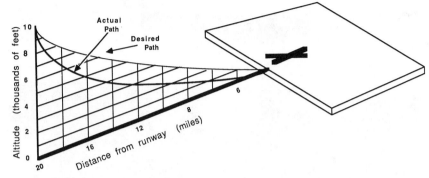

Figure 4.4.   Comparison of the approach path flown by pilots during a night visual
approach with the desired altitudes. Altitude is in thousands of feet; distance from the runway is in miles. (After Kraft, 1978.)

tive action. Such reports confirm the validity of the simulator studies
and support the hypothesis that an error in the visual estimation of
altitude played a major role in the pattern of nighttime accidents
(Kraft, 1978).

These data should raise questions in the mind of the reader. Since
all aircraft are equipped with altimeters, why would a pilot rely on
visual estimates of height during a critical phase of landing? A possible answer is related to the fact that landing an aircraft is perhaps
the most demanding task faced by pilots. During approach and landing, pilots must carefully monitor the speed of the aircraft, adjust the
power settings of the engines, steer the aircraft in three-dimensional
space, respond to instructions from the ground controller, and be
alert for other aircraft in line with the see-and-avoid principle. Given
these multiple responsibilities, it is understandable that pilots may
assign a lower priority or even fail to check the altimeter if they feel
confident that visual estimates of altitude are accurate. When faced
with multiple responsibilities, we typically set priorities and direct
our attention to those events which we assume pose the greatest
threat under the circumstances.

This situation is similar to that described above in which drivers
of automobiles are confident that they can see as well at night as
during the day and do not take the necessary precautions to compensate for the degradation in their ability to recognize hazards. A common factor in both of these situations is the dual nature of the visual
process and the fact that the orientation mode is carried out without
awareness. In the case of pilots, they are misled into believing that

their ability to estimate altitude visually is as accurate at night as during daylight. In view of this unjustified self-confidence, and when faced with a number of highly demanding tasks, it is understandable that they may not confirm their visual estimates of altitude by reference to the altimeter.

Immediately after Kraft's research was completed, commercial airlines instituted corrective measures by informing the pilots of the conditions under which a false estimate of altitude might be encountered. As a consequence, some airlines have adopted a procedure in which the copilot is required to monitor the altimeter during approach and to call out the altitudes at regular intervals to the pilot, whose attention is directed outside the cockpit. These measures along with other precautions have effectively eliminated inadvertent visual overestimation of altitude as a factor contributing to nighttime landing accidents in commercial aviation. For his contribution to air safety, Dr. Kraft has received awards from the International Air Safety Foundation and the American Psychological Association.

The effectiveness of Kraft's research is based both on the identification of a source of misinformation in flying and the effective dissemination of this information to pilots. Both of these steps are essential in public safety. Whenever our sensory systems do not normally inform us directly about hazards in our environment, it is necessary to communicate this information to the public through education. Unfortunately there are many hazards in our society of which we are not normally aware through our senses, such as carbon monoxide gas produced by internal combustion engines, radiation hazards from the medical use of X rays, and high blood pressure. Thanks to effective education, the public is now more aware of these hazards. Dissemination of information regarding the hazards of night visual approaches has been particularly successful and serves as a reminder of the necessity and effectiveness of human factors engineering and public education.

Visual–Vestibular Interaction: Spatial Disorientation and Motion Sickness

In the early days of aviation, pilots who flew into clouds would frequently become disoriented. They could not determine whether the plane was flying straight or turning, whether the wings were level with respect to the ground, or in some cases even if the aircraft was right side up or upside down. Failure to maintain proper spatial orientation when the ground was obscured was originally thought to result from a lack of diligence or an avoidable pilot error which could be overcome if the pilot were more attentive or tried harder. One of the pioneers in military aviation was convinced that pilots could not possibly maintain their orientation when the ground was not visible and was sent to a hospital on two separate occasions to determine if he was sane!

We now know that reliable spatial orientation in an aircraft when the ground is not visible is an impossible task if pilots must rely exclusively on their senses. The reason is related to the fact that spatial orientation is not determined by vision alone, but rather by the interaction between vision and the vestibular system. Most of us are not aware of our vestibular system because it operates without our conscious knowledge, rarely exhibits deficiencies, and is located completely inside the bones of the skull (near the organ of hearing). It informs us about the position of our head and when it is moving. This is accomplished by means of the response of vestibular receptors to the movement of fluids in a manner analogous to what would happen if we were to fasten a piece of thread to the bottom of a glass of water, as illustrated in Figure 4.5. If the glass is not moving, as in Figure 4.5 (A), the thread will point upward. If the glass is moved to the right, the water will pile up on the left side of the glass due to its inertia and bend the thread to the left in the direction opposite to the movement (B). This illustrates how the vestibular system actually works. Movement of fluid bends hairlike cells in the direction *opposite* to body motion; these cells then send nervous impulses to the brain to signal movement of the head.

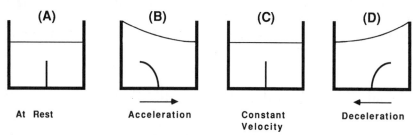

Figure 4.5.   Schematic illustration of the response of the vestibular receptors. (A), at rest; (B), acceleration to the right; (C), constant velocity; (D), deceleration. Note that the position of the hair cells which signal movement are the same during rest and constant velocity, and that the bending (and sensory signal) is in opposite directions during movement to the right, depending upon the direction of the accelerative force.

The complication with this system can be illustrated by considering what occurs when the movement is slowed down or decelerated, as illustrated in Figure 4.5 (C). In this case the fluid shifts to the right and bends the hair cells in the *same* direction as the movement of the body. The signal sent to the brain is that the head is moving in a direction opposite to the bending of the hair cells. Even though the head movement is to the right, the vestibular system is signalling motion to the left. This is a common situation which is encountered whenever a vehicle in which we are traveling slows down. If our eyes were closed and we had no other information about our body movement we would in fact feel that we are moving in the opposite direction. Similarly if we are moving to the right and suddenly stopped (D) the inertia of the fluids will continue to move and bend the hair cells to the right, with the result that the vestibular system signals motion to the left even though the body is actually stationary!

A false signal also occurs when we are moving at a *constant* speed. In this case, the fluid is level and the hair cells are vertical, the same as is the case when we are not moving. If we were to rely on the vestibular system alone for information, we would have the false impression that we were motionless.

These examples illustrate the fact that the vestibular system signals the correct motion of our bodies only when our body speed is increasing or when we have not been moving for several seconds. Under other possible conditions, the signal from the vestibular system is incorrect.

Many airplane accidents occurred before the source of the false signals from the vestibular system was properly appreciated. The solution to the problem is that pilots must *never* rely on sensations from their vestibular systems nor from the pressure exerted on their bodies. The expression "one cannot fly by the seat of the pants" reflects the possibility of erroneous sensations from the vestibular system or from body pressure when the ground is not visible. Pilots must learn to rely on their instruments and to disregard their body sensations no matter how compelling they might be. Fortunately, history has vindicated our hapless military pioneer.

Thanks to recent advances in our understanding of the mechanisms of spatial orientation, we can now reanalyze the problem of disorientation in aircraft in a more general context. We are not ordinarily aware of the many instances in our daily lives when false signals are sent from the vestibular system. When we slow down in an automobile, we do not have the impression that we are moving backwards, as would be the case if we relied completely on our vestibular system. The visual impression of movement normally corrects or overrides the vestibular signal. This is an example of *visual–vestibular interaction*, a process by which the visual and vestibular signals interact to inform us accurately about the movement of our bodies. In effect, spatial orientation is a joint function of the interaction between the visual and vestibular systems. However, when the vestibular system is activated in the absence of normal visual inputs, as occurs regularly in aircraft, erroneous sensations may result.

The normal pattern of interaction between the visual and vestibular signals is that the visual scene moves in a direction opposite to head motion. When we move our heads to the right, the visual scene moves to the left, and vice versa. This relationship is extremely well learned because it occurs literally thousands of times in our daily lives. However, a serious problem occurs when the normal expected pattern of visual and vestibular signals is altered in a moving vehicle. Consider a pilot flying under conditions where the ground is not visible. If the aircraft moves to the right, the visual scene provided by the inside of the cockpit will not move in the opposite direction, as is typically the case in the majority of the individual's previous experiences, but rather, in the same direction. This is an example of a *visual–vestibular mismatch*; the relationship between the visual scene and the vestibular signals is different from what is normally encountered. The visual information signals no motion but the vestibular signal and the pressures from the seat indicate motion to the right.

This situation poses a dilemma for pilots. Because vision provides most of the information about the external world, we tend to rely on visual information. However, the inside of the aircraft provides no information about vehicle motion because it is subject to the same motion as the pilot and, therefore, will always be stationary with respect to the pilot. If pilots close their eyes, they may receive erroneous signals from the vestibular system and from body pressure. The solution to this problem is to deliberately ignore both the view of the cockpit and the vestibular signals and rely on the interpretation of instruments.

Spatial Disorientation

Serious problems may be encountered when pilots rely on their sensations rather than the information from instruments. A dramatic case occurred in 1978, when a Boeing 747 aircraft crashed into the ocean during takeoff from Bombay, India, on a dark night. Investigations assigned the probable cause of the accident to the failure of the pilot to correctly interpret the information from the attitude indicator (Fitzgerald, 1985). This was fortunately an extremely rare event in the history of commercial aviation, but it does serve to remind us that under stress we often become less efficient both at disregarding our habitual modes of perception and at utilizing skills which were learned at later stages of our lives.

A less serious situation arises when pilots report that they feel disoriented, even though they know from their instruments that this is not the case. For example, after completing a turn, the pilot may feel that the plane is still banked, even though the instruments indicate that the aircraft's wings are level. This illusion, referred to as the "leans," may persist for a half hour or more but will disappear suddenly when the ground is again visible (Benson, 1978a). Most probably, this disorientation results from a visual–vestibular mismatch.

Disorientation occurs occasionally in commercial aviation, but the consequences are rarely serious because most aircraft are crewed by two pilots and equipped with automatic piloting equipment. However, disorientation is a serious problem in military aviation. A successful fighter pilot deliberately pushes his aircraft to its performance limits, which exacerbates the mismatch between the visual and vestibular systems. Many fighter planes have only a single pilot, who is often in situations where transfer to automatic equipment is not tactically feasible. As an aid to prevention of spatial disorientation in high-performance aircraft, Malcolm, Money, and Anderson (1975) have proposed that an image of a ground-stable horizon be projected onto the instrument panel. This artificial horizon would be coupled to and assume the same position as the artificial horizon in the attitude indicator, but it would be much larger. The rationale behind this system is that the larger artificial horizon, referred to as the *Malcolm horizon*, provides a more direct input to the spatial orientation system in a manner analogous to the role of visual contours in everyday life. It is well known that the effectiveness of visual contours in maintaining spatial orientation is related to their size, so that the large artificial horizon should serve as a more natural spatial orientation stimulus, which should be processed more automatically and more quickly than the information from the small, conventional instruments. This system, which is consistent with our current knowledge of the nature of visual–vestibular interaction, is currently undergoing field testing ("Peripheral Vison," 1984).

The role of earth-stable visual cues in preventing disorientation is illustrated by an incident in which a fighter pilot, flying above the clouds at a high altitude, became severely disoriented. He asked the ground controller at what altitude the ground would be visible and immediately descended below the clouds. As soon as the ground was visible, his disorientation symptoms disappeared. Ground-stable contours, which appear to move *against* head motion, as is normally the case, are an effective antidote against disorientation.

The interaction of visual and vestibular cues is dramatically illustrated by accidents involving the takeoff of aircraft from carriers. Because the short length of carriers does not permit aircraft to attain flying speeds under their own power, they are propelled off the end of the carrier deck by powerful launching equipment. A number of accidents occurred during this process in which the pilots put the nose of the aircraft downward and crashed into the water. Malcolm Cohen, an aviation psychologist now at NASA's Ames Research Center, has explained this effect in terms of the distortion of the direction of "down." Ordinarily, we perceive down in terms of both gravitational and visual cues. In an aircraft at night, the visual cues are absent, and when it is launched from a carrier, the direction of down is altered. As a result of the inertia of the body during a launching, the pilot feels as if he is tilted backward (Figure 4.6), so that the perceived attitude of an actually level aircraft is that it is pitched backwards (Benson, 1978a). In some cases, pilots apparently responded to this illusion by pitching the plane forward and were unable to discover their error before crashing into the water. This type of illusion can occur whenever gravitational forces are suddenly altered. Figure 4.6 also illustrates the case in which sudden deceleration creates an illusion of leaning forward.

Motion Sickness

Most of us have been motion sick at one time or another and are familiar with its symptoms. Motion sickness has been known for centuries to crews and passengers on ships. Some individuals become ill in automobiles or airplanes, and many theories have been proposed to explain these distressing symptoms. Recently, an explanation has been proposed which suggests that both spatial disorientation and motion sickness result from a visual–vestibular mismatch (Benson, 1978b, Reason, 1974, Reason & Brand, 1974). A passenger in the cabin of a ship will be subject to a mismatch whenever the ship moves, since the visual scene moves with, rather than against, body motion. Procedures which are recommended to combat seasick-

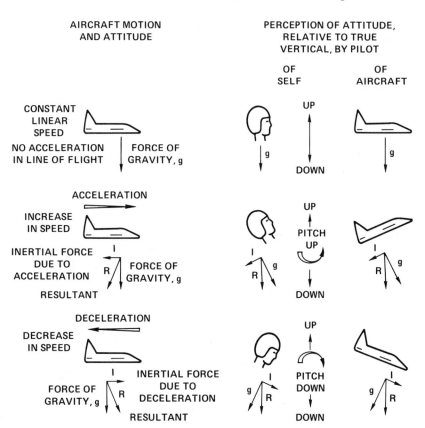

Figure 4.6.   Diagram illustrating the relationship between acceleration and perceived attitude. Note that the aircraft is flying level in all cases. (After Benson, 1987b.)

ness, such as closing ones eyes or observing the stable horizon, serve to reduce this mismatch. Analysis of the conditions which result in car sickness are also consistent with this hypothesis. Passengers report fewer symptoms when riding in the front rather than the back seat of an automobile. This has been attributed to the fact that the view from the rear seat includes more of the interior of the car, which will move *with* the motion of the vehicle and produce a visual–vestibular mismatch. Reading in an automobile also increases the percentage of the visual scene which moves with vehicle motion, and this also exaggerates symptoms in susceptible individuals. As with spatial disorientation, measures which increase the number and size of visual contours which move *with* head motion tend to prevent motion sickness. When passengers on a ship view the horizon, they frequently report that motion sickness is eliminated or reduced.

A particularly interesting manifestation of motion sickness that occurs in flight simulators is *simulator sickness* (McCauley, 1984). Some pilots, who rarely become ill in actual flight, report that they become motion sick in the simulator. This phenomenon is interpretable in terms of the mismatch hypothesis. Although the visual contours accurately represent those which are normally encountered in actual flight, the vestibular cues are absent. In effect, the lack of appropriate vestibular cues creates a visual–vestibular mismatch. Support for this interpretation comes from the observation that the pilots with the most actual flying experience are more likely to experience motion sickness in a simulator. For the more experienced pilots, the absence of vestibular cues represents a greater mismatch compared with previous experience than would be the case for novice pilots. It is interesting to note that experience either in real flight or in a simulator reduces sickness for that particular condition but increases the probability of discomfort in the other condition. In effect, experience with a particular pattern of interaction provides a baseline of normal "expectations" so that any deviation then becomes a mismatch. This interpretation is consistent with the familiar observation that passengers on a ship are more likely to become ill than the more experienced crew and that susceptibility to the ship's motion diminishes with exposure. When returning to land, mild symptoms of motion sickness may be experienced at first *(mal de débarquement)*.

Illusions of spatial orientation and the conditions which lead to motion sickness nicely illustrate the importance of the normal pattern of interaction between visual and vestibular cues. False information from either sense will normally be compensated by the other. However, in the absence of either normal visual or vestibular inputs, false or atypical information from the other modality may result in spatial disorientation, motion sickness, or both.

Research on these problems is currently under way in a number of laboratories, and it would be inaccurate to suggest that we completely understand spatial disorientation and motion sickness. However, the results to date are encouraging because they have identified common elements in a variety of normal and abnormal phenomena. As we understand these basic mechanisms, we will be in a better position to propose ameliorative procedures.

Spatial disorientation and motion sickness illustrate a common theme in human factors engineering. Because vision is the dominant sense among humans, any change in the pattern of visual inputs that interferes with well-practiced habits may cause difficulties. This is a reoccurring theme in this chapter. When we are transported passively in vehicles at speeds which exceed those encountered in self-loco-motion, our visual systems may not be adequate, for the variety of reasons outlined in this chapter. Interference with the normal operation of our sensory systems in aviation is of particular interest because of the normal coupling of vision and the vestibular system in spatial orientation. It is hoped that the description of the basic mechanisms underlying these problems will not only help the reader to understand the basis of the difficulties encountered to date but also serve to aid in the solution of problems, such as those associated with space flight, which are certain to arise in the future. As technology advances, the demands on humans and our need to understand our capabilities and limitations will undoubtedly increase. For example, one of the most serious problems in the manned space program is the debilitating motion sickness experienced during the initial stages of weightlessness (Reason, 1974). Scientists concerned with the problem suspect that a mismatch between the part of the vestibular system which responds to changes in position and that which is sensitive to movement may be responsible.

Perception of Motion

One of the most important dimensions of vision is the perception of motion. In order to interact with the environment, it is essential that we know when we and the objects in the environment are stationary or moving and, if in motion, how fast and in which direction we or the observed objects are moving. This may strike the reader as a strange statement, because except in rare instances there are very few problems with motion perception on earth. However, in the aviation environment there are many instances in which errors or illusions of motion perception are encountered. There are two different kinds of motion—perception of the motion of our own bodies and perception of the motion of objects such as other aircraft.

Self-Motion. The possibility of errors or illusions of self-motion was introduced in the discussion of the vestibular system. In the absence of vision of the outside world, our perception of self-motion is correct only when we are accelerating or have not been moving for a few seconds. Because of the limitations of the vestibular system, vision of the external world is essential to accurate self-motion perception. In the aviation environment, it is possible to determine only roughly how fast one is moving by reference to the outside world, and it is essential to rely on instruments to ascertain the speed of the aircraft.

Object Motion.   It is important that pilots know in what direction and how fast other aircraft are moving. This is a particularly difficult visual task at night. As an example, consider what happens when a pilot views a light from an aircraft at night. Every time the pilot's own aircraft changes speed, the viewed light will appear to move. If the other light is actually stationary, for example, a star, planet, or light from the ground or a ship, it may appear to the pilot to be moving, and it could look the same as the light from another aircraft. If the light is actually from another aircraft, the illusory motion could distort the true motion of the aircraft and mislead the pilot, who is trying to avoid a possible collision. This illusory sensation, referred to as the *oculogyral* illusion, rarely occurs on earth, but it is very common in aircraft at night or when lights are viewed against a background of a clear sky or clouds (Benson, 1978a, Post & Leibowitz, 1985). Since these situations are very common in aviation, there are many opportunities for false perceptions of the movement or speeds of other aircraft. A particularly dangerous situation occurs in close formation, nighttime military flights in which the pilots rely on the lights from their neighboring aircraft for guidance. Under this condition, motion of either the neighboring aircraft or one's own will result in the perceived movement of a fixated light. As with most such illusions, this is particularly dangerous because the false sensation is indistinguishable perceptually from the real situation. As pointed out above, the most dangerous perceptual errors are those about which we are not normally aware.

Limitations of Vision during Flight

Because vision is almost always accurate on earth, the natural tendency is to rely on the sense of vision during flight. It is clear however that in the aviation environment this can be dangerous. Vision is not always reliable in detecting the presence of other aircraft; it is essentially useless for perceiving self-motion in the absence of ground cues; it is subject to errors in the perception of velocity and height during nighttime or other degraded observation conditions;

and object motion perception is unreliable at night and during other impoverished observation conditions. The essential message is that pilots must be made aware of the capabilities and limitations of their visual systems and apprised of the fundamental differences between vision while self-locomoting on the ground and when in an aircraft. They must appreciate the importance of disregarding their own sensations in certain situations no matter how compelling they may be, and to rely on instruments whenever their own perceptual systems are subject to illusory or erroneous sensations.

Concluding Remarks

The study of the capabilities and limitations of the visual system in aviation is an important and challenging problem which has multiple payoffs. For the aviation community, knowledge of situations in which pilots may not be aware of hazards or may misperceive the environment is a matter of life and death. Countless accidents occurred before the characteristics and peculiarities of our sensory systems in the demanding aviation environment were fully appreciated. For the basic researcher, the aviation environment provides a natural laboratory which makes it possible to test the extent of our understanding of sensory systems. The close relationship between operational considerations and the search for scientific fundamentals has historically been fruitful for both groups. This should be even more important in the future, as the demands on humans in aviation and space pose new challenges for the engineering, medical, and behavioral sciences.

References

Allen, M. J. (1970). *Vision and highway safety*. Philadelphia: Chilton.

Benson, A. J. (1978a). Spatial disorientation (Chap. 20) and Spatial disorientation in flight (Chap. 21). In G. Dehnin, G. R. Sharp, & J. Ernsting (Eds.), *Aviation medicine* (Vol. 1, pp. 405–467). London: Tri-Med Books.

Benson, A. J. (1978b). Motion sickness (Chap. 22). In G. Dehnin, G. R. Sharp, & J. Ernsting (Eds.), *Aviation medicine* (Vol. 1, pp. 468–493). London: Tri-Med Books.

Boyce, P. R. (1981). *Human factors in lighting*. New York: Macmillan.

Fitzgerald, J. M. (1985). *Findings and conclusions, air crash disaster near Bombay, India, January 1, 1978*. U.S. District Court Western District of Washington at Seattle, MDL No. 359.

Gregory, R. L. (1978). *Eye and brain*. New York: McGraw Hill.

Kraft, C. L. (1978). A psychophysical contribution to air safety: Simulator studies of visual illusions in night visual approaches. In H. Pick, H. W. Leibowitz, J. R. Singer, A. Steinschneider, & H. W. Stevenson (Eds.), *Psychology from research to practice* (pp. 363–385). New York: Plenum.

Leibowitz, H. W., & Owens, D. A. (1986). We drive by night. *Psychology Today, 20,* #1, 54–58.

Leibowitz, H. W., Post, R. B., Brandt, T., & Dichgans, J. (1982). Implications of recent developments in dynamic spatial orientation and visual resolution for vehicle guidance. In A. Wertheim, W. A. Wagenaar, & H. W. Leibowitz (Eds.), *Tutorials on motion perception* (pp. 231–260). New York: Plenum.

Leibowitz, H. W., & Shupert, C. L. (1984). Low luminance and spatial orientation. *Proceedings of the tri-service aeromedical research panel, Fall, 1984.* Pensacola, Florida: Naval Aeromedical Research Laboratory.

Malcolm, R., Money, K. E., & Anderson, P. J. (1975). Peripheral vision artificial display. *AGARD Conference Proceedings No. 145 on Vibration and Stress in Advanced Systems* (B20-1-B20-3).

McCauley, M. E. (1984). *Simulator sickness: Proceedings of a workshop.* Washington, DC: National Academy Press.

Peripheral vision horizon display (PVHD). (1984). *Proceedings of a Conference Held at NASA-Ames Research Center, Dryden Flight Facility, Edwards. CA, March 1983.* NASA conferences publication No. 2306.

Post, R. B., & Leibowitz, H. W. (1985). A revised analysis of the role of efference in motion perception. *Perception, 14,* 631–643.

Reason, J. R. (1974). *Man in motion.* New York: Walker.

Reason, J. R., & Brand, J. J. (1974). *Motion sickness.* London/New York: Academic Press.

Sekuler, R., and Blake, R. (1985). *Perception.* New York: Knopf.

Shinar, D. (1978). *Psychology on the road.* New York: Wiley.

Information Processing

5

Christopher D. Wickens
John M. Flach

Introduction

The use of analogy or metaphor is a powerful heuristic of science. That is, scientists approach new, mysterious phenomena by comparing them to things that are familiar, things that are understood. For psychologists, the human–computer analogy has proven to be a powerful stimulus for generating research and theories about human performance. It has been particularly useful to engineering psychologists in building models of how humans interact with systems such as aircraft, ships, and computers themselves. These models by their nature require a common language for describing the behavior of both humans and machines.

The human–computer analogy forms the foundation for the study of human information processing. However, other analogies have also contributed in shaping theories of human performance. Norbert Wiener's (1948) cybernetic hypothesis—the analogy of man to servomechanism—has increased awareness of the closed-loop, goal-seeking nature of human behavior. Information theory has contributed a

Human Factors in Aviation

111

number of useful metaphors for characterizing human performance, including the concept of channel capacity—so important to early models of attention and to the theory of signal detectability—which has provided a means for modeling cognitive aspects of thresholds. Finally, the analogy of the human to economic systems has contributed the idea of resources as a mechanism for modeling humans' flexibility in allocating attention across multiple tasks. As research on human information processing is reviewed in this chapter, the impact of each of these analogies will be apparent.

A principal feature of information processing models is the assumption of a series of stages or mental operations which occur between stimuli and responses. Much of the research is directed at isolating and then characterizing each of these stages. Primary attributes of a stage include its capacity (how much information?), its duration (how long can information be stored?), and its form of representation (how is information coded?). Figure 5.1 shows a typical four-stage information processing model.

The first stage in Figure 5.1 is the sensory store. It is assumed that there is a separate sensory store for each sensory modality. In the sensory store, physical energy (e.g., light) is transformed into neural energy (e.g., response of rods and cones). Information is represented

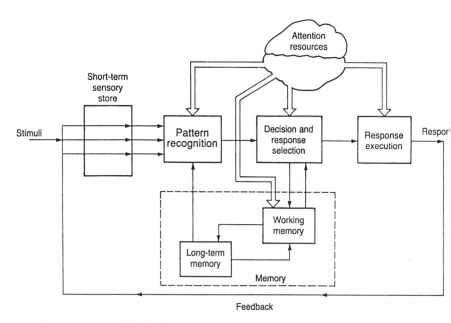

Figure 5.1. A model of information processing.

in the sensory store in terms of physical features. For example, the text on this page is represented in your visual sensory store, not as words or letters, but simply as a pattern of dark shapes against a white background. This information lasts only briefly (less than 1 second for visual sensory store) and does not require attention resources.

The second stage, pattern recognition, is probably the most important yet least understood of all the stages. It is at this stage that the "booming, buzzing confusion" of physical stimulation in the sensory stores is integrated into meaningful elements. At this stage of processing, for example, the pattern of dark shapes from this page are recognized as words and ideas, the pattern of stimulus-flow from the ground outside the aircraft is integrated as a particular aircraft elevation and airspeed, or the pattern of sounds is recognized as a particular message. This pattern recognition process involves mapping the physical codes of the sensory store into semantic or meaningful codes from memory. This mapping is very complex in that many different physical codes may all map to a single memory code (e.g., a, A, the sound "a"), and a single physical code may map to different memory codes. Perceptual processes are often limited by the supply of attention resources. For example, it would be easy to become so engrossed in landing that you fail to "hear" radio conversations. However, the communications are entering auditory sensory store and may even receive deeper analysis. This becomes apparent when your attention is "captured" by the mention of your call sign. At other times, perceptual processes may proceed well without attention, as when we process cues from the visual field to move about in a room, as our full attention is directed to thinking or talking.

The next stage is the decision and response selection stage. At this stage, a stimulus has been recognized and a decision must be made as to what to do with it. A number of options are available at this point. The information can be stored for use at some future date, it can be integrated with other available information, or it may initiate a response. Each of these options will generally be associated with potential costs and benefits which must be considered in choosing among them.

If the option chosen at the decision stage is to initiate a motor response, the response execution stage translates this intention into a coordinated sequence of motor commands. This stage interprets what may be a generally specified intention (e.g., walk or execute a flare in landing) into precisely sequenced muscle commands. The resulting responses, by way of the feedback loop, then become input to the sensory stores, which can be interpreted and entered as data relevant to selecting the next response.

In addition to the processing stages, the human information processing model contains three ways to store information: sensory store (mentioned earlier), working memory, and long-term memory. Working memory represents the information currently being used by the information processor. To use the computer metaphor, it is the "active program" running in the central processing unit. Long-term memory represents information available to the information processor, but not currently in use. Long-term memory is the storehouse of all accumulated knowledge.

An enormous amount of research has been generated by the information processing approach to human performance, and it would be impossible to thoroughly review this research in a single chapter. The aim of this chapter, therefore, is to provide the reader with a small sampling of research which both typifies the information processing approach and which has significance for applications to aviation. For a more extensive review of the information processing approach to cognitive psychology, Lachman, Lachman, and Butterfield (1979) is recommended. For applications of the information processing approach to human factors, texts by Wickens (1984a) and Kantowitz and Sorkin (1983) are good sources.

Perception

Perception involves the association of meaning to sensory stimulation. It is the process through which the marks on this page are associated with words and ideas. It is the process through which the geometry of the visual scene (e.g., apparent shape of the runway) is associated with states of the aircraft (e.g., above or below the correct glideslope). Two issues which are central to research on perception are (1) the problem of signal detection—how much energy or change must be present in the stimulus for humans to detect the stimulus or change, and (2) the problem of selection—how the human selects or abstracts from the "booming, buzzing confusion" of stimuli those which are relevant to the task at hand.

Signal Detection

As the air traffic controller scans the busy display section, a potential conflict situation develops; will he or she detect it (Bisseret, 1981)? The pilot searches the cloud-obscured world for a glimpse of the airport; when will it be seen? These are problems of signal detection. There are four possible outcomes in any signal detection task: (1) a signal (e.g., conflict situation or airport) can be present and the human can detect it (HIT); (2) a signal can be present and the human can fail to detect it (MISS); (3) the human can think the signal is present when, in fact, a signal is not present (FALSE ALARM); and (4) the human can correctly observe that no signal is present (COR-RECT REJECTION). The likelihood that each of these possible outcomes will occur is a function of sensitivity and response bias.

Sensitivity is an index of the human's ability to distinguish the signal (e.g., radio communication, radar signal, other aircraft) from noise (e.g., static, engine noise). Sensitivity will be determined by properties of the receptor system (e.g., vision and audition are limited in terms of the frequencies which they can detect), by the skill of the observer, and by properties of the environment or communication channel (e.g., amount of background noise). When sensitivity is high, the human will be very likely to detect a stimulus that is present and will be unlikely to respond to a stimulus that is not; that is, the probability of HITS and CORRECT REJECTIONS will be high, and the probability of MISSES and FALSE ALARMS will be low.

Response bias is an index of the human's decision-making crite-rion; that is, the human's tendency to respond "yes" or to respond "no." Response bias will be a function of the value of each of the four alternative outcomes and the expectancy or likelihood of a sig-nal being present. For example, in high-traffic areas the presence of other aircraft is more likely and detecting them is very important. Thus, in this phase of a mission the probability of detecting other aircraft when they are present (HITS) will be high. However, there will also be an increased probability that a speck on the windscreen will be mistaken as a signal (FALSE ALARM). When a signal is im-portant and likely, then humans should adjust the response bias so that the probability of HITS and FALSE ALARMS will be relatively high and the probability of MISSES and CORRECT REJECTIONS will be relatively low. When a signal is not important and when it is un-likely, the response bias should be adjusted so that the probability of HITS and FALSE ALARMS will be relatively low and the probability of MISSES and CORRECT REJECTIONS will be relatively high. Expe-rienced signal detectors typically do adjust their response bias as im-portance and event probability dictates. For example, Bisseret (1981) found a difference between experienced and novice air traffic con-trollers in adjusting response bias to detect impending collision situ-ations.

For human factors applications, it is important to differentiate the relative contributions of sensitivity and response bias to detection performance in optimizing the human–machine interface. Signal detection theory (SDT) accomplishes this differentiation by examining the trade-offs between HITS (e.g., seeing the aircraft when it is present) and false alarms (e.g., seeing the aircraft when it is not present). Any variable that both increases the probability of a HIT and decreases the probability of a FALSE ALARM (e.g., filtering radio static) affects sensitivity. Any variable that increases both the probability of HITS and FALSE ALARMS affects response bias. Thus, in evaluating displays for detection tasks, data must be collected on both the HIT and FALSE ALARM rates. The goal in the design of new displays should be a gain in sensitivity, since changes in response bias simply trade off one source of error (MISSES) for another (FALSE ALARMS).

An important detection problem with relevance to aviation is the vigilance decrement. That is, when a human operator is required to monitor a display for long durations, there is a decrease or decrement in HIT rate as time passes (particularly if the signal rate is low). This decrement has been attributed to changes in sensitivity resulting from fatigue (Broadbent, 1971) or memory load (Parasuraman, 1979) and to changes in bias resulting from changes in arousal (Welford, 1968) or to changes in expectancy (Baker, 1961). The particular contribution of each of these factors to the vigilance decrement will likely vary from task to task (Parasuraman & Davies, 1984; Wickens, 1984). One solution to the vigilance decrement which can ease the operator's memory load, increase arousal, and increase expectancy is to artificially increase the signal rate by introducing "false signals" which are similar to real signals (Baker, 1961; Wilkinson, 1964).

Selection

Most people, when first exposed to the task of flying an aircraft, are overwhelmed by the vast array of instruments which must be processed. Experienced pilots, on the other hand, have little difficulty monitoring their instruments. What are the fundamental limits on humans' ability to process information and how are these limits affected by experience and processing strategies? This is the problem of selection or perceptual attention.

In situations such as the aircraft cockpit, there are numerous sources of information which must be sampled periodically. How do pilots decide when to attend to a particular display? This question has been addressed by a number of researchers (Moray, 1978, 1981; Senders, 1964; Sheridan, 1972). Wickens (1987) suggests four conclusions based on this research.

First, sampling is guided by knowledge about the statistical properties of the environment. These statistical properties include frequency of events on a particular display and correlation between displays. Displays in which events occur at high frequencies will be sampled more often than displays in which events occur at low frequencies. For example, Senders (1966) cites Air Force research which indicated that the directional gyro is the most frequently sampled instrument. Also, operators are less likely to consecutively sample two displays that are highly correlated than two displays that have low correlations (Allen, Clement, & Jex, 1970; Cuqlock, 1982). Sampling a second display that is highly correlated with the first display provides little new information, whereas sampling a second display that has a low correlation with the first display provides more information. Senders (1966) shows that the frequency of transitions between the airspeed indicator and the directional gyro—two uncorrelated instruments—are high for ground-controlled approaches. Above and beyond simple statistical relations, pilots' sampling behavior will be guided by their knowledge of the coupling of systems within the aircraft. As Senders (1966) explains, "it seems reasonable to assume if, on observation of the altimeter, an error is observed between that which is displayed and that which is desired, the next observation should be on the vertical speed indicator in order to observe the cause of the change in altitude (p. 105)." In diagnosing faults or errors it is often better to transition between normally correlated displays to localize the source of the problem (Moray, 1981).

Second, human memory is imperfect and sampling reflects this fact. Memory limitations result in a tendency to sample displays more often than should be needed if there was perfect memory of the display status obtained in the previous sample. Also, people occasionally forget to sample a particular display source when it is one of many that must be monitored. In their analysis of 270 pilot-error experiences in reading and interpreting instruments, Fitts and Jones (1947) attributed 11% to forgetting-errors (failing to check or refer properly to an instrument before takeoff or during flight). Moray (1984) cautions that forgetting to sample instruments will be increasingly likely as dedicated electromechanical displays that are always visible are replaced by menu-driven CRT displays in which particular displays must be requested.

Third, human sampling improves when a preview of events which are likely in the future is presented. This preview provides a "planning horizon" to guide sampling. Thus, comprehensive preflight planning in which waypoints and potential errors are considered should result in a pilot who is less likely to make sampling errors. Ability to use this information, however, declines when the number of information sources is large (Tulga & Sheridan, 1980).

Fourth, human sampling is affected by high stress, which restricts the number of cues that are sampled. Those few cues which are sampled tend to be those that the pilot perceives to be most important. Emphasis here is on "perceives to be." The pilot's perception of importance will not always reflect the true situation. For example, in 1972 an Eastern Airlines L-1011 flight crashed into the Florida Everglades when the crew became preoccupied with an unsafe landing-gear indication and failed to monitor the critical altimeter readings, which showed the plane gradually descending to ground level (Wiener, 1977).

In general, the sampling behavior of a well-trained operator will approach an optimal strategy based on consideration of the costs of missing an event. However, limitations will arise due to limited memory and stress. Several design guidelines can be distilled from research on sampling behavior. First, displays which are sampled most frequently should be located centrally, such as the directional gyro and the gyro horizon displays (Senders, 1966). Second, displays that are sampled sequentially should be located close together. This guideline is difficult to implement since the sampling strategy may change depending on whether the pilot is operating under normal conditions or is attempting to diagnose a fault. And finally, the design should be such that the important displays are also the most salient, particularly at times of high stress. This will help ensure that the pilot's perception of importance agrees with the actual state of the world.

Another important question with regard to selection is how much information can be processed in a single sample? There are two aspects to this question. First, when multiple relevant stimuli are present, how many can be processed at the same time? This is the question of divided attention. Second, when both relevant and irrelevant stimuli are present, can processing be dedicated to only the relevant stimuli? That is, can processing of irrelevant stimuli be avoided? This is the question of focused attention.

Spatial proximity is a critical dimension which determines whether visual stimuli are processed together (in parallel) or processed individually (serially). Research by Broadbent (1982) indicates that "information that is within 1° of visual angle of a focused target will be likely to receive some processing in parallel with the focused stimulus" (Wickens, 1984, p. 257). For auditory stimuli, pitch appears to be an important dimension of proximity which determines whether stimuli are processed together or separately (Treisman, 1964).

Thus, one general guideline for design is that stimuli which need to be processed together should be close together in space, while stimuli that should be treated separately should be relatively distant. However, there is another important dimension—meaning. Treisman (1964) has found that people tend to process meaningfully related material together. Spatial proximity does not guarantee that stimuli will be processed together, particularly if the material is not perceived to be related. Both Neisser and Becklan (1975) and Fischer, Haines, and Price (1980) have shown that spatial superposition of two displays does not increase the ability to monitor the two information sources. In fact, Fischer et al. (1980) showed that pilots flying with head-up displays that superimpose information from the instruments on the view through the windscreen were slower to detect obstacles on the runway than were pilots flying with conventional head-down instruments.

A technique for integrating stimuli both spatially and in terms of meaning involves the use of object displays. In an object display, multiple stimuli are combined as attributes of a single object. The artificial horizon is an example of an object display in which orientation of the symbolic plane with respect to the horizon is used to present information about both pitch and roll (Taylor, 1987). Woods, Wise, and Hanes (1981) have developed an object display for nuclear control rooms which combines information for eight critical safety parameters into an octagon. Carswell and Wickens (1987) have found that an object display (triangle) is superior to separated displays (bar graphs) in a laboratory process control task which required the subject to integrate several sources of information to detect a system fault. Thus, for tasks that require operators to combine information from multiple stimuli in order to make a single decision, displays which integrate these stimuli as dimensions of a single object should be considered.

All of the research on perception discussed above and, in fact, most of the research on perception done by information processing psychologists has focused on artificial, instrument-type displays of information. However, an important source of information to pilots in addition to their instruments is the optical transformations, or "flow field," which is provided by visual contact with the outside world. Gibson (1966, 1979) has hypothesized that patterns within this flow field carry information which specifies important states of the aircraft (e.g., altitude, heading, velocity). For example, during an approach to landing, texture in the visual field will appear to flow out from an isolated stationary point. Objects above this point will flow upward toward the horizon and objects below this point will flow downward, disappearing at the bottom of the windscreen (see Nagel, this volume, Figure 9.7). This is the aimpoint. It specifies the heading of the airplane with respect to the earth's surface. In a proper approach the aimpoint will be located at the heading of the runway. Analysis of human abilities to extract information from this optical flow field is an important challenge to aviation psychologists. It has important implications for the design of visual flight simulators and instruments which utilize computer-generated imagery. Use of patterns which naturally occur in optical flow fields in the design of graphic displays may provide a familiar context (i.e., compatible with previous experiences) for integrating multiple sources of information regarding aircraft motion. For a review of candidate sources of information relevant for flight control, Warren (1982) is recommended. Also, Langewiesche (1944) provides an intuitive description of visual referents to pilots in guiding their craft.

Linguistic Factors in Perception

Cognitive psychologists have studied the human ability to understand and verify perceived information. Such information may be relayed by voice commands or through printed messages and must then be compared with a preexisting model of the state of the world. The combination of perception, comprehension, and verification constitutes an information processing sequence that is relevant to the performance of nearly every task and is of particular interest to us in the context of aviation. A pilot follows this sequence, for example, when completing a series of procedures on his checklist or when responding to queries from air traffic control (ATC). In designing messages to be presented to the pilot, systems engineers and controllers need to bear in mind certain difficulties, intrinsic to the area of cognition, that may hinder the pilot's ability to comprehend. The following discussion centers on the comprehension of verbal instructions.

Context Provision.   Information is always more easily understood if the reader or listener knows what it pertains to before rather than after the message is presented (Bransford & Johnson, 1972). In this way, the right mental model can be activated to interpret the message appropriately. This mental model will frequently provide an economic framework for storing the details of an otherwise complex message. Difficulties the student pilot has in understanding radio messages from ATC may result, for example, because they fail to have a good mental model of how the ATC system works, and therefore do not always interpret a message in the right context. Simpson and Williams (1980) have argued that a pilot's understanding of synthesized voice messages (e.g., "fuel low") will be improved if the message is surrounded by added voice context ("your fuel is low").

Logical Reversals. Comprehension is hindered whenever a reader or listener is required to logically reverse the meaning of a statement in order to translate from a physical sequence of words to an understanding of what is intended. An example is the use of *negatives.* We comprehend more rapidly that a particular light should be "on" than that it should be "not off." A second example of logical reversals is *falsification.* It is more quickly understood that a statement should be true than that it should be untrue or false.

Experiments by Clark and Chase (1972) examined the experimental analog of a pilot who reads a verbal instruction (e.g., "Check to see that switch x is closed") and verifies the statement either against the actual state of the switch or against his own mental representation of the state. The statement may be either affirmative ("switch x is closed") or negative ("switch x is not open"). Furthermore, it may be either true, agreeing with the most likely position of the switch, or false. From their research, Clark and Chase drew two important conclusions, both having direct implications for the design of procedural checklists:

1. Statements that contain negatives invariably take longer to verify than those that do not. Therefore, where possible, instructions should contain only positive assertions (e.g., "Check to see that the switch is on") rather than negative ones ("Check to ensure that the switch is not off").

2. Whether a statement is verified as true or false influences verification time in a more complex way. If the statement contains no negatives (is positive), then true statements are verified more rapidly than false ones. However, if statements contain negatives, then false statements are verified more rapidly than true ones. Hence, these results suggest that proper phrasing of instructions for most rapid comprehension should avoid negatives and be structured so that the instructions agree with the most likely state of the system. For example, if a switch is normally in an up position, the instruction should read: "Make sure that the switch is up."

Absence of Cues.   The dangers inherent when operators must extract information from the absence of cues are somewhat related to
the recommendation to avoid negatives in instructions. Fowler
(1980) makes this point in his analysis of an aircraft crash near Palm
Springs, California. He notes that the absence of an R symbol on the
pilot's airport chart in the cockpit was the only indication that the
airport did not have radar. Since terminal radar is something pilots
come to depend upon and the lack of radar is highly significant,
Fowler argues that it is far better to call attention to the absence of
this information by the presence of a visible symbol. In general, the
presence of a symbol should be associated with information that an
operator needs to know, rather than with certain expected environmental conditions. People simply do not easily notice the absence of
things.

Order Reversals.   Instructions are often intended to convey a
sense of ordered events in time, as in a procedure checklist (procedure X is followed by procedure Y). When instructions are meant to
convey a sense of order, it is important that the elements in the instructions be *congruent* with the order of events (DeSoto, London, &
Handel, 1965). The problems with order reversals would dictate that
procedural instructions should read, "Do A, then do B," rather than
"Prior to B, do A," since the former preserves the actual sequencing
of events in the ordering of statements on the page.

Mental Model

It should become apparent in reading this section on perception
that a person's ability to gather information is critically influenced
by that person's knowledge state or mental model of a task. This
knowledge includes information about the value or importance of
particular stimuli, about the statistical relations between stimuli, and
is part of the context that determines the meaning of stimuli. For example, it is clear that the experienced pilot's knowledge about the
correlations among displays and the functional relationships among
aircraft systems results in efficient sampling of information. It is also
true that the lack of such a model is a principal reason that the novice is overwhelmed by the seemingly vast array of instruments. The
mental model is shaped by perceptions, and perceptions are in turn
shaped by the mental model. Thus, perception is a dynamic, cyclic
process. One danger in using the traditional information flow diagrams, such as shown in Figure 5.1, is that these diagrams tend to

mask this cyclic, dynamic nature of information processing (Neisser, 1976).

Memory

Information that is perceived, interpreted, and comprehended usually results in action. However, the pilot may choose to remember the information for some time before the action is taken, for example, while working to obtain more information that will either confirm or disconfirm the earlier information. In such cases, the characteristics of human working memory—the system that must retain this information until its translation to action—becomes important. The properties of working memory and long-term memory—the more permanent store of facts—is discussed below.

Working Memory

Working memory is the system employed when a pilot hears a navigational waypoint and then must enter it with a keyboard (Loftus, Dark, & Williams, 1979). It is also used when the pilot or controller must recall the relative position of blips on a radar scope after a brief scan (Moray, 1984). In fact, these two examples illustrate two different *codes* used in working memory. Verbal information is normally maintained in working memory using an acoustic–phonetic rehearsal. Spatial information (regarding locations, orientations, and velocities of things in space) is normally maintained in working memory using a visual code. Research suggests that visual codes are less easily rehearsed than verbal codes (Goettl, 1985). Regardless of the type of code, the capacity of working memory is quite limited, and its demands for the pilot's limited resources are high. These limits should be of concern to both the designer and the user of aviation systems.

The maximum number of unrelated items that can be maintained in working memory when full attention is devoted to rehearsal ranges from about 5 to 9. Miller (1956) refers to this limit as the "magic number 7 ± 2." Lists that exceed this limit are likely to have one or more items forgotten or transposed before recall takes place. This limit is important to consider when voice messages are relayed, as well as in the design of computer menus or procedures manuals that list sets of options. Within a given menu or list, the number of options should not exceed the 7 ± 2 limit of working memory. If more options than this must be presented, then they should be configured hierarchically into related clusters. This clustering of related materials takes advantage of a principle, referred to as *chunking*, that can functionally expand the limits of working memory.

Chunking results when two or more stimulus items have been associated in past experience. These items can, therefore, be stored as a single "chunk" and in this form occupy only a single space in working memory. For example, if a pilot becomes familiar with the call letters of his aircraft (Aztec 237), the digits 237 will become associated into a single chunk requiring only one, as opposed to three, spaces in working memory.

Chunking of material that may not be familiar can also be induced by putting gaps or breaks between strings of unrelated digits or letters. Wickelgren (1964) found that chunks of three or four letters or digits between gaps was best. The message "234 9187" would be better retained than "23491 87." It is also important, where possible, to choose breaks that are meaningful to the human operator. Thus, it would make sense to present a navigation coordinate as 40 ⌐ 37, not as 4037.

Working memory is more likely to treat dimensions of a single object as a single chunk than the same dimension of several objects. As an example of this phenomenon, Yntema (1963) found that subjects showed better memory for a small number of objects that had a large number of attributes than for many objects which had only a few attributes. For example, in an air traffic control problem, the altitude, airspeed, heading, and size of two aircraft would be better retained than the altitude and airspeed of four aircraft, even though in each case eight items are to be held in working memory (Harwood, Wickens, Kramer, Clay, & Liu, 1986). Thus, when operators must retain information about multidimensional "objects" (e.g., several engines, each with several critical parameter values), this information will be better remembered when the operator is given responsibility for monitoring many attributes of a smaller number of objects, rather than the converse.

The principal cause of forgetting or of loss of information from working memory is *interference*. That is, information to be stored in working memory becomes confused or replaced either by information that was previously stored *(proactive interference)* or by new information *(retroactive interference)*. Unless actively rehearsed, information in working memory will generally be forgotten within about 10 to 20 seconds. In the remainder of this section, four steps will be suggested that may reduce forgetting due to interference.

1. Distribute the material to be held in memory over time. In this

way the proactive interference from previous items that are no longer relevant will be reduced. In their study of memory for aviation-relevant materials, Loftus et al. (1979) concluded that a minimum of 10 seconds should elapse between the presentation of different independent instructions to the pilot from ATC.

2. Reduce similarity between items. A string of similar-looking items (QOGDUQUDUG) will create more interference, and thus more confusion and forgetting, than a string of different-looking ones (XPOLNTSKUA). Because verbal material is normally rehearsed using an acoustic code, similar-sounding items will also lead to greater interference. Thus, the string EGBZCDT will lead to more errors in recall than will the string KFEYWMU (Conrad, 1964). Acoustic similarity will create interference even when the material is presented visually. Yntema (1963) also found that when several attributes of an object must be held in working memory, retention is best if each attribute has a distinct, identifiable code such that the similarity between codes is reduced. For example, in an air traffic control problem, altitude might be coded in terms of raw feet (4,100), heading in terms of compass direction (315), and airspeed in 100-knot units (2.8). Furthermore, the displayed information to be stored could be made physically different in other respects (e.g., different colors or sizes). This distinction would maintain each code's unique appearance, would maximize the differences between items, and so would reduce the potential for interference. Using aircraft navigational and transponder ID information, the study by Loftus et al. (1979) found better memory when some material was represented in strings ("four two seven two") and other material was represented in chunks ("thirty-five twenty-seven"). The use of different physical formats reduced similarity and resulted in less interference.

3. Eliminate unnecessary redundancy. This is a second way to maximize differences between items that must be stored in working memory. Tversky (1972) had noted that perceived similarity between items is determined both by the number of features two things have in common and the number of features that are different. When the ratio of common to distinct features is high, perceived similarity will be high and the potential for interference will be increased. For example, when an air traffic controller must deal with several aircraft from one fleet, all possessing highly similar identifier codes (e.g., AI3404, AI3402, AI3403), it is difficult to maintain their separate identity in working memory (Fowler, 1980). In this example, interference could be reduced by deleting the shared features 340, and using only the codes AI4, AI2, AI3.

4. Minimize within-code interference. As noted earlier, informa-

tion can be stored in working memory using either verbal or spatial codes. Research suggests that acoustically coded, verbal information will be more harmed by concurrent activity that is also verbal or phonetic, while spatially coded information will be more harmed by concurrent spatial activities (Goettl, 1985). Hence, task environments that must impose high loads on the memory for verbal information should be designed to minimize the need for a lot of extra voice communication (speaking or listening), as this will disrupt the verbal code. In contrast, task environments with high demands for manipulating and recalling spatial information (e.g., the ATC environment) should try to reduce the use of visual coding for other tasks (e.g., by using voice recognition and synthesis technology instead; Wickens, Sandry, & Vidulich, 1983).

Long-Term Memory

Two classes of information can be distinguished in long-term memory—semantic and episodic. *Semantic memory* represents memory for meaning—What is the meaning of a word or how you ride a bike, tie your shoes, or fly a plane. These types of information would be referred to as semantic memories. *Episodic memory* represents knowledge about specific events, for example, what happened on your recent flight to Oshkosh. Most common amnesias affect episodic memories, but do not affect semantic memory.

An important question about semantic memory is how knowledge is organized in memory. This question is thought to be particularly important in designing interfaces between humans and knowledge-based information systems (e.g., computerized data bases such as card catalogs). It is assumed that the operator's ability to locate and use information will be more efficient if the computer's knowledge base is organized in a fashion consistent with the operator's (Durding, Becker, & Gould, 1977). For example, Roske-Hofstrand and Paap (1985) used an analytic technique known as *multidimensional scaling* to uncover the pilot's mental representation of aircraft systems. This representation was then used as a basis for designing a computerized menu system, whereby the pilot could obtain relevant information about each aircraft system. The structure of the menu produced in this fashion proved to be much more compatible and user-friendly than was the conventional menu organization.

Episodic memory is important for accident and critical event investigations. Here the pilot or air traffic controller is asked to recall what happened at such and such a time. Research on eyewitness testimony (Loftus, 1979) indicates that episodic memories can be quite plastic. Loftus and Palmer (1974), for example, studying eyewitness testimony of simulated events, demonstrated vividly how much the recall of these episodes could be biased by the phrasing of questions asked about the events. It is also well documented that our memory for what actually happened in an episode is heavily influenced by our expectations of what *should* happen in a logical world. When the expectations and wishes disagree with what actually did happen, the expectations and wishes often rule memory.

Decision Making

A pilot's judgment and decision-making abilities are critical to air safety. Analysis of FAA reports by Jensen and Benel (1977) suggested that errors in pilot judgment accounted for over 50% of pilot fatalities during the period from 1970 to 1974. Yet despite this importance, pilot decision making has received only a minimum degree of research interest (for exceptions see Buch, 1984; Buch & de Bagheera, 1985; Jensen, 1981; Lester, Diehl, & Buch, 1985). This neglect is even more surprising in light of the growing amount of solid theory-based research in the psychology of decision and choice (see Einhorn & Hogarth, 1981; Kahneman, Slovic, & Tversky, 1982; Pitz & Sachs, 1984 for recent reviews). Our discussion focuses upon conclusions regarding human strengths and limitations in decision making that have been drawn from general research. Where possible these factors are illustrated in the framework of aviation-related tasks, but for the most part their actual investigation in an aviation context has not been carried out.

There are three general characteristics that define the decision-making task. First, the pilot must evaluate several sources of information in assessing the situation or understanding the current state of the "world." This assessment forms the basis for choosing an appropriate action. Second, the information the pilot deals with is probabilistic. The cues used for situation assessment may be unreliable (e.g., a weather forecast predicts a 20% chance of thunderstorms), and the projected consequences of an action into the future are uncertain. This probabilistic element means that the right decision can often produce an unfortunate outcome ("bad luck") and the wrong decision can often "luck out." Third, the elements of value and cost underlie most decisions. For example, the pilot may have to balance the benefit of continuing a flight through bad weather and satisfying the passengers' need to reach their destination on time against the potential greater cost of an accident.

Figure 5.2 presents a general model of human decision making that highlights the information processing components which are relevant to decision making. To the left of the figure, environmental cues are sampled to obtain a situation assessment or diagnosis of the state of the world that calls for a decision. An accurate assessment often requires perception of a large number of cues—radar pictures, weather forecasts, visual topographic features, fuel consumption, engine status, airport capabilities, and so forth. These cues in turn must be interpreted against a knowledge base in long-term memory to accurately construct a mental model or diagnosis of the situation. Possible alternative hypotheses that describe the situation are generated from long-term memory, held in working memory, and compared against the cues. As we shall see, this construction process is hampered both by limits of attention (are relevant cues processed?) and by biases in long-term memory.

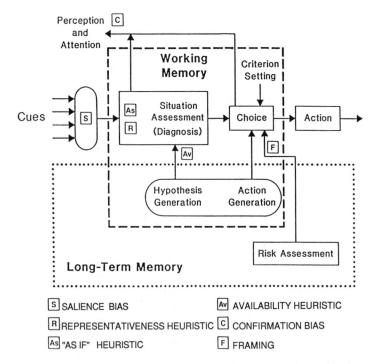

Figure 5.2.   A model of decision making. Biases and heuristics, denoted by letters surrounded by a square, are discussed in the text.

Assuming that the assessed situation is identified as a problem that requires some action, the pilot must then generate plausible alternative courses of action to take. For example, the pilot may ask, "Do I continue my approach, fly around while seeking more information, or turn back to an alternate airport?" Each proposed course of action may have a different anticipated set of possible outcomes, depending upon the diagnosed state of the world. Furthermore, all of these outcomes will have potential values associated with them (or costs, which may be defined as negative values). The *expected value* of an outcome is its true value multiplied by the probability that it might occur. When values cannot be expressed in monetary terms they are called *utilities*. The pilot's *choice* or decision should be that which produces the most positive, or least negative, expected utility. As indicated in the figure, this critical choice point involves the process of *risk assessment*—the subjective evaluation of the probability of different outcomes—and the assessment of the utilities of these outcomes, as this information is retrieved from long-term memory.

Finally, the figure indicates that at any stage these operations may trigger the decision to seek more information in order to better assess the situation or evaluate the consequences of an action. In the following pages, we outline some of the behavioral findings with regard to human strengths and limitations in this interactive process. The squared-in letters within the figure indicate particular sources of bias or heuristics that are identified and discussed as the elements of the decision process are described in more detail below.

Situation Assessment

In setting the stage for our discussion of cue perception and situation assessment, it is appropriate to consider two different aviation scenarios. In the first, a pilot flying instrument flight rules (IFR) has become completely disoriented. Not only are glimpses of the now unfamiliar terrain below intermittent and cloud obscured, but the navigational information itself may be unreliable because of a suspected instrument malfunction. The situation to be assessed is "Where am I?" In the second scenario, the pilot senses, through a series of warning indicators and gauge readings, that one of the engines may be malfunctioning, but the nature of the malfunction is not an obvious one with which he is familiar. The situation to be assessed here is the diagnosis of what is wrong with the engine.

In situation assessments such as these, psychologists have found that problem solvers and troubleshooters often engage in heuristics or mental rules of thumb that help them reach a diagnosis without expending too much mental effort (Kahneman et al., 1982; Rasmussen, 1981). While such heuristics often work adequately, the fact that they are shortcuts may prevent the decision maker from obtaining the most accurate information. They may, therefore, sometimes lead the decision maker to a false understanding. These sources of bias and error in situation assessment are the focus of the following discussion.

Cue Seeking.   Searching the environment for critical cues in the first stage of situation assessment, is limited by characteristics of human attention, as discussed earlier in this chapter. It is apparent, for example, that decision makers do not necessarily process all of the information that is available to them (Wickens, 1984a), particularly when they are under time stress (Wright, 1974). Given that stress often causes a "tunneling of attention" when monitoring multi-element displays (Hockey, 1970), it is reasonable to assume that this tunneling would have the same restricting influence on the processing of multiple cues to assess the situation. For example, in attempting to diagnose a faulty engine, a pilot may focus on only a small number of physically salient symptoms, ignoring critical cues that might provide even more diagnostic information concerning the nature of the fault (such perceptual tunneling has been considered responsible, in part, for the disaster at Three Mile Island). This bias toward *salience*, at the expense of information content, is indicated by S in Figure 5.2.

Research has also found that the decision maker's cue-seeking behavior is heavily guided by the hypothesis that may already have been tentatively chosen. This tendency, known as the *confirmation bias* (C in Figure 5.2), describes the bias to seek (and therefore find) those sources of information that confirm what we already believe to be true (Mynatt, Doherty, & Tweney, 1977; Wason & Johnson-Laird, 1972). Thus, disoriented pilots who are trying to establish their location over the ground may first posit that they are in a certain location and then focus attention on ground features that are consistent with that location, while ignoring (or discounting) those that are inconsistent. As Wason and Johnson-Laird have noted, the best way to test whether a hypothesis is true is to seek information which, if found, will *falsify* the hypothesis rather than confirm it.

While, in general, people process only a limited number of sources of independent information when testing or confirming a hypothesis, these limitations are removed (or at least are greatly lessened) to the extent that the information sources are *correlated*. Thus, the skilled pilot can rapidly diagnose the current state of an aircraft from the six crucial instrument readings because of the typical pattern of correlation that is observed between these readings. For example, a positive rate-of-climb is correlated with an increase in altimeter reading; a change in attitude predicts a change in heading, and so forth. In the same way, extensive familiarity with the patterns of symptoms produced by particular aircraft malfunctions will allow the pilot to interpret rapidly the potentially large number of cues indicating their status. For example, the failure of the suction pump will cause a failure of gyro instruments (artificial horizon and heading indicator), resulting in a correlated change in these two instrument readings.

Hypothesis Formulation and Testing. People typically try to understand a situation by matching in working memory the pattern of cues seen in the environment with a mental representation of the typical or *representative* pattern for a particular situation as recalled from long-term memory (R in Figure 5.2). We may think of this memorized pattern as a hypothesis of the proposed state. If the hypothesis matches the data, then the situation is diagnosed (Tversky & Kahneman, 1974). A limitation of this heuristic results from the fact that a particular pattern of cues may not be a perfectly diagnostic indicator of the true state of the world. For example, to the lost pilot, the 60° intersection of a freeway with a road below may be consistent with several different ground locations, just as a pattern of low oil pressure and high engine temperature could be symptomatic of a variety of causes of engine failures.

To ensure an accurate diagnosis, the decision maker should first think of a reasonable number of possible hypotheses, in order to make sure that as many situations are covered as possible. An extensive program of research by Gettys and his colleagues (summarized in Gettys, 1983) suggests, however, that faced with problem-solving situations, people generate only a small fraction of possible hypotheses (relative to the number of plausible ones), even as they remain overly confident that their list is exhaustive.

Second, those hypotheses that the decision maker generates should be the most probable or likely ones. For example, suppose a pilot has formed two alternative hypotheses concerning the diagnosis of an electronic system failure, one of which occurs 10 times more frequently than the other. In such a case, the pilot's initial hypothesis concerning the cause of the malfunction should indicate the more frequently occurring failure. Yet, people do not accurately use the probability or "base rate" frequency information to guide their choice in this way (Kahneman et al., 1982). Instead, when generating the few hypotheses from memory, they use what is described as the *availability* heuristic (*Av*; Tversky & Kahneman, 1974), in which a hypothesis is considered most likely if it is most available in memory. However, the most available hypothesis in memory may not be the most probable, but rather the one that was most recently experienced, or the simplest one, since simple hypotheses are easier to remember than complex ones (Fontenella, 1983; Tversky & Kahneman, 1974).

There is a second sense in which people fail to use probability information appropriately in diagnosis, and this relates to *cue reliability*. Clearly, some cues are quite reliable: the visual sighting of a distinct ground landmark or the smell of smoke in the cockpit. For others the reliability may be somewhat less: instrument readings or views of the same landmarks through the haze. Still other cues may have a reliability that is at best marginal—a message spoken by another pilot heard through static, an instrument reading that is notoriously unstable, or the sense of vertical obtained through vestibular cues. Yet, when integrating a number of information sources that vary in their reliability, people follow what is sometimes referred to as the "as if" heuristic (*As* in Figure 5.2; Wickens, 1984). In the extreme, this amounts to treating all information sources *as if* they were of equal reliability or, to a lesser degree, failing to "devalue" those information sources of lower reliability to an extent that is optimal (Johnson, Cavanagh, Spooner, & Samet, 1973; Kahneman & Tversky, 1973; Schum, 1975).

Instead of using cue reliability as a basis for choosing their hypothesis, people more often focus attention most heavily on those cues that are physically salient (loud, bright, recent, centrally visible, and easy to interpret; Wallsten & Barton, 1982), and those that are likely to confirm the hypothesis that was already tentatively formed (*S* and *C*, respectively, in Figure 5.2). If those cues, by chance or by design, also happen to be quite reliable, then the assessment of the situation will likewise be accurate; but if they are not reliable, and their indicated diagnosis is wrong, then even the best-intended decision of what action to take may lead to disaster because it will be based on a faulty assessment of the world.

Decision Formulation

Once an assessment of the situation is made, a decision must then follow as to what action to take. Of course, the decision may simply involve the choice to seek still more information, as indicated by the top loop in Figure 5.2. In all cases, the decision maker should choose the course of action with the most favorable expected outcome—the highest expected utility. Sometimes this course of action is simple, if the situation is diagnosed with certainty ("I'm sure that my fuel is about gone"), and there is no question about the best action ("I must land in the nearest field below rather than going further"). However, at other times the choice of possible actions is far less clear-cut. This may occur either because the situation assessment leaves some uncertainty to be resolved in the pilot's mind ("There is an 80% chance that my fuel is gone, but because I haven't flown very far since I refueled, there is a 20% chance that my fuel gauge may be in error") or because the consequence of the pilot's choice of actions cannot be predicated with certainty ("If I try an emergency landing here, I *believe* my chances of survival are high, but I am not certain").

Formally, this state of affairs may be represented in terms of the decision matrix shown in Figure 5.3. In this example, two states of the world, with different subjective probabilities, are shown across the top, and two potential courses of action are shown down the sides. (Of course, in a real-world decision problem, there may be a greater number of both states of the world and of potential actions.) The decision maker should optimally assign probabilities to each state of the world as we have seen above. Each action then, when taken in the presence of one or the other state of the world, can generate one or more potential *outcomes*. In the case of the example here, the possible outcomes of a decision to land might be a safe landing in the nearby field, with the unpleasant aspects of getting the aircraft out again, or a disastrous landing in the same place; a decision to continue might result in a safe flight to the final destination or the potential disaster of running out of fuel short of the field and with a less-feasible landing place. Each of these outcomes has a *utility*, a positive or negative consequence to the decision maker that can be assigned some relative value, and a *probability*, or expected frequency of occurrence. Together, the utility and the probability serve to define the *risk*, and the human should optimally choose that action with the lowest expected risk. Formally, the expected risk of an action is computed as the expected risk of each outcome—its utility times its probability—summed across states of the world. These calculations are shown to the right of Figure 5.3, in which it is clear that the emergency landing has the lowest expected risk and, hence, is the decision that should be made. Here again, human performance has been found to be adversely affected by certain biases and limitations.

STATE OF THE WORLD

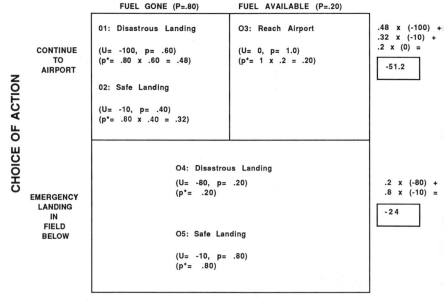

Figure 5.3.   A decision matrix representation of pilot decision making. p, absolute probability of a given outcome; p*, contingent probability of an outcome, given the state of the world.

To begin with, even the basic rows and columns in the decision matrix may not be set up optimally. As we have noted, the diagnosis estimating the probability of the possible system states may be in error. Because of the confirmation bias, the diagnosis will probably show a far greater confidence or estimated probability of the most likely hypothesis than is warranted. Second, Gettys (1983) has found that, as in hypothesis generation, people generate only a small fraction of the feasible problem-solving actions that may be appropriate in a given situation.

Even assuming that an adequate matrix is set up, arriving at an optimal decision still requires that the risks (probability × utility) of the different outcomes be accurately assessed. Here again, experiments show that people are not skilled at assessing the probability of different outcomes and their resulting risks (Fischoff, 1977; Kahneman et al., 1982; Slovic, 1984), although it is not entirely clear what kind of biases these problems will demonstrate. On the one hand, people clearly overestimate the frequency of very rare positive events

(Pitz, 1965). This bias explains why gambling and lotteries are pursued—because the low-probability payoffs are perceived as occurring more frequently than they do. On the other hand, peoples' estimates of the frequency of different kinds of unpleasant or negative events appear to be influenced very much by the availability heuristic described above (Tversky & Kahneman, 1974). Highly available events, because they are salient and well publicized, are overestimated (fatal aircraft accidents fall into this category), while less-salient events are greatly underestimated (near misses or nonfatal accidents; Slovic, 1984). Collectively, the effect of these biases on the decision matrix such as that shown in Figure 5.3 cannot be entirely predicted.

To this analysis, two further important findings should be added. The first is based on a general theory of choice, put forward by Tversky and Kahneman (1981), which describes the influence of problem framing (F in Figure 5.2). While the entire theory is relevant to the concept of risky decision making, its most critical aspect for this discussion is the assertion that the choice between two actions, one a risk and the other a sure thing, will depend very much upon whether the problem is framed as a choice between gains or between losses. Of course, in our critical analysis of pilot decision making, the choice is often between losses. Here, Tversky and Kahneman observe that people are biased to choose the risky loss rather than the certain loss, even when the expected loss resulting from the former is greater. For example, consider the pilot who must choose between turning back in the face of potentially bad weather (with the certainty of missing a critical appointment and disappointing the passengers), and continuing on (with a chance of getting through safely and on time but also with a small chance of suffering a major disaster). The choice is clearly one between negatives: a sure loss versus an uncertain probability of disaster. Tversky and Kahneman have shown that people have a bias to favor the risky choice. This risk-seeking tendency is reversed, however, when the choice is framed as one between gains, and here the sure-thing alternative is favored. In the previous example, we might suppose that if the pilot could frame the same decision as one between ensuring that lives are saved (the option to turn back) and probably keeping an appointment (the option of going ahead), the bias would swing toward the sure-thing turn-back option.

The second bias that is relevant in choosing actions is a well-documented tendency toward overconfidence in forecasting. In a general sense, people overestimate the likelihood that their predictions of the future will be correct. Here again, one may account for the "can do," or "it won't happen to me" bias of a pilot choosing to undertake a risky option. Studied repeatedly by Fischoff (1977), this bias is accounted for by peoples' inherent dislike of uncertainty.

Decision Quality

The preceding litany of limitations in human diagnosis and decision making suggests that the human operator is nothing more than a "bundle of biases" waiting for the inevitable disaster to occur. Yet the outstanding safety record in commercial aviation belies this conclusion, and there are a number of possible reasons why. In the first place, bad decisions are usually correctable and do not invariably lead to instant failure. Most aircraft systems are designed with enough redundancy to guarantee that corrections are possible. Hence, the accident rate surely underestimates the frequency of poor pilot judgment. Second, there are a number of other variables in addition to strict information processing limitations that can influence pilot decision making. Intuition and lore (but not formal research) indicate that personality variables will influence a pilot's risk-taking tendency (Lester & Bombaci, 1984), while differences in cognitive style undoubtedly also play some role in the diagnosis–decision sequence. For example, Gettys (1983) has found that individuals who show divergent thinking generate more possible actions.

Finally, the role of expertise and training in pilot judgment must be mentioned. The most apparent difference between the expert and novice lies in the long-term memory store of information. The expert can more automatically interpret patterns of environmental cues to reach a rapid and accurate assessment (Ebbeson & Konecki, 1980; Phelps & Shanteau, 1978; Wickens et al., 1987) and undoubtedly has a greater store of hypotheses and actions that can be generated in the search for a solution. Ironically, however, the experimental evidence does not strongly support the conclusion that expertise reduces the magnitude of biases, the dependence on heuristics, or the overall qualities of decision making (Brehmer, 1981; Fischoff, 1977; Irizarry & Knapp, 1986; Wickens et al., 1987). In particular it may well be that greater experience in successful flying will increase the overconfident forecast of "it couldn't happen to me," with the consequence of further suppressing the risk estimates for undesirable events (Fischoff, 1977).

While the issue of training judgment skills has been discussed in some detail as a worthwhile enterprise (Jensen, 1981), there have been few efforts to directly implement such programs. Buch (1984; Buch & de Bagheera, 1985) demonstrated the success of a fairly direct, prescriptive program of "dos" and "don'ts" in air judgment, developed by Embry-Riddle. She found that those who had undergone such training were much less likely to grant requests from "confederate" passengers to engage in unwise or unsafe procedures than was a control group who had not (e.g., fly low over a particular house to "get a closer look" or fly farther over water than gliding distance to land). However, the extent to which this training had any more general influence on improving judgmental characteristics and reducing biases could not be determined.

In conclusion, it would seem that as long as judgment errors remain a significant cause of accidents, and potential causes of these errors have been documented in laboratory research, then further knowledge of the cause of these errors in the air and the potential means of training them away should be of paramount importance to research in aviation psychology.

Selection of Action

The aviation environment is often a time-critical one. When aircraft are flying at supersonic speeds, or are close to the ground, differences in as little as a fraction of a second to which the pilot can respond to new information can make the difference between safety and disaster. Furthermore, the time pressure of the airborne environment may cause errors in carrying out even simple actions. The issue of how people respond to information under time stress has been studied extensively by psychologists over the past four decades in the paradigm of the *choice reaction-time task*. This paradigm studies the actions typical of a pilot who suddenly perceives an obstacle directly in the flight path (an unexpected stimulus) and must rapidly choose and execute a response (e.g., pull up, down, left, or right, depending upon the aspect of the obstacle). We describe below the various factors that psychologists have identified for the choice reaction-time paradigm which will influence the speed of responding to unexpected environmental events or which will increase the likelihood that the wrong response will be chosen. These factors are discussed in more detail in Wickens (1984a).

Information Transmission

Employing the concepts of information theory developed by Shannon and Weaver (1949), psychologists in the 1950s reasoned that unexpected environmental events could be *quantified* in terms of the amount of information that they conveyed. Events that are perfectly predictable in time and identity convey no information. The lesser degree to which an event can be predicted, the greater its information content. Information theory describes the information H_i conveyed by an event i appearing in context X, with a probability P_i/X as $H_i = \log_2[1/(P_i/X)]$.

Information increases if there are more possible events that can occur in a given context. Thus for example, the information conveyed to the air traffic controller by hearing a plane squawk its ID will be greater if there are a large number of planes on the display than if there are few, since in the former case, the probability of any given plane calling will be less (equal to the reciprocal of the number of planes). A direct change in the context, X, in which the same event could occur, also changes the information. The information conveyed by a weather report of thundershowers will be greater in the context of winter than in summer. Finally, the average information conveyed by a *series* of such events is simply the average of the information of each event, weighted by its respective probability of occurrence.

Using information theory to quantify the information conveyed by an event or series of stimulus events H_s, Hick (1952) and Hyman (1953) established that the time to respond to stimuli was a linear function of the information conveyed by those stimuli. This relation, known as the Hick–Hyman law stated that RT = $(a + b) H_s$.

Examples of the direct application of information theory in the aviation environment have involved quantifying the information conveyed by turbulence on disturbance input in a manual control task (Baty, 1971) or by messages occurring with various probabilities in a communications task.

The prospects of the Hick–Hyman law to offer a predictive model of exactly how fast a pilot or controller will respond to different stimuli are quite attractive. However, in practice there are often too many other variables that cannot be described by information theory which will affect reaction time in less quantifiable ways. Some of these are described below. Nevertheless, even in less-controlled environments, the Hick–Hyman law still provides the qualitative prediction that events of high information content will be responded to more slowly than those of low information content.

Preparation

Reaction time will be faster to events for which we are prepared. Such preparation may either be carried by a warning as to *what* stimulus may be present (e.g., the alert from ATC to watch out for a possible contact below and to the right) or for *when* a stimulus might occur. As an example of this temporal preparation, Danaher (1980) describes the avoidance of a midair collision between two aircraft over Detroit as attributable in part to the fact that the pilot of one of the airplanes was prepared by the controller to make an evasive response just before the other aircraft came into view through the clouds.

The Speed–Accuracy Trade-off

It is well known that when one is pressured to respond more quickly, the chance of making an error increases, a phenomenon formally known as the speed–accuracy trade-off (Pachella, 1974; Wickelgren, 1977). The direct relevance of the speed–accuracy trade-off to aviation environments is threefold:

1. The trade-off is of critical importance, because those periods in which time stress is greatest (i.e., approach to landing, decisions during takeoff, or, for the air traffic controller, the saturated airspace) are also those in which the consequences of an error are least forgiving.

2. In designing and comparing systems, it should be realized that any system characteristic that produces *slower* responding will also probably be that which is more likely to produce greater errors under speed stress. It is for this reason that engineering psychologists rightfully pay close attention to differences of only a fraction of a second when comparing or evaluating system components. The fraction of a second might not have any impact on overall system performance— but the increased chance of error certainly could.

3. There are certain important variables that *drive* people to trade speed for accuracy. One variable that we have of course noted already is time pressure. A second related one is *arousal*. Conditions or stimuli that increase the level of arousal will lead to faster, but less accurate, responding (Posner, 1978). For example, auditory stimuli tend to be more arousing than visual, and hence loud auditory alarms or alerts in the cockpit may be more likely to be responded to in error. A third variable is *preparation*. If we expect a particular stimulus and are thus prepared to trigger the appropriate response, we will respond more rapidly when the expected stimulus occurs; but also, if a different stimulus occurs, we will be more likely to make the prepared response. This response will now of course be in error. Finally, a different sort of variable that appears to drive the speed–accuracy trade-off is *age*. Strayer, Wickens, and Braune, (1987) have reported that the increase in age from 20 to 60 brings

about a disposition for slower but more accurate responding, a trend which probably serves the older pilot to advantage in many circumstances.

Stimulus–Response Compatibility

Response time is affected by the spatial relationships between stimuli and responses. Some spatial arrangements result in faster responses than others. For example, if two side-by-side lights are to be responded to with two key presses, faster reaction times will be obtained if the left key is assigned to the left light and the right key is assigned to the right light (Cotton, Tzeng, & Hardyck, 1980; Simon, 1969). Fitts and Seeger (1953) examined a number of somewhat more complex stimulus response arrangements and demonstrated that certain spatial arrangements led to faster responses than others. Fitts and Seeger (1953) also examined the interaction of compatibility and practice. They found that while practice could improve reaction times for incompatible mappings, performance failed to reach the levels found for compatible mappings. Loveless (1963) notes that, under conditions of stress, there is a danger that highly compatible responses will be erroneously substituted for correct but incompatible responses.

To a great extent, stimulus–response compatibility is guided by expectancies or internal models of how the world behaves; that is, humans have a model of the world which leads them to associate certain responses with certain stimuli. When the stimulus–response configuration is congruent with these expectations, then performance will be both faster and more accurate. In the context of stimulus–response compatibility these expectations are referred to as population stereotypes. For example, Americans associate an upward position of a light switch with lights on, and Europeans associate an upward position with lights off. These associations result from an internal model constructed from past experiences. Loveless (1963) reviews compatibility and population stereotypes in display–control relations.

The design of most military helicopters is an example where the principle of stimulus–response compatibility is violated. In these helicopters, altitude information is presented to the right of the instrument display, but controlled with the left hand, while airspeed information is presented to the left, yet controlled using the right hand. Research suggests that this configuration results in poorer performance than would a more compatible arrangement (Hartzell, Dunbar, Beveridge, & Cortilla, 1982).

In addition to the spatial arrangements of stimuli and responses, there is also evidence for a compatibility effect which may be attributed to the central processing codes used for representing stimuli and responses. Greenwald (1970) referred to this relationship as ideomotor compatibility. Research has shown that when stimuli and responses are in the same modality (e.g., verbal response to auditory stimulus), reaction times are faster and are less influenced by variations in information content or extra task loading (Greenwald, 1979; Greenwald & Shulman, 1973). Additional research, both in the laboratory and in an aircraft simulator, indicates that tasks which use verbal working memory are served best by auditory inputs, while spatial tasks are better served by visual inputs (Vidulich & Wickens, 1982; Wickens et al., 1983).

Stimulus Sequencing

The previous discussions have focused on the factors that will affect the speed of one response to one of many possible stimulus events. There are times however when the pilot or controller must make repeated responses to a sequence of events, and then the nature of the timing between events becomes more critical. An obvious example is in the execution of repeated yoke responses to changes in error of pitch and role in flight control. In the increasingly automated cockpit such stimulus sequencing is involved in keyboard data entry as well. While factors related to stimulus timing are extensively discussed by Wickens (1984a), four of these are briefly enumerated here.

1. *Interstimulus interval.* As stimuli requiring responses are placed too closely together (i.e., less time to respond to each stimulus alone), the response time to each will be longer, and/or the error rate will increase.

2. *Repetition effect.* In general, people respond faster to a stimulus that repeats itself than to one that does not. The exception will occur only if the rate of responding is extremely fast (e.g., more than two responses per second, as in typing).

3. *Decision complexity advantage.* Humans are better able to process information delivered in the format of a smaller number of complex decisions per unit time than in the format of a larger number of simpler decisions (Alluisi, Muller, & Fitts, 1957; Broadbent, 1971).

This bias is referred to as the *decision complexity advantage* (Wickens, 1984). Several applied studies extend this finding to suggest that the information transmission rates of human–machine systems can be improved by designs that require the human to make a few complex decisions rather than many simple ones (Deininger, Billington, & Riesz, 1966; Miller, 1981). Thus, for example, when paging through a hierarchically organized computer menu to retrieve a piece of information, each "level" of the menu should incorporate a fairly large number of alternatives (but not more than seven due to limits on working memory) in order to offer a reasonably complex decision. One way of implementing the decision complexity advantage in keyboard design is through the use of "chording" keyboards, since each chord can convey much more information than a single keystroke (Gopher & Eilam, 1979; Wickens, 1984a). The chord has a particular advantage for data entry in the airborne environment because it does not require visual feedback (Gopher & Eilam, 1979).

4. *Preview.* Performance in serial reaction-time tasks often improves when subjects are allowed to preview upcoming stimuli. Investigations of typing and keyboard data entry performance indicate that benefits of preview result from providing both advanced information and from allowing the typist to respond to chunks of information from several stimuli (Herson & Hillix, 1965; Shaffer, 1973; Shaffer & Hardwick, 1970).

Dual-Task Performance

Many aviation environments impose concurrent demands on the pilot. Some of these demands are measurable tasks, as when the pilot moves the yoke while talking to ATC, or when the controller listens to the pilot while scanning the visual display. Other activities are covert—planning, problem solving, and decision making for example—but may be just as demanding for the operator's limited attention resources as the more observable activities. The usefulness of descriptions of the components of information processing presented on the previous pages depends very much upon knowing how these components are affected when attention is diverted to concurrent tasks. In this section we consider two major variables that affect the ability to perform multiple tasks concurrently: their difficulty and their structure.

Task Difficulty.   Many of a pilot's tasks have been described as "automated"—highly practiced activities that demand little atten-

tion. This concept of performance automation has been represented
in the framework of the *performance–resource function* (PRF),
shown in Figure 5.4. The function represents the relation between
the amount of effort, attention, or resources invested in performing a
task, and the quality of its performance. The figure indicates that performance generally gets better, or at least does not get worse, as more
resources are invested. However, the more automated a task becomes, the fewer resources are required to obtain a perfect level of
performance (shown as the level portion of curve B). The figure
shows that Task B is more automated than Task A.

The concept of automation, as reflected in the PRF, is important in
three respects: it has implications for performance measurement, it
describes differences in task difficulty, and it describes practice.
First, as indicated in Figure 5.4, the level of performance obtained
when all resources are invested (i.e., single-task performance) will
not necessarily reveal all that is important to know about the task. In
the case of Figure 5.4, both tasks show equivalent levels of performance, yet that performance on Task B can be achieved with a much
smaller investment of resources, leaving more resources available for
other activities. Hence, it becomes important to measure not only the
level of performing a primary task, but its *resource cost* or *mental
workload*, a concept that is elaborated in Chapter 10. This resource
cost can be assessed by examining performance on a concurrent task.
As more "residual resources" are available for the primary task (A),
performance on the concurrent secondary task will be improved. For

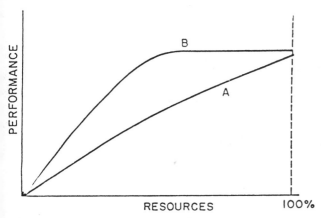

Figure 5.4.   A performance–resource function.

example, Dougherty, Emery, and Curtin (1964) compared different aircraft instrument layouts and obtained results that were entirely consistent with the pattern shown in Figure 5.4. No differences were observed in single-task performance, but differences appeared with the increased demand imposed by a digit readout task. Jex and Clement (1979) have reported a linear inverse relation between the subjective difficulty of different flight dynamics and the measure of secondary-task performance.

Second, the difference between two PRFs may very well be attributed to differences in the information processing demands imposed by the task. It is possible to identify a number of task characteristics that will increase resources demanded to obtain a given level of performance. Several of these variables are listed in Table 5.1. Unfortunately, the effects of each of these manipulations on the performance of a concurrent task may depend very much upon the information processing structure of that task—for example, whether it is visual or auditory, perceptual or motor, and so forth. This is because humans appear to possess more than a single kind of attentional resource, and an increase in demand of one task will have a more harmful effect on performance of a concurrent task if the two demand the same rather than different resources. This issue is dealt with below.

Third, the differences between the two curves in Figure 5.4 may also represent the difference between the skilled and novice performer on a given task. In general, practice at a task will increase its level

Table 5.1. Variables That Will Increase Task Difficulty

Encoding	Degrading noise
	Visual clutter
	Stimulus similarity and confusability
Memory	Number of items retained
	Phonetic and semantic confusability
	Retention duration
Response	Response frequency
	Response complexity
	Degree of choice
	Stimulus–response incompatability
	Degree of precision
Continuous control	Control order
	Control bandwidth
	Gain (too high or too low)
	System time-delays

of performance and reduce its resource demands. However, the benefits of practice on resource demands will vary as an increasing function of the *consistency* of components in the task (Schneider, 1985; Schneider, Dumas, & Shiffrin, 1984; Schneider & Shiffrin, 1977). Practice on tasks whose components are consistent, such as the invariant sequence of actions called on to execute a particular route or emergency procedure, will have a much greater influence on reducing resource demands than will practice on tasks whose components may vary or change from trial to trial. Continued practice on consistent tasks produces the gradual development of *automatic processing*.

Task Structure.   The previous section suggests that with a sufficient level of practice on the right kind of task, performance *can* be carried out in a resource-free fashion, avoiding interference with any concurrent task. In fact, however, such perfect time-sharing will not necessarily occur. Even two tasks with minimal resource demands may interfere if they compete for common processing *structures*. For example, no matter how automated the processing of two different visual symbols may be, perceiving them both at the same time will still be difficult if they are presented simultaneously at widely separated regions of the visual field. Nor can one understand speech while talking as clearly as while one is silent.

Recent models of attention have allowed the psychologist to predict when the information processing structure of two tasks will be such that they will interfere, even when their resource demands are slight. On the one hand, one can clearly identify physical constraints in the human's perceptual and motor "hardware" that will guarantee interference. For example, two visual displays with high-acuity demands separated by more than 2° will be difficult to perceive at once. Listening to two voices at once will produce acoustic masking, and any pair of tasks that require one hand (or finger) to be in two different places at the same time will obviously lead to a loss in performance of one or the other.

It is also possible, however, to go beyond these strict peripheral limitations of sensory–motor hardware and describe how tasks may compete for more specific processing resources within the brain itself (Navon & Gopher, 1979; Wickens, 1984b).

Table 5.2 shows one scheme for labeling or identifying processing structures within the brain that correspond to separate resources (Wickens, 1984b). This version of the multiple resources model makes two assertions: (1) to the extent that two tasks share common

Table 5.2.   Multiple Resource Model

Dichotomous dimension	Examples
Processing modalities	
Auditory vs. visual	ATC communications and auditory alerts vs. instrument scanning or out-of-cockpit monitoring
Voice vs. manual control	ATC communications vs. flight control or keyboard entry
Processing codes	
Verbal vs. spatial	Processing navigational coordinates, radio frequencies or understanding conversations vs. tracking or maintaining spatial orientation
Processing stages	
Perceptual and cognitive (working memory) vs. response	Instrument scanning, rehearsing, listening, calculating, and predicting vs. speaking, switch activation, or manual control

levels on any of the three dichotomous dimensions in Table 5.2, time-sharing will be less efficient; (2) to the extent that an increase in resource demand occurs at the level of a dimension shared by another task, there will be increasing interference between the two.

The three dichotomous dimensions and the relevant data pertaining to these for time-sharing are as follows.

1. *Processing modalities.* This dimension explains data that show it is easier to time-share an auditory and a visual task than two auditory or two visual tasks. Of course, to some extent this difference may be accounted for in terms of peripheral interference, since a pair of visual inputs will often compete for foveal vision, and a pair of auditory tasks may produce peripheral auditory masking. When experimental conditions are controlled to ensure that this peripheral competition does not occur, the effects of intramodality resource competition are reduced, but still generally observed (e.g., Rollins & Hendricks, 1980; Wickens, 1980; Wickens et al., 1983). In aviation, the dichotomy of modality-defined perceptual resources suggests that the heavy visual workload that characterizes the in-flight environment could be off-loaded by the increased use of voice display. However, two important cautions should be noted before the decision is made to display information auditorily. The first is that certain kinds of tasks are incompatible with auditory displays, particularly those portraying spatial analog information. Any advantages of presenting

such information auditorily may well be offset by the incompatibility (Wickens et al., 1983). Second, while verbal messages (digits and words) are more compatibly presented via speech than print, the transient characteristics of the speech mode make it important that messages of some length should be provided with a redundant "visual echo."

2. *Processing codes.* The second dichotomy of the multiple resource model, that defined by processing codes, distinguishes information that is mostly spatial and analog in nature from that which is verbal and linguistic. As such, the dichotomy distinguishes the *perception* of speech and print from that of graphics, motion, and auditory analog information (tone pitch and location); the *working memory* for verbal linguistic information from that for spatial information; and voice *responses* from spatially guided manual responses (e.g., those used in tracking and flight control). Because the spatial–verbal distinction is also assumed to have a brain hemispheric basis, the dichotomy also distinguishes between left- and right-handed control. The implications for the spatial–verbal dichotomy in working memory have been described earlier in this chapter. As pertains to perception, the dichotomy suggests that a mixture of graphics and digital or verbal displays will be a more nearly optimal format for displaying multitask information than will a homogeneous display (Boles & Wickens, 1987). The implications for response design are twofold. On the one hand, it points to the advantage of a mixture of voice and manual control over an all-manual multitask control configuration (Wickens, Zenyuh, Culp, & Marshak, 1985). (This guideline pertains as long as the voice-controlled task is not an inherently spatial task such as tracking.) On the other hand, it argues that when two tasks must be performed manually, performance will still be better if control is distributed across two hemispheres. Thus, for example, simultaneous responses to a key press task and a continuous tracking task will be improved if each is given by different hands rather than a single hand via a configuration in which the keypad is mounted on the movable control stick (Carswell & Wickens, 1985). The latter configuration of course reflects the design of the hands-on throttle and stick (HOTAS), used in many high-performance aircraft.

3. *Processing stages.* The third resource-defining dimension is that of processing stages. The data here, reviewed by Wickens (1980), suggest that two tasks both demanding either response processes or perceptual or cognitive processes (e.g., decision making, working memory, information integration) will interfere with each other to a greater extent than will a perceptual or cognitive task and a response

task. Thus, the rehearsal of information in working memory, or solving a mental arithmetic problem, will be time-shared more efficiently with a well-learned pattern of switch activation (a response process) than with a perceptual search operation, or with the reading of new information from a display, given that the response switch and the perceptual tasks are of equal resource demand.

An advantage of the multiple resource model as depicted in Table 5.2 is its usefulness in predicting performance in complex multitask situations. Tasks may be coded in terms of their level of demand on different dimensions of the model. Then "penalty points" can be subtracted to the extent that two or more tasks impose a common simultaneous demand on a given resource (North, 1985). Such a technique has proven reasonably successful in predicting the global level of task interference (Derrick & Wickens, 1984; Gopher & Braune, 1984).

Conclusion

In this chapter, we have reviewed representative research generated by the information processing approach to human cognition and demonstrated some implications of this research for the design of safe, comfortable, and efficient aviation systems. In essence, we have addressed what basic research on information processing has to offer human factors professionals who must design aviation systems. In conclusion, however, we would like to borrow a theme from Franklin V. Taylor (1957) and ask this question: what does applied research have to offer the basic study of human information processing?

The information processing approach has not been without its critics. It has been accused of playing 20 questions with nature and losing (Newell, 1973). The essence of this criticism is that the science has become too segmented along the line of specific experimental tasks. That is, one group is studying the infinite permutations on choice reaction time tasks, another group is studying memory search tasks, still another focuses only on tracking tasks—and very little information is exchanged among these groups. Thus, the science has produced an enormous catalog of information about a few rather esoteric laboratory tasks, yet has contributed very little to our understanding of how humans function outside the laboratory in real-world settings. In pursuing answers to our 20 questions we have missed the big picture. Implicit in this criticism is the belief that human information processing is a complex system which will never be understood as a sum of its component parts. For example, the constructs of attention and internal models may exist only as emergent properties of this complex system; that is, these constructs may not be localized within a particular component but arise as a result of interactions among components.

It is likely that the future success of the information processing approach will rest on its ability to deal with this criticism. There is a need for human factors specialists to widen their perspective beyond the relatively simple tasks that currently dominate research—to increase the complexity of experimental tasks and to incorporate more ecologically valid sources of information. This is where applied research has much to contribute to the basic science of cognitive psychology. The tasks of the pilot or the air traffic controller provide exactly the level of complexity that is needed in order to begin the task of integrating the answers to our 20 questions into a comprehensive understanding of human cognition. In addition, advances in computer technology allow these tasks to be studied in well-controlled simulated environments. These environments provide an ideal compromise between the need for experimental control and the need for ecological validity.

In conclusion, the information processing paradigm has contributed both knowledge and tools relevant for understanding human performance in aviation systems. The study of human performance in aviation systems provides an excellent opportunity for us to better understand general issues related to human cognition in complex environments.

Acknowledgments

Much of the writing of this chapter was carried out while the first author was supported by a grant from NASA-Ames Research Center (NASA-NAG2-308). Sandra Hart was the technical monitor.

References

Allen, R. W., Clement, W. F., & Jex, H. R. (1970). *Research on display scanning, sampling, and reconstruction using separate main and secondary tracking tasks* (NASA CR-1569). Washington, DC: NASA.

Alluisi, E., Muller, P. I., & Fitts, P. M. (1957). An information analysis of verbal and motor response in a force-paced serial task. *Journal of Experimental Psychology, 53,* 153–158.

Baker, C. H. (1961). Maintaining the level of vigilance by means of knowledge of results about a secondary vigilance task. *Ergonomics, 4,* 311–316.

Baty, D. L. (1971). Human transinformation rates during one-to-four axis tracking. In *Proceedings of the Seventh Annual Conference on Manual Control* (NASA SP-281). Los Angeles: University of Southern California and Washington, DC: U.S. Government Printing Office.

Bisseret, A. (1981). Applications of signal detection theory to decision making in supervisory control. *Ergonomics, 24,* 81–94.

Boles, D., & Wickens, C.D. (1987). Display formatting in information and non integration tasks. *Human Factors, 29,* 395–406.

Bransford, J. D., & Johnson, M. K. (1972). Contextual prerequisites for understanding: Some investigations of comprehension and recall. *Journal of Verbal Learning and Verbal Behavior, 11,* 717–726.

Brehmer, B. (1981). Models of diagnostic judgment. In J. Rasmussen & W. Rouse (Eds.), *Human detection and diagnosis of system failures.* New York: Plenum.

Broadbent, D. E. (1971). *Decision and stress.* New York and London: Academic Press.

Broadbent, D. E. (1982). Task combination and selective intake of information. *Acta Psychologica, 50,* 253–290.

Buch, G. (1984). An investigation of the effectiveness of pilot judgment training. *Human Factors, 26*(5), 557–564.

Buch, G., & de Bagheera, I. J. (1985). Judgment training effectiveness and permanency. In R. S. Jensen & J. Adrion (Eds.), *Proceedings of the Third Symposium on Aviation Psychology.* Columbus: Ohio State University.

Carswell, C. M., & Wickens, C. D. (1985). Lateral task segregation and the task-hemispheric integrity effect. *Human Factors, 27,* 681–694.

Clark, H. H., & Chase, W. G. (1972). On the process of comparing sentences against pictures. *Cognitive Psychology, 3,* 472–517.

Conrad, R. (1964). Acoustic comparisons in immediate memory. *British Journal of Psychology, 55,* 75–84.

Cotton, W., Tzeng, O., & Hardyck, C. (1980). Role of cerebral hemispheric processing in the visual half field stimulus response compatibility effect. *Journal of Experimental Psychology: Human Perception and Performance, 6,* 13–23.

Cuqlock, V. B. (1982). *A behavioral assessment of the weights applied to redundant cues.* Unpublished doctoral dissertation, University of Illinois, Urbana-Champaign.

Danaher, J. W. (1980). Human error in ATC system operations. *Human Factors, 22,* 535–546.

Deininger, R. L., Billington, M. J., & Riesz, R. R. (1966). The display mode and the combination of sequence length and alphabet size as factors of speed and accuracy. *IEEE Transactions on Human Factors in Electronics, 7,* 110–115.

Derrick, W. L., & Wickens, C. D. (1984). *A multiple processing resource explanation of the subjective dimensions of operator workload* (Tech. Rep. EPL-84-2/ONR-84-1). University of Illinois Engineering Psychology Laboratory.

DeSoto, C. B., London, M., & Handel, S. (1965). Social reasoning and spatial paralogic. *Journal of Personal and Social Psychology, 2,* 513–521.

Dougherty, D. J., Emery, J. H., & Curtin, J. G. (1964). *Comparison of perceptual workload in flying standard instrumentation and the contact analog vertical display* (Janair Tech. Report D.228-421-019). Fort Worth, TX: Bell Helicopter Co.

Durding, B. M., Becker, C. A., & Gould, J. D. (1977). Data organization. *Human Factors, 19,* 1–14.

Ebbeson, E. D., & Konecki, V. (1980). On external validity in decision-making research. In T. Wallsten (Ed.), *Cognitive processes in choice and decision making* (pp. 21–45). Hillsdale, NJ: Erlbaum Associates.

Einhorn, H. J., & Hogarth, R. M. (1981). Behavioral decisions theory: Processes of judgment and choice. *Annual Review of Psychology, 32,* 53–88.

Fischer, E., Haines, R., & Price, T. (1980). *Cognitive issues in head-up displays* (NASA Technical Paper 1711). Washington, DC: NASA.

Fischoff, B. (1977). Perceived informativeness of facts. *Journal of Experimental Psychology: Human Perception and Performance, 3,* 349–358.

Fitts, P. M., & Jones, R. E. (1947). Psychological aspects of instrument display: Analysis of 270 "pilot-error" experiences in reading and interpreting aircraft instruments. In H. W. Sinnaiko (Ed.) (1961), *Selected papers on human factors in the design and use of control system* (pp. 359–396).

Fitts, P. M., & Seeger, C. M. (1953). S–R compatibility: Spatial characteristics of stimulus and response codes. *Journal of Experimental Psychology, 46,* 199–210.

Fontenella, G. A. (1983). *The effect of task characteristics on the availability heuristic for judgments of uncertainty* (Report No. 83-1). Houston, TX: Rice University, Office of Naval Research.

Fowler, F. D. (1980). Air traffic control problems: A pilot's view. *Human Factors, 22,* 645–654.

Gettys, C. F. (1983). *Research and theory on predecision processes* (Tech. Rep. TR 11-30-83). Norman: University of Oklahoma, Department of Psychology.

Gibson, J. J. (1966). *The senses considered as perceptual systems.* Boston: Houghton Mifflin.

Gibson, J. J. (1979). *The ecological approach to visual perception.* Boston: Houghton Mifflin.

Goettl, B. P. (1985). The interfering effects of processing code on visual memory. *Proceedings of the 29th Annual Meeting of the Human Factors Society.* Santa Monica, CA: Human Factors Society.

Gopher, D., & Braune, R. (1984). On the psychophysics of workload: Why bother with subjective measures? *Human Factors, 26*(5), 519–532.

Gopher, D., & Eilam, Z. (1979). Development of the letter shape keyboard. In C. Bensel (Ed.), *Proceedings, 23rd Annual Meeting of the Human Factors Society.* Santa Monica, CA: Human Factors.

Greenwald, A. (1970). A double stimulation test of ideomotor theory with implications for selective attention. *Journal of Experimental Psychology, 84,* 392–398.

Greenwald, A. G. (1979). Time-sharing, ideomotor compatibility and automaticity. In C. Bensel (Ed.), *Proceedings, 23rd Annual Meeting of the Human Factors Society.* Santa Monica, CA: Human Factors.

Greenwald, H., & Shulman, H. (1973). On doing two things at once: Eliminating the psychological refractory period affect. *Journal of Experimental Psychology, 101,* 70–76.

Hartzell, E. S., Dunbar, S., Beveridge, R., & Cortilla, R. (1982). Helicopter pilot response latency as a function of the spatial arrangement of instruments and controls. *Proceedings of the 18th Annual Conference on Manual Control* (pp. 345–364). Dayton, OH: Wright–Patterson Air Force Base.

Harwood, K., Wickens, C., Kramer, A., Clay, D., & Liu, Y. (1986). Effects of display proximity and memory demands on the understanding of dynamic multidimensional information. *Proceedings of the 30th Annual Meeting of Human Factors Society* (pp. 786–790). Dayton, OH: Human Factors.

Hershon, R. L., & Hillix, W. A. (1965). Data processing in typing: Typing rate as a function of kind of material and amount exposed. *Human Factors, 7*, 483–492.

Hick, W. E. (1952). On the rate of gain of information. *Quarterly Journal of Experimental Psychology, 4*, 11–26.

Hockey, G. R. (1970). Signal probability and spatial location as possible bases for increased selectivity in noise. *Quarterly Journal of Experimental Psychology, 22*, 37–42.

Hyman, R. (1953). Stimulus information as a determinant of reaction time. *Journal of Experimental Psychology, 45*, 423–432.

Irizarry, V., & Knapp, B. (1986). A preliminary investigation of problem solving and judgmental strategies of expert military intelligence personnel. In *Proceedings, Psychology in the Department of Defense* (pp. 393–397). Colorado Springs, Colorado: United States Air Force Academy.

Jensen, R. J. (1981). Prediction and quickening in prospective flight displays for curved landing and approaches. *Human Factors, 23*, 333–364.

Jensen, R. S., & Benel, R. A. (1977). Judgment evaluation and instruction in civil pilot training (Final Report FAA-RD-78-24). Springfield, VA: National Technical Information Service.

Jex, H. R., & Clement, W. F. (1979). Defining and measuring perceptual–motor workload in manual control tasks. In N. Moray (Ed.), *Mental Workload and Its Theory and Measurement* (pp. 125–178). New York: Plenum.

Johnson, E. M., Cavanagh, R. C., Spooner, R. L., & Samet, M. G. (1973). Utilization of reliability measurements in Bayesian inference: Models and human performance. *IEEE Transactions on Reliability, 22*, 176–183.

Kahneman, D., Slovic, P., & Tversky, A. (Eds.) (1982). *Judgment under uncertainty: Heuristics and biases.* New York: Cambridge University Press.

Kahneman, D., & Tversky, A. (1973). On the psychology of prediction. *Psychological Review, 80*, 251–273.

Kantowitz, B. H., & Sorkin, R. D. (1983). *Human factors: Understanding people–system relationships.* New York: Wiley.

Lachman, R., Lachman, J. L., & Butterfield, E. C. (1979). *Cognitive psychology and information processing.* Hillsdale, NJ: Erlbaum Associates.

Langewiesche (1944). *Stick and rudder.* New York: McGraw-Hill.

Lester, L. F., & Bombaci, D. H. (1984). The relationship between personality and irrational judgment in civil pilots. *Human Factors, 26*(5), 565–572.

Lester, L. F., Diehl, A. E., & Buch, G. (1985). Private pilot judgment training in flight school settings: A demonstration project. *Proceedings of the Third Symposium on Aviation Psychology.* Columbus, OH: Ohio State University.

Loftus, E. F. (1979). *Eyewitness testimony.* Cambridge, MA: Harvard University Press.

Loftus, E. F., & Palmer, J. C. (1974). Reconstruction of automobile destruction: An example of the interaction between language and memory. *Journal of Verbal Learning and Verbal Behavior, 13*, 585–589.

Loftus, G. R., Dark, V. J., & Williams, D. (1979). Short-term memory factors in ground controller/pilot communications. *Human Factors, 21*, 169–181.

Loveless, N. E. (1963). Direction of motion stereotypes: A review. *Ergonomics, 5*, 357–383.

Miller, D. P. (1981). The depth/breadth trade-off in hierarchical computer menus. In R. Sugarman (Ed.), *Proceedings, 25th Annual Meeting of the Human Factors Society* (pp. 296–300). Santa Monica, CA: Human Factors.

Miller, G. A. (1956). The magical number seven plus of minus two: Some limits on our capacity for processing information. *Psychology Review, 63,* 81–97.

Moray, N. (1978). Strategic control of information processing. In G. Underwood (Ed.), *Human information processing.* New York: Academic Press.

Moray, N. (1981). The role of attention in the detection of errors and the diagnosis of errors in man–machine systems. In J. Rasmussen & W. Rouse (Eds.), *Human detection and diagnosis of system failures* (pp. 185–198). New York: Plenum.

Moray, N. (1984). Attention to dynamic visual displays in man–machine systems. In R. Parasuraman & R. Davies (Eds.), *Varieties of attention* (pp. 485–512). New York: Academic Press.

Mynatt, C. R., Doherty, M. E., & Tweney, R. D. (1977). Confirmation bias in a simulated research environment: An experimental study of scientific inference. *Quarterly Journal of Experimental Psychology, 29,* 85–95.

Navon, D., & Gopher, D. (1979). On the economy of the human processing system. *Psychological Review, 86,* 254–255.

Neisser, U. (1976). *Cognition and reality: Principles and implications of cognitive psychology.* San Francisco: Freeman.

Neisser, U., & Becklan, R. (1975). Selective looking: Attention to visually specified events. *Cognitive Psychology, 7,* 480–494.

Newell, A. (1973). You can't play 20 questions with nature and win. In W. G. Chase (Ed.), *Visual information processing.* New York: Academic Press.

North, R. (1985). A workload index for iterative crewstation evaluation. *NAECON Proceedings* (pp. 868–872). Dayton, OH.

Pachella, R. G. (1974). The interpretation of reaction time in information processing research. In B. H. Kantowitz (Ed.), *Human information processing: Tutorials in performance and cognition* (pp. 431–482). Hillsdale, NJ: Erlbaum Associates.

Parasuraman, R. (1979). Memory load and event rate control sensitivity decrements in sustained attention. *Science, 205,* 924–927.

Parasuraman, R., & Davies, D. R. (Eds.). (1984). *Varieties of attention.* Orlando, FL: Academic Press.

Phelps, R. H., & Shanteau, J. (1978). Livestock judges: How much information can an expert use. *Organizational Behavior in Human Performance, 21,* 209–219.

Pitz, G. F. (1965). Response variability in the estimation of relative frequency. *Perceptual and Motor Skills, 21,* 867–873.

Pitz, G., & Sachs, N. (1984). Judgment and decision: Theory and application. *Annual Review of Psychology, 35,* 139–163.

Posner, M. I. (1978). *Chronometric explorations of the mind.* Hillsdale, NJ: Erlbaum Associates.

Rasmussen, J. (1981). Models of mental strategies in process plant diagnosis. In J. Rasmussen & W. B. Rouse (Eds.), *Human detection and diagnosis of system failures* (pp. 241–258). New York: Plenum.

Rollins, R. A., & Hendricks, R. (1980). Processing of words presented simultaneously to eye and ear. *Journal of Experimental Psychology: Human Perception and Performance, 6,* 99–109.

Roske-Hofstrand, R. J., & Paap, K. (1985). Cognitive network organization and cockpit automation. In *Proceedings of the Third Symposium on Aviation Psychology.* Columbus: Ohio State University.

Schneider, W. (1985). Training high-performance skills: Fallacies and guidelines. *Human Factors, 27*, 285–300.

Schneider, W., Dumas, S. T., & Shiffrin, R. M. (1984). Automatic and control processing and attention. In R. Parasuraman & D. R. Davies (Eds.), *Varieties of Attention* (pp. 1–33). New York: Academic Press.

Schneider, W., & Shiffrin, R. M. (1977). Controlled and automatic human information processing I: Detection, search, and attention. *Psychological Review, 84*, 1–66.

Schum, D. (1975). The weighing of testimony of judicial proceedings from sources having reduced credibility. *Human Factors, 17*, 172–203.

Senders, J. (1964). The human operator as a monitor and controller of multidegree of freedom systems. *IEEE Transactions on Human Factors in Electronics, HFE-5*, 2–6.

Senders, J. W. (1966). A reanalysis of the pilot eye-movement data. *IEEE Transactions on Human Factors in Electronics, HFE-7*, 103–106.

Shaffer, L. H. (1973). Latency mechanisms in transcription. In S. Kornblum (Ed.), *Attention and Performance IV*. New York: Academic Press.

Shaffer, L. H., & Hardwick, J. (1970). The basis of transcription skill. *Journal of Experimental Psychology, 84*, 424–440.

Shannon, C. E., & Weaver, W. (1949). *The mathematical theory of communications.* Urbana: University of Illinois Press.

Sheridan, T. (1972). On how often the supervisor should sample. *IEEE Transactions on Systems, Sciences, and Cybernetics, SSC-6*, 140–145.

Simon, J. R. (1969). Reactions towards the source of stimulation. *Journal of Experimental Psychology, 81*, 174–176.

Simpson, C., & Williams, D. H. (1980). Response-time effects of alerting tone and semantic context for synthesized voice cockpit warnings. *Human Factors, 22*, 319–330.

Slovic, P. (1984). Facts vs. fears: Understanding perceived risk. Paper presented at a Science and Public Policy Seminar.

Strayer, D., Wickens, C. D., & Braune, R. (1987). Adult age differences in the speed and capacity of information processing. II. An electrophysiological approach. *Psychology & Aging, 2*, 70–78.

Taylor, F. V. (1957). Psychology and the design of machines. *American Psychologist, 12*, 249–258.

Taylor, R. M., (1987). Workload management in military cockpits: Present insights. In *Proceedings of Symposium on Cockpit Aids in Military Aircraft*. London: Royal Aeronautical Society.

Treisman, A. (1964). Verbal cues, language, and meaning in attention. *American Journal of Psychology, 77*, 206–214.

Tulga, M. K., & Sheridan, T. B. (1980). Dynamic decisions and workload in multitask supervisory control. *IEEE Transactions on Systems, Man, and Cybernetics, SMC-10*, 217–232.

Tversky, A. (1972). Elimination by aspects: A theory of choice. *Psychological Review, 79*, 281–299.

Tversky, A., & Kahneman, D. (1974). Judgment under uncertainty: Heuristics and biases. *Science, 185*, 1124–1131.

Tversky, A., & Kahneman, D. (1981). The framing of decisions and the psychology of choice. *Science, 211*, 453–458.

Vidulich, M. D., & Wickens, C. D. (1982). The influence of S-C-R compatibility and resource competition on performance of threat evaluation and fault diagnosis. In R. E. Edwards (Ed.), *Proceedings, 27th Annual Meeting of the Human Factors Society* (pp. 223–226). Santa Monica, CA: Human Factors.

Wallsten, T. S., & Barton, C. (1982). Processing probabilistic multidimensional information for decisions. *Journal of Experimental Psychology: Learning, Memory, and Cognition, 8*(5), 361–383.

Warren, R. (1982). *Optical transformation during movement: Review of the optical concomitants of egomotion,* (Tech. Rep. AFOSR-TR-82-1028). Air Force Office of Scientific Research.

Wason, P. C., & Johnson-Laird, P. N. (1972). *Psychology of reasoning: Structure and content.* London: Batsford.

Welford, A. T. (1968). *Fundamentals of skill.* London: Methuen.

Wickelgren, W. A. (1964). Size of rehearsal group in short-term memory. *Journal of Experimental Psychology, 68,* 413–419.

Wickelgren, W. (1977). Speed–accuracy tradeoff and information processing dynamics. *Acta Psychologica, 41,* 67–85.

Wickens, C. D. (1980). The structure of attentional resources. In R. Nickerson & R. Pew (Eds.), *Attention and Performance VIII* (pp. 63–102). Hillsdale, NJ: Erlbaum Associates.

Wickens, C. D. (1984a). *Engineering Psychology and Human Performance.* Columbus, OH: Charles Merrill.

Wickens, C. D. (1984b). Processing resources in attention. In R. Parasuraman & D. R. Davies (Eds.), *Varieties of Attention.* Orlando, FL: Academic Press.

Wickens, C. D. (1987). Attention. In P. Hancock (Ed.), *Human factors in psychology.* Amsterdam: North Holland Publishing.

Wickens, C. D., Sandry, D., & Vidulich, M. (1983). Compatibility and resource competition between modalities of input, central processing, and output: Testing a model of complex task performance. *Human Factors, 25,* 227–248.

Wickens, C. D., Stokes, A., & Barnett, B. J. (1987). *Componential analysis of pilot decision making.* University of Illinois Aviation Research Laboratory Technical Report ARL-87-41 SCEEE-87-1.

Wickens, C. D., Zenyuh, J., Culp, V., & Marshak, W. (1985). Voice and manual control in dual-task situations. *Proceedings, 29th Annual Meeting of the Human Factors Society* (pp. 1093–1097). Santa Monica, CA: Human Factors.

Wiener, E. L. (1977). Controlled flight into terrain accidents: System-induced errors. *Human Factors, 19,* 171.

Wiener, N. (1948). *Cybernetics.* Cambridge, MA: The Technology Press.

Wilkinson, R. T. (1964). Artificial "signals" as an aid to an inspection task. *Ergonomics, 7,* 63–72.

Woods, D., Wise, J., & Hanes, L. (1981). An evaluation of nuclear power plant safety parameter display systems. In R. C. Sugarman (Ed.), *Proceedings, 25th Annual Meeting of the Human Factors Society* (pp. 110–114). Santa Monica, CA: Human Factors.

Wright, R. E. (1974). Aging, divided attention, and processing capacity. *Journal of Gerontology, 36,* 605–614.

Yntema, D. (1963). Keeping track of several things at once. *Human Factors, 6,* 7–17.

Human Workload in Aviation

6

Barry H. Kantowitz
Patricia A. Casper

Introduction

This chapter is intended for the reader who would like to know
more about the human factors of workload in aviation without necessarily becoming an instant human factors expert. Since no special
background in experimental psychology, industrial engineering, control engineering, or the like, is assumed, the chapter omits some of
the detailed technical points—especially those requiring some
knowledge of mathematics and psychological theory—that qualified
human factors experts find interesting and useful. Nonetheless, we
believe it is possible to explain the fundamentals of workload, including some problems associated with the concept, to an audience
that is motivated by practical considerations. Since the first com-
mandment of human factors is "Honor thy user" (Kantowitz & Sorkin, 1983), it is important for human factors specialists to
communicate to users directly in language that is simpler and less
contaminated by jargon than the language normally used in professional journals and reports.

Human Factors in Aviation
Copyright © 1988 by Academic Press, Inc.
All rights of reproduction in any form reserved.

Still, it will be necessary for the reader to learn something of the tools and theories used in human factors. While we shall try to explain these as simply and clearly as we can, assuming that the reader has minimal human factors background, these new concepts will create mental workload for the reader. We believe that the conclusions of human factors experts cannot be evaluated without some knowledge of the procedures used by these experts. Thus, we ask the reader to avoid skimming over what might at first appear to be an esoteric discussion of, say, a model of attention or a difficulty with establishing subjective rating scales of workload. These discussions are necessary to understand how human factors can help the aviation industry.

Let us now preview the path taken in this chapter. First, we briefly discuss the importance of human workload in aviation systems. This provides the motivation for the following section on defining and measuring workload, a complex issue indeed. The most abstract section of this chapter relates workload to the psychological concept of attention and suggests how theories of attention can help solve some of the problems in defining and measuring workload. This is followed by a selective review of empirical workload studies using a variety of measurement techniques. Finally, the chapter ends with a brief discussion of prospects for workload research and its pragmatic application to the aviation industry.

Why Workload Is Important

Safety

The aviation industry is proud of its safety record and takes aggressive action to maintain the public perception that aviation, especially commercial air transport by certified carriers, is safe. Pilot error (Hurst & Hurst, 1982) is an important component of safety, as is the possibility of human error in other aviation subsystems such as air traffic control and maintenance. Even if some divine power could guarantee that all mechanical and electrical systems used in aviation were 100% reliable, there would still be accidents due to human error.

Human factors research has amply demonstrated that workload is an important determinant, although not the only relevant factor, in causing human error (Kantowitz & Sorkin, 1983, chapters 2, 6, & 19). The human is most reliable under moderate levels of workload that do not change suddenly and unpredictably. Extremes of workload increase the likelihood of human error. When workload is excessive, errors arise from the inability of the human to cope with high information rates imposed by the environment. When workload is too low, the human is bored and may not attend properly to the task at hand, also leading to error.

The modern jet aircraft presents a complex and variable environment to its human operator. Flight-deck automation (see below) offers the opportunity to decrease pilot workload enough to induce boredom and even sleep. Attempts to prevent pilot error by additional regulation, both federal and corporate, have increased the complexity of the environment and increased pilot workload. Different phases of flight present different workloads for the flight crew. Workload is further modified by factors not under the control of the crew, such as weather, visibility, traffic density, and communication requirements, to name but a few.

Safety depends upon reducing human error. Human error depends upon both the amount and stability of workload. Since the jet aircraft presents variable amounts of workload at variable times, there is ample opportunity for pilot error.

Crew Size

Crews of two pilots are now routinely flying wide-bodied jet aircraft without flight engineers. Has this reduction in crew size from three to two been achieved at the cost of higher crew workload? If so, does this imply that present crew workloads are excessive?

This issue was heavily debated, and a presidential task force upheld certification of two-pilot crews, although it is not completely clear that the flight engineer is necessarily gone forever (Wiener, 1985). Adding a third crew member does not reduce workload by one-third, since the need for communication among crew members may be increased. Furthermore, if overall crew workload requirements are moderate, the third crew member may be too underloaded, which can increase human error.

Automation

Automation offers the potential for both decreasing and increasing crew workload. Tasks once performed by the crew can now be allocated to automatic devices; this is intended by designers to reduce crew workload. However, the crew is still responsible for the operation of the automatic device, and this introduces monitoring requirements that increase workload. While automation often results in a net decrease in crew workload, opportunities for system error may not decrease correspondingly, since automation can introduce large delays between the performance of a crew action and its ultimate effect. For example, an incorrect entry of a waypoint on an inertial navigation system may not become apparent until hours later. This long delay decreases the probability of human error being detected and fixed.

A survey of more than 100 B-767 pilots from three airlines reflects both sides of the effects of automation (Curry, 1984). When asked if "automation reduces overall workload," 47% agreed and 36% disagreed. Similarly, 53% agreed and 37% disagreed that "automation does not reduce overall workload, since there is more to keep watch over." Nevertheless, 79% agreed that "I use the automatic devices a lot because I find them useful." Part of this division may depend upon which seat the pilot flies. Captains agreed more, and first officers disagreed more, that "automation frees me of much of the routine, mechanical parts of flying so I can concentrate more on 'managing' the flight."

Human factors specialists call the systematic decisions about which tasks should be assigned to the human and which to automatic equipment *allocation of functions*. Allocation of functions is a traditional human factors responsibility, and many rules of thumb and techniques have been developed to help decide how automation should be implemented. These details are beyond the scope of this chapter, but see a chapter by Kantowitz and Sorkin (1986) in the *Handbook of Human Factors* for additional information. However, one of the better solutions to allocation of functions allows allocation to be changed dynamically as environmental demands change. Thus, the pilot can enable or disable flight-deck automation as he or she sees fit. Control is passed to automation only when this is desired by the pilot. The importance of allowing the pilot to make this determination can be seen in the following quotation from an airline check-pilot (Wiener, 1985, p. 88): "I am willing to fly it as long as it has the yellow button (autopilot disengage). I can always turn it back into a DC-9." This decision will be influenced by pilot workload.

The converse function of allowing the automation to decide whether or not the pilot should be in the loop is technically feasible but has been only minimally implemented in aircraft. For example, stick pushers that automatically take over control of the aircraft to prevent a stall represent an allocation of functions decision whereby automation overrides human control. Pilots' reluctance to allow automation to control their operations is understandable. Since pilots have the ultimate responsibility for the safety and operation of the aircraft, according to Federal Aviation Regulation 91.3(a), they feel that they should also have the ultimate control.

In general, people are more comfortable and under less stress when they believe they control a situation, even if, in fact, this control is lacking. Psychologists call this situation *perceived control*, and many experiments document its positive benefits in minimizing effects of stressful situations (Glass & Singer, 1972). Perceived control can be illustrated by a commonplace example. Imagine you are at the dentist having a tooth filled. Have your dentist agree to stop drilling if you raise your right hand. The stress, especially for people who are afraid of visits to the dentist, will be less, due to your perceived control of the situation. Even if you never raise your hand to test your control (this is why it is called *perceived* control), you will still feel better. Part of the reluctance to have automation override pilots may be due to pilots wanting perceived control. However, part of the reluctance may be justified by inappropriate implementation. Wiener (1985) cites the dangers of stick pushers, including a crash at Terre Haute, Indiana, of a Fairchild Metro whose stall warning system first sounded an alarm and then activated a stick pusher with 60 pounds of force to lower the nose. It is hard to tell how many pilots' complaints about allocation of functions to automatic devices are due to loss of perceived control and feelings of being "along for the ride" versus accurate knowledge that such automation decreases system reliability.

Automation can also alter crew workload by changing the format of traditional controls and displays. The use of CRT (cathode ray tube) displays in the cockpit is but one example of new display technology. As computerized displays become dominant, there is a tendency to display information in digital, rather than analog, format since computers are more readily programmed to display numerical data. (A traditional watch with minute and hour hands is an analog display; a newer watch with a liquid crystal display that presents numbers is a digital display.) Even automobiles are now available with digital speedometers. This display format is not always optimal. Human factors scientists have distinguished between two kinds of display readings: check-readings are used when only an approximate knowledge of some internal parameters is required. For example, you don't need to know the precise temperature of the coolant in the radiator of your car, and so a check-reading is sufficient to determine if temperature is cold, normal, or overheated. Quantitative readings are required when precise information such as a heading or a navaid frequency setting is needed. Analog displays are much better for check-reading than are digital displays because they can be check-read more quickly and with less workload (Hanson, Payne, Shively, & Kantowitz, 1981).

Certification

As aircraft manufacturers are well aware, new aircraft must pass a series of federal tests before they can be placed into commercial transport service. Federal Aviation Regulation 25 deals with crew workload. As we shall see, it is commendably vague:

> FAR 25.771 Pilot Compartment
> (a) Each pilot compartment and its equipment must allow the minimum flight crew (established under 25.1523) to perform their duties without unreasonable concentration or fatigue.
>
> FAR 25.1523 Minimum Flight Crew
> The minimum flight crew must be established so that it is sufficient for safe operation, considering
> (a) The workload on individual crew members.
>
> FAR 25 Appendix D
> Criteria for determining minimum flight crew. The following are considered by the Agency in determining the minimum flight crew under 25.1523:
> a. Basic workload functions. The following basic workload functions are considered:
>   (1) Flight path control
>   (2) Collision avoidance
>   (3) Navigation
>   (4) Communications
>   (5) Operation and monitoring of aircraft engines and systems.
>   (6) Command decisions.
> b. Workload factors. The following workload factors are considered significant when analyzing and demonstrating workload for minimum flight crew determination:
>   (1) The accessibility, ease, and simplicity of operation of all necessary flight, power, and equipment controls . . .
>   (2) The accessibility and conspicuity of all necessary instruments and failure warning devices such as fire warning, electrical system malfunction, and other failure or caution indicators. The extent to which such instruments or devices direct the proper corrective action is also considered.
>   (3) The number, urgency, and complexity of operating procedures with particular consideration given to the specific fuel management schedule . . .

These regulations are quoted to make a specific point. Nowhere does FAR 25 specify how workload is to be measured or even how workload is defined. (This may be a positive feature for reasons that will become evident later.) While FAR 25 establishes workload as an important factor for certification, it refrains from telling us what workload is. The typical engineering specification is far more precise, but when the human enters the equation we do well to avoid a foolish search for precision where none exists. This is the central focus of human factors as a profession: to wed the qualitative understanding of human functioning to the engineering precision required in complex systems. There are some areas of human factors, manual control, for example, where reasonable approximations of human functioning can be expressed with mathematical precision. Alas, as we turn to mental functioning in general, and workload in particular, such precision has not yet been achieved except in limited instances that often are hard to generalize to practical situations. The remainder of this chapter explains how the human factors professional tries to meet the goals of FAR 25 by studying workload.

Defining and Measuring Workload

The previous discussion carefully avoided a precise definition of workload. You were probably able to understand the discussion based upon your own private everyday usage of the term *workload*. While this is satisfactory for everyday conversation, scientific usage demands a more exact definition for technical terms (Kantowitz & Roediger, 1984). A tremendous variety of definitions of workload have been used by researchers and practitioners (Hart, 1985; Kantowitz, 1985a; Moray, 1979). Indeed, one of the editors of this volume has remarked that so many reviews of workload have been published that we will soon need a review of reviews (Wiener, 1985). This chapter is not intended as a review of reviews, and so we refrain from listing all the definitions of workload proposed to date. This also permits us to escape from the unprofitable task of deciding whose definition of workload is best. There is no empirical technique for proving a definition. Definitions are not correct or incorrect but rather more or less useful. Ultimately, individuals must decide which definition of workload will be most helpful in accomplishing their own goals. So we concentrate upon discussing problems and advantages of certain classes of definitions, especially as these relate to techniques for measuring workload empirically, instead of dogmatically asserting some specific definition of workload.[1]

Physical versus Mental Workload

Physical workload is a straightforward concept. It is easy to define and measure in terms of energy expenditure. Traditional human factors texts (e.g., McCormick & Sanders, 1982) tell us how to measure human physical work in kilocalories and oxygen consumption. Very light physical workload is defined and measured as an expenditure of energy less than 2.5 kilocal/minute and oxygen consumption under 0.5 liters/minute. Very heavy work calls for expenditures exceeding 12.5 kilocal/minute and 2.5 liters/minute. This physical workload scale is intuitively sensible and matches our notions of work learned in freshman physics, where we gaily rolled steel balls down inclined planes. Unfortunately, measures of physical workload are becoming less and less relevant in aviation, where hydraulic systems and other devices have been allocated the function of exerting large forces that once were the responsibility of the human operator. While it is still possible for a pilot to become physically fatigued, especially during an emergency when some of the mechanical systems fail, it is far more likely for designers to worry about mental, rather than physical, overload.

It is natural for designers to want a metric for mental workload that offers the simplicity and elegance of earlier metrics used to establish and calibrate physical workload. Alas, the truth is that such a metric is neither currently available nor even on the horizon (Kantowitz, 1985a). We may never be able to create a meaningful and valid scale for mental workload equivalent to kilocalories per minute in terms of its utility, generality, and formal measurement properties. Mental workload is not nearly as tidy a concept as physical workload, and viewing it primarily as an analogy to physical workload is bound to lead to disappointment.

There is, however, some cause for optimism. A number of scientists are working hard to create useful measures of mental workload using the various techniques discussed below. The problem they are having is that few of the measures reliably agree with each other. It

---

[1]A precise definition is given by Kantowitz (1986), but its technical details are beyond the scope of this chapter: "Workload is an intervening variable, similar to attention, that modulates or indexes the tuning between the demands of the environment and the capacity of the operator."

is quite common to read a report of an experiment or flight simulation that tested several measures of mental workload only to find that many of them failed to discriminate among experimental conditions. In order to discuss what the human factors expert can (and cannot) contribute to this issue, we must first review some of the more common methods used to measure mental workload. These include subjective ratings, secondary tasks, and biocybernetic indices.

Subjective Ratings

This method of measuring mental workload has been the most widely used, most likely due to its ease of use. Operators are simply asked to rate how hard they feel they have worked in a particular task either during or after the task has been completed. The method has the advantages of being nonintrusive and easy to implement. On the other side of the coin, however, its disadvantages include the lack of a theoretical framework, difficulties in comparing results between experimenters using different rating scales, and the problem of ratings yielding relative rather than absolute results. Last but certainly not least is the problem of applying valid statistical tests to data obtained from subjective ratings.

Data sets of this type are called ordinal because there are only ordinal relationships among set members, for example, greater than, less than, or equal to. When numbers are arbitrarily assigned to points along a subjective rating scale, they cannot be manipulated mathematically in the same straightforward way as data that describe a numerical relationship between points on a continuum, like reaction time, or skin temperature, for example (ratio or interval data). As an example, suppose that three runners (A, B, and C) have just completed a marathon, and runner A finished in 1:30:10, runner B in 1:30:20, and runner C in 1:50:40. An ordinal scale would simply describe the finishers as first, second, and third, and would not reflect how far apart the runners finished. An interval scale, however, would take into account the elapsed time between finishers and would accurately reflect the fact that runner B was a lot closer to runner A than to runner C. Subtraction of the times for the three runners gives us an accurate picture of who finished closer to whom, while if we were to attempt this with the ordinal data (the numbers 1, 2, and 3) we could conclude nothing about the spacing of the runners. Some of the subjective rating methods we describe have attempted to eliminate this scaling problem, as we shall see.

Cooper–Harper Scales.   The oldest of the three rating scales that we discuss is the Cooper–Harper scale, originally designed to measure the handling qualities of aircraft. Cooper and Harper (1969) had pilots arrive at ratings through the use of a binary decision tree containing increasingly specific questions, until a final rating between 1 and 10 could be reached. Although there is still uncertainty about whether anything more than an ordinal scale is achieved, the scale has been hardy enough to generate several modifications, including one developed for workload by Wierwille and Casali (1983), which has been used successfully a number of times in a variety of experiments.

SWAT Ratings.   A second subjective technique, with solid footings in the study of psychometric analysis, is the Subjective Workload Assessment Technique (SWAT), used quite extensively by researchers at the Air Force Aerospace Medical Research Laboratory. SWAT ratings are based on three major factors: time load, mental effort, and psychological stress, each of which is rated on a 3-point scale, yielding 27 ($3 \times 3 \times 3$) basic scale points. Conjoint measurement techniques are then applied to create a unitary measurement scale having interval properties. Although some researchers are confident of the mathematical validity of this method (Shingledecker, 1983), others have raised serious questions concerning the fulfillment of assumptions underlying the procedure (Boyd, 1983).

Weighted Bipolar Ratings.   The Human Performance Group at the NASA-Ames Research Center has achieved good results by combining ratings from several unweighted scales into a single weighted measure of workload. Pilots are repeatedly asked to choose which of a pair of subscales contributes more to their overall mental workload, until all possible pairs of subscales have been compared. The number of times a particular subscale was preferred to other subscales is its weight. When all of the subscale ratings are obtained, they are multiplied by their appropriate weights and added together to give the total overall workload. Recent results using this weighted rating appear to indicate that the subjective workload of particular flight subtasks (e.g., fly at a constant altitude or fly at a constant heading) can be linearly combined to predict subjective workload for combinations of subtasks (Kantowitz, Hart, Bortolussi, Shively, & Kantowitz, 1984).

Secondary Tasks

The secondary-task paradigm imposes an additional task on the operator in addition to the main task (flying, in our case) and measures performance on the extra task. Decrements in performance of the secondary task are thought to indicate increased mental workload in the primary task. Although one of the more preferred methods in laboratory settings, due to its objectivity and strong theoretical foundation, the secondary-task method has its disadvantages. It is obtrusive in operational settings, and, like the subjective rating technique, there are serious problems in comparing data from different experiments using different secondary tasks.

In order to correctly use and interpret results from experiments using this method, a few initial assumptions must be met (see Kantowitz, 1985a). If one is indeed trying to measure "spare" capacity, it must be made certain that enough capacity has been given to the primary task that it is performed as well in the dual-task condition as it is in isolation. This requirement is met by including single-stimulation control conditions where both the primary and the secondary tasks are performed alone. With these conditions one can tell if decrements occur in primary-task performance in the dual-task condition (an undesirable result) as well as in secondary-task performance (an indicator of increased primary-task workload). It is also useful to include at least two levels of difficulty of the secondary task, in order to make inferences about the internal system architecture. With only one level of the secondary task it is impossible to tell if no changes in secondary-task performance reflect no changes in workload or a secondary task that is too easy. Later in this chapter experiments are presented illustrating the utility of the secondary-task technique and how the use of a good theory can minimize the problem of deciding which secondary task to use in an experiment.

Biocybernetic Measures

Perhaps the most potentially unobtrusive class of mental workload indices is the biocybernetic, or physiological, group of measures. These include dependent variables such as heart rate, pulse wave velocity, skin temperature, electromyogram, evoked potentials, magnetic evoked potentials, and pupil diameter (see Wierwille, 1979). Most experiments do not include all of these indices at once, possibly because there is no one theory of workload that successfully explains how all of these psychophysiological measures are correlated.

The biocybernetic measures of mental workload are superior to subjective ratings in their objectivity, and they are superior to secondary tasks in their unobtrusiveness. Increases in an operator's stress level can be detected by these measures when the operator is subjectively unaware of a rise in workload, and without the costly disruption of primary-task performance.

These highly useful tools have a set of related drawbacks, however. As you can imagine, the continuous monitoring of physiological functions generates an enormous amount of data—often embedded in a great deal of biological noise—that must usually be analyzed off-line after an experiment is completed. Even when the analyses are complete and enough data points have been obtained, the lack of a sound theoretical framework makes interpreting the results a difficult task. Biocybernetic measures of mental workload show the most promise when combined with behavioral measures that have a stronger base in theory.

Other Metrics

Not all researchers attempt to measure mental workload using the three techniques outlined above, although they are by far the most popular. Some scientists administer only one task and interpret decrements in performance of the task as indicators of increased mental load (Albanese, 1977). While this method appears to be simple to use and to interpret, it equates workload with performance and seems poor in detecting changes in mental workload for a task associated with low to medium levels of mental workload.

Others in the field have used the observational method to measure mental workload (Hurst & Rose, 1978b). Although similar to the subjective rating technique, it is less frequently used. An observer monitors the behavior of another person engaged in a task and subjectively rates the degree of stress reflected by the worker. Later in this chapter we present an example of a study in the air traffic control industry using this technique.

Attention and Workload

As we have stated in the preceding discussion, there are many ways to define and measure mental workload. It is not astonishing that these many ways do not always agree with each other. Thus, the practitioner has the problem of deciding which index of mental workload to use. Similarly, the experimenter has the problem of explaining the relationships among different measures of mental workload. Conceptually there is a single tool that can help accomplish both goals: a good theory of mental workload (Kantowitz, 1985a). Theory helps us to fill in the gaps of missing data, and theory can explain why different measures of mental workload are not perfectly correlated. Since workload is such a multidimensional concept (Hart, 1985), there are quite a few alternative starting points for developing relevant theory. We have selected the psychological concept of attention as the starting point for a theory of mental workload.

Attention refers to our ability to do more than one thing at the same time. Many experiments have shown that our ability to attend to several sources of information simultaneously is severely restricted (e.g., Broadbent, 1971). As a first approximation, we can regard the human as a *limited-capacity channel* who can only transmit a small amount of information per second. Whenever this small amount (on the order of 10 bits/second, where 1 bit is the information in the toss of a fair coin and also the smallest unit of information in computer memory) is exceeded, people make errors. So according to this model of attention, a pilot who must process information that exceeds his channel capacity will make mistakes. Perhaps an analogy will make this important point clearer. An airport can land only so many planes per hour. This is its landing capacity. If there is a need to land planes in excess of this capacity, holding patterns must be assigned to augment the storage capability of the system. If this is consistently required, the airport would try to expand its landing capacity, perhaps by adding an extra runway.

The limited-capacity model states that the human is similar to an airport with only one runway. At one time psychologists thought this runway was very short and could handle only a single aircraft at one time; this was known as the single-channel model of attention. Now we know that the mental runway is long enough to hold more than one aircraft under certain circumstances, analogous to landing one propjet quickly after another. However, it is possible for one cognitive function to take up all the runway space if it requires lots of mental calculation, analogous to landing a heavy, wide-bodied jet with a turbulent wake that prevents even lighter craft from landing too soon behind it.

There are not many possibilities for increasing the channel capacity of a pilot, although extensive training may sometimes give the impression that this has happened. The best human factors specialists can do is to arrange the format and content of the tasks to be performed so they are most compatible with the information processing capabilities of people. Then no channel capacity is wasted by being used to transform incompatible information.

One particular theory of attention (Figure 6.1) that we find especially helpful when talking about mental workload is called a *hybrid processing model* because it combines two important pathways for information flow (Kantowitz & Knight, 1976). In a *serial* model, like the original limited-channel model, information flows directly from one box (or *stage*, as the boxes are technically termed) into the next. Each successive stage cannot do anything until it receives the output from the preceding stage. Thus, information flows like a row of dominoes arranged adjacently; knocking down the first domino propagates a chain reaction down the row until finally the last one topples. In a *parallel* model, information can be worked upon by more than one stage at a time. So a stage need not wait until preceding stages are finished. The hybrid model states that human informa-

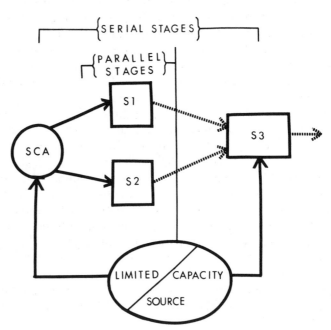

Figure 6.1.   The hybrid attention model proposed by Kantowitz and Knight (1976). S1 and S2 represent perceptual processing stages that operate in parallel. S3 represents the "bottleneck" in human information processing, a serial output stage. SCA is a static capacity allocator whose operation exceeds the scope of this chapter.

tion processing starts out parallel but ends up serial. We can process several types of incoming events at once, but we can only output responses or actions, such as adjusting a throttle or throwing a switch, serially.

Although the hybrid model may appear to be quite abstract, it makes some useful predictions about practical situations. For example, it tells us that if we want to minimize mental load, we should concentrate upon the human output stage rather than the input stage. Responses are very expensive consumers of capacity. The human is good at taking in several sources of information provided a response to each one is not required. So the ideal control panel for an air traffic controller should have several displays but only a single output device.

Selective Review of Empirical Workload Studies

Pilot Workload

Task Distribution.   The distribution of responsibility in flight and air traffic control may well be one of the most important factors influencing workload. The duties operators are assigned to are important in determining how hard they will be working and at what times during the course of the task (e.g., flight segment) they will be most taxed. It comes as no great surprise that most empirical studies find higher overall levels of mental workload for the pilot than for the copilot or navigator (Hart & Hauser, 1987; Roscoe, 1978). Anyone who has ever driven a car filled with friends or relatives knows that it is the person whose hands are on the wheel who must make any last-minute decisions in order to control the vehicle, no matter how much the backseat driver tries to help out. Not all measures of mental workload detect such differences, however. In an interesting study conducted aboard the NASA C-141 Kuiper Airborne Observatory, Hart and Hauser (1987) evaluated several different measures of pilot and copilot workload, including subjective ratings (Hart, 1982b) and heart rate.

The pilots' subjective ratings of overall workload and stress were found to vary significantly across flight segments, with the highest ratings occurring after takeoff and landing segments, as indicated by the U-shaped curve in Figure 6.2. No differences in subjective ratings of overall workload or stress were found between pilots and copilots. This result is palatable if one things back to the driving example just

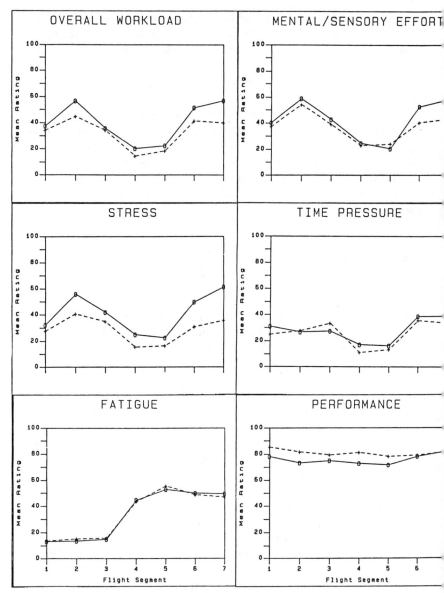

Figure 6.2.   Average bipolar ratings by flight segment for pilots (solid line) and copilots (dashed line). (From Hart, Hauser, & Lester, 1984.)

mentioned—the mother-in-law in the back seat is sure to report being under as much stress as the poor husband who is driving through rush hour traffic in downtown Chicago. For both pilots, reported fatigue levels increased significantly during the course of the flights, while mental effort ratings increased or decreased with different flight segments. The correlations between heart rate, workload, and stress were high for both pilots, but were higher for the pilot than the copilot.

The mean heart rate of the pilot controlling the aircraft (81 beats/minute) was found to be higher than that of the pilot responsible for navigation and communications (68 beats/minute). Heart rate also varied significantly between flight segments (see Figure 6.3). For the pilot there was an increase in heart rate during the landing phase of flight, and for both pilots and copilots, heart rates were faster during preflight and takeoff than at altitude portions of flight.

The results of the Hart and Hauser (1987) study provide further evidence of the divergence of subjective and objective measures of mental workload. The heart rate measure detected workload differences between the pilot and the copilot, while the subjective measures did not. Discrepancies like this are common in workload studies, and they support the idea that workload is a dynamic and complex phenomenon not totally described by any one particular measure. This problem is readdressed later in this section.

Our previous discussion of delegation of responsibility was by no means meant to trivialize the duties of the navigator. The navigator

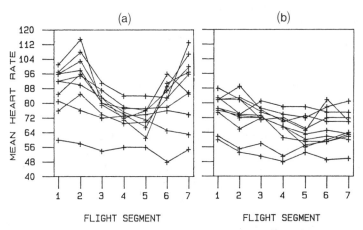

Figure 6.3.   Mean heart rate (averaged across 11 flights) by flight segment and position: (a), pilot; (b), copilot. (From Hart, Hauser, & Lester, 1984.)

has stress periods also, during flight segments involving communications with the tower, frequent instrument-check calls, map checks, and out-of-cockpit visual scanning during low-terrain flights. Sanders, Simmons, Hofmann, and DeBonis (1977) conducted an in-flight study attempting to measure and categorize the visual workload of copilots and navigators during low-level flights in a UH-1 helicopter. Results showed that the majority of the navigator's time (91.4%) was spent alternately looking at the hand-held map and looking out of the aircraft. A total of 5.5% of visual time was spent on instruments and warning lights, while only 3% was devoted to the visual free-time task. If the navigator is to be expected to help the pilot more, new maps and better navigational aids should be developed in order to reduce the amount of time a navigator must spend looking out of the cockpit, thus allowing more time to help the pilot monitor the instruments.

Subjective versus Objective Measures.   In the search for practical estimates of pilot workload, objective measures have been too often replaced by subjective measures, despite convincing laboratory evidence that objective measures should accurately reflect workload differences between simulated flight segments. The abandonment of objective measures is disturbing for two reasons. First, as discussed previously, there is some uncertainty associated with the interpretation of subjective ratings, especially when ratings are compared between laboratories. Confirmation of subjective results with objective ones would increase our confidence in both types of measures. Second, it is not clear if the failure to find reliable objective measures has been due entirely to deficiencies in these measures or in part to an inability to program simulated flight scenarios that really do require different levels of pilot workload. Significant subjective measures of workload could perhaps reflect pilots' expectations about what the workload should be for different segments, not what it actually is.

A series of experiments at the NASA-Ames Research Center using a general aviation trainer (GAT) and secondary-task techniques was successful in helping to save objective measures of pilot mental workload from the theoretical and empirical scrap heap. Convinced that earlier failures with objective methods were due to the use of a simple reaction-time secondary task (the reader is encouraged to refer back to the section on defining and measuring mental workload), Kantowitz, Hart, and Bortolussi (1983) gave pilots flying the GAT either a two- or four-choice auditory secondary task. Pilots responded to the secondary task by pushing a helicopter trim switch in the appropriate direction depending upon the pitch of a tone. Each pilot flew easy and hard flight scenarios that had been constructed using earlier rating data (Childress, Hart, & Bortolussi, 1982).

Figure 6.4 shows the error on the flying task (the primary task) as a function of the choice level of the secondary task. The most important finding was that performance on the flight task was not changed by the addition of a secondary task to measure workload.

Figure 6.5 shows performance on the secondary tone task as a function of flight segment. The vertical axis shows transmitted information in bits per second, a measure that takes both speed and accuracy into account. Higher scores indicate better performance. The figure indicates that performance on the tone task was worst during

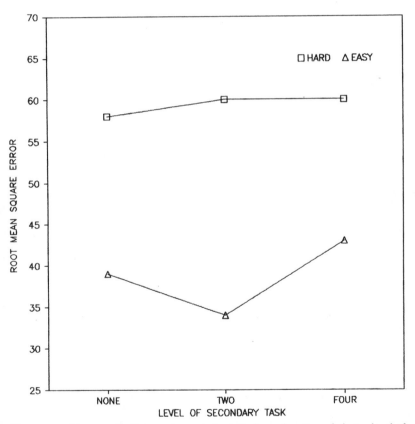

Figure 6.4.   Error on the flying primary task plotted as a function of choice level of the secondary tone task. (From Kantowitz, Hart, & Bortolussi, 1983.)

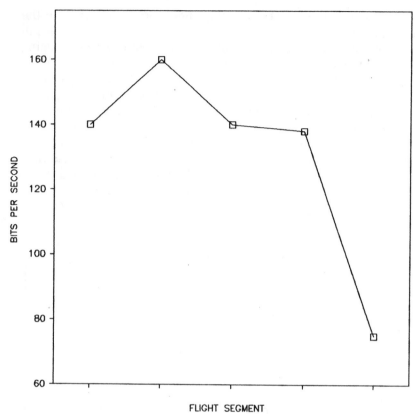

Figure 6.5.   Performance on the secondary tone task for different flight segments. The ticks on the horizontal axis represent points on the approach to the San Jose airport. The first tick marks the start of the approach near Gilroy, California, 26 miles southeast of San Jose airport. The last tick is from the middle marker to the touchdown at the airport. (From Kantowitz, Hart, & Bortolussi, 1983.)

the flight segment from the middle marker to landing, reflecting that workload on the flight task was the greatest during this part of the flight and that less attention was available for the secondary task. The result of greater objective workload levels during the landing phase of flight supports subjective ratings of high workload during landing.

Subsequent experiments using the GAT and the methodology just outlined were directed at the problem of constructing standardized flight scenarios (Kantowitz et al., 1984). Flight tasks were divided into groups varying in complexity, involving combinations of from

one to three subtasks. Both secondary task and subjective rating results were successful in building prespecified levels of workload.
The GAT experiments have shown two important things: (1) it is
possible to measure workload objectively and (2) the use of standardized flight scenarios requiring known levels of workload is necessary
if results from different laboratories are to be compared.

The Role of Memory.   As was found in many of the experiments
just mentioned, the components of a flight scenario are closely
linked with levels of pilot mental workload. Berg and Sheridan
(1984) studied simulated flight scenarios emphasizing either short- or
long-term memory tasks in their overall execution. In short-term
memory (STM), or working memory, a limited number of items to be
remembered (e.g., letters, numbers, or words) are stored by rehears-
ing them until they are no longer needed or until they have been
transferred into permanent storage, or long-term memory (LTM).
Once items are in LTM they need not be rehearsed to be remembered, but they can only be accessed using the correct "retrieval
cue." In Berg and Sheridan's experiment, four highly experienced
Air Force pilots flew a flight simulator on two different flights: one
that consisted of a number of small maneuvering tasks (STM-depen-
dent) and one that required less maneuvering but required the pilot
to remember a number of tasks prior to the time they were to be performed (LTM-dependent). Results showed that subjective workload
was not statistically different among the different flight segments;
however all measures of workload were significantly different for the
STM and LTM versions of the flight, with performance on the STM-
dependent flight being consistently rated higher than the LTM version. Objective measures of flight performance also reliably distinguished between the two types of flight. If minimization of pilot
workload is the goal, then flight scenarios placing heavy demands on
the pilot's short-term memory should be traded for those that use the
less costly storage of long-term memory. Another alternative would
be to assign heavily memory-dependent tasks to a computer.

Unexpected Events.   Another common finding in studies of pilot
mental workload is that sudden, unexpected, or emergency events in
flight can cause subjective measures of workload to increase and objective measures of the quality of performance to decrease (Sperandio, 1978). To improve hazard detection, as well as target detection,
Gabriel and Burrows (1968) have suggested training pilots to systematically scan the areas of their visual field. These researchers trained

a number of pilots to scan the instruments on the panel as well as the view from the windows in a designated order and with increasing speed. In a later intruder detection test, the trained pilots were much better at detecting advancing intruders than were pilots who had not undergone training. This type of instruction could be invaluable in reducing the number of midair collisions, especially in low-altitude military missions. Gabriel and Burrows concluded that training in visual scanning can be effectively used to increase the amount of time a pilot devotes to processing extra-cockpit information.

If training pilots how to organize their visual scanning can improve their detection performance, perhaps training could also help them deal more effectively with emergency situations. Unexpected events disrupt the normal execution of a flight "script" and cause pilots to ad lib the next course of action as they are engaged in flying the plane. Johannsen and Rouse (1983) studied the planning behavior, workload, and objective performance of nine professional pilots flying an HFB-320 Hansa Jet simulator in three types of flight situations: normal, abnormal, and emergency. All three scenarios consisted of phases starting with cruise and ending with touchdown, but the abnormal and emergency scenarios forced the pilots to deal with unexpected events. In the abnormal flight the pilots were informed at some prespecified time into the mission that the runway had been closed temporarily for snow removal and they should enter a holding pattern or attempt to land at an alternate airport. The emergency scenario was characterized by the failure of the right engine at a certain point during the flight.

Johannsen and Rouse found that the emergency scenarios were associated with the highest workload levels and the greatest number of performance errors, while the abnormal flights resulted in slightly higher average depth of planning ratings. They defined *depth of planning* as "level of detail which can range from broad and sketchy to specific and concrete" (1983, p. 269). Similar to the results of the Kantowitz et al. experiment, the landing phase of the flight scenario produced the highest values of depth of planning, performance errors, and workload. Further examination of the results of the experiment suggested that the presence of an autopilot affected the pilot's planning behavior, with more planning occurring with the autopilot for the emergency situations than in the abnormal situations. Johannsen and Rouse have offered the explanation that the engagement of the autopilot in emergency situations allows the pilot to spend more time planning, while in abnormal situations such planning is not required, since all the pilot has to do is wait for the abnormal situation to resolve itself.

Single- versus Dual-Task Training.   Perhaps surprisingly, in light of the results of the earlier study done by Gabriel and Burrows, there has been some debate concerning the validity of single- versus dual-task measures to predict later flight simulator performance. As you recall, Gabriel and Burrows were able to improve pilot performance in a simulator task by giving them pretraining in a related time-sharing task. It is intuitively obvious to most people that the way to get better at something is to practice doing it over and over again. If you can't practice on the same task you're training for, the best substitute is something that resembles your "test" task, either in its components or overall complexity. As a hypothetical example, if Bobby Rahal wanted to polish up his racing skills before the Indianapolis 500, but was prevented from going out on the track because of rain, he could go down to the local video parlor and wisely invest some time improving his visual–manual coordination on one of the more well-known racing games. The time spent in the arcade would be immensely more valuable in assuring him a win at the track than, say, sitting in a stationary car and practicing turning the steering wheel.

In an effort to test the ideas just outlined, Damos and Lintern (1981) had 57 nonpilots perform either one or two one-dimensional compensatory tracking tasks followed by instruction and then testing in a Singer–Link general aviation trainer. It was found that dual-task correlations with later simulator performance increased across trials of practice, while single-task correlations dropped steadily, except for two single-task trials that were given after earlier dual-task trials. The authors speculate that the increased predictive validity of the final two single-task trials could be attributed to a transfer of strategies learned on earlier dual-task trials. Thus, dual-task performance was a better predictor of later performance in a simulated flight task than single-task performance, as had been suspected.

Air Traffic Controller Workload

Task Distribution.   Although it is difficult to find as many empirical studies that have measured air traffic control (ATC) workload as have measured pilot workload, the body of available literature suggests that ATC jobs require the same, if not greater, levels of mental workload as piloting an aircraft. The ATC worker must monitor and instruct several planes at once and is responsible for preventing mishaps such as near misses or collisions. It is no wonder that accounts in the popular press inform us daily of the high incidence of ulcers, hypertension, and related nervous disorders that plague this segment of the population. Objective evidence of the ATC worker's condition of overload has been surfacing lately in the form of takeoff and landing delays (Kreifeldt, 1980), and the FAA is actively seeking to reorganize the ATC system to distribute workload more equilaterally. One of the more feasible system structures would place radar displays, called *cockpit displays of traffic information* (CDTIs), in the cockpit and allow pilots to have complete knowledge and increased control over their position in the airspace. CDTI would effectively decrease ATC workload while giving pilots a more complete picture of the traffic situation.

A series of studies at NASA-Ames Research Center was conducted to determine the possible effects of CDTIs on both pilots and ATC workers (see Kreifeldt, 1980). Professional pilots and controllers either flew simulators equipped with CDTIs or participated in a simulated ATC task. The tasks were coordinated so that pilots and controllers performed their scenarios simultaneously, making the simulation as realistic as possible. Results of these experiments indicated that CDTI use was associated with increased levels of reported manual workload for the pilots (Hart, 1982a), reflecting their exercise of freedom to control their aircrafts' position more precisely. Although the pilots' verbal workload remained fairly stable, less verbal workload was observed for the controllers, though this finding is inconsistent with a later study by Hart (1982a). The pilots reported their visual workload to be higher when using CDTIs than when centralized ATC was used, although associated performance decrements were not observed. Spacing between successive planes was found to be "tighter" and less variable when the CDTIs were in use. Preference ratings indicated that pilots preferred distributed management, while controllers preferred centralized management. This is not surprising in light of the fact that many psychological experiments cite a lack of perceived control over a situation as a cause of increased levels of stress (Fisher, Bell, & Baum, 1984). This may explain why both the pilots and the controllers preferred the management system that gave them the most control over the air traffic situation. From this series of studies it appears that the implementation of CDTIs could be a viable solution to the problem of ATC workload. By placing the air traffic information directly in the hands of the people who control the planes, not only are the pilots happier but ATC workers would have more time to engage in other tasks that require their expert knowledge.

Air Traffic Control Subtasks. Just as the components of a flight scenario are crucial in determining pilot mental workload, the subtasks associated with ATC work are also vital in measuring the amount of mental exertion experienced by controllers on the job. The stress and mental workload of air traffic controllers in 13 major airport radar control rooms was objectively studied by Hurst and Rose (1978a), who employed two experienced controllers at each facility to observe and record 28 measures of job tasks thought to be related to controller stress. It was found that the time spent monitoring, but not communicating with, aircraft under control accounted for 15% of controllers' time, while peak levels of air traffic accounted for 12%. It appears that although monitoring objectively presents itself as a task with low associated workload, the internal cognitive activity it requires is quite expensive in terms of behavioral resources. As has been previously found (Hurst & Rose, 1978; Philip, Reiche, & Kirchner, 1971), the duration of radio communications also reliably predicted behavioral responses. Peculiarly though, the amount of standby time was positively correlated with behavioral activity. An explanation offered by the authors alluded to the anticipation of impending control involvement as being responsible for the increased behavior during standby.

Summary and Conclusion

From the brief review of aviation workload literature presented in the preceeding pages it is possible to draw several conclusions. First, there is much to be gained from conducting well-controlled experiments in the laboratory. Not only can applied problems be solved, but a carefully designed experiment can test the robustness of the theories psychologists use to guide their search for answers to scientific questions. The whole process from the initial question to the final answer can be made more efficient when a good theory is used as a flashlight in the darkness. Second, the factors found to have an influence on mental workload (task distribution, memory, and unexpected events) all highlight the problem presented to human factors experts in aviation today—the proper assignment of tasks to human and machine (Kantowitz & Sorkin, 1987). Chapters 13 and 11, this volume, address the problems of cockpit automation and task allocation, so these issues are not discussed at any length here. Suffice it to say that the experiments just reviewed are valuable tools for the design engineer faced with assigning tasks to each component of the human–machine system.

Prospects

Workload Research

The reader who has come this far with us now understands why determining pilot workload is so difficult. The easy solutions (e.g., asking for ratings on a scale of 1 to 10) are used because they are easy, not because they yield good answers. The hard solutions (e.g., measuring ratings, 9 secondary tasks, and 14 biocybernetic indices simultaneously) are too cumbersome and yield internally inconsistent results. Where then will scientists turn for future workload research?

We believe there is only one correct answer to this question. Researchers will be forced to turn to theory in order to define and measure workload. Past atheoretical efforts, of the kind that were sufficient to answer questions about physical workload, are not adequate to deal with human cognitive functions. While we prefer a theoretical framework derived from models of attention, this is not the only viable approach. Pilot workload will be studied from as many points of view, including problem solving, decision making, psycholinguistics, signal detection theory, and the like, as scientists have theories about human behavior. A full and complete understanding of pilot workload will require general models that are applicable to many facets of human behavior.

This prediction contrasts with past approaches to studying workload. Researchers have been more concerned with trying to develop a simple metric that characterizes mental workload in the same way that oxygen consumption measures physical workload. We believe that this traditional approach has gone about as far as it can. There is no "magic bullet" for measuring mental workload. Researchers will understand pilot workload when they understand human information processing.

We hasten to add that this does *not* imply that human factors has little to contribute to pragmatic applications. The workload problems of today will not wait until scientists develop perfect models. Fortunately, even incomplete models are useful in developing practical specifications.

Pragmatic Applications

The flying pilot has little concern for abstract theories of human behavior and cognition. He or she wants to know if the aircraft of the future will optimize pilot workload. Our response is ambiguous: yes and no.

Let us start with the "no" portion of our answer. As this chapter has documented, one of the most important determinants of pilot workload is phase of flight. This is true regardless of the specific aircraft, its flight-deck configuration, or its crew size. Different phases of flight present different crew workload. A flight deck that is optimized for the lowest level of crew workload will be inadequate for the highest level. This problem is not necessarily solved by optimizing for the highest level. Recall that workload can also be too low. A flight deck that is optimized for the most difficult phases of flight may produce insufficient workload for some other phases.

Designers tend to be more concerned with excessive, rather than insufficient, levels of crew workload. Flight-deck automation is seen by designers as a way to reduce workload, although as we have noted earlier, automation is a mixed blessing. The flight deck of the future will be more and more like the control room of a factory or a nuclear power plant (Kantowitz, 1977). Computers and CRT displays have already displaced traditional displays and controls; this trend will continue until even the yoke disappears. Eventually the aircraft will take off, fly, and land by itself without the need for human intervention. The pilot will be as useful as the engineer of a subway train. What is the role of the operator in such a highly automated system?

It is unlikely that the pilot will be eliminated, any more than will the operator of a nuclear power plant. Our society believes that humans should have ultimate responsibility for control of complex systems even if inserting the human degrades overall system performance most of the time. The human is still the ultimate back-up system. While machines that are overloaded fail abruptly, people degrade gracefully under excessive levels of workload. Thus, it seems prudent to include human operators, even if only as the subsystem of last resort that can "pull the plug." Furthermore, there are also strong political forces to keep humans employed.

But when the human is primarily along just for the ride, the chances for a human-induced error greatly increase. For extremely sophisticated automated systems, one might even argue that, at least on a statistical basis, a better design decision might be to remove the human operator entirely. But this solution, although in some cases technically correct, seldom prevails. It is far more likely that a redundant operator will remain as part of the system. Pilots have already reacted to automation by voicing fear of losing their manual flying skills. There will be future accidents due to pilots trying to program their way out of trouble, instead of deactivating automation and flying under manual control.

Thus, we predict that the future significant problems of workload will relate to *inadequate*, not excessive, workload. Human factors experts will be required to devise methods for keeping the operator awake and actively involved in ways that the pilot considers meaningful. Perhaps this will involve more simulator time. When automation can fly more efficiently (e.g., more accurately, with less fuel use) than humans, there will be strong incentives for pilots to keep hands off the manual controls. While human factors as a discipline has some of the knowledge required to anticipate and solve these workload problems, current trends in automation create concern that this knowledge be applied and expanded. It would be tragic and ironic if our current efforts to measure pilot workload succeeded, only to be faced with a new generation of aircraft where pilot workload was so low that nobody bothered to measure it at all.

This need not happen. To be forewarned is to be forearmed, which leads us to the "yes" portion of the answer to our question about optimizing pilot workload. We know that pilot workload is determined by the cognitive demands placed on the crew. Most research and design effort to date has been directed at detecting (and then eliminating or minimizing) excessive crew workload. We are on the threshold of determining which cognitive functions can be combined and which cannot. All this is in the spirit of FAR 25 (cited earlier in this chapter) that directs the flight crew "to perform their duties without unreasonable concentration or fatigue." The danger is that unthinking reliance on this directive could create a situation where no cognitive demands were placed on the crew. Our very success in eliminating crew workload, extrapolated too far, can create a more dangerous situation than existing designs. Fortunately, the same research that helps define excessive cognitive demands can also be used to define appropriate cognitive demands. All that is needed is a modest change to FAR 25.771 to make it direct the flight crew to perform their duties with reasonable concentration.

Human factors has a rapidly improving technology for measuring reasonable concentration and appropriate levels of pilot workload. Perhaps a small portion of the resources now being used to study excessive workload should be diverted to two complementary issues. First, there is the issue of measuring and establishing standards for minimal levels of cognitive demands. Second, there is the related problem of sudden transitions that move the operator from a minimal level (or from an unreasonably low level) of cognitive demand to an excessive level. Such an excessive level could arise in many ways, ranging from a cockpit emergency within the pilot's control to an external event such as another aircraft on a collision course when the pilot has only partial control. We anticipate the problems of excessive pilot workload being ultimately solved by a combination of improved workload measurement techniques and automation. It is time to get started on the next important problem: insufficient cognitive demands in future aircraft and flight operations.

Acknowledgments

Preparation of this chapter, as well as our research (the NASA GAT Experiments), was supported by Cooperative Agreement NCC 2-228 from the National Aeronautical and Space Administration, Ames Research Center. S. G. Hart was the NASA Technical Monitor.

References

Albanese, R. A. (1977). Mathematical analysis and computer simulation in military mission workload assessment. In *Proceedings of the AGARD conference on methods to assess workload* (AGARD-CP-2166).

Berg, S. L., & Sheridan, T. B. (1984). Measuring workload differences between short-term memory and long-term memory scenarios in a simulated flight environment. *Proceedings of the Twentieth Annual Conference on Manual Control* (pp. 397–416). Moffett Field, CA: NASA-Ames Research Center.

Boyd, S. P. (1983). Assessing the validity of SWAT as a workload measurement instrument. In *Proceedings of the Human Factors Society 27th Annual Meeting* (pp. 124–128). Norfolk, VA: Human Factors Society.

Broadbent, D. E. (1971). *Decision and stress.* New York: Academic Press.

Childress, M. E., Hart, S. G., & Bortolussi, M. R. (1982). The reliability and validity of flight task workload ratings. In *Proceedings of the Human Factors Society 26th Annual Meeting* (pp. 319–323). Seattle, WA: Human Factors Society.

Cooper, G. E., & Harper, R. P., Jr. (1969). *The use of pilot rating in the evaluation of aircrafts handling qualities* (NASA TN-D-5153). Moffett Field, CA: NASA-Ames Research Center.

Curry, R. E. (1984). What pilots like (and don't like) about the new cockpit technology. *Proceedings of the Twentieth Annual Conference on Manual Control* (NASA CP 2341; pp. 199–215). Moffett Field, CA: Ames Research Center.

Damos, D. L., & Lintern, G. (1981). A comparison of single- and dual-task measures to predict simulator performance of beginning student pilots. *Ergonomics, 24,* 673–684.

Fisher, J. D., Bell, P. A., & Baum, A. (1984). *Environmental psychology* (2nd ed.). New York: Holt, Rinehart & Winston.

Gabriel, R. F., & Burrows, A. A. (1968). Improving time-sharing performance of pilots through training. *Human Factors, 10,* 33–40.

Glass, D. C., & Singer, J. E. (1972). *Urban stress.* New York: Academic Press.

Hanson, R. H., Payne, D. G., Shively, R. J., & Kantowitz, B. H. (1981). Process control simulation research in monitoring analog and digital displays. *Proceedings of the Human Factors Society 25th Annual Meeting* (pp. 154–158). Rochester, NY: Human Factors Society.

Hart, S. G. (1982a). *Effect of VFR aircraft on approach traffic with and without cockpit displays of traffic information.* Paper presented at the 18th Annual Conference on Manual Control. Dayton, OH.

Hart, S. G. (1982b). Theoretical basis for workload assessment research at NASA-Ames Research Center. In M. L. Frazier & R. B. Crombie (Eds.), *Proceedings of the Workshop on Flight Testing to Identify Pilot Workload and Pilot Dynamics* (AFFTC-TR-82-5). Edwards Air Force Base, CA.

Hart, S. G. (1985). Theory and measurement of human workload. In J. Zeidner (Ed.), *Human productivity enhancement.* New York: Praeger.

Hart, S. G., Hauser, J. R. (1987). Inflight application of three pilot workload measurement techniques. *AeroSpace and Environmental Medicine, 58,* 402–410.

Hart, S. G., Hauser, J. R., & Lester, P. T. (1984). Inflight evaluation of four measures of pilot workload. In *Proceedings of the 28th Annual Meeting of the Human Factors Society* (pp. 945–949). Santa Monica, CA: Human Factors Society.

Hurst, K., & Hurst, L. (Eds.). (1982). *Pilot error: The human factors.* New York: Jason Aronson.

Hurst, M. W., & Rose, R. M. (1978a). Objective workload and behavioral response in airport radar control rooms. *Ergonomics, 21*(7), 559–565.

Hurst, M. W., & Rose, R. M. (1978b). Objective job difficulty, behavioral responses and sector characteristics in air route traffic control centers. *Ergonomics, 21*(9), 697–708.

Johannsen, G., & Rouse, W. B. (1983). Studies of planning behavior of aircraft pilots in normal, abnormal, and emergency situations. *IEEE Transactions on Systems, Man, and Cybernetics, SMC-13*(3), 267–278.

Kantowitz, B. H. (1977). Ergonomics and the design of nuclear power plant control complexes. In T. O. Kvalseth, (Ed.), *Arbeidsplass og miljobruk av ergonomiske data* (pp. 177–195). Trondheim, Norway: Tapier.

Kantowitz, B. H. (1985a). Channels and stages in human information processing: A limited analysis of theory and methodology. *Journal of Mathematical Psychology, 29*(2), 135–174.

Kantowitz, B. H. (1985b). Mental work. In B. M. Pulat & D. C. Alexander (Eds.), *Industrial ergonomics* (pp. 31–38). Institute of Industrial Engineering.

Kantowitz, B. H. (1986). Mental workload. In P. A. Hancock (Ed.), *Human factors psychology.* Amsterdam: North Holland.

Kantowitz, B. H., Hart, S. G., & Bortolussi, M. R. (1983). Measuring pilot workload in a moving-base simulator: I. Asynchronous secondary choice-reaction task. In *Proceedings of the Human Factors Society 27th Annual Meeting* (pp. 319–322). Norfolk, VA: Human Factors Society.

Kantowitz, B. H., Hart, S. G., Bortolussi, M. R., Shively, R. J., & Kantowitz, S. C. (1984). Measuring pilot workload in a moving-base simulator: II. Building levels of workload. *Proceedings of the Twentieth Annual Conference on Manual Control* (NASA CP 2341, Vol. II; pp. 359–371). Moffett Field, CA: NASA-Ames Research Center.

Kantowitz, B. H., & Knight, J. L. (1976). Testing tapping timesharing: II. Auditory secondary task. *Acta Psychologica, 40,* 343–362.

Kantowitz, B. H., & Roediger, H. L. (1984). *Experimental Psychology* (2nd ed.). St. Paul, MN: West Publishing.

Kantowitz, B. H., & Sorkin, R. D. (1983). *Human factors: Understanding people–system relationships.* New York: Wiley.

Kantowitz, B. H., & Sorkin, R. D. (1987). Allocation of functions. In G. Salvendy (Ed.), *Handbook of human factors* (pp. 355–369). New York: Wiley.

Kreifeldt, J. G. (1980). Cockpit displayed traffic information and distributed management in air traffic control. *Human Factors, 22*(6), 671–691.

McCormick, E. J., & Sanders, M. (1982). *Human factors in engineering and design* (6th ed.). New York: McGraw-Hill.

Moray, N. (Ed.). (1979). *Mental workload.* New York: Plenum.

Philip, W., Reiche, D., & Kirchner, J. H. (1971). The use of subjective rating. *Ergonomics, 14,* 611–616.

Roscoe, A. H. (1978). Stress and workload in pilots. *Aviation, Space, and Environmental Medicine, 49*(4), 630–636.

Sanders, M. G., Simmons, R. R., Hofmann, M. A., & DeBonis, J. N. (1977). Visual workload of the copilot/navigator during terrain flight. In *Proceedings of the Human Factors Society 21st Annual Meeting* (pp. 262–266). San Francisco, CA: Human Factors Society.

Shingledecker, C. A. (1983). Behavioral and subjective workload metrics for operational environments. In *Sustained intensive air operations: physiological and performance aspects.* Neuilly-sur-Seine, France: AGARD Conference Proceedings No. 338.

Sperandio, J. C. (1978). The regulation of working methods as a function of work-load among air-traffic controllers. *Ergonomics, 21,* 195–202.

Wiener, E. L. (1985). Beyond the sterile cockpit. *Human Factors, 27*(1), 75–90.

Wierwille, W. W. (1979). Physiological measures of aircrew mental workload. *Human Factors, 21,* 575–594.

Wierwille, W. W., & Casali, J. G. (1983). A validated rating scale for global mental workload measurement. In *Proceedings of the Human Factors Society 27th Annual Meeting* (pp. 129–133). Norfolk, VA: Human Factors Society.

Group Interaction and Flight Crew Performance

7

H. Clayton Foushee
Robert L. Helmreich

Introduction

The focus of this chapter is upon the group performance process as it affects crew effectiveness in multipilot operations. This task is a classic small group performance situation where a number of social, organizational, and personality factors are relevant to flight safety. In this chapter, we will review these factors and research that supports this conclusion. We begin by briefly providing some of the historical context surrounding pilots and the type of individuals who populate the profession. Consider the following example from a contemporary social history (Wolfe, 1979):

> Anyone who travels very much on airlines in the United States soon
> gets to know the voice of *the airline pilot* . . . coming over the intercom

Human Factors in Aviation

. . . with a particular drawl, a particular folksiness, a particular down-home calmness that is so exaggerated it begins to parody itself (nevertheless!—it's reassuring) . . . the voice that tells you, as the airliner is caught in thunderheads and goes bolting up and down a thousand feet at a single gulp, to check your seat belts because "it might get a little choppy" . . . the voice that tells you (on a flight from Phoenix preparing for its approach into Kennedy Airport, New York, just after dawn): "Now folks, uh . . . this is the captain . . . ummmm . . . We've got a little ol' red light up here on the control panel that's tryin' to tell us that the *landin'* gears're not . . . uh . . . *lockin'* into position when we lower 'em . . . Now . . . I don't believe that little ol' red light knows what it's talkin about—I believe it's that little ol' red light that iddn' workin' right" . . . faint chuckle, long pause, as if to say *I'm not even sure all this is really worth going into—still, it may amuse you* . . . "But . . . I guess to play it by the rules, we oughta *humor* that little ol' light . . . so we're gonna take her down to about, oh, two or three hundred feet over the runway at Kennedy, and the folks down there on the ground are gonna see if they caint give us a *visual* inspection of those ol' landin' gears"—with which he is obviously on intimate ol'-buddy terms, as with every other working part of this mighty ship—"and if I'm right . . . they're gonna tell us everything is *copacetic* all the way aroun' an' we'll jes take her on in" . . . and, after a couple of low passes over the field, the voice returns: "Well, folks, those folks down there on the ground—it must be too early for 'em or somethin'—I 'spect they still got the *sleepers* in their eyes . . . 'cause they say they caint tell if those ol' landin' gears are all the way down or not . . . But, you know, up here in the cockpit we're convinced they're all the way down, so we're jes gonna take her on in . . . And oh" . . . *(I almost forgot)* . . . "while we take a little swing out over the ocean an' empty some of that surplus fuel we're not gonna be needin' anymore—that's what you might be seein' comin' out of the wings—our lovely little ladies . . . if they'll be so kind . . . they're gonna go up and down the aisles and show you how we do what we call 'assumin' the position'" . . . another faint chuckle *(We do this so often, and it's so much fun, we even have a funny little name for it)* . . . and the stewardesses, a bit grimmer, by the looks of them, than *that voice*, start telling the passengers to take their glasses off and take the ballpoint pens and other sharp objects out of their pockets, and they show them *the position*, with the head lowered . . . while down on the field at Kennedy the little yellow emergency trucks start roaring across the field—and even though in your pounding heart and your sweating palms and your boiling brainpan you *know* this is a critical moment in your life, you still can't quite bring yourself to *believe* it, because if it were . . . how could *the captain*, the man who knows the actual situation most intimately . . . how could he keep on drawlin' and chucklin' and driftin' and lollygaggin' in that particular voice of his—

Well!—who doesn't know that voice! And who can forget it!—even
after he is proved right and the emergency is over.

That particular voice may sound vaguely Southern or Southwestern,
but it is specifically Appalachian in origin. It originated in the mountains of West Virginia, in the coal country, in Lincoln County, so far up
in the hollows that, as the saying went, "they had to pipe in daylight."
In the late 1940's and early 1950's this up-hollow voice drifted down
from on high, from over the high desert of California, down, down,
down, from the upper reaches of the Brotherhood into all phases of
American aviation. It was amazing. It was *Pygmalion* in reverse. Military pilots and then, soon, airline pilots, pilots from Maine and Massachusetts and the Dakotas and Oregon and everywhere else, began to talk
in that poker-hollow West Virginia drawl, or as close to it as they could
bend their native accents. It was the drawl of the most righteous of all
the possessors of the right stuff.[1]

Those associated with the aviation profession have long been familiar with the profile so ingeniously depicted by Tom Wolfe in the
preceding passage. Most of us are familiar with the common stereo-
type of the pilot as a fearless, self-sufficient, technically qualified,
and slightly egotistical individual, whose job description calls for the
defiance of death on a regular basis. Aviation lore is rich with descriptions of such "white scarf and goggles" individuals operating
fabric-covered machines held together with bailing wire by "the seat
of their pants." Indeed, there is a grain of truth in these stereotypes
derived from the early days of aviation when flight was not routine,
and the dangers associated with the piloting profession were considerable, and it is also probably true that the characteristics of the "the
right stuff" were not only functional but a prerequisite. These characteristics were much admired and became not only essential elements of the informal pilot culture which were passed from
generation to generation of pilots but they were also institutionalized
in regulations governing pilot performance, as well as in policies
guiding pilot selection criteria. They are so much a part of the culture that they are still with us in an age where flight operations are
routine and aviation is by far the safest mode of commercial transportation.

Equipment reliability in the formative years of aviation was minimal, and a pilot's savvy and skill were very often the only reliable

resources. Over the years, aeronautical engineers have done a remarkable job of solving the reliability problem, to the extent that each generation of aircraft promises not only better performance and safety but also reduced pilot workload. While the decreasing percentage of accidents due to hardware problems is a testament to this increased reliability, the percentage of accidents due to human error has not exhibited the same steady downward trend. Although estimates vary, even conservative figures attribute about 65% of all accidents worldwide to the human error category.

This state of affairs has placed increasing pressure upon those concerned with pilot performance to isolate those individual characteristics associated with the right stuff. Traditionally, human factors specialists and psychologists dating back to World War II (see Melton, 1947, for a review of this research) have focused their efforts upon the identification of technical or "stick-and-rudder" skills and the personality characteristics associated with the perceptual skills necessary for the job, as well as the emotional stability required for operations in stressful circumstances. The focus was, and continues to be, almost entirely on the individual pilot and the pilot's technical proficiency.

To minimize the human error problem, another strategy that was a direct result of the limitations and imperfections of individual humans was used: the development of multipiloted aircraft. By this means, individual pilot workload could be reduced, thereby, at least theoretically, providing an important safeguard against human error. Yet, this system of redundancy has failed to provide an adequate safeguard in many cases. It has failed too often because captains have not heeded the warnings of subordinate crew members. It has failed because crew members who possessed adequate information have, for some reason, not provided it. In fact, a review and analysis of jet transport accidents worldwide during the period 1968 to 1976 (Cooper, White & Lauber, 1979) revealed more than 60 in which breakdowns of the crew performance process played a significant role. Although individual pilot performance remains an important research topic, these occurrences suggest that more emphasis needs to be placed on crew performance.

It should also be noted that the technical proficiency standards and the accompanying pilot selection criteria were developed largely for single-pilot operations and were more or less maintained for multipilot operations. In many ways this is somewhat paradoxical. The flight of a sophisticated multipilot transport aircraft is a highly structured group performance situation where a number of interpersonal factors are relevant to crew effectiveness. It has been suggested that those characteristics associated with the right stuff are "the wrong stuff" as far as effective group function is concerned, and therein lies the paradox. Since so much value has been placed upon personality characteristics such as self-sufficiency, machismo, and bravery, we may be selecting individuals who tend to keep to themselves, communicate less than the average person, and are not very good at sharing responsibility with others—not exactly the characteristics one would look for when trying to put together a group that functions well. Both the culture and the system have contributed to this circumstance. Since the culture has fostered the myth of the brave, maverick, pilot, individuals possessing such characteristics have gravitated toward the profession in greater numbers. In addition, our selection criteria weight these characteristics more heavily, and for some piloting jobs this may be entirely appropriate. For example, when selecting pilots for high-performance, single-seat fighter aircraft, it may be highly desirable to look for the brave maverick, since such a profile is probably related to survival in the demanding air-to-air combat environment. A fighter pilot assignment is among the more glamorous—the demand far exceeding the supply of such jobs—so only the best and the brightest make it to these positions, while the rest tend to get transport assignments. However, airlines want the best and the brightest too, and once again the demand for these lucrative positions has traditionally exceeded the supply. Thus, those individuals who have spent their formative professional years working alone and who may be dispositionally less suited to working in groups have been thrust into this group performance environment in large numbers.

Groups in the Operational Environment

Webster's New Collegiate Dictionary (1961) defines *cockpit* as "a region noted for many conflicts." Although this definition does not specifically apply to aircraft cockpits, it is interesting to note how often interpersonal phenomena can affect air transport operations. We have previously noted that the cockpit crew is a highly structured, small group in which a number of sociopsychological, personality, and group interactional variables are related to crew effectiveness. The complexities of the operational environment—aircraft systems—and the sheer volume of information that must be processed (often in brief periods of time) mandate highly coordinated team performance. Rigorous company hiring practices, employment conditions, and regulations requiring frequent checking and retraining have together assured that each individual crew member is a highly skilled professional. However, in situations where a high level of team work is required, the individual skills of team members are often not enough to assure effective performance. Jones (1974) illustrated this point nicely in a classic study of professional athletic teams. He found that teams with better athletes seem to win more often—not a very surprising finding. What was interesting about this study is that the strength of the talent—performance relationship seemed to depend on the amount that a particular sport requires teamwork. Jones found that 90% of baseball team effectiveness was predictable from the skills of the individual players (batting averages, fielding effectiveness, earned-run averages, etc.). However, in basketball teams only 35% was predictable from individual player statistics (scoring averages, field goal percentages, rebounds, etc.). In explaining this result, the author noted that team success in basketball was much more critically dependent on interpersonal relations and teamwork than in baseball.

Despite the fact that studies of group performance have implicated many variables (see Hare, 1972; McGrath & Altman, 1966, for reviews), group performance problems have received relatively little attention in the aviation research and training communities until recently. Awareness of these types of pilot performance problems is gradually increasing, but unfortunately, this heightened awareness has been stimulated in large part by a series of tragic accidents.

An L-1011 went down at night in the Florida Everglades in 1972 killing 99 passengers and crew members. The accident sequence was initiated by a burned-out light bulb in the system indicating that the landing gear was down and locked; a problem which occupied all three crew members' attention to the extent that no one noticed that the autopilot had become disengaged. The sad result was that the aircraft slowly drifted down into the swamp without anyone noticing. An ironic part of the accident scenario was that the air traffic controller noticed on his radar display that the aircraft was losing altitude and queried the flight crew by asking, "how are things comin' along out there?" The crew, of course, probably thought that he was inquiring about the landing-gear problem and responded by saying that everything was alright. In short, the accident probably would have been prevented had the controller simply directed his observation toward the loss of altitude in a precise manner, but of course, it could have been prevented in many other ways. Nonetheless, the most interesting aspect of this accident is that *no one* was actually flying the aircraft, and the system of redundancy (both in the air and on the ground) that we alluded to earlier was nonexistent.

In 1978, a DC-8 crashed several miles short of the Portland airport after running out of fuel. Again, a burned-out bulb denied the crew a "green light" on one of the landing gear, and again, the crew became preoccupied with trying to diagnose the problem and decide on a strategy. The captain in this case was particularly concerned with allowing the flight attendants enough time to teach the passengers how to "assume the position." The cockpit voice recording indicates that the flight engineer was concerned about the amount of time this was taking and the increasingly critical fuel situation, making several observations to the captain that were repeatedly ignored. The U. S. National Transportation Safety Board (NTSB), a government organization whose major responsibility is the investigation of transportation mishaps, made the following observations in its report of the accident that resulted (NTSB, 1979b):

> The Safety Board believes that this accident exemplifies a recurring problem—a breakdown of cockpit management and teamwork during a situation involving malfunctions of aircraft systems in flight. To combat this problem, responsibilities must be divided among members of the flightcrew while a malfunction is being resolved. . . .
>
> Admittedly, the stature of a captain and his management style may exert subtle pressure on his crew to conform to his way of thinking. It may hinder interaction and adequate monitoring and force another crewmember to yield his right to express an opinion. (pp. 26–27)

In 1982, a B-737 experienced difficulty taking off in a snowstorm in Washington, D.C., failed to maintain an adequate rate of climb, and crashed into the 14th Street Bridge. The cockpit voice recorder again tragically documented the cause as a breakdown in the group process. The copilot made repeated subtle advisories that something did not appear quite right (engines set at substantially less than normal takeoff thrust due to a partially ice-blocked probe causing false, high thrust readings on the engine gauges), and these advisories were, for whatever reasons, not attended to by the captain. This message again did not go unnoticed by the NTSB, which recommended that pilot training include "considerations for command decision, resource management, role performance, and assertiveness," in implying that the primary cause was the copilot's lack of assertiveness and possibly a general hesitancy among subordinates to question superiors forcefully.

The three accidents cited above, as well as many others, have common characteristics. In each case, there was nothing seriously wrong with the aircraft that crashed except for a relatively minor mechanical problem that tended to occupy crew members' attention. Likewise, each crew member was highly skilled in the technical aspects of aircraft operations and certified fit under the voluminous regulations governing pilot skills and qualifications. In each case, someone either on the flight deck or the ground had access to information which would have prevented the accident, but for various reasons, this information was not properly acted upon by the group.

Accidents such as these and research delving into the group process have prompted some to adopt a rather pessimistic view of the process. "It is tempting to conclude that 'the group effectiveness problem' will not be solved in the forseeable future and to recommend to decision-makers that in the meantime they use groups as infrequently as possible" (Hackman and Morris, 1975, p. 46). Theoretically, pooling the abilities of a number of highly skilled individuals should result in a better product. Most would argue that two heads are better than one, but this is often not the case. The group process is slow, cumbersome, and often very inefficient. It simply takes two or three individuals longer to decide on a course of action than it would for a single individual to go ahead and do it. Many psychologists (e.g., Steiner, 1972) have referred to this as the *process loss* inherent in group activity. However, in noting the inherent problem with groups, some (e.g., Hackman and Morris, 1975) are also quick to point out that the likelihood of catching errors is still greater and that inefficiency associated with the process is clearly justified in any situation where freedom from errors is paramount.

Yet, the group process rarely results in error-free performance, as we have attempted to demonstrate, because this system of redundancy often breaks down. Sometimes it breaks down because of a lack of cohesion within the group, interpersonal strife, and a resultant inability of group members to coordinate their actions. However, it can also break down because of too much cohesion. Respected psychologist Irving Janis (1972) has, for example, attributed massive foreign policy fiascos, such as Britain's appeasement toward Hitler prior to the outbreak of World War II and the Bay of Pigs invasion during the early days of John F. Kennedy's presidency, to a phenomenon in close-knit groups known as *group think*. In such groups, a "clubby feeling of we-ness" seems to develop, which often prohibits group members from introducing or entertaining unsettling information for fear of upsetting the group.

In the following section, we review many of the factors affecting the group process. We also discuss some of the reasons why group phenomena have traditionally received little attention.

Classifying Group Performance Factors

Although there are myriad factors affecting the group performance process, they can be roughly sorted into three large classes—input, process, and output variables. Input variables refer to the personal characteristics individuals bring into the group, characteristics of the group itself, and factors related to the environment or the task performance situation in which the group is functioning. Process variables refer to the dynamics of group interaction or how group members communicate with each other in order to coordinate their individual actions. Outcome variables are those related to how well the group performed the task, as well as other outcomes indicating how group members feel about each other and what they have learned about each other as a result of the interaction. Variables and their interrelationships are portrayed in Figure 7.1.

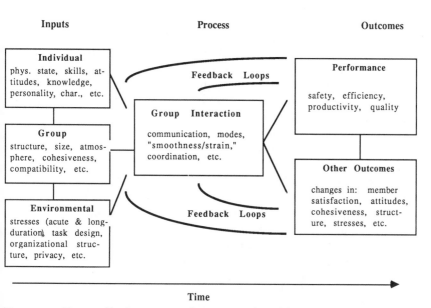

Figure 7.1.   Factors affecting group performance. (Adapted from McGrath, 1964.)

Input Factors

There are three types of input variables: individual, group, and environmental factors which are all interrelated as the figure implies. Individual-level input factors refer to the patterns of individual skills, physical state, attitudes, and personality characteristics that each group member brings to the task performance situation. Individual skills, of course, affect the level of competence and the resources that the group has at its disposal. Performance and motivational implications are often attached to physical state variables such as fatigue. Personality and attitudinal factors affect how group members actually work together. For example, studies of the effects of different styles of leadership on overall group effectiveness (e.g., Fiedler, 1967) have concentrated heavily on the effect of such global personality dimensions as task orientation and relationship orientation (we discuss these dimensions in greater detail later). Organizations have utilized personality inventories for years as a means of screening individuals, but these efforts have usually been more directed toward screening out "psychopathology" rather than selecting for the characteristics associated with effective group function.

Group-level input factors include dimensions such as group size, prior history, structure, composition, and cohesiveness. Does the group have an adequate number of people to perform the task without under- or overworking individual members? The prior history of the group is important because in groups where members already know each other, knowledge and expectations cultivated from their prior experiences can significantly facilitate or inhibit the function of the group. Composition is simply the collection of all the individual input characteristics within the group, and it is a very strong predictor of overall group cohesiveness (do the personalities and skills of individual group members blend so that they identify strongly with each other and get along well?). Structural factors include the *role structure* of the group, a psychosociological term referring to the rights and responsibilities of particular group members in their respective positions and how well these roles are defined. For example, is the group highly structured with an inviolate chain of command, such as in cockpit crews and many other managerial situations, or is the role structure undefined, as in a group of volunteers getting together for the first time to work on a charitable project? Cohesiveness refers to the level of mutual liking within the group. It also affects the overall stability of the group, and if the level of cohesiveness within the group is low, attrition and dissatisfaction are common problems.

Environmental input factors include characteristics of the task itself, the reward structure, and other situational aspects such as the level of stress inherent in the performance of the task. Task design factors, for example, whether the task is highly automated or predominately manual, are important, but how they affect group interaction is not well understood. In addition, factors related to the attractiveness of the task and its basic reward structure are also important. The level of stress associated with task performance, or in the environment, is also an influence with significant interactional and performance implications.

All of the above input factors are closely interrelated, and it is difficult to predict how they will manifest themselves in combination. Most studies examining the influence of group input characteristics have consisted of isolated manipulations of one or two factors, and such research has been criticized because the results have lacked consistency (e.g., Foushee, 1984). One of the major reasons for this inconsistency may well be the complicated interrelationships among the various factors.

Group Process Variables

Some of the least understood and least studied, but perhaps most important, factors are those related to the actual process of group interaction. What is the nature of the mechanism that allows a group to work together in a task performance situation? How is responsibility delegated, how often do group members communicate with each other, what is the style of their interchange? Do communication patterns originating at the bottom of the chain of command differ from those beginning at the top and directed downward? The communications process is the most outward and measurable manifestation of the process of group interaction, and it is a vital one. We will provide research evidence from actual cockpit crews that demonstrates the pivotal nature of these process variables.

It has been observed that most studies of group performance have ignored process variables (e.g., Foushee, 1984; Hackman & Morris, 1975). Instead, group investigations have generally concentrated upon direct links between input and output factors (performance). This may be another reason why the literature on group performance displays so much inconsistency. For example, it is entirely possible that such direct links are rare—more commonly, we might expect input factors to exert their influence on process variables such as communication. In turn, these process variables are likely to influence the quality of group performance, as Figure 7.1 illustrates.

Output Variables

When speaking of output factors, the focus is usually on the dimensions associated with task performance (quality, time necessary for performance, number of errors, etc.). Performance is clearly critical, but there are also other outcomes as a result of group interaction in a performance situation. For example, in a group performing an attractive task at very high levels of competence, it would be expected that overall group cohesion would evolve to high levels. We also learn a considerable amount about other group members as a result of working together on a task, and these are definable outcomes just as is performance quality. It is important to note these other products of group interaction, because if the group is one which is expected to perform together in the future, these other outcomes feed back and modify various group input and process variables (Figure 7.1). We have mentioned how cohesiveness can be affected by group performance. Similarly, patterns of member knowledge and skill, attitudes, motivation, task characteristics, stress, the reward structure, and other input factors are modified depending on prior performance outcomes.

This feedback process is another area where laboratory research in the group domain has failed to account for important factors that influence the performance of real groups in the real world. It is likely, for example, that input and process variables may not predict as much about performance in the early stages of a group's lifetime, but after frequent exposure and experience with different types of performance outcomes, these "feedback loops" have modified input characteristics that will substantially influence subsequent outcomes. Unfortunately, we do not know very much about group performance over time, because the typical laboratory studies of groups utilize college students as subjects, brought together in artificial groups for a short period of time in a laboratory environment to work on a task that has little or nothing to do with performance in a real-world setting. It has been said (e.g., Helmreich, 1975) that psychologists have "sterilized" research to the extent that potential consumers of the findings, such as pilot training organizations, do not really pay attention to them.

Input Variables and the Flight Crew Process

In this section, we highlight some of the input variables that have been shown to influence the process of flight crew interaction. Space considerations preclude a complete discussion, so we concentrate upon personality characteristics, on attitudes related to leadership styles, and on the flight-deck role structure.

Group member personality characteristics and their effect upon group interaction and performance have been, traditionally, one of the more heavily studied areas in group research. In this domain, leadership studies have concentrated on the identification of "profiles" that are associated with successful leadership. Fiedler (1967) and his coworkers undertook an ambitious program to identify those profiles most pertinent to effective group function. It is impossible to detail the findings of this program here, but briefly stated, Fiedler identified two basic types of leadership profiles—task-oriented and group-oriented—that were tied to performance in a complicated fashion. Task-oriented leaders are characterized as those who are primarily concerned with performance. Group-oriented leaders are conceptualized as those who are primarily concerned with the feelings and needs of other group members.

As in most research in this area, the type of leadership that was most effective was not readily apparent—it was heavily dependent upon the type of group and the task with which the group was charged. In groups with highly structured tasks and powerful leader positions, such as the cockpit crew, task-oriented leaders performed better as long as interpersonal relationships within the group remained relatively good. Group-oriented leaders performed better in groups where leader–member relations were relatively poor. (This is the type of research finding that is very difficult to implement in formulating management policy.) Moreover, while these data are interesting, they are also intuitively paradoxical. It would seem logical to assume that group-oriented leaders, over time, would more often find themselves in situations characterized by good interpersonal relations, since their primary interest is supposed to be group member relationships. Conversely, it would be expected that task-oriented leaders more often find themselves in groups with problems in leader–member relations because of their lack of interest and possible insensitivity to these factors. Although these data may be valid for the situations tested, it is likely that group-oriented leaders less frequently find themselves in situations characterized by poor interpersonal relationships, thus the relative frequency of this pattern may be low.

One possible reason for this seemingly paradoxical set of research findings is that group-oriented and task-oriented profiles have usually been treated as mutually exclusive patterns. In other words, group-oriented leaders are treated as if they are only concerned with interpersonal relationships and not very concerned with task performance. Likewise, task-oriented leaders have been viewed as if they are only concerned with task performance and not terribly cognizant of the feelings of group members. However, there is a substantial amount of recent research evidence that would seem to indicate that these two profiles should not be viewed as if they were mutually exclusive (e.g., Blake & Mouton, 1978; Spence & Helmreich, 1978). Spence and Helmreich (1978) have conducted considerable research that argues persuasively for the idea that task orientation and group orientation are independent. In short, one's standing on task orientation has no bearing on whether one is relatively "high" or "low" in group orientation and vice versa. Thus, it is entirely possible to possess high levels of both, low levels of both, or to be high on one dimension and low on the other.

Blake and Mouton (1978) have conducted managerial training in a variety of environments (including airline pilot training) using a framework known as the *managerial grid*. Figure 7.2 illustrates that the grid pattern essentially incorporates the notion that the best (9,9 managers) leadership profile for all situations is found among individuals who possess relatively high levels of "concern for people" (group orientation) and "concern for performance" (task orientation). This does not imply that managers who are high in one and low in the other are necessarily bad or ineffective in all situations—simply that the most adaptive profile combines both dimensions. For example, it has been suggested that "low-task, high-group" oriented managers are quite effective in routine situations, but not as effective in performance situations with high task demands. Likewise, "high-task, low-group" oriented managers are assumed to be quite effective in situations with high task demands, but perhaps not as effective in day-to-day operations.

The finding that both sets of characteristics can be present in a single individual is considerably more appealing to decision makers concerned with group performance, because it suggests that such individuals can adapt to many different types of performance situations. Previous approaches (e.g., Fiedler, 1967) have speculated that managers should be assigned to situations more in keeping with their particular managerial style. Unfortunately, this is not practical in many situations, but perhaps even more problematic is the fact that most management situations are dynamic and in constant evolution, influenced by continuing change in membership, member relations, task motivation, and the like.

With respect to the flight deck, as in most performance situations, it has usually been assumed that task orientation is strongly related

The Grid®

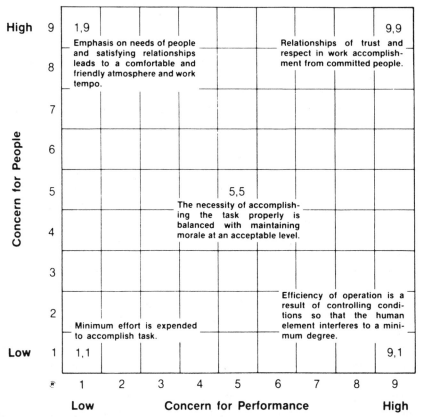

Figure 7.2.   The "managerial grid." (Courtesy of Scientific Methods, Inc.)

to performance and that group orientation is essentially unrelated. However, Helmreich (1982) has presented data which suggest otherwise. In a study of air carrier pilots, both task and group orientations were significant predictors of the group process variable of crew coordination.

As previously suggested, the incident and accident record has also implicated the lack of an effective interpersonal orientation as a cause of breakdowns in the group process variable of information exchange. Subordinate crew members complain that captains are at times so insensitive and intimidating that they hesitate to speak up even in potentially dangerous situations. We have identified the extent of this problem, in part, through a confidential data base, the Aviation Safety Reporting System (ASRS), which is a joint endeavor of NASA and the Federal Aviation Administration. This data base (which currently contains over 80,000 reports submitted by pilots, air traffic controllers, and other members of the aviation community since 1976) has proven to be an invaluable tool for the identification of significant problem areas.

An example of this type of behavior is illustrated in a copilot report to ASRS (Foushee, 1982, p. 1063). Air traffic control had issued a speed restriction which was repeatedly ignored by the captain. After several attempts had been made by the copilot to convey the information, the captain responded by saying, "I'll do what I want." Air traffic control inquired as to why the aircraft had not been slowed, advised the crew that they had almost collided with another aircraft, and issued a new clearance which was also disregarded by the captain despite repeated clarification by the copilot. Following the last advisory from the copilot, the captain responded by telling the copilot to "just look out the damn window."

The inherent danger of such situations is that subordinate crew members can become *conditioned* not to speak up after running into captains such as the one in the preceding report. Consistent behavior of this sort by captains (while not usually as blatant as in this example) may have contributed to the development of a normative pattern of what constitutes "appropriate copilot behavior," and there is a strong likelihood that this behavioral norm will transfer to situations where there is no reason for member input to be suppressed.

Another report from a copilot to ASRS illustrates this phenomenon. This report described a situation where air traffic control had instructed the flight to level off at 21,000 feet. As they reached their assigned altitude, the copilot noticed that the captain was climbing through it. The copilot mentioned it to the captain, "but not forcefully enough and he did not hear me." The copilot mentioned it again and pointed to the altimeter at which point the captain stopped the climb and descended back to the assigned altitude. Assigned altitudes are extremely critical in dense air traffic environments, and strict adherence to these altitudes is necessary because of the likelihood that other aircraft are assigned to adjacent airspace. Because of this, the copilot was extremely concerned about the incident and summed up the reasons for its occurrence in the following insightful manner:

> The captain said he had misread his altimeter and thought he was 1000 ft. lower than he was. I believe the main factor involved here was

my reluctance to correct the captain. This captain is very "approach-able" and I had no real reason to hold back. It is just a bad habit that I think a lot of copilots have of double-checking everything before we say anything to the captain. (Foushee, 1982, p. 1063).

It should come as no great surprise that this situation can produce, and has produced, disastrous consequences. In a 1979 crash of a northeastern commuter carrier (NTSB, 1980), the first officer failed to take control of the aircraft when the captain apparently passed out at the controls. The captain was a company vice-president, and the first officer was a recently hired pilot still on probation. The captain, according to reports, had a gruff personality and was observed to be visibly upset on the day of the accident. Further, this captain apparently had a history of not acknowledging cockpit communications. Clearly, the group dynamics of that particular situation were not conducive to the first officer's assumption of control. It would appear that had the first officer not been intimidated, the accident might not have occurred. In another accident (NTSB, 1979a), a twin-jet slid off the end of the runway after crossing the outer marker approximately 60 knots over the appropriate speed. Although the captain was apparently oblivious to the excessive speed, evidence indicates that the first officer knew but could only muster a sheepish comment about the possible presence of a tail wind. The Washington, D. C., B-737 accident, which we have already discussed, had similar characteristics.

It is reasonable to assume that the development of a strong group norm of shared responsibility will increase the probability that subordinate crew members will function more effectively in critical instances. Obviously, the captain's leadership style is an important component for the establishment of such a norm, but it is by no means the only component, and it would be a mistake to infer that personality characteristics, alone, dictate flight-deck behavior. As we have mentioned previously, it is the combination of input factors that influence behavior and also make it difficult to predict.

The strong role structure (chain of command) of the flight deck is a group-level input factor and is also a powerful predictor of flight crew interaction. In the airlines, position is largely a function of seniority and experience, so that the person in charge is usually the most experienced and so on down the chain of command. In multipilot, military operations, for example, pilots are officers, and flight engineers are enlisted personnel. When the role structure is well defined, as it usually is in flight-deck crews, it governs how subordinates interact with superiors and explains, in part, why subordinates are sometimes so hesitant to speak up. Sometimes it is not so well defined. In the military, the aircraft commander is not necessarily the senior officer on the flight deck. In the civilian sector, the recent demise of some air carriers has precipitated the hiring, by prosperous, expanding airlines, of formerly "senior captains" who go to the bottom of the seniority list (usually to the flight engineer position) for their new employer. Such "role reversals" can be equally disruptive to crew coordination by raising questions as to who is really in charge. Role structure problems can also extend to the part of the group working in important supporting roles on the ground. We mentioned previously the case of the air traffic controller in the Everglades accident asking the flight crew how everything was going instead of probing more directly about the aircraft's altitude loss. One potential explanation of this rather indirect inquiry is that, traditionally, pilot positions carry higher prestige than air traffic controller jobs, and this role differential causes some air traffic controllers to tread lightly in their professional interactions with pilots.

Apparently, the reluctance to question superiors or assume control is not an isolated problem. In an investigation conducted by Harper, Kidera, and Cullen (1971) at a major air carrier, captains feigned subtle incapacitation at a predetermined point during final approach in simulator trials characterized by poor weather and visibility. In that study, approximately 25% of these simulated flights "hit the ground" because the first officers did not take control.

Attitudes, as input factors, also affect the group process and subsequent performance. Helmreich, Foushee, Benson, and Russini (1986) asked supervisory pilots at an airline to provide a list of their most effective cockpit managers along with a list of their most ineffective. Volunteer pilots in this airline then completed a survey of their attitudes toward effective cockpit crew coordination. In this study, over 95% of the subject pilots were correctly classified (whether they were good or bad managers) by their attitudes toward cockpit crew coordination. Effective managers tended to feel that they were not infallible and encouraged other crew members to question their actions whenever necessary. They reported a recognition of the need for sensitivity to others feelings and the necessity of verbalizing intentions so that all crew members were aware of the necessary information. Ineffective managers tended to advocate a more authoritarian style of management, leaned more toward the right stuff profile, and were not as quick to acknowledge their own personal limitations.

In sum, there is little question that flight crew interaction and behavior is strongly affected by many of the input factors that affect groups in task-related environments. Our attention is now turned to the relationship between process variables and performance.

Flight Crew Process Variables and Performance

Researchers in the aviation environment are perhaps more fortunate than many of our laboratory research colleagues. The rapid advancement of simulator technology has provided an ideal laboratory for the study of group process variables. It is now feasible to simulate realistically virtually every aspect of the aircraft operational environment (complete with realistic auditory, visual, and motion cues) to the point where actual trips can be "flown" in a simulator, and these "flights" are almost indistinguishable from those in the airplane. Due to the high degree of simulator fidelity, it is possible to conduct controlled studies of group process variables with almost complete confidence that the results generated in the simulator are strongly (if not completely) representative of the real world (see Lauber & Foushee, 1981). Moreover, the simulator allows the study of situations that are too dangerous to perform in an actual aircraft.

The best example of this use of simulation was provided by H. P. Ruffell Smith (1979) in a study which was not originally designed as an investigation of group process, but which provided strong evidence for the importance of the group performance dimension. In that study, B-747 crews were asked to fly a highly realistic simulated flight from New York to London. Because of an oil-pressure problem, the crew was forced to shut down an engine. Since the trip to London could not be completed with a failed engine, the crew had to decide where to land the airplane, and the decision was further compounded by a hydraulic system failure, poor weather, less than ideal air traffic control, and a cabin crew member who consistently requested assistance from the cockpit crew at inopportune moments. The Ruffell Smith study allowed the examination of flight crew performance in a completely comparable and controlled setting, and there were marked variations in the performance of the crews. Perhaps the most salient aspect of this flight simulation study was the finding that most problems were related to breakdowns in crew coordination, not to a lack of technical knowledge and skill. "High-error" crews experienced difficulties in the areas of communication, crew interaction, and integration. For example, some of the more serious errors occurred when the performance of an individual crew member was interrupted by demands from other crew members. Other performance deficiencies were associated with poor leadership and the failure of the flight crew to exchange information in a timely fashion.

A classic example of how the crew coordination process can break down was seen in the simulation and provides an interesting case study. Since the scenario involved a high gross weight takeoff followed by an engine shutdown and subsequent diversion, it was necessary for the crew to dump fuel to get the aircraft weight down to a permissible landing weight. The fuel-dump is a high workload procedure and requires a high level of coordination. The following is a brief synopsis of how poor coordination led to considerable difficulty, including a landing weight 77,000 pounds over the maximum allowable, on a short, wet runway:

> After the captain decided that it would be necessary to dump fuel the captain and first officer decided that 570,000 lbs. was the correct landing weight. The decision was made without consulting either the flight engineer or any aircraft documentation.
>
> The flight engineer then calculated a dump time of 4 minutes and 30 seconds and this was accepted by the captain without comment, although it was approximately one-third the actual time required. Without prompting, the flight engineer then recalculated the dump time, and arrived at the nearly correct figure of 12 minutes.
>
> However, instead of dumping for 12 minutes, the engineer terminated the dumping procedure after only three minutes, possibly because he reverted to his initial erroneous estimate, or because he may have misread the gross weight indicator. Unsatisfied, he again started to recalculate, but was interrupted by the failure of the No. 3 hydraulic system (part of the scenario).
>
> During the next eight minutes, the flight engineer was subjected to high workload but then noticed that the gross weight was much too high and decided to refigure the fuel. During that time, he was subjected to further interruptions and did nothing more about the fuel until the captain noticed that the gross weight indicator read 647,000 lbs. and decided to make an over gross weight landing. A minute and a half later, the flight engineer rechecked the fuel as part of the landing checklist and became concerned about the gross weight. He spent a minute and a half rechecking calculations and announced that the aircraft gross weight computer must be in error. Two minutes later, the simulator was landed at 172 kts. with only 25 degree flaps, 1000 ft./minute sink rate, and 77,000 lbs. over correct weight.
>
> During the 32 minutes between the decision to dump fuel and the landing, there were 15 interruptions to the flight engineer's specific tasks concerning determination of the proper amount of fuel dumped in light of conditions, runway length, etc. Nine of these interruptions came directly or indirectly from the captain.

Because of these interruptions, the flight engineer was never able to complete and verify his fuel calculations and dump times before he was interrupted. The flight engineer was overloaded in large part because of poor prioritization. The captain, whose job it was to set priorities did nothing to resolve the situation, and the engineer did nothing to provide feedback to the captain on the situation. (Lauber, 1984, pp. 20–21)

One of the most significant group process variables is reflected by the information flow within the group. The measurement of relational communication has been utilized over the years by a number of researchers in various paradigms (e.g., Bales, 1950; Mark, 1970). In studies that have examined the relationship between group process variables and performance effectiveness, careful analyses of the communications process have often proven fruitful. Lanzetta and Roby (1960) monitored and recorded all communications during a group performance task. Their study found that this particular measure of group interaction predicted task success better than such measures as member knowledge and skill. These authors suggest, in a quote that might as easily have come from one of the NTSB accident reports, that "the way the group 'utilizes' its resources and the procedures it employs for communicating essential information are as important, if not more important than 'knowledge' of the problem for determining its performance" (p. 146).

In a separate investigation designed to look at the group process, Foushee and Manos (1981) analyzed the cockpit voice recordings from the Ruffell Smith (1979) simulation study, utilizing a technique adapted from Bales' (1950) interaction process analysis. Several interesting relationships emerged from the Foushee and Manos study, and these data are displayed in Table 7.1.

Overall, there was a tendency for crews who communicated less not to perform as well, but the type or quality of communication played an even more pivotal role. There was a negative relationship between crew member observations about flight status and errors related to the operation of aircraft systems. In short, when more information was transferred about aspects of flight status, fewer errors appeared which were related to such problems as mishandling of engines, hydraulic, and fuel systems, the misreading and missetting of instruments, the failure to use ice protection, and so forth.

It would appear that information exchange of this sort facilitates the development or coordination of strategies through the assurance that all members have access to the relevant information. However, there may be a negative side to the complete coordination or sharing of strategic plans unless group norms specifically allow for the processing of discrepant information. As Janis (1972) has pointed out,

Table 7.1. Selected Relationships between Flight Crew Communication and Errors

Type of communication		Type of error					
	Navigation	System operations	Flying	Tactical decisions	Communication	Flying skill	Total
Crew member observations							
Commands		-.51	-.64				
Response uncertainty	.68						
Agreement						.56	-.61
Acknowledgment		-.61		-.52			-.68
Tension release		-.53			.51		
Frustration/anger	.53		-.51				
Embarrassment	.53						
Pushes	.54						

group processes often lead to situations where information discrepant with the group's strategic course of action is ignored or de-emphasized, even when it is critically relevant. This can occur not only in groups where interpersonal relations are strained, but also in groups where there is too much agreement.

In other areas of information exchange, Foushee and Manos found a negative relationship between aircraft systems errors and acknowledgments of information provided by other crew members. In crews in which commands, inquiries, and observations were frequently acknowledged, these types of errors were less apparent. Acknowledgments were also related to fewer errors overall. It appeared that acknowledgments served the important function of validating that a certain piece of information had, in fact, been transferred. These types of communication also seemed to serve as reinforcements to the input of other crew members. This relationship suggests that communication patterns can serve to increase member effort and motivate further participation in the group process.

Commands were associated with a lower incidence of flying errors, such as problems with power settings, neglect of speed limits, altitude deviations, and the lack of formal transfer of control between captain and first officer. Often communications of this type seem to assure the proper delegation of cockpit duties and facilitate coordination and planning. Yet, it should be noted that the overuse of imperative statements may have negative consequences. The use of commands provides a very good illustration of the effect of varying interpersonal styles. An identical piece of information can be related to other crew members in one of several different ways. For instance, a communication such as "Ask air traffic control for a higher altitude," which would constitute a command, could also be relayed as an observation ("I think we should ask air traffic control for a higher altitude") or as an inquiry ("Why don't we ask air traffic control for a higher altitude").

Foushee and Manos also found evidence for higher rates of response uncertainty, frustration or anger, embarrassment, and lower rates of agreement in crews who tended to make more errors. Despite the fact that these correlational data do not allow inferences of causation, it is safe to infer that discord related to the commission of errors, whether cause or effect, may be related to crew coordination deficiencies downstream.

In addition to the importance of communication style, the precision of communication plays a pivotal role. The ASRS data bank contains a number of incidents in which each pilot thought he or she knew what the other meant or intended to do when, in reality, he or she did not. One report to ASRS described a situation where a critical alarm went off in the cockpit followed by immediate diagnostic actions by the crew. Shortly thereafter the alarm silenced, leading the captain to believe that it was probably a false warning. After landing, the captain discovered that the circuit breaker for the alarm system had been pulled by the flight engineer, that it was not a false warning, and that the warning could have been potentially serious. The flight engineer stated that he had asked the captain if he wanted the warning inhibited, and since there was no reply, he assumed he was complying with the captain's wishes (Foushee, 1982).

Input, Process, and Output Relationships

In order to demonstrate the power of the group level of analysis and the extent of input, process, and output relationships in flight crews, a recent full-mission simulation study may serve as a good example. We discuss not only the results of this study in some detail but also some of the associated methodology, in order to illustrate how state-of-the-art flight simulators can serve as experimental laboratories with almost complete applicability to real-world settings.

In this study, Foushee, Lauber, Baetge, and Acomb (1986) examined the performance of fully qualified, twin-jet transport crews in a highly realistic setting. The experiment was done by NASA at the request of the U. S. Congress, which was concerned with the potential effects of pilot fatigue and circadian dysrhythmia (jet lag), but as we seek to demonstrate, the results of the study had substantial implications for group performance. Interestingly enough, this congressional request was stimulated, in large part, because of an almost complete lack of research in actual operational settings—another example of how decision makers are often hesitant to base policy on laboratory research findings. Thus, the emphasis of this study was on realism and the search for any behavioral and performance changes that might be "operationally significant" (having substantial implications for safety), such as differences in decision making and crew coordination. Of less concern were those aspects of individual pilot performance related to mechanical skills (e.g., stick-and-rudder performance).

Since the primary objective of the study was to assess the operational significance of exposure to various types of flight and duty cycles, subjects were selected either before or after they had completed a 3-day trip (see Graeber, Chapter 10, this volume for more details on fatigue research). The target trips in this study consisted of high-density, short-haul airline operations—averaging 8 hours of on-duty time per day, and five takeoffs and landings, with at least 1 day (usually the last) averaging close to eight takeoffs and landings and a 13-hour duty day. Crews in the "post-duty" condition flew the simulation as if it were the last segment of a 3-day trip, while subjects in the "pre-duty" condition flew the scenario after a minimum of 2 days off-duty (usually 3), as if it were the first leg of a 3-day trip. All simulator sessions occurred in the early evening to control for time-of-day effects. Ten crews were run in each condition (40 pilots), and all were volunteers, currently flying the aircraft which was simulated in airline operations.

Due to the emphasis upon operational realism, the experiment incorporated everything that airline pilots would experience on an actual flight, to the extent that this was possible. This included complete air traffic control (ATC) services, including background transmissions between ATC and other aircraft. They also had radio access to complete weather information, company maintenance, and flight dispatch. When crews arrived at the simulation facility, they met with a flight dispatcher who provided them with weather information, flight plans, and other paperwork necessary for a trip. The weather information for the vicinity of flight revealed a frontal system passing through with low ceilings and visibilities. This included the departure airport which was still acceptable for takeoff, but nearing the legal limit. The airplane was relatively heavy, and the longer runway at the departure airport was closed, which meant that the airplane was dispatched with a minimum, but legal amount of fuel. Because of this and the poor weather, which increased the probability of diversion, crews should have been concerned about the amount of fuel (possibility of extra fuel needed for a diversion), and as in the real world, crews had the option of requesting additional fuel from the flight dispatcher. However, this had implications for the number of passengers and baggage on board, and if more fuel was requested (prudent under the circumstances), baggage had to be off-loaded.

After the crew had preflighted the aircraft and received clearance to pushback and taxi, ATC issued a special weather observation indicating that the weather had deteriorated. The operational implications were that takeoff was still legal, but landing was not, and this meant crews were legally required to obtain a "takeoff alternate" (necessary in case mechanical problems forced a quick return for landing). As in all of the operational events programmed into the

simulation, some crews realized this necessity and acted appropriately, while some did not. Once airborne, a relatively low-activity, routine segment was planned in order to allow crews to relax so that
their behavior would more closely approximate actual flight behavior. Most of the performance measures were taken after the end of
this routine segment.

The high-workload phase of flight was initiated when crews began
their approach to the destination airport. When they received standard weather information for their arrival, they discovered that the
weather was poor and required a complicated, instrument approach.
Further, there was a substantial crosswind on the active runway that
was close to the legal limit. As they continued their approach and
contacted the tower for landing clearance, they were advised that the
winds were higher (3 knots over the legal limit of 10 knots). Again,
some crews realized this and executed the required missed approach,
and some did not. In any event, all crews, whether they realized that
landing was illegal or not, were forced to execute a missed approach,
because those who continued did not have visual contact with the
ground at *decision height* (a legal minimum altitude for each approach at which point the runway must be visible). During the
missed approach, crews received a "System A" hydraulic failure.
The implications of this malfunction were many: (1) landing gear
and flaps had to be extended manually; (2) braking effectiveness was
reduced, which meant increased stopping distances; and (3) a 15°
flaps approach was dictated (30–40° is the norm).

Crews were then faced with a number of complicated decisions
and procedures. They had to figure out where they were going to
land, since the original destination did not have legal landing conditions, and in some cases there was only a limited amount of fuel (remember the beginning of the scenario and the original dispatch with
minimum fuel). They had to diagnose the failure, realize the implications, and secure the failed system. Since higher approach speeds
and reduced braking effectiveness were primary problems, clearly
the most desirable alternate landing site, under the circumstances,
was one with a relatively long runway. Unfortunately, this did not
exist due to weather in the general vicinity (this was consistent with
the initial weather briefing crews received prior to the flight in dispatch) and limited fuel. The only reasonable alternate was an airport
with acceptable weather but with a relatively short runway (5,800 ft)
that was wet, sloping downhill, and in the middle of mountainous
terrain. Moreover, manual gear and flap extension is a time-consuming process that requires a fair amount of preplanning. In short, this

simulation was one requiring a high level of crew coordination to execute it effectively—a good test of the group process. It should also be pointed out that some of the features of this scenario are similar to those seen in past incidents and accidents.

The results of the Foushee et al. study revealed that, not surprisingly, post-duty crews were more fatigued than pre-duty crews. They had significantly less sleep and rated themselves significantly more tired than did the pre-duty crews. However, a fascinating and somewhat counterintuitive pattern of results emerged on the crew performance measures. During each run, a qualified supervisory pilot (check-pilot) rated each crew on a number of dimensions specific to important aspects of crew performance in this particular simulation scenario. In a number of these areas, post-duty (tired) crews were rated as performing significantly better than pre-duty (rested) crews, particularly on those measures that were operationally significant. They were rated better on approach planning, planning for the implications of the System A hydraulic failure, and on the execution of the emergency procedures. In fact, there were no cases on any of these rating dimensions where pre-duty crews were rated better than post-duty crews.

A similar pattern was evident on measures related to aircraft handling. Specifically, measures related to the stability of aircraft handling were taken from the simulator computer and analyzed for the last few minutes of final approach after the System A failure. It should be recalled that this was the culmination of the scenario, where crews were forced to land on a short runway with less than normal braking effectiveness, at higher speeds, after having just completed manual gear and flap extension procedures—in short it was the point in this simulated flight where aircraft stability was most important. Post-duty crews executed more stable approaches than did pre-duty crews. Specifically, pre-duty crews landed at higher speeds, were sinking faster, and deviated more, vertically and laterally, from the normal approach path.

The error data were also very interesting. Errors were broken down into three classes according to severity. Type I errors were regarded as relatively minor and having no serious safety connotations. Type II errors were more serious, but not necessarily dangerous, and Type III errors were regarded as highly serious, with adverse effects upon flight safety (although not necessarily serious enough to cause a crash). In terms of the more serious Types II and III errors, pre-duty crews tended to commit more errors than did post-duty crews.

If you think about how crews are often rostered, there is an important difference between crews at the beginning of the duty cycle and crews at the end of a trip, in addition to the fatigue factor. Obviously, after 3 days of flying with someone, you know a considerable amount about his or her operating characteristics, personality, and communication style. If you are a copilot, you know a lot about when and how an aircraft commander or captain likes to be assisted. If you are the person in charge, you know more about how your subordinates supply information and how to best elicit their input. As everyone knows, there is wide variation in human interaction, and the more you know about someone, the better you are able to tailor your behavior to the needs of the interaction. In an effort to control for this factor, some crews were assigned to conditions differentially. In some cases, post-duty crew members from different trips were assigned as a simulation crew, so they had not necessarily flown together recently. Likewise, pre-duty crews were assigned to the simulation from the ranks of individuals who had just finished a trip together, but had been off-duty for 3 days. All of the data were then reanalyzed, based on who had flown together recently or not (forgetting about the fatigue factor), and a very striking pattern of results emerged. The performance differences became stronger. As Table 7.2 indicates, crews who had flown together made significantly fewer errors than crews who had not, particularly the more serious types of errors—the Type II and Type III errors. This same pattern was true for all of the performance data we collected. Recent operating experience appears to be one of those group-level input factors that strongly affects crew performance.

Examination of the flight crew communication patterns in the Foushee et al. study, as group process variables, suggests that they are, in fact, moderating the relationship between input factors (fatigue and recent operating experience or prior history) and output

Table 7.2.   Crew Errors as a Function of
Recent Operating Experience

Type of error	Crews who had	
	Not flown together	Flown together
Type I	1.22	1.50
Type II	4.78	2.20*
Type III	5.67	1.30**
Total	11.67	5.00**

*$p < .04$. **$p < .009$.

factors (performance). Crews who had flown together communicated significantly more overall, and these differences were in logical directions in light of the significant performance variations. As in the Foushee and Manos (1981) study which found commands associated with better performance, captains in crews that had flown together issued more commands, but so did copilots (even though the frequency of copilot commands was relatively low). This probably indicates a better understanding and division of responsibility between the two crew members. There were more suggestions made in crews that had flown together, and more statements of intent by each crew member, also indicating more willingness to exchange information.

Another replication of the Foushee and Manos results showed acknowledgments again associated with better performance. There were many more acknowledgments of communications by both captains and first officers who had flown together (we have already discussed that acknowledgments probably serve to reinforce the communications process). A particularly interesting finding was the presence of more disagreement exhibited by first officers who had flown with the same captain during the preceding 3 days. This suggests that increased familiarity may be, at least, a partial cure to the previously cited hesitancy of subordinates to question the actions of captains.

There was significantly more nontask related communication in crews who had not flown together, which may well indicate that they spent more time attempting to get to know each other. There was also significantly more tension release among crews who did not previously fly together. Also interesting was the presence of more frustration among captains who had not flown with the same copilot before.

In presenting these data, we are not trying to suggest the creation of permanent crews. There are also negative aspects associated with flying with the same person all of the time, such as complacency, boredom, and so forth. It could well be that continued flying with the same individuals would ultimately lead to a reversal of this pattern—worse performance associated with increased familiarity. Unfortunately, no research presently exists to substantiate this possibility, and it is not known how much familiarity might lead to this reversal. The point to be made here is that a collection of highly qualified individuals does not necessarily constitute an effective team. All of the crew members in this simulation study were technically qualified, yet substantial performance differences existed that were attributable to the group process.

A Note on Aviation System Safety

The reader should bear in mind that the results of the Ruffell Smith (1979), Foushee and Manos (1981), Foushee et. al. (1986), and other empirical studies in this area are based upon realistic flight simulations, where high levels of crew workload precipitated by carefully controlled events no doubt contributed to the crew performance problems reported herein. These levels of workload and stress are characteristic of many accident scenarios, but they are infrequently encountered in day-to-day operations. While the results of these studies may be disturbing to some, the remarkable overall safety of the system should be stressed. Fortunately, the problems discussed here rarely lead to accidents, which is a testament to overall system redundancy. It should be comforting to note that since accidents are so infrequent, they make terrible research criteria for judging crew performance, and it is a credit to the industry that the primary research and training concern is upon those aspects of performance which under some circumstances can have dramatic consequences. Attention is now turned to methods aimed at the facilitation of this process.

Addressing the Issue

Hackman and Morris (1975) suggest that the best way to effect meaningful change in group performance is to concentrate on input factors. Thus, it is proposed that group performance strategies can be made more task-appropriate by modifying the group's norms, that member effort and coordination can be increased by task redesign, and that the level and utilization of group member knowledge and skill can be improved by altering the composition of the group.

It was previously noted that the existence of group performance problems is becoming more salient both to the air carrier industry and to the military. Several airlines, stimulated by this awareness, are beginning to address these issues in their training programs, and at least one major air carrier has made a substantial investment in a comprehensive program of "cockpit resource management" training for all of its pilots. The Military Airlift Command of the U. S. Air Force is now implementing group training and plans to expand these efforts to the entire fleet. The remainder of this discussion focuses on some of the techniques utilized in this program and whether they may be expected to facilitate the group performance process.

Altering Group Norms

As we discussed in the beginning of this chapter, much of the attitudinal structure of professional pilots is well established, having
evolved during a time when aviation was not routine and the dangers of flight were considerable. We mentioned that reliance upon
others was perhaps negatively related to longevity in "the old days."
While it is easy to visualize such individuals functioning effectively
as fighter or test pilots, it is more difficult to view them as "good
team players." In the past, airlines themselves did little to discourage
captains from functioning in this manner. The 1952 guidelines for
pilot proficiency-checks at a major airline explicitly stated that the
first officer should not correct errors made by the captain (H. W. Orlady, personal communication, March 20, 1983). To this day, the
Federal Aviation Regulations governing pilot qualifications deal almost exclusively with the acquisition and maintenance of individual
pilot proficiency.

Despite the fact that the aviation environment has changed considerably, these attitudes and norms for behavior are ubiquitous, and an
attempt is being made to alter the normative structure of the flight
crew in some training programs. One method—the use of videotape
feedback and diagnosis of task-specific behaviors—is being employed
in an effort to correct certain ineffective task performance strategies
associated with excessive task orientation and insensitivity to others.
In one program, crews are asked to fly a full-mission simulation
(LOFT; we discuss other training benefits of LOFT in the next section) that is videotaped from start to finish. Following these simulated flights, crew members view the tape with an instructor and
discuss such aspects of the group process as the effects of interpersonal styles, the appropriate delegation of responsibility, and how
the role structure can inhibit the input of subordinate flight crew
members. From a theoretical standpoint, this approach may very
well produce some tangible change. Duval and Wicklund (1972), in
their theory of objective self-awareness, found that self-focusing stimuli often force objective appraisals of oneself that may lead to attitude and behavior change. An interesting study illustrates how self-
focusing manipulations can induce heightened objectivity. Pryor,
Gibbons, Wicklund, Fazio, and Hood (1977) conducted a study in
which college students were asked to write down their SAT scores.
Half the subjects did this in front of a mirror and half without the
mirror. The actual scores of these students were then checked using
records in the university registrar's office. The results of this study

indicated that subjects sitting in front of the mirror reported their scores significantly more accurately than those not in front of the mirror. Anecdotal evidence from programs utilizing videotape as self-focusing stimuli is suggestive of a positive impact, with crew members expressing surprise at their behavior during the videotaped flights. It is easy to discount feedback from others indicating that your behavior is inappropriate, but it is not so easy to discount it if you see it for yourself. Video feedback is, for many people, the only opportunity they will ever have to observe themselves in action as others do.

Another prevalent technique within the industry is the use of seminars as a means of providing information aimed at altering the normative structure of flight crews. These seminars are frequently offered as part of the training required for promotion from junior crew member to captain. The philosophy underlying this approach, as well as other feedback approaches, is that heightened awareness will produce tangible behavior change. It is not presumed that the personality structures of individuals can be altered in a short period of time. Personality is the result of years of development and it is completely unreasonable to assume that a series of seminars and exercises will alter predispositions that have developed over a lifetime. However, it is felt that the pilot socialization process has not generally produced patterns consistent with teamwork. Thus, it is argued that pilots are often not aware of how subtle factors can compromise group function. The educational content generally places a heavy emphasis on material related to the role of interpersonal styles and the effects of certain types of behavior on coworkers. Group exercises, personality assessment, feedback techniques, role-playing, case studies, and interpersonal encounter drills, are frequently employed.

It may surprise some to discover that these programs are proving to be popular in airlines that have implemented them. However, serious questions are usually raised as to their long-term effectiveness. It is probably true that these interventions provide short-term insight, but long-term change is no doubt dependent on periodic exposure and reinforcement. Unfortunately, few organizations are providing their personnel with this type of training on a recurrent basis. Perhaps more disturbing is the absence of research dealing with the evaluation or relative efficacy of such programs. Many principles and techniques that are being "preached as the gospel" in such programs are in need of further study.

Increasing Member Effort and Coordination

Raising individual member effort and coordinating these efforts is another means of increasing group productivity. One method suggests that restructuring tasks, in a way that requires coordinated performance from all group members, will result in increased member effort by necessity and will produce normative change. Since flight training has traditionally emphasized individual skills, most pilots have had very little realistic experience with high-workload or emergency situations that require teamwork. Moreover, equipment reliability and automation have rendered most flight tasks routine; high-stress emergency situations are relatively rare. Yet, as has been mentioned, this lack of experience may be a factor when crews are faced with nonroutine situations, a view that is supported by the incident and accident record.

While it makes little sense to change substantively the task of flying most modern aircraft considering the remarkable safety record of the present system, it may be logical to restructure the training task. Many airlines are beginning to utilize a technique known as line-oriented flight training (LOFT, or mission-oriented simulator training, MOST, in the Air Force; e.g., Lauber & Foushee, 1981) in which crews fly a complete trip in a high-fidelity simulator. However, unlike the real world, LOFT scenarios are usually designed to include emergency situations which require the coordinated actions of all crew members for success. LOFT or MOST scenarios are usually very similar to those we have described in the simulator experiments presented in this chapter. These flights occur in real time, and no intervention is made by the instructor regardless of the actions of the crew. LOFT is a learning experience in which errors are usually made. However, since effective group function in this environment is by definition the management of human error, LOFT provides highly effective crew coordination training. Just as it is necessary to practice landing skills in order to gain and maintain aircraft-handling proficiency, it is necessary to practice crew coordination skills in order to assure good flight crew performance. LOFT provides the vehicle by which these skills, now recognized as important, are practiced and maintained. Some air carriers provide LOFT training every 6 or 12 months, and this approach may be a more viable way of producing long-term behavior change.

As Hackman and Morris (1975) suggest, the amount of effort group members put into a task is also heavily affected by the normative structure of the group. It has been noted that factors inherent in the role structure of the flight crew, while necessary for the effective co-ordination of responsibilities, sometimes serve to decrease the effort expenditure of subordinate crew members. By changing the norms of the group and reinforcing the importance of coordinated perfor-mance, the malady some refer to as "captainitis" may begin to sub-side, and subordinate crew members may find it easier to have sufficient input into the group process. If these programs accomplish nothing else, they may be beneficial by simply heightening aware-ness of the importance of leadership styles that encourage the input of all team members. By "legitimizing" this input or making it a part of the group's values, it is reasonable to expect some increase in member motivation, at least in the short term. The legitimization of the importance of group interactional factors in the maintenance of crew coordination should not be underestimated. Now that organiza-tions have accepted the importance of these factors, the way has been paved for acceptance and perhaps change by the people in the system.

Changing Group Composition

Altering the group's composition may be the most effective and perhaps the most difficult means for improving group effectiveness. Yet, it is an inescapable fact that successful group performance is heavily dependent upon the individual skills and characteristics of members, and efforts aimed at the recruitment of qualified individu-als has always been one of the favored means of producing the de-sired result. There is very little question that most airline pilots are highly skilled in the technical aspects of their job, but there is con-cern about their function as team members. We have discussed the fact that in the United States the labor pool is composed heavily of pilots whose formative years were spent in high-performance, single-seat military aircraft, and we suggested that pilots with this type of experience may bring an individualistic emphasis to the multipilot cockpit. For individuals such as these, learning team skills can only be accomplished slowly and painfully. One obvious solution, which could be implemented during the hiring process, would be the selec-tion of individuals who possess the skills associated with good lead-ership or team function.

For the airline industry, this approach has obvious drawbacks, at least in the near term. Clearly, it does not address the needs of the present pilot population, since past selection criteria have not encompassed these abilities. Helmreich (1982) has recently reported work with a new airline in which both group orientation combined with goal orientation were among the desirable selection criteria for new pilots, but it is too soon to draw any inferences about the success of such selection practices.

The most practical approach for most organizations is to focus upon changing pilot attitudes and experiences in this domain. The techniques discussed above such as LOFT, seminars, and feedback are aimed at increasing the skills associated with group function in flight crew members through an increasing awareness of the importance of these factors. It should be stressed that this is neither a small nor short-term task. The open treatment of issues related to one's interpersonal competence can be very anxiety provoking for some individuals. No matter how well this type of training is conducted, certain people will be resistant to change, provoking some critics of these programs to argue that the very individuals who need to improve will not benefit because they are the ones likely to be threatened. On the other hand, carriers that have undertaken resource management training programs report that after exposure to this training, peer pressure often facilitates change among those initially unreceptive to the program.

Future Tasks and Directions

It is customary to close discussions such as these with solemn predictions of the future, and we have no intention of violating this time-honored tradition. It should be noted, however, that most predictions about changes in the aviation system over the past few years have been strikingly inaccurate, and our forecasts should be regarded in this light.

It does appear safe to predict that, once having become aware of the critical importance of group interaction patterns for the safety and effectiveness of flight, the system will never again ignore these issues. It also seems likely that increased emphasis will be placed on training programs to increase crew coordination and effectiveness.

As we have noted, however, the overall effectiveness of these programs has never been assessed through systematic research. There is a consensus judgment that they are effective, at least for some pilots some of the time, but this is hardly a substitute for empirical evidence. The lack of research data is not entirely due to a failure of expertise or motivation on the part of aviation researchers; rather it is an indication of the sensitivity of the topic of evaluation and the apprehensions of participants that information regarding performance in this area could be used to threaten their status as active pilots (see Helmreich, Hackman, & Foushee, 1988 for a complete discussion of this topic). For example, when implementing training in this area, one major air carrier agreed with its union that no evaluation of cockpit resource management performance would be undertaken at that time. This program has LOFT as a core component, and crew behavior is videotaped to be used in the feedback process. However, after tapes are reviewed with the instructor during debriefing, they are immediately erased, thus destroying a potentially invaluable data base that could be used in assessing the effectiveness of such training. Of course, some of the pilots' concerns about videotapes "falling into the wrong hands" are not entirely without merit.

In order to obtain the essential data, a research strategy will have to be developed that simultaneously protects individual participants and permits collection of systematic records of group process variables and performance both prior to intervention and at periodic intervals after completion of training. This will necessarily involve the cooperation of organizations, regulatory agencies, and the pilots themselves. It would appear to be a difficult, but attainable, goal.

Given validation of the effectiveness of training in crew coordination and resource management (an outcome that we both believe is highly likely), the critical research task becomes the determination of the relative effectiveness of different instructional techniques and the development of more effective ones. Certainly, none of the courses currently in use represents the ultimate in instructional content or methodology. As courses develop, it will be imperative to determine the most important content areas and to evaluate the relative impact and retention levels produced by different techniques and media.

We are convinced that the type of hands-on experience gained through the enactment of mission scenarios (as in LOFT and MOST) can produce the most powerful and lasting type of behavioral change. It is not clear, however, that it is necessary to employ a multimillion dollar simulator with six-axis motion system, wrap-around visual representation, sound effects, and high-fidelity re-creation of operational parameters in order to enhance the crew coordination process. It is possible that lower-fidelity simulation using interactive video workstations and video recording of behavior might provide much of the needed training at a lower cost. In any event, these are the types of issues that can be pursued profitably in research.

Regulation of Resource Management

At the present time, the training associated with resource management and the simulator experience associated with LOFT are entirely nonpunitive. By this we mean that individuals are free to make mistakes without placing their licenses in jeopardy. On the other hand, given the demonstrated relationships between effective crew coordination and safety, it would be a logical extension of the current emphasis on training in this area to require demonstrated proficiency in cockpit resource management as a condition of gaining or maintaining a license to operate in multipilot aircraft (just as demonstrated proficiency is now required in technical areas). At this time, however, the evaluation methodologies and behavioral criteria are not sufficiently refined to guarantee valid or fair assessment of crew coordination. The development and validation of such methodologies is an attainable goal for aviation psychology and is a goal with high potential value (e.g., Helmreich et al., 1988). However, checking for effective crew coordination also implies a wholesale reevaluation of regulations governing pilot proficiency.

Should formal evaluation in the area of resource management be mandated at some future time, we feel that it is essential to maintain or even increase the separation between training and evaluation. The opportunity to explore behavioral options without prejudice is critical. People in almost all situations learn valuable lessons from their own mistakes, and many of the benefits of resource management training would undoubtedly be lost if such training were conducted in a formal evaluation environment.

We cannot speak confidently about the likely outcome of serious research scrutiny of resource management training, the impact of resource management concerns on future crew selection practices, or the direction that evaluation procedures will take in the years to come. Nonetheless, we do feel that even the limited insights into the domain of crew coordination achieved to date have contributed to the ever-increasing safety of the aviation system.

References

Bales, R. F. (1950). *Interaction process analysis: Theory, research, and application.* Reading, MA: Addison-Wesley.

Blake, R. R., & Mouton, J. S. (1978). *The new managerial grid.* Houston: Gulf.

Cooper, G. E., White, M. D., & Lauber, J. K. (Eds.). (1979). *Resource management on the flight deck* (NASA Conference Publication 2120). Moffett Field, CA: NASA-Ames Research Center.

Duval, S., & Wicklund, R. A. (1972). *A theory of objective self awareness.* New York: Academic Press.

Fiedler, F. E. (1967). *A theory of leadership effectiveness.* New York: McGraw-Hill.

Foushee, H. C. (1984). Dyads and triads at 35,000 feet: Factors affecting group process and aircrew performance. *American Psychologist, 39,* 885–893.

Foushee, H. C. (1982). The role of communications, socio-psychological, and personality factors in the maintenance of crew coordination. *Aviation, Space, and Environmental Medicine, 53,* 1062–1066.

Foushee, H. C., Lauber, J. K., Baetge, M. M., & Acomb, D. B. (1986, August). *Crew performance as a function of exposure to high-density short-haul duty cycles* (NASA Technical Memorandum 88322). Moffett Field, CA: NASA-Ames Research Center.

Foushee, H. C., & Manos, K. L. (1981). Information transfer within the cockpit: Problems in intracockpit communications. In C. E. Billings & E. S. Cheaney (Eds.), *Information transfer problems in the aviation system* (NASA Technical Paper 1875; pp. 63–71). Moffett Field, CA: NASA-Ames Research Center.

Hackman, J. R., & Morris, C. G. (1975). Group tasks, group interaction process, and group performance effectiveness: A review and proposed integration. In L. Berkowitz (Ed.), *Advances in experimental social psychology* (Vol. 8, pp. 45–99). New York: Academic Press.

Hare, A. P. (1972). Bibliography of small group research: 1959–1969. *Sociometry, 35,* 1–150.

Harper, C. R., Kidera, G. J., & Cullen, J. F. (1971). Study of simulated airline pilot incapacitation: Phase II, subtle or partial loss of function. *Aerospace Medicine, 42,* 946–948.

Helmreich, R. L. (1982, August). *Pilot selection and training.* Paper presented at the meeting of the American Psychological Association, Washington, DC.

Helmreich, R. L. (1975). Applied social psychology: The unfulfilled promise. *Personality and Social Psychology Bulletin, 1,* 548–561.

Helmreich, R. L., Foushee, H. C., Benson, R., & Russini, W. (1986). Cockpit resource management: Exploring the attitude–performance linkage. *Aviation, Space and Environmental Medicine, 57,* 1198–1200.

Helmreich, R. L., Hackman, J. R., & Foushee, H. C. (1988, in preparation). *Evaluating flightcrew performance: Policy, pressures, pitfalls, and promise* (NASA Technical Memorandum). Moffett Field, CA: NASA-Ames Research Center.

Janis, I. L. (1972). *Victims of groupthink: A psychological study of foreign policy decisions and fiascos.* Boston: Houghton Mifflin.

Jones, M. B. (1974). Regressing group on individual effectiveness. *Organizational Behavior and Human Performance, 11,* 426–451.

Lanzetta, J. T., & Roby, T. B. (1960). The relationship between certain group process variables and group problem-solving efficiency. *Journal of Social Psychology, 52,* 135–148.

Lauber, J. K. (1984). Cockpit resource management in the cockpit. *Air Line Pilot, 53,* 20–23, 38.

Lauber, J. K., & Foushee, H. C. (1981). *Guidelines for line-oriented flight training, (Vol. 1)* (NASA Conference Publication 2184). Moffett Field, CA: NASA-Ames Research Center.

Mark, R. A. (1970). *Parameters of normal family communication in the dyad.* Unpublished doctoral dissertation, Michigan State University.

McGrath, J. E. (1964). *Social psychology: A brief introduction.* New York: Holt, Rinehart & Winston.

McGrath, J. E., & Altman, I. (1966). *Small group research: A synthesis and critique of the field.* New York: Holt, Rinehart & Winston.

Melton, A. W. (1947). *Army air force aviation psychology program.* Report No. 4, Apparatus Tests: Washington, DC: Defense Documentation Center.

National Transportation Safety Board. (1972). *Aircraft accident report. Eastern Air Lines, Inc. L-1011, N310EA, Miami, Florida, December 29, 1972* (Report No. NTSB-AAR-73-14). Washington, DC: Author.

National Transportation Safety Board. (1979a). *Aircraft accident report. Allegheny Airlines, Inc. BAC 1-11, N1550, Rochester, New York, July 9, 1978* (Report No. NTSB-AAR-79-2). Washington, DC: Author.

National Transportation Safety Board. (1979b). *Aircraft accident report. United Airlines, Inc. McDonnell-Douglas DC-8-61, N8082U, Portland, Oregon, December 28, 1978* (Report No. NTSB-AAR-79-7). Washington, DC: Author.

National Transportation Safety Board. (1980). *Aircraft accident report. Air New England, Inc. DeHavilland DHC-6-30, N383EX, Hyannis, Massachusetts, June 17, 1979* (Report No. NTSB-AAR-80-1). Washington, DC: Author.

National Transportation Safety Board. (1982). *Aircraft accident report. Air Florida, Inc. Boeing B-737-222, N62AF, Collision with 14th Street Bridge, Near Washington National Airport, Washington, D.C. January 13, 1982* (Report No. NTSB-AAR-82-8). Washington, DC: Author.

Pryor, J. B., Gibbons, F. X., Wicklund, R. A., Fazio, R., & Hood, R. (1977). Self-focused attention and self-report validity. *Journal of Personality, 45,* 513–527.

Ruffell Smith, H. P. (1979). A simulator study of the interaction of pilot workload with errors, vigilance, and decisions (NASA Technical Memorandum 78482). Moffett Field, CA: NASA-Ames Research Center.

Spence, J. T., & Helmreich, R. L. (1978). *Masculinity and femininity: Their psychological dimensions, correlates, and antecedents.* Austin, TX: University of Texas Press.

Steiner, I. D. (1972). *Group process and productivity.* New York: Academic Press.

Webster's new collegiate dictionary. (1961). Springfield, MA: Merriam.

Wolfe, T. (1979). *The right stuff.* New York: Farrar, Straus & Giroux.

Flight Training and Simulation

8

Paul W. Caro

Introduction

Training is the systematic modification of behavior through instruction, practice, measurement, and feedback. Its purpose is to teach the trainee to perform tasks not previously possible or to a level of skill or proficiency previously unattainable. Flight training involves use of resources that may include instructional personnel, operational aircraft, simulators and other representations of aircraft, printed and graphic media, classrooms and practice areas, and a variety of other specialized aids and devices, depending upon the tasks to be trained. It also involves management and control of these resources to assure their effective and efficient utilization, as well as management and control of resources needed to produce courseware and other materials utilized during training.

Flight Simulator Design and Use

The modern aircraft simulator is an extremely important resource in most flight-training programs beyond the private pilot certification level. This review addresses the evolution of aircraft simulators as a

Human Factors in Aviation

flight-training resource, the significance of realism in the regulation of simulator design and use by the Federal Aviation Administration, and the importance of human learning processes in the efficient use of flight simulators. A review of simulation and its value in training prepared by the National Academy of Sciences Committee on Human Factors Working Group on Simulation may be consulted for additional information (Jones, Hennessy, & Deutsch, 1985).

Evolution of Flight Simulators

Early Pilot Training.   In the "good old days," pilots learned to fly in airplanes, not in simulators as is often the case today. Not a lot was known then about how skills are learned, and pilot training was largely a process of self-instruction—and survival. In the French Foreign Legion during World War I, for example, pilot training consisted primarily of lectures on the ground and solo practice in single-seat airplanes. An instructor did not fly with a student until the student had mastered basic airplane maneuvers and had completed a solo cross-country flight. Each trainee was responsible for finding the cues necessary for aircraft control and working out and practicing responses to those cues that would result in surviving each flight. Trainees could figure out the consequences of their responses, but without an instructor on board, little guidance was available to keep them from making mistakes while they learned. Under such trial-and-error learning conditions, many airplanes were damaged and frequently trainees were killed. (An illuminating firsthand account of flight training in the French Foreign Legion Aviation Section in 1917 was provided by Major Charles J. Biddle, 1968, in letters written to family and friends during his own flight training.)

Not all pilot training was conducted solo. The Wright brothers gave dual instruction to would-be pilots, but the brothers did little more than function as safety pilots while their trainees learned to fly through trial and error, much the same as was done in the Foreign Legion. Resources that could make flight training more efficient were beginning to emerge. The Foreign Legionnaires discovered that a plane with little or no fabric on its wings made a pretty good ground trainer. In it, pilots could learn about aircraft handling while taxiing, without becoming airborne. Other more imaginative people were attempting to advance the technology of flight training by building training devices that would simulate flying.

We sometimes think that simulators were invented by pilots. That is not true. The need to provide training, even when operational equipment could not be used for that purpose, has been around for a long time in many areas of activity. For example, the U. S. Army resorted to simulation when horses were not available to train cavalry troops. Those horse "simulators" were made of wood and barrels on which troopers could "ride." Figure 8.1, a sketch of one of these horse simulators, is based upon an old photograph. Similarly, early flight-training devices were developed in part because dual-control training aircraft were not available, and solo flight training was inefficient and presented unacceptable risks to trainees and equipment.

Realism in Simulator Design.   One might debate whether the Army's wooden horses were horse simulators or generic trainers, that is, whether they simulated a horse or a more general class of animals that included mules and donkeys. The evidence suggests that the Army was attempting to make them look as much like a horse as available resources would permit because it was thought that a high degree of realism was necessary in training.

The concept that realistic appearance is necessary to assure that training received in a simulator will transfer to operational equipment underlies the design and use of training simulators even today. The concept is based upon a theory developed by an early American psychologist, Edward L. Thorndike (1931). His *common elements*

Figure 8.1.   A horse simulator sketched from an old photograph.

theory suggests that transfer will occur to the extent that a simulator and the equipment simulated share common elements. A later theorist, Charles E. Osgood (1949), developed the concept *transfer surface,* based upon an extension of the common elements theory. Using Osgood's transfer surface, one could map an assumed relationship between elements or features of a simulator and the equipment simulated. Where there is one-to-one correspondence, according to Osgood, transfer of training will be positive and high. Less than one-to-one correspondence will yield decreasing transfer to the point that none will occur when the correspondence is zero. From these theories, it was an easy step to assume that physical correspondence between a simulator and the aircraft or equipment simulated was the key to transfer of training. For this reason, the evolution of flight simulation became primarily a matter of technological advancement to make simulators more realistic, accurate, and comprehensive representations of a particular system. Some people refer to realistic flight simulators as being "high fidelity."

Early Flight Simulators.   In 1929, Edwin A. Link introduced the forerunner of modern flight-training simulators (Figure 8.2). The influence of the then-current theories concerning realism and training effectiveness are evident in its design. Although the Link trainer was used primarily to teach instrument flight, the device was made to

Figure 8.2.   Early link trainer. Photo provided by the Singer Company, Link Flight Simulation Division.

look like an airplane, complete with wings and tail. Even when Link later added a hood to his design, to make a more realistic instrument flight simulator, the wings and tail were retained. This basic design, complete with wings and tail, was used widely in military flight-training programs during World War II. The airplane-like appearance of the Link trainer had practical advantages. Professor Ralph E. Flexman (1983, personal communication) of the University of Illinois has commented:

> I remember in my early "Link training," a single instructor would watch up to four trainees simply by noticing what they were doing via the motion system—like stalling, spinning, turning, rough movements, etc. The wings and tail gave an interpretable perspective for him, and the student knew it, so he tried harder, knowing he couldn't cheat.

Instructors can still monitor students' simulator performance—even though modern simulators do not have wings and tails—in up to four devices at a time in the case of the Army's multiple-cockpit UH-1 helicopter simulator (the synthetic flight-training system, SFTS, designed by the Human Resources Research Organization in 1965; Caro, Isley, & Jolley, 1975). Special instructor station displays are now used for such monitoring.

Following World War II, our understanding of human learning processes had evolved to the point that the need for the realism that characterized early flight-training equipment was questioned. The relevance of some simulator features to the training objectives, such as external structures of the airplane, was not obvious, so such features were omitted; however, realism inside the cockpit or in the simulated flight characteristics was not questioned. The only limitations in those areas were imposed by the state of the simulation engineering art and the cost of reaching the limits. Even then, it was not possible to simulate a particular aircraft with high realism. The Link trainer of the early postwar era was a training device that simulated the instrument environment. It responded to pilot manipulation of flight controls with many of the characteristics of airplanes, and it permitted realistic practice of instrument navigation tasks, but it did not simulate a specific aircraft. It should be considered, therefore, an instrument flight simulator rather than an aircraft simulator.

Modern Aircraft Simulators. In the 1950s, simulators became increasingly important due to the rapidly increasing complexity of aircraft and corresponding increases in the complexity and cost of pilot training. It was reasoned that more realistic simulators would produce increased transfer. Attempts were made to develop devices whose features corresponded precisely to features of specific aircraft. In this way, the modern aircraft simulator was born, at least conceptually. Because of engineering limitations at the time, these simulators were more realistic in cockpit appearance and switch functions than in flight characteristics. Nevertheless, they were quite useful for the practice of emergency procedures that could not be practiced safely in flight. The Air Force began to rehearse strategic combat missions in these early simulators, and other applications of simulator training began to emerge. Extra-cockpit visual displays appeared during the same period, so training conducted in the new simulators was not limited necessarily to flight under simulated instrument conditions. Motion simulation also was included in these simulators, but motion was not new, having been included in the design of some of the earliest flight-training devices (see Figure 8.2). Many advances in the simulation engineering state of the art applicable to training simulation also were made during this period by aircraft developers who were beginning to use simulation to solve aircraft design problems.

As the increased potential training value of simulators was recognized, evidence for transfer of simulator training to operational equipment became the critical issue in their use. Pilot training became increasingly influenced by Thorndike's common elements theory, which provided an objective basis for designing transfer into simulators. Aircraft-specific simulators began to replace generic training devices in an increasing number of training programs. Generic flight trainers continued to be used, however, because realistic aircraft simulators were more costly. Their use was limited to training generic tasks such as instrument flight procedures and general aircraft control, but they continued to play an important role in pilot training. For example, one generic trainer for twin-engine light airplanes, the GAT-II (built by the Link Flight Simulation Division of the Singer Company), was demonstrated to provide effective training in instrument flight and aircraft control. Even though it had no visual display, the general aircraft control training received in that particular device was shown to reduce by about half the time required for subsequent transition training involving visual flight maneuvers and landings (Caro, Isley, & Jolley, 1973).

With the introduction in the mid-1960s of digital computers, more faithful simulation of flight dynamics and aircraft system performance became possible. Reliance on Thorndike's common elements theory to assure the effectiveness of simulator training increased with the availability of technology required to produce more realistic simulators. Many pilots believed that, if a simulator did not look, feel, smell, and bounce around like the aircraft simulated, its transfer-of-training value had to be low. Consequently, realism became an increasingly important factor in simulator design, and training programs that incorporated realistic aircraft simulators generally were judged to be superior to those that did not. In fact, by the late 1970s, training in realistic simulators with elaborate and realistic visual, motion, and sound systems began to be accepted as a partial substitute for training in aircraft. The U. S. military services increased their use of flight simulators substantially, and the Federal Aviation Administration (FAA) placed heavy emphasis on the value of realistic simulators in its regulation of commercial aviation.

The FAA and Simulator Training

Acceptance of Training in Simulators.   The FAA is charged by law to prescribe standards for the certification of civil aviation pilots. In meeting this responsibility, the FAA places high value on simulators for the training and checking of pilots. The increased use of simulators for training, particularly outside the U. S. Department of Defense, is in large part a result of the value the FAA places upon simulators. The FAA historically has placed an almost uncritical reliance on realism as a criterion for adequate simulator capabilities.

The fact that simulators can provide more in-depth, efficient, safer, and less expensive training and checking than is possible in airplanes has been acknowledged by the FAA for many years. As early as 1954, Federal Aviation Regulations (FARs) allowed air carrier pilots to use simulators for all but four of the tasks required for recurring proficiency checks. Checks in the aircraft were required for tasks where visual cues outside the cockpit were judged critical to performance (e.g., circling approach). In 1973, the FARs were amended to permit extensive use of simulators for initial certification checks of airline transport pilots. By 1978, improvements in visual systems and aerodynamic simulation techniques permitted selective approval of certain simulators with visual systems for landing tasks; the FARs were amended in 1980 to allow the use of these simulators for recency-of-experience qualification in landings.

The air carrier industry advocated developing rules to permit total simulation, that is, to permit experienced pilots to complete all of their initial training and checking for particular aircraft in high-realism simulators. This was due, in part, to the training benefits available through high-realism simulation and, in part, to the cost benefits of training in simulators instead of aircraft—benefits that were magnified by rapidly escalating fuel prices during the 1970s. Consequently, in 1980, the FAA published an Advanced Simulation Plan that defined specifications for simulators to be used for total training and checking, and thus made the concept of total simulation an operational reality. The plan, described in FAR Part 121, Appendix H, incorporates three major sets of criteria for simulators that may be used for different levels of training. The criteria correspond to phases in an overall plan for upgrading simulators to meet the most sophisticated training requirements. The phases are designated I, II, and III. Each phase describes a level of simulator realism that is progressively more demanding. Total training and checking are permitted by the FAA only with Phase II and III simulators, the difference being that Phase III simulators may be used by pilots with less experience than those who use Phase II simulators. A Phase II simulator is shown in Figure 8.3. Note that it bears little external resemblance to the aircraft being simulated.

Figure 8.3.   A Phase II flight simulator.

Realism and Training Credit. The specifications embodied in the Advanced Simulation Plan were developed without the benefit of a front-end analysis of training and other behavioral support requirements. Such an analysis was deferred so that the air carrier industry could reap the benefits of total simulation as soon as possible. In the absence of front-end analysis data, the most convenient simulator design criterion was realism. In 1984, the FAA undertook the delayed front-end analysis (Gilliom et al., 1985). Although the results generally supported the need for high levels of realism in simulators to be used for certification checking, it also found that Phase II and III simulation requirements that related to realism in the visual field of view and dimensions of motion could be relaxed.

Long before publication of Part 121, Appendix H, the FAA had recognized and set standards for two additional types of simulators, termed *visual* and *nonvisual*. These devices had lesser realism requirements than were specified in Part 121, Appendix H, although they were required to represent a specific airplane type and to have a motion system. Nonvisual simulators provide the least realism and are given the least training and checking credit. Phase III simulators provide the most realism and are given the most training and checking credit. Thus, over the past 30 years, the FAA has promoted the use of flight simulators by providing regulatory guarantees that if a simulator meets specified standards for realism, then that simulator may be used to satisfy certain regulatory requirements for pilot training and checking. Table 8.1 presents a synopsis of the principal simulator realism requirements specified by the FAA.

Devices without motion systems are classified by the FAA as training devices rather than simulators and are given relatively little training and checking credit. In 1987, however, the FAA issued Advisory Circular No. 120–45 defining Advanced Training Devices (Airplane Only). Advanced Training Devices are simulators which meet specific realism standards but have no motion or visual display systems. Training for specified procedures and maneuvers may be accomplished in Advanced Training Devices, but pilot performance on most of the maneuvers must be checked in a simulator approved for checking these maneuvers or in the aircraft. (For a review of simulator motion in flight training see Caro, 1979.)

The underlying rationale for the FAA's reliance on realism in simulation is simple and understandable. When the FAA issues a pilot certificate, the issuing inspector, in effect, is stating that he or she has witnessed the applicant's performance across a broad spectrum of piloting tasks and that the applicant is competent to perform the

Table 8.1.   Federal Aviation Administration Simulator Fidelity Requirements[a]

Type of simulator	Visual system[b]	Motion system[c]	Aerodynamic programming	Aural
Nonvisual	N/A	3 DOF	Representative data[d]	None
Visual	45° FOV Night 300 ms dynamic response	3 DOF	Representative data[d]	None
Phase I	All visual simulator requirements	3 DOF	Specific flight test data to include ground effect, ground handling, ground reaction	None
Phase II	75° FOV Dusk/night Ground and air hazards	6 DOF Buffets and bumps on the ground and in the air	All Phase I requirements Brake and tire failure dynamics, crosswind/shear, effects of runway contaminants	Precipitation and airplane noises Crash
Phase III	All Phase II requirements Day/dusk/night Wet/snow-covered runways Color	All Phase II requirements	All Phase II requirements Flight test data for buffet motions Modeling for icing, reverse thrust, aeroelastics, nonlinear sideslip	All Phase II requirements Communication static Engines Airframes

[a]The following features are required for nonvisual, visual, Phase I, Phase II, and Phase III simulators: (a) full-scale cockpit mock-up; (b) functionally accurate circuit breakers; (c) aerodynamic programming for thrust and drag effects; (d) automatic instrument response to control inputs; (e) functionally accurate communications and navigation equipment; (f) operational major aircraft systems; (g) accurate rates of change for instrument readings and control forces; and (h) accurate control forces and degree of control travel.
[b]FOV, horizontal field of view.
[c]DOF, degrees of freedom.
[d]Data derived from engineering predictions for the airplane's performance.

duties authorized by the certificate. When the performance is witnessed in a simulator, the FAA inspector still must be able to make this statement before a certificate is issued. Consequently, when a simulator is used for pilot performance evaluations, the piloting skills witnessed must be either identical to the skills the applicant would evince with the actual equipment or approximations that the inspector judges will transfer to the actual equipment without further practice or training. The FAA relies upon simulator realism as a major factor in assuring the accuracy of such judgments.

Learning Processes and Simulator Training

Is the realism demanded by the FAA and other users of simulators necessary to effective training and performance checking? Realism is necessary if one relies upon it, as the FAA has tended to do, to assure the success of training or if the simulator is used as a surrogate airplane for training and performance evaluation; however, studies involving simulators of intentionally low realism (simulators the FAA would classify as training devices) have demonstrated that effective training can be conducted in them (Grimsley, 1969). In fact, for most procedural tasks, training in low-realism simulators has enabled pilots to perform as well in aircraft as pilots trained in high-realism simulators or even in aircraft (Prophet & Boyd, 1970). In these studies, the low-realism simulators had training value equal to that of very high-realism simulators.

Cues.   Based on these results, one might question the validity of the common elements theory of transfer. How can transfer take place in the absence of high realism? The key lies in the concept of *cues.* Pilots depend upon cues to assess the status and condition of their aircraft, to initiate actions, to guide their performance, and to signal when an action should be altered or ended. The concept of cues and the distinction between a cue and a stimulus are important aspects of simulation and flight-training technology. Stimuli are the bases for cues, but a stimulus is not a cue by itself. A stimulus is a physical object or event that can activate a sense organ. The illumination of an indicator light on an instrument panel is a stimulus sensed by the eye. Movement of a control wheel provides pressure sensed by nerves in a pilot's hand and arm. The training task is to learn the meaning of such stimuli and to derive pertinent information from them so that the proper response can be made.

As these meanings are learned, stimuli become cues. In other words, a cue is a stimulus that has acquired meaning. A panel caution light, for example, conveys information that is understood by the pilot. An important goal of pilot training is to learn the informational content—the cueing value—of task-relevant stimuli so that precise actions can be taken. This role of cues, as opposed to stimuli, has a major implication for simulator design and use. The cue information available in a particular simulator, rather than stimulus realism per se, should be the criterion for deciding what skills are to be taught in that simulator.

Discriminations.   Skilled pilot performance is dependent upon making appropriate responses to cues. The two most important training considerations concerning cueing are how one learns to interpret cues and how one develops and selects the correct responses to be made to those cues. Interpreting cues and selecting appropriate responses involve a process called discrimination. Discrimination is the recognition that a given stimulus or response has a meaning different from that of another stimulus or response. Although two panel lights may be physically identical and have the same stimulus effect upon the pilot's eyes, they may have quite different meanings; therefore, the pilot must discriminate between these lights and make a unique response to each.

Discriminations are not simple, easily learned processes. The more complex the skill, the larger the number of moment-to-moment discriminations that must be made. As task complexity increases, discriminations may depend upon very subtle differences in entire patterns of numerous stimuli. The discriminations that must be learned when practicing landings in a new aircraft or during cockpit resource management training could be numerous and complex. The principal difference between a novice and an expert pilot performing complex tasks is that the expert has learned to discriminate subtle stimulus differences that a novice cannot. He or she also can translate subtle meanings of such stimuli into equally subtle control movements or other responses.

Generalizations.   Another concept important to an understanding of training is generalization. Generalization refers to the use of previously learned skills in situations that are different from the situations in which the skills were learned. For example, engine run-up procedures learned in a low-realism cockpit mock-up can be generalized to (that is, performed in) a high-realism simulator or an actual airplane even though physical stimuli may vary among the three cockpits. Instruments may be of different sizes or configurations; visual displays may resemble geometric patterns more than real-world scenery or can use symbols to represent objects; and platform motion systems may be restricted to accelerations of brief duration and movements of small distances. But because the meanings of cues present in the mock-up are similar to the meanings of corresponding cues present in the aircraft, the procedures can be performed in either setting even though the settings differ considerably with respect to actual stimuli. In fact, all cues learned in simulators can be generalized to aircraft to the extent that the cues have the same meaning in both simulator and aircraft. And, further, training in the simulator can concentrate on cues and responses that will generalize to the aircraft and its mission. To the extent that appropriate cues and responses cannot be represented in a particular simulator due to technology or cost limitations, the skills associated with them must be learned in the classroom, in other devices, or in the aircraft itself.

Training in Low-Realism Simulators.   About the time aircraft simulators (as opposed to generic trainers) were being introduced, the U. S. Army developed a very high-realism procedures trainer, Device 2-C-9, for a new twin–turbine-powered aircraft and contracted for an assessment of its training value (Figure 8.4). Knowledge of human learning processes was used to construct a low-realism mock-up of the same aircraft (Figure 8.5), and its training effectiveness was assessed along with that of the more expensive Army device. The mock-up was made of plywood, dowel rods, and photographs at a cost of about $30. Physically, it was unlike the aircraft it simulated;

Figure 8.4.   Device 2-C-9, a cockpit procedures trainer simulating the OV-1 aircraft.

Figure 8.5. Low-cost OV-1 cockpit mock-up.

however, it contained stimuli that could serve as cues to the same procedural tasks that could be practiced in the Army's high-realism trainer. Further, responses to cues that were required in the aircraft could be practiced in the mock-up, either actually or symbolically. The training program used with the mock-up emphasized the discriminations that were to be learned and the meaning, or cue value, of the physical features of the mock-up. It also called the trainee's attention to the generalizations that would be required in order to perform correctly in the aircraft after training in the mock-up.

The trainees were Army pilots qualified to receive transition training for the new airplane. None had previous turbine-powered aircraft experience. Three equally experienced groups of pilots were used during the evaluation of the training effectiveness of the two devices. One group was trained entirely in the trainer developed by the Army, one group in the mock-up, and one in the aircraft itself. Each group received ground school instruction relevant to the tasks they were being trained to perform.

Following training in the trainer or the mock-up, each group was given a performance test in the aircraft, and its performance was compared with the group trained only in the aircraft. The results are summarized in Figure 8.6. The groups trained in the trainer and in the mock-up made about the same number of errors during each training trial. On their first attempt to perform the procedures in the aircraft, which occurred after five training trials in the respective device, their performance was about equal to the performance of the group who had received all five training trials in the aircraft. The transfer-of-training value of these two simulators was essentially equal in spite of their wide discrepancy in realism and cost. Further, training in either device was essentially as effective as training in the aircraft.

Both of the devices used in this study were simulators, not generic trainers. That is, they were designed to present precisely the cues

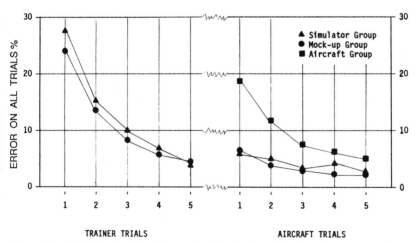

Figure 8.6.   Training data for pilots trained in Device 2-C-9 (simulator group), the low-cost trainer (mock-up group), and the aircraft. (From Prophet & Boyd, 1970).

Figure 8.7.   Low-cost U-21 cockpit procedures trainer.

(not necessarily the stimuli) and response opportunities appropriate to a specific aircraft. Generic trainers should not be expected to result in the very high levels of transfer shown here, because the discriminations appropriate to a specific aircraft cannot be learned easily in generic trainers. The value of a generic trainer is more or less proportional to the extent of its cue and response similarity to the aircraft in which posttraining performance is intended to generalize. The greater the dissimilarity, the more difficult it becomes to train the discriminations that will be required in the posttraining aircraft.

Another low-realism simulator is shown in Figure 8.7, although it is somewhat more realistic than the mock-up just discussed. (It cost about $4,300, including material and labor.)[1] This simulator is a procedures trainer for the Army U-21 (Beech King Air) turbine-powered airplane. None of the instruments or controls in this device is real.

---

[1]The costs cited in this chapter do not take inflation into account, so the devices pictured in Figures 8.5 and 8.7 would cost more to build today. The costs are cited only to indicate an order of magnitude of cost for low-realism simulators that can be used to provide effective training.

They are either photographs, molded plastic, or plywood painted to resemble airplane components. Unlike the mock-up in Figure 8.5, the panel and annunciator lights function on this device, a few in response to movement of specific controls, as they would in the aircraft. When it was found that the wiring requirements were too complicated for the carpenters who built this simulator, switches were provided so an instructor could turn lights on and off as appropriate to trainee control movements and system conditions. Except for these lights, the simulator had no dynamic features (Caro, Jolley, Isley, & Wright, 1972). But it was unlike any other airplane simulator in that the instruments had pointers that could be positioned manually. During engine start procedures, when the trainee advanced the condition lever to the high-idle position, he or she also reached over to the N_1 indicator and set the pointer to 70%. Because in actual aircraft the pointer rises automatically to 70% in response to movement of the condition lever to the high-idle position, the trainee's action in the simulator involved the unnecessary intermediate step of manually setting the pointer. During subsequent performance in the aircraft, the intermediate steps learned in the simulator rapidly disappeared because they were no longer useful. During the first trial in the aircraft, the trainee moved the condition lever to the high-idle position, reached over and touched the N_1 indicator, and verified that it read 70%. During the second trial, the trainee only pointed to the N_1 indicator. By the third trial, the overt intermediate steps had dropped out, and the trainee's performance was totally appropriate to the aircraft.

Mediation.   The intermediate steps performed in the U-21 simulator just described are known technically as *mediators;* that is, they come between, or mediate the link between, stimuli, cues, and responses. A mediator is not necessarily an overt act such as physically positioning a pointer. A mediator can be a word, phrase, or thought that helps a trainee connect a cue with a response or associate meaning with a particular stimulus. A verbal or other symbolic response can even substitute in training for an action that is overt in the aircraft.

Another U-21 simulator is shown in Figure 8.8. The device is 4 : 10 scale and is printed on a single sheet of paperboard, ready to be cut out and assembled as shown (Caro et al., 1972). Pilots with no prior turbine aircraft experience, using only the aircraft flight manual, have learned the procedures associated with ground operation of the U-21 aircraft using this simulator. In doing so, they made exten-

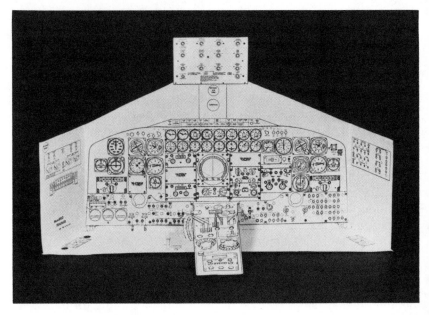

Figure 8.8.   U-21 cockpit procedures trainer made of paper.

sive use of verbal mediation to discriminate stimuli, to establish cue meanings, to practice operation of the aircraft's controls, and to anticipate generalizations that would occur during subsequent practice in the aircraft. Through mediation, demonstrable transfer of training can be obtained by mental rehearsal of discriminations to be learned, controls to be activated, and switches to be positioned. In a carefully structured and administered training program, such training can be as effective and efficient as actually performing the procedures involved.

Although computer-based training (CBT) is beyond the scope of the present discussion, it is worth noting the central role that the concept of mediation plays in CBT. Through mediation, the trainee can substitute touching a computer-based representation of, for example, a toggle switch for the actual act of moving the switch in the aircraft. In this way, the trainee can learn quite readily to operate rather complex systems by having them simulated on the computer display screen. Several computer-based aircrew training programs developed by Seville Training Systems make extensive use of the computer terminal as a low-cost simulator of aircraft systems and, through mediation, provide training in the operation of those systems. An example of CBT simulation of an aircraft fuel system, taken from a CBT lesson, is shown in Figure 8.9.

Although low-cost simulators can be effective in training, higher-cost devices also are needed in a total training program. Low-cost devices can be used to train selected tasks that can be represented realistically at low cost, but many tasks involved in flight training cannot be trained in simulators that represent so few cues and responses. Complex tasks that are more dependent upon variable rather than fixed procedures and upon crew coordination, timing, and situational considerations cannot be practiced efficiently in such simple devices. Most aircrew training programs recognize this fact and incorporate mission simulators that simulate all—or nearly all—of the features of an aircraft and its environment, as well as devices such as cockpit procedures trainers that simulate only a subset of those features. Regardless of the complexity of the tasks to be trained or the realism and completeness of the simulation of those tasks, the learning processes involved in efficient simulator training are the same. The manner in which the simulator is used in training must

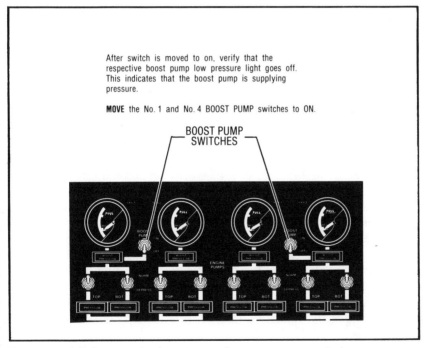

Figure 8.9.   A fuel system simulator presented on a computer terminal.

attend explicitly to cues, discriminations, generalizations, and mediators if the intended aircrew skills are to be developed. (For further information about the importance of learning processes in aircrew training, see Caro, Shelnutt, & Spears, 1981; and Spears, 1983.)

Development and Delivery of Flight Instruction

The efficiency of flight training is determined largely by the simulator and other resources available and by the extent to which the learning processes reviewed above are employed in their use. The effectiveness of flight training is determined largely by the content and organization of the training program, the skill of its delivery to trainees, and the extent to which its quality is controlled and maintained. The training must enable every aircrew member to acquire knowledge about the aircraft and its many complex systems that is required to respond appropriately to unexpected equipment failures, environmental factors, traffic conditions, or events involving other crew members or passengers.

Training Program Development

Need for Precision in Training.   The Kemeny Commission report on the accident at Three Mile Island was critical of the operators of that nuclear power plant and noted that, among other deficiencies, the content of training provided to control-room operators was imprecise and was not based upon detailed and systematic analysis of the operators' tasks (Kemeny, 1979). Available training-program development technology had not been employed, the commission noted. The same criticism could be made of a large portion of the flight training conducted throughout the world. Its content often is based upon tradition and upon instructors' judgments and unique experiences rather than upon detailed, systematic analyses of piloting tasks. Documented audit trails between flight-training program content and training requirements seldom exist, typically because the training requirements have been vaguely defined, and the training, therefore, cannot address the requirements with any precision. Such programs characteristically rely on lectures delivered by flight instructors who are free to select the course content they judge to be appropriate to the vaguely defined requirements. The expertise of these instructors often is limited to the subject matter being taught. They usually lack a working knowledge of instructional and learning processes and efficient methods of use of aircraft simulators and other available training resources.

Operators of imprecisely defined aircrew training programs cannot demonstrate the relevance and adequacy of their course content with respect to known training requirements and, therefore, might be judged culpable in the event of errors committed by aircrews they trained. These operators would be hard pressed to build a legal defense against a charge that their training is inappropriate, should they be required to do so. Because procedures do exist whereby the necessary precision in defining training-program content can be obtained, as the Kemeny Commission noted, it would be difficult to defend the adequacy of a training program that is not derived through those procedures.

These operators also face a technical problem. Imprecisely defined training programs cannot be packaged for efficient delivery, cannot be made available economically to small groups or individual pilots when needed, and cannot be controlled easily or standardized from one administration to another. The advantages obtained by controlling training through computer-managed and computer-based training, advantages that are increasingly affordable because of recent developments in computer and videodisc technologies, cannot be realized readily, if at all, in imprecisely defined training programs. Further, without clear definition of training requirements and objectives, the adequacy of pilot knowledge and performance at the end of training cannot be measured precisely. Regardless of the extensive experience and good intentions of the instructors and check-pilots involved, evaluations of pilot knowledge and performance will be more a function of the individuals conducting the assessments rather than of the performance of the pilots assessed. This outcome has been demonstrated in training programs where the validity and reliability of nonobjective flight grading systems have been studied (Caro, 1968).

Procedures for Instructional Systems Development. Many flight-training organizations, including several major airlines, have adopted systematic procedures for developing training programs in order to define training content precisely and to organize and control the subsequent delivery of training. These procedures help assure that the scope and content of the training pilots receive is sufficient to their needs. Because every hour of training costs money, these procedures also help control training costs by eliminating unneeded content and by packaging required content for convenient and cost-effective delivery. The procedures are varied and have been given a variety of names—Instructional Systems Development (ISD), Systems Approach to Training (SAT), Specific Behavioral Objectives (SBO), to name a few. These procedures involve detailed and systematic analysis of the tasks for which training is to be provided and equally detailed and systematic definition of the knowledge and skills necessary to the performance of those tasks. Following these procedures, it is possible to define training requirements, select training resources, prepare instructional lessons, train instructors, and produce pilots with the skills required to perform the jobs given them. Without such procedures, the risk of omitting critical content or including incorrect or unnecessary material in training programs is much greater.

A number of models of these procedures have been developed for instructional developers to follow when analyzing training requirements and designing and developing training programs. Several of the models have been applied in flight training. One of the most complete is being used currently by Seville Training Systems to develop aircrew training programs for the U. S. Air Force. The Seville Instructional Systems Development Model is presented in Figure 8.10. An examination of the figure indicates the complexity of the effort involved in designing and developing a training program of the magnitude required to train the aircrews of modern aircraft.

How good are these procedures for defining and developing training programs? They are very good, but only when employed by people trained to use them. When skillfully used, they can produce lean and efficient training, with content that is both necessary and sufficient for the aircrew performance requirements. When used by people whose only expertise is in the subject matter to be trained, however, these procedures are of little help and, in fact, are typically misused. United Airlines, whose procedures are similar to those outlined in Figure 8.10, has made very good use of detailed and systematic procedures for aircrew training program development, and the training programs they have produced over the past two decades are widely recognized as excellent. Their training is lean—there is no "fat" or "nice-to-know" information. In fact, they are so lean that questions were raised concerning whether they contained enough information and practice. In 1980, an independent consulting organization undertook a study for United to examine the adequacy of their pilot training programs. About 6,000 United pilots were surveyed, and detailed interviews were conducted with about 200 of them. Not a single instance was found in which a United pilot had been unable to perform adequately due to an omission of technical information

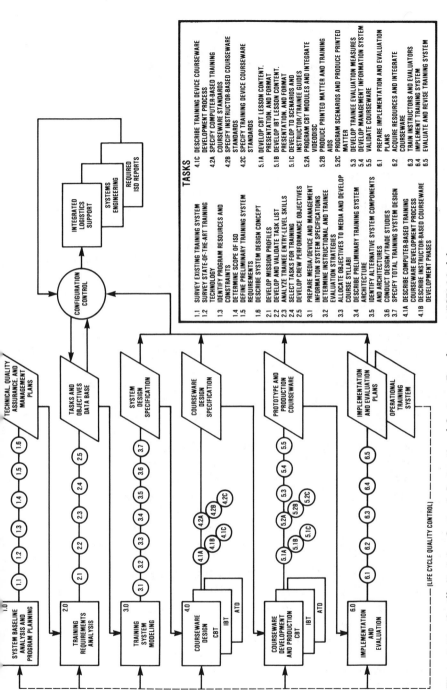

TASKS

1.1	SURVEY EXISTING TRAINING SYSTEM
1.2	SURVEY STATE-OF-THE-ART TRAINING TECHNOLOGY
1.3	IDENTIFY PROGRAM RESOURCES AND CONSTRAINTS
1.4	DETERMINE SCOPE OF ISD
1.5	DEFINE PRELIMINARY TRAINING SYSTEM REQUIREMENTS
1.6	DESCRIBE SYSTEM DESIGN CONCEPT
2.1	DEVELOP MISSION PROFILES
2.2	DEVELOP AND VALIDATE TASK LIST
2.3	ANALYZE TRAINEE ENTRY-LEVEL SKILLS
2.4	SELECT TASKS FOR TRAINING
2.5	DEVELOP CREW PERFORMANCE OBJECTIVES
3.1	PREPARE MEDIA/DEVICE AND MANAGEMENT INFORMATION SYSTEM SPECIFICATIONS
3.2	DETERMINE INSTRUCTIONAL AND TRAINEE EVALUATION STRATEGIES
3.3	ALLOCATE OBJECTIVES TO MEDIA AND DEVELOP COURSE SYLLABI
3.4	DESCRIBE PRELIMINARY TRAINING SYSTEM ARCHITECTURE
3.5	IDENTIFY ALTERNATIVE SYSTEM COMPONENTS AND ARCHITECTURES
3.6	CONDUCT DESIGN/TRADE STUDIES
3.7	SPECIFY TOTAL TRAINING SYSTEM DESIGN
4.1A	DESCRIBE COMPUTER-BASED TRAINING COURSEWARE DEVELOPMENT PROCESS
4.1B	DESCRIBE INSTRUCTOR-BASED COURSEWARE DEVELOPMENT PHASES
4.1C	DESCRIBE TRAINING DEVICE COURSEWARE DEVELOPMENT PROCESS
4.2A	SPECIFY COMPUTER-BASED TRAINING COURSEWARE STANDARDS
4.2B	SPECIFY INSTRUCTOR-BASED COURSEWARE STANDARDS
4.2C	SPECIFY TRAINING DEVICE COURSEWARE STANDARDS
5.1A	DEVELOP CBT LESSON CONTENT, PRESENTATION, AND FORMAT
5.1B	DEVELOP IBT LESSON CONTENT, PRESENTATION, AND FORMAT
5.1C	DEVELOP TO SCENARIOS AND INSTRUCTOR/TRAINEE GUIDES
5.2A	PROGRAM CBT MODULES AND INTEGRATE VIDEODISC
5.2B	PRODUCE PRINTED MATTER AND TRAINING AIDS
5.2C	PROGRAM SCENARIOS AND PRODUCE PRINTED MATTER
5.3	DEVELOP TRAINEE EVALUATION MEASURES
5.4	DEVELOP MANAGEMENT INFORMATION SYSTEM
5.5	VALIDATE COURSEWARE
6.1	PREPARE IMPLEMENTATION AND EVALUATION PLANS
6.2	ACQUIRE RESOURCES AND INTEGRATE COURSEWARE
6.3	TRAIN INSTRUCTORS AND EVALUATORS
6.4	IMPLEMENT TRAINING SYSTEM
6.5	EVALUATE AND REVISE TRAINING SYSTEM

Figure 8.10. Seville Training System's Instructional Systems Development (ISD) Model.

during training. Clearly, United's program development procedures were working well. United is not unique, however. Many other examples could be given of the success of systematic program development procedures in pilot and other training.

The Instructor

The instructor is an important element in effective flight training, but an element that is not always managed well. Instructor selection is sometimes based upon seniority, personality, or position within an organization rather than instructional skills. Often, instructors receive no training related to instructional processes and techniques or effective resource utilization. They typically are burdened with other tasks that interfere with instructional duties. In part, mismanagement of this important element of the total flight-training process is due to a lack of knowledge about instructor qualifications and effective instructional techniques.

Instructor Selection.   The more effective instructors are selected from among volunteers who seek the assignment. The selection of instructors can best be made by experienced instructors on the basis of personal knowledge of the selectee's qualifications as an aircrew member and judgments as to his or her maturity, emotional stability, and ability to maintain favorable working relationships with peers and students. Such knowledge can be gained in part through prior observation of the selectee's performance during periodic requalification training or flight performance checks. The more effective instructors typically are aircrew members who have served in operational positions and are judged by themselves as well as their peers to have performed well above average in those assignments.

No empirical evidence exists indicating that flight-rated personnel are required for simulator and classroom training; however, in an analysis of differences between flight-training programs judged relatively effective or ineffective (Caro et al., 1981), the programs judged more effective employed flight-rated personnel in the dual role of flight and ground school instructors. In the more effective programs, the same instructors were scheduled to conduct both flight and simulator instruction for a given student. Programs in which the roles of simulator–classroom instructor and aircraft instructor were assigned to separate individuals were judged less effective, as were those in which nonrated personnel were permitted to conduct ground school instruction. Programs using flight-rated personnel, particularly to instruct in simulators, may be more effective because rated instructors are better able to provide mediational instruction which compensates for any lack of physical realism in the devices. The experiences of flight-rated instructors enable them to provide supplemental information about flying and airborne system operation, thus creating training situations that have greater realism and functional similarity to operational tasks, and to provide mediational instruction that helps integrate classroom, simulator, and aircraft training. Rated instructors also improve the credibility of training and promote its acceptance. For example, inclusion of only "need-to-know" information in training, such information having been identified through application of detailed and systematic instructional systems development procedures, may appear too restrictive to some trainees. If so, rated instructors can give credibility to the training. Additionally, use of rated instructors in simulators may be viewed as a manifestation of management recognition of the importance of the training.

These implied criteria for instructor selection have not been validated, and no formal studies are known to have established a relationship between instructor abilities, experience, or personality and flight instructional effectiveness. These criteria, however, can serve to identify and eliminate marginal performers, those not wanting to instruct, and others who probably would do a poor job.

Instructor Training. The structure and content of flight instructor training programs vary widely. Training ranges from a check-ride in the aircraft and, if training in a simulator is involved, a checkout on the device's instructor console, to a comprehensive program including training in instructional technology, instruction on how and when to employ available resources, and the conduct of training under the supervision of a qualified instructor.

Following the introduction in 1973 of simulators into the flight training conducted at the U. S. Coast Guard Aviation Training Center, a comprehensive and formal flight instructor training program was instituted. That program can serve as a useful model for the development of other instructor training programs. The program consisted of four phases. During the first phase, the instructor trainees went through the instructional program they were to teach to assure that their performance of all aircrew tasks conformed to specified standards. During the second phase, the trainees observed the administration of the course to two students, noting particularly (1) operation of the simulator and other ground school resources, (2) employment of simulator instructional support features, (3) use of instructor job aids (e.g., lesson guides, grade slips), and (4) techniques of in-flight instruction. Concurrently, they were tutored by an instructional technologist concerning application of principles of instruction to the training they would conduct. During the next phase, the trainees conducted selected portions of the training they were preparing to teach, with a qualified instructor role-playing as a student and presenting common student problems. Following each training period, trainees' performances (and those of their "students") were critiqued to give them a better understanding of their actions and how to improve them. Finally, each trainee was assigned two incoming students to train under supervision. Thus, the final phase was supervised "practice teaching," during which the trainee continued to be critiqued as necessary by the supervising instructor.

In the Coast Guard instructor training program, progress in instructional skills development was necessary for the instructor trainee's advancement. The trainee's workload was managed so that the demands of collateral duties did not detract from his or her studies. Commensurate with the importance placed on instructor training by the Coast Guard, job evaluation reports of the newly qualified instructor reflected the evaluation of his or her performance in the instructor training course.

It is not just initial instructor training that influences the competency of flight instructors but also the adequacy of the continuation training they receive. To maintain their effectiveness, instructors require regularly scheduled continuation training designed to refresh, refine, update, and expand their instructional capabilities. Training specialists and program development personnel, as well as senior flight instructors, should be employed to provide this training on an individual or group basis. Included also should be supervised instructor workshops, seminars, and bull sessions designed to encourage instructor communication about personal experiences with various instructional techniques. Individualized remedial training should be provided to address deficiencies identified in an instructor's performance during routine evaluations of his or her instructional skills.

Quality Control of Training

An important adjunct to effective and efficient flight training is a quality control system. The system must include continuing examination of the training program developmental process, as well as the products of that process, by a person or staff organizationally independent of the process. The responsibilities of the quality control staff are to assure the quality of training programs under development, to assist the program development and administrative staff in achieving quality products, and to verify that finished products are responsive to the training requirements. Quality control encompasses two phases in the life of a training system: formative and summative.

Formative Quality Control.   The purpose of formative quality control is to ensure that the training program under development will meet the desired standards when the program is implemented in the training environment. This means that the training program should be at the outset technically current and correct, standardized in form and content, instructionally efficient and effective, and precisely tailored to training requirements. Assuring that the training program meets these criteria requires monitoring the quality of both developmental processes and products throughout the analysis, design, development, production, and validation activities.

During the analysis, design, and production activities, quality control focuses on four requirements:

1. *Standards.* Standards provide guidance to the instructional developer, criteria for review of the procedures and products throughout development, and criteria for evaluation of the training system as a whole. *Process* standards define how various steps of the process are to be performed. *Product* standards define the desired characteristics of interim as well as final products.

2. *Training.* Analysis, design, and production personnel must learn the standards and develop the skills and discipline required to produce quality products. They must be provided continual assistance and on-the-job training.

3. *Review.* Systematic reviews of the developing training system determine whether products resulting from the analysis, design, and production activities meet the defined standards. When found acceptable, the products proceed to the next stage. If unacceptable, the products must be recycled through the appropriate development or production processes and revised as necessary.

4. *Measurement.* The quality control staff must collect data regarding conformance and nonconformance to process and product standards. Information derived from these data must be used to improve processes and products.

A critical portion of formative quality control is the use of course material *tryouts.* Tryouts, which involve individuals and small groups of persons representative of the population for which the training is intended, are conducted after lessons have been reviewed for content, structure, and conformance to standards. They are used to identify faults that went undetected in the design and development process and to measure how well course materials satisfy lesson and course objectives. Tryouts go beyond issues of face validity (the question of whether or not course materials appear to be instructionally effective). Instead, they must establish content validity (the question of whether or not course materials actually impart the particular knowledge and skill which they intend to impart).

Summative Quality Control. Installation and implementation of the training system marks the beginning of the summative quality control process. Summative quality control involves an initial comprehensive analytic and empirical examination of the completed training program, as well as ongoing review of the training throughout the period of its use. The analytic evaluation seeks information of an administrative and pragmatic nature. Verification must be obtained that instructors are prepared adequately and trained to do their jobs, and that all system resources are in place and functioning properly. The empirical evaluation consists of the conduct of training for a group of students (i.e., the exercise of the training system in its entirety) and the measurement of student achievement against stated training objectives. The purpose is to determine that course graduates are trained adequately and can perform the operational job, and if not, to provide data that point to the areas within the training in need of revision.

Quality control does not end with the completion of the analytic and empirical examinations. A permanent set of procedures involving periodic analytic reexamination of the training system and empirical evaluation of student achievement must be implemented as an element of the training system to ensure that the system will remain technically current and responsive to the objectives. Further, the objectives of the training must be subjected to periodic review to assure they remain responsive to possibly changing training requirements. Ongoing quality control is a watchdog activity involving both analytic and empirical efforts, the results of which feed back into the developmental process, thus creating yet another cycle of analysis, design, development, test, and revision.

Current Trends in Flight Training

Flight training has continued to change since the early flights of the Wright brothers. Some of the changes were described earlier in this chapter. Presently, three significant changes are taking place in flight training, and a fourth can be expected in the not-too-distant future. They involve training and performance evaluation capabilities designed into operational aircraft, new approaches to cockpit crew coordination and resource management training, the use of computers and videodiscs to individualize the academic portions of flight training, and application of artificial intelligence to future academic, simulator, and possibly in-flight training.

Embedded Training and Testing

Embedded training and testing refers to hardware or software features of operational equipment (e.g., an aircraft and its various systems) provided specifically for purposes of operator training and assessment. Embedded training involves use of operational equipment in a training, that is, nonoperational, mode. Embedded testing may involve recording and scoring performance during training or operational use of the equipment.

Embedded training is a relatively new concept in flight training, but one that will find increasing applications as cockpit designs incorporate more programmable function controls and displays. Applications involve software that permits aircraft electronic systems to operate independently of ongoing events or to simulate events consistent with scenarios designed for training. Through programming, these systems can simulate operational events such as hostile electronic countermeasures or own-ship weapons effects. Embedded training features of an aircraft may be designed for use on the ground or during flight, although on-the-ground applications will rarely be economical or efficient. Examples of embedded training include:

1. *Mission rehearsal.* Tasks associated with suspected threats can be rehearsed in response to on-board sensors that are stimulated artificially when the aircraft "flies" within range of simulated hostile forces.

2. *Air-to-air combat.* Computer-generated imagery representing aerial targets can be displayed on a head-up display (HUD) or on the pilot's visor via a helmet-mounted display device. Such imagery can provide visual simulation of threat aircraft with the dynamics of a specific adversary weapons system, and the simulated aircraft image can interact with own-ship flight. Weapons traces and effects can be included in the computer-generated imagery.

3. *Air-to-ground weapons delivery.* This application is similar to the air-to-air application, except that images of ground targets can be

generated in electro-optical displays and superimposed upon the pilot's displays of the terrain. Alternatively, artificial stimulation of onboard sensors can simulate ground-target signatures.

Embedded testing is not a new concept in aviation, although its applications have been limited, typically because pilots tend to resist systems that permit their operational performance to be monitored, recorded, or scored. In-flight recorders of performance data found on all large commercial aircraft illustrate an embedded testing system. These flight recorders are used for pilot performance assessment only in instances of accident or incident investigations, although they could be used for a variety of other purposes. Gun cameras used to determine air combat kills also illustrate embedded testing systems.

Embedded testing in aircraft is limited only to the extent that performance of the aircraft and each of its systems can be recorded in flight and interpreted in relation to objective criteria when the recordings are replayed. Information recorded can include everything viewed by a pilot on a HUD or cockpit display or heard through his headset, including target and weapons information. Such recordings can be replayed later on aircraft displays or on ground-based display devices, permitting operational skills to be evaluated following an actual or simulated mission.

Cockpit Resource Management Training

Many mishaps involving crew-served aircraft have been attributed to aircrew performance failure. Perfectly sound aircraft have flown into the ground or have been allowed to fly unsafely by well-trained and experienced personnel. The L-1011 that flew into the ground near Miami (the cockpit crew was distracted by a failed indicator light) and the DC-8 that ran out of fuel over Portland (the cockpit crew was distracted by a presumed landing-gear malfunction) are illustrative. Factors in such accidents include aircrew preoccupation with minor mechanical problems, failure to delegate tasks and assign responsibilities, failure to set priorities, failure to communicate intent and plans, failure to utilize available data, and inadequate monitoring of other crew members' performance.

Training in aircraft operations alone has proved insufficient to preclude such mishaps. As a consequence, various airlines, with the encouragement and assistance of NASA, have developed training programs that address situational, sociopsychological, and other factors that influence aircrew performance. These programs have become known as "cockpit resource management" (CRM) training. It is probable that pilots of all crew-served aircraft will receive CRM training in the future. In fact, the U. S. Air Force's Military Airlift Command has mandated CRM training for all MAC aircrews, and the FAA is likely to require civil aircraft crews and FAA flight examiners to receive CRM training.

Individualization of Instruction

The nature of in-flight training and the size of most aircraft cockpits dictate that pilots be trained one at a time. It is only during advanced stages of training—where mission tasks are practiced—that crew training becomes feasible. The airlines' use of simulators for line-oriented flight training (LOFT) and the military counterpart, mission-oriented simulator training (MOST), are examples of crew training, but even here, crews are trained one at a time. By contrast, academic portions of flight training traditionally have been taught to groups, with the rate of student progress fixed by the instructor. Recent advances in microcomputers, interactive videodiscs, and programming techniques for computer-based and computer-managed instruction have made it both economical and convenient to individualize the academic portion of flight training. It is now feasible to provide interactive, individualized learning experiences via machines under student control. The instructional systems development processes described earlier in this chapter define instructional content in sufficient detail for it to be formatted for computer and videodisc presentation interactively with a student.

Although it is unlikely that academic instructors will have no role in future flight training, their traditional role as lecturers is diminishing. Instructors' future involvement will place more emphasis upon their utility as information resources, discussants, and role models, and lesson presentation will be under computer management or control. Although automation of instruction is expensive, the benefits of individualized training are substantial and can be highly cost effective. Not the least of these benefits is the control computer-based training permits over the content and sequence of training. The combination of tools currently available for training—systematic procedures for specification of the training to be delivered and microcomputers for control of the delivery process—virtually dictate that individualization of academic training will become common, particularly in higher-volume flight-training programs.

Artificial Intelligence

Artificial intelligence (AI) is a term currently used to describe computer programs that (1) apply rules rather than follow routines, (2) "learn" through experience, and (3) solve problems not anticipated by the programmers, knowledge engineers, and subject matter experts who developed them; thus they emulate the behavior of an expert. AI is expected to perform many functions of human experts in the design and operation of future manned and unmanned vehicles, air defense weapons, social and health care organizations, and other complex systems. AI has yet to have a significant impact on aircrew training, but its influence is forthcoming.

Two likely areas of AI impact are training program development and individualization of instructional delivery. The instructional systems development procedures illustrated in Figure 8.10 are expert intensive, particularly in the analysis, design, and development phases. AI offers the potential for enhanced training by replacing the expert instructional developer with an intelligent computer that will extract information describing system operations from appropriate data bases and formulate it into a flexible and interactive instructional system adaptable to students' unique backgrounds, learning styles, and limitations. Similarly, present computer-based instructional delivery systems permit sophisticated branching and remediation based on student response patterns, but they do not mimic the skills of an expert tutor by, for example, adapting simulations or task difficulty levels to trainee performance, identifying and correcting misconceptions, or choosing examples and analogies to explain complex issues. Nor do they address mediational processes or accommodate variances in student perceptions, as would an expert tutor. Future AI instructional development and delivery systems will do these things.

Acknowledgments

The section of this chapter titled "The FAA and Simulator Training," including Table 8.1, was adapted from Gilliom et al., 1985. The author gratefully acknowledges the assistance in the preparation of this chapter of Robert P. Fishburne, Jr., Wallace W. Prophet, and William D. Spears.

References

Biddle, C. J. (1968). *Fighting airman: The way of the eagle*. New York: Doubleday.

Caro, P. W. (1968). *Flight evaluation procedures and quality control of training* (Tech. Report 68-3). Washington, DC: The George Washington University, Human Resources Research Office.

Caro, P. W. (1979). The relationship between flight simulator motion and training requirements. *Human Factors, 21,* 493–501.

Caro, P. W., Isley, R. N., & Jolley, O. B. (1973). *Research on synthetic training: Device evaluation and training program development* (Tech. Report 73-20). Alexandria, VA: Human Resources Research Organization.

Caro, P. W., Isley, R. N., & Jolley, O. B. (1975). *Mission suitability testing of an aircraft simulator* (Tech. Report TR-75-12). Alexandria, VA: Human Resources Research Organization.

Caro, P. W., Jolley, O. B., Isley, R. N., & Wright, R. H. (1972). *Determining training device requirements in fixed-wing aviator training* (Tech. Report 72-11). Alexandria, VA: Human Resources Research Organization.

Caro, P. W., Shelnutt, J. B., & Spears, W. D. (1981). *Aircrew training devices: Utilization* (Tech. Report AFHRL TR-80-35). Brooks AFB, TX: Air Force Human Resources Laboratory.

Gilliom, D. C., Spears, W. D., DeMuth, H. J., Eddy, P. P., Hanley, D. E., Holmbeck, G. E., & Fishburne, R. P., Jr. (1985). *A systematic determination of skill and simulator requirements for Airline Transport Pilot Certification* (DOT/FAA/VS-84-1, DOT/TSC-FAA-85-1). Washington, DC: U. S. Department of Transportation, Federal Aviation Administration.

Grimsley, D. L. (1969). *Acquisition, retention, and retraining: Group studies on using low-fidelity training devices* (Tech. Report 69-4). Washington, DC: The George Washington University, Human Resources Research Office.

Jones, E. R., Hennessy, R. T., & Deutsch, S. (Eds.). (1985). *Human factors aspects of simulation.* Washington, DC: National Academy Press.

Kemeny, J. G. (1979). *The President's Commission on the accident at Three Mile Island. The need for change: The legacy of TMI.* Washington, DC: U. S. Government Printing Office.

Osgood, C. E. (1949). The similarity paradox in human learning: A resolution. *Psychological Review, 56,* 132–143.

Prophet, W. W., & Boyd, H. A. (1970). *Device-task fidelity and transfer of training: Aircraft cockpit procedures training* (Tech. Report 70-10). Alexandria, VA: Human Resources Research Organization.

Spears, W. D. (1983). *Processes of skill performance: A foundation for the design and use of training equipment* (Tech. Report NAVTRAEQUIPCEN 78-C-0113-4). Orlando, FL: Naval Training Equipment Center.

Thorndike, E. L. (1931). *Human learning.* New York: Century.

Human Error in Aviation Operations

9

David C. Nagel

[Airplanes] will be used in sport, but they are not to be thought of as commercial carriers.

Octave Chanute (1904)

Introduction

Despite this faulty prediction, a "human error" by one of the revered pioneers of aviation, worldwide scheduled airline passenger traffic grew in 1985 to more than 850 billion passenger miles (World Aviation Directory, 1986). Despite the extraordinary number of miles flown, commercial air travel is among the safest forms of transportation. Figure 9.1 shows the number of aircraft accidents known to have occurred during the 24-year period from 1959 to 1983. Worldwide, about two accidents occur (defined either by any aircraft hull loss or by one or more fatalities) for every one million departures. United States carriers do better than this by more than a factor of two. These average ranges equate to about 20 major accidents worldwide per year, of which about five occur to U. S. air carriers (Sears, 1986). Airline accidents are thus very rare events. Events with such low probabilities of occurrence can produce wide apparent variations in the accident rate from year to year. The year 1984, for example, was nearly accident free; in 1985, well more than the expected number of accidents occurred. Overall, accident rates for major carriers,

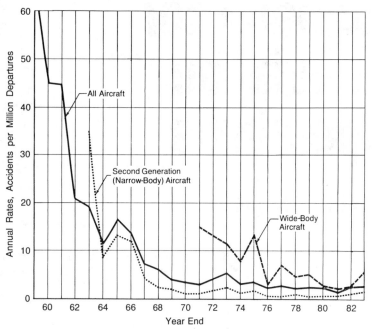

Figure 9.1.   Total scheduled air carrier accidents, worldwide, 1959–1983. (Excludes sabotage, military action and operations, turbulence and evacuation injury.) Second generation includes 727, 737, DC-9, BAC 111, Trident, F-28, and VC-10 aircraft. Wide-body includes 747, DC-10, L-1011, and A300 aircraft. (Boeing Commercial Airplane Company, 1985.)

particularly those in the United States, have shown a steady decline for many years, a decline that can no doubt be attributed to better equipment, better operating procedures, and better training practices. However, it is clear that the *rate* of improvement of safety has slowed significantly and substantially during the last decade.

Accident rates are substantially greater for other classes of aircraft operations. Figure 9.2 shows accident rates from 1977 to 1982 for three classes of operations: business aviation, corporate aviation, and scheduled air carriers (here normalized by the number of hours flown rather than the number of departures). The rates for other forms of air traffic (pleasure flying is the least safe of all statistically) are more than an order of magnitude worse than corporate aviation, and very nearly the rates, on an hourly basis, that one can expect driving an automobile.

Although the overall record for airlines is excellent, certain aspects of these data are unsettling. For instance, humans are implicated as

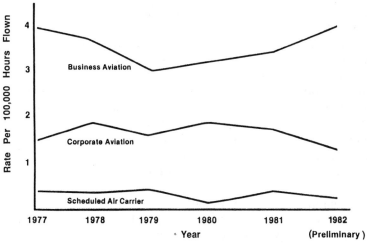

Figure 9.2. Annual accident rates for air carriers, corporate and business aviation, 1977–1982.

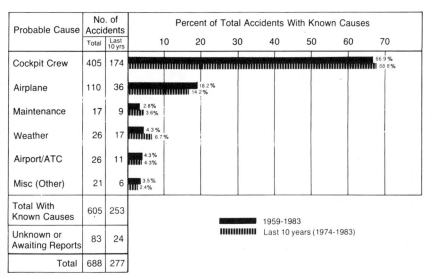

Figure 9.3. Causal factors for air carrier accidents, 1959–1983: worldwide jet fleet, all operations. (Excludes sabotage, military actions, turbulence and evacuation injury.) "Airplane" includes airframe, aircraft systems, and powerplant.

the "causal factors" in well more than one-half of all aircraft accidents. Figure 9.3 illustrates the data for air carrier operations, again for a 24-year period (Boeing, 1985). For air carriers, about two-thirds of all accidents are attributable to the cockpit crew. For general aviation, the rates are even more disproportionate; almost 9 out of 10 accidents are attributable to human causes. Although not illustrated by the data in the first several figures, human error has played a progressively more important role in accident causation as aircraft equipment has become more reliable. Figure 9.4 illustrates this trend. Billings and Reynard (1984) have aptly termed this problem the last great frontier in aviation safety. Can the problem of human error be solved?

The problem of human error in aviation has turned out to be a difficult one both to understand and to solve. Part of the reason for this is that the human is so complex that the understanding of behavior is not nearly as advanced as that of physical phenomena. Another is that accidents are often catastrophic; typically, little information is available from which to piece together a complete or comprehensive picture of causality. Nonetheless, we are beginning to learn a great deal about the causes of human error. What we know suggests that

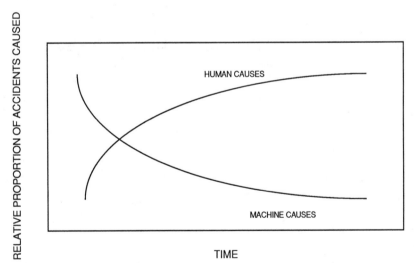

Figure 9.4.   Trends in the causality of accidents. As aircraft and systems have become more reliable over time, the relative proportion of accidents attributed to human error has systematically increased. (International Civil Aviation, Organization, 1984.)

errors are neither random nor mysterious. They seem to be lawful in the sense that they are predictable and that most humans (even experts) tend to make errors that follow certain patterns under a variety of circumstances. Substantial progress has been made over the past few years of understanding the nature and root causes of human error. The hope is that through this understanding can come control. Thus, as safe as flying has become, we have reason to believe that levels of safety may be increased, perhaps dramatically, over what they are today.

Methods of Studying Error

What methods are available to study errors, to learn about their causes, and to explore methods of reducing or eliminating the incidence or severity of human error in a complex, operational system like the air transportation system? Generally, there are four approaches. First, and most straightforward, is direct observation. Skilled observers place themselves in the operating environment and simply watch and record what pilots and crewmembers do as they go about their flying tasks. For these methods to be effective, the observer must be an expert in the intricacies of the piloting task as well as have a well-tuned appreciation for the kinds of errors that may occur. Curry (1985) and Wiener (1985), both pilots as well as trained human factors professionals, have successfully used direct observational methods to study the ways in which airline crews use, or in some cases misuse, automated cockpit systems. These methods can yield a wealth of information concerning the type, frequency, and cause of errors in airline operations. There are, on the other hand, fundamental problems with observation in the natural setting. For one, the observer may make errors (of observation) themselves. It is also possible that the presence of the observer may alter the behavior of the observed. Finally, the observer cannot control all the variables that might be of interest; the power of the naturalistic approach is also its fundamental scientific weakness. Despite these practical and theoretical problems, direct observation continues to be one of the best ways to develop a systematic understanding of errors made in natural settings.

A second approach, accident data and postaccident analysis, can also provide useful data, although as has been noted, too often the information record is incomplete. Notwithstanding these difficulties, the science and technology of accident investigation is advanced; in the United States, the National Transportation Safety Board (NTSB) has the overall responsibility to review the facts that surround major civil aviation (and other transportation system) accidents and to issue a formal finding of causality. Again, humans are often implicated as providing the primary or other causal factors; what is typically missing from such analyses is any indication as to why the errors were made in the first place. Indeed, the data often appear inexplicable. More will be made of this later in the chapter.

Other methods' and systems that have been developed to collect information from the operational setting rely on a third approach, the self-report. Aviation incident reporting systems are in operation in the United States, the United Kingdom, Australia, and other countries. In the United States, the primary locus of reporting is the Aviation Safety Reporting System (ASRS), developed and operated by NASA for the Federal Aviation Administration (Reynard, Billings, Cheaney, & Hardy, 1986). The ASRS has been in operation for more than a decade; 60,000 reports made by pilots, controllers, and others have been collected, analyzed, and archived. A large number of these are available for study by research professionals, members of the operating industry, and regulatory or other investigatory bodies such as the NTSB. Figure 9.5 illustrates the main operational characteristics of the ASRS. The system is closely monitored by an advisory group

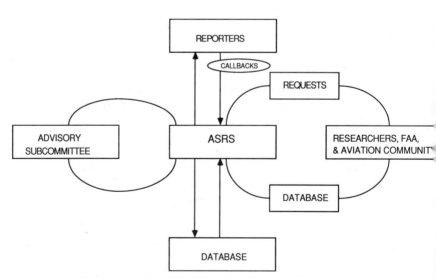

Figure 9.5.   The U.S. Aviation Safety Reporting System (ASRS) process. Advisory subcommittee includes government, industry, and labor.

that represents most of the major organizations involved in aviation operations in the United States. Important aspects of the system are confidentiality and immunity from prosecution for the reporter in cases other than those involving some criminal act; thus, there is an incentive to report. These are important features of any system designed to collect and analyze operational data. Similar systems that do not have these features often fail to access those most likely to provide useful information concerning the "how" and "why" of human error, the incident reporters themselves. Data from the ASRS have proven to be a practical and indispensible source of information for the operational community and the scientist alike. In the case of the ASRS, hundreds of "alert bulletins" have been issued to appropriate agencies and organizations, bulletins which have resulted in a variety of actions that have themselves had measurable effects on aviation safety in the United States. In some cases, modifications to the Federal Aviation Regulations (FARs) have resulted from ASRS data and analyses. The ASRS data base has also been used to conduct in-depth studies of particular interest, such as the effects that the introduction of highly automated aircraft is currently having on the nature and character of aviation operations. What relationship do these incident reports bear to accidents?

Billings (1981) has argued that at least several categories of aircraft accidents involving operational and human factors are subsets of populations of incidents that contain the same elements. In other words, incidents of the kind and type that are reported to the analysts of the ASRS are representative of those which under unusual and unfortunate circumstances underlie accidents. Table 9.1 shows

Table 9.1.   Frequency Distribution of Air
            Safety Reporting System
            (ASRS) Reports by Problem
            Origin

Problem origin	Percentage of reports received
Air traffic control function	40
Flight crew function	41
Aircraft structure or subsystem	3
Airport and subsystem	4
Publications/procedures	2
All other classes of problems	10
	100

the percentages of ASRS incident reports that reflect pilot and controller error. These, as well as other similarities of the incident and accident records, strongly suggest that errors reported as incidents are, indeed, similar to actions that cause accidents, although the incidents occur with much greater frequency. In the large majority of operational cases, incidents are kept from turning into accidents because of the many redundancies and other safeguards that are built into our aviation systems; these safeguards mitigate the effects of errors which are apparently quite common in aviation operations. Incident reporting has one major advantage relative to accident analysis; because of the manner in which the ASRS was designed, it is possible to query the incident reporter prior to report de-identification. Because of this feature, it is possible to learn more about *why* errors are made as well as something of the circumstances in which they are made.

The voluntary reporting feature of the ASRS and all other incident reporting systems is a drawback as well as a strength. The problem is that reports are not made on a purely random basis. Certain individuals (perhaps those more safety conscious) may report more often than others. Certain operational conditions (new regulations or safety assurance programs, for example) may induce people to report more frequently in some geographical areas or during certain periods than in others. These sampling characteristics make quantitative analysis of the incident record difficult. Thus, we may learn a great deal about what errors are occurring but not necessarily be able to determine much about how often errors occur.

Finally, error may be studied in the laboratory and in simulators. The advantages of the laboratory setting are straightforward; the many and complex conditions which often confuse and confound the natural operational environment can be controlled or eliminated in the laboratory. Behavior can be stripped to its most elemental aspects and the root causes of errors dissected to yield predictive models of causality. The disadvantages of the laboratory approach mirror just this simplicity; the fundamental nature of the typical laboratory experiment is its undoing—with experts, errors often only become apparent in the complex and high-workload conditions that reflect actual operating conditions. Ruffell Smith (1979) showed convincingly that operational conditions must be reproduced very carefully for trained pilots of aircraft to begin to reveal the kinds of errors which lead to aircraft accidents and which show up in the incident data base of the ASRS. To do so, Ruffell Smith used what has since become an indispensible tool to the human factors discipline:

full mission flight simulation. Modern simulators, which reproduce virtually all of the operational complexity of actual line flight, can provide the best of the carefully controlled laboratory setting and the rich complexities of the airways. Such simulators are used increasingly to understand errors and their causes.

Information from studies using all these methods are used in the remainder of this chapter to illustrate both the diversity and regularity of errors made by the human element within the aviation system and to describe the causes of human error in aviation operations. As Green and Taylor (1979) have aptly described it, "the thesis here is that accidents happen for reasons, but that there are not as many reasons as there are accidents." It has become increasingly clear that human errors may be demystified, errors which to the lay public often seem to be "puzzling [aspects of] human behavior" (Witkin, 1986).

A Model of Error

The Need for a Theory

The need for a model or theory of human error becomes clear when we begin to look in detail at accident or incident statistics. Table 9.2, for example, shows a recent and comprehensive analysis by Sears (1986) of airline accident statistics for a 24-year period from 1959 to 1983. In all, Sears examined in detail 93 major accidents

Table 9.2. Significant Accident Causes and Percentage Present in 93 Major Accidents

Cause of accident	Presence (%)
Pilot deviated from basic operational procedures	33
Inadequate crosscheck by second crew member	26
Design faults	13
Maintenance and inspection deficiencies	12
Absence of approach guidance	10
Captain ignored crew inputs	10
Air traffic control failures or errors	9
Improper crew response during abnormal conditions	9
Insufficient or incorrect weather information	8
Runway hazards	7
Air traffic control/crew communication deficiencies	6
Improper decision to land	6

worldwide. He developed a classification system with the categories shown to help in conceptually organizing the data. Indeed, the particular method used by Sears can be extremely useful in the operational setting. For example, the major cause category is shown at the top of Table 9.2: "Pilot deviated from basic operational procedures." The fact that more than 30 of the 93 major accidents may be attributed to a failure of the flight crew to follow standard operating procedures may suggest that better training methods or better methods of selecting crew members are needed. As useful as the classification is, however, it says very little about why crew members often apparently fail to follow procedures or how one might train or select to reduce error in following procedural protocols. Failure to know in detail why a human error occurs makes the development of a solution strategy both difficult and inefficient.

Another problem with most classification schemes is that they are merely descriptive of behavior, not predictive. To develop solutions to the problem of human error, whether they be better equipment, better selection policies for flight crews, or better training, we must be able to predict with some certainty what conditions in flight are the most likely to cause the types of errors which contribute so disproportionately to aviation accidents and incidents. A word on prediction is warranted. By the ability to predict error, I mean generally the ability to recreate situations (perhaps in the laboratory or in a simulator) where it may be anticipated that certain kinds of errors will occur with significant regularity. It should not be assumed that the existence of a predictive model of human error would necessarily allow the flight crews or flight controllers themselves to reduce the incidence of error (though this may be true in certain cases) nor that errors can be predicted with 100% certainty. Nonetheless, even though imperfect, a detailed knowledge of conditions under which errors will occur can enable us to design aviation systems and procedures and to select and train crews in such a manner as to significantly reduce vulnerability to error.

Finally, if our search for solutions is to be at all efficient, it is unwise to ignore or discard decades of systematic research in the behavioral and life sciences. Put simply, an adequate model for classifying human error should properly tie back into the rich experimental and theoretical literature on human behavior if we are ultimately to make much sense of the complex operational data of the type we have been examining.

A Simple Error Model

Since human behavior is complex, it might seem that a comprehensive theory that would satisfy our criteria would necessarily mirror this complexity. Many models, classification schemes, taxonomies, or other systems to describe human error have been developed (e.g., Rouse & Rouse, 1984; Singleton, 1972); many of these are comprehensive and most quite complex. None that I have examined fully meet the three criteria noted above, although a number satisfy two of the three, to one degree or another. Although a complete model of error may ultimately be complex, it has proven feasible to develop a reasonably simple outline or framework for error within which it is possible to capture much of the richness of cockpit behavior and at the same time begin to meet the other criteria noted above. I term this framework an *information–decision–action* model of piloting. In spirit, it has been inspired by information processing models of human performance (e.g., Card, Moran, & Newell, 1983). It asserts that cockpit behavior can be thought of as reflecting three basic stages. In the first of these, the acquisition, exchange and processing of information is the key activity. In the second stage, decisions are made and specific intents or plans to act are determined. Finally, in the third stage, decisions are implemented and intents acted upon. The three stages take place in the context of goals, which are established by the flight crews, their companies through operational protocols, or in some cases by the specific context of the flight. Although the establishment of goals may in itself be a complex, multistage process, a simplifying assumption here is that the flight crews are both highly skilled and experienced and that their rational intentions are not to commit errors. In other words, we ignore the possibility of dishonorable intentions or inappropriate high-level goals. Although the stages are not constrained to occur in the exact sequence described, a moment's reflection should suggest that most purposive, skilled behavior in a somewhat constrained environment like the airplane cockpit can reasonably be described in terms of this simple stage model of behavior. Just as clearly, our model framework cannot do justice to the full complexity and richness of the human experience. It does not immediately offer much insight into those kinds of behaviors that we consider creative, whimsical, or emotionally driven, for example. As discussed here, the model also assumes good will on the part of the human elements of the system; irresponsible behavior is discounted. Nonetheless, as I hope to show, the bare framework outlined can begin to lead to a very useful understanding of why errors are made and the circumstances that both increase and decrease the likelihood that they will occur.

Toward Error-Resistant Systems

There are, generally speaking, three approaches to reducing the incidence and severity of human error in any complex human–machine system. First, errors may be avoided through the careful and informed design of controls, displays, operational procedures, and the like. The likelihood that humans will make mistakes can also be reduced through selection and training. Selection focuses on the artificial parts of the system, training, on the human. It is clear that these reduce, but do not eliminate, the incidence of error. Distinct from selection and training is the attempt to design systems which are tolerant of error. To a degree, of course, this is done today in aviation through the use of multiple crew members and other redundancies which significantly reduce the probability that any given error will lead to an accident. In the past few years, however, it has become clear that the development of error-tolerant automation may allow the achievement of significantly safer flight operations and in some cases perhaps eliminate entire classes of error. In designing error tolerance, it is explicitly accepted that errors will occur; automation is used to monitor the human crew and to detect errors as they are made. The crew may then be warned or, in certain cases, the monitors may be designed to take control and mitigate the errors before they affect safety of flight. Although we are a long way from deploying such systems on a routine basis, the promise of error-tolerant technology is being demonstrated in the laboratory. Some features of the Boeing 757 and 767 aircraft represent a beginning in these directions. If a pilot of one of these aircraft enters a destination into the flight management computer that is incompatible with the entered fuel load, an alert points this out to the two crew members. More is described of this revolutionary approach to reducing the consequences of pilot error in the latter part of this chapter.

Information Acquisition and Processing Errors

Information and Skilled Performance

Once a complex skill like flying an aircraft is mastered through a long and arduous training process, the proficient performance of that skill is critically dependent on an adequate and timely flow of information. Aircraft pilots must continually maintain an awareness of their situation if they are to conduct a safe flight; breakdowns in this situational awareness caused by faulty acquisition and processing of information represent one of the most serious human factors problems in aviation operations. The pilot must maintain an awareness, for example, of where the aircraft is geographically, what its current performance state is, its altitude, power setting, configuration, and relationship to other aircraft. The pilot must (1) be mindful of verbal communications and instructions from air traffic control personnel, (2) be aware of the environment, and (3) systematically monitor for and anticipate changes in weather that might affect his or her performance and that of the aircraft. Information to maintain an appropriate awareness of the flight situation is obtained visually, through the windows of the aircraft and from instruments, aurally from other crew members within the cockpit and from air traffic controllers over radio channels, and through the vestibular senses.

Although the human is an exquisite processor of information by almost any measure, all of these means of acquiring information are subject to error. Thus, it is not only possible but likely that pilots will suffer lapses in their ability to maintain an adequate theory of the situation (Bohlman, 1979). Failures to do so can result in serious consequences affecting the safety of flight.

Information is also the grist of decisions. Most systematic treatments of the process of making optimal decisions emphasize the importance of the proper seeking and processing of information prior to the actual decision-making step. The timely flow of information often also is important in triggering appropriate actions, both the continuous manual control and discrete actions, which a pilot must make to manage a safe flight. Thus, information is critical in each stage of skilled performance. Much of the effort of early aviation psychologists and human engineers was directed to the problem of understanding the details of processing of information in flight and to the design of displays and other equipment and operating protocols designed to improve this processing.

What happens when information processing breaks down in flight? Billings (1981) examined a sample of more than 12,000 incident reports submitted to NASA's ASRS; more than 73% of all reports submitted contain evidence of a problem in the transfer of information within the aviation system. Approximately 85% of these involved aural information transfer, and 15% involved visual problems of one sort or another. From this, we might conclude that information transfer problems, particularly of the auditory variety, are quite common in aviation; subsequent studies of the ASRS data suggest that the problem is an ongoing one.

Over the past decade, catastrophic encounters of aircraft with severe weather conditions, while fortunately rare, have highlighted the need for appropriate and timely information in maintaining safe flight. Some years ago, while attempting a takeoff from the airport in New Orleans, the pilot of a Boeing 727 encountered a severe windshear. Because of the severe nature of the condition, the pilot was unable to maintain adequate airspeed and the aircraft crashed, causing the loss of life of all aboard and serious destruction and additional loss of life on the ground. More recently, the crew of a Delta L1011 on approach to Dallas–Ft. Worth Airport encountered a similar windshear; again, because of the severity of the shear, the crew eventually were unable to maintain airspeed and crashed short of the runway. Again, the loss of life was enormous. There is some question in both cases of whether the crews of the aircraft had adequate information to make a reasonable determination of the potential severity of the weather hazard. In both cases, they only became aware of the magnitude of the shear once it had been encountered, and in both cases they (or their aircraft) were unable to respond quickly and appropriately enough to avert a crash. Also in both cases, however, the particular weather conditions which caused the shears (microbursts associated with thunderstorms) were localized; if the crews had obtained and had acted upon information about the nature and severity of the weather hazards in both locations, both tragic accidents could have been averted. In the remainder of this section, we examine information acquisition and processing in flight and the kinds of errors associated with various conditions of flight.

Visually Guided Flight

Many aircraft approaches every day are made under visual conditions. This means that the primary means of guidance and control of the aircraft is through the eyes of the pilot. Countless successful landings made visually attest to the adequacy of visual information in allowing pilots to control the attitude, vertical speed, and the point at which their aircraft touches down. We know a great deal about the specific kinds of information that are critical to successful visual landing performance, and we are beginning to understand some of the limitations of visually guided flight during conditions of less than perfect visibility.

Scientists generally distinguish between static and dynamic visual cues when they talk about visual landings. *Static cues* are those which allow pilots to maintain the proper aircraft attitude and glideslope. *Dynamic cues* refer to elements of the visually expanding scene which appear to the pilot to move radially from a focus—the so-called aimpoint, or point at which the aircraft would touch down if it were to remain on a straight course.

Static cues include the perceived shape, size, and location of the runway in the windscreen; they refer to information extractable from a view of the runway at an instant in time. For example, the subtended visual angle formed by the touchdown zone of the runway in the foreground and the horizon in the distance will remain constant as the aircraft nears the runway, provided that the aircraft is maintained on a constant angle glideslope. Thus, by using this visual angle and controlling the aircraft in such a manner to keep it constant during an approach, a pilot can in theory maintain the aircraft on the appropriate constant glidepath.

Using the dynamic visual cues of scene expansion and visual flow described above, pilots can also control the point at which the aircraft impacts the runway, since a continuous referent exists from which the actual impact point can be compared to the desired impact point in the touchdown zone of the runway. Figure 9.6 illustrates the static and dynamic visual cues available to the pilot during a normal visual approach.

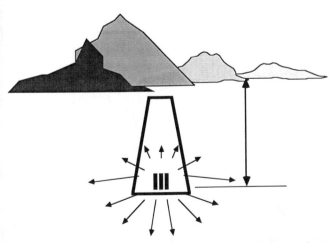

Figure 9.6.   Dynamic and static visual cues in a simplified landing scene.

There are, of course, both procedural and perceptual complications to all of this. First, at most airports, landings are typically made under air traffic control conditions; in addition to the purely perceptual task of visually guiding and controlling the aircraft, the pilot communicates with and receives instructions from a controller. The instructions may include the visual acquisition and tracking of other traffic and clearances to land on specific runways. Thus, the visual task is often more complex than our simple analysis might suggest.

I have described the visual cues used by pilots in the approach to land because it is precisely this flight maneuver which, statistically, is the most hazardous of all and which is subject to the greatest incidence of human error. Thus, although pilots become quite familiar, proficient, and comfortable with visually guided landings through the course of their training, it has become clear that the margins of safety are small and the potential for error very great, even among very experienced pilots. Figure 9.7, for example, shows the percentage of scheduled airline accidents distributed by the phase of flight. Approach and landing accidents comprise nearly 50% of all airline accidents; yet, these segments constitute a very small percentage of total flight time. As interesting is the fact that the approach and landing accidents are more reliably caused by human error than those of any other phase of flight (nearly 75%). What is known about the source of these errors?

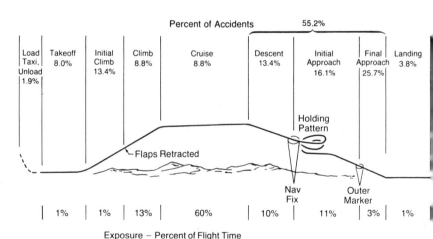

Figure 9.7.   Air carrier accidents distributed by phase of flight, 1959–1983: worldwide jet fleet, all operations. (Excludes sabatoge and military action). Exposure percentage based on an average flight duration of 1.6 hours. (Boeing, 1985.)

Conrad Kraft (1978), formerly a psychologist with the Boeing Company, undertook a study of approach and landing errors following a series of accidents involving Boeing aircraft that took place in the mid-1960s. Using ingenious simulation techniques, Kraft determined that under certain nighttime visual conditions involving a reduction in the number and quality of visual cues, pilots often misjudged glidepaths and touchdown points in ways that almost exactly reproduced the conditions which had preceded the actual accidents. Kraft subsequently termed such approaches *black hole landings*, since they were characterized as occurring at airports which had few if any lights in the area surrounding the airport environment; under such circumstances, the only visual cues available for aircraft guidance are those provided by the airport, runway, and touchdown zone lights. Interestingly, pilots typically misjudged their approaches in a very systematic fashion; they tended to land short of the runway. Such errors turn out to be characteristic of reduced visibility accidents, whether the reduction in visibility is caused, as in Kraft's studies, by a lack of visual information or a reduction in the available information caused by meteorological conditions such as haze or fog.

Kraft went on to show that pilots behaved as though they were misusing the static visual cues normally adequate to safely guide an aircraft to the proper touchdown zone. Specifically, rather than keep the visual angle formed by the touchdown zone in the foreground and the horizon constant, they behaved as though they kept the angle constant between the touchdown zone in the foreground and the far end of the airport runway. If this visual angle is kept constant, a circularly curved glideslope results which is concave upward; given the normal variability of a visually flown approach, such a glideslope may bring the aircraft dangerously close to the ground well short of the actual runway.

During the past decade, several investigators have thoroughly explored performance-limiting and error-producing factors during the visual approach and landing. A consistent picture emerges. Mertens, in a series of studies (1978, 1981), convincingly showed that human pilots systematically underestimate the angle of a slanted surface under certain circumstances. Perrone (1984), working at the Ames Research Center, developed a mathematical model which predicts Mertens' quantitative results and offers a simple geometric explanation for when inaccurate slant estimation will occur.

Dynamic visual cues, too, seem subject to bias. Studies of pilots' abilities to judge aimpoint in a simplified visual simulation show that humans consistently have more difficulty and make larger errors when judging vertical rather than horizontal position of the aimpoint (Ferrante, 1979) and that, under certain circumstances, they may exhibit a significant bias toward reporting the aimpoint as higher in the visual field than it actually is (Ahumada, 1981; Knott, 1983). In actual flight, such biases would lead to lower than desired glidepaths and, in conjunction with the errors shown to be associated with static visual landing cues, offer a comprehensive explanation of the accident data.

The lesson from all this is that the visual sense, although adequate for aircraft guidance when visual information is excellent, may mislead when the quality of the information degrades for a variety of reasons. The errors which occur are systematic; under conditions of reduced visibility, the misperception of both static and dynamic visual cues leads pilots to fly low approaches. If severe enough, these errors can and do cause accidents. Despite the fact that our visual sense is not completely reliable, pilots often tend to rely on it more than on their instruments; in many approach and landing accidents, primary flight display equipment which would indicate the presence of guidance errors during the final approach has been found to have been functioning normally. Our direct senses are often compelling indicators of the state of the world, even when they are in error.

Disorientation

Although uncommon in commercial aviation operations, pilot disorientation can often occur in both military and civilian flight. Disorientation in flight is a complex phenomenon, but again one which has been thoroughly studied over the past decade or two. In general, disorientation is the result of interactions among the visual systems, the vestibular system—that sensory system which signals head movements in three-dimensional space—and the proprioceptive mechanisms which detect and process gross movements of the body. Illusions of motion, and the disorientation which results from uncorrelated information from the various sensory systems (your vestibular system suggests that you are rotating but your eyes say otherwise), result from four characteristics of the human sensory apparatus: finite thresholds; the mechanical dynamics of the vestibular system and particularly the semicircular canals, which signal rotary movement; compensatory eye movements; and other compensatory eye reflexes. Finite thresholds suggest that some movements, though perhaps detectable visually, will not be sensed by the semicircular canal receptors. Canal dynamics produce greater sensitivity and a different time course of sensation for some motions than for others. Compensatory eye movements, which can include both rotational as well as positional changes, can sometimes suggest visual movement opposite that of the actual movement of the body, or of the aircraft. Again, though complex, conditions under which illusions and disorientation will occur are well understood (e.g., Howard, 1982) and predictable. In general terms, they occur often in high-performance aircraft subject to rapid and high-g maneuvers and during conditions of reduced visual information. Among general aviation pilots not skilled in the use of instruments, flight into clouds can result in severe disorientation and sometimes tragic consequences. As with visual errors associated with the approach and landing, disorientation conditions are both compelling and avoidable if pilots are properly educated to the hazards and trained to either avoid the precursor conditions or to properly use flight instrumentation to provide guidance information.

Instrument-Assisted Guidance

Flight instruments are intended to provide information to assist, or in some cases replace, the use of natural visual cues in aircraft guidance and control. Instruments which indicate aircraft attitude, heading, airspeed, vertical speed, and altitude have been available since very early days in aviation. In recent years, electronic displays indicate the geographical position of the aircraft, pictorial representations of the major aircraft systems, and other forms of visual information to keep the pilot informed and aware of his flight "situation."

That aircraft could be flown entirely with artificial information was dramatically demonstrated when James Doolittle took off on September 24, 1929, in an aircraft with the cockpit covered, flew 20 miles, and landed at almost the exact spot where he had taken off, all using an attitude indicator called the Sperry Horizon. A number of demonstrations over the past several decades have shown that an aircraft can be flown safely using a closed-circuit television camera to replace the natural visual cues seen through the windscreen.

Despite the fact that flight instruments have been in use for more than a decade, no general agreement exists concerning how they should display information to the pilot. For dynamic displays, for example, the question of what should move on the display is the most controversial issue in display design (Roscoe, 1968), an issue which has not been fully resolved today. For attitude indication, it was early argued that the display should be thought of as a "porthole through which the pilot views a symbolic analog of the real horizon" (Johnson & Roscoe, 1972). Known as an "inside-out" display, the moving horizon is common even today in contemporary flight instruments. "Outside-in" displays are also in use, however, and even some in which some elements of the display perform in an inside-out fashion while others move as though outside-in. As might be gathered, pilots occasionally confuse and misinterpret display motions.

The psychologist Paul Fitts was among the first to systematically study errors made in the interpretation of display information (Fitts & Jones, 1947). The investigation involved 270 errors made by pilots in reading and interpreting flight instruments. A tabulation of these errors follows.

Display-related errors	Control-related errors
Incorrect interpretation	Control substitution
Legibility problems	Adjustment errors
Substitution errors	Memory errors control reversals
Undetected failures	Unintentional activation
Illusions, disorientation	Anthropometry-related errors
Failures to monitor	

Using the moving horizon attitude indicator, pilots made 19 reversal errors in angle of bank that resulted in a control movement that aggravates rather than corrects an undesirable bank angle. Although this error occurs in relatively small numbers, it may have serious effects if it leads to pilot disorientation or a flight condition such as a spin from which recovery is difficult.

A number of attempts have been made to articulate display principles to reduce or eliminate display-related errors. After reviewing the evidence for performance and errors, Roscoe (1968) has described six rules of display design. Although the experimental evidence favoring the use of such rules is often compelling, there is yet to emerge a common industry practice in all cases. For example, in the *principle of the moving part*, Roscoe suggests that the part of a display that represents the aircraft should move against a fixed scale or referent rather than having the referent move against a fixed index representing the aircraft. This principle applied to the attitude indicator would suggest that the horizon should remain level while the aircraft symbol moves in reference to it. Nonetheless, one today finds displays which use both the inside-out and outside-in characteristics. It has been shown that, indeed, pilots can learn to use either kind of display. They may even adapt from one display type to another, although the potential for interpretative errors and disorientation increases whenever the display skills are not overlearned or the pilot finds himself in a highly stressful situation (Roscoe, 1968). Precisely because the human is so adaptable, it has been difficult to reach a consensus on display design principles based on rigorous empirical evidence.

The newer electronic display technologies have significantly increased designers' flexibility in presenting artificial visual information to the flight crew. Pictorial rather than symbolic displays are finding their way increasingly into the cockpit. Again, principles are being discovered which when properly applied reduce the potential for misinterpretation of display information. McGreevy and Ellis (1986) investigated the use of perspective in displays designed to depict the relative spatial locations of "ownship" and other air traffic in a given three-dimensional airspace. They found that, relative to two-dimensional depictions using symbolic tags to indicate the altitude dimension, three-dimensional displays employing perspective lead to spatial interpretations on the part of pilots that are significantly less error prone. Pilots also state more confidence and respond more quickly to in-flight conflict situations when using the perspective displays. McGreevy and Ellis went on to study and specify the specific perspective laws which yield minimal perceptual errors. It appears that errors are minimized when the human is allowed to make the fewest number of transformations to match an internal, cognitive representation of the situation. Information in displays which exhibit this characteristic appear to be interpreted both more quickly and in a more error-free fashion. Thus, the scientific basis for display design is rapidly becoming both mature and useful on a practical basis.

Errors in Communication

Although pilots obtain much of the information necessary for flight through the visual sense, verbal communications are an important source of situational awareness. As noted before, commands from air traffic controllers help pilots to avoid other traffic and to navigate through often crowded terminal areas and en route sectors. They often serve as an important source of information about weather and other potential flight hazards. Within multicrewed aircraft, effective communication patterns among crew members are, as we will see, important precursors to effective decisions. Communication clearly serves in a central role in the creation and maintenance of situational awareness.

The process of communication is complex and subject to error. In the ASRS data base, verbal information transfer problems account for roughly 85% of all reported information transfer incidents (see Table 9.3). Monan (1983, 1986) has described many of the incidents reported to the ASRS staff that can properly be characterized as reflecting problems of communication. In some cases, the imprecision of natural language coupled with the expectancies of the situation can lead to serious misinterpretations of controller instructions. In visual meteorological conditions with the airport in sight, crews are often too quick in expecting clearance to descend and land. In some cases, controllers saying, "you will be cleared for a visual approach" has been interpreted too hastily as, "you have been cleared for a visual approach." Also common are transpositions of numbers representing tower frequency or, in some cases, runway designations. During particularly high-workload conditions, flight crews sometimes forget entirely to request tower clearances to land.

The results of communication errors in aviation can lead to serious impacts on margins of safety. Incident reports, again exemplified by

Table 9.3. Frequency Distribution
of Information Transfer
Problems During
Aircraft Operations[a]

Message medium	Frequency
Aural information transfer	
Radio	6834
Interphone	855
Voice	450
Telephone	438
Tape recording	19
	8616
Visual information transfer	
Video/CRT	587
Instruments	416
Publications	309
Charts	203
	1515
All media	10131

[a]From Billings, 1981.

those found in the ASRS data base, describe hundreds of traffic conflicts, narrowly missed midair collisions, unnecessary go-arounds, and aborted takeoffs. Again, such errors tend not to be random, especially when viewed in the aggregate. Monan (1986) suggests that many of the ASRS incidents reflect a failure in a structural process designed to point out communication errors to the involved participants, pilot, and controller. The structural process, the act of a controller actively listening to the pilot's response to an ATC clearance, is termed by Monan, *hearback*, and is intended to provide a necessary redundancy to an imprecise system. In many ASRS incidents, this hearback is frequently missing from controller–pilot–controller dialogue. As Monan (1986) notes, "Pilots heard what they expected to hear, heard what they wanted to hear and frequently did not hear what they did not anticipate hearing—amendments to just-issued clearances." Such incidents and observations by trained observers such as Captain Monan point out the active as opposed to passive nature of communication; listeners do not merely register incoming messages but rather contribute actively to the process of synthesizing the received communication. There exists an extensive literature dealing with the particular conditions likely to accompany serious errors of communication. Among the most complete accounts is that of Fromkin (1980).

Among the best of possible measures to counter the possibility of mishearing or mispeaking is to employ redundancy, as in the hearback procedure noted above. Precision, and the maintained awareness of the dangers of imprecision in communication, may also be an important antidote to the potential for error. Foushee and Manos (1981) analyzed cockpit voice recordings from a full mission simulation study designed to investigate the role of crew interaction factors in flight safety. A number of interesting findings emerged, all relevant to the problem of effective communication. Overall, there was a clear tendency for crews who communicated less not to perform as well in making critical inflight decisions, but the specific patterns of communication also played an important role. For example, when relatively more information was transferred among crew members concerning flight status, fewer errors were made related to the operation of aircraft systems. Crew members who acknowledged other crew members' communications were also less likely to make flight errors. Mitigated communication styles ("I think we should ask air traffic control for a higher altitude" rather than "Ask air traffic control") were also precursors to more errors on the average than were more command-oriented styles. As with many aspects of performance in flight, factors such as fatigue can also lead to communication patterns that are less precise and effective. Perhaps the best countermeasure is constant vigilance concerning the potential for error in the entire process of communication, whether it is between pilot and controller or pilot and first officer.

Errors in Deciding

On January 14, 1982, an Air Florida B737 attempted a takeoff from the National Airport in Washington, D.C., during a heavy snowstorm. The flight crew of the aircraft apparently were unaware of or ignored the buildup of ice and snow on the aircraft, including that which made a critical measurement system on board the aircraft provide erroneous indications of engine power during the takeoff roll. Consequently, the crew attempted the takeoff at roughly three-quarter engine power settings, could not sustain flight, and crashed into a roadway bridge across the Potomac seconds after attempting lift-off. The crash occurred due to a combination of a lack of thrust and airspeed and the increased drag and decreased lift caused by the accumulation of ice and snow on the 737's wings and fuselage.

Why had the crew, as NTSB investigators later found, failed to perform the customary (and required) "walkaround" of the aircraft, which would have undoubtedly revealed the extent of the ice and snow buildup? Why did the crew fail to attempt a takeoff abort, once it had become apparent (to at least the copilot) during the takeoff roll that the aircraft was not accelerating sufficiently to make a safe takeoff?

The simple answer to these questions is that the crew made a series of bad decisions, both in planning the takeoff operation well before the crash and during the last few seconds prior to crashing into the crowded commuter-filled bridge across the Potomac. This answer is unsatisfying; it does not tell us why such apparently flawed decisions were made by two men trained to make expert decisions under both normal and emergency situations. The more educated answer is both more interesting and disturbing. It suggests that the decision errors made by the crew reflect decision and judgment tendencies that we all exhibit, to a degree, in our day-to-day lives.

Decisions under Uncertainty

An important element in many real-life situations is that the decision maker never has complete information and that nature is always, to a degree, random, though we may have (or think we have) estimates of how probable or likely various outcomes are. When this is the case, decisions are said to be made under conditions of uncertainty; this simply means that the decision maker cannot be absolutely sure of the outcome of the decision. This uncertainty characterizes the conditions under which we make many decisions every day.

Early on, decision theorists developed optimum ways of making decisions under conditions of uncertainty. The methods are optimal in the sense that their use will maximize the outcome or payoff to the decision maker, provided he or she is consistent in the use of the decision rules. The word *payoff* may alert the reader to a peculiarity of the optimal or rational decision models. Such methods were originally developed for decisions in which the outcomes could be measured in terms of something objective and quantifiable, like money. Later, the models were broadened by suggesting that any decision in which the utility of the outcome could be quantified or measured in some fashion, even subjectively, could be made using the prescriptive rules and would, over the long run, result in the best possible outcomes for the decision maker.

Although optimal and rational decision methods work well when certain ground rules are met, they turn out to be very poor descriptions or models of how actual decisions are made in the real world, even by experts. Optimal methods assume (1) that the various decision outcomes can be quantified and scaled in terms meaningful to the decision maker, (2) that the probabilities or likelihoods associated with outcomes of the various decisions are known to the decision maker, (3) that the decision maker is perfectly sensitive and responsive to new information about the situation, and (4) that he or she consistently and rationally acts in such a fashion to produce optimal results. There is one thing that the optimal models do not assume: that optimal decisions always lead to good or desirable outcomes. Because of the randomness of nature, decisions made optimally will sometimes lead to undesirable outcomes.

How do real decision makers compare to these criteria of rationality? First, a growing body of literature suggests that real decision makers behave in significantly different ways than the process implied by the normative models. To recap the above, according to the normative theories, the decision maker is assumed to identify all relevant courses of action, identify fully the consequences that may arise as a result of choosing each option, assess the likelihood of the various consequences being realized, and through some integration process that considers all the information in a rational fashion, identify the best option. In other words, the whole process is assumed to be quite serial and exhaustive. However, human decision makers, particularly experts, appear not to act this way. Klein and his colleagues (1985), for example, have shown that experts often act as though they quickly assess the pattern of a decision situation and immediately make a categorization of the situation that leads to a decision. They do not carefully consider all possibilities and then perform some sort of mental computation to arrive at the decision. Dreyfus and Dreyfus (1984) have argued that only novices tend to make decisions in the careful analytical fashion suggested by the normative decision models. They, too, suggest that real-world experts tend to behave in what can only appear to be much more impulsive ways than implied by the theories.

In addition, whether expert or not, decision makers tend to use a small number of rules of thumb, or heuristics, in making their decisions (Tversky & Kahneman, 1973); they tend not to respect the required principles of probability and statistics. They tend to be inconsistent with respect to preferences, to fail to consider all the possible decision and outcome options (Slovic, Fischof, & Lichtens, 1978), to be inconsistent in dealing with risk (Lopes, 1983), to be overly subject to the situational context in which the decisions are made (Tversky & Kahneman, 1981), and to have inappropriate levels of confidence in their own decisions (Einhorn & Hogarth, 1978). This last characteristic tends to make them persevere long after the available evidence suggests that they should adopt a different strategy than the one they have chosen. Those who have systematically looked at experts as well as naive decision makers have found that expertise does not guarantee optimality; experts tend to make the same errors as do the rest of us under certain circumstances (Nisbett & Ross, 1980).

Some Decision Heuristics: The Air Florida 90 Accident

Nisbett, Krantz, Jepson, and Dunda (1983) describe some additional statistical principles that should be followed if one is making optimal decisions under uncertainty. For example, generalizations from specific instances of events should be made more confidently when they are based on a larger number of instances, when the instances represent an unbiased sample, and when events are less, rather than more, variable. The judged likelihood of an event should somehow take into account the *a priori* probability that the event will occur, and not just the immediate circumstances surrounding it. Tversky and Kahneman have shown convincingly that people use heuristics in making decisions that make them overlook such important statistical variables as sample size, prior probabilities, and critical correlations.

They suggest that, when faced with real decision situations, people use a small number of heuristic principles to arrive at predictions about what will happen and to make decisions about plans and actions. For example, *representativeness* is the name Tversky and Kahneman give to the tendency to judge the likelihood that event A arises from process B, based on the similarity of A to B. In other words, if enough of the perceived characteristics of a situation resemble an experience from the past, people will tend to judge the new situation as having the same outcome as they experienced before, irrespective of how likely it may be on an absolute basis. Judging situations in this fashion, without regard for how likely events are on an absolute basis, can lead to serious errors of prediction.

Another rule of thumb described by Tversky and Kahneman is known as the *availability rule*. Availability suggests that events are judged as being more or less likely dependent on the ease with which instances can be remembered. Clearly, use of the availability rule can ignore important information about the likelihood of particular sets of outcomes, since decisions will depend more on characteristics of the human memory system than of the situation at hand. People simply seem to not reason statistically about problems which require such reasoning for optimality.

With these simple rules in mind, let us reexamine the series of decisions leading up to the Air Florida disaster. First, the decision not to examine the aircraft for ice and snow prior to takeoff is enigmatic; performance of a walkaround should be standard procedure in such situations. To understand how this lapse happened, it may be enlightening to consider the prior experience of the pilot and first officer. As the name might imply, as an airline, Air Florida had not had much experience with winter conditions. The pilot and first officer had rarely encountered such conditions (though there is some evidence that the first officer had enough cold weather experience to be more aware than he seems to have been of the potential dangers); their judgment of the likelihood of an icing condition was thus dangerously biased by the lack of availability of analogous situations in their memories. Similarly, after they had made the ill-fated decision to begin their takeoff roll, their ability to imagine that their engine power readings were improper because of accumulations of ice or snow may have been impaired by the overwhelming representativeness of their current takeoff conditions to successful takeoffs in the

past: engines spooling up, power indications appearing to correspond appropriately, no exceptional warning signals, and so forth.
From the cockpit voice recorder, it is possible to determine that they
did indeed notice that the throttle settings that normally corresponded to takeoff power had, during the takeoff roll, led to engine power
instrument readings well in excess of normal takeoff thrust. Rather
than imagining the readings to be faulty, the pilot's comments indicate clearly his judgment that the apparent increase in power must
be due to what were for him unusually cold conditions. In other
words, he apparently thought that the engines were more efficient in
the cold!

Finally, although it is apparent from the voice recordings that the
first officer indicated on at least three separate occasions that he was
aware that the takeoff roll was not normal, he failed to take any action to abort the takeoff; nor did the captain heed his admittedly
somewhat oblique queries and warnings. The captain's behavior displays the instance of a heuristic described earlier; once having made
a decision, people persevere in that course of action, even when evidence is substantial that the decision was the improper one. The failure of the first officer to override the captain in some fashion
illustrates another common failure, though this time not a failure of
judgment. It is well known that people often improperly defer to authority figures, even when it is clear that they have embarked on an
unwise course of action (Foushee, 1984). Also, as suggested before,
most all of us are more confident in our decisions than we typically
have any right to be. This tendency reinforces the reluctance of others to attempt to change our minds—and our decisions.

Debiasing

Given that pilots, like the rest of us, may tend to depart from optimum decision practices, particularly under conditions of time pressure or other stress (Einhorn & Hogarth, 1981), how might
operational decision making be improved to prevent the occurence of
tragedies such as the Air Florida accident? Individuals may be
warned about the possibility of bias, without specifying its nature;
they may have described for them the direction and extent of biases
that have been known to occur, or they may simply be better trained
so that their inherent biases (e.g., those based on a preponderance of
experience with warm weather operations) may be properly balanced
by experience with a broader range of conditions (even if only simulated). With modern flight simulators capable of reproducing a wide

range of operational conditions, such training can be extremely effective in alerting the crew to deal effectively with unlikely events (Lauber & Foushee, 1981). Nisbett et al. (1983) suggest that formal training in statistics can also improve individuals' tendencies to properly evaluate information and thus to not fall prey to heuristic-based errors.

A fundamentally different approach to that of prior training of flight crews to reduce or eliminate improperly biased decision tendencies is the use of automated decision aids at the time that decisions are required. Woods (1986) has reviewed approaches to decision aiding (most in a nonaviation context) and concluded that most developed to date worsen, rather than improve, decision performance. In many of these approaches, the human decision maker is used only to gather data and to implement decisions made, in effect, by a computer program or machine. A skeletal depiction of the organization and function of such a system is shown in Figure 9.8(a). In such systems, humans often adopt one of two strategies: always accept or always reject the machine recommendation. In either case the combination of human plus machine does significantly worse than theory would suggest. In some cases the combination can do significantly worse than either the man or machine acting alone! An improved decision-aiding architecture is shown in Figure 9.8(b). Here the computer gathers information, presents it in such a fashion to properly bias the human, and suggests a range of alternatives (remember than humans are often poor at generating all relevant or possible outcomes). The human is then left to make the decision. That such an approach to decision aiding may lead to significant improvements in performance is suggested by some recent work of Tversky and Kahneman on the importance of decision framing; they show in convincing fashion that people's judgment preferences can be radically altered by the manner in which germane information is presented or, in other words, by the manner in which the decision question is framed (Tversky & Kahneman, 1981). This result suggests, at minimum, that if one knew how to properly frame the situation, it would be possible to significantly shift decision tendencies in the desired directions. Unfortunately, for the most part, we do not as yet know how to do this.

Machine-aided human decision making is a relatively new approach to bettering decision performance in complex human–machine systems. Although current evidence suggests that such systems should work in such a fashion that allows the human in the system to be the final decision agent, beyond that little is known specifically

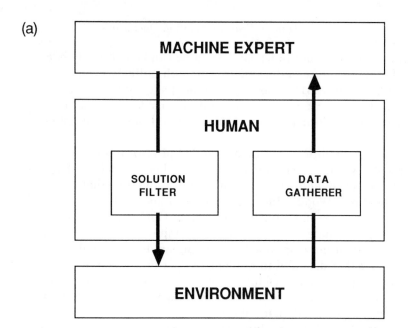

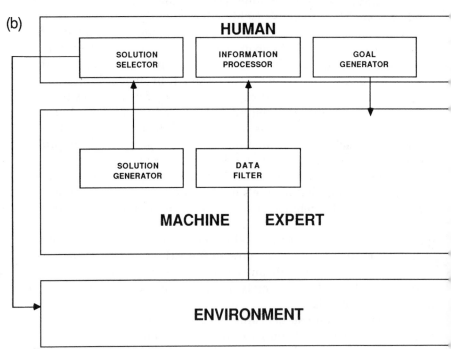

Figure 9.8. Two decision-aiding architectures: (a) limited rate for human decision maker; (b) improved version with more active role for human decision maker.

with respect to the design and use of these kinds of systems. Further development is likely to proceed slowly, even in the relatively restrictive context of aviation operations. Clearly, such a system would necessarily embody significant expertise regarding not only the contingencies of aircraft performance under an immense variety of operational conditions, but also of the kinds of bias and decision failures to be expected of the human. Decision aiding will doubtlessly be an active topic of research in the future. Until then, better methods of training seem to be the only practical solution to the problem of decision errors.

Action Errors

Much of what is observable in human behavior falls into the general category of action. Although we have been stressing in our simple model for the understanding of error the precursors of actions, the acquisition and processing of information, and the making of decisions and forming of intents, actions themselves are subject to error, even if the intent is correct. Norman (1981) calls such errors of action *slips*: those actions in which one thing is intended but another done. Errors made earlier in the chain of behavior are simply termed *mistakes*.

In this section, I discuss errors made during the "output" processes of the skilled performer, the expert pilot. Thanks to psychologists like Don Norman, slips, like other kinds of errors, are slowly being understood to be normal components of behavior and predictable consequences of the ways in which humans process information. As with errors in decision making, slips and other output errors tend to highlight the interdependence of the various stages of behavior. As we will see, the elements of gathering and processing of information are key factors in determining under what circumstances slips may be expected to occur.

Slips tend to be discrete acts: activating a switch, entering data with a keystroke, or speaking a word. As aircraft become more highly automated, and the manual control skills of the pilot are displaced by aircraft systems (autopilots) which perform the general guidance and control functions associated with management of the flight path, discrete actions—and slips as key error modes associated with the discrete actions—seem to be assuming increasing importance in the causation of incidents and accidents. Nonetheless, pilots still manually fly even the most highly automated aircraft, if only to maintain their flying skills in the case that they are called on if the automatics fail. Much is known about the limits of manual control; failures to adequately control aircraft in the face of flight path disturbances such as severe weather or the failure of aircraft equipment are sometimes the final errors made by pilots. Since control has been discussed extensively in the chapter by Baron, I touch only on one particularly interesting aspect of manual control, an aspect that compellingly points up the importance of information and the integrated nature of human behavior.

Information and Control

When manually piloting an aircraft, pilots invariably are trying to achieve some performance goal: adherence to a 3° glideslope, level flight, constant bank-angle turn, or so on. In other words, there is some desired output. In order to create this output, the pilot executes continuous control actions such as manipulations of the wheel and column, the rudder pedals, and throttles. Typically, there is some indication, either via the pilot's flight instrumentation or through natural visual or motion cues, of whether the actual behavior of the aircraft is that which the pilot intends. Deviations from the intended behavior, either because the wrong control inputs have been made or because other influences such as turbulence have disturbed the flight path, are termed *control errors*. Such control errors are nominal and cannot be avoided; when they become very large or the aircraft is very close to the ground, major control errors can threaten the safety of flight.

In a sense, then, manual flight control consists of matching the desired with the actual. A quantitative measure of how well the pilot can do this is given by a metric the control theorists call the *bandwidth of the human controller*. The bandwidth of the controller is simply a measure of the frequency region over which the result of the control activity is a close approximation of the intended behavior of the aircraft. Large bandwidths correspond to high frequencies; this simply means that the pilot is able to respond to increasingly rapid disturbances. High bandwidth also corresponds to quick as well as rapid response. A fascinating aspect of human control behavior is that the bandwidth that a given human pilot can achieve is very much a function of both the degree to which the control skill is practiced and the nature of information provided to the pilot about the state of his aircraft and the world outside.

McRuer, Clement, and Allen (1980) illustrate different degrees of the ability to control a system through use of a simple block diagram of the control situation (Figure 9.9). When the pilot is given information only about the direction and size of his control error, he is said to be engaged in *compensatory control*; he can only compensate for an error whether the result of a previous control movement made incorrectly or a disturbance outside the aircraft. Most attitude indicators and flight directors give rise to compensatory control, since the pilot creates control inputs to maintain a particular attitude or flies to minimize the difference between a commanded path and an actual one as indicated by the flight instrument. *Pursuit control*, on the other hand, occurs when the pilot can see separate dynamic indications of, for example, the flight path as well as some indication of where his aircraft is relative to this desired path. Interestingly, the ability to preview or to independently monitor commanded versus actual state variables provides a significant benefit to the control process; the same pilot when performing in pursuit mode may exhibit control bandwidths that are as much as 50% greater than when information is only available to support compensatory control (McRuer et al., 1980). This greater bandwidth can immediately translate into smaller control errors since the pilot is able to respond both more quickly and precisely. Note again that the only difference between the compensatory and pursuit modes is the degree and kind of information

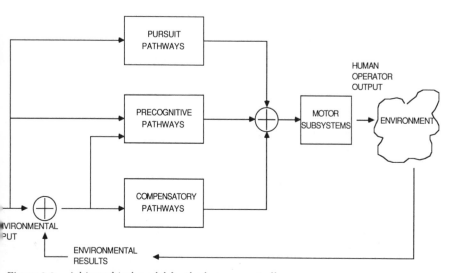

Figure 9.9.   A hierarchical model for the human controller.

displayed to the pilot; neuromuscular or other structural factors inherent to the task remain constant.

An even more precise form of control is possible. *Precognitive control* is said to occur in those circumstances when the pilot is completely familiar with the control or handling characteristics of the aircraft and is given a preview of desired paths and possible disturbances (McRuer et al., 1980). Given these conditions, the pilot is able to execute control movements that are properly timed and sequenced and of the proper magnitude such that even higher control bandwidths are possible, as much as three times that achievable in the purely compensatory mode.

In summary, the ability of a pilot to manually control an aircraft is fundamentally limited by the handling qualities and characteristics of the aircraft as well as basic neuromuscular capabilities of the human. Practice—and increasing skill—can significantly improve performance by allowing higher degrees of control. Just as significant is the provision of information which allows the pilot to anticipate and plan ahead. Thus, the provision of information of the right kind can greatly reduce control errors made even by the most highly skilled pilots. Conversely, without the proper information, even the most highly skilled pilot may be helpless to effect adequate control.

Other factors may dramatically influence control errors. Inattention or improper instrument scanning behavior can result in imprecise control, as can high levels of mental workload. As with many aspects of piloting, repeated practice can create the fundamental skill levels adequate for safe flight. Distractions, high workload levels, fatigue, and other factors may reduce the effective skills to levels where the margins of safety are adversely affected.

Action Slips

As noted earlier, slips are errors made in carrying out an intention. We all make such errors. Driving absentmindedly in the direction of work on the weekend instead of the intended grocery store has happened to all of us at one time or another. Can we predict when such erroneous actions will tend to occur? In a seminal paper, Norman (1981) described a variety of types of slips and the conditions under which they are most likely to occur. In a later report (Norman, 1983), he suggested simple principles that system designers can use to minimize the occurence of slips among skilled performers such as pilots.

In talking about slips, Norman refers to certain learned patterns, or *schemas*, as central to the understanding of when slips become likely. A schema is a sequence of linked behaviors that, through repeated performance or deliberate training, becomes somewhat automatic. Driving to work in the morning becomes quite automatic for many of us, even though if examined closely, it represents a complex set of behaviors. Norman sees much of our more practiced behavior as representing the selective and serial activation of many such schemas or patterns; in skilled behavior, specific schemas are activated at appropriate times. For example, when landing a modern airliner, a specific sequence of steps is appropriate. Although deviations may occur to the nominal sequence because of unusual circumstances (for which other more appropriate schemas may have been learned), each landing tends to resemble the others more often than not. Slips occur when the inappropriate schema is activated or triggered. *Mode errors* are said to occur, for example, when a situation has been misclassified; for example, a pilot may think that the autopilot is in one mode when in fact it is in another. *Capture errors* occur when a sequence being performed is similar to another more frequent or better-learned sequence, and the stronger schema "captures" control of the behavior. In some cases, the intention itself may become forgotten at some intermediate stage of action, but the action sequence, once initiated, is continued, perhaps to an inappropriate conclusion. Again, such errors are both possible and likely for skilled, highly trained performers such as pilots. Other slips may occur when the information that a pilot may normally use to activate a particular action sequence is either ambiguous or undetected. Norman calls such slips *description errors*, since they occur when the appropriate action is not sufficiently described by the system instrumentation. Banks of identical displays or switches invite description errors in which the pilot performs the correct operation on the wrong item (e.g., raising the landing gear rather than flaps after landing).

Norman suggests several design principles to minimize the occurrence of slips. First, the state of the system should always be made unambiguously clear to the system user; this will minimize the occurrence of mode errors. Second, different classes of actions should have dissimilar command sequences; this will make capture and description errors less likely. Actions should be reversible whenever possible; whenever the consequences of an action are particularly significant, the action should be made difficult to do, thus tending to prevent unintentional performance. Finally, systems should be made consistent to the operator. Consistency minimizes the demands on human memory (though consistency can also lead to overly similar action sequences in certain cases).

Although Norman's work was primarily conducted in the context of human interaction with computers, much of it is becoming increasingly relevant to the piloting of modern aircraft. Indeed, as aircraft become more and more automated, pilots are relegated increasingly to functions of management and monitoring, what Sheridan (Chapter 2, this volume) has termed *supervisory control*. In such systems, actions become discrete and can often be displaced in time from the consequences of action. Thus, at the same time that automation may be making flight more efficient, it may be enabling entirely new forms of error. Particularly pernicious are those errors made at a time significantly displaced from the consequences. The pilot who keys in incorrect waypoints to a flight management computer at the beginning of a flight may under certain circumstances not become aware of the error until disaster strikes. It has been suggested that the tragic conclusion to Korean Airline Flight 007 was the result of a programming error of just this type (Wiener, 1985). As an unintended consequence of new forms of automation, therefore, an increasing potential for slips in skilled piloting may ultimately reduce, rather than enhance, levels of flight safety.

Such is not necessarily the case, however. Automation can be designed to have just the opposite effect. Norman (1983) suggests as a general design principle that systems should be made insensitive to errors, since, he argues, we know that people will make them. John Hammer (1984) and colleagues at the Georgia Institute of Technology have further suggested that systems be designed that are not only insensitive to but *tolerant* of error. In a sense, such systems would necessarily be embodied with an expectancy of the kinds of errors that might occur. Because of recent advances in the computer science field known as artificial intelligence, it is no longer beyond the realm of possibility to consider developing such systems. Hammer, for example, has developed a relatively simple system capable of monitoring the behavior of skilled pilots in a general aviation aircraft simulator and detecting errors automatically as deviations from a model of flight procedures. These results have laid the basis for an entirely new approach to the development of advanced aircraft with error-tolerant cockpits; if successful, such designs could significantly increase levels of operational safety.

Concluding Thoughts

It should be clear by now that no completely adequate understanding of human error exists but that significant progress is being made to achieve that understanding. Even our simple framework for discussing error in a systematic fashion should help the reader to better understand the basis for error in the operation of a complex system such as the national airspace system and that the solutions to the error problem must be developed in just such a "systems context." Working on any one component of the system, whether it be the pilots, the machinery, or any of the other human actors, is bound to fail at some level. All these components are interdependent, and changes in any one eventually are reflected in the others. For just this reason, attempts to increase levels of aviation safety solely through the use of automation, as is sometimes suggested, cannot succeed.

This latter point deserves some expansion. The logic of the suggestion seems clear enough: if the human is the cause for the majority of aviation accidents, why not eliminate the source of vulnerability, if only for those kinds of aircraft operation where it might be conceivably done. The answer, in truth, is nearly as straightforward: we cannot eliminate the human (even if we wanted to) because we cannot begin to automate systems well enough to eliminate all those roles that the human pilot currently fills. In fact, at this time, there exists a significant debate within—and without—that field of computer science known as artificial intelligence about whether artificial systems will ever be developed that can function as intelligently as the human (Denning, 1986). If nothing else, it has become clear from this debate that the goal of truly artificial intelligence is nearly as distant as it has been elusive.

On the other hand, it is becoming clear that the technology that has been developed can and must play an increasingly significant role in helping to deal with the problem of human error. I mentioned in an earlier section of this chapter that certain advances in artificial intelligence can provide the basis for a new kind of automation: that which monitors the human and assists the pilot in his role by detecting errors as they are made. The potential for this to dramatically improve safety is heightened by the accident statistics we examined earlier. Nearly a third of the errors that in retrospect led to air carrier accidents over the past several decades may be traced to procedural origins. A reasonable near-term goal is the dramatic reduction of such procedural errors.

Progress, too, is being made in the understanding of how to aid humans to make better decisions, both through training and through machine facilitation or management of the decision process. Although the effective enhancement of the decision-making process of the pilot will no doubt be a slow process (primarily because the general skill level among professional pilots at least is as high as it is today), clearly there exists substantial room—and hope—for improvement. Finally, the understanding of the abilities and limitations of the human as a processor of information can lead to significant insights concerning how best to manage the flow of information in the cockpit and among all segments of the aviation operating system. Since advances in automation and information technology have given the aircraft designer so much flexibility in determining how information may be presented, the hope that this can be done with much greater effectiveness than at present is neither idle nor unwarranted.

I have described the prognosis for improving levels of safety with some optimism. There is also the darker side of this picture. First, although airline deregulation has not yet had the dire consequences that some have predicted for air travel (Nance, 1986), we would not do well to be excessively complacent in this regard. Unprecedented numbers of aircraft and changes in the pilot population are creating conditions that suggest caution. Many in the industry are concerned about the declining experience base of the professional pilot population; with some justification it is felt that this loss of aggregate experience can only have deleterious effects on the margins of safety in the system. Greater numbers of aircraft must mean that the potential for midair conflicts will be greater; unless better separation assurance systems are developed fast enough to keep pace with the growth in traffic, levels of safety in crowded airspace will be depressed. Some of the effects of deregulation are clear, others more subtle. For example, since the era of deregulation began, airlines have been much freerer to establish arrival and departure schedules that reflect public preferences than at any time in the past. The net effect of this is that more aircraft arrive and depart at certain peak times of the day than at others, and more and more airlines attempt to service airport hubs associated with the greatest demands. What may make perfect sense economically may not make the most sense from the perspective of safety. As large airlines strive to stay competitive and small lines strive merely to survive, the indirect expenses of operation (such as safety and maintenance) will inevitably receive the dispassionate scrutiny of financial experts; downward pressures may eventually be felt in system reliability.

Finally, automation, which as we have seen can have a very positive effect on both efficiency and safety, can also have a depressing effect on safety. As pilots are removed from an active role in flying the aircraft, more and more incidents that can only be termed "loss of situational awareness" are reported. The reports are particularly prominent when the automatic systems either fail to perform as the pilots expect them to or, sometimes, fail to perform at all. In these moments, when pilots are not fully aware of their aircraft or of the airspace around them, the system is most vulnerable.

Thus, there is cause for some optimism, but also signs that we must be vigilant. The continued, though slowing, rate of improvement in the overall level of safety is itself cause for optimism; it is clear that modern technology can have salutary influences on levels of system performance. It seems just as clear that changing conditions warrant renewed attention to the resistent problem of human error; the progress that is being made suggests that we may be on the threshold of being able to make significant—and perhaps revolutionary—changes in the direction of greater safety for the flying public and for those whose livelihoods depend on the continued integrity of the national airspace system.

References

Ahumada, A. J., Jr. (1983). Vertical row aimpoint estimation. Unnumbered NASA Technical Memorandum.

Billings, C. E. (1981). Information transfer problems in the aviation system. NASA Technical Paper 1875.

Billings, C. E., & Reynard, W. D. (1984). Human factors in aircraft incidents: Results of a 7-year study. Aviation, Space, and Environmental Medicine, 960–965.

Boeing Commercial Airplane Company (1985). Statistical summary of commercial jet aircraft accidents, worldwide operations, 1959–1984.

Bohlman, L. (1979). Aircraft accidents and the theory of the situation. In Resource management on the flight deck. Proceedings of a NASA/industry workshop. NASA Conference Proceedings 2120.

Card, S., Moran, T., & Newell, A. (1983). The psychology of human–computer interaction. Hillsdale, NJ: Lawrence Erlbaum.

Chanute, O. (1904). Attributed in C. Cerf & V. Navasky (Eds.), The experts speak: The definitive compendium of misinformation. New York: Pantheon Books.

Curry, R. E. (1985). The introduction of new cockpit technology: A human factors study. NASA Technical Memorandum 86659. Moffett Field, CA: NASA-Ames Research Center.

Denning, P. (1986). The science of computing: Will machines ever think? American Scientist, 74, 344–346.

Dreyfus, H., & Dreyfus, S. (1984). Mind over machine. New York: Free Press.

Einhorn, H. J., & Hogarth, R. M. (1978). Confidence in judgment: Persistence in the illusion of validity. Psychological Review, 85, 395–416.

Einhorn, H. J., & Hogarth, R. M. (1981). Behavioral decision theory: Processes of judgment and choice. Annual Review of Psychology, 32, 55–88.

Ferrante, F. (1979). Detection of visual movement through expanding gradient cues. Master's thesis. San Jose State University, CA.

Fitts, P. M., & Jones, R. H. (1947). Analysis of factors contributing to 460 "pilot error" experiences in operating aircraft controls. In H. W. Sinaiki (Ed.), *Selected papers on human factors in the design and use of control systems.* New York: Dover.

Foushee, H. C. (1984). Dyads and triads at 35,000 feet. *American Psychologist, 39,* 885–893.

Foushee, H. C., & Manos, K. L. (1981). Information transfer within the cockpit: Problems in intra-cockpit communications. In C. E. Billings & E. S. Cheaney (Eds.), *Information transfer problems in the Aviation system.* NASA Technical Paper 1875.

Fromkin, V. A. (1980). *Errors in linguistic performance: Slips of the tongue, ear, pen, and hand.* New York: Academic Press.

Green, R. G., & Taylor, R. H. (1979). The psychologist in aircraft accident investigation. In *Human factors aspects of aircraft accidents and incidents.* AGARD Conference Proceedings No. 254.

Hammer, J. (1984). An intelligent flight management aid for procedure execution. *IEEE Transactions on Systems, Man, and Cybernetics, SMC-14,* 885–888.

Howard, I. P. (1982). *Human visual orientation.* Chichester: Wiley.

International Civil Aviation Organization (1984). *Accident prevention manual* (1st ed.). ICAO Doc 9422-AN/923.

Johnson, S. L., & Roscoe, S. N. (1972). What moves, the airplane or the world? *Human Factors, 14,* 107–129.

Klein, G. (1985). *Hyper-rationality.* Unpublished manuscript.

Knott, K. (1984). *Simulated night landing approaches and aim point performance under aerosol and electronically generated fog displays.* Master's thesis, San Jose State University, CA.

Kraft, C. L. (1978). A psychophysical contribution to air safety: Simulation studies of visual illusions in night visual approaches. In H. A. Pick, H. W. Liebowitz, J. E. Singer, A. Schneider, & H. W. Stevenson (Eds.), *Psychology: From research to practice.* New York: Plenum Press.

Lauber, J. K., & Foushee, H. C. (1981). *Guidelines for line-oriented flight training* (Vols. 1 and 2). NASA Conference Proceeding 2120.

Lopes, L. (1983). Some thoughts on the psychological concept of risk. *Journal of Experimental Psychology, 9,* 137–144.

McGreevy, M., & Ellis, S. (1986). The effect of perspective geometry on judged direction in spatial information instruments. *Human Factors, 28,* 439–456.

McRuer, D., Clement, W., & Allen, W. (1980). *A theory of human error.* NASA Contractor Report 166313. Moffett Field, CA: NASA-Ames Research Center.

Mertens, H. (1978). Comparison of the visual perception of a runway model in pilots and non-pilots during simulated night visual landings. *Aviation, Space, and Environmental Medicine,* 457–460.

Mertens, H. (1981). Perception of runway image shape and approach angle magnitude by pilots in simulated night landing approaches. *Aviation, Space, and Environmental Medicine,* 373–386.

Monan, W. P. (1983). *Addressee problems in ATC communications: The call sign problem.* NASA Contractor Report 166462. Moffett Field, CA: NASA-Ames Research Center.

Monan, W. P. (1986). *Human factors in aviation operations: The hearback problem.* NASA Contractor Report 177398. Moffett Field, CA: NASA-Ames Research Center.

Nance, J. J. (1986). *Blind trust.* New York: Morrow.

Nisbett, R., & Ross, L. (1980). *Human inference: Strategies and shortcomings of social judgment.* Englewood Cliffs, NJ: Prentice-Hall.

Nisbett, R. E., Krantz, D. H., Jepson, C., & Dunda, Z. (1983). The use of statistical heuristics in everyday reasoning. *Psychological Review, 90,* 339–363.

Norman, D. A. (1981). Categorization of action slips. *Psychological Review, 78,* 1–15.

Norman, D. A. (1983). Design rules based on analyses of human error. *Communications of the ACM, 26,* 254–258.

Perrone, J. A. (1984). Visual slant misperception and the 'black hole' landing situation. *Aviation, Space, and Environmental Medicine,* 1020–1025.

Reason, J. T. (1986). Current errors in process environments: some implications for the design of intelligent support systems. In E. Hollnagel, G. Mancini, & D. Woods (Eds.), *Intelligent decision support in process environments.* Berlin: Springer-Verlag.

Reynard, W. D., Billings, C. E., Cheaney, E., & Hardy, R. (1986). *The development of the NASA aviation safety reporting system.* NASA Reference Publication No. 1114.

Roscoe, S. N. (1968). Airborne displays for flight and navigation. *Human Factors, 10,* 321–332.

Rouse, W. B., & Rouse, S. H. (1984). Analysis and classification of human error. *IEEE Transactions on Systems, Man, and Cybernetics, SMC-13,* 539–549.

Ruffell Smith, H. P. (1979). *A simulator study of the interaction of pilot workload with errors, vigilance, and decisions.* NASA Technical Memorandum 78482.

Sears, R. L. (1986). *A new look at accident contributions and the implications of operational and training procedures.* Unpublished report. Boeing Commercial Airplane Company.

Singleton, R. T. (1972). Techniques for determining the causes of error. *Applied Ergonomics, 3,* 126–131.

Slovic, P., Fischof, B., & Lichtens, S. (1978). Behavioral decision theory. *Annual Review of Psychology, 28,* 1–39.

Tversky, A., & Kahneman, D. (1973). Availability: A heuristic for judgment frequency probability. *Cognitive Psychology, 5,* 207–232.

Tversky, A., & Kahneman, D. (1974). Judgment under uncertainty: Heuristics and biases. *Science, 211,* 453–458.

Tversky, A., & Kahneman, D. (1981). The framing of decisions and the psychology of choice. *Science, 211,* 453–458.

Wiener, E. L. (1985a). Beyond the sterile cockpit. *Human Factors, 27,* 75–90.

Wiener, E. L. (1985b). *Human factors of cockpit automation: A field study of flight crew transition.* NASA Contractor Report 177333. Moffett Field, CA: NASA-Ames Research Center.

Witkin, R. (1986, January 19). Almost perfect is a failing grade. *New York Times,* p. 10.

Woods, D. (1986). Paradigms for intelligent decision support. In E. Hollnagel, G. Mancini, & D. Woods (Eds.), *Intelligent decision support in process environments.* Berlin: Springer-Verlag.

World Aviation Directory, Volume 1. (1986, summer). Washington, DC: News Group Publications.

Aircrew Fatigue and Circadian Rhythmicity

10

R. Curtis Graeber

Introduction

Tiredness is experienced by all of us almost every day of our lives. It varies in its intensity but is a familiar, sometimes welcome feeling which is rarely given serious thought. Often we are free to take time to sleep or rest; if not, we may find that our effectiveness is diminished, but not our safety. Unfortunately, this is not the case for those who fly airplanes.

Since the infancy of aviation, pilots have been keenly aware of the dangers lurking in the shadow of fatigue. Charles Lindbergh came close to not completing his 1927 New York to Paris flight when he fell asleep and woke to find himself slowly descending toward the cold Atlantic. Wiley Post was so concerned about the potential sleep loss and fatigue associated with crossing time zones that he totally readjusted his daily living pattern before departure to match Moscow time, the midway point of his pioneering global flight (Post & Gatty, 1931).

Although the greatest fear may be that of falling asleep at the controls, most pilots recognize that the less extreme effects of fatigue can jeopardize flight safety just as seriously. All too often a pilot returns in the evening from a long trip, only to land "wheels up" because he forgot to lower the landing gear. Similar tales attributed to crew fatigue are common among today's commercial and military flight crews. The following report to NASA's Aviation Safety Reporting System (ASRS) from a captain of a wide-body commercial jet is typical:

> Landed at [a large midwestern] airport without landing clearance, discovered when switching radios to ground control. Had very early final contact with approach control (20 mi. out at 7000 ft.). [Causal factors included] my involvement in monitoring an inexperienced first officer, crew fatigue, cockpit duties and procedures at requested changeover point. However, the primary factor was crew fatigue caused by late night departure (0230 local time), inability to rest prior to departure (both pilots attempted afternoon naps without success), long duty period (11.5 hrs duty time with enroute stop at JFK), also, my primary concentration on flying by first officer with low heavy aircraft experience. Also, very clear weather made traffic conditions readily apparent, reducing my awareness of ATC needs. . . . Both pilots were having trouble throughout the let down and approach phases of this last leg of the trip remembering altitudes cleared to, frequencies, and even runway cleared to.

Reports such as this are neither isolated nor rare. In 1980 Lyman and Orlady analyzed the ASRS data base for air transport crew error reports that were directly attributed to fatigue. They found that 77 (3.8%) reports qualified out of the 2006 received since 1976 (Lyman & Orlady, 1980). The authors were careful to point out, however, that this relatively small proportion most likely underestimated the frequency of fatigue-related errors because fatigue is frequently a personal experience. While one crew member may attribute an error to fatigue, another may report a more directly perceived cause such as inattention or miscommunication. This could also result from the common belief that fatigue is not an acceptable excuse for an error because flying when tired is so much a part of the pilot profession. When Lyman and Orlady included all reports that mentioned factors directly or indirectly related to fatigue, the number increased to 426, or 21.2%. Not surprisingly, the fatigue-related incidents tended to occur more frequently between midnight and 0600 hours and during the descent, approach, and landing phases of flight. The significant implications of these data for flight safety lie in the fact that the large majority of these reports consisted of substantive, potentially unsafe incidents, and not just minor errors in airmanship.

Since 1980, air transport error reports directly associated with fatigue have continued to increase in the ASRS data base. An additional 261 such reports were received from crew members during the 4-year period from July 1980 through July 1984. Similarly, the United Kingdom's corresponding safety reporting system (CHIRP) received 52 reports citing problems of sleep, fatigue, and rostering during its first 18 months of operation since 1983.

Why should such potentially unsafe situations ever arise among professional flight crews? Numerous explanations can be put forth, from poorly designed duty schedules or unanticipated operational delays, to pilots who report for duty without proper rest. This chapter explores the various factors which contribute to fatigue or sleepiness in the cockpit, focusing on those which stem from our basic biological heritage. Recent scientific advances in our understanding of such factors is explored in search of helpful hints for preventing the problem. The importance of these factors for improving flight safety and maintaining operational efficiency may be increasing with our rapid progress in flight-deck automation and its potential for inducing boredom on long flights, particularly in two-person crews.

Nature of the Problem: The Limits of Endurance

The Biological Clock

In the early days of aviation, fatigue was viewed primarily as a function of total flight time and workload intensity. Such a view was certainly reasonable given that most flying was accomplished during the day. With the advent of frequent night flying and transoceanic aircraft, the need has arisen for a more comprehensive view of pilot fatigue. Flight time and workload cannot account for the increases in fatigue experienced by crews operating throughout the night or across multiple time zones. The additional factor of biological rhythmicity must be considered. Similarly, the effectiveness of flight crew rest time cannot be separated from the influence of the internal biological clock which programs our bodies to behave differently at different times of the day. A brief review of some key physiological concepts should provide the necessary background to understand why this is so.

Telling time is a skill most of us learn at an early age, often before we learn to read. Clocks make it easy to mark the passage of time and to anticipate when certain events are likely to occur. Thus, clocks help us plan for appropriate and effective action. Similarly, our vertebrate ancestors were able to survive and evolve partly because of their instinctive ability to tell time and plan ahead for periodic environmental events. Evidence of this innate biological clock is seen in the tidal movements of fish and crustaceans, in the seasonal migration of birds, and in the hibernation habits of certain mammals. Most of all it is reflected in the sleep–wake cycles and daily feeding habits of all animal life.

Humans are no exception. As part of our evolutionary heritage, we have inherited a biological clock (in fact, maybe two, but more about that later). It is the source of the *circadian rhythms* which are known to exist throughout human physiology. These rhythms have a period of *about* 24 hours (*circa*, about; *dies*, day) and are seen as measurable and stable daily fluctuations—sometimes greater than 50% of the daily mean—in variables such as body temperature, blood pressure, heart rate, sensory acuity, adrenal gland output, brain neurotransmitter levels, and cell division (Luce, 1971; Moore-Ede, Sulzman, & Fuller, 1982). They are both ubiquitous and persistent but should not be confused with the recently discredited theory of "biorhythms" (Brown, 1982; Klein & Wegmann, 1980).

Circadian rhythms are also manifested in a variety of human behaviors when measured by standard techniques at different times of day. Undoubtedly a number of these contributed to the circadian variation shown in Figure 10.1 for experienced pilots flying F-104 simulators (Klein et al., 1970). Significant rhythmic variations can be seen in overall flying skill and in each independent flight parameter as a function of the time of day, with poorer performance prevailing during the early morning hours.

Circadian Desynchronization

Before the widespread use of electric lights, humans typically lived in harmony with their circadian system, working during the day and sleeping at night; however, this pattern is much less common today. Each year increasing numbers of shiftworkers must work at times that conflict with their circadian rhythms. Pilots in particular must be able to perform safely and effectively at various times of the day or night. Additional stress results from the substantial irregularity of flight crew duty hours in comparison to those of industrial shiftworkers. As Figure 10.2 shows, this is true even for those short-haul crews whose trip patterns cross no more than one time zone. There are wide daily variations in the number and timing of flights

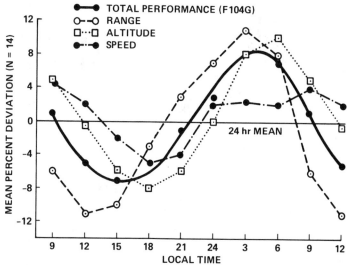

Figure 10.1. Circadian rhythm in mean performance of 14 experienced military pilots on an F-104G simulator. Based on standard 24-minute flights at 300 miles/hour in a circular pattern (25 mi radius) at 2500 feet with a 200 miles/hour wind which changed direction continuously through 360° twice during each flight. Performance is displayed as percentage of the 24-hour mean deviation from preset flight parameters. Total performance = sum of the three performance variables. From "Circadian Rhythm of Pilot's Efficiency and Effects of Multiple Time Zone Travel" by Klein et al., 1970, *Aerospace Medicine, 41*, p. 125. Copyright 1970 by the Aerospace Medical Association. Reprinted by permission.

both within and between such trips, requiring crews to frequently alter their work–rest schedules.

Given the evolutionary legacy and pervasiveness of circadian rhythmicity, it is not surprising that most pilots have difficulty countering its influence. One is tempted to paraphrase a well-worn comment on aviation, "If God had intended for man to work or sleep at any hour of the day or night, He would have disconnected his clock!" Unfortunately, the technology for overcoming this human handicap lags far behind that for overcoming our lack of wings.

While the body clock is inherently capable of monitoring the passage of time, it differs from most clocks in that its period is flexible (within a very limited range) and must therefore be properly set, or synchronized, before it can accurately predict the timing of periodic environmental events. This synchronization is accomplished through entrainment by external sychronizers or zeitgebers (time givers),

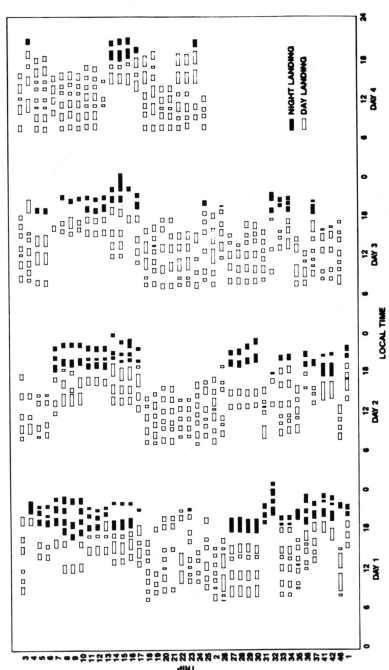

Figure 10.2. Sequence of flight segments for selected short-haul trips flown within the eastern United States by twin-jet aircraft operated by two commercial carriers. Most trips were 3 or 4 days in length and were selected for a study of fatigue among short-haul crew members.

which themselves are cyclic, usually with a period of 24 hours. For animals, cycles such as sunrise–sunset, ambient temperature, and food availability are important zeitgebers. For humans, social time cues such as interpersonal communication, work schedules, or group activities are more important, partly as a result of our widespread use of artificial lighting (Moore-Ede et al., 1982; Wever, 1979).

When an individual flies from one time zone to another, his or her body clock and the rhythms it controls must resynchronize to the local geophysical and social zeitgebers of the destination time zone. Eastward flights shorten the day and require a phase advance, while westward flights lengthen the day and require a phase delay. The impairment of well-being and performance experienced after transmeridian flight is in large part the result of the circadian system's inability to adjust rapidly to sudden shifts in the timing of its zeitgebers. In effect, the system resists changes in its timing and stability. Consequently, complete resynchronization of the biological timing system can often take up to several days.

The number of time zones crossed determines the extent of the phase shift and can also influence the direction of shift. For example, intuitively it should not make any difference whether the body clock's period is lengthened or shortened by 12 hours after a flight across 12 time zones. Either process should be equally effective in resetting it. Accordingly, if fewer than twelve time zones are crossed in the westward direction, resynchronization is accomplished more rapidly by a phase delay similar to the zeitgeber shift. The situation is quite different after eastward flight. Instead of advancing the biological clock to match the shortened daylength of eastward flight, many travelers' rhythms exhibit a counterintuitive and complementary phase delay after crossing only eight or nine eastward time zones, that is, some of their circadian rhythms adjust by lengthening their periods across 15 hours until they "lock onto" destination time (Gander, Myhre, Graeber, Andersen, & Lauber, 1985; Klein & Wegmann, 1980). As a result, some rhythms are advancing (e.g., adrenal hormones), while others (e.g., body temperature) are delaying to reach the same realignment with the new local zeitgebers. This phenomenon, known as resynchronization by partition, can probably be attributed to the entrainment properties of the biological clock, which has a natural tendency to lengthen its period beyond 24 hours (Wever, 1979).

The same tendency may also be responsible for the well-documented directional asymmetry in resychronization rate. In all studies where comparisons can be made, subjects' rhythms readjust faster after westward flight than after eastward flight, regardless of the variable under study (Aschoff, Hoffman, Pohl, & Wever, 1975; Graeber, 1982; Klein & Wegmann, 1980). Furthermore, this asymmetry occurs irrespective of the relative direction of flight (outgoing or homegoing) or whether the flight takes place during the day or night (Klein, Wegmann, & Hunt, 1972b). It would not be surprising that this biological advantage, coupled with the avoidance of flying into sunrises, may be responsible for the preference of many pilots to fly westward rather than eastward, especially when operating globally (Preston & Bateman, 1970).

Normally, when we are living at home, our circadian system resembles a finely tuned symphony, each rhythm rising and falling, not at the same time, but at its own prescribed time in harmony with one another. This internal synchronization does not persist after transmeridian flight. Even though our myriad circadian rhythms are timed by only one or two clocks, they all do not resynchronize together. Different rhythms adjust to the new zeitgebers at different rates, some lagging more than others. As a result, the jet lag which flight crews experience is symptomatic of both external desynchronization (when the timing of their circadian rhythms is not appropriate for local time) and internal desynchronization (when their readjusting internal rhythms are no longer in phase with each other). A third component is the sleep loss that results from the combined influence of both types of desynchronization.

Sleep and Sleepiness

The nature of the biological clock has been studied most thoroughly in time-isolation laboratories where all external zeitgebers are either removed or carefully manipulated. Such control allows the clock to reveal its natural operating characteristics uncontaminated by time cues, that is, to free run. Under such conditions the human circadian system consistently behaves as if it is controlled by not one, but two biological clocks. Volunteer subjects living in temporal isolation for several weeks start out sleeping and waking on a 24-hour schedule but soon spontaneously begin to lengthen their "day" up to as long as 48 hours without any awareness of doing so (Colin, Timbal, Boutelier, Houdas, & Siffre, 1968; Wever, 1979); however, their circadian rhythm of body temperature increases its period only slightly, to about 25 hours, and remains there despite the much longer rest–activity cycle.

Such lengthening of the subjective day reveals an important fact for understanding the problems of shifted sleep–wake cycles in aviation. Usually we go to sleep late in the evening soon after the temperature rhythm begins to decline and wake up in the morning just after it begins to rise, but free-running subjects with their longer "days" go to bed at varying phases of the temperature cycle and thereby enable us to examine the influence of the circadian rhythm on sleep. Their data indicate that the duration and quality of sleep differ depending on when sleep occurs within the body temperature cycle.

As shown in Figure 10.3, these subjects sleep for longer periods when they go to sleep near the temperature peak and for much shorter periods when they retire near the temperature trough. Thus, contrary to most expectations, it is the timing of sleep, not the amount of time awake, that is the critical factor controlling sleep duration in this situation. Also, dream (known as rapid eye movement, or REM) sleep appears to be coupled to the temperature trough, so that the timing of REM sleep within the sleep period again depends on when sleep occurs. Going to sleep near the peak results in most REM sleep occurring in the second half of the sleep span, whereas going to

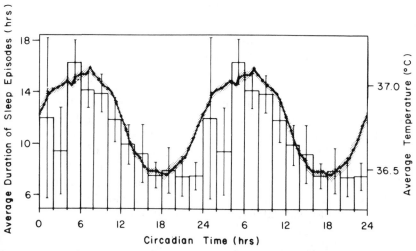

Figure 10.3. Sleep duration as function of the time of sleep onset in relation to the phase of the circadian body temperature rhythm in free-running subjects living in a time isolation environment. From "Human Sleep: Its Duration and Organization Depend on Its Circadian Phase" by Czeisler et al., 1980, *Science, 210*, p. 1264. Copyright 1980 by the American Association for the Advancement of Science. Reprinted by permission.

sleep near the low point in temperature results in a shift of REM sleep to the first half of the sleep span (Czeisler, Weitzman, Moore-Ede, Zimmerman, & Knauer, 1980; Zulley, Wever, & Aschoff, 1981).

Why are such findings important for planning crew rest? One reason is that they explain why sleep at certain body clock times can be more disturbed and less refreshing than sleep at the usual (i.e., home) body time. Conversely, they also explain why crew members sometimes report sleeping for extremely long durations after crossing several time zones. While pilots often attribute such lengthy sleeps to being excessively tired, it is likely that the timing of the sleep in relation to a crew member's altered circadian cycle helps to prolong sleep beyond its usual limit.

Another implication of this research concerns the optimal duration of layovers for obtaining crew rest. There is little doubt that the amount of sleep obtainable, even under ideal environmental circumstances, will depend on when sleep is attempted. If sleep is attempted when the body temperature rhythm is rising, the crew member will have considerably more difficulty getting to sleep and, if successful, will usually awaken within a relatively short time. Consequently, the timing of a layover and the adequacy of the accommodations for obtaining sleep at any local time of day may be more critical than layover length for assuring proper rest before departure.

Just as sleep is partly controlled by our biological clock, sleepiness is also influenced by the internal timing system. As shown in Figure 10.4, there is a consistent rhythmic pattern in our tendency to fall asleep, even during the daytime hours when individuals are living in accordance with their normal routines (Richardson, Carskadon, Orav, & Dement, 1982). These findings are based on the Multiple Sleep Latency Test (MSLT), a procedure designed to measure a person's physiological sleepiness by removing the usual types of external stimuli and activities that often maintain alertness during the day. Subjects are put to bed in a quiet, dark room and instructed to close their eyes and try falling asleep. The test is terminated after the first 90 seconds of EEG-validated sleep or after 20 minutes if no sleep occurs.

In this soporific environment both old and young subjects fall asleep most quickly at two distinct, but remarkably consistent, times within a 24-hour period (Figure 10.4). Notice that they also recover from the mid-afternoon period (about 1530 hours) of maximal daytime sleepiness (i.e., short sleep latencies) to reach a peak of alertness between 1930 and 2130 hours. This peak is equivalent to that

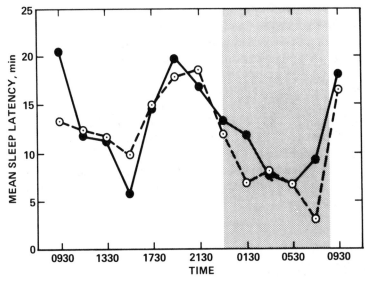

Figure 10.4.   Mean sleep latencies for eight young (mean age 21 yr) and ten old (mean age 70 yr) subjects who received the MSLT during the day followed by four brief awakenings at 2-hour intervals during the night (shaded). After 15 minutes of being kept awake, the latency to return to sleep was measured. From "Circadian Variation in Sleep Tendency in Elderly and Young Subjects" by Richardson et al., 1982, *Sleep, 5* (suppl. 2) p. s82. Copyright 1982 by Raven Press. Reprinted by permission.

exhibited at 0930 in the morning just after a night's sleep. Since essentially no rest is provided by the MSLT procedure, this dramatic recovery is clearly spontaneous and provides strong evidence for the controlling influence of the biological clock over our underlying levels of sleepiness.

While many experts do not necessarily equate sleepiness with fatigue, the former is viewed by most aviation professionals as the most operationally significant aspect of fatigue. A recent analysis of single-vehicle road accidents in rural Texas strongly supports this view. When the incidence of such accidents was tabulated by time of day, a distinct peak was found to occur at 1500 hours for drivers over 46 years of age (Langlois, Smolensky, Hsi, & Weir, 1985). This peak rose gradually from a morning low at 1000 hours and then smoothly descended to an evening low at 1900 hours, a pattern remarkably similar to the inverse of the MSLT curves in Figure 10.4. The accident rate rose and fell with the predicted increases and decreases in daytime sleepiness.

The operational implications of these data should be obvious to anyone concerned about aviation safety and flight crew performance efficiency. The soporific qualities of the cockpit during long flight segments, particularly at night over water, are well known to experienced pilots. Fortunately, the MSLT data reveal that these periods of maximal sleepiness are reliably predictable. Consequently, crew members should be able to anticipate these periods and plan for their occurrence. This should be especially easy for short-haul pilots whose circadian rhythms are not disturbed by the crossing of multiple time zones.

After the review of some current data on sleep loss and fatigue, the relevance of these findings to flight crews will become more apparent to the reader, as will their potential application for the improved management of crew rest.

Short-Haul Operational Studies

Background

As part of a comprehensive program examining fatigue in line operations, our laboratory has been conducting a series of field studies on commercial flight crews. Most previous studies have focused on long-haul crews by using sleep logs and self-ratings of fatigue before and after flight. Small sample sizes and the lack of the appropriate baseline and recovery data have limited their applicability towards interpreting the effects of different schedules (Graeber, Foushee, & Lauber, 1984).

Only one study has seriously attempted to determine the effects of short-haul flying. Klein and his colleagues (Klein, Bruner, Kuklinski, Ruff, & Wegmann, 1972a) monitored eleven B-737 crews across 3-day trips consisting of a 0600–1400 schedule or a 1200–2300 schedule. Focusing on standard physiological stress, they found flight-related increases in pulse and breathing rate comparable to those reported for other moderate workload activities (e.g., intense administrative work or driving a car for a long distance). Since the amount of increase remained at 15–20% over rest values throughout the trip, they concluded that there was no accumulation of stress. Supplementary data on urinary stress hormones generally supported this finding in that any increases in concentration were directly related to increases in workload. Despite the lack of cumulative effects, the study did find that stress hormones were elevated during each night's sleep, thereby suggesting that the psychophysiological impact of short-haul trips is substantial enough so as not to dissipate overnight.

Unfortunately, the generalizability of these findings to other short-haul operations may be limited by the young age of the German crews (captains' average age was 32.2 years, first officers' average age was 26.8 years) and by the relatively undemanding number of flight segments (three to five per day). The importance of the latter factor was pointed out by Ruffell Smith (1967), who reported similar increases in heart rate in captains flying short-haul flights in Trident aircraft. Although lacking data on cumulative effects, he emphasized that the highly variable heart rates seen during approach and landing warranted the inclusion of the number of daily flights as a stress factor in designing cockpit crew schedules.

Field Study Design

A major objective of our work is to determine the psychological and physiological responses of individual pilots to short-haul flight schedules, with an emphasis on documenting circadian rhythms, sleep, and subjective state. The monthly schedules of two U. S. carriers were scanned to identify trips which included some combination of early morning or late evening departures, long duty days, many segments, long en route layovers, or minimal overnight rests. Crews assigned to these trips were then contacted and asked to volunteer as anonymous participants, and 85% agreed to do so.

While field research offers the advantage of operational face validity, the inherent richness of uncontrolled variables can often threaten its scientific usefulness. The study's scope and size had to be sufficient, in terms of subjects and flights, to provide meaningful conclusions that would be applicable to most short-haul jet transport operations. Consequently, we spent 2 years studying 74 pilots flying a total of 731 flight segments across 40 different trips in DC-9 and B-737 aircraft throughout the eastern United States. These trips lasted 3 or 4 days and included up to eight landings per day (Figure 10.2). Duty schedules consisted primarily of daytime flights with early morning departures, late afternoon and evening flights, or a switch from one type of schedule to the other within a trip. Total daily duty time ranged from 1 to 14 hours but usually equalled 10 or more hours (Figure 10.5) with the average flight lasting approximately 1 hour. Trips were distributed throughout the seasons in a wide variety of weather conditions, with each pattern including one or more days of flying in high-density airspace. Crew members ranged in age

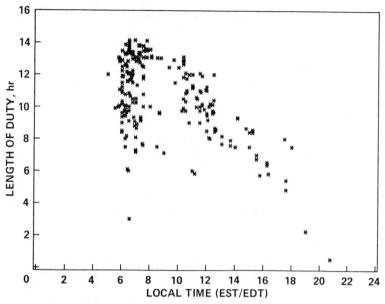

Figure 10.5.   Length of duty days sampled in NASA short-haul field study as a function of on-duty start time.

from 25 to 56 years, with captains averaging 46 years and copilots averaging 36 years.

Data collection began up to 2 days prior to departure and lasted up to 3 days post-trip. Subjects wore a small solid-state monitor that recorded heart rate, rectal temperature, and wrist activity every 2 minutes around the clock. In addition, they maintained a daily log to document sleep and other activities along with ratings of mood and fatigue every 2 hours. Information was also obtained on experience, life-style, personality, and sleep habits. Operational data was gathered by a trained cockpit observer.

Sleep Loss, Sleep Quality, and Fatigue

Short-haul pilots are vulnerable to fatigue for a variety of reasons, some individually determined and others more operationally driven. Several important findings have already emerged regarding both types of factors (Gander, Graeber, Foushee, Lauber, & Connell, 1988; Graeber, 1985). In general, we found that short-haul crews became more fatigued as they progressed through a trip. As Figure 10.6 shows, most of the increase in fatigue occurred after Day 1 of flying

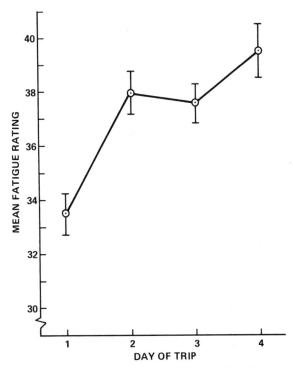

Figure 10.6.   Mean subjective fatigue ratings (± SE) for 74 short-haul crew members
on successive days of a 3- or 4-day trip. Means are based on ratings
made on a 100 mm analog scale (from 0 = alert to 100 = drowsy) every
2 hours throughout the day whenever subjects were awake.

followed by a more gradual increase on Day 4. Although this might
suggest that fatigue would be even greater on the last day of a 4-day
trip than on the last day of a 3-day trip, statistical analysis did not
support such a conclusion—4-day trips did not appear to be any
more tiring than 3-day trips. Furthermore, there was no significant
difference between 3- and 4-day trips in the mean fatigue rating on
the third duty day.

Together, these findings suggest that flight crews may be able to
pace themselves or somehow anticipate at the beginning of a trip the
fatigue they will experience over the length of the trip. Consequently, they may feel equally tired at the end of trips of different scheduled lengths. This is not to say that trip length is not an important
operational factor contributing to fatigue. For instance, it is possible
that trips of 5 or 6 days would have produced further increments in
fatigue, as the trend in Figure 10.6 suggests. The concept of pacing

also underscores the potential crew rest problems associated with requesting additional duty when crew availability is compromised by
weather or mechanical breakdowns. Substantially more fatigue might
be experienced on Day 4, when a crew flying a scheduled 3-day trip
is asked unexpectedly on Day 3 to fly one more day.

One obvious reason for anticipating such an outcome is the
amount of sleep loss experienced during trips. As Figure 10.7 shows,
the crew members reported sleeping about an hour less per night
during layovers than at home. Particularly striking is the shorter
amount of sleep obtained at home during the night before reporting
for duty (wake-up, Day 21). These pilots went to bed at their usual
time and therefore did not compensate for waking up unusually early the next day in order to report on time. As a result, they typically
began the trip with a sleep deficit, some of which was reduced on
the first layover night (wake-up, Day 22). A similar behavior pattern
also explains a substantial amount of the sleep loss that accumulated
during the trips. The crews went to sleep slightly later (about 30
minutes) and woke up considerably earlier (about 75 minutes) on
trips compared to at home. As is discussed later, this change in the

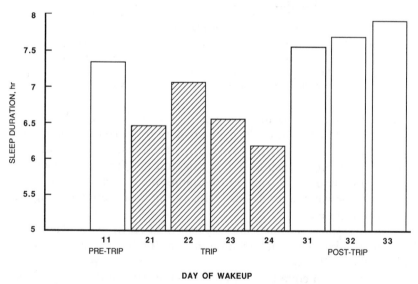

DAY OF WAKEUP

Figure 10.7.   Mean self-reported sleep durations during successive short-haul trip
days (21 to 24) compared to sleep at home before (Day 11) and after the
trip (Days 31 to 33). Values are plotted according to the day of wake-up,
so that the duration for Day 21 represents sleep obtained at home on the
night before reporting for duty (N = 74).

timing of sleep represents the combined effects of individual pilot behavior and the impact of overnight rest scheduling.

The crew members' sleep is not only shorter but also more fragmented during trips than at home. This source of sleep loss was documented in the report of significantly more awakenings (about 50%) during hotel layovers than during the two prior nights at home. The actual number of awakenings was most likely higher than reported since individuals are usually not aware of brief transient arousals or else do not remember them upon arising. Since such sleep disruption is known to produce less restful sleep and increased levels of daytime sleepiness (Stepanski, Lamphere, Badia, Zorick, & Roth, 1984), it is not surprising to find that the crews also rated their trip sleep as poorer than sleep at home either before or after the trip (Figure 10.8). The validity of these sleep ratings is supported by the fact that high levels of activity and heart rate during sleep were significantly correlated with poorer sleep ratings. Higher activity levels were also associated with shorter sleep durations, while higher heart rates were recorded when sleep was more fragmented. Thus, both the subjective and objective measures of sleep quality reinforce the finding of poorer sleep during layovers.

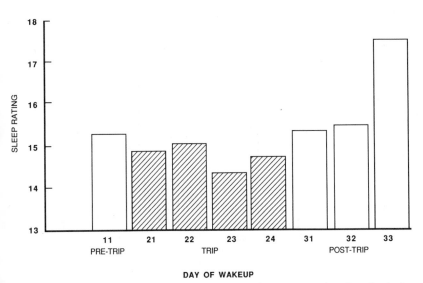

Figure 10.8.   Mean subjective sleep-quality ratings during successive short-haul trip days compared to sleep at home before and after the trip. Ratings are based on the combined answers to four questions, each according to a 5-point scale (4 = poorest quality, 20 = highest quality).

Compensating for Fatigue

Further evidence for the increases in fatigue and sleep loss during short-haul trips was seen in the incidence of napping both during and after the trip. As shown in Figure 10.9, the frequency of napping began to increase on the second day of the trip and reached a sharp peak during the first day home. These naps, plus the return to pretrip sleep durations, support the conclusion that the trips induced enough sleep loss to elicit compensatory sleep when crew members were able to obtain it.

The other approach to counteracting sleep loss is to mask fatigue by inducing a more alert state through stimulation. The use of caffeine and tobacco for this purpose is legendary among flight crews (McFarland, 1941). Thus, it is not too surprising to find that these pilots drank significantly more caffeinated beverages during trips compared to home and did so primarily during the first few hours after waking or during the late evening. Furthermore, their average daily intake increased as the trip progressed, reaching the highest level on the last day of a 4-day trip. Although only 16.7% of the subjects

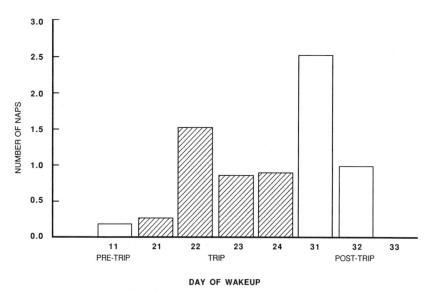

Figure 10.9.   Mean number of self-reported naps during successive short-haul trip days compared to days at home before and after the trip. For each subject, the number of daily naps was normalized with respect to the mean daily number of naps for that subject across the entire study.

smoked during the study, for those that did, the incidence of smoking also increased gradually with successive days on the trip, so that an average increment of over 50% was observed by the fourth day of duty.

The off-duty use of alcohol to aid relaxation and sleep is common practice among flight crews in most types of operations. In this regard, the influence of trips on alcohol consumption was particularly noteworthy. Subjects drank significantly more alcohol while on trips than at home. Since alcohol was consumed only in the evening, this was true for all days except the last day, when the evening was spent at home. Higher intake of alcohol was significantly correlated with higher heart rates, but not activity, during sleep; however, it is difficult to determine whether this relationship reflects an effect of alcohol on the cardiovascular system or whether both increases are due to the stresses that Klein et al. (1972a) showed to be associated with short-haul flight operations. The impact of alcohol on crew rest deserves further attention because of the known potential for alcohol to disturb REM sleep and thereby detrimentally affect sleep quality (Knowles, Laverty, & Kuechler, 1968; Yules, Lippman, & Freedman, 1967).

Operational Factors

The analysis of operational variables has so far been limited to scheduling factors and their impact on layover sleep and subjective fatigue. Correlational statistics revealed that the number of daily flight segments was the one factor consistently related to sleep quality. Flying more segments led to increased sleep duration and more restful sleep that night, as measured by lower heart rates and activity during sleep, and higher sleep-quality ratings after wake-up. These relationships were valid for increases up to six or seven flights per day. Two additional findings support the interpretation that the intensity of the duty day has more impact on sleep quality than does length of the duty day. First, the number of daily flight hours, but not duty hours, was significantly associated with longer sleep durations. Second, poorer sleep ratings were correlated with increases in the amount of en route stopover time (i.e., duty time minus flight time). In other words, less demanding duty days were accompanied by shorter and poorer sleep that night.

The timing of layover sleep on trips was also related to duty schedules. In contrast to the pre-trip night at home, crew members went to bed earlier if they had an early report day, but still not early enough to compensate for sleep loss in the morning. They also got up later if they got off duty later the previous night or reported later the next day. Because a higher number of flight segments was associated with later morning report times and longer layovers, it is likely that at least part of the positive relationship between sleep duration and intensity of prior duty may be attributable to the scheduling of relatively later departures the following day.

Similar analyses of the subjective fatigue ratings given at the end of the duty day (2000 to 2400 hours) failed to reveal any significant relationships with such scheduling parameters as duty times, flight hours, daily segments, or en route stopovers. The only trends that approached significance were for earlier on-duty times and a higher number of flight segments to be associated with higher fatigue ratings. While the lack of significant relationships may seem surprising compared to the sleep findings, it should be noted that some of the effects of scheduling on perceived fatigue would result from the impact on post-duty sleep and therefore would not manifest themselves until the next morning.

Individual Attributes

Individual attributes have typically been ignored in previous attempts to examine crew fatigue. It now appears that such factors may influence considerably how well a pilot sleeps and how rested he feels. Perhaps the most unexpected finding is the relationship between personality and the impact of trips on crew members. Both fatigue ratings and various measures of layover sleep quality were correlated with the results of personality questionnaires. One of these, the Personal Attributes Questionnaire (Spence & Helmreich, 1978), has been used extensively in the group performance context (see Foushee & Helmreich, Chapter 7, this volume). It yields scores on "instrumentality" (I) as well as "expressiveness" (E). Those who score high on the former tend to be very performance or goal oriented, decisive, and capable of getting the job done. Those who score high on the latter are more group oriented and tend to be sensitive to the needs of others, warm in interpersonal relationships, and communicative. Those who score high on both scales (I + E) are more effective in group problem-solving situations and tend to adapt better when the situation calls for flexibility.

Statistical analyses revealed that crew members who scored high on I + E also reported significantly less overall fatigue on trips and exhibited fewer negative mood changes. Of course, one interpretation of such results might be that they are self-fulfilling because a subject's personality could influence his own self-assessments of mood and fatigue. This interpretation is less applicable to the interaction of personality with sleep. Again, those who scored high on I + E had significantly shorter sleep durations and lower heart rates during sleep. Similarly, those who were more work oriented exhibited higher sleep-quality ratings.

Age is an individual attribute that is often debated as to its effects on pilots. While age was significantly correlated with fatigue at the end of the duty day, the trend of increasing age being associated with reduced sleep quality (i.e., more awakenings, higher heart rates and activity) failed to reach significance. Recent findings indicating poorer sleep in older long-haul aircrews (Graeber, 1986) suggest that a more in-depth examination of some of the older short-haul crew members (i.e., over 50 years) may reveal similar age-related sleep disturbances. Exercise is another individual factor currently receiving considerable attention among crews. Their interest may have practical consequences, since there was some indication that subjects who exercised both at home and on trips manifested less effects of trips on heart rate during sleep than did those who did not exercise or who exercised only at home. This would suggest that the former group may sleep better on layovers. Finally, analysis of the general health data revealed that subjects who reported increases in gastrointestinal problems on trips also experienced poorer sleep on trips as measured by quality ratings and heart rate.

Lessons Learned

The results which have been described still await further clarification from more in-depth analyses of such factors as specific types of trips, in-flight operational events, and individual patterns of responding. For instance, fatigue and sleep disruption might be considerably worse after flying all day in instrument flight rules (IFR) conditions and performing instrument approaches into small airports. Traffic density represents a similar, potentially important operational consideration. Because all 4-day trips were flown by one carrier and most of the 3-day trips by another, differences between the two airlines (e.g., crew meals, stable cabin crews) may have to be explored more thoroughly. Likewise, the interindividual variability seen in the physiological measures argues for the importance of examining why certain crew members adapted either very well or very poorly to the trips.

In spite of the need for further analyses, some clear lessons have emerged. First, and most important, the results reveal that short-haul crews experience sleep loss despite overnight rests that meet the regulatory and contractual requirements for time off-duty and quality of accomodations. While such findings might be expected for short-haul crews who fly predominantly at night, they are somewhat surprising for crews who operate primarily during daylight. Of course, the study trips were specifically chosen for their demanding characteristics and therefore probably represent the more difficult portion of the short-haul scheduling continuum. Nevertheless, they reflect the realities of today's operating conditions and cannot be considered extreme by U. S. standards.

From the operational perspective, it is important to realize that the timing of trips and not necessarily the length of the duty day or the number of segments flown appears to contribute more to the development of fatigue. Although it could be argued that part of the sleep loss and consequent fatigue was due to the crew members' own behavior, there is sound scientific evidence to support the hypothesis that flight crews may have difficulty adjusting their sleep habits to obtain home-equivalent sleep during layovers (much of this evidence was described in the earlier section of this chapter). Consequently, it is not surprising that these pilots did not go to sleep early enough to compensate for early morning departures. Nor should it be surprising that they stayed up later on trips than when living under the social control of the home and family environment. These findings are consonant with the well-documented tendencies of humans to lengthen their subjective day beyond 24 hours. The fragmentation of sleep reported by many crew members may very well be related to the type of stress response reported in European short-haul crews (Klein et al., 1972a).

More surprising, perhaps, is the positive relationship between the intensity of a day's duty and the length and quality of sleep that night. In some ways this finding supports the preference of most crews to keep flying with brief en route stopovers. Also, the suggestion that crews may somehow learn to pace themselves has implications for down-line schedule changes. It would be advisable to notify crews about the potential for such requests as soon into their scheduled trip as possible so they can "reprogram" themselves to anticipate their reactions to a more extended flight schedule.

The area of individual attributes offers a rich potential for future crew selection procedures to obtain crews who may be less affected by flying that demands short-haul schedules. The implications for career health maintenance, employee satisfaction, and operational safety and efficiency make this subject worthy of further exploration. Likewise, there are indications that certain life-styles and trip-related behavior patterns may improve a pilot's ability to cope with such flight schedules. These suggest the possibility of training crew members about the use of countermeasures to minimize the impact of line flying on themselves.

Before leaving this discussion, there remains the important issue of the operational significance of fatigue and sleep loss in short-haul crews. Can fatigue detrimentally affect safety and operational efficiency in standard operations? The ASRS record suggests that it can; however, there is recent evidence that these effects can be ameliorated to some extent. A full-mission simulator study was conducted by Foushee and his colleagues (1986) in parallel with the field work just described. Although the simulator crews may not have been as tired as many of the field study crews, the results support the view that increased crew coordination resulting from several days flying together can substantially reduce the effects of fatigue on the flight deck.

Long-Haul Operational Studies

Circadian Desynchronization

Most long-haul flight operations add a second dimension to the problem of aircrew fatigue. While short-haul trips can require long duty days, early report times, or night flying, long-haul trips frequently include transmeridian flights as well, and thereby impose the additional burden of circadian desynchronization. The operational significance of this factor has not been clearly identified; however, its likely impact on performance is underscored by the consistently higher accident rate for long-haul versus short-haul commercial sectors. While short- and medium-range jet aircraft performed 3.34 times more landings and takeoffs worldwide than long-range aircraft during the years 1979–1985 inclusive, their loss ratio was only 1.38 times that of the long-range fleet (192:139). The latter's operational total loss ratio (based on sectors flown) was 2.83 times that of the combined short- and medium-range fleet (Caesar, 1986). Similar statistics describe the record for the prior 20 years. While numerous other adverse circumstances (e.g., more difficult handling characteristics, unfamiliar and poorly equipped airports, language problems, etc.) undoubtedly contributed to this difference, there is little doubt that the impact of time zone changes on crew performance was a significant factor. Of the total aircraft losses since 1959, 75% have been the result of cockpit crew error (Caesar, 1986).

Almost all research about the effects of multiple time zone flight on circadian rhythms has been carried out on nonpilot subjects flying as passengers. Typically, measurements have included some combination of heart rate, body temperature, urinary hormones, and performance on laboratory tasks. While recent reviews of this literature are available elsewhere (Graeber, 1982; Klein & Wegmann, 1980), some important findings have emerged about the basic mechanisms that underlie jet lag. Nevertheless, there is substantial reason to question whether passenger results are generalizable to the international flight crew population. In contrast to passengers, flight crews usually have many years of experience crossing multiple times zones. They actively perform duties during flight, are familiar with the destination locale, and rarely stay in the new time zone for more than 2 days. In fact, crews often experience repeated multiple time zone changes within the same trip pattern. Also, most passenger studies have focused on readily available student subjects, whereas flight crews are typically older males with a concentration in the 45–60 year age range. All these factors can be expected to alter the effects of transmeridian flight but not so much as to eliminate the incongruity between the pilot's body clock and that of the local time zone.

The resulting circadian desynchronization can have a variety of effects on the individual crew member, including disturbances in manual flying skills. Using the same type of F-104 flight simulator scenario described earlier (see Figure 10.1), Klein and his colleagues compared the performance of twelve German fighter pilots before and after they experienced a westward flight as passengers across eight time zones on a scheduled airline (Klein et al., 1970). The simulator regimen, shortened to 12 minutes, was repeated every 2 hours for 25 hours starting at 0900 on days 1, 3, 5, and 8 after arrival. After 17 days in the United States, the pilots returned to Germany, where they repeated the simulator test procedure starting 22 hours after completion of the eastward flight.

As Figure 10.10 shows, there were clear directional differences in the amount of postflight performance disruption and in the rate of recovery in the new time zone. Overall simulator performance was substantially more affected after the eastward return flight (-8.5% decrement for 24-hour mean) than after the westward outbound

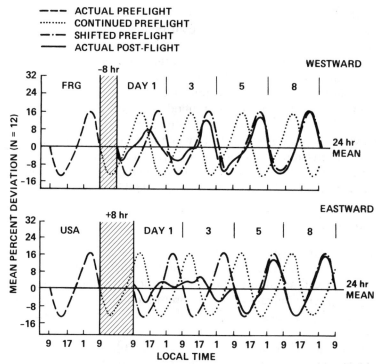

Figure 10.10.   Mean performance rhythms for 12 pilots on a F-104G simulator before and after westward and eastward flights across eight time zones. The preflight rhythm has been duplicated during the postflight period to allow comparison with expected performance under conditions of no time zone adjustment versus immediate total adjustment. Except for 12-minute simulated flight durations, all specifications are as in Figure 10.1. From "Circadian Rhythm of Pilot's Efficiency and Effect of Multiple Time Zone Travel," by Klein et al., 1970, *Aerospace Medicine, 41,* p. 125. Copyright 1970 by the Aerospace Medical Association. Reprinted by permission.

flight (-3.3% decrement). Also, the amplitude and phase of the circadian performance rhythm adapted more quickly to the destination zeitgebers after westward flight.

While this study is the first to demonstrate an operationally significant effect of multiple time zone transitions and time of day, it leaves many questions unanswered. Because the subjects were transported military fighter pilots unaccomstomed to transmeridian flight, their performance data represent more an estimate of the effects of time shifts on raw flying skill than an estimate of the effects on flying in line operations. The aviation record in general indicates that poor decision making and crew coordination are considerably more responsible for accidents and unsafe incidents than are deficiencies in aircraft handling (Cooper, White, & Lauber, 1979). It is therefore significant that laboratory evidence and studies on long-haul passengers have shown that time zone shifts produce significant decrements in cognitive ability and mood (Graeber, 1982). Unfortunately, there have been no such studies in operating international flight crews. Work is currently underway to address this critical issue using full-mission simulation coupled with field monitoring of pilots' circadian rhythms and sleep during layovers (Graeber, Foushee, Gander, & Noga, 1985; Graeber et al., 1984).

Sleep and Sleepiness

The issue of fatigue and sleep loss dominates any discussion with flight crews about the effects of international transmeridian operations. While circadian rhythmicity and desynchronization affect a multitude of physiological and behavioral functions, it is the subjective feeling of fatigue paired with an inability to sleep that crews complain about the most.

A study by Carruthers and his colleagues (1976), though limited to one crew, revealed how this issue can translate to diminished performance on the flight deck during long-haul operations. They carried out electrophysiological (EEG) recordings on a crew operating a B-707 from Buenos Aires to London via Madrid and Paris. Their data, collected during the 9-hour transatlantic flight segment, represent the best objective evidence of microsleep and superficial sleep patterns in pilots functioning in the cockpit. During the early morning hours (0400–0600 GMT), while the airplane was cruising on autopilot, all five on-duty crew members displayed various brain wave patterns characteristic of sleep or extreme drowsiness, including sleep spindles and increased 12–14 Hz activity with mass EEG synchronization. While such sleepiness may not be uncommon at that time of night during long overwater flights, the authors caution that their observations may be attributable in part to cumulative sleep loss caused by unusually warm weather in Buenos Aires for several days before departure.

In order to examine the issue of crew rest during layovers in new time zones, an international group of researchers, government agencies, and airlines recently cooperated to study the sleep and wakefulness of operating B-747 crews during their first outbound layover of a long-haul trip pattern (Graeber, 1986). Standard polysomnographic nocturnal sleep recordings were carried out at four homebase locations: San Francisco, London, Frankfurt (Cologne), and Tokyo. After awaking, the volunteer crew members underwent the previously described multiple sleep latency test (MSLT) every 2 hours for 12 hours, thus providing an objective measure of their physiological sleepiness throughout the waking day.

The same procedures were repeated at the destination sleep laboratory after crews had operated a flight across seven, eight, or nine time zones. European and Japanese crews flew to San Francisco, while U. S. crews flew from there to London or Tokyo. The only difference from the homebase recording procedure was the freedom each crew member had to choose when he would try to sleep within the 25–48 hours before the return flight. MSLTs were administered on even GMT hours whenever the subject was awake.

A total of five eastward or westward flight schedules were studied with approximately 12 crew members participating in each. The results were remarkably consistent despite the cultural disparity among the crew samples. Most subjects were able to obtain adequate sleep during the layover either by sleeping efficiently at selected times or by sleeping less efficiently but staying in bed longer than usual. Sleep quality decreased slightly in most cases. Many of the observed alterations in sleep stages and quality were predictable from known relationships between circadian rhythmicity and sleep, for example, the decreased amounts of REM sleep that were recorded following eastward flights; however, most of the changes were not as extensive as one might expect from this literature (see earlier review). For certain groups, there were no statistically significant changes in sleep-stage percentages or latencies despite the substantial time zone shift. It is unclear whether this outcome was due to some type of career adaptation developed in response to repeated transmeridian flying, or whether it represents a statistical artifact resulting from some of the relatively low homebase sleep durations used for comparison.

One clear result did emerge regarding the direction of flight. Sleep quality decreased more after eastward flights than after westward flights. This directional difference can be seen by comparing the patterns of sleep shown in Figures 10.11 and 10.12. Sleep was much more variable and fragmented after eastward night flights (Figure 10.11) than after westward flights (Figure 10.12) over an equivalent number of time zones. The consequences of this more prominent disruption were reflected in the subsequent measures of daytime sleepi-

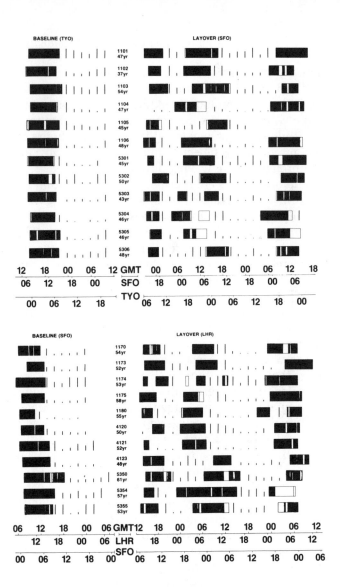

Figure 10.11. Sleep–wake patterns for individual B-747 crew members from two airlines during homebase recordings and after eastward night flights. Vertical lines represent sleep latency tests, the height of each being proportional to the time taken to fall asleep (maximum = 20 min). Black rectangles represent EEG-validated sleep; open bars represent time in bed while not asleep.

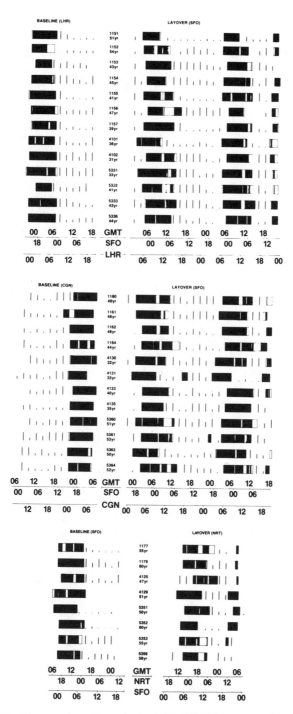

Figure 10.12. Sleep–wake patterns for individual B-747 crew members from three airlines during homebase recordings and after westward flights. All representations as in Figure 10.11.

ness; however, the mean circadian sleepiness rhythm (as measured by the MSLT) often persisted on homebase time after arrival in the new time zone, so that at least part of the increased sleepiness observed after eastward flights may represent the increase usually exhibited at that GMT hour.

As described earlier, other behavioral and physiological variables are also more disrupted after eastward flights, presumably due to the difficulty humans have in shortening their day. In this regard, it is interesting to note that the westbound crews resembled the short-haul crews in that they did not compensate for an early morning report time by going to bed earlier at home on the night before the trip departed (Wegmann et al., 1986). Thus, sleep both before and after transmeridian flight represents another example where the characteristics of the body clock affect, in a predictable fashion, the ability of crews to adjust to work demands.

A wide range of individual differences in sleep quality and efficiency (i.e., percentage of time in bed when the subject was asleep) was observed among these long-haul crews. For example, in the U. S. group, layover sleep efficiency varied from 54.6% of 9.8 hours to 90.0% of 16.2 hours. The number of spontaneous awakenings during a single layover sleep period ranged from fewer than 10 to more than 50 (Dement, Seidel, Cohen, Bliwise, & Carskadon, 1986). Although part of this variability surely represents the statistical noise common to any sampling procedure, there is reason to believe that some of the differences can be attributed to identifiable individual factors.

Age was one such factor that significantly affected sleep quality. In confirmation of Preston's (1973) limited observations, older crew members experienced less total sleep as well as poorer quality sleep (Dement et al., 1986; Nicholson, Pascoe, Spencer, Stone, & Green, 1986). The results further indicate that this enhanced decrement occurs predominantly in those crew members who are over 50 years old. These findings, together with those of the short-haul field study, strongly suggest that it would be prudent to consider the effects on sleep when discussing the impact of age on pilot fitness for duty.

Circadian type is another factor which may explain some of the individual variability. The evidence supporting this possibility comes from the Japanese crew members who were divided into morning- or evening-types, based on a standard questionnaire. When their MSLT data were separately averaged, the two types displayed about a 2-hour difference in the time of maximal sleepiness at home and more dramatic differences in their sleepiness patterns during layovers (Sasaki, Kurosaki, Mori, & Endo, 1986). Again this finding supports the short-haul field study in that it underscores the potential usefulness of factors related to personality and life-style as predictors of individual reactions to multiple time zone flights.

Two other aspects of the MSLT results have important implications for crew rest and flight-deck performance. First, there was a striking similarity among the daytime sleep latency curves reported for the homebase condition. The average curves for each group closely matched each other as well as those reported for nonpilot populations (see Figure 10.4). Thus, they all exhibited a gradual increase in sleepiness throughout the day, reaching a maximum during the late afternoon, and followed by a gradual decline into the evening. Despite the sampling limits imposed by irregular layover sleep–wake patterns, these sleepiness rhythms appeared to persist on homebase time after the time zone transition (Dement et al., 1986; Nicholson et al., 1986; Sasaki et al., 1986; Wegmann et al., 1986). This apparent stability of the sleepiness curve suggests that crews may be able to use it to predict when they could fall asleep more readily and thereby develop better strategies for sleeping or napping while away from home. Conversely, it could also be used proactively to forewarn crews about when sleepiness would be more likely to to occur on the flight deck so they could prepare themselves accordingly.

A second important aspect of the MSLT stems from the objectivity it provides in assessing sleepiness or fatigue. Before each MSLT, subjects were required to complete two self-rated estimates of sleepiness, a Stanford Sleepiness Scale and a 10-cm analog scale. Linear regression analysis of all 56 crew members revealed that the subjective estimates did not predict sleepiness as objectively measured by the MSLT procedure (Dement et al., 1986). This finding implies that crew members on duty are probably not able to reliably assess their own current state of fatigue and, therefore, are not aware of when they are most at risk for increased sleepiness and reduced vigilance. Conversely, it also suggests that sometimes they may not be as sleepy as they feel or say they are. In either case, crew members and flight operations managers should be aware of the underlying flaw in assuming that crews can monitor their own fitness for duty in this regard. Finally, it is interesting to note that, contrary to the MSLT results, crew members were able to reliably estimate their total sleep time during layover, thus supporting the validity of the sleep log data obtained in the previously discussed short-haul study (Dement et al., 1986).

Operational Implications and Recommendations

Although the international layover sleep study may be limited by sample size, the simplicity of the trips studied, and the use of sleep laboratories as layover sites (except in Tokyo), its findings provide an operationally sound framework for addressing the issue of long-haul crew rest and for developing more effective ways to study sleep-related problems in human performance.

The project's principal investigators agreed by consensus that eastward flying crews could substantially improve their chance of obtaining good layover sleep by adhering to a more-structured sleep schedule (Graeber, Dement, Nicholson, Sasaki, & Wegmann, 1986). In the study, many subjects went to bed immediately after arriving on an overnight flight. They fell asleep more quickly than during the homebase testing, but slept a relatively short amount of time. They then tended to awake at a time corresponding to the late morning of their home time. The timing of the next major sleep varied considerably, with some individuals delaying sleep until it coincided with their usual bedtime at home. Similar wide-ranging differences occurred in the second night's sleep. It was recommended that crews should instead limit their sleep immediately after arrival and prolong the subsequent wakeful period to end about the normal local time for sleep. Proper sleep scheduling during the first 24 hours of the layover is particularly critical, and crew members should therefore develop the discipline to terminate their initial sleep even though they could sleep longer. This process would increase the likelihood that sleep immediately preceding the next duty period would be of adequate duration for long-haul operations.

As a corollary, the investigators noted that, unless layover sleep is arranged in a satisfactory manner by an appropriate sleep–wake strategy, increased drowsiness is likely to occur during the subsequent long-haul flight. As they point out, other research (Mullaney, Kripke, Fleck, & Johnson, 1983; Naitoh, 1981; Nicholson et al., 1985) suggests that, under acceptable operational circumstances, limited-duration naps can be a helpful strategy to improve alertness for a useful period of time. Consequently, controlled napping on the flight deck could be an important strategy if operationally feasible. Although there are no data bearing directly on this issue, it would seem reasonable that flight safety during the critical phases of flight (letdown, approach, and landing) would benefit if naps were taken by one crew member at a time for about an hour during overwater flight segments at cruise altitude.

It is this author's opinion that it is more important to have an alert, well-performing crew member available upon descent than to have a tired, error-prone individual who has the dubious distinction of having fought off sleep during several boring hours of cruising over the ocean. Of course, the argument against this view is that sudden arousal from a nap, as might occur due to an emergency, would result in a serious performance decrement that could threaten safety. A variety of studies have shown that this sleep inertia effect depends upon several variables: the amount of prior wakefulness, the amount of sleep obtained (especially slow-wave sleep), the sleep stage awakened from, the time of day, and the type of task being tested (Dinges, Orne, & Orne, 1985; Naitoh, 1981). Indeed, if an in-flight emergency called for immediate action on the part of a suddenly awakened crew member, there may be reason for concern, since laboratory tasks reveal that reaction time deficits persist during the first 5 to 10 minutes after awakening and that further deficits in cognitively demanding performance tasks can last up to 30 minutes. However, given the relative rarity of in-flight emergencies during cruise versus the disturbingly high percentage of accidents and incidents occurring during approach and landing (Eastburn, 1985), the sleep-inertia argument seems out of proportion to the nature of the problem revealed by the operational record. Furthermore, most problems that develop during cruise do so gradually and offer the luxuries of time, altitude, and clear skies to troubleshoot and solve. This is much less often the case for operational problems that develop on descent into the potential weather conditions and crowded airspace that typically surround an international destination airport.

Is Automation the Answer?

Behavioral Effects of Fatigue and Sleep Loss

One approach for reducing potential operator error is to remove the human as much as possible from the operation. To many in the aviation industry, today's rapid advancements in automation technology offer the promise of accomplishing this objective on the flight deck. How will such improvements interact with the impact of fatigue and circadian desynchronization on crew performance? The answer to this question awaits the realistic test that only flight operations can provide. Nevertheless, there is considerable evidence to suggest that increased automation may exacerbate the potential for problems in certain situations while reducing it in others. While the goal of increased automation is to reduce pilot workload while simultaneously improving flight safety and efficiency, its converse effect is to increase crew boredom and encourage overreliance on automated systems.

Some insight can be gained by reviewing the known effects of sleep loss and fatigue on human performance. Table 10.1 divides these into four categories related to psychomotor skill, sensory–perceptual awareness, cognitive ability, and affective state. While the individual entries reveal that these categories are not mutually exclusive, a cursory inspection of the diversity of effects should increase the concern of even the most optimistic automation advocate.

Performance Requirements in Automated Aircraft

The nature of these concerns is related to the altered role of the pilot. For instance, automation brings with it an increased requirement for keyboard entries before and during flight. Depending on the aircraft, these entries can include navigational waypoints, ascent and approach routes, radar headings, control surface settings, engine power settings, and weight and balance information. The increased potential for "finger" errors is obvious, but the actual entries, includ-

Table 10.1.   Effects of Fatigue and Sleep Loss on Flight Crew Performance

Performance category	Effects
Reaction time: Increased	Timing errors in response sequences Less smooth control Require enhanced stimuli
Attention: Reduced	Overlook/misplace sequential task elements Preoccupation with single tasks or elements Reduced audiovisual scan Less aware of poor performance
Memory: Diminished	Inaccurate recall of operational events Forget peripheral tasks Revert to "old" habits
Mood: Withdrawn	Less likely to converse Less likely to perform low-demand tasks More distracted by discomfort More irritable "Don't care" attitude

ing errors, are often not as obvious to the crew as a misset "bug" on a gauge or an incorrect setting on a mechanical dial. In highly automated aircraft, the entries, which are often buried within levels of computer displays, can be recalled on demand but are not constantly in view. Because many incorrect entries can meet the logical requirements of the software and be within the flight parameters of the aircraft, the onus is often on the crew to discover the incongruities.

This requirement raises the parallel need for crews to continuously monitor not only their own computer entries but also the performance of a growing number of automated systems controlling such functions as engine parameters, fuel flow, flight guidance, and cabin environment. While the computerization of the cockpit has enabled designers to provide additional ways for warning crews about malfunctions and procedural lapses, the result can often foster the attitude that the aircraft will tell you when something is wrong. It is not surprising that vigilance and attention to procedural details begin to appear less critical when color CRTs and computer-generated voices are there to protect you. Another consequence of increased automation results from the reduction in manual flying experience and the potential for diminished flying proficiency. When this effect is coupled with the growing complacency that may develop as crews rely more on automated systems, there is reason for concern about their ability to operate the aircraft when systems fail or when unexpected changes in traffic or weather conditions require the crew to revert to less-automated flight regimens, particularly near terminal areas.

Finally, there remains the issue of cognitive demands placed on flight crews. Flight computers are untiring machines that obediently follow the rules of logic and sequential processing. Unfortunately, the appropriate crew response to various flight situations is not always the one which such processing would recommend. Humans have the unique ability to weigh both the strictly logical argument and the importance of other variables in making any decision. Even in normal operations, much of the information that crews must consider is not readily available to the computer (e.g., each other's experience and opinions, low-level weather, turbulence, air and ground traffic, company needs, and cabin problems). When the abnormal occurs, it is the pilots who must retain the ability to develop creative solutions to unpredictable or novel problems. The availability of automated information systems to aid in this process may certainly be helpful, but they are not a replacement for the experience and judgment of the crew.

All of these performance requirements involve various mixtures of the skills and abilities listed in the first column of Table 10.1. Of course, fatigue and sleep are nothing new to aviation and neither are the performance losses associated with them. The critical issue is the change that automation is bringing about in the crew's job requirements. Many of the stimulating and rewarding aspects of flying may be eroded as less and less manual flying is called for, or even permitted, by individual carriers. By reducing workload and providing precision information processing, on-board computers have eliminated many sources of crew error, but they have simultaneously increased the subtlety of error detection. The increased use of radio transmitted datalinks and stored navigational data bases may help to decrease the dependency on crew keyboard entries and thus the opportunity for input errors. Therefore, crews then become even less familiar with the input procedures necessary when en route flight plans must be altered unexpectedly.

In summary, the computerized cockpit may exceed the capacity of the conventional cockpit to trap the tired crew member into performing incorrectly or not at all. When you are tired, there is always the temptation to conserve energy and let someone, or something, else do the job. It is reasonable to expect that the resident expertise and compelling displays of highly automated flight-deck systems will heighten this tendency, especially because ordinary in-flight procedures will require less crew member involvement. Added to this performance threat is the impact of automation on crew complement.

Currently, all next-generation aircraft are being designed for two-pilot crews. While many short-haul aircraft have been flying for years under this configuration, there has been little experience in long-haul flight operations. In fact, currently almost all extended-range operations (ETOPS) on two-man aircraft, B-767 or A-310, include a third "relief" pilot. It is common knowledge among international carriers that crew members occasionally nap while cruising over water, and, as discussed earlier, such naps may be helpful. While there may be little reason for concern in a three-person cockpit, the possibility of only one crew member being awake in an automated cockpit is less comforting to many. Another aspect of the reduced crew complement in long-haul operations relates to the changes in mood that accompany transmeridian flying. When there are only two individuals available to interact, there is no one else to turn to when disagreements develop or attitudes suffer. This may have serious implications for crew coordination. The final factor to be considered is the extension of range that is accompanying the progess in automation. The B-747-400 and the MD-11 will have ranges extending beyond 14 hours. While it appears that most carriers will assign at least one extra crew member to such flights, the increase in boredom and time zones crossed can only be expected to multiply the concerns already raised.

What approaches can be taken to address these concerns? One suggestion may be to develop in-flight procedures that will keep the crew involved and interacting with the computers on board. By stimulating activity and motivating the crew, appropriate procedures can overcome some of the boredom associated with long flights. In a way, this approach is the opposite of the Multiple Sleep Latency Test described earlier in that its aim would be to mask the crew's physiological sleepiness in a soporific environment. A related suggestion would be to take further advantage of the computer capacity and CRT displays of the cockpit to periodically stimulate the crew's alertness and performance readiness. There are already anecdotes about crew members who pass the time as computer hackers during long flights. A more radical suggestion may be to have the computer monitor certain performance parameters for each crew member and use the results to alert the crew when rest is needed. Perhaps onboard training would relieve some of the boredom. Would the availability of computerized training problems during overwater flight segments be inadvisable if they were programmed as secondary to operational displays? Finally, the availability of demonstrably effective crew bunks for extra crew members may be particularly desirable on proposed long-range routes, instead of requiring crew rest to be taken in a passenger seat.

These suggestions are merely intended to provide stimulation for taking a positive approach to the issue of fatigue and automated long-haul flying. The challenge of the new technology is to find ways of capitalizing on its strengths, so that crews can function more safely and not to be fooled into believing that its sophistication will compensate for the reality of our daily need for sleep and rest.

Acknowledgments

I thank Captains William Frisbie and Harry Orlady, Dr. Cheryl Spinweber, and Ms. Linda Connell for their helpful comments and suggestions.

References

Aschoff, J., Hoffman, K., Pohl, H., & Wever, R. (1975). Re-entrainment of circadian rhythms after phase shifts of the Zeitgeber. *Chronobiologia, 2,* 23–78.

Brown, F. M. (1982). Rhythmicity as an emerging variable for psychology. In F. M. Brown & R. C. Graeber (Eds.), *Rhythmic aspects of behavior* (pp. 3–38). Hillsdale, NJ: Erlbaum.

Caesar, H. (1986). Long-term statistics and their impact on safety management and operational procedures. *Proceedings of the 39th International Air Safety Seminar* (pp. 11–23). Arlington, VA: Flight Safety Foundation.

Carruthers, M., Arguelles, A. E., & Mosovich, A. (1976). Man in transit: Biochemical and physiological changes during intercontinental flights. *Lancet, 1,* 977–980.

Colin, J., Timbal, J., Boutelier, C., Houdas, Y., & Siffre, M. (1968). Rhythm of the rectal temperature during a 6-month free-running experiment. *Journal of Applied Physiology, 25,* 170–176.

Cooper, G. E., White, M. D., & Lauber, J. K. (1979). *Resource management on the flight deck* (NASA Conference Publication 2120). Washington, DC: NASA.

Czeisler, C. A., Weitzman, E. D., Moore-Ede, M. C., Zimmerman, J. C., & Knauer, R. S. (1980). Human sleep: Its duration and organization depend on its circadian phase. *Science, 210,* 1264–1267.

Dement, W. C., Seidel, W. F., Cohen, S. A., Bliwise, N. G., & Carskadon, M. A. (1986). Sleep and wakefulness in aircrew before and after transoceanic flights. *Aviation, Space and Environmental Medicine, 57* (12, suppl.), B14–B28.

Dinges, D. F., Orne, M. T., & Orne, E. C. (1985). Assessing performance upon abrupt awakening from naps during quasi-continuous operations. *Behavior Research Methods, Instruments, and Computers, 17,* 37–45.

Eastburn, M. W. (1985). Are training, operational and maintenance practices improving the safety record? *Proceedings of the 38th Annual International Air Safety Seminar* (pp. 11–24). Arlington, VA: Flight Safety Foundation.

Foushee, H. C., Lauber, J. K., Baetge, M. M., & Acomb, D. B. (1986). *Crew factors in flight operations: III. The operational significance of exposure to short-haul air transport operations* (NASA Technical Memorandum 88322). Moffett Field, CA: NASA-Ames Research Center.

Gander, P. H., Graeber, R. C., Foushee, H. C., Lauber, J. K., & Connell, L. J. (1988). *Crew factors in flight operations: II. Psychophysiological responses to short-haul air transport operations* (NASA Technical Memorandum 89452). Moffett Field, CA: NASA-Ames Research Center.

Gander, P. H., Myhre, G., Graeber, R. C., Andersen, H. T., & Lauber, J. K. (1985). *Crew factors in flight operations: I. Effects of 9-hour time-zone changes on fatigue and the circadian rhythms of sleep/wake and core temperature* (NASA Technical Memorandum 88197). Moffett Field, CA: NASA-Ames Research Center.

Graeber, R. C. (1982). Alterations in performance following rapid transmeridian flight. In F. M. Brown & R. C. Graeber (Eds.), *Rhythmic aspects of behavior* (pp. 173–212). Hillsdale, NJ: Erlbaum.

Graeber, R. C. (1985). Sleep and fatigue in short-haul flight operations: A field study. *Proceedings of the 38th International Air Safety Seminar* (pp. 142–148). Arlington, VA: Flight Safety Foundation.

Graeber, R. C. (Ed.). (1986). Sleep and wakefulness in international aircrews. *Aviation, Space and Environmental Medicine, 57* (12, suppl.), B1–B64.

Graeber, R. C., Dement, W. C., Nicholson, A. N., Sasaki, M., & Wegmann, H. M. (1986). International cooperative study of aircrew layover sleep: Operational summary. *Aviation, Space and Environmental Medicine, 57* (12, suppl.), B10–B13.

Graeber, R. C., Foushee, H. C., & Lauber, J. K. (1984). Dimensions of flight crew performance decrements: Methodological implications for field research. In J. Cullen, J.

Siegrist, & H. M. Wegmann (Eds.), *Breakdown in human adaptation to stress*, vol. 1, (pp. 584–605). Boston: Martinus Nijhoff.

Graeber, R. C., Foushee, H. C., Gander, P. H., & Noga, G. W. (1985). Circadian rhythmicity and fatigue in flight operations. *Journal of the University of Occupational and Environmental Health (Japan)*, 7 (suppl.), 122–130.

Klein, K. E., Bruner, H., Holtmann, H., Rehme, H., Stolze, J., Steinhoff, W. D., & Wegmann, H. M. (1970). Circadian rhythm of pilots' efficiency and effects of multiple time zone travel. *Aerospace Medicine, 41*, 125–132.

Klein, K. E., Bruner, H., Kuklinski, P., Ruff, S., & Wegmann, H. M. (1972a). *The evaluation of studies of flight personnel of the German Lufthansa on the question of stress during flights on the short European routes* (DFVLR Institute of Flight Medicine Report DLR 355-74/2). Bonn: DFVLR. (Translation NASA Technical Memorandum 76660, 1982. Washington, DC: NASA.)

Klein, K. E., Wegmann, H. M., & Hunt, B. I. (1972b). Desynchronization of body temperature and performance circadian rhythm as a result of outgoing and homegoing transmeridian flights. *Aerospace Medicine, 43*, 119–132.

Klein, K. E., & Wegmann, H. M. (1980). *Significance of circadian rhythms in aerospace operations* (NATO AGARDograph No. 247). Neuilly sur Seine: NATO AGARD.

Knowles, J. B., Laverty, S. G., & Kuechler, H. A. (1968). Effects of alcohol on REM sleep. *Quarterly Journal of Studies on Alcohol, 29*, 342–349.

Langlois, P. H., Smolensky, M. H., Hsi, B. P., & Weir, F. W. (1985). Temporal patterns of reported single-vehicle car and truck accidents in Texas, U. S. A. during 1980–1983. *Chronobiology International, 2*, 131–146.

Luce, G. G. (1971). *Body time.* New York: Pantheon Books.

Lyman, E. G., & Orlady, H. W. (1980). *Fatigue and associated performance decrements in air transport operations* (NASA Contract NAS2-10060). Mountain View, CA: Battelle Memorial Laboratories, Aviation Safety Reporting System.

McFarland, R. A. (1941). Fatigue in aircraft pilots. *New England Journal of Medicine, 225*, 845–855.

Moore-Ede, M., Sulzman, F., & Fuller, C. (1982). *The clocks that time us.* Cambridge: Harvard University Press.

Mullaney, D. J., Kripke, D. F., Fleck, P. A., & Johnson, L. C. (1983). Sleep loss and nap effects on sustained continuous performance. *Psychophysiology, 20*, 643–651.

Naitoh, P. (1981). Circadian cycles and restorative power of naps. In L. C. Johnson, D. I. Tepas, W. P. Colquhoun, & M. J. Colligan (Eds.), *Biological rhythms, sleep and shift work* (pp. 553–580). New York: Spectrum.

Nicholson, A. N., Pascoe, P. A., Roehrs, T., Roth, T., Spencer, M. B., Stone, B. M. & Zorick, F. (1985). Sustained performance with short evening and morning sleeps. *Aviation, Space and Environmental Medicine, 56*, 105–114.

Nicholson, A. N., Pascoe, P. A., Spencer, M. B., Stone, B. M., & Green, R. L. (1986). Nocturnal sleep and daytime alertness of aircrew after transmeridian flights. *Aviation, Space and Environmental Medicine, 57* (12, suppl.), B43–B52.

Post, W., & Gatty, H. (1931). *Around the world in eight days.* London: Hamilton.

Preston, F. S. (1973). Further sleep problems in airline pilots on world-wide schedules. *Aerospace Medicine, 44*, 775–782.

Preston, F. S., & Bateman, S. C. (1970). Effect of time zone changes on the sleep patterns of BOAC B.707 crews on world-wide schedules. *Aerospace Medicine, 41*, 1409–1415.

Richardson, G. S., Carskadon, M. A., Orav, E. J., & Dement, W. C. (1982). Circadian variation in sleep tendency in elderly and young subjects. *Sleep, 5* (suppl. 2), s82–s94.

Ruffell Smith, H. P. (1967). Heart rate of pilots flying aircraft on scheduled airline routes. *Aerospace Medicine, 38,* 1117–1119.

Sasaki, M., Kurosaki, Y., Mori, A., & Endo, S. (1986). Patterns of sleep-wakefulness before and after transmeridian flight in commercial airline pilots. *Aviation, Space and Environmental Medicine, 57* (12, suppl.), B29–B42.

Spence, J. T., & Helmreich, R. L. (1978). *Masculinity and femininity: Their psychological dimensions, correlates, and antecedents.* Austin: University of Texas.

Stepanski, E., Lamphere, J., Badia, P., Zorick, F., & Roth, T. (1984). Sleep fragmentation and daytime sleepiness. *Sleep, 7,* 18–26.

Wegmann, H. M., Gundel, A., Naumann, M., Samel, A., Schwartz, E., & Vejvoda, M. (1986). Sleep, sleepiness, and circadian rhythmicity in aircrews operating on transatlantic routes. *Aviation, Space and Environmental Medicine, 57* (12, suppl.), B53–B64.

Wever, R. (1979). *The circadian system of man.* New York: Springer-Verlag.

Yules, R. B., Lippman, M. E., & Freedman, D. X. (1967). Alcohol administration prior to sleep. *Archives General Psychiatry, 16,* 94–97.

Zulley, J., Wever, R., & Aschoff, J. (1981). The dependence of onset and duration of sleep on the circadian rhythm of rectal temperature. *Pfluegers Archiv, 391,* 314–318.

PART THREE

HUMAN FACTORS IN AIRCRAFT DESIGN

Pilot Control   11

Sheldon Baron

Introduction

The importance of flight control to the development of aviation is difficult to overestimate. As noted by McRuer and Graham (1981) in their short history of the subject, even Wilbur Wright recognized the centrality of the stability and control problem and held the opinion that once the ability to "steer and balance" reliably could be achieved, the age of flying machines would arrive. These authors have also pointed out that flight control is a systems problem involving the characteristics of the aircraft, the sensing of information necessary for control, the appropriate control laws, and the mechanisms for generating the appropriate control forces and moments. Of course, superimposed upon all of these are the goals of the mission to be accomplished.

In the early days of aviation, virtually all of the functions and systems involved in flight control were provided by the human pilot. However, the evolution and advances in aviation that resulted in current advanced aircraft have been accompanied and to some extent stimulated by an ever increasing use of automation to both replace and complement functions originally performed by the human pilot. The aforementioned reference provides an informative and very readable overview of developments in the field along with some key theoretical advances that supported that development.

In this chapter, we focus on the human aspects of the flight control problem, sharing with McRuer and Graham a systems viewpoint. That is, the problem is not seen primarily from a human-centered perspective but, rather, from one that emphasizes the entire pilot–vehicle system and the environment in which it operates. This viewpoint has proven extremely successful in terms of measuring human performance, developing theories to describe and predict that performance, and applying those theories and data to real problems of flight control (and other control tasks).

I begin with an overview of flight control tasks and a discussion of basic approaches to analyzing their problems. Then, fundamental capabilities and limitations of the human controller are discussed. This is followed by a discussion of mathematical models for closed-loop control analysis. Continuous control is, at present, unique among human tasks in the degree to which it has been quantified and modeled. The discussion here includes outlines of the two modeling approaches that dominate the field and an indication of the range of applications possible, including some very briefly described illustrative examples. Next, the implications of changes in the control task resulting from increasing uses of automation are discussed briefly. In the chapter's final section, future areas of concern and research are addressed.

Nature of the Aircraft Control Problem

Flying an airplane, be it for military, commercial, or purely personal reasons, is a goal-oriented human activity. Inevitably, it involves deciding on routes and flight paths to follow, selecting appropriate motion parameters (course and speed) for guiding the aircraft so as to traverse those routes, and controlling the aircraft to maintain it on the chosen paths in a safe and stable fashion. All this must be accomplished by the pilot under constraints imposed by both the limits of aircraft capability and conditions of the environment (weather, terrain, other traffic, etc.) and while performing other supportive tasks such as systems monitoring and communication. This is, fundamentally, a very complex task. The manner in which it is, or must be, accomplished by the pilot is, to a great extent, determined by the motion characteristics of the aircraft itself. It is also significantly dependent upon other factors such as the pilot–vehicle interface and the degree and character of automation. We therefore describe briefly some important aspects of those characteristics.

The pilot controls or governs the motion of the aircraft to achieve and maintain the desired path by trimming it appropriately, by executing large preprogrammed or open-loop maneuvers where significant changes in location (position and orientation) and path are needed, and by continuous closed-loop control to maintain the desired path (i.e., precision tracking of, or disturbance regulation about, the path). The ability to trim the aircraft in various steady equilibrium flight conditions is related to the static characteristics of the aircraft. These characteristics should be such as to allow the pilot to establish an equilibrium flight condition and then leave the aircraft essentially unattended, in a control sense, for periods of time required to perform other activities or to relax. Good static characteristics are also a prerequisite of good dynamic behavior. The dynamic characteristics of an aircraft are those that govern its motion when it has been disturbed from equilibrium, either deliberately by a control input or inadvertently by a disturbance; these are critical to accomplishing both the open-loop maneuvering and the closed-loop tasks necessary to flight. The important subject of flying, or handling, qualities is concerned directly with the relation of the aircraft's static and dynamic characteristics to the ease with which the pilot can exercise the various aspects of control so as to accomplish his or her mission.

The main concern of this chapter is the continuous closed-loop control tasks which are usually the most demanding for the pilot. Figure 11.1 gives a general illustration of such a task. The pilot is shown to sense (or observe) information about the vehicle (from displays and other cues), interpret and structure that information so as to determine the appropriate action, and then execute the basic control manipulations. The manner in which this is accomplished by the pilot (or, at least, is analyzed by control engineers) is, in large measure, related to more detailed aspects of the aircraft motion which are discussed below.

The aircraft moves in three-dimensional space and has, from the standpoint of its basic dynamic response, six degrees of freedom: it can translate linearly in three ways (forward–backward, left–right, up–down) and it can rotate angularly about three separate axes. The motions of the airplane are actually determined by the action of a va-

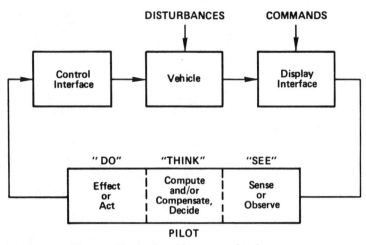

Figure 11.1.   Human pilot in closed-loop control task.

riety of aerodynamic, gravitational, and thrust forces and moments, some of which can be controlled by the pilot using the control manipulators. For conventional, fixed-wing aircraft, there are four basic controls (elevator, aileron, rudder, throttle). With these, and changes in configuration, the pilot can introduce control moments about three axes (pitch, roll, and yaw) and control forces along the aircraft's forward–aft body axis (through thrust–drag modulation). Clearly, for complete control of all six degrees of freedom, there must be interaction or coupling among motions. The most familiar examples of this are motions in which the pilot rotates the aircraft to orient its lift force so as to produce appropriate sideways and normal accelerations (e.g., bank-to-turn). Because such coupling both slows and complicates response, advanced high-performance aircraft are now being designed to provide direct or independent six-degrees-of-freedom control (see Citurs, 1984).

Although there is some inevitable coupling among all six degrees of motion of the aircraft, some interactions are quite strong while others may be virtually negligible, when one considers the motions relative to an axis system fixed to the aircraft. This is especially true for the relatively small motions that occur in successful closed-loop control about an equilibrium flight condition. A great deal of the analysis of aircraft control problems (and, indeed, the very structuring of the pilot's control task) takes advantage of this simplifying fact, as it allows the total aircraft motion to be divided into two types, longitudinal and lateral. Longitudinal motions are those motions that take place in the aircraft's plane of symmetry—a vertical plane passing through the center of gravity of the aircraft; lateral motions are those that take place outside this plane. Thus, longitudinal motions are forward, vertical, and pitching motions; lateral motions are sideward, rolling, and yawing motions. The elevator and the throttle are the principal mechanisms for controlling longitudinal motions, whereas the aileron and rudder are the prime lateral controls in conventional aircraft.

Figure 11.2 illustrates a longitudinal and a lateral control example, namely the use of pitch control to climb or descend and the use of bank control to turn. The diagrams are simplified considerably in terms of aircraft response in that they leave out important scaling variables (such as speed) and even more by the omission of all contributions to pitch and roll accelerations other than those of the control inputs; the latter simplification removes inherent feedback that would otherwise exist within each diagram as well as cross-feeds from variables not included in the individual diagrams. However, the simplified structures allow us to capture essential features of the two control problems and to point out some very important control considerations without undue complications.

The diagrams in Figure 11.2 show that important aircraft state variables (e.g., pitch rate, pitch, and altitude) are related by time integra-

(a)

ELEVATOR
(Pitch
Acceleration
Input)

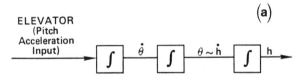

Altitude Control via Elevator Input; θ = Pitch,
$\dot{\theta}$ = Pitch Rate, $\dot{h}$ = Sink/Climb Rate, h = Altitude.

(b)

AILERON
(Roll
Acceleration
Input)

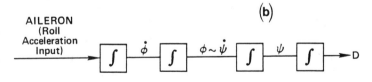

Lateral Deviation Control via Aileron Input;
ϕ = Bank, $\dot{\phi}$ = Bank Rate, ψ = Heading, $\dot{\psi}$ = Heading Rate,
D = Lateral Displacement.

Figure 11.2. Longitudinal (a) and lateral (b) control tasks. ($\int$ Denotes time integration.)

tion processes. Thus, for example, one obtains velocity by an integration of acceleration and position by an integration of velocity. An extremely important consideration in flight control (or other dynamic control tasks) is the number of integrations between the control input and the output or state variable to be controlled. This number is called the control order of the system: in a zero-order system, the output is directly proportional to the input; thus, for example, in a first-order system, the input results in (commands) a rate-of-change of position.

Referring to Figure 11.2, we see that the elevator input creates a control pitching moment which acts as a pitch acceleration command. Two integrations yield the pitch angle. Because the rate-of-change of altitude is proportional to the pitch angle, an additional (appropriately scaled) integration yields a variation in altitude. Similarly, the aileron generates a bank acceleration command, via a rolling moment, which after two integrations results in a bank angle. Changes in bank angle generate a turning rate and a subsequent change in heading that ultimately leads to a deviation in lateral position. In terms of control order, the control of altitude with elevator and lateral deviation with aileron involve third- and fourth-order control systems, respectively. However, attitude (pitch and roll) control with the respective inputs is a second-order control problem, as shown here.

The importance of control order is that, in general, the higher the order, the longer the time between control input and output response and, additionally, the more complicated the required control-input time sequence to generate a given output response. These characteristics are illustrated in Figure 11.3. In the upper half of the figure (a), the response to a unit step after integration is shown for unity gain systems; not only does the output become more complicated as a result of additional integrations, but the time to reach unity value increases. Thus, a unit-step command to a first-order system requires 1 second for the output to reach that value, a second-order system requires approximately 1.5 seconds, and so on. Figure 11.3b illustrates the complexity of control manipulation required as control order is increased. To interpret this figure, one works backwards from the output. Thus, to change the output from one constant value to another (with a linear transition) requires one change in direction of control for a first-order system, two directional changes for a second-order system, and so forth. Put another way, for the systems shown in Figure 11.2, to change altitude or heading from one constant value to another, using a continuous control applied in open-loop fashion, would require the complicated control manipulation

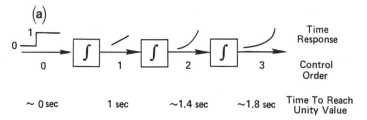

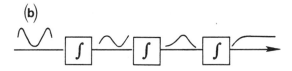

Response To a Step Input as a Function of Control Order

Change in Input Complexity With Control Order

Figure 11.3.   The effects of control order.

shown on the left of Figure 11.3b. To change lateral deviation would require an even more complicated sequence in which the pilot would be required to change the direction of the control input four times.

The splitting of the flight control problem from one involving control of six basic motions to two problems (longitudinal and lateral) of controlling three basic motions is a significant simplification and decomposition of the task. Further progress along these lines is possible and indicated by the discussion above. It was noted that the response of translation variables to the control inputs was slower than that of the rotation variables. More generally, it can be shown by examining the basic modes of response in the longitudinal and lateral submotions that, for conventional aircraft, there tends to be a separation of responses by time (and frequency) into fairly rapid (high-frequency) motions associated with rotation about the center of mass and significantly slower (low-frequency) motions associated with translation of the center of mass. For example, in the longitudinal response there often exist two basic oscillatory responses, the short-period mode and the phugoid mode. For typical flight conditions, the short-period mode governs changes in pitch angle (and angle of attack), whereas the phugoid affects primarily altitude and airspeed. A typical ratio of short-period to phugoid natural frequencies is on the order of 60 (McRuer, Ashkenas & Graham, 1973). These considerations, along with those concerning the difficulties of direct control of high-order systems, suggest that it may be both desirable and possible to decompose further the pilot's control task by separating it into short-term ("rapid") and long-term ("slow") control problems.

In its most simplifying interpretation, the time (or frequency) separation allows one to consider, in isolation, single-input, single-output attitude tracking or disturbance regulation tasks. These control tasks are fundamental to all aspects of aircraft control and guidance and are, therefore, of extreme importance. If pilots are to perform the fast control tasks, it is essential that they become highly skilled in their execution so that their control responses are virtually automatic. On the other hand, because these tasks can be continuously demanding of pilot attention and their automation and/or augmentation is simplest to accomplish, they are generally the first candidates for some form of automatic control.

If one considers control of translation variables, the time separation inherent in the responses still allows for some hierarchical decomposition of the task. In terms of classical methods of feedback control analysis, this takes the form of a nesting of control loops with response times progressively slower as one moves from "inner" to "outer" loops. An example of a nested loop for pilot control of altitude (at constant speed) as compared to a simple loop for the task, is given in Figure 11.4. In this figure, the blocks labeled Y_p represent pilot actions. Note that the nested loop separates the pilot's task into one of generating an appropriate pitch command based on the observed altitude error and an elevator control input based on the pitch error; thus, the inner loop is just a single-input, single-output pitch attitude tracking loop.

The desirability for such a nested-loop structure or some comparable alternative stems in large measure from the difficulties inherent in control of high-order systems, as noted above. It is difficult to establish or prove whether or not the pilot actually adopts such a structure, but there are two features it embodies that will be inherent in any successful control implementation for such a system: first is the decomposition of the overall task into subtasks, each with a well-specified objective; second is the need to observe intermediary state variables in addition to the main variable being controlled. Basically, one cannot expect the pilot to construct the complicated sequences needed for control of third-, or higher, order systems based solely on the observation of a single output. This would inevitably require numerous differentiations and other computations too difficult to manage. By providing the pilot with displays of the intermediate variables, it is possible to both structure the problem into simpler ones and to allow him or her to construct control "laws" from sim-

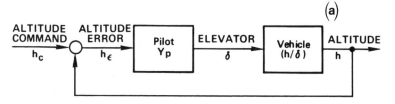

h/δ Denotes Vehicle's Altitude–Response to Elevator Input

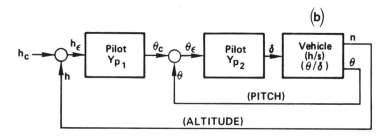

θ/δ   Denotes Pitch (θ) Response to Elevator; θ_c = Pitch Command, θ_ε = Pitch Error

Figure 11.4.   Comparison of simple (a) and nested (b) loops for altitude control.

pler combinations of observed (or estimated) variables. These ideas
will be reflected in the discussion of pilot models presented below.

Analysis Methods

The previous discussion indicates the complexity of flight control.
This is a problem not only for the pilot but also for the designer or
analyst who is concerned with determining the human's capability of
accomplishing the requisite control tasks as well as with devising
methods for assisting or augmenting that capability where necessary.
We have seen that several simplifications are possible, both in terms
of actual control and analysis, through problem decomposition. This
decomposition is abetted by assuming that the control tasks involve
"small" perturbations from steady-equilibrium flight conditions.
However, the major import of this assumption, which is quite reasonable for cases in which the flight condition is maintained by
closed-loop control, is that it allows a vast array of well-developed
analysis techniques to be employed, namely those that can be used
for linear, time-invariant systems. These techniques (and the mitigat-
ing assumption) have proven to be the cornerstone of flight control
analysis and design both for automatic and manual control systems.

The early developments built heavily on the experience gained in the study of servomechanisms. They relied principally on methods that allow one to transform the analysis problem from one involving differential equations to one involving algebraic equations. Moreover, the methods also "transform" the problem from the time domain to other domains in which graphical methods of analysis, as well as increased intuitions, are possible. The key idea in this approach is the system transfer function.

Without getting into the details, we note that the *system transfer function* is a convenient means of capturing the invariant, system-inherent aspects of the input–output response of a system. It is, in general, a ratio of polynomials in the transform variable, thus providing the algebraic description of the system. The most complete treatment of the application of transfer-function methods to aircraft control problems is given by McRuer, Ashkenas, and Graham (1973).

A concept closely related to that of the transfer function is that of frequency response. The response of a linear time-variant system to a sinusoidal input of a given frequency is, in steady state, a sinusoid of the same frequency but with different amplitude and a shift in phase. Because of linearity, the response to a sum of sinusoids of different frequencies is the sum (or superposition) of the responses to the individual sine waves comprising the input. Frequency-response methods are more powerful than might be first supposed because rather arbitrary inputs and responses can be decomposed into their component frequencies by Fourier analysis methods. Thus, it becomes possible to obtain very useful and insightful characterizations of a system by considering its frequency response, which can be represented as an amplitude ratio and a phase difference, as illustrated for four systems in Figure 11.5. The amplitude ratio at a given frequency is just the ratio of the amplitudes of the respective sinusoid components of the output and input; the phase is actually the phase difference between the output and input. Thus, for example, the rate-command (pure first-order) system tends to attenuate the amplitude of the input, the more so the higher the frequency. On the other hand, the output lags the input by a constant 90° regardless of the frequency of the input (thus, the "delay" associated with integration). When a feedback loop is closed around the basic rate-command system, it is possible to obtain a flatter response at low frequencies, which is desirable for command following, while retaining attenuation at higher frequencies, which is useful for filtering out unwanted noise. In addition, low-frequency phase lag is reduced substantially. This system tends to combine the desirable properties of position-and-rate-command systems. The reader is again referred

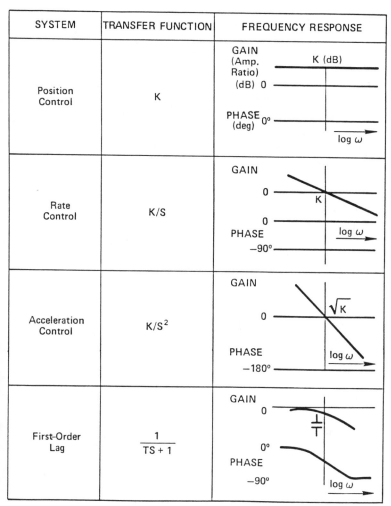

Figure 11.5.   Frequency response for four basic systems.

to McRuer, Ashkenas, and Graham (1973) for detailed treatments.

In the late 1950s and early 1960s, a different approach to control problems emerged, undoubtedly stimulated by the advent of high-speed computers. This approach was then referred to as *modern control theory*, and it was the basis for a number of significant developments. In terms of aircraft control (and pilot-modeling) developments, the key aspects of the approach (which distinguished it from the previous "classical" transform methods) were (1) a shift toward time-domain analysis; (2) a shift toward state–space descriptions of systems, with a corresponding emphasis on internal behavior as opposed to the emphasis on input–output behavior of transform techniques; (3) an increased emphasis on optimization of an explicit performance metric as a control goal rather than on more qualitative control characteristics such as stability and response time; and (4) a consequent need to consider estimation of the state of the system as an integral part of the control process. The state–space approach is inherently a loop-independent analysis in that it usually doesn't rely on a prespecified loop structure any more explicit than the feedback structure implied in Figure 11.1. Instead, the most prominent and useful techniques attempt to find linear feedback laws that are linear combinations of the state variables (or their estimates).

It should be noted that each approach to control systems analysis and design has advantages, and they have many features in common. Moreover, it is often possible to move between methods and/or incorporate or describe features of one within the context of the other. For example, it is possible to interpret linear feedback laws in terms of equivalent-loop transfer functions (see Kleinman & Baron, 1971). This is to be expected insofar as they address the same phenomenon. Nonetheless, the two methods have different philosophical bases and have led to different insights and implementations in both automatic and manual control.

Human Control

Factors Affecting Human Control Performance

Because the human pilot is so flexible and adaptive and so heavily influenced by his or her surroundings, a host of factors or variables will affect closed-loop flight control performance. It is useful for discussion to separate these influences into four categories: task variables, environmental variables, procedural variables and pilot-centered variables (McRuer & Krendel, 1974).

The task variables include the aircraft (and related system) dynamics, the displays, the controls, the external inputs (be they command or disturbance inputs), and the performance requirements. These factors are of dominant importance to the system designer interested in system performance, aircraft flying qualities, control and display design, and pilot workload.

The environmental variables are the factors in the physical environment of the pilot that may impact performance, largely because of physiological reasons. These include temperature, ambient illumination, vibration, "noise," acceleration, and the like. Many of these factors are of little direct concern in flight control systems analysis because they are assumed to be maintained at nominal desirable levels by some sort of environmental control system. Three exceptions to this that are often relevant to high-performance military aircraft involve concern with the impact on manual control performance of vibration, acceleration, and the debilitative effects of cumbersome protective gear. These aspects of the environment can have important direct effects on perception and manipulation, in addition to those information processing effects that result from the mental stress they impose on the pilot. Therefore, understanding and being able to account for the effects of the environments on pilot control response can be quite important in system design. Because of space limitations, the effects of these environmental variables on manual control are not discussed here; the reader is referred to Levison and Houck (1975) and Levison and Muralidharan (1982) for further information.

Procedural variables are those that can affect performance via the procedures imposed on, or employed in, the task environment in which that performance is observed (e.g., the nature of instructions, the training schedule, etc.). In manual control systems analysis, these variables have been important mainly in relation to the collection of data in experimental situations. Appropriate experimental protocols are a necessity if meaningful data involving human subjects are to be obtained. For most design purposes, one usually assumes that the pilots are fully trained and highly motivated and that appropriate procedures are employed to attain this lofty condition.

The last set of variables to be considered are the pilot-centered variables which encompass those characteristics that the pilot brings to the control task. These are a major component of the human factors portion of the analysis of closed-loop control and are discussed in the next section.

Characteristics of the Human Controller

The manual flight control tasks that tend to be of greatest interest in system design and evaluation generally require a high degree of skilled performance from the pilot. Well-trained and motivated pilots bring to such tasks a collection of capabilities and limitations that affect greatly the level of performance that is attainable with the pilot–vehicle system. Indeed, the process of acquiring a skill in performing a given task may be thought of as one of enhancing and sharpening the capabilities for performing that task while learning to minimize the task-specific degrading effects of one's inherent limitations.

The characterization and quantification of those capabilities and limitations that are relevant to human control performance is a central problem in predicting that performance, and therefore it is also a problem in the design and evaluation of pilot–aircraft systems. The problem, though quite difficult, is manageable because a limited number of characteristics tend to dominate control performance and also because the demands of the tasks themselves tend to constrain the range of acceptable behaviors, thereby reducing variability in individual pilots and between pilots. Below, we discuss briefly some of the basic capabilities and limitations of human controllers that can have a significant impact on performance in flight control tasks.

The most significant capability that humans bring to control tasks is the ability to adapt to substantial variations in situations and conditions. Indeed, adaptive control is epitomized by skilled humans performing manual control tasks. With training, and proper feedback, pilots are capable of adapting their control strategies to a wide range of task variables, that is, to changes in aircraft dynamics, input characteristics, and performance requirements. They are also capable of compensating for their own limitations and for changes in environmental variables. It should be noted that, though extensive, this adaptive capacity is not unlimited, and certain types of adaptation are more demanding of human resources than are others. Indeed, this can lead to another more subtle form of adaptation, namely a trade-off between performance and workload or stress. In what follows, we see specific evidence of some of the more important forms of human controller adaptation both in the human performance data that are presented and in the models that capture or predict human control performance. More detailed discussions and data can be found in the manual control literature (e.g., McRuer et al., 1965; McRuer & Krendel, 1974; Baron, 1984b).

The human controller also has a truly remarkable and general ability to take account of the predictable rules and regularities in the environment and to translate them into appropriate control responses (motor commands). We have in mind here a capacity to "optimize" one's response to a particular situation or environment rather than adapting it to different ones. A very interesting aspect of this capability is that prediction can operate either in terms of deterministic responses or statistical rules. With respect to aircraft control, three aspects of predictive compensation are particularly important: (1) prediction of the effects of system dynamics, (2) input signal prediction, and (3) preprogramming.

Prediction of the Effects of System Dynamics. In formulating and executing the motor commands required to control the aircraft, the pilot must utilize knowledge about the transmission properties of the muscle system, the limbs, and any external devices (most importantly the aircraft) being controlled, so that the desired output will be produced. An important component of skill acquisition is the building up of these models for the particular flying task of concern, and its fidelity or accuracy is one key to successful performance. All of the literature on the effects of manipulating the dynamics being controlled, differences between position, rate, and acceleration control systems, and so forth, can be thought of as studies of the success at building up such an internal model (see Poulton, 1974). A more detailed account of prediction based on stored representations is presented in Kelley (1968).

Input Signal Prediction. In a tracking experiment in which a simple, pure-gain system is to be controlled, performance, as measured in terms of error score, improves with practice. Under these conditions, in which learning the control operation is relatively trivial, the improvements in performance are mainly attributable to learning the deterministic or statistical properties of the input signal. This capability is important for pilots in performing either disturbance regulation or precision tracking tasks when the input is at all predictable.

Preprogramming. The ultimate capacity for predictive compensation is embodied in the human ability to formulate, in advance, a controlling sequence relatively independent of the ongoing stimulus conditions. The psychologist refers to the development of *motor programs*, while the control engineer uses the term *open-loop behavior.* (McRuer, Jex, Clement, & Graham, (1967) call this *precognitive behavior.*) Preprogramming can exist at many levels of specificity, ranging from prediction and extrapolation of a relatively constant-velocity segment of a random signal to the formulation and execution of a lazy-eight maneuver. The difference is one of degree. In all cases, preprogramming refers to the ability to take a given set of initial conditions and to operate at a higher level of control for a varying period of time. One has a model of the desired consequences of the movement sequence and can modify or correct an ongoing sequence to bring it closer to the intended goal and still be operating in a relatively preprogrammed mode. This behavior is important for generating large amplitude maneuvers.

These very special capabilities of the human controller are offset, to some extent, by a set of limitations that tend to degrade human performance. Some of these limitations (time delay, noise, band-width limitations) are so fundamental that they are operative in the simplest control tasks. Others (limited capacity, limited task under-standing, nonlinearities, the effects of stress, fatigue, etc.), become relevant as tasks become more complex or impose special circum-stances. This hierarchy of limitations also reflects, to a degree, our ability to quantify them. Here, we discuss those limitations that come into play most frequently in the analysis of flight control tasks as performed by skilled pilots, namely time delay, noise, bandwidth, and capacity limitations and nonlinearities. Although these limita-tions may themselves be relatively invariant across tasks, their effects on performance are highly task dependent. This causes difficulty for analytical or empirical approaches to predicting pilot performance that do not separate the quantification of fundamental and inherent limitations from their closed-loop performance effects.

Time Delay. Human response to a stimulus takes time, so there is an inevitable delay between the appearance of the stimulus and the generation of the response. These delays are measured in every dis-crete choice task, but they are also observed in continuous control tasks. In general, the amount of the delay observed will depend on the complexity of the task (and, for continuous control, on the meas-urement technique). There is, however, a fundamental or residual de-lay associated with sensory and neural pathway transmission times and basic central processing time. For continuous control this delay is on the order of 150 to 250 milliseconds.

Noise. Humans exhibit an inherent randomness in their response that is reflected in a variety of ways but most notably in the variabili-ty of that response. This randomness may arise from a number of sources, such as unpredictable fluctuations in control strategy, errors in observation or control manipulation that can only be described statistically, fluctuations in attention, and so forth. A major area in which this phenomenon has been studied extensively is in human detection of signals in noise. Signal detection theory as applied to the human observer has been able to characterize and measure hu-man performance in such tasks in terms of a signal-to-noise ratio that includes a noise that is intrinsic to the human (Green & Swets, 1966). In the context of aircraft control, we may postulate that each input variable or cue used by the pilot has associated with it a noisy perceptual process, and one aspect of piloting skill is to learn to effi-ciently extract the time course of these variables from this noisy representation. In addition, we can assume that there is some noise associated with the motor output of the human controller, but the literature suggests that this is a lesser source of human randomness.

Bandwidth Limitations.   The pilot's control inputs to the aircraft are generally inserted by limb movements. Such movements are intrinsically limited in their response characteristics, particularly in terms of the rapidity of the response that can be generated. A great deal of study of the human neuromuscular system has been conducted, and fairly detailed mathematical models that are appropriate for analyzing continuous control tasks have been developed for it (see McRuer & Krendel, 1974). These models range from the relatively simple to the highly complex, but, in essence, they capture the fact that the limbs have significant difficulty in following (or generating) movements with a frequency content greater than about 1 to 1.5 Hz.

Nonlinearities.   There are a number of basic nonlinearities in perception (or observation) and in motor output that may be relevant to particular control tasks. The most prominent of these involve thresholds in perception and saturations of response capability (e.g., a limit on the maximum force that can be generated). In many cases, the effects of these limitations can be avoided by appropriate design of the display and control systems. However, there are situations where the impact is unavoidable (e.g., threshold effects in the perception of cues from the external world) and, therefore, where the limitations must be considered in predicting performance.

Limited-Capacity, Single-Channel Operation.   It is widely accepted that the human behaves as a limited-capacity, single-channel operator. While coordinated motor commands are possible and common in skilled performance, it is rare to find an operator performing independent input and output activities simultaneously without some loss in performance quality on one or the other activity. This postulate underlies much current human information processing research and leads directly to a consideration of attention management. Given limited attentional capacity, the operator learns to allocate the available capacity in accordance with task demands; one can expect performance with respect to unattended variables to degrade accordingly. A major aspect of flight control in which the effects of this limitation are overt and have a significant impact is in the visual scanning required in multivariable monitoring and control. This scanning behavior has been the subject of considerable research

(Senders, 1983), and accounting for it, and other attention-sharing behavior, has been a major focus in the efforts to predict pilot performance in complex flight tasks.

Measurement of Human Control Performance

The dynamic performance of a control system, or element, is assessed by considering the following factors: (1) stability, (2) response to desired inputs, (3) response to unwanted inputs, (4) accuracy, (5) insensitivity to parameter changes, and (6) power or energy demands (Wolkowitch et al., 1962). System analysts have relied on a wide variety of measures (singly and in combination) to evaluate these various aspects of performance. There are no universal measures that can be applied to human performance measurement, but a combination of time-domain measures, frequency-domain measures, and pilot–model-related measures have proven useful for a range of purposes. The most significant of these are discussed in the following paragraphs.

Time-domain measures have a long history of use for performance measurement and as performance criteria in both control system analysis and experimental psychology. Virtually all of these measures are concerned with deviations from some desired response or value, or in other words, with performance errors (or "error scores"). It is worth pointing out that in multivariable situations no single error score will tell the entire story. Further, as was noted previously, power or energy demands are an important aspect of control system performance; in terms of human operator performance this implies that measures of control input, such as root-mean-square control deflections, are often as significant as measures of error and should therefore be measured routinely. In short, in flight control tasks it is useful to measure all major output and control variables, if possible.

There is a need in analyzing human control to obtain performance measurements other than error or control statistics. It is sometimes the case that these measures are not sufficiently sensitive to the changes in pilot response behavior that accompany changes in aircraft configuration or other variables of interest. Moreover, these measures do not, in themselves, reveal the human controller's strategy or the ways in which information is being processed. In order to detect changes and to understand the corresponding pilot behavior, it is frequently necessary to compute additional metrics of response behavior. Frequency-domain measures can provide a detailed look at the pilot's response, as well as an indication of the relative stability of various closed-loop configurations. Therefore, they have great potential with respect to both discriminating and understanding the effects of system and operator changes. Of special importance and value are measures of pilot describing-functions and remnant spectra.

The describing-function is a measure, in the frequency domain, of the linear relationship between the input stimuli available to the pilot and the pilot's control actions. It is defined as a frequency response (an amplitude ratio and phase difference of the output and the input signals at component input frequencies). In a sense, the describing-function is a measure of the pilot's control strategy, since it provides a rule relating control response to perceptual input. In general, however, not all of the pilot's response will be accounted for by the linear describing-function, and that portion which is not is called the *remnant*. The remnant spectrum is a measure of the stochastic portion or noisiness of the pilot's response as well as of any nonlinear aspects of that response. The dominant methods of modeling pilot–vehicle performance, discussed below, have been developed and/ or based on these frequency-domain measures of pilot response. The models provide a mechanism for interpreting the measures in terms of the component aspects of the pilot's response (sensory–perceptual, information processing, and motor) and in relation to pilot workload.

The measurement of pilot describing-functions requires that the task be essentially linear and time invariant over the measurement interval. A statistically stationary input is also necessary, and for most studies it is desirable that the input be random (or random appearing). These constraints obviously limit the tasks that can be investigated if these measures are to be made. However, their value for analysis of human performance suggests that flight control tasks that can be so approximated should be considered wherever possible.

It is important to emphasize that the performance measures discussed above are task dependent. That is, they provide descriptions of response behavior that pertain, in general, only to the control context in which they are measured. Because of the adaptive nature of the human controller, these measures can be expected to vary with factors such as aircraft dynamics, performance criteria, and available sensory cues. To help avoid this problem, it can be useful to augment the other measurements with measures or estimates of the parameters of an explicit model for the pilot's response. Such parameters may be more-sensitive indicators of a change in response resulting from a change in simulator configuration than are overall system performance measures. They also can have more diagnostic and interpretive value than error scores and are more likely to be of value in extrapolating the data to new situations than are the nonparametric frequency-domain measures discussed above.

Data

To gain an appreciation of skilled control performance as might be exhibited by human pilots, we present some experimental data col-

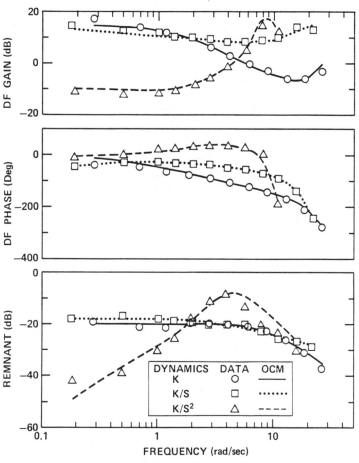

Figure 11.6.   Experimental and model (OCM) frequency response curves. Experimental results are indicated by symbols, model results by smooth curves. Model results are matched to data.

lected in three fundamental, but important, control tasks. These data also illustrate the performance measures described above.

Figure 11.6 (Levison, 1982) presents pilot describing-functions (DF) and remnant spectra for position, rate, and acceleration control system (see Figure 11.5), that is, zero-, first-, and second-order control systems, respectively. It can be seen that the describing-functions (i.e., the control strategies) adapt dramatically to the changes in system character. These adaptations are consistent with the basic requirements for good closed-loop control, discussed below. Perhaps more impressive is the fact that these data (and "score" data not shown here) are matched quite closely by an optimal control system with limitations that correspond to those of the human. This observation provides a powerful means for modeling human control performance, but it also is testimony to the high level of skill that can be obtained by humans through proper training.

The remnant spectra are the portion of the pilot's control output that is not linearly correlated with the input. The shapes of these spectra clearly depend on system dynamics, but it is difficult to develop significant insights directly from these curves. It is often more revealing to reflect the remnant back to the subject's input and normalize it with respect to the mean-squared values of that input. In this way, the remnant spectrum can be viewed as a noise associated with observation. This tends to make the results more consistent and leads to the most useful model for remnant developed to date (Levison et al. 1969). In addition, when used in conjunction with models for remnant, the remnant spectra, so reflected, can provide useful clues as to what perceptual variables are most important to the controller. Such an analysis reveals that for position control, the operator relies primarily on error information; for acceleration control, error-rate information is of prime importance; and for rate control, both error and error rate are used to a substantial degree.

Modeling the Pilot–Vehicle System

Manual Control Models

The expansions of operational envelopes and mission requirements for flight vehicles that have occurred in the past two to three decades, and the resulting increases in task difficulty and pilot workload, have stimulated a strong need for systematic means of analyzing the pilot–vehicle system and predicting closed-loop performance. This has been particularly true for problems involving the assessment of aircraft handling qualities and in the design and evaluation of advanced control and display systems. This, in turn, has led to a substantial effort aimed at developing quantitative engineering models for the human pilot performing closed-loop manual control tasks. Not surprisingly, the majority of the models developed for this purpose have been based on methods from control theory that have been applied to inanimate systems. We refer to this class of models as *control-theoretic models*, to distinguish them from psychologically based models (Pew & Baron, 1983).

Within the framework provided by a control-theoretic perspective, there is still much room for a variety of approaches to human performance modeling, and many models have been proposed. (For reviews of some of the models see Pew, Baron, Feehrer & Miller, 1977; Rouse, 1980; Sheridan & Farrell, 1974). Although many of these models have interesting and useful features, it is fair to say, in the light of passing time, that the manual control field has been and is dominated to a great extent by two types of models; namely, the quasilinear describing-function model and the state–space, optimal control model (OCM).

The describing-function and optimal control approaches to modeling human performance have several aspects in common. They both concentrate on the prediction of total (pilot–vehicle) system performance. As a result, they tend to focus on issues relating to system response and information requirements rather than on the "knobs and dials" questions of more traditional human engineering. This imposes a need for characterizing human limitations in terms appropriate to the control analysis context. They both also view the human operator as an information processing and control–decision element in a closed loop (sometimes referred to as the cybernetic view of the human). Both modeling approaches anticipate that trained human operators will exhibit many of the characteristics of a "good," or even optimal, inanimate system performing the same functions in the loop. Finally, both approaches make extensive (albeit different) use of the frequency-domain measures of control performance mentioned above. However, despite these similarities, it is the author's view that the describing-function models and the OCM differ significantly both from a theoretical–conceptual standpoint and in terms of methods and potential range of application.

The describing-function approach to modeling the pilot–vehicle system uses classical frequency-domain methods and relies heavily on the structuring of control loops as discussed above. Based on analysis and prior data, *form* of pilot equalization is predicted and, then, a set of adjustment rules are used to determine the parameters of that form. Detailed quantitative prediction of performance is not the strong point nor the focus of this approach. Rather, the quasilinear describing-function models have been aimed primarily at (1) determining the conditions, or vehicle or system designs, necessary for satisfactory closed-loop performance and pilot workload and (2) determining appropriate piloting technique. In particular, a major focus has been the analysis of aircraft flying or handling qualities. Many investigators have made contributions to the data base and the theory underlying describing-function models, but the major developments and applications in flight control can be attributed to McRuer and his colleagues (McRuer & Jex, 1967; McRuer & Krendel, 1957, 1974; McRuer et al., 1965).

The OCM, on the other hand, is a time-domain model for human–machine systems that is based on state–space ideas and optimal control. Instead of focusing on loop structures and corresponding equalization forms, the OCM starts from a consideration of the task, its performance criteria, and the pilot's inherent information processing and control constraints. It then predicts analytically the optimal strategy and the corresponding human and system performance. This leads to a model for the pilot that comprises the following: (1) an "equivalent" perceptual model that introduces human "observation noise" and time delay and, thereby, translates displayed variables into noisy, delayed *perceived* variables; (2) an information processing model that consists of an optimal estimator and predictor and generates the best estimate of the system state based on the perceived data; (3) a set of "optimal gains," chosen to optimize a performance metric that expresses task requirements; and (4) an equivalent "motor" or output model that accounts for "bandwidth" limitations (frequently associated with neuromotor dynamics) and the inability to generate noise-free control inputs. This structure is described in detail in Kleinman, Baron, and Levison (1971). A fairly recent review of the model and its application, along with several key references, may be found in Baron and Levison (1980).

Figure 11.6 illustrates the OCM's validity for three simple but important systems: rate, position, and acceleration command systems. In the figure, measured and theoretical human controller describing-functions and remnant spectra are compared. It can be seen that the model reproduces the characteristics of the subjects with remarkable fidelity over the entire frequency range of interest in manual control. In general, the OCM has proven capable of predicting or matching human performance with considerable fidelity in a variety of tasks. It has several other intrinsic advantages as a tool for pilot–vehicle analysis. Of perhaps greatest importance is that the OCM's explicit (and validated) model for information processing behavior, along with its models for human limitations, permit extension to tasks related to flight management. In addition, the fact that the OCM is a time-domain model allows it to be applied quite naturally to tasks in which the vehicle dynamics, or any other aspect of the task, varies with time (Baron 1976). Thus, the OCM is potentially applicable to a much wider range of flight control and flight management problems than is the describing-function methodology.

Some Applications of Pilot Models

Pilot models have been employed to analyze a wide range of problems related to flight control. These include display and control system analysis, flight director and stability augmentation system design, analysis of vehicle handling qualities, analysis of the limits of piloted control, analysis of pilot workload, and the determination of flight simulator requirements. A useful alternative way of categorizing these applications, that emphasizes the pilot–vehicle systems problems addressable by models of the human controller, is to relate them to flight-test problems, design problems, and simulator planning problems. This was done by McRuer and Krendel (1974) and more recently by Ashkenas (1984). Each of these references provides three tables that illustrate quite succinctly the broad scope of application of pilot modeling. Ashkenas (1984) also provides a reference list by application category.

Here, a few specific applications of pilot modeling will be presented and discussed briefly. Results are presented only for application of the OCM because of the author's own involvement with that model. The goal is to give the reader a general sense of the scope and nature of these applications rather than to provide specific results. Details, omitted here for brevity, can be found in the original sources.

Attitude Regulation for a High-Performance Aircraft.   The OCM has been used to analyze manual attitude regulation in cruise of high-performance aircraft in several studies (Baron, 1981; Levison & Junker, 1977; Levison, Tanner & Triggs, 1973). The basic task considered in these studies was nulling of small attitude errors (pitch and roll) about a wings-level operating point. In the studies, which were

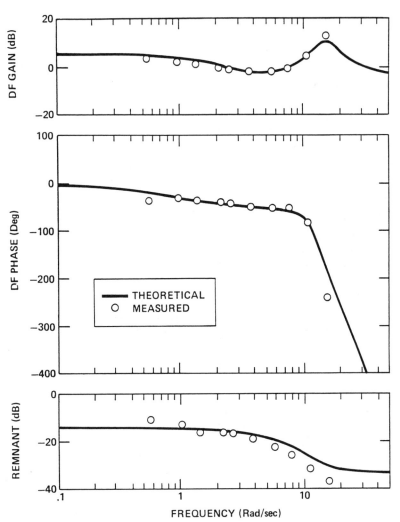

Figure 11.7.   Comparison of predicted and measured frequency-domain characteristics
for a simulated high-performance aircraft pitch-tracking task.

aimed at display analysis and simulator cueing requirements, the
model was used to plan and analyze experiments that provided both
a measurement-rich environment and a meaningful control task.

Figure 11.7 shows the comparison of describing-functions (DF) and
remnant spectra for the pitch axis. It can be seen that predictions are
in close agreement with the data. In addition, the predicted mean-

squared error and control scores for both pitch and roll control tasks were remarkably close to those measured in the experiment (Baron, 1976). This was accomplished using model parameters selected a priori on the basis of the laboratory data for different control dynamics and different subjects.

Display Analysis.   Because of the explicit perceptual modeling and information processing structure of the OCM, it is particularly well suited to the development of systematic methods for analyzing cockpit displays and information requirements (Baron & Levison, 1975, 1977; Hoffman, Kleinman, & Young, 1976). The model permits one to analyze many fundamental display-related issues such as the following in a quantitative manner (Baron & Levison, 1977):

1. Is status information adequate to achieve requisite performance with acceptable workload?
2. Will additional information improve performance and reduce workload, or will it degrade the situation because of increased monitoring and processing load?
3. Do the advantages of display integration (reduced scanning and attention sharing) outweigh those associated with the improved scaling available with separated displays?
4. Does given command information integrate status information effectively? If not, how does one design appropriate flight director laws?
5. What performance and workload levels can be achieved with a display that is perfectly integrated and scaled (an idealized display).

Here, we discuss a case where the OCM was used to analyze vertical situation displays for landing approach to landing of a STOL aircraft (Baron & Levison, 1972). We present just a few of the results to illustrate how overall system performance can be analyzed as a function of relevant environmental, system, or pilot-related parameters.

For this problem, system error-scores predicted by the OCM can be related to a more meaningful measure of mission performance, namely, the probability of a missed approach. Missed approach, in the longitudinal plane, can be defined in terms of category II "window" specification to be the case where height errors exceed 3.7 m or airspeed errors exceed 2.6 m/s. The model can be used to compute the probability of a missed approach as a function of any system or human-related parameter. Figure 11.8 shows these probabilities as a function of gust intensity, that is, the degree of turbulence.

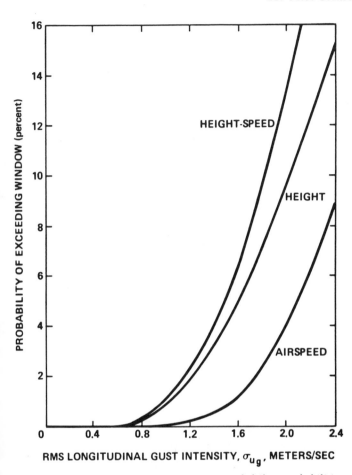

Figure 11.8.   Effect of gust intensity on approach failure probabilities.

Figure 11.9 shows the predicted probability of a missed approach as a function of the relative attention of the pilot to the longitudinal control task. For this figure, the probability of a missed approach has been computed by averaging over all possible gust intensities, thereby removing gust level as a factor. Attention level has been shown to be related to the observation-noise component of the OCM (Levison, Elkind, & Ward, 1971). It is therefore possible, by examining sensitivity to a single model parameter related to observation noise, to examine trade-offs between attentional demand and performance. For this application, the model predicts that if the pilot operates consistently at a nominal attention level, the overall probability of a missed ap-

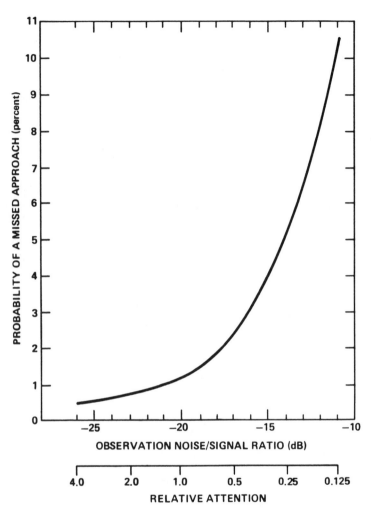

Figure 11.9.   Effect of attention on probability of missed approach.

proach is about 1%. Note, however, that performance degrades fairly rapidly as attention to the longitudinal control task is reduced (as might be necessitated, e.g., by an increased demand for lateral control or by the need to perform other activities).

The overall reliability of the system might be improved (either through improved performance or reduced workload) by providing the pilot with appropriate display augmentation. To investigate this possibility, the effect of adding a flight director display was ana-

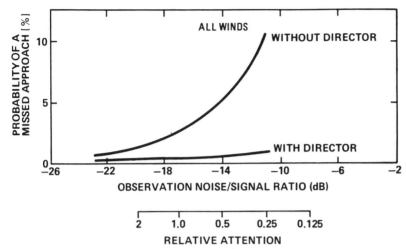

Figure 11.10.   Effect of display augmentation (flight director) and attention on missed approach.

lyzed. Figure 11.10 shows the result in terms of missed approach probability as a function of relative attention to the longitudinal control task. The director improves both performance and workload. The largest improvement is at the lower levels of attention, that is, in the region of attention in which the pilot is likely to be operating, owing to the demands of other tasks.

Handling Qualities.   A major application of pilot modeling has been in the analysis of vehicle handling qualities. This has been a particular area of emphasis for the quasilinear describing-function models (Ashkenas, 1984), but it has also been treated in the OCM framework (e.g., Hess, 1977; Levison, 1980). The underlying theme in this work is that if the vehicle has poor handling qualities it will require that the pilot adapt to them in a manner that is undesirable from the pilot's viewpoint, thereby resulting in a corresponding degradation in pilot opinion. Therefore, if one can determine empirically, or otherwise, the correlation between pilot subjective opinion and the parameters of a closed-loop pilot model, one has the basis for predicting vehicle handling qualities using pilot modeling techniques. This has been accomplished to a degree sufficient for some applications. In the quasilinear context, it turns out that the main concern is usually with the amount of "lead" required by the pilot, as reflected in the describing-function. In the OCM, the important parameter is the attention level (or observation-noise–signal ratio) necessary to achieve the prescribed performance objectives. In both cases, the basic notion is one of not requiring excessive pilot workload to achieve desired performance.

Levison (1980) suggested three possible schemes whereby model predictions of performance and pilot workload could be combined to predict pilot ratings: (1) pilot rating is determined by the performance achievable at some particular level of workload; (2) pilot rating is determined by the attention or workload required to achieve some criterion level of performance; (3) pilot rating is a continuous function of both performance and workload, and the pilot operates at a workload so as to minimize the numeric value of his rating (i.e., achieve the minimal (best) rating). He then generated performance–workload predictions (similar to Figure 11.9) with the OCM for eight vehicle configurations of a large transport aircraft executing an approach to landing. From these he was able, in turn, to predict pilot ratings and to compare them with corresponding ratings obtained experimentally in a simulation study (Rickard, 1976). The result is shown in Figure 11.11. It can be seen that the different model results are in quite good agreement among themselves and with the experimental data. Statistical analyses reveal that, with one exception, model predictions of rating are within one standard deviation of the subject mean rating; and the exception is only slightly greater than that criterion.

Changes in the Flight Control Problem

Aircraft control problems have changed significantly in recent years and will continue to do so in the future. The changes result primarily from advances in automatic control technology, which have opened up the possibilities for major changes in aircraft configuration and increasingly demanding mission profiles requiring, for example, nap-of-the-earth high-speed flight or curved, decelerating landing approaches. Advances in computers, materials, and propulsion are likely to accelerate existing trends. These developments impact significantly all aspects of flight control analysis, development, and implementation.

In terms of analysis, it is important to recognize that the traditional response modes, as well as the techniques used to analyze and design control systems, discussed above, may be of limited relevance in the future. In particular, aircraft with unconventional configurations

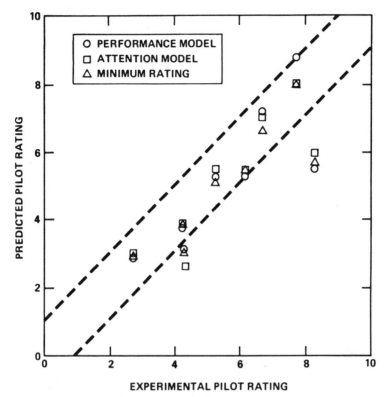

Figure 11.11. Predicted versus experimental pilot ratings.

and significant degrees of control augmentation can have many more, and very different, basic response characteristics. In addition, linear analysis may be of much more limited value, particularly in certain flight regimes of interest, such as high angle of attack. As a result, the role of simulation in control system design and development will continue to expand.

From the perspective of the pilot's role and tasks, the changes are, and will be, major. The need for continuous manual control on the pilot's part will continue to diminish and may ultimately vanish. Where such a need remains, there may be significant problems either because of the inherent difficulty of the particular control task or because the pilot will be used as a backup, thereby introducing serious questions regarding takeover of control and skill retention. The major impact of the changes is that the pilot will be principally a flight manager and supervisory controller who is interacting more with computers than with the vehicle itself. Moreover, with increases in computer capacity and advances in artificial intelligence, the pilot may be faced with interacting with systems exhibiting much more "intelligence" than that of current automation. This remains a control problem, but one of a very different character than that discussed in the previous sections.

The changes also have a direct impact on the nature of the devices that will be used by pilots to exercise their control responsibilities. For continuous control tasks, new "sticks" that are appropriate for six-degrees-of-freedom control and/or environments involving high accelerations will be employed. For management and supervision, control inputs are usually discrete and will involve quite different devices. Some of the possibilities for control input, and associated human factors issues, are discussed later in this section.

Models for Flight Management and Supervision. The changing nature of the pilot's control task to one emphasizing flight management and supervision imposes a need for new approaches to modeling the pilot–vehicle system. Various modeling approaches have been, and are being, explored (e.g., Lane, Streib, Glenn, & Wherry, 1980; Siefert, 1979), but the one most relevant to this discussion involves an extension of the ideas and submodels employed in the OCM so as to incorporate a much wider range of piloting tasks within an integrated framework. One particular example of this approach is a model called PROCRU (procedure-oriented crew model; Baron, Muralidharan, Lancraft, & Zacharias, 1980).

PROCRU was developed with a view toward providing a tool for systematic investigation of questions concerning the impact on performance and safety of procedural and system design changes and of the allocation of resources in the cockpit. The model has individual models for each crew member (pilot flying, pilot not flying, and second officer) and covers a range of crew activities including monitoring, continuous and discrete control, situation assessment, decision making, and communication. Though implemented only for the approach-to-landing task, the model is general in concept and can be extended to other flight tasks.

PROCRU is analogous to person-in-the-loop simulation and provides the same kind of performance information as would be available from such simulations. It provides a means for investigating a large number of variables in a relatively cost-effective and enlightening manner and could provide a useful adjunct to the simulations. However, it should be noted that the overall model has not been validated with human performance data, though some of its important component models have been so validated.

Human Engineering Considerations in Advanced Control[1]

Perhaps the major human factors concern of pilots in regard to introduction of automation in the cockpit is that, in some circumstances, operations with such aids may leave the critical question, Who is in control? unanswered. There are two dimensions to this concern:

1. Automation, and particularly "intelligent" systems, may take away control initiatives.
2. Intelligent systems are likely to be complex and difficult to understand. They may draw on data that are largely unobserved by the crew. For this reason, they may evaluate and choose among alternatives whose characteristics and utilities are not directly available to the crew. Given time and workload constraints, the crew may not be able to approve system choices before implementation is required.

The concern is legitimate. Unlike current autopilots and fault detection and reporting systems, which operate on "simple" inputs, generate easily verifiable outputs, and produce predictable consequences when disabled, more intelligent automated systems have the potential for quickly manipulating large quantities of diverse data, executing rule and knowledge-based algorithms beyond the immediate comprehension of the crew, and effecting significant and unseen changes in remote aircraft subsystems. These systems must, of course, be designed in ways that allow the crew to remain "in the loop." How to accomplish that remains an extremely difficult problem.

In addition to the issue of control responsibility, a host of questions related to human engineering of system–crew interfaces arise in connection with increased automation and the change in the crew's primary role from one of active continuous controllers to that of supervisors. Many of these are classical questions, but they take on added significance in the light of expanding technological opportunities for information acquisition, processing, and display. With respect to control inputs, the following questions are significant: What methods or techniques of information input are most consistent with

[1]This material is drawn from Baron and Feehrer (1985) and is principally the work of Dr. Carl Feehrer.

goals of rapid, accurate, and reliable performance by the crew? Which provide the lowest average increase in workload?

Obvious alternatives for inputting control information (or requests) are (1) keyboards and function buttons, (2) voice input, and (3) touch-sensitive displays. Although the merits of technological alternatives associated with such questions cannot be judged without a reasonably specific concept of the function(s) to be performed by an automated system, the general desirability and undesirability of certain of the alternatives can be summarized.

Keyboards and Function Buttons. The value of function buttons and keyboards as input devices is undeniable. Their significance is unequivocal and virtually instantaneous, and their use conserves space. At the same time, they have at least three obvious disadvantages that are difficult to design away:

1. They present opportunities for human error, particularly during conditions of high workload. Such errors, when they occur, may not be immediately obvious. This is especially true when lengthy inputs are made via keyboard.

2. It is difficult, if not impossible, for the operator to accomplish other tasks while pressing buttons or keys. If the input task cannot be deferred, the pilot has the choice of accepting the risks that go with a division of attention, deferring the competing task(s) or adding an increment to the workload of another crew member. None of these alternatives may be acceptable in some circumstances.

3. Current cockpit layouts require that the operator remain head down while accomplishing most button keyboard inputs. Again, depending on circumstances, the input task may be accomplished only at a cost in performance in other competing tasks. There have been instances (see Baron & Feehrer, 1985) where crews already well into the approach phase chose, probably inappropriately, to type revised coordinates into their automatic system rather than fly to the coordinates manually, thereby risking critical losses in awareness of external environmental factors. The context in which these events were recalled suggested a latent "trap," namely, the typical degree of success experienced with the automatic system may actually have prevented consideration of hand-flown corrections to the flight path.

Voice Input. It may not be surprising that, despite increasing use of function buttons and keyboards for input of information (e.g., in navigation), one of the most desired modes for transmission of information under most circumstances is voice. It is the mode very likely to be preferred for communications both within the cockpit—that is, between the crew and onboard "intelligent" systems—and for up and down-links between the aircraft and the ground control.

The preferences of the pilots for voice mode seem to have largely to do with the naturalness and efficiency with which voice communications can be carried on and, perhaps more importantly, with the fact that voice transactions can be completed in parallel with the performance of ongoing control and monitoring functions.

When one goes beyond simple word recognition systems into a consideration of speech-understanding technology, some of the difficulties inherent in that enterprise should be noted. For example, changes in the characteristics of the voice under stressful conditions might pose a severe problem. The most desirable system requires a conversational mode mediated by natural language for most crew–system interaction, under any but the most routine circumstances. This is significantly beyond current voice technology.

It is important when assessing the potential utility of voice or synthetic speech as an input–output mode to consider that a virtue which verbal outputs may not share with, for example, a warning light or horn or even printed copy, is persistence. The warning light or horn typically remains on until the condition it signals is attended to. A printed message is somewhere in the cockpit until it is disposed of. But human memory for the content of spoken messages is typically short. If the full potential of systems that will employ voice or speech synthesis techniques is to be realized, methods which permit rapid crew access to the content of previous transmissions must be developed.

Touch-Sensitive Displays.   Although major disadvantages of touch-sensitive displays are that they, like buttons and keyboards, generally require the user to remain head down and to concentrate carefully on his or her task, there may be an off-setting advantage in the application of this technology to input of navigation map-based information. Depending upon the scale(s) of the map(s) used and the accuracy of specification requirements for a given maneuver, one can imagine a crew member actually pointing at map locations rather than keying in coordinates in order to trigger route planning or re-planning computations by an intelligent system. Or, pointing and keying modes might be intermixed in such a way that global desires were initially imparted to the system via touch control panel and then final tuning of plans proposed by the system accomplished via keyboard.

Concluding Remarks

Flight control by human pilots is one of the most studied and well understood of human activities. Quantitative models have been developed to describe and predict human control performance and workload, and these have been applied to study a wide range of significant problems such as aircraft handling qualities, display and control system design and analysis, and simulator design and use. These models do not replace human-in-the-loop simulation as a development tool, but instead are complementary to simulation, flight testing, and to more conventional human factors analyses.

Despite the high level of understanding of human control that has been attained and the accomplishments alluded to above, there are a number of challenging problems and areas for research that remain or are arising. The evolution of aircraft, control and display systems, and mission requirements are imposing new problems in control. Thus, we have innovative aircraft configurations with different dynamic characteristics (especially when highly augmented), new types of control (including six-degrees of-freedom controls), different paths to fly, and so forth. These new systems are not wholly understood, to say the least, and there have been persistent difficulties in design, with pilot-induced oscillations, excessive pilot workload, and inadequate pilot–vehicle interfaces. There is a need for both data and for extension of the predictive capability of pilot models for such tasks.

With the increasing costs associated with simulation and training of flight control skills, it has become desirable to use models to assist in specifying simulators and in defining or monitoring training programs. In this area, a major limitation is the lack of adequate models for the way in which flight skills are acquired or learned.

The future concern most often raised in connection with modeling and understanding the pilot in the aircraft control loop is the changed and changing nature of the pilot's task owing to the introduction of substantial amounts of automation. Thus, the roles of flight management and supervisory control (monitoring, decision making, interacting with intermediary computers) are becoming dominant in many pilot–vehicle-display applications. As might be expected, the data and models needed for understanding these roles are not at all up to the standards of those for manual flight control tasks and are clearly in need of further development.

In summary, the changing, not fully understood nature of flight tasks, the costs associated with aircraft development and production as well as with those of training operational personnel, and the history of unanticipated pilot–vehicle-interface problems arising in development all argue for the need for systematic, crew-centered design techniques. These techniques must be capable of addressing the problems of the crew in the total system context of mission, vehicle, environment, automation, displays, and the like. Although much work remains, the lessons learned in analyzing manual flight control and some of the modeling techniques that have emerged from that endeavor can provide a sound foundation for the development of suitable analytical and experimental methods for the problems of interest.

References

Ashkenas, I. L. (1984). Twenty-five years of handling qualities research. *Journal of Aircraft, 21*(5), 289–301.

Baron, S. (1976). A model for human control and monitoring based on modern control theory. *Journal of Cybernetics and Information Sciences, 4*(1), 3–18.

Baron, S. (1981). *A pilot/vehicle model analysis of the effects of motion cues on Harrier control tasks* (Technical Report 4814). Cambridge, MA: Bolt Beranek and Newman, Inc.

Baron, S. (1984a). A control theoretic approach to modelling human supervisory control of dynamic systems. In W. B. Rouse (Ed.), *Advances in man–machine systems research, 1*, (pp. 1–47). Greenwich, CT: JAI Press.

Baron, S. (1984b). Adaptive behavior in manual control and the optimal control model. In O. G. Selfridge, E. L. Rissland, & M. A. Arbib (Eds.), *Adapative control of ill-defined systems* (pp. 51–737). New York: Plenum.

Baron, S. (1985). *Human performance models for assessment of simulator effectiveness* (Technical Report 5869). Cambridge, MA: Bolt Beranek and Newman, Inc.

Baron, S., & Feehrer, C. (1985). *An analysis of the application of AI to the development of intelligent aids for flight crew tasks* (NASA Contractor Report 3944). NASA-Langley Research Center.

Baron, S., Lancraft, R., & Zacharias, G. L. (1980). *Pilot/vehicle model analysis of visual and motion cue requirements in flight simulation* (Contractor Report 3312). Moffett Field, CA: NASA-Ames Research Center.

Baron, S., & Levison, W. H. (1972). *A manual control theory analysis of vertical situation displays for STOL aircraft* (Technical Report 2484). Cambridge, MA: Bolt Beranek and Newman, Inc.

Baron, S., & Levison, W. H. (1975). An optimal control methodology for analyzing the effects of display parameters on performance and workload in manual flight control, *IEEE Transactions on Systems Man and Cybernetics,* SMC-5(4), 423–430.

Baron, S., & Levison, W. H. (1977). Display analysis with the optimal control model of the human operator. *Human Factors 19*(5), 437–457.

Baron, S., & Levison, W. H. (1980). The optimal control model: Status and future directions. In *Proceedings of the international conference on cybernetics and society* (pp. 90–101). Cambridge, MA.

Baron, S., Muralidharan, R., Lancraft, R., & Zacharias, G. (1980). *PROCRU: A model for analyzing crew procedures in approach to landing* (Contractor Report CR-152397). Moffett Field, CA: NASA-Ames Research Center.

Citurs, K. D. (1984). *Controller requirements for uncoupled aircraft motions* (Technical Report 84-306). Dayton, OH: Wright–Patterson Air Force Base, Flight Dynamics Laboratory, Air Force Wright Aeronautical Laboratories.

Green, D. H., & Swets, J. A. (1966). *Signal detection theory and psychophysics.* New York: Wiley.

Heffley, R. K., Clement, W. F., Ringland, R. F., Jewell, W. F., Jex, H. R., McRuer, D. T., & Carter, V. E. (1981). *Determination of motion and visual system requirements for flight training simulators* (Technical Report 546). Ft. Rucker, AL: U.S. Army Research Institute for the Behavioral and Social Sciences.

Hess, R. A. (1977). Prediction of pilot opinion ratings using an optimal pilot model. *Human Factors, 19*(5), 459–475.

Hoffman, W. C., Kleinman, D. L., & Young, L. R. (1976). *Display/control requirements for automated VTOL aircraft* (Contractor Report 158905). : NASA-Langley Research Center.

Kelley, C. R. (1968). *Manual and automatic control.* New York: Wiley.

Kleinman, D. L., & Baron, S. (1971). *Manned vehicle systems analysis by means of modern control theory* (Contractor Report 1753). : NASA, Electronics Research Center.

Kleinman, D. L., Baron, S., & Levison, W. H. (1971). A control theoretic approach to manned-vehicle systems analysis. *IEEE Transactions on Automated Control AC-16*(6) 824–833.

Lane, N. E., Strieb, M. I., Glenn, F. A., & Wherry, R. J. (1980). *The human operator simulator: An overview.* Proceedings of the Conference on Manned Systems Design, Freiburg, W. Germany.

Levison, W. H. (1980) *A model-based technique for predicting pilot opinion ratings for large commercial transports* (Contractor Report 3257). : NASA-Langley Research Center.

Levison, W. H. (1982). The optimal control model for the human operator: Theory, validation and application. In *Proceedings of the Workshop on Flight Testing in Identifying Pilot Workload and Pilot Dynamics.* Edwards Air Force Base, CA.

Levison, W. H. (1983). *Development of a model for human operator learning in continuous estimation and control tasks* (Technical Report 5331). Cambridge, MA: Bolt Beranek and Newman, Inc.

Levison, W. H., Baron, S., & Kleinman, D. L. (1969). A model for human controller remnant. *IEEE Transactions on Man–Machine Systems, MMS-10*(4).

Levison, W. H., Elkind, J. I., & Ward, J. L. (1971). *Studies of multi-variable manual control systems: A model for task interference* (Contractor Report 1746). Moffett Field, CA: NASA-Ames Research Center.

Levison, W. H., & Houck, P. D. (1975). *Guide for the design of control sticks in vibration environments* (Technical Report 74-127). Dayton, OH: Wright–Patterson Air Force Base, Aerospace Medical Research Laboratory.

Levison, W. H., & Junker, A. M. (1977). *A model for the pilot's use of motion cues in roll-axis tracking tasks* (Technical Report 77-40). Dayton, OH: Wright–Patterson Air Force Base, Aerospace Medical Research Laboratory.

Levison, W. H., & Muralidharan, R. (1982). *Analysis of manual control tasks in support of the chemical defense program* (Technical Report 5168). Cambridge, MA: Bolt Beranek and Newman, Inc.

Levison, W. H., Tanner, R. R., & Triggs, T. J. (1973). Evaluation of factual displays for flight control. In *Proceedings of the Ninth Annual Conference on Manual Control.* Cambridge, MA.

McRuer, D. T., Ashkenas, I. L., & Graham, D. (1973). *Aircraft dynamics and automatic control.* Princeton, NJ: Princeton University Press.

McRuer, D. T., & Graham, D. (1981). Eight years of flight control: Triumphs and pitfalls of the systems approach. *Journal of Guidance and Control, 4*(4) 353–362.

McRuer, D. T., Graham, D., Krendel, E. S., & Reisner, W. (1965). *Human pilot dynamics in compensatory systems* (Technical Report 65-15). Dayton, OH: Wright–Patterson Air Force Base, Flight Dynamics Laboratory.

McRuer, D. T., & Jex, H. R. (1967). A review of quasi-linear pilot models. *IEEE Transactions on Human Factors in Electronics, 8*(3), 231–249.

McRuer, D. T., Jex, H. R., Clement, W. F., & Graham, D. (1967). A system analysis theory for displays in manual control (Technical Report STI 163-1). Hawthorne, CA: Systems Technology, Inc.

McRuer, D. T., & Krendel, E. S. (1957). *Dynamic response of human operators* (Technical Report 56-524). OH: Wright Air Development Center.

McRuer, D. T., & Krendel, E. S. (1974). *Mathematical models of human pilot behavior* (AGARDograph No. 188). North Atlantic Treaty Organization, Advisory Group for Aerospace Research and Development.

Pew, R. W., & Baron, S. (1983). Perspectives on human performance modelling. *Automatica, 19*(6), 663–676.

Pew, R. W., Baron, S., Feehrer, C. E., & Miller, D. C. (1977). *Critical review and analysis of performance models applicable to man–machine systems evaluation* (Technical Report 3446). Cambridge, MA: Bolt Beranek and Newman, Inc.

Poulton, E. C. (1974). *Tracking skill and manual control.* London: Academic Press.

Rickard, W. W. (1976). Longitudinal flying qualities in the landing approach. In *Proceedings of the Twelfth Annual Conference on Manual Control.* Cambridge, MA.

Rouse, W. B. (1980). *Systems engineering models of human–machine interaction.* New York: North Holland.

Seifert, D. J. (1979). *Combined discrete network–continuous control model of man–machine systems* (Technical Report AMRL-TR-79-34). Dayton, OH: Wright-Patterson Air Force Base, Aerospace Medical Research Laboratories.

Senders, J. W. (1983). *Visual scanning processes.* Netherlands: University of Tilberg Press.

Sheridan, T. S., & Ferrell, W. R. (1974). *Man-machine systems: Information, control and decision models of human performance.* Cambridge, MA: MIT Press.

Wolkowitch, J. R., Magdelano, R., McRuer, D. T., Graham, D., & McDonnell, J. (1962). *Performance criteria for linear constant coefficient systems with deterministic inputs* (Technical Report 61-501). Dayton, OH: Wright–Patterson Air Force Base, Aeronautical Systems Division.

Aviation Displays

12

Alan F. Stokes
Christopher D. Wickens

Introduction

Aircraft displays are the pilot's window on the world of forces, commands, and information that cannot be seen as naturally occurring visual events or objects. As aircraft grow in complexity and technology provides the capability of offering more and more information, the pilot's senses can become overloaded with information (Statler, 1984). The limits of attention may be rapidly exceeded by the proliferation of warning indicators, status displays, flight path displays, air traffic control data links, meteorological information, navigational information, and communications data. While a strong case can be made for the pilot's need to know about much of this, it is essential to consider how the information should be displayed and formatted in a way that offers the pilot the most automatic and compatible representation of the current and future state of the aircraft and the environment.

This chapter examines the relationship between emerging technologies and information overload in the cockpit. The first two sections

Human Factors in Aviation

address developments in the display of two important categories of information: that pertaining to flight control and that pertaining to navigation. Then, four different emerging technologies in the design of displays are discussed—innovations concerning the physical location of displayed elements and the use of voice, color, and pictures. Finally, the chapter concludes with a brief discussion of the relationship between displays and automation.

Flight Path Displays

An important dichotomy in the display of information relevant to flight control can be drawn between *status displays,* which tell the pilot the current state of the aircraft, and *command displays,* which tell the pilot how he or she should control the aircraft. In aviation, status displays are represented by the traditional instrument panel that provides status information about the rate of climb, altitude, bank, heading, and so forth. One drawback of the status display is that extra cognitive computations are often required to translate a knowledge of the current state of the aircraft into a decision as to what the appropriate control action should be to change that state according to the desired flight path. The objective of the command display is for a computer algorithm to make these predictive calculations directly and thus provide the pilot with information stating exactly what control inputs are required.

Command displays become progressively more important with larger, more sluggish aircraft. The high inertia of the class of wide-bodied jets (such as the B-747, DC-10, or L-1011) means that a control input delivered at one time will not effectively alter the rate of change of flight path position until a few seconds later, and the delay until a new flight path position is reached may be still longer. Hence, effective control must be achieved by responding to the *predicted* error rather than to the current error. An optimum source of error prediction is the rate of change and acceleration of the present error. However, acceleration, in particular, is not a variable that the human eye is well equipped to perceive (Fuchs, 1962; McRuer et al., 1968) nor one that the brain can easily compute (Gottsdanker, 1952; Waganaar & Sagaria, 1975). Techniques of display quickening and prediction have been developed as command displays to help overcome these perceptual and cognitive limitations.

Quickening

As we have noted, if the pilot of a sluggish aircraft inputs a control correction on the basis of the current size of an error rather than its rate of change or acceleration, the response may be too late. Quickening provides a direct presentation of the velocity and acceleration of system state (Birmingham & Taylor, 1954, 1958; Kelley, 1968). This technique is classically accomplished by adding the higher derivatives (velocity and acceleration) of the error (or aircraft state) directly onto the error position with some relative weighting. Using this algorithm, the pilot tracks or nullifies an error symbol that moves ahead of the actual state of the aircraft. From the pilot's point of view, a system of lower order (fewer time integrations) is being tracked.

The principle of quickening forms the basis of the *flight director display* in aviation. In the flight director, various higher-derivative signals of a controlled dimension, such as glidepath deviation, are combined to produce a command target signal for the pilot to match. The command does not represent the true zero-error flight path, but instead represents a signal which, if used as the basis for control, will produce successful guidance along the flight path.

Because quickening (and the flight director) amounts to lowering the order of tracking control, this results in a reduction of display error. However, the quickened display will not necessarily reduce system error. Poulton (1974) has carefully articulated many of the shortcomings of quickened displays. Under certain circumstances, such displays may provide operators with a false sense of security because they believe that error is nullified (as the display of quickened error suggests), when in fact considerable system error may be present. Furthermore, the quickened display does not leave the pilot with a true indication of the exact state of the system. Such an indication may be essential in a sudden emergency, and so it is desirable also to have an additional indicator of true system state. This indicator is present in the predictive display.

Predictive Displays

Predictive displays, an alternative to quickening, provide information concerning how to respond, without sacrificing the presentation of accurate information about the current aircraft state. The predictive display offers the pilot one or more symbols depicting the future state of the aircraft, inferred from certain assumptions concerning the pilot's future control activity (see Figure 12.1). The precise form of these assumptions may vary, but two are typical: the pilot will hold the control at its current value for a set duration of time and then return it to neutral or the control will exponentially return to its neutral value from the current setting. The predictive information may be based upon a fast-time model of the aircraft dynamics that is con-

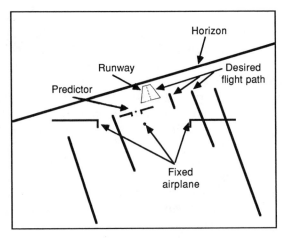

Figure 12.1.   A typical predictor display used by Jensen (1981), with one future point. The
predicted aircraft symbol is shown off to
the left, and banked more to the left than
the present indicator labeled "fixed airplane." The predictive display also shows
the future command inputs represented
by the desired flight path. From "Prediction and Quickening in Perspective Flight
Displays for Curved Landing Approaches"
by R. S. Jensen, 1981, *Human Factors, 23,*
p. 358. Copyright 1981 by the Human
Factors Society, Inc. Reprinted by permission.

tinuously iterated to generate future states (Kelley, 1968). Alternatively, since the predictive information is typically based upon the
derivatives of the current aircraft state, which the pilot is asked to
perceive while controlling the aircraft, predictive estimates may be
determined directly by these derivatives (Gallagher, Hunt, & Williges,
1977; Jensen, 1981). Taking derivatives of slowly changing quantities
can lead to relatively noisy displayed signals. Therefore, an alternative is to drive the derivative portions of the display with variables
related directly to the control surfaces, since these correspond
closely to the desired derivative values. In aviation control, for example, bank angle provides a good approximation of the first derivative
(rate-of-change) of heading, while aileron position provides a good
approximation of its second derivative (acceleration).

Using either basis for the predictive algorithm, predictive displays
have been demonstrated unequivocally to be useful (Grunwald, 1981;

Jensen, 1981; Kelley, 1968; Palmer, Jago, & DuBord, 1981), and these have been incorporated into the horizontal situation display of the Boeing 757 and 767 cockpits (see Figure 12.7, bottom). Their benefit is, of course, directly proportional to the accuracy of prediction, and this accuracy in turn, is a joint function of the frequency and magnitude of disturbance inputs and of the time-constant of the system. The accuracy of prediction will always decrease as time being predicted increases into the future, and the useful predictive interval into the future will be shorter if the input disturbance is greater and the system time-constant is shorter. Systems of high inertia and therefore long time-constants, such as wide-bodied aircraft, will allow relatively longer predictive intervals and will be little influenced by the magnitude of high-frequency disturbances. Systems with relatively short time-constants may also have accurate and therefore long predictive spans if operating in a noise-free environment (e.g., spacecraft in outer space). On the other hand, combinations of short time-constants and high-amplitude or high-frequency disturbance inputs will render the valid prediction interval considerably shorter for such vehicles as light aircraft flying through turbulence.

Unfortunately, predictive displays lack spatial economy and, despite their benefit to performance, may add display clutter and increase visual workload (Murphy, McGee, Palmer, Paulk, & Wempe, 1978; Yeh & Wickens, 1984). A predictive display of a one-dimensional control task must add a second dimension to depict time. When two-dimensional tasks are to be predictive, fairly demanding spatial graphics techniques must be employed, and these often require considerable on-line computing power. Nevertheless, advances in microprocessor technology have made practical predictor displays increasingly feasible. Jensen (1981) demonstrated the value of a predictor display (shown in Figure 12.1) for landing approaches. Kelley (1968) developed a design for a six-degrees-of-freedom predictive display for representing the motion of space vehicles, and Grunwald (1981) showed the utility of a 3-D flight predictor. Leffler (1982) gives an illustration of a possible predictor display for takeoff performance that combines real-time performance modeling with a synthetic voice alert. The system would comprise a monitor that used aircraft acceleration, air and ground speed, engine performance, and runway length to model likely takeoff performance and so facilitate an early abort decision if necessary.

More recently Filarsky and Hoover (1983) described a command flight path display undergoing flight testing for the Naval Air Development Center. This display uses a fully integrated pictorial format. Hawkins, Reising, and Gilmour (1984) also reported a study of advanced fighter-aircraft display concepts in which predictive information is presented pictorially by computer-generated graphics. The prediction is based upon real-time computation of future navigational position using present system status variables. Known as TFM, for tactical flight management, the computational part of the system at present uses latitude, longitude, altitude, and time to predict the aircraft's path. Hawkins et al. (1984) and Hawkins, Reising, Lizza, and Beachy (1983) present this information on a vertical situation display CRT as a three-dimensional "path-in-the-sky," showing the future track of the aircraft if the pilot does not override the TFM system (see Figure 12.2). The TFM system also takes a step beyond conventional predictor displays by using color to provide an estimate of uncertainty as to the aircraft's future position.

Navigational Displays

To achieve effective navigation, the pilot must rely upon a map of the terrain and integrate information on the map with that from other

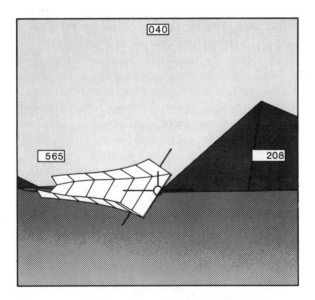

Figure 12.2.   Predictor display showing highway in the
              sky, developed at the Crew Systems Develop-
              ment Branch, Flight Control Division, Flight
              Dynamics Laboratory, Wright–Patterson Air
              Force Base, Ohio.

instruments or with the view of the outside world. Microprocessor technology now makes it possible for maps, charts, and traffic diagrams to be displayed on a CRT. Such computer-driven displays have two major advantages over conventional paper maps: they are less cumbersome to manipulate physically, and they have the potential to augment information in novel format, taking advantage of the computer's flexible graphics capabilities. Computer-driven maps or navigational displays have been implemented in a range of aircraft, and it is likely that further-improved systems will become more widely used in the future.

Human interaction with maps and geographical information is, of course, influenced to some extent by certain biases. For example, we tend to cognitively "distort" the world into a north–south–east–west grid, dealing less easily with directions between these 90° axes (Wickens, 1984). This bias is shown by pilots as well as nonpilots (Loftus, 1978). Our perception of distance on maps is influenced by the amount of visual clutter within (Thorndyke, 1980), and the advantages of spatial maps rather than "route lists" or verbal commands depends very much on the task at hand. Navigation, for example, favors route lists, and planning favors maps. These cognitive issues in navigation are discussed in detail by Wickens (1984).

During the early part of this decade, NASA undertook a research program on a display concept whose objective was to present the pilot with visual information pertaining to the location and heading of other aircraft in the surrounding airspace. Such a concept, referred to as the *cockpit display of traffic information,* or CDTI, was intended to increase the pilot's situational awareness, thereby both enhancing flight safety, by contributing to the early resolution of potential traffic conflicts, and increasing the efficient use of airspace. The CDTI is a CRT display showing the relative positions of the host aircraft and other air traffic, as well as heading relative to waypoints or route markers. Conventionally the CDTI is a "track-up" or inside-out moving map display with the host aircraft shown as a fixed symbol around which the display moves (O'Connor, Jago, Baty, & Palmer, 1980).

The CDTI display may be integrated with a TCAS (Traffic Alert and Collision Avoidance System), in which case collision-avoidance instructions are output, making this a command display (Klass, 1981; Lester & Quan, 1983). In the absence of the TCAS however, the CDTI is quite explicitly a status display and *not* a command display, as there is no intention of relieving the air traffic controller of the primary responsibility for maintaining safe separation in the airspace. In fact, one concern over implementation of the CDTI is the fear that its presence might give the pilot greater autonomy and opportunity to question or ignore air traffic control commands. Additionally, some concern has been expressed that the CDTI may actually increase the pilot's visual workload and distract from critical out-the-window scanning (Smith & Ellis, 1982). Nevertheless, the research program on the CDTI concept is important, because it represents an entirely new integration of display concepts that did not need to be bound by prior traditions and habits (a limitation in redesign of conventional pilot flight instruments).

Considerable research effort at NASA has been devoted to determining the optimal format of the CDTI. Since its presence in the cockpit may well lead to an increase in visual workload, there is an obvious need to present only needed information in a coherent format compatible with the pilot's mental model of the situation. A sur-

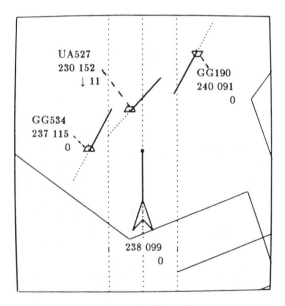

PLAN-VIEW DISPLAY

Figure 12.3.   Prototype of CDTI. From "Perspective Traffic Display Format and Air Pilot Traffic Avoidance" by S. Ellis, M. McGreevy, and L. Hitchcock, 1987, *Human Factors, 29*, p. 61. Copyright 1987 by the Human Factors Society, Inc. Reprinted by permission.

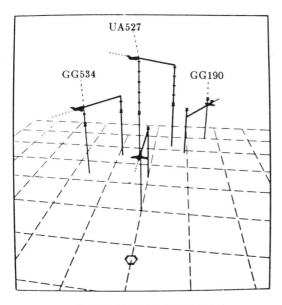

PERSPECTIVE DISPLAY

Figure 12.4.   Three-dimensional perspective format
of CDTI. From "Perspective Traffic
Display Format and Air Pilot Traffic
Avoidance" by S. Ellis, M. McGreevy,
and L. Hitchcock, 1987, *Human Factors, 29,* p. 61. Copyright 1987 by the
Human Factors Society, Inc. Reprinted
by permission.

vey by Hart and Wempe (1979) investigated pilots' subjective
evaluations of CDTI symbology. This information contributed to the
design of symbols for a plan-view CDTI, depicted in Figure 12.3.
Geometric coding is used to represent altitude above and below the
own-ship's altitude.

   Researchers have established the clear benefits of the predictor information in the CDTI for both the pilot's and other aircraft. Such information allows for more optimal corrections in the face of potential
conflicts with a two-dimensional CDTI representation (Palmer, 1983).
However, Smith and Ellis (1982) found that pilots tended to implement only two-dimensional collision-avoidance maneuvers (i.e.,
turns) rather than climbs or descents when using the two-dimensional predictor. To address this issue, Ellis and McGreevy (1983)
and Ellis, McGreevy, and Hitchcock (1987) examined a three-dimen-

sional perspective display of the airspace, as depicted in Figure 12.4. They found that this perspective allowed the pilot to maneuver earlier out of conflict situations and to use the vertical dimension more frequently in carrying out those maneuvers.

Display Organization and Configuration: The Visual Overload Problem

Aviation designers have sought ways to address the visual workload problem imposed by the multidial cockpit, in which scores of separate indicators, each requiring foveal vision for precise reading, are displayed across a wide panel. Information from one cannot be extracted unless it is fixated, precluding information extraction from somewhere else. This situation forces a serial mode of information intake that is clearly detrimental to performance and safety under conditions of stress and high information overload. The search for solutions has taken several paths, each of which is discussed in some detail. The first two paths have involved restructuring the spatial layout of the display panel and have taken opposite approaches.

The head-up display concept has attempted to bring more information into the fovea, while the use of peripheral displays has the objective of relieving foveal vision. Other approaches have attempted to exploit voice, color, and pictorial representations, and a final approach has been an effort to automate displays by making them callable or configurable on command.

Head-Up Displays (HUD)

The head-up display, or HUD, used in many military aircraft is an extension of the conventional attitude display indicator (ADI) or artificial horizon. Like the ADI, the HUD presents attitude information, but this information is projected onto a transparent screen behind the windshield or onto the windshield itself in the pilot's line of sight. It is often accompanied by the projection of related instrument information (e.g., airspeed, altitude). The intended purpose of such projection is, of course, to allow the pilot to take in information on the HUD instruments without taking his eyes off the outside scene. Research issues in the design of the HUD, many of which are comprehensively reviewed by Egan and Goodson (1978), can typically be subdivided into two categories. The first concerns the effects of the symbology of the HUD itself, independent of its location. The second relates to the positioning of the HUD. What are the actual benefits or potential costs of superimposing instrument information on the outside scene, and what optical and attentional variables must be considered to maximize these benefits?

HUD Symbology. Despite the existence of military standards, there has been little standardization in the format and symbology of aviation HUDs. These tend to differ between different aircraft types. Even within NATO, the horizon symbol used on British military aircraft is inverted with respect to that used on U.S. aircraft. One focus of research in this area has been on the specification of attitude information, because such information as knowing the direction of the horizon is of critical importance for a pilot flying in unusual attitudes during air-to-air combat (Taylor, 1982, 1984). Taylor (1984) reports a series of human factors experiments concerned with the pitch-scale display, and concludes that the results of these experiments support converging evidence from recent studies in the psychology of perception (Hoffman, 1980; Navon, 1977). This evidence suggests that macroscopic or global features of complex multidimensional stimuli are processed more rapidly than detailed components of the whole. He therefore recommends that HUD design follow the established Gestalt principles of perceptual organization such as proximity, similarity, and closure (Pomerantz & Kubovy, 1986).

A second research focus concerns the problem of HUD display clutter. A study by Oppitek (1973) found that 11 of 17 pilots turned off the HUD "at critical phases of a mission because it interfered with their performance" (p. 26). Out of this concern, Josefowitz, North, and Trimble (1980) integrated user comments from experienced Navy and Air Force pilots and experimental and analytical data to provide a set of recommendations concerning the use of symbology and color on multisensor displays including HUDs. At present, aviation HUD formats rely upon symbolic codes and alphanumeric information that is monochrome rather than colored because of the perceptual distortions that may result when colored HUD information is perceived against the background of changing hues. The computer-generated symbology usually takes the form of pictographs or abstract symbols. Since HUD formats differ from the backup panel instrumentation, difficulty may be experienced in switching between the HUD and the traditional instrument panel (Schmit, 1982).

HUD Optics and Attention. In theory, the location of symbology on a HUD, rather than on the control panel below, allows for two advantages: visual scanning need not be required between the two information sources and, through optical techniques, the HUD instrumentation may be presented at the same apparent distance (optical infinity) as the outside world through a projection device known as a Fresnel lens. This device collimates the light rays from the symbology, projecting them to the eyes as parallel rays. This projection characteristic is assumed to eliminate the need for the visual reaccommodation that is necessary if the pilot shifts focus from the instrument panel to the outside world. In fact, subjects do not invariably accommodate to infinity in viewing collimated displays (Hull, Gill, & Roscoe, 1982; Norman & Ehrlich, 1986).

In spite of the apparent attractiveness of this concept, many important issues with regard to HUD optics remain to be fully resolved. In particular, despite the optics of the Fresnel lens, some characteristics of the HUD may be unambiguously perceived as near, and the potential conflicting influence of two of these sources of nearness has yet to be determined (Roscoe, 1984). On the one hand, visible scratches or dust on the windscreen will "pull" visual accommodation to a much nearer focal level than the topical infinity projected by the Fresnel lens (Benel, 1980; Owens, 1979). On the other hand, other perceptual cues of depth, such as binocular disparity, convergence, and relative motion, clearly signal the closeness of the HUD combining glass. The combined effect of these cues may serve to negate the efforts to pull accommodation to optical infinity through the Fresnel lens.

The potential conflicts between "near" and "far", and their dependence upon basic perceptual cues, also highlights the role of attention. Here, one potential advantage of the HUD is an improvement in the pilot's ability to divide attention between the two information sources, processing information on one, while monitoring for events on the other. Much of the systematic work on attention in HUDs has been carried out in a program of research at NASA-Ames Research Center. This program has focused upon three important issues pertaining to the position (head-up vs. head-down) and accommodative distance of the HUD instrument domain relative to the far domain outside the aircraft: (1) the ability to focus attention on one domain without distraction or clutter from the other, (2) the ability to process information in parallel from both domains, and (3) the ability to switch attention between domains.

Fischer (1979) and Naish (1964) have examined the effects of the presence of information at one depth on the ability to extract information at the other; that is, the ability to focus attention. In this regard, their findings closely replicate those of the laboratory study by

Neisser and Becklan (1975). The presence of information at either distance did not harm information extraction at the other.

If information processing along one channel is unaffected by events on the other, does this mean that processing between the two channels is serial rather than parallel? This hypothesis was supported in a simulator investigation by Fischer, Haines, and Price (1980), who examined the pilot's ability to detect an unexpected obstacle on a visually simulated runway while flying with or without a HUD. Some of the pilots failed even to notice the object, a large aircraft partially on the runway. When detected, reaction time to detect the plane was actually longer with the HUD than with the conventional head-down display. To account for these results, it may be assumed that the attentional world was partitioned between near and far channels, on the basis of optical and motion cues. Then, in the serial processing mode, pilots focused on the near, while filtering out far, information. These findings tend to support Neisser and Becklan's (1975) conclusion that parallel processing of information from two visual scenes may not occur, even when these are superimposed in visual space. Of course, such serial processing occurs with head-down displays as well. However, in these conditions pilots presumably are aware that they *must* sample, since physical constraints on peripheral vision prevent outside information from registering while they are head-down. Therefore, fairly rigid and optimal scanning strategies will be invoked to check the far domain of the outside world. This optimal sampling may break down when scanning is no longer required in the HUD.

If a serial processing mode is indeed in effect, then the critical question to be asked concerns the physical distinctions (visual angle and accommodative distance) between the near and far domains that either facilitate or disrupt this switching action. A set of simulator experiments by Weintraub, Haines, and Randle (1984, 1985) examined this issue by requiring subjects to switch attention either from the near to the far or from the far to the near domain, in order to cross-check HUD instrument information with runway closure information. The authors concluded that the positioning of the instrumentation, head-up or head-down, had little effect on the speed of attention switching, so long as it was presented at optical infinity (i.e., at the same accommodative distance as the far domain of the simulated runway). Decreasing the accommodative distance of HUD information did indeed retard attention switching, but only by a tenth of a second, a delay that is probably not significant in operational environments.

In conclusion, experimental data suggest that HUD positioning may not facilitate parallel processing, may actually harm it, and will have relatively little effect on attention switching. Yet HUD research is far from complete. For example, the studies by Weintraub et al. (1984, 1985) were carried out with static stimuli, thereby eliminating the dynamic motion information that may serve to enhance the definition and discrimination of the near and far domain channels. The selective aspects of visual attention and their implications for superimposed displays remain poorly understood.

Peripheral Displays

Even with the use of HUDs, panel space for additional instrumentation is very limited. Increasing the density of symbology on HUDs and head-down CRT displays gives rise to clutter. What's more, the processes of eye movement, accommodation, and convergence set limits on the rate of information acquisition in the conventional (foveal) instrument scan (Wulfeck, Weisz, & Raben, 1958). Visual sensitivity decreases as the image is displaced further from the fovea of the eye, but peripheral vision may still be a useful, underutilized resource, especially for the detection of motion and luminosity (Leibowitz, 1986; Vallerie, 1968). Indeed, as much as 90% of visual stimulation is obtained, without conscious effort, from the peripheral visual field (Malcolm, 1984). If there are visual tasks which can be assigned to peripheral vision, more central visual-processing resources should, in theory, be freed to improve performance in normal situations or to manage high-workload or stressful situations.

Peripheral Display Implementation.   A number of display systems, such as the para-visual director (PVD), the peripheral command indicator (PCI), and the Malcolm horizon, have been designed for peripheral vision. Except for the Malcolm horizon, they incorporate the rate-field principle suggested by Majendie (1960) for use in instrument landing aids. Rate-field displays typically use real or apparent motion, a horizontal or vertical rippling-effect in peripheral vision, for example, to alert the viewer to variations in rate-of-change. In the PVD this is achieved by rotating a black-and-white "barber's pole" (Vallerie, 1968; see Figure 12.5). This concept was successfully tested as an approach and landing aid in a KLM DC-8 (Reede, 1965). The PCI is a similar device combining two concentric rotating barber's poles to produce a moiré pattern giving apparent motion in any direction. The motion was controlled by quickened flight director signals (Fenwick, 1963). The same principle under-

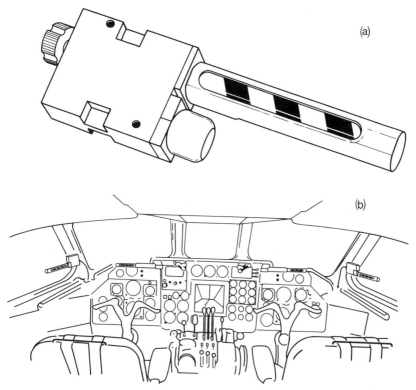

Figure 12.5.   Paravisual flight director (PVD): a, closeup of PVD; b, positioning of
PVDs in the cockpit. (From Vallerie, 1967.)

lying these early devices was later explored experimentally using
ripple patterns on small strip indicators (Roscoe, 1980). This work
underpins the development of the HOVERING display, a CRT-pre-
sented rate-field display for vertical takeoff aircraft (Roscoe, Tatro, &
Trujillo, 1984a,b).

The Malcolm horizon serves the function of a conventional foveal-
vision attitude indicator but projects a narrow line of laser-generated
light across the instrument panel (Knotts, 1983; Malcolm, 1984; Tilden, 1983). This horizon line is readily perceived in peripheral vision during instrument flight and does not require eye fixation and
attention during the panel scan. The Malcolm horizon has been test
fitted in a range of simulators, and in Canadian Armed Forces and
USAF aircraft (Hammond, 1983; Malcolm, 1984; McNaughton, 1983;
Nims, 1983).

Performance Effects of Peripheral Displays.   A number of experiments have shown that while instruments in foveal vision are being used, useful tracking information can be obtained through peripheral vision (Chorley, 1961; Fenwick, 1963; Holden, 1964; Majendie, 1960; Moss, 1964a,b). Peripheral vision may be useful in multiaxis tracking (Allen, Clement, & Jex, 1970) and in both second- and third-order tracking tasks (Moriarity, Junker, & Price, 1976).

An early series of laboratory experiments by Brown, Holmquist, and Woodhouse (1961) comparing the PVD, two other peripheral vision displays, and an orthodox ILS (instrument landing system) display, showed that peripheral displays could give rapid response times to sudden changes. Where central displays are close together, there may be little need for visual switching, and peripheral displays may not lead to any significant increase in performance. However, where the display format requires appreciable visual switching, peripheral displays can give significant improvements in second-order tracking performance (Vallerie, 1967, 1968). Airspeed and localizer tracking error can be reduced by the use of "ripple-strip" rate-fields, but some control reversals may occur where there is ambiguity over display movement–control movement relationships (Swartzendruber & Roscoe, 1971). The latter study did not display the rate-fields peripherally and so can throw no light on Vallerie's speculation concerning the function of peripheral displays in reducing the time-sharing burden of centrally displayed multiple information sources. Rate-field displays may be valuable as redundant auxiliary displays alongside standard primary indicators, and they may serve an alerting function, giving early warning of the direction of changes and directing attention to the appropriate central display (Roscoe, 1980). Rate-field peripheral display techniques have demonstrated considerable potential, and the present movement toward electronic display technologies may make these easier to implement. Recent attention, however, has focused on the Malcolm horizon.

Dual-task performance may be improved by the presence of the peripherally displayed horizon, with tracking error being reduced and mental arithmetic speed and accuracy being increased (Bellenkes, 1984; Gawron & Knotts, 1984). A production version of the Malcolm horizon has been shown to provide improved pitch control in a full-motion simulator, though heading and airspeed deviations did not improve and, in fact, became worse on a high-workload segment involving secondary flight tasks (Gillingham, 1983). It is well known that stress can result in attentional tunneling and an increase in the number of peripheral signals missed (Broadbent, 1971; Bursill, 1958; Kahneman, 1973; Teichner, 1968; Williams, 1985, 1986), and there appears to be some prima-facie evidence of this effect in experience with the Malcolm horizon. A study by Malcolm revealed that, while pilots coped with more emergencies for longer periods with the peripheral vision horizon than without it, "many of [the pilots] said that it had failed just when things began to get interesting. When they were taken back into the simulator, they were invariably surprised to find the display still running" (Malcolm, 1984, p. 236).

It could still be the case, however, that some peripheral display applications have so much potential performance benefit over traditional display techniques that even degraded performance will be superior to that obtainable with orthodox displays. Individual differences may be an important factor in shaping stress response to peripheral displays (Malcolm, 1985, personal communication), and further research might, for example, consider the role of such factors as field dependence and independence (Witkin, Goodenough, & Karp, 1967) in this connection.

Auditory Displays

If the visual channel is overloaded, there are obvious advantages in allocating some tasks to other sensory channels (Doll, Folds, & Leiker, 1984). Replacing traditional visual indicators with auditory signals such as bells, beepers, and electronic tones reduces the need for visual instrument scanning, thereby allowing the user to devote more attention to other visual tasks. Indeed, the amount of information transmission required in modern aircraft is such that the number of auditory displays has increased to the point where auditory clutter may rival visual clutter. However, significant advances in speech synthesis technology are expanding the range and flexibility of auditory display systems.

Auditory systems possess a number of characteristics which can make them preferable to the visual mode even when vision is not overburdened. Auditory signals alert the user quickly, irrespective of head position or eye fixation, and appear to do so faster than visual displays. They therefore lend themselves particularly well to the transmission of cautions, alerts, and warnings. Pilots' responses to taped voice warnings are faster than to similar warnings presented visually (Lilliboe, 1963). Indeed, most aircraft auditory displays to date are used to convey warning messages of various types. Auditory displays also have the advantage that they do not require the user, once alerted, to adjust his gaze in order to receive the message. They are therefore valuable in situations where the user must maintain eye fixation at a particular point in order to perform most effectively.

Auditory displays can also be useful in situations where vision is likely to be degraded. Auditory perception is less affected by high-g forces or anoxia than visual perception, for example. Darkness, bright sunlight, glare, or vibration may inhibit vision, particularly when CRT displays are used (Deatherage, 1972). Other advantages of auditory displays are equally pragmatic—they may be cheaper than equivalent visual displays and require little or no instrument panel area.

Auditory displays do, however, possess certain limitations that also need to be considered. As pointed out, overuse of auditory displays can lead to auditory clutter. Auditory displays are by their nature intrusive and distracting and may therefore sometimes disrupt concentration (Patterson, 1982). Pilots sometimes consider speech displays to be noisy, strident, and intrusive (Butler, Manaker, & Obert-Thorn, 1981; Randle, Larsen, & Williams, 1980). Mellen (1983) points out that computer-generated speech presents data in serial form and as such may not be optimal for presenting comparison data. For this and related purposes a parallel display may be better, that is, visually scanned multiple information sources such as side-by-side gauges or indicators.

The use of voice for display of text that is longer than simple warnings (e.g., "fuel low") leads to further potential costs relative to a printed display. Since the voice is transient, if the message is long, parts of it may be forgotten after or during transmission, whereas a printed message can be referred to as often as necessary until all components are encoded (Williges & Williges, 1982).

Advances in synthesized speech technology have given auditory displays considerably greater flexibility than was previously possible. They have, for example, made it possible to expand caution and warning applications beyond simple alerts to include more complex diagnostic information and instructions for corrective action. With this new versatility, however, it becomes necessary to determine the relative advantages of speech and nonspeech (e.g., tones) auditory systems in differing functional contexts.

When information of any complexity must be presented, verbal messages, whether spoken or printed, are certainly superior to nonverbal auditory signals, since the amount of information that can be conveyed by bells, tones, and other simple codes is clearly very limited. Current military standards specify a limit of four absolutely discriminable auditory signals in a system (MIL-STD-1472C, 5.3). Even with simple messages such as alerts, however, a number of studies indicate that voice messages may be superior. Visual displays, when combined with a voice warning, provide shorter response times than when combined with a nonspeech (tonal) warning (Kemmerling, Geiselhart, Thornburn, & Cronburg, 1969; Mellen, 1983). Voice warnings have the potential to be more flexible and informative than simple tone warnings, since they not only alert the user to the existence of the problem but simultaneously provide more cues as to its nature and thereby assist the user in taking immediate action (Bertone, 1982). The use of speech is also likely to be more effective in conditions of high workload and stress, when the meaning of coded signals may be forgotten (Edman, 1982). Of course, the most common application of auditory messages, that is, for cautions and warnings, can sometimes be expected to be accompanied by stress.

The relative simplicity of nonspeech signals, however, makes their use advantageous under certain conditions. Synthetic speech may be masked in ambient noise to a greater extent than a warning tone, bell, or buzzer, depending upon the characteristics of the noise. Furthermore, if speech signals are already in use, it may become necessary to avoid overlap or duplication of this form of auditory signal (Edman, 1982). Unfortunately, little empirical data exist to support the above recommendations (Simpson, McCauley, Roland, Ruth, & Williges, 1985), and in the absence of such studies, they must be treated as rules of thumb.

Nonspeech Displays

A large array of nonspeech auditory displays is presently used in aircraft, including bells, whistles, horns, buzzers, clackers, and various electronic tones. All these may vary in intensity, pitch, and duration. Patterson and Milroy (1979) found that pilots could learn to identify at least 10 auditory signals but tended to forget the meaning of them over time. Doll and Folds (1986) evaluated the complete set of auditory signals in the F-4D, the F-15, and F-16 fighter aircraft and in the C-5 and C-141 transport aircraft. They found that a large number of nonspeech signals were used but that there was relatively little standardization between aircraft. They point out that this could itself lead to confusion over the meanings of the different signals. However, even within an aircraft, some of the signals resemble each other to a degree which suggests that these may be dangerously confusing, particularly in high-workload or stressful situations. It is surprising to find, for example, that in a modern aircraft like the F-16, the ground proximity warning (usually indicating a need to raise the nose) and the high angle-of-attack warning (usually indicating the need to lower the nose) both use an 800 Hz tone. These sorts of problem are compounded by the fact that the acoustic characteristics of the signal often tend to be a poor guide to the urgency of the message it is intended to convey. Doll and Folds suggest that research needs to focus upon a few main areas. Two of these are concerned with the reduction of nonspeech signal loudness and improvements in signal distinctiveness and "masking resistance," but they also recommend research into the effects of concurrent auditory warning signals on performance.

Speech Displays

Potential display applications of speech technology include advisories (of, for example, traffic and terrain conditions), status information (such as fuel levels), and warnings (Mellen, 1983). Further possibilities include commands, feedback from control inputs, and answers to user queries (Simpson et al., 1985). All of these types of information lend themselves to aural presentation, although in some circumstances a visual display may be equally effective or even superior.

Warnings.   A number of early applications of speech technology have been in warning displays. The F-16 fighter, for example, has a master warning light accompanied by a synthesized voice announcing "warning, warning—warning, warning." The F-15 fighter has a range of warning messages which direct attention to visual displays and also announce the presence of engine fires or adverse fuel states, for example. Warnings must be received quickly, irrespective of eye fixation or workload, and they should be sufficiently brief so as to lend themselves to aural transmission. Hilborn (1975) found that pilots preferred speech messages for conveying warnings but preferred visual displays for other information.

Commands and Advisories.   A number of researchers have expressed practical objections to the use of speech in transmitting information less critical than warnings. The use of voice messages to provide both advisories and actual warnings could impair detection of the latter (Hakkinen & Williges, 1984; Simpson et al., 1985). The use of an alerting cue to announce warning messages might circumvent this problem, but further research is needed to ascertain this. Pilots themselves have expressed a preference for visual presentation of advisory information and for using speech messages only to transmit more urgent information (Williams & Simpson, 1976). The possibility of adverse interactions between display elements underscore the necessity for a global consideration of display components as they function together.

Sex, Naturalness, and Intelligibility.   A large number of variables influence the intelligibility of synthesized speech. These include the method of speech generation, the similarity to human speech, speech rate, voice pitch, and volume. Contextual factors such as ambient noise level and frequency are also important, as are linguistic factors such as the size of the vocabulary set and the choice of vocabulary. Early (tape-based) auditory displays used a female voice (Doll et al., 1984), but female speech may be less intelligible than male speech in a cockpit environment (Fairbanks, 1958; House, Williams, Hecker, & Kryter, 1965; Smith, 1983). Simpson and Navarro (1984), however, using two modern synthesis methods, found that the sex of the speaker did not contribute significantly either to intelligibility or to user confidence ratings. Synthesized speech need not sound natural at all, and it has been argued that it *should* be perceived as distinct from human speech. This may prevent confusing the machine message with flight crew speech or radio transmissions and provide an immediate cue as to message content (Brown, Bertone, & Obermeyer, 1968; Simpson & Williams, 1980; Simpson, 1980; Voorhees, Bucher, Huff, Simpson, & Williams, 1983). Actual performance data to confirm this hypothesis are lacking, however (Simpson & Navarro, 1984), and in fact, synthesized speech has generally been observed to be less intelligible than human speech. Luce, Feustel, and Pisoni (1983) found evidence to suggest that the use of synthesized speech decreases efficiency of short-term memory, in particular the functions of encoding and rehearsal.

Each word in a synthesized speech signal can be apprehended, but the meaning of the message as a whole may still be missed (Edman, 1982). The linguistic context inherent in a message provides cues that limit the range of possible interpretations that can be assigned, but the linguistic context factors in comprehension appear to trade off with the length of the total message and the words within the message. For example, the effect of word length was studied by Simpson (1976), who found that the presence of redundant words in a message only improved intelligibility when the key words were monosyllabic, but there was no significant difference for sentences consisting of polysyllabic key words. Hart and Simpson (1976) reported that sentences composed of two polysyllabic words were more readily recognized and recalled than sentences composed of two monosyllabic words, but full-sentence messages tended to be more intelligible still. The meaning of a voice message is typically not comprehended until the message is nearly completed (Simpson & Marchionda-Frost, 1984). Reducing the number of redundant words (non-key words) would keep the message short. However, the elimination of context words decreases message intelligibility, increases listener response times (Simpson, 1976), and imposes a greater cognitive load (Hart & Simpson, 1976). Simpson and Williams (1980) measured system response time—the total time elapsed from the onset of the message to completion of listener response. In this case, the presence of redundant context words failed to produce a significant difference in total response time. The effect may be related to message complexity, however.

A different approach to the problem of decreasing response time is to increase the rate of speech without eliminating vocabulary. Simpson and Marchionda-Frost (1984) found no impairment in intelligibility of synthetic speech transmitted at the high rate of 178 words per minute (wpm). However, pilots in the study preferred the more moderate rate of 156 wpm. Conversely, subjects found a slower than normal rate (123 wpm) to be distracting and time consuming (also see Voorhees et al., 1983). While the authors recommend the moderate rate, further study is needed to demonstrate whether the subjective reservations expressed about the faster rate are ever reflected in performance data and, if so, under what circumstances.

Speech and Nonspeech Combinations.   Auditory displays can alert the pilot irrespective of eye fixation, but attention may not be shifted quickly enough to apprehend the initial part of message (Bertone, 1982). The problem becomes acute in critical messages such as warnings, the major application of current speech displays. To address this problem, a nonspeech alerting tone has been recommended by many researchers, including Bertone (1982), Burrows (1963), Burrows and Travis (1959), Woodhead (1957), Brown et al. (1968), Erlick and Hunt (1957), and Licklider (1961). Empirical support for this recommendation is, however, ambiguous. Simpson and Williams (1980) found that alerting tones before voice warning messages can significantly increase response times. However, in this study all the messages were warning messages, and the alerting cue may have been redundant. Where both critical and noncritical information is presented auditorily, however, alerting cues before warning messages result in better detection of emergency messages (Hakkinen & Williges, 1984). Bucher, Karl, Voorhees, and Werner (1984) found that semantic alerts (such as "Attention!" "Danger!" or "Advisory") were no more effective than nonspeech alerting tones, although both were superior to having no alert at all.

Speech displays are in their infancy, but technical developments have already permitted advances in the quality of the sound signal and in vocabulary size. Developments in natural language processing and airborne artificial intelligence promise a greatly expanded role for speech displays in the future.

Color Displays

The aesthetic appeal of color is strong, as a number of researchers have emphasized (Christner & Ray, 1961; Greenstein & Fleming, 1984). Color can also contribute to image realism. For both reasons color can enhance the presentation of information and gain user acceptance for display systems. The usefulness of color in displays goes beyond aesthetic and realism considerations, however. Humans can recognize about 9 distinct colors (Jones, 1962) and discriminate between some 24 when hue, luminosity, and saturation are varied (Feallock, Southard, Kobayashi, & Howell, 1966). Color, therefore, has the potential to exploit more of the available information channels in the human visual system (Thorell, 1983). Furthermore, it is processed rapidly and relatively automatically (Dick, 1970; Ellis & Chase, 1971).

Historical Background and State of the Art

Color has been used in cockpits since before the Second World War in simple applications such as coding control knobs and levers. This has tended to be largely a matter of adhering to population stereotypes, traditional industry practices, and conventions. Increasingly, however, pilots must monitor an ever-growing volume of information, a challenge that is being partly met, and partly created, by the introduction of CRT displays and other electro-optical flight instruments. The use of these displays has generated a new set of problems and possibilities connected with color coding. The newer literature on the subject focuses largely upon CRT applications, reevaluating the use of color in diverse applications, from terrain maps through symbology to pictographs.

Color CRT displays are currently in operational use for a number of civil aircraft—the Boeing 757, 767, and the European Airbus A310, for example. Development work on all-electronic flight decks, the so-called glass cockpit, is at an advanced stage. In 1970, however, the U.S. Air Force ruled against the use of color CRT displays because the degree of luminance and contrast then possible was inadequate under the conditions of high ambient illumination present in the cockpit of bubble-canopy fighters. Despite intensive research development, the use of color displays was again rejected—this time by the U.S. Navy—as late as 1978. The problem of luminosity has to some degree been mitigated by more recent technological developments, however. By 1983, the French company Dassault was flying the Mirage 2000 with a color display with full military certification. A number of U.S. Air Force aircraft are presently flying with experimental color displays, and further technological advances are likely to hasten operational applications in the near future (Byrd, 1986). While technical work has focused upon three-gun shadow-mask color CRT systems, flat panel displays, LED, and liquid crystal technologies, a comprehensive human factors program concerned with the introduction of color displays has been initiated at the Naval Air Test Center in Maryland (Silverstein, Merrifield, Smith, & Hoerner, 1984). Indeed, the numerous human factors questions relating to the functional use of color in displays are as pressing as the technical questions and in many ways less well researched.

Functional Applications of Color

In aviation, both the volume and rate of information transmission tend to be high, and most human factors attention has been given to the use of color to enhance the representation and organization of data. Color-coding schemes, for example, can facilitate the location and processing of displayed information, reduce confusion resulting from visual clutter and high workload, and improve performance (Krebs, Wolf, & Sandvig, 1978; Mays, 1983). Color has proved effective where a great deal of information must be presented in a dense format (Kopala, 1979), as it groups data into larger categories of information more efficiently processed in short-term memory. Maps also benefit from the broad categorization powers of color (Rogers, Spiker, & Cicinelli, 1985; Spiker, Rogers, & Cicinelli, 1985). Indeed, color coding may be the single most effective type of coding available, being superior to size, shape, or brightness in identification tasks and significantly reducing search times (Christ, 1975).

Color coding lends itself to two types of application. The first relates to quantitative display formats which present data in specific increments—interval or ratio scales. In this type of application, colors can categorize the data and aid processing by representing numerical ranges. A clear example of this can be seen in the airspeed indicator, a dial-type instrument in which numerical data are presented against a background of color bands. These indicate appropriate airspeed ranges for turbulent and nonturbulent air, as well as flap operating ranges and maximum permissible speed. The use of color in displays of this sort appears to be most effective as a redundant code.

In contrast, qualitative color displays classify data by type or condition and are often used to convey status information. Diagrammatic representations of aircraft fuel states are an example of this. The use of color in such displays aids visual search for specific items in a diverse set. Color can also be used to separate and contrast different elements in a display that cannot be separated in space—thereby improving symbol visibility—and as an aid to selective attention by highlighting particular display elements. In this capacity color serves as an attention cue for the operator who cannot possibly monitor all instruments simultaneously. As such it is less intrusive and distracting than devices such as flashing lights or auditory signals and, for noncritical information, may be superior.

The actual choice of colors to represent different display elements may be based upon the use of environmental color, traditional codes, and population stereotypes (Reising & Calhoun, 1982).

Environmental color refers to color coding that, rather than being wholly symbolic, suggests the actual appearance of features in the environment. Thus blue represents the sky on an attitude indicator or artificial horizon, and brown represents the ground.

Traditional color refers, for example, to the use of red, amber, and green codes for danger, caution, and advisory information, respectively. Red, for example, is customarily used for the VNE (velocity never exceed) line on airspeed indicators, for the revolution limit on tachometers, and for the failure flag on VOR (radio beacon) instruments. Reising and Calhoun recommend that these codes should continue to be used on CRTs and to have the same semantic significance (red to denote hostile missile flight envelopes, enemy aircraft, etc.).

Unfortunately, little published literature discusses the extent to which these and other color-coding conventions do in fact represent actual population stereotypes. This lack of data has been compounded by the fact that stereotyping has yet to be adequately defined. Bergum and Bergum (1981) showed that even a color thought to have strong associations carries several meanings, such as "stop," "danger," and "hot," for the color red. Other strong associations included "caution" for yellow, "go" and "safe" for green, and "cold" for blue, but many associations were weaker and more ambiguous: purple was assigned the meaning "far" in a third of responses, while orange received nearly equal ratings for "near" and "far."

Full versus Partial Color

Although designers may feel tempted to utilize a full range of colors, this may increase visual clutter (Mays, 1983; Teichner, 1979). Burnette (1984) points out that in color-coded displays it is necessary to maintain absolute color discrimination in all ambient illumination conditions. Suggested limits on the number of colors desirable within a single display have ranged from ten (Teichner, 1979) or twelve (Speicher et al., 1985) down to three or four (Bauwman, Leebeek, & Padmos, 1978; Murch & Huber, 1982). As Narborough-Hall (1985) indicates, however, the optimum number of colors will vary with the type of display used and the presence or absence of other coding dimensions; maps and other displays using a variety of codes may be able to accommodate a larger number of colors than more simple displays.

Performance Effects of Color

The aesthetic preference for color noted earlier has not always been reflected in actual task-performance data. Research results concerning the functional effectiveness of color coding have in fact been somewhat variable and context dependent. Some studies, certainly, have found that color coding improves performance. Oda (1977) found that color decreased the time taken to analyze antisubmarine warfare tactical displays. Kopala (1979) tested flight performance and threat detection using two kinds of visual threat display: one with shape coding only and one with both shape coding and redundant color coding. Redundant color coding significantly reduced both response time and error rate, an effect that increased with display density. In fact, the response-time gap between the least- and most-dense display was nearly eliminated when redundant color was used. Christ (1975) reported that the use of color coding under dual-task conditions generally improved performance on search tasks but had a variable effect on identification tasks.

Color does not invariably lead to performance improvements, however. Performance on simulated military missions, for example, was not significantly affected by color in the visual display (Kellogg, Kennedy, & Woodruff, 1983; Way & Edwards, 1983); there is evidence to suggest that color may give no advantage in a simple nondegraded, well-formatted display (Calhoun & Herron, 1981) and in some circumstances may lead to no redundancy gain (Kanarick & Petersen, 1971; Najjar, Patterson, & Corso, 1982; Simon & Overmyer, 1984). Indeed, color coding which is irrelevant or which varies independently of other features may actually interfere with processing of other dimensions (Carter, 1979; Carter & Cahill, 1979; Lehtio, 1970; Morgan & Alluisi, 1967; Stone, 1969).

Thus, the effects of color on task performance appear to be very situation specific. Color coding may be most effective where the display is not formatted, the symbol density is high or legibility degraded, where relevant information must be discriminated, and where prevailing population stereotypes are utilized (Krebs et al., 1978). Redundant color coding is likely to enhance performance only above a certain threshold of display complexity and when viewing time is limited (Reising & Calhoun, 1982). The skill level of the user may also influence color display effectiveness (Mays, 1983).

It should be noted that most of the studies of color effectiveness have not fully represented the dynamic multitask conditions found in the real world of the aircraft pilot. Also, display formats used in these studies have tended to consist of simple graphics rather than the more advanced computer-generated imagery formats now in use in some crew stations. These complex,information-rich formats are likely to require more visual organization than can be provided by other forms of coding, such as brightness and shape (Reising & Calhoun, 1982). Much of the recent research that has investigated color in aviation-relevant environments has done so in the context of a simultaneous evaluation of pictorial representations. These studies are now described.

Pictorial Display Formats

Pictures and pictorial schematics integrate information from diverse instruments or symbols into a single display. Pictures tend to display information in a meaningful way that is compatible with mental models of the world, condensing information into readily recognized gestalts in which interrelationships are clear. However, there is evidence that a redundant combination of pictorial-schematic and verbal information is more effective than either element alone (Booher, 1975; Fitter & Green, 1979; Kamman, 1975; Krohn, 1983).

Conversely, unfamiliar pictorial schematics requiring interpretation may be no more effective than text or voice (Hawkins, Reising, & Gilmour, 1983).

The potential of pictorial displays has long been recognized by researchers in aircraft instrumentation. Grether discussed pictorial versus symbolic aircraft displays just after World War II (Grether, 1947), and during the 1960s the principle of pictorial realism in displays was expounded as one of a number of display principles advanced to guide design (Carel, 1961; Roscoe, 1968). The objective is to make the static representation of aviation displays conform as much as possible to the real-world configuration of the displayed item. A more recent effort has been directed toward the integration of the multiple dimensions of displayed information into holistic geometric objects (Beringer, Howard, & Jenkins, 1986; Wickens, 1987). The potential of pictorial approaches to cockpit display design could not be fully realized until the present, however, when technological developments give the option of displaying monochrome or color pictures and schematics that can be rapidly changed and updated under software control.

Hawkins et al. (1983), in a study using the tripartite color system discussed earlier, found that pilots favored full-color pictorial formats in head-down displays, but preferred head-up displays (HUDs) to be monochrome because of obscuration of the external view by color displays. Performance (in terms of success or failure in avoiding tactical threats) was better with the full-color displays; however, large variations in performance were found. In a follow-on study involving both head-up and vertical situation displays (Hawkins et al., 1984), color versions were rated more favorably than their monochrome counterparts. Ratings for tactical threat displays alone tended to be better still for color and worse for monochrome. This may be because tactical threats are varying elements in a rapidly changing three-dimensional space. Displaying these in color-coded pictorial form is likely to be of even greater help to the pilot in forming a mental representation of the situation than is, for example, the presentation of the hydraulic system which, as a fixed system, may be relatively well internalized by the pilot. Hawkins et al. (1984) also reported that pilots' flight path tracking performance and response

Figure 12.6.   Pictorial format status displays used by Stollings (1984).

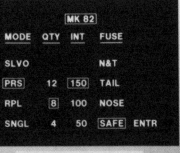

STORES MANAGEMENT

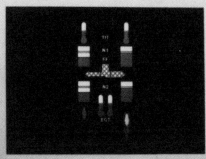

ENGINE STATUS

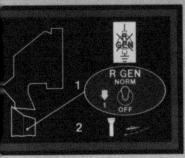

HYDRAULIC ADVISORY

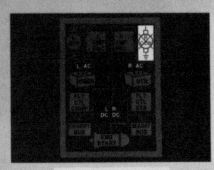

HYDRAULIC STATUS

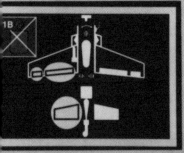

ELECTRICAL ADVISORY

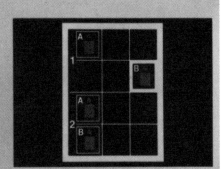

ELECTRICAL STATUS

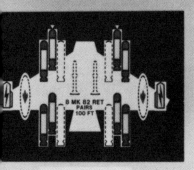

STORES STATUS

FUEL STATUS

times were superior when using the full-color pictorial displays. Switch errors were reduced by over 20%, and pilots' verbal responses tended to be more complete and correct when the color displays were in use.

These results were confirmed in a study reported by Stollings (1984), who also compared traditional alphanumeric formats with pictorial formats (see Figure 12.6). Response latencies were not influenced by format type, but error rates were. When the display presentation was of short duration, the color-graphic format was superior to either of the other display types. The longer the presentation, the less difference was found. Stollings' results suggest that pictorial displays in color are likely to be more effective when workload is high and the view outside the aircraft is making the heaviest attentional demands—the case in many phases of a fighter mission. In these experiments, however, the duration of presentation of displays was extremely short by operational, if not laboratory, standards—as low as 63 milliseconds. In practice, longer durations of around 500 milliseconds characterize eye-fixation times for primary flight, navigation, and engine instruments (Harris & Christhilf, 1980). At these durations format effects were appreciably weaker.

The preceding studies have to be evaluated in the light of their function as part of a software and hardware development process largely aimed at Air Force requirements. It seems possible, for example, that a pictorial display designed with color in mind would, if shown in monochrome, perform less well than a display designed from the outset as an optimal monochrome display. A comprehensive evaluation of the performance effects of the different display variables remains to be done. At present it remains unclear what contribution is made to performance by pictorial form and what by color itself. It is not clear whether greater performance benefits could be achieved using some alternative set of pictorial forms, perhaps even in monochrome, or whether redundant text–picture combinations could be made to give optimal performance in the operational setting as they have in laboratory experimentation. At present there appears to be no published criteria for the initial design of pictorial-schematic representations of different forms of information, and in many cases this is left to intuition and guesswork. Finally, it is important to note that in none of the head-down displays investigated was the presence of redundant color found to be harmful. By and large, color appears to be an attribute that can be employed when it is useful, but ignored when it is not.

Advanced Cockpits

At the Air Force Flight Dynamics Laboratory, researchers are currently pursuing the ultimate objective of pictorial realism by designing a "virtual" or "super cockpit" for fighter aircraft (Furness, 1986). One approach to this would be to present a holographic display projected into the cockpit space. The display would be viewable in 3-D from all head positions (Hopper, 1986). Current conceptions for the super cockpit, however, are to use helmet-mounted displays in order to create a complete multisensory spatial awareness of the aircraft's altitude in space relative to the ground and to other potential airborne threats. By using the helmet-mounted display and sensors that react to head position and eye fixation, the displayed representation is freed from the physical constraints of the instrument panel. By capitalizing on auditory localization, the super cockpit will attempt to integrate auditory with visual presentation in order to present the most ecologically natural representation of three-dimensional space that is possible.

Finally, an example of a less-ambitious effort to exploit color and pictorial representation, but one that is presently further along in terms of airborne implementation, is found in the Boeing 757, 767, and European Airbus and A310 cockpits. Figure 12.7 depicts the electronic attitude director indicator (ADI) and horizontal situation indicator (HSI), while Figure 12.8 presents a configuration of the engine indication and crew-alerting system (EICAS) from the Boeing cockpit. These displays have gone beyond the constraints of conventional electromechanical instruments in three important directions. First, they have systematically exploited color coding, for instruments such as the ADI and HSI in Figure 12.7. Green, for example, is used to indicate flight-mode displays, magenta indicates command information, and so forth. Second, they have taken advantage of the flexibility of the electronic display to present a mixture of pictorial, numeric, and text formats, as shown on the EICAS displays of Figure 12.8. Third, and of greatest importance, the displays are configurable, that is, pilot commands can call up different displays or configurations in the same physical location. The horizontal situation indicator, for example, may be configured in a map mode, a planning mode, two instrument landing system modes, or two VOR (radio beacon) modes, while the system status display may be configured to indicate the status of various systems and subsystems.

The Boeing cockpit represents a substantial advance in the level of

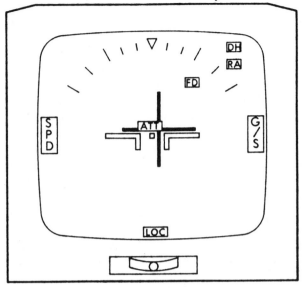

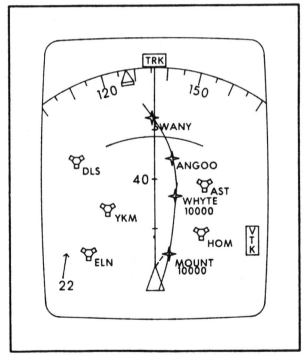

Figure 12.7.   An electronic attitude display indicator (top)
and horizontal situation indicator (bottom) on
the Boeing 757 and 767 aircraft.

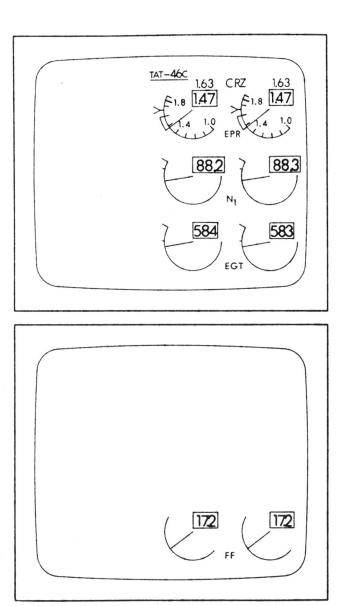

Figure 12.8.   Engine indication and crew-alerting system in the
Boeing 757 and 767 cockpit.

sophistication and automation in commercial air transport displays, and many of these innovations are welcomed incorporations of new technology. Yet the introduction of automation in display technology, as in other areas of aircraft automation, brings with it some problems as well. While Wiener addresses this issue more fully in this volume (see Chapter 13), we touch briefly on the issue from a display's perspective in closing the present chapter.

Display Automation: Decluttering and Configuration

We have referred before to the problems in aviation displays arising from display clutter. For example, Abbott et al. (1980) investigated a CDTI system under realistic workload conditions and found that the problem of display clutter emerged as a major factor in pilots' subjective evaluations of the system. Egan and Goodson (1978) report similar pilot complaints concerning HUDs, while Thorndyke (1980) notes that unnecessary symbology on maps distorts the estimates of distance between two points. Decluttering is an automation option proposed to address the problem by enabling items of information or display that are not relevant for a particular task to be temporarily removed.

Much of the recent research on decluttering has been carried out in paradigms dealing with map interpretation which are not necessarily of direct relevance to aviation problems. Nevertheless, in these environments the benefits of different decluttering options in target location and enumeration tasks have been firmly established (Regal & Knapp, 1984; Schultz, Nichols, & Curran, 1985). Further research however needs to address the problem of decluttering where more complex interpretive tasks are involved. Rather than locating and identifying symbols—tasks which benefit from decluttering—the operator must build a mental model of a system using the relationship between, and the semantic properties of, the displayed symbols.

The decision to allow a pilot to choose what and how much information should be displayed on a particular panel may well decrease visual workload, but it may impose unwanted workload costs on two other pilot resources: those related to memory and to responses. On the one hand, the pilot must now *remember* what is *not* being currently displayed and how to obtain it if needed. Continuous visual presence of an instrument or dial in the nonautomated cockpit is a strong reminder that it needs to be inspected. This reminder is eliminated by the configurable display concept. When the number of options to be displayed are few, the problem is not serious; but when, as in the multimode displays of the advanced fighter aircraft, there are numerous options that must be assessed by computer-based menus that are both broad and deep, the issue is far from trivial. Getting "cognitively lost" in a computerized menu system while trying to maintain situational awareness in the air may spell disaster.

On the other hand, even assuming that the pilot knows what information needs to be inspected and how to find it, he must still actively select that option. Such requirements naturally lead the display designer directly to the issue of what response medium provides the best channel for interacting with these configurable displays. Obvious candidates such as keyboards, touch panels, voice, and even visual fixation (Calhoun, Janson, & Arbak, 1986) have been compared as potential media for the display selection interface. These options are discussed in more detail in Stokes, Wickens, and Kite (1985).

The substantial problems of cognitive and response load associated with configurable displays in the modern fighter aircraft have led systems designers to seek a more radical level of automation as a solution—to let an intelligent on-board computer decide how displays should be configured and what should be seen at what time. A recent Air Force program, known as the Pilot's Associate program, has begun to examine the issues related to automation of displayed information. The program has the broader goal of providing an intelligent computer-based system to assist the fighter pilot with critical tactical and information management decisions during periods of high workload. An important component of this program therefore focuses on the automated display of information—knowing what the pilot needs to know and when he needs to know it.

It is apparent from the preceding that the needs of the civilian and military pilot may often be quite different and that the level of display automation provided should probably differ accordingly. In fact, this very distinction highlights what should be the paramount force guiding the designer of aviation displays as newer technologies are introduced and refined: displays must serve the pilot, and not the other way around.

Acknowledgments

This chapter was written under support of a grant from General Motors 84-Pri-G/W-1539. Brian Repa was the technical monitor. The authors would like to acknowledge the contributions of Kirsten Kite in helping retrieve and organize the literature in this area.

References

Abbott, T. S., Mowen, G. C., Person, L. H., Jr., Keyser, G. L., Jr., Yenni, K. R., & Garren, J. F., Jr. (1980). *Flight investigation of cockpit-displayed traffic information utilizing coded symbology in an advanced operational environment* (NASA Tech. Paper n. 1684). Hampton, VA: NASA-Langley Research Center.

Allen, R. W., Clement, W. F., & Jex, R. H. (1970). *Research on display scanning, sampling, and reconstruction using separate main and secondary tracking tasks* (NASA CR-1569).

Bauwman, A. G., Leebeek, H. J., & Padmos, P. (1978). *The conspicuousness and discriminability of red, green, and yellow symbols on a penetron display* (Report IZF). Soesterberg, The Netherlands; Institute for Perception TNO.

Bellenkes, A. H. (1984). Dual-task time-sharing using a projected attitude display (Tech. Rep. AD-A150789: NAMRL-1310). Pensacola, FL: Naval Aerospace Medical Research Laboratory.

Benel, R. A. (1980). Vision through interposed surfaces: Implications for vehicle control. *Human Factors in Transport Research* (pp. 328–336), Ergonomics Society, London and New York: Academic Press.

Bergum, B., & Bergum, J. (1981). Population stereotypes: An attempt to measure and define. *Proceedings of the 25th Annual Meeting of the Human Factors Society.* Santa Monica, CA: Human Factors Society.

Beringer, D. B., Howard, F., & Jenkins, J. (1986). Putting information in the visual periphery: It beats a pointed stick in the eye. *Proceedings of the 30th Annual Meeting of the Human Factors Society* (pp. 613–617). Santa Monica, CA: Human Factors Society.

Bertone, C. M. (1982). Human factors considerations in the development of a voice warning system for helicopters. In *Behavioral Objectives in Aviation Automated System Symposium* (pp. 133–142). Warrendale, PA: Society of Automotive Engineers.

Birmingham, H. P., & Taylor, F. V. (1954). *A human engineering approach to the design of man-operated continuous control systems* (Report No. NRL-4333). Washington, DC: Naval Research Lab.

Birmingham, H. P., & Taylor, F. V. (1958). Why quickening works. *Automation and Control, 8,* 16–18.

Booher, H. R. (1975). Relative comprehensibility of pictorial information and printed words in proceduralized instructions. *Human Factors, 17,* 266–277.

Broadbent, D. E. (1971). *Decision and stress.* New York: Academic Press.

Brown, J. E., Bertone, C. M., & Obermeyer, R. W. (1968). *Army aircraft warning system study* (U.S. Army Technical Memorandum 6–68). Aberdeen Proving Ground, MD: U.S. Army Engineering Laboratories.

Brown, I., Holmquist, S., & Woodhouse, M. (1961). A laboratory comparison of tracking with four flight director displays. *Ergonomics, 4,* 229–251.

Bucher, N. M., Karl, R., Voorhees, J., & Werner, E. (1984). Alerting prefixes for speech warning messages. *Proceedings of the National Aerospace and Electronics Conference (NAECON)* (pp. 924–931). New York: IEEE.

Burnette, K. T. (1984). Multi-color display design criteria. In *Proceedings of the National Aerospace and Electronics Conference (NAECON)* (pp. 1348–1363). New York: IEEE.

Burrows, A. A. (1963). Aircraft warning systems: argument, evidence, and design (Douglas Aircraft Co., Engineering Paper. No. 1587). *Fifteenth IATA Technical Conference,* Lucerne, Switzerland.

Burrows, A. A., & Travis, M. N. (1959). *Aircraft warning, cautionary and advisory systems* (ASCC W. P. 10, Project 3) RAF Institute of Aviation Medicine.

Bursill, A. E. (1958). The restriction of peripheral vision during exposure to hot and humid conditions. *Quarterly Journal of Experimental Psychology, 10,* 113–129.

Butler, F., Manaker, E., & Obert-Thorn, W. (1981). *Investigation of a voice synthesis system for the F-14 aircraft* (Report No. ACT-81-001). Bethpage, NY: Grumman Aerospace Corporation.

Byrd, J. D. (1986). Aircraft color CRT experience. *Proceedings of the IEEE 1986 National Aerospace Electronics Conference* (NAECON), Vol 1 (pp. 173–176). New York: IEEE.

Calhoun, G. L., & Herron, S. (1981). Computer-generated cockpit engine displays. *Proceedings of the 25th Annual Meeting of the Human Factors Society* (pp. 127–131). Santa Monica, CA: Human Factors Society.

Calhoun, G. L., Janson, W. P., & Arbak, C. J. (1986). Use of eye control to select switches. *Proceedings of the 30th Annual Meeting of the Human Factors Society* (pp. 154–158). Santa Monica, CA: Human Factors Society.

Carel, W. L. (1961). *Visual factors in the contact analog* (Report R61ELC60). Ithaca, NY: General Electric Advanced Electronics Centre.

Carter, R. C. (1979). Visual search and color coding. *Proceedings of the 23rd Annual Meeting of the Human Factors Society* (pp. 369–373). Santa Monica, CA: Human Factors Society.

Carter, R. C., & Cahill, M. C. (1979). Regression models of search time for color-coded information displays. *Human Factors, 21,* 293–302.

Chorley, R. A. (1961). *The development of the Smiths paravisual director.* Lecture presented to the Bristol Branch of the Royal Aeronautical Society (R.I.D. 597), Smiths Industries, Ltd., England.

Christ, R. E. (1975). Review and analysis of color coding research for visual displays. *Human Factors, 17,* 542–570.

Christner, C. A., & Ray, H. W. (1961). An evaluation of the effect of selected combinations of target and background coding on map reading performance. Experiment V. *Human Factors, 3,* 131–146.

Deatherage, B. H. (1972). Auditory and other sensory forms of information presentation. In H. P. VanCott & R. G. Kinkade (Eds.), *Human engineering guide to equipment design* (pp. 123–160). Washington, DC: U. S. Govt. Printing Office.

Dick, A. O. (1970). Visual processing and the use of redundant information in tachistoscopic recognition. *Canadian Journal of Psychology, 24,* 133–140.

Doll, T. J., & Folds, D. J. (1986). Auditory signals in military aircraft: Ergonomic principles versus practice. *Applied Ergonomics, 17,* 257–264.

Doll, T. J., Folds, D. J., & Leiker, L. (1984). *Auditory information systems in military aircraft: Current configurations versus the state of the art.* Brooks Air Force Base, TX: USAF School of Aerospace Medicine.

Edman, T. R. (1982). Human factors guidelines for the use of synthetic speech devices. *Proceedings of the 26th Annual Meeting of the Human Factors Society* (pp. 212–216). Santa Monica, CA: Human Factors Society.

Egan, D. E., & Goodson, J. E. (1978). *Human factors engineering for head-up displays: A review of military specifications and recommendations for research* (Monograph 23). Pensacola, FL: Naval Aerospace Medical Research Laboratory.

Ellis, S. H., & Chase, W. G. (1971). Parallel processing in item recognition. *Perception and Psychophysics, 10,* 379–384.

Ellis, S. H., & McGreevy, M. W. (1983). Influence of a perspective cockpit traffic display format on pilot avoidance maneuvers. *Proceedings of the 27th Annual Meeting of the Human Factors Society (pp. 762–766). Santa Monica, CA: Human Factors Society.

Ellis, S. H., McGreevy, M. W., & Hitchcock, R. J. (1987). Perspective traffic display format and air pilot traffic avoidance. *Human Factors, 29,* 371–382.

Erlick, D. E., & Hunt, D. P. (1957). *Evaluating audio warning displays for weapon systems* (AD-118 189). Dayton, OH: Wright–Patterson AFB, Aeromedical Laboratory.

Fairbanks, G. (1958). Test of phonemic differentiation—the rhyme test. *Journal of the Accoustical Society of America, 30,* 596–600.

Feallock, J. B., Southard, J. F., Kobayashi, M., & Howell, W. C. (1966). Absolute judgment of colors in the Federal Standards System. *Journal of Applied Psychology, 50,* 266–272.

Fenwick, C. (1963). Development of a peripheral vision command indicator for instrument flight. *Human Factors, 5,* 117–128.

Filarsky, S. M., & Hoover, S. W. (1983). *The command flight path display.* Warminster, PA: Naval Air Development Center.

Fischer, E. (1979). *The role of cognitive switching in head-up displays* (NASA Contractor Report 3137). Washington, DC: NASA.

Fischer, E., Haines, R., & Price, T. (1980). *Cognitive issues in head-up displays* (NASA Tech. Rep. #1711). Washington, DC: NASA.

Fitter, M. J., & Green, T. R. G. (1979). When do diagrams make good computer language? *International Journal of Man–Machine Studies, 11,* 235–261.

Fuchs, A. (1962). The progression regression hypothesis in perceptual motor skill learning. *Journal of Experimental Psychology, 63,* 177–192.

Furness, T. A., III. (1986). The super cockpit and its human factors challenges. *Proceedings of the 30th Annual Meeting of the Human Factors Society* (pp. 48–52). Santa Monica, CA: Human Factors Society.

Gallagher, P. D., Hunt, R. A., & Williges, R. C. (1977). A regression approach to generate aircraft predictor information. *Human Factors, 19,* 549–556.

Gawron, V., & Knotts, L. (1984). A preliminary flight evaluation of the peripheral vision display using the NT-33A aircraft. *Proceedings of the 28th Annual Meeting of the Human Factors Society* (pp. 539–541). Santa Monica, CA: Human Factors Society.

Gillingham, K. K. (1983). Evaluation of the Malcolm horizon in a moving-base flight simulator. In *Peripheral Vision Horizon Display (PVHD)* (NASA CP-2306). Washington, DC: NASA.

Gottsdanker, R. M. (1952). Prediction-motion with and without vision. *American Journal of Psychology, 65,* 533–543.

Greenstein, J. S., & Fleming, R. A. (1984). The use of color in command control electronic status boards. *Proceedings of the NATO Workshop: Color coded vs. monochrome displays* (pp. 5.1–5.10). Farnborough, England:

Grether, W. (1947). *Discussion of pictorial versus symbolic aircraft instrument displays* (Memorandum Report, Serial No. TSEAA-694-8B). Dayton, OH: Wright-Patterson AFB.

Grunwald, A. J. (1981). Predictor symbology in computer-generated perspective displays. In J. Lyman & A. Bejczy (Eds.), *Proceedings of the 17th Annual Conference on Manual Control* (NASA-JPL Pub 81-95) (pp. 81–95).

Hakkinen, M. T., & Williges, B. H. (1984). Synthesized warning messages: Effects of an alerting cue in single- and multiple-function voice synthesis systems. *Human Factors, 26,* 185–195.

Hammond, L. B. (1983). Peripheral vision horizon display testing in RF-4C aircraft. In *Peripheral vision horizon display (PVHD)* (NASA, CP-2306) (pp. 97–102). Washington, DC: NASA.

Hart, S. G., & Simpson, C. A. (1976). Effects of linguistic redundancy on synthesized cockpit warning message comprehension and concurrent time estimation (NASA TMX 73, 170). *Twelfth Annual Conference on Manual Control* (pp. 309–321).

Hart, S. G., & Wempe, T. E. (1979). *Cockpit display of traffic information: Airline pilots' opinions about content, symbology, and format* (NASA Tech. Mem. No. 78601). Moffett Field, CA: NASA Ames Research Center.

Hawkins, J. S., Reising, J. M., & Gilmour, J. D. (1983). Pictorial format display evaluation. *Proceedings of the National Aerospace and Electronics Conference (NAECON)* (pp. 1132–1138). New York: IEEE.

Hawkins, J. S., Reising, J. M., & Gilmour, J. D. (1984). Information interpretation through pictorial formats. Society of Automotive Engineers (pp. 4.148–4.153).

Hawkins, J. S., Reising, J. M., Lizza, G. D., & Beachy, K. A. (1983). Is a Picture Worth 1000 words—Written or Spoken? *Proceedings of the 27th Annual Meeting of the Human Factors Society* (pp. 970–972). Santa Monica, CA: Human Factors Society.

Hilborn, E. H. (1975). *Human factors experiments for data link* (Final Report FAA-RD-75-170). Cambridge, MA: Department of Transportation Systems Center.

Hoffman, J. E. (1980). Interaction between global and local levels of a form. *Journal of Experimental Psychology: Human Perception and Performance, 6,* 222–234.

Holden, K. J. (1964). Instrument displays for blind flying. *J. Roy. Aero. Soc., 68,* 833.

Hopper, D. G. (1986). Dynamic holography for real-time 3-D cockpit display. *Proceedings of the IEEE 1986 National Aerospace & Electronics Conference (NAECON)* (pp. 66–172). New York: IEEE.

House, A. F., Williams, C. E., Hecker, M. H. L., & Kryter, K. D. (1965). Articulation testing methods: Consonantal differentiation with a closed-response set. *Journal of the American Statistical Association, 37,* 158–166.

Hull, J. C., Gill, R. T., & Roscoe, S. N. (1982). Locus of the stimulus to visual accommodation: Where in the world, or where in the eye? *Human Factors, 24,* 311–319.

Jensen, R. S. (1981). Prediction and quickening in perspective flight displays for curved landing approaches. *Human Factors, 23,* 333–364.

Jones, M. R. (1962). Color coding. *Human Factors, 4,* 355–365.

Josefowitz, A. J., North, R. A., & Trimble, J. (1980). Combined multisensor displays. In G. E. Corrick, E. C. Haseltine, & R. T. Durst, Jr. (Eds.), *Proceedings of the 24th Annual Meeting of the Human Factors Society* (pp. 17–21). Santa Monica, CA: Human Factors Society.

Kahneman, D. (1973). *Attention and effort.* Englewood Cliffs, NJ: Prentice-Hall.

Kamman, R. (1975). The comprehensibility of printed instructions and the flowchart alternative. *Human Factors, 17,* 183–191.

Kanarick, A. F., & Petersen, R. C. (1971). Redundant color coding and keeping-track performance. *Human Factors, 13,* 245–248.

Kelley, C. R. (1968). *Manual and automatic control.* New York: Wiley.

Kellogg, R. S., Kennedy, R. S., & Woodruff, B. R. (1983). Comparison of colour and black-and-white visual displays as indicated by the bombing performance in the 2B35 TA-4J flight simulator. *Displays, 4,* 106–107.

Kelly, D. H. (1974). Color names of very small fields varying in duration and luminance. *Journal of the Optical Society of America, 64,* 983.

Kemmerling, P., Geiselhart, R., Thornburn, D. E., and Cronburg, J. G. (1969). *A comparison of voice and tone warning systems as a function of task loading* (Technical Report ASD-TR-69-104). Dayton, OH: Wright-Patterson AFB, U.S. Air Force, ASD.

Klass, P. J. (1981). FAA selects collision avoidance system. *Aviation Week and Space Technology*, June 29th, pp. 31–32.

Knotts, L. H. (1983). Extracts from the Test Plan for In-Flight Evaluation of the NT-33A Peripheral Vision Display. *Peripheral Vision Horizon Display, Proceedings of a Conference* (NASA Conference Publication 2306) (pp. 103–109). Washington, DC: NASA Scientific and Technical Information Branch.

Kopala, C. J. (1979). The use of color-coded symbols in a highly dense situation display. *Proceedings of the 23rd Annual Meeting of the Human Factors Society* (pp. 397–401). Santa Monica, CA: Human Factors Society.

Krebs, M. J., Wolf, J. D., & Sandvig, J. H. (1978). *Color Display Design Guide* (Report ONR-CR213-136-2F). Office of Naval Research.

Krohn, G. S. (1983). Flowcharts used for procedural instruction. *Human Factors, 25,* 573–581.

Leffler, M. F. (1982). Advanced technology in the flight station. Behavioural Objectives in Aviation Automated Systems Symposium, *Proceedings P-114, Society of Automotive Engineers* (pp. 97–101). Warrendale, PA:

Lehtio, P. K. (1970). The organization of component decisions in visual search. *Acta Psychologica, 33,* 93–105.

Leibowitz, H. W. (1986). Recent advances in our understanding of peripheral vision and some implications. *Proceedings of the 30th Annual Meeting of the Human Factors Society* (pp. 605–607). Santa Monica, CA: Human Factors Society.

Lester, P. T., & Quan, E. E. (1983). The cockpit display of traffic information and threat alert and collision avoidance system integration: A review. *Proceedings of the Second Symposium on Aviation Psychology* (pp. 69–75). Columbus, Ohio:

Licklider, J. C. R. (1961). *Audio warning signals for air force weapon systems* (WADD Technical Report No. 60-814, Contract No. AF33(616)-5611). Bolt Beranek and Newman, Inc., Behavioral Sciences Laboratory, Aerospace Medical Laboratory, Wright-Patterson Air Force Base, OH.

Lilliboe, M. L. (1963). *Final Report: evaluation of Astropower, Inc. auditory information display installed in the VA-3B airplane* (Technical Report ST 31-22R-63; AD-831823). Patuxent River, MD: U.S. Naval Air Station, Naval Test Center.

Loftus, G. R. (1978). Comprehending compass directions. *Memory and Cognition, 6,* 416–422.

Luce, P. A., Feustel, T. C., & Pisoni, D. B. (1983). Capacity demands in short-term memory for synthetic and natural speech. *Human Factors, 25,* 17–32.

Majendie, A. M. A. (1960). Para-visual director. *Journal of the Institute of Navigation* (London) *13,* 447–54.

Malcolm, R. (1984). Pilot disorientation and the use of a peripheral vision display. *Aviation, Space, and Environmental Medicine, 55,* 231–238.

Mays, J. A. (1983). The need for color in displays. *Proceedings of the Society for Information Display 1983 International Symposium: Digest of Technical Papers.*

McNaughton, G. B. (1983). Personal experience with the PVHD and opinion of situations in which a wide field of view (FOV) might be helpful. *Peripheral Vision Horizon Display (PVHD).* Proceedings of a Conference held at NASA Ames Research Center, Edwards, CA.

McRuer, D. T., Hofmann, L. G., Jex, H. R., Moore, G. P., Phatak, A. V., Weir, D. H., & Wolkovitch, J. (1968). *New approaches to human-pilot/vehicle dynamic analysis* (AFFDL-TR-67-150). Dayton, Ohio: Wright–Patterson AFB, Air Force Flight Dynamics Laboratory.

Mellen, G. (1983). Speech technology for avionic computers. *Proceedings of the IEEE National Aerospace and Electronics Conference* (pp. 404–408). New York: IEEE.

Morgan, B. B., & Alluisi, E. A. (1967). Effects of discriminibility and irrelevant information on absolute judgments. *Perception and Psychophysics, 2,* 54–58.

Moriarity, T. E., Junker, A. M., & Price, D. R. (1976). Roll axis tracking resulting from peripheral vision motion cues. *Proceedings, 12th Annual Conference on Manual Control* (NASA TMS-73-170). Washington, DC: U.S. Govt. Printing Office.

Moss, S. M. (1964a). Tracking with a differential brightness display: I. Acquisition and transfer. *Journal of Applied Psychology, 48,* 115–122.

Moss, S. M. (1964b). Tracking with a differential brightness display. II. Peripheral tracking. *Journal of Applied Psychology, 48,* 249–254.

Murch, G. M., & Huber, J. (1982). Colour—the logical step. *New Electronics, 15,* 31–32.

Murphy, M. R., McGee, L. A., Palmer, E. A., Paulk, C. H., & Wempe, T. E. (1978). Simulator evaluation of three situation and guidance displays for V/STOL aircraft zero-zero landing approaches. *Proceedings of the 1978 IEEE International Conference on Cybernetics and Society* (pp. 563–571).

Naish, J. M. (1964). Combination of information in superimposed visual fields. *Nature, 202,* 641–646.

Najjar, L. J., Patterson, M. J., & Corso, G. M. (1982). Redundancy in coding of a visual display as assessed by a signal detection paradigm. *Proceedings of the 26th Annual Meeting of the Human Factors Society* (pp. 586–588). Santa Monica, CA: Human Factors Society.

Narborough-Hall, C. S. (1985, July). Recommendations for applying colour coding to air traffic control displays. *Displays,* 131–137.

Navon, D. (1977). Forest before trees: The presence of global features in visual perception. *Cognitive Psychology, 9,* 353–383.

Neisser, V., & Becklan, R. (1975). Selective looking: Attention to visually specified events. *Cognitive Psychology, 7,* 480–494.

Nims, D. F. (1983). *Peripheral vision horizon display (PVHD) on the single-seat night attack A-10* (NASA CP-2306). Proceedings of a Conference held at NASA-Ames Research Center, Edwards, CA.

Norman, J., & Ehrlich, S. (1986). Visual accommodation and virtual image displays: Target detection and recognition. *Human Factors, 28,* 135–151.

O'Connor, S., Jago, S., Baty, D., & Palmer, E. (1980). *Perception of aircraft separation of pilot preferred symbology on a cockpit display of traffic information* (NASA-Ames Research Center, Report No. 81172). Moffett Field, California: NASA.

Oda, D. J. (1977). *The benefits of color in an airborne integrated tactical display system.* Lockheed California Company, Burbank, CA. SIO Conference, San Diego, CA.

Oppitek, E. W. (1973). *Head-up display study* (AFAL-TR-73-215). Wright-Patterson AFB, OH: Air Force Avionics Laboratory, Air Force Systems Command.

Owens, D. A. (1979). The mandelaum effect: Evidence for an accommodative bias toward intermediate viewing distances. *Journal of the Optical Society of America, 69,* 646–652.

Palmer, E. (1983). Conflict resolution maneuvers during near-miss encounters with cockpit traffic displays. *Proceedings of the 27th Annual Meeting of the Human Factors Society* (pp. 757–761). Santa Monica, CA: Human Factors Society.

Palmer, E., Jago, S., & DuBord, M. (1981). Horizontal conflict resolution maneuvers with a cockpit display of traffic information. *Proceedings of the 17th Annual Conference on Manual Control* (Caltech JPL Pub. 81–95). Pasadena, CA: Caltech Jet Propulsion Lab.

Patterson, R. D. (1982). *Guidelines for auditory warning systems on civil aircraft* (Civil Aviation Authority Paper 82017). London, UK

Patterson, R. D. & Milroy, R. (1979). *Existing and recommended levels for auditory warnings on civil aircraft*. Medical Research Council Applied Psychology Unit, Cambridge, UK.

Pomerantz, J. R., & Kubovy, M. (1986). Theoretical approaches to perceptual organization. In K. R. Boff, L. Kaufman, & J. P. Thomas (Eds.), *Handbook of Perception and Human Performance, Vol II* (pp. 36-1/36-46). New York: Wiley.

Poulton, E. C. (1974). *Tracking skill and manual control*. London: Academic Press.

Randle, R. J., Jr., Larsen, W. E., & Williams, D. H. (1980). *Some human factors issues in the development and evaluation of cockpit alerting and warning systems* (NASA-RP-1055). Moffett Field, CA: NASA-Ames Research Center.

Reede, C. H. (1965). "KLM—Research on the Lowering of Weather Minima for Landing of Aircraft," *De Ingenieur 77* (No. 11, LI-13). Royal Aircraft Establishment, Library Translation No. 1250.

Regal, D., & Knapp, B. G. (1984). *An aid for improved information prosystem failures*. New York: Plenum.

Reising, J. M., & Calhoun, G. L. (1982). Color display formats in the Cockpit: Who needs them? *Proceedings of the Human Factors Society* (pp. 397–401). Santa Monica, CA: Human Factors Society.

Rogers, S. P., Spiker, A., Cicinelli, J. (1985). Luminance contrast requirements for legibility of symbols on computer generated map displays in aircraft cockpits. In R. S. Jensen & J. Adrion (Eds.), *Proceedings of the Third Symposium on Aviation Psychology* (pp. 175–182). Columbus, OH: Ohio State University, Department of Aviation.

Roscoe, S. N. (1968). Airborne displays for flight and navigation. *Human Factors, 10*, 321–332.

Roscoe, S. N. (1980). *Ground-referenced visual orientation with imaging displays* (Final Report Oct 1979–Sept 1980, BEL-80-3/AFOSR-80-3). Washington, DC: Air Force Office of Scientific Research, Bolling AFB.

Roscoe, S. N. (1984). Judgments of size and distance with imaging displays. *Human Factors, 26*, 617–629.

Roscoe, S. N., Tatro, J., & Trujillo, E. (1984a). Display technology and the role of human factors. *Proceedings of the Sixth Advanced Aircrew Display Symposium* (pp. 126–136).

Roscoe, S. N., Tatro, J., & Trujillo, E. (1984b). The role of human factors in VTOL aircraft display technology. *Displays*, 149–153.

Schmit, V. P. (1982). *Factors affecting the allocation of attention and performance in cross-monitoring flight information displays* (NATO AGARD Conference Proceedings No. 329) (pp. 20-1 to 20-5). Advanced Avionics and the Military Aircraft Man/Machine Interface, Blackpool, UK.

Schultz, E. E., Nichols, D. A., & Curran, P. S. (1985). Decluttering methods for high-density computer-generated graphic displays. *Proceedings of the 29th Annual Meeting of the Human Factors Society* (pp. 300–304). Santa Monica, CA: Human Factors Society.

Schutz, H. G. (1961). An evaluation of methods for presentation of graphic multiple trends. Exp. III. *Human Factors, 3*, 108–119.

Silverstein, L. F., Merrifield, R. M., Smith, W. D., & Hoerner, F. C. (1984). A systematic program for the development and evaluation of airborne color display systems. *Proceedings of the Sixth Advanced Aircrew Display Symposium* (pp. 3–44). Patuxent River, MD: Naval Air Test Center.

Simon, J., & Overmyer, S. (1984). The effect of redundant cues on retrieval time. *Human Factors, 26*, 315–322.

Simpson, C. A. (1976). *Effects of linguistic redundancy on pilots' comprehension of synthesized speech* (NASA TMX 73170), 294–308.

Simpson, C. A. (1980). *Synthesized voice approach callouts for air transport operations* (NASA CR-3300). Menlo Park, CA: Psycholinguistic Research Associates.

Simpson, C. A., & Marchionda-Frost, K. (1984). Synthesized speech rate and pitch effects on intelligibility of warning messages for pilots. *Human Factors, 26*, 509–517.

Simpson, C. A., McCauley, M. E., Roland, E. F., Ruth, J. C., & Williges, B. H. (1985). System design for speech recognition and generation. *Human Factors, 27*, 115–141.

Simpson, C. A., & Navarro, T. (1984). Intelligibility of computer-generated speech as a function of multiple factors. *Proceedings of the 1984 National Aerospace and Electronics Conference* (NAECON) (pp. 932–940). New York: IEEE.

Simpson, C. A., & Williams, D. H. (1980). Response-time effects of alerting tone and semantic context for synthesized voice cockpit warnings. *Human Factors, 22*, 319–320.

Smith, C. (1983). Relating the performance of speech processors to the bit error rate. *Speech Technology, 2*, 41–53.

Smith, J. D., & Ellis, S. R. (1982). Effect of perceived threat on avoidance maneuvers selected while viewing cockpit traffic displays. *Proceedings of the 26th Annual Meeting of the Human Factors Society* (pp. 772–776). Santa Monica, CA: Human Factors Society.

Spiker, A., Rogers, S., & Cicinelli, J. (1985). Selecting color codes for a computer-generated topographic map based on perception experiments and functional requirements. In R. S. Jensen & J. Adrion (Eds.), *Proceedings of the Third Symposium on Aviation Psychology* (pp. 151–158). Ohio State University, Department of Aviation.

Statler, I. C. (1984). Military pilot ergonomics. *Proceedings, AGARD Aerospace Medical Panel Symposium on Human Factors Considerations in High Performance Aircraft* (pp. 13–23). Williamsburg, VA: North Atlantic Treaty Organization.

Stokes, A., Wickens, C. D., & Kite, K. (1985). *A review of the research on aviation display technology* (Final Contract Report ARL-Tr-85-2/Gm-85-1). Savoy, IL: University of Illinois, Institute of Aviation.

Stollings, M. N. (1984). *Information processing load of graphic versus alphanumeric weapon format displays for advanced fighter cockpits* (Technical Report AFWAL-TR-84-3037). Dayton, OH: U.S. Air Wright-Patterson Air Force Base, U.S. Air Force Flight Dynamics Laboratory.

Stone, G. C. (1969). Response latencies in matching and oddity performance effects of format stimulus and demand variables. *Perceptual and Motor Skills, 29*, 219–232.

Swartzendruber, L. E., & Roscoe, S. N. (1971). Rate-field displays. In S. N. Roscoe (Ed.), *Aviation psychology*. Ames: Iowa State University Press.

Taylor, R. M. (1982). *Human factors aspects of aircraft head-up display symbology: The presentation of attitude information*. Electronic Displays 1982, Session 3, Display Applications. Conference Proceedings (pp. 41–61). Network Exhibitions Ltd., Buckingham, UK.

Taylor, R. M. (1984). *Some effects of display format variables on the perception of aircraft spatial orientation*. Paper presented at the NATO AGARD Aerospace Medical Panel Symposium on "Human Factors Considerations in High Performance Aircraft," Williamsburg, VA.

Teichner, W. H. (1968). Interaction of behavioral and physiological stress reactions. *Psychological Review, 75,* 271.

Teichner, W. H. (1979). Color and visual information coding. *Proceedings of the Society for Information Display, 20,* 3–9.

Thorell, L. G. (1983). *Introduction to Color Vision. Advances in Display Technology III.* Bellingham, WA: SPIE-International Society for Optical Engineering.

Thorndyke, P. W. (1980). *Performance models for spatial and locational cognition* (Tech. Rep. No. R-2676-ONR). Washington, DC: Rand Corporation.

Tilden, T. V. (1983). Using the peripheral vision horizon display. *Proceedings of the Aerospace Engineering Technology Conference* (pp. 275–278). Society of Automotive Engineers, Warrendale, PA.

Vallerie, L. L. (1967). *Peripheral Vision Displays* (NASA CR-808). Washington, DC: NASA.

Vallerie, L. L. (1968). *Peripheral Vision Displays, Phase II Report* (NASA CR-1239). Washington, DC: NASA.

Voorhees, J. W., Bucher, N. M., Huff, E. M., Simpson, C. A., & Williams, D. H. (1983). Voice interactive electronic warning system (VIEWS). *Proceedings of the IEEE/AIAA 5th Digital Avionics Systems Conference* (pp. 3.5.1–3.5.8). New York: IEEE.

Waganaar, W. A., & Sagaria, S. D. (1975). Misperception of exponential growth. *Perception and Psychophysics, 18,* 416–422.

Way, T. C., & Edwards, R. E. (1983). Simulator evaluation of color in pictorial flight displays. *Society for Information Display International Symposium: Digest of Technical Papers* (188–189).

Weintraub, D. J., Haines, R. F., & Randle, R. J. (1984). The utility of head-up displays: Eye-focus vs. decision times. *Proceedings of the 28th Annual Meeting of the Human Factors Society* (pp. 529–533). Santa Monica, CA: Human Factors Society.

Weintraub, D. J., Haines, R. F., & Randle, R. J. (1985). Head-up display (HUD) utility, II: Runway to HUD transitions monitoring eye focus and decision times. *Proceedings of the 29th Annual Meeting of the Human Factors Society* (pp. 615–619). Santa Monica, CA: Human Factors Society.

Wickens, C. D. (1984). *Engineering psychology and human performance.* Columbus, OH: Merrill.

Wickens, C. D. (1987). Attention. In P. Hancock (Ed.), *Human factors in psychology.* Amsterdam: North Holland.

Williams, L. J. (1985). Tunnel vision induced by foveal load manipulation. *Human Factors, 27,* 221–227.

Williams, L. J. (1986). Peripheral information extraction: Cognitive load effects. *Proceedings of the 30th Annual Meeting of the Human Factors Society* (pp. 611–612). Santa Monica, CA: Human Factors Society.

Williams, D. H., & Simpson, C. A. (1976). A systematic approach to advanced cockpit warning systems for air transport operations: Line pilot preferences. In *Proceedings of the Aircraft Safety and Operating Problems Conference* (NASA SP-416) (pp. 617–644). Norfolk, VA: NASA-Langley Research Center.

Williges, B. H., & Williges, R. C. (1982). Structuring human/computer dialogue using speech technology. In *Proceedings of the Workshop on Standardization for Speech I/O Technology* (pp. 143–151).

Witkin, H. A., Goodenough, D. R., & Karp, S. A. (1967). Stability of cognitive style from childhood to young adulthood. *Journal of Personality and Social Psychology, 7,* 291–300.

Woodhead, M. (1957). *Effects of bursts of loud noise on a continuous visual task.* Royal Navy: (RNP no. 57/891).

Wulfeck, J. W., Weisz, A., & Raben, M. W. (1958). Vision in military aviation (USAF: WADC TR. 58-399) Dayton, OH: Wright-Patterson Air Force Base.

Yeh, Y. -Y., & Wickens, C. D. (1984). The dissociation of subjective measures of mental workload and performance (Final Report EPL-84-2/NASA-84-2). Champaign, IL: University of Illinois, Department of Psychology, Engineering-Psychology Laboratory.

Cockpit Automation

13

Earl L. Wiener

Introduction

Cockpit automation is a subject that evokes considerable controversy among users, manufacturers, and regulatory agencies. As in other applications—for example, manufacturing—automation is regarded at one extreme as a servant, relieving the human operator of the tedium of momentary control, freeing him or her for higher cognitive functions. At the other extreme it is viewed as reducing the status of the human to a "button pusher," and stripping the job of its meaning and satisfaction. Many see cockpit automation as a great boon to safety, removing human error at its source and replacing fallible humans with virtually unerring machines. The critics view automation as a threat to safety, replacing intelligent humans with devices that are both dumb and dutiful, a dangerous combination.

There appears to be ample evidence to support both positions; however, as usual, the truth undoubtedly lies somewhere between the extremes. On the positive side, the new digitally based equipment is extremely reliable, generally works "as advertised," and offers opportunities to reduce flight time and costs, navigate more precisely (laterally and vertically), operate power plants more efficiently, and augment highly imperfect human monitoring ability with a variety of warning and alerting systems. On the negative side, the digital systems seem to invite new forms of human error in their operation, often leading to gross blunders rather than the relatively minor errors which characterize traditional systems. Furthermore, the equipment does not appear to live up to its expectations in reducing crew workload or increasing time available for extra-cockpit scanning (Curry, 1985; Wiener, 1985c), since while the manual tasks may be declining, monitoring and mental workload have increased. The mixed feelings of 166 pilots, B-757 in this case, about automation can be seen in Figure 13.1. They were asked in a questionnaire by Wiener (in progress) to state their degree of agreement or disagreement with a series of statements. Figure 13.1 shows one example. If nothing else, these results should prompt us to be cautious about speaking of "pilot opinion" as if pilots were a monolithic group.

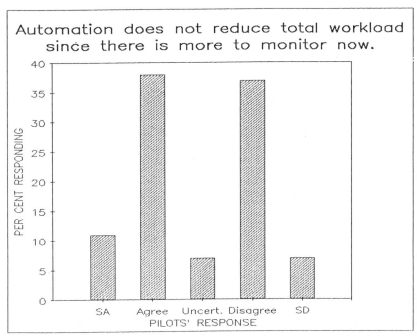

Figure 13.1.   Responses to one of 36 questions asked of a sample of 166 B-757 pilots. Crew members could respond on five-point scale from "strongly agree" (SA) to "strongly disagree" (SD). These data reflect the diversity of opinion on a crucial aspect of cockpit automation. (Wiener, in progress.)

Undoubtedly the march toward automation will continue, despite the protests of many pilots that things have already gone too far and of human factors specialists who would prefer to solve the problems through research before seeing more equipment introduced. The era of the "glass cockpit" (displays driven by computer graphic systems) is upon us, and the technology seen in the Boeing 757/767 and Airbus A-310/320 is just a beginning. Already a joint Lockheed–NASA project has produced a design and simulator for an advanced technology cockpit for the turn of the century (see Figure 15.15, Sexton, this volume). Military applications are advancing even more rapidly (Air Force Studies Board, 1982).

New information technologies, generically referred to as *artificial intelligence* (AI), are being actively researched for their applicability in the cockpit. Where these technologies will take us is difficult to say. The adherents are already speaking of "pilot's associates" and "electronic crew members" (Chambers & Nagel, 1985). Just at a time when the airline industry and unions are adjusting to two-pilot crews on wide-body aircraft, there is discussion of the single-pilot crew, aided by intelligent computer systems. Others are less impressed by the promise of AI and see it as another technological flash in the pan—if anything, an opportunity to place between the human crew and their vehicle yet another layer of authority which may be both undependable and undecipherable. Most in the human factors community are maintaining a cautious attitude, eager to see a few good examples of what AI can do to assist flight crews, particularly in civil air transport aircraft.

Official Concern

By the mid-1970s, concern over automation within the aviation industry, government, and the unions was growing. Edwards (1977) was the first to alert the human factors profession to the problems in piloting automated airliners. The Subcommittee on Transportation, Aviation, and Weather of the House of Representatives Committee on Science and Technology issued a report (U.S. House of Representatives, 1977) which identified cockpit automation as one of the leading safety concerns for the decade ahead. A similar concern was voiced in a report of the Senate Subcommittee on Aviation of the Committee on Commerce, Science, and Transportation (U.S. Senate, 1980). Congress directed NASA to look into the matter, and research programs were undertaken at NASA-Ames Research Center on human factors in cockpit automation, focusing on the air carrier environment, and at NASA-Langley with emphasis on general aviation.

In 1979, Renwick Curry and the author undertook to define the automation problem and survey the state of the art (Wiener & Curry, 1980), and a joint NASA–industry workshop sought to outline research needs (Boehm-Davis, Curry, Wiener, & Harrison, 1983). Two field studies of the introduction of highly automated aircraft followed, Curry (1985) on the B-767 and Wiener (1985c) on the MD-80 (DC-9 Super 80), and a current study by the author on the B-757 (Wiener, in progress).

By the early part of the 1980s a number of critical incidents and accidents intensified concern about human error in operating the rapidly advancing equipment, and in 1983 the president of the Air Line Pilots Association (ALPA) appointed a task force on automation, as did the National Transportation Safety Board (NTSB) soon after. In 1983 ALPA held a special symposium, entitled "Beyond Pilot Error," in which discomfort over automation played a prominent role (Nagel, 1983; Wiener, 1983a).

Definitions

In control theory, *automation* is an ill-defined term that generally means replacing human functioning with machine functioning. It is no easier to define in the cockpit environment; in fact in our early work on the project at NASA-Ames, a considerable amount of time went into trying to determine just what is meant by the term.

The following is not an airtight definition that would satisfy all but an attempt to bring some meaning to the word. By *cockpit automation* we generally mean that some tasks or portions of tasks performed by the human crew can be assigned, by the choice of the crew, to machinery. This usually refers to control-type functions such as flight path guidance, power plant, or environmental control. The word *automatic* in this environment can also refer to computational support, as in the example of a thrust computer indicator which computes engine power ratings for various phases of flight, and it can refer as well to designs which allow procedures to be omitted by the crew. Thus, if raising the landing gear also turns off the "no smoking" light in the cabin, that event is often said to occur automatically.

The other general use of the term automation refers to cockpit warning and alerting systems. In a sense, these may be thought of as the machine monitoring the human. For example, the MD-80 has an elaborate set of voice warnings called the central aural warning system (CAWS). To take one example, if the plane accelerates past the

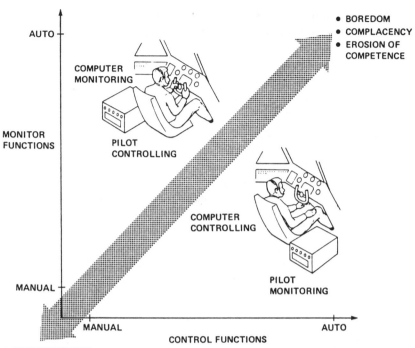

Figure 13.2. Two dimensions of automation: control functions and monitoring functions. (From Wiener & Curry, 1980.)

placard speed for flap retraction with the flaps still deployed, a female voice alerts the crew.

One possible way of defining the degree of automation, at least subjectively, is to see each design as a point in two-dimensional space, as in Figure 13.2. The two axes represent the degree of automation of control functions and warning functions, going from fully manual (or mental) to fully automatic. In the manual extreme on both axes, the design would likely lead to fatigue, high workload, and failures in detecting critical conditions. At the other extreme—a high degree of automation of both the control and monitoring functions—there are presumed problems of boredom and complacency (also an ill-defined, though much-used term in aviation) and concern for skill loss. Table 13.1 summarizes some of the advantages and disadvantages of automation in human–machine systems. The presumption that automation of either function, particularly the control function, leads to the reduction in workload has been questioned recently (see Curry, 1985; Wiener, 1985c; Wiener & Curry, 1980).

Table 13.1.   Some Generalizations about Advantages and
              Disadvantages of Automating Human–Machine
              Systems[a]

Advantages

Increased capacity and productivity
Reduction of manual workload and fatigue
Relief from routine operations
Relief from small errors
More precise handling of routine operations
Economical utilization of machines (e.g., energy management)
Damping of individual differences (narrower tolerances)

Disadvantages

Seen as dehumanizing; lower job satisfaction; consumer resistance
Low alertness of human operators
Systems are fault intolerant—may lead to larger errors
Silent failures
Lower proficiency of operators in case of need for manual takeover
Over-reliance; complacency; willingness to uncritically accept results
False alarms
Automation-induced failures
Increase in mental workload

Questionable

Overall workload reduced or increased?
Total operational cost increased or decreased?
Training requirements increased or decreased?
Reduction in crew size?

Unknown

Capital acquisition costs
Use of common hardware (e.g., standard mainframe computers)
Maintenance costs
Extent of redundancy necessary and desirable
Long-range safety implications
Long-range effect on operators and other personnel (including physical and mental
    health, job satisfaction, self-esteem, attractiveness of job to others entering field)
Long-range implications for collective bargaining
Implications for civil liability (e.g., software error resulting in an accident)

[a]From Wiener & Curry, 1980.

Incidents and Accidents

More Automation: The Ground Proximity Warning System

A number of accidents and incidents in recent years have been
laid at the doorstep of automation, again not failures of the equipment so much as human error in its operation and monitoring. Undoubtedly the best known case was the crash in the Florida

Everglades of an L-1011 in 1972 (NTSB, 1973), which caused concern over the ability of the crew to detect and deal with an inadvertent autopilot disconnect. This accident, along with others that followed, brought a new term for an old problem: *controlled flight into terrain* (CFIT) (Ruffell Smith, 1968; Wiener, 1977).

The CFIT accidents occurring in the 1970s generated yet another automatic device, the ground proximity warning system (GPWS). The Congressionally mandated GPWS introduced its own problems, mainly an intolerably high false alarm rate; however, later models reduced (but did not eliminate) this undesirable feature and also produced improvements in mode annunciation. In the earlier models, the crew could not tell what mode was responsible for the alert. The GPWS is still controversial—its false alarm rate is the source of frequent incident reports to NASA's Aviation Safety Reporting System (ASRS). Many pilots complain that a false GPWS "pull-up" advisory could cause a collision with an aircraft above them, though to date there has been no accident or serious incident attributable to the GPWS. Even with its faults, there is strong evidence that the GPWS has achieved its purpose, and CFIT accidents which plagued the industry in the 1970s have virtually disappeared—automated out of existence, one might say (Loomis & Porter, 1981).

The GPWS should alert us to some important truths about automation in the cockpit:

1. Every time a problem is solved by technology, a new one may be created.
2. In any warning system, one can expect false positives (false alarms) and false negatives (missed critical signals), and the designer must design the filter logic to strike a balance. If the system is designed to be "sensitive," that is have a high detection rate, then it will have a high false alarm rate, and vice versa. There is no perfect system which can detect all true events and filter out all false events.
3. Although the mandate of safety equipment by a law-making body may speed things along, premature introduction of the equipment may also create problems. The emergency locator transmitter (ELT) was another unfortunate example of the folly of Congressional intervention in aircraft design.

Representative Cases

A more comprehensive list and discussion of automation-related incidents and accidents can be found in Wiener and Curry (1980) and Wiener (1985a), but here are a few representative cases:

1. While in navigation mode, the aircraft turned the wrong way over a checkpoint. Although the wrong turn was immediately noticed, the aircraft turned more than 45° before the pilot took action.

2. On a U.S. air carrier departing Sydney for Honolulu, the crew entered north rather than south latitude into the inertial navigation system (INS) as its initial position at the gate. This resulted in a gross track error that was detected about 100 miles after departure.

3. While climbing to altitude, the crew of a DC-10 flying from Paris to Miami programmed the flight guidance system to climb at a constant vertical speed. As altitude increased, the autopilot dutifully attempted to comply by constantly increasing the pitch angle, resulting in a high-altitude stall, loss of over 10,000 feet of altitude before recovery, and damage to the empennage that was not discovered until after the plane crossed the Atlantic and landed in Miami (NTSB, 1980). A similar incident occurred shortly after the B-767 was introduced in line service, but recovery was initiated as a stall was approached.

4. A DC-10 landed at Kennedy Airport, touching down about halfway down the runway and about 50 knots over target speed. A faulty autothrottle was probably responsible for the overspeed condition, which was never detected by the flight crew, who apparently were not monitoring the airspeed. Serious damage to the aircraft occurred when it overran the end of the runway (NTSB, 1984).

5. Numerous cases have been reported of MD-80s failing to capture the target altitude during climb or descent and continuing through the altitude. These are usually due to a design feature of the flight guidance system, in which the capture maneuver is discontinued if the crew touches the vertical speed control once altitude capture has been annunciated but prior its completion.

6. In 1981 a DC-10 crashed into Mt. Erebus in Antarctica. Although the causes are still controversial (see Mackley, 1982; Mahon, 1984; Vette, 1983), the accident was primarily due to incorrect navigational data that was inserted into a ground-based computer in the airline's navigation section, then loaded by the flight crew from the flight plan into the on-board INS. The INS dutifully flew the preprogrammed course into the mountain (New Zealand Royal Commission, 1981). There had been no opportunity for intervention on the part of the crew, who unknowingly transferred an incorrect waypoint from one computer system to another.

7. In 1984, Spanish airlines came under criticism for lax navigation along the crowded North Atlantic tracks. Safety experts blamed "finger trouble," meaning keyboard errors in loading navigation

points into the automatic navigation systems (Carley, 1984).

8. On September 1, 1983, a Korean Airlines B-747 (KAL Flight 007) was shot down by Soviet interceptors over the Sea of Japan near Sakhalin Island, USSR. It was more than 300 miles south of course (Stein, 1983; Feaver, 1983). The cause of such a gross navigational error remains in question and may never be known since the flight recorders were not recovered. Conspiracy theorists claim that the overflight of Russian territory was deliberately planned by the CIA for reconnaissance purposes, or at least that the United States did nothing to stop the deviation, recognizing a possible intelligence bonanza (Johnson, 1984; Mann, 1984; Pearson, 1984). (For an excellent review of books on the subject, and some conspiracy debunking, see Sayle, 1985). Other speculations suggest an overly aggressive policy toward fuel conservation which encouraged KAL pilots to take shortcuts on the Anchorage–Seoul routes (Rohmer, 1984). Another conspiracy advocate (St. John, 1984) advanced the theory that the Soviets had by some unknown electronic system beamed a signal to the B-747's INS and directed the plane over Kamchatka to do away with a passenger, Congressman Larry McDonald, a friend of the John Birch Society and sworn enemy of Communism. The fuel conservation theory is at least plausible and cannot be so easily dismissed as the spy plane allegations. However, in all likelihood the track deviation was due to improper programming of the INS (International Civil Aviation Organization [ICAO], 1983; Machado, 1984; Wiener, 1985a). Probably the most authoritative of the plethora of KAL Flight 007 books (Hersh, 1986) supports this view. Finally, in their report, ICAO darkly concluded, "Each of the postulations [to explain the navigational error] assumes a considerable degree of lack of alertness on the part of the entire flight crew, but not to a degree that is unknown in international civil aviation" (ICAO, 1983, p. 3).

9. In February 1985, a B-747 bound from Taipai to Los Angeles at 41,000 feet suffered a slowly developing power loss in its number 4 engine. As the engine power deteriorated, the autopilot attempted to compensate for the rightward yaw but eventually ran out of rudder authority; the aircraft rolled to the right, and the nose fell through to an almost vertical dive. The crew had become preoccupied with the mechanical failure and apparently did not monitor the flight instruments or attempt to prevent the loss of control. The plane was recovered at 9,500 feet. An animation derived by the NTSB from the flight data recorder is shown in Figure 13.3.

Numerous airline pilots began to voice their doubts about the march of cockpit automation (Hopkins, 1983; Manning, 1984; Melvin, 1983; Oliver, 1984). In an interview with the chairman of the

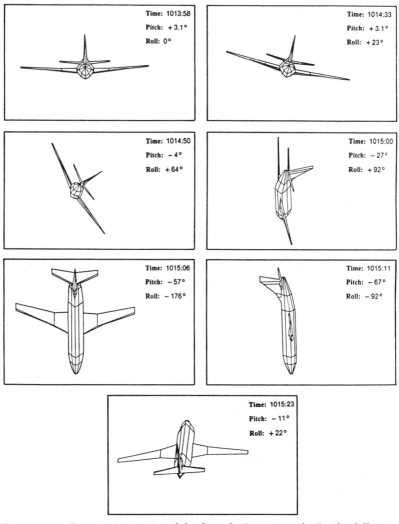

Figure 13.3.   Computer animation of the dive of a B-747 over the Pacific, following
loss of power at 41,000 feet. (From NTSB, 1986.)

ALPA Automation Task Force (Peterson, 1984), Captain Mel Hoagland expressed grave reservations about the wisdom of "the rage to
automate." In another paper he states, "In some cases the forces driving technology have caused the design of automated systems which
compromise the ability of the pilot to fulfill his responsibilities for
the safety of the airplane under his command" (Hoagland, 1984,
p. 155).

As a result of these and other incidents, and the promise that more automation was on the way both in the cockpit and in ground-based air traffic control (ATC) systems (Wiener, 1980, 1983b), concern was growing by the mid-1980s. Machado (1984, p. 5), writing of the loss of KAL Flight 007, leaves us with a disturbing question: "Is this destruction the consequence of man's absolute confidence in the robots he has built, and is this a warning on the danger of the coming robotics era?"

On Balance

While it is important to recognize the potential problems of flight-deck automation, it is equally important to maintain a balance. First, one must recognize that the dramatic incidents and accidents, such as those described above, are extremely rare. Furthermore, automation is continually working to the advantage of safety and economy of flight. Also, with the emphasis on the exotic devices such as flight guidance systems, autothrottles, and long-range navigators, it is easy to forget the less spectacular equipment that is quietly and efficiently doing its job day in and day out.

A good example is the yaw damper. With the introduction of the jet engine came the swept-wing aircraft. This in turn created a hitherto unknown hazard, the Dutch roll maneuver, which could result from an uncoordinated yaw (not unlike a skid in an automobile) at high altitude. This is prevented by an automatic device that controls the rudder and damps any tendency to yaw, totally relieving the crew of this concern. The pilots turn it on and forget about it. It is all one could ask for in a workload-reducing mechanism.

The list of such devices is endless. True, many have limited authority, and hence could probably at worst simply fail to do their jobs. The yaw damper damps yaw and does nothing else, so there is negligible potential for trouble. Our focus in this chapter remains on those devices which have high authority and opportunity for error at the human interface and, therefore, are critical to flight safety. But as we discuss the automation "problem," let us keep a proper balance by recalling that during every flight, a host of automatic devices are at work. On rare occasions, due primarily to errors at the human interface, they can be a source of serious trouble, but the majority of the time, cockpit automation is indeed the servant of the human crew. Gannett concludes: "The final report card on the results of the most recent application of digital technology and human performance principles to air transports will not be available for several years. It is firmly believed that in the long run the benefits far outweigh the costs" (1982, pp. 93–94).

Why Automate?

Why has this rapid automation of pilot functions occurred? Flight-deck automation did not await the microprocessor revolution. Long before the transistor or silicon chip, even before rudimentary digital systems, analog devices such as autopilots, flight directors, and various alerting devices were playing a significant role in automatic flight. Rapid developments in the digital world, especially recent advances in microprocessors and display systems, hastened the process.

The author has identified eight principal reasons behind flight-deck automation. The first three were discussed in Wiener and Curry (1980):

1. Availability of technology
2. Safety
3. Economy, reliability, and maintenance
4. Workload reduction and certification of two-pilot transport aircraft
5. More precise flight maneuvers and navigation
6. Display flexibility
7. Economy of cockpit space
8. Special requirements of military missions

Available Technology

Aviation has always been a leader, not only in developing required technology but in exploiting advances made elsewhere. As digital technology developed, aircraft and avionics designers, airlines, and pilot groups were eager to put it to work in the cockpit. The increased speed and capabilities of jet aircraft, the explosive growth of air traffic, the complexity of the regulatory environment, the unbearable costs of an accident, and the recognition of human limitations spurred designers and operators to seek machine assistance. The rapid digitalization of cockpits designed in the 1970s brought what Wiener and Curry (1980) called promises and problems. The promises were immediately realized; the problems were not fully recognized until recently. It also brought a dangerous new design concept, which might be called "Let's just add one more computer."

Concern for Safety

Much has been written about the changing nature of the pilot's task and the resulting safety implications. Comparing the task of flying modern jet aircraft to flying the propeller planes of the 1950s is not a simple matter. Certainly modern aircraft require more skillful handling due to their speed (both longitudinal and vertical), weights, and criticality of flight regimes. In addition to the changes in the aircraft themselves, there has been a never-ending escalation in regulatory requirements—Federal Aviation Regulations (FARs), company procedures, and now municipally imposed noise-abatement procedures. At the same time, the modern aircraft brought high reliability of power plants, avionics, and advanced navigation devices. But as surely as nature abhors a vacuum, as the jet plane became mechanically simpler, other demands, including regulations and procedures, rushed in to occupy the flight crews, often as a result of specific accidents. For example, a speed limit of 250 knots below 10,000 feet was imposed as a result of the Staten Island, New York, collision of 1960. Designers responded to pilot error by attempting to remove the error at its source, that is, to replace human functioning with device functioning—in their view, to automate human error out of the system. But there were two flaws in this reasoning: (1) the devices themselves had to be operated and monitored by the very humans whose caprice they were designed to avoid, thereby relocating but not eliminating human error; and (2) the devices themselves had the potential for generating errors that could result in accidents.

Economy

In 1978 the price of a gallon of jet fuel in the United States was about 38¢; by 1979 it had nearly doubled, and by 1980 it was about $1.00. The forecast, fortunately incorrect, was for the price to go to $1.25 in 1981, which would have been a catastrophe for airlines in the United States as well as other Western countries. The average price at this writing has dropped below 70¢ but is on the rise again. Obviously, planes had to be flown more fuel-economically, within the constraints of the ATC systems, airport bottlenecks, unpredictable weather, and safety and regulatory demands. More precise vertical and lateral navigation was required as well as more efficient power plant control, and these were beyond the bandwidth of the human pilots, who were already flying about as economically as their systems permitted. Automation of control functions would be needed, and the avionics and airframe industry was quick to respond. Thrust computers and performance management systems provided the pilots with more precise information on power settings and vertical navigation; autothrottles provided more precise means of holding these settings, or holding desired airspeeds or Mach. Autonavigators permitted precise navigation over the earth's surface so that planes could fly through oceans of air rather than along rivers (airways). Today we have reached the point of diminishing returns for fuel conservation through cockpit automation, pending modernization of the ATC system.

Reducing flight time also saves money by reducing flight crew pay. Autothrottles reduce engine wear and along with autobrakes make for more precise touchdowns and smoother decelerations, resulting in less brake wear. In addition, digital systems are more easily maintained and have generally higher reliability, though they have some annoying and puzzling properties, such as sudden failure often followed by sudden recovery, that baffles pilots and maintenance personnel alike. Apocryphal lists of circuit breakers to pull to restore computer power can now be found in Boeing 757/767 pilots' flight bags. But overall, dispatch reliability (fraction of time a scheduled aircraft is available for a trip) of the advanced technology aircraft has been higher than that of their earlier counterparts.

Workload Reduction and Crew Complement

A principal rationale for cockpit automation has been the assumption that workload is reduced, achieving three objectives:

1. Pilots prefer to be relieved of much of the routine manual controlling and mental computation in order to have time to supervise the flight more effectively and to perform optimally in an emergency.
2. At lower altitudes, especially in terminal areas, it is essential that pilots spend less time with their "heads in the cockpit" and more time doing what no presently certified airborne device can do—scan for other aircraft.
3. Airlines have demanded, and are now receiving, wide-body aircraft that are flown by two-pilot crews. For two pilots to perform tasks previously performed by three, workload must be reduced. To achieve this, designers look to automation.

The definition, let alone the measurement, of workload is a problem which baffles human factors specialists. The mental workload dimension further confounds this issue. Pilots recognize that the new aircraft call for more programming, planning, sequencing, alternative selection, and more "thinking," or in psychological terms, more cognitive processing. Field studies on the MD-80 (Wiener, 1985c) indicate that pilots see some reduction in the total workload but probably less than claimed by the manufacturers during the certification process. Designers emphasized reducing manual workload, not accounting adequately for mental workload. As for more time to look for other traffic, pilots generally are unimpressed with the claims for automation. Their attitude is that the automatic devices demand constant attention, "scanning," as they call it. While crews may be relieved of certain head-in-the-cockpit duties such as maintaining airspeed, which an autothrottle does quite competently, each device creates its own scanning demand.

These questions were at issue during the certification of the MD-80 and the B-767/757 as two-pilot aircraft (O'Lone, 1980). In the mid-1970s the U.S. airlines and manufacturers proposed that in future aircraft cockpits, automation could reduce the workload to the point where only two crew members would be required. Many had already questioned the importance of the flight engineer, in view of the mechanical simplicity of jet aircraft and the fact that two-engine jets (DC-9, B-737, etc.) were being flown quite safely by two-pilot crews. Some airlines had, as contract concessions, carried a third pilot in the B-737. Evidence for and against the relative safety record of two-pilot and three-pilot crews was advanced and refuted by the various parties to the dispute and ended as a hopeless statistical stalemate.

The issue was drawing to a head in 1979 as two seemingly unrelated events were transpiring: the DC-9-80 (MD-80) was about to roll off the assembly line in Long Beach, California, and a presidential campaign was heating up. Hoping for ALPA's support, candidate Ronald Reagan promised to impanel a presidential commission to study the two- versus three-pilot cockpit, should he be elected. The economic stakes were high—McDonnell Douglas probably could not have sold the Super 80 as a three-pilot plane, and thus the future of the company rested very much on the plane's certification for two pilots. The designers based their case on automation (Smith, 1978). The Super 80 provided the short- and medium-haul carrier with a sophisticated flight guidance system and advanced avionics package of the sort previously seen only in wide-body transports (Ropelewski, 1981). The eyes of the world aviation community were on the presidential task force. Although not bound by U.S. decisions, foreign airlines and manufacturers would certainly be influenced by the outcome.

After extensive hearings, the task force upheld the FAA's certification of the two-pilot Super 80 and made the even more sweeping decision that future aircraft, including wide-bodies, could be designed and certificated for two pilots, brightening the future of the new Boeing products (President's Task Force on Aircraft Crew Complement, 1981). Thus the flight engineer will likely go the way of the airline navigator and radio operator. As the aging B-707s, B-727s, and DC-8s are retired, they will be replaced by two-pilot models. The new wide-bodies, such as the B-747-400, the MD-11, and the A-340, will have two-pilot cockpits.

Fortunately we have not yet experienced a loss of a two-pilot, wide-body aircraft in which the accident might be attributed to automation or excessive workload (or even perceived to be). If and when this unhappy event occurs, who knows what will be said about the missing third crew member? It may be premature at this time to say the final benediction over the flight engineer. While the presidential task force may now be ancient history, we can never be sure that the issue is dead. Too many people stand ready to resuscitate it at a moment's notice.

More Precise Flight Maneuvers and Navigation

Another vitally important issue is the conservation of that dwindling and essentially irreplaceable commodity, airspace. Forecasts for the remainder of this century predict a marked increase in the number of flights, and virtually no increase in the number of airports (Hoffman & Hollister, 1976). In 1984, flight delays in the United States increased 80%, due partly to the residual effects of the controllers' strike of 1981 but principally to congestion in the terminal areas ("FAA planning new procedures," 1984) that arose to some degree as a by-product of the Airline Deregulation Act of 1978. That legislation gave birth to the hub-and-spoke system, with highly compacted airline schedules occurring at certain times each day at the hubs.

More economical use of the airspace, with no compromise in safety, requires packing planes closer together through more-precise lateral, vertical, and longitudinal (speed) navigation, less-rigid airway and approach and departure structure, and effective metering and spacing of aircraft arrivals. Such precise navigation is clearly beyond human capabilities; thus, flight-deck as well as ground-based automation is required. Area navigation, already mentioned, increases the programming and monitoring demands on the crews and ATC personnel. Microwave landing systems (MLS), which are under development, will permit curved final approach paths instead of the traditional straight-in localizer. These will be highly economical of the airspace around airports but will demand intricate programming and careful monitoring by the flight crews.

With the possible reduction of vertical separation in the high-altitude sectors from 2,000 to 1,000 feet, there will be a greater demand on the crew to capture and maintain their assigned altitude and a greater importance attached to the automatic level-off features of flight guidance systems, as well as automated altitude alerting systems. Altitude deviations ("busts") are a common problem as yet unsolved by automated altitude alerters and flight guidance systems.

Display Flexibility

The extreme flexibility of "soft displays" (software-generated) allows the designer to display information in formats never used before—symbols, colors, text, 3-D graphics, perspective views, enhanced images (such as radar returns), map overlays, and the like. Equally important, they permit pilots to configure their instrument panels and displays as they see fit. With soft displays pilots can select or deselect features according to their own style of flying and their desire for information, a development consistent with one of the principles proposed by Wiener and Curry (1980, p. 1009): "Desires and needs for automation will vary with operators and with time for any one operator. Allow for different 'styles' (choice of automation) when feasible."

But with flexibility come problems. We have seen a tendency for proposed soft displays to become a jungle of clutter, of ill-considered symbols and text, or a dazzling presentation of colors. Little wonder that pilots are now referring to the modern instrument panel as "Pacman" and "Ataris." The attitude of too many computer experts is "we can do it, so let's throw it up on the display—it can't hurt anything." Thus it will fall to human factors practitioners to persuade designers to return to the fundamental question: what information does the operator need, and in what form (or forms) should it be displayed?

Finally, we might take note of the striking similarity between the conceptualized cockpit and the office of the future, as seen by comparing Figure 13.4 with Figure 15.15 (Sexton, this volume). The cockpit is starting to resemble an office and the office a cockpit. This is an example of what biologists call *convergent evolution*, whereby disparate systems begin to resemble each other over time. Why does

Figure 13.4.   An office architect's concept of a future office. (Courtesy of Environetics International.)

convergent evolution occur? Because the separate systems are attempting to solve the same problem using roughly the same resources. What is the common problem here? Essentially it consists of information management, communication, decision making, and supervisory control.

The works of scholars of office automation confirm this commonality. For example, in a recent study of the transition of the French banking system from manual to computer-based operations, Adler (1984) reports findings strikingly similar to those reported in the field studies of aircrew transition by Curry (1985) and Wiener (1985c).

Economy of Cockpit Space

Digital systems allow not only display flexibility but control flexibility as well, resulting in economy of another vanishing resource, cockpit space, or "real estate" as pilots and designers call it. Computer-driven controls and displays, for example, multifunction keyboards, have great potential for conserving real estate. But once again, multifunctionality, as another form of flexibility, can lead to problems, and it will demand careful attention from the human factors engineers.

Special Requirements of Military Missions

The special demands of military combat missions have accelerated the interest in cockpit automation (Air Force Studies Board, 1982). The requirement for flexibility is again one of the drivers. A modern fighter–bomber is capable of a variety of missions involving a multitude of weapons, countermeasures, and reconnaissance devices. One of the tasks of the crew is to select the weapon for the job, once the aircraft is airborne and approaching the target, and then to deliver it, often in a high-g maneuver. At the same time the crew must operate systems to protect their plane from enemy fire, as well as perform other tasks such as communication and target acquisition. Such missions require a high degree of automation, as these multiple tasks are well beyond unaided human capability. To a far greater extent than in transport aircraft, the military pilot has become essentially a programmer, monitor, decision maker, and systems manager.

Current Issues in Automation

The Changing Nature of Piloting

It should be clear by now that to discuss automation we must examine the rapidly changing nature of the flying task, which resulted from two developments: (1) the increasing complexity of the environment in which pilots fly—an environment congested with aircraft, demands, regulations, and procedures; and (2) a vast number of computer-based devices at the pilots' fingertips, replacing the demand for manual control and mental arithmetic. Modern aircraft also contain an array of warning and alerting systems (the machine monitoring the pilot) which are a subject of considerable controversy. These devices remind, suggest, or demand that pilots take action (e.g., altitude alerters, the "pull up" message of the GPWS), warn them of deviations (e.g., the excessive-airspeed clacker), warn them of unacceptable configurations (e.g., "flap overspeed" on the MD-80), and even take action on their own (e.g., autoslats and stick pushers, which are designed to break stalls if pilot intervention has not relieved the problem).

Who's in Charge Here?

Not surprisingly, the pilots are concerned. The last example is a good one, for it exemplifies what pilots fear in the automation movement, that decisions will actually be implemented without their consent. One airline captain (Melvin, 1983, p. 320) warns of the danger of stick pushers. His fears may be justified by events in the 1980s. A Fairchild Metro crashed in a steep nose-down attitude shortly after takeoff from Terre Haute, Indiana. The Metro has a stall warning system that gives an aural alert upon recognizing an impending stall, then activates a stick pusher with a 60-pound force to lower the nose to avoid the stall. Two other incidents of pilots having to overpower or deactivate stick pushers have recently been examined by the NTSB ("NTSB urges review," 1984).

But an even more fundamental question is being asked: who is in charge now, the human or the machine? This is not a simple question, and it is certainly not merely a matter of pilots' self-esteem being threatened by the advance of the machine age. The question goes to the very heart of the nature of piloting, the seemingly divided authority between human and machine, and mainly, what is the role of the pilot as minder of equipment that is not only increasingly sophisticated but increasingly autonomous. In a field study on the MD-80 with a major airline (Wiener, 1985c), pilots have remarked about being "along for the ride." The problem is not one of insufficient workload, although boredom and complacency are often mentioned, but a strong sense of being "out of the loop." Similar complaints have been voiced about other highly automated aircraft. A B-767 captain remarked to the author, "I know I'm not in the loop, but I'm not exactly out of the loop. It's more like I'm flying alongside the loop." Pilots and observers have been alarmed at the tendency of crews to attempt to "program their way out of trouble" with the automatic devices rather than shut them off and revert to manual flight. As a result of his field studies on the B-767, Curry (1985) recommended that crews be given "turn-it-off training."

Pilots are worried about a possible erosion of skills due to overuse of automation, but they are more concerned about their perceived loss of control—that the machines are taking over and making decisions on their own, as in the case of the stick pusher. On the other hand, it could be argued that there is nothing more serious than a stall, and the stick pusher is designed to save the aircraft when all else has failed; since the human crew has not responded to the stall warnings and indications, the device takes over by default. It is the ultimate backup. We can only remark that if pilots perceive a surrender of authority to present-day automation, the introduction of artificial intelligence in the cockpit may face an even stormier resistance.

Manual Reversion

Considerable and well-deserved concern has been expressed in the aviation community over how quickly and effectively the crews can transition from automatic to manual flight when suddenly required to do so. A similar concern has been expressed about the air traffic controller, whose job may soon become increasingly automated. The fear is that crews and controllers, during automatic operation, may lose contact with the momentary progress of the flight and may falter when required to reenter the loop. Unfortunately, there is little research to turn to. This will undoubtedly be a focal point of human factors research in the years to come. The good news is that now there are research-oriented full-mission simulators available to human factors scientists so that they can adequately study this problem.

Blunders Made Easy

Also of great concern is the fact that automated devices, while preventing many forms of errors, seem to invite others. As mentioned previously, it appears that automation tunes out small errors and creates the opportunities for large ones (Bergeron, 1981; Wiener, 1985a). A familiar household example of this property of digital devices is the digital alarm clock. Unlike the analog alarm clock, with which one could easily make 10- and 15-minute errors, the digital clock can be set very precisely, but it operates on a 24-hour cycle; thus one can inadvertently set a wake-up time at PM instead of AM. With the introduction of the digital clock, small errors were eliminated, but a new blunder was born: the precise 12-hour error. Bergeron (1981) showed that general aviation pilots made more serious navigational errors in a simulator with an autopilot than without.

Another disconcerting property of digital flight guidance and navigation systems is that programming errors introduced early in the flight, even before takeoff, may not come to fruition under hours later (e.g., an incorrectly loaded waypoint).

Many airlines have attacked the blunder problem as a training matter. The importance of training for the conduct of automated flight cannot be overemphasized, but all too often training departments become dumping grounds for problems created by cockpit design and management. Because of the vulnerability of the modern systems to blunders, especially in programming, or more generally to what Wiener and Curry (1980) have called "set-up errors," aggressive approaches (in addition to training) must be considered, and considerable research on error causation and prevention is needed. Just to name a few approaches:

1. Designing the systems to be less cordial to error at the human interface rather than depending on training and correct operation. If human factors engineering is done properly at the conceptual and design phase, the price is high, but it is paid only once. If training must compensate for poor design, the price is paid every day.
2. Designing systems to be less vulnerable once an error is made ("error tolerant").
3. Providing error-checking mechanisms. (These may depend on more intelligent on-board computers.)
4. Designing the overall system in which aircraft operate, mainly ATC systems, to be less vulnerable to error.

The last recommendation may be particularly difficult, as trade-offs between resource usage and safety may be required (e.g., 1,000 vs. 2,000 foot separation in the high-altitude sectors; Feazel, 1984). But in other cases, some rather simple and inexpensive redesign may do the job. For example, the automatic navigation system of the Boeing 767 allows the crew to establish waypoints by loading three-letter station identifiers ("ICAOs"). It occurred to the author that a heavily traveled route in the southwestern United States passed over or near two VORs (navigation stations) with identical names—Las

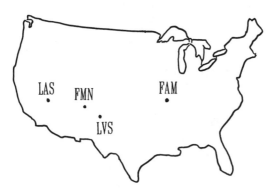

Figure 13.5.   Map of the United States with pairs of possibly confusing VOR identifiers. (From Wiener, 1985b. Reprinted with permission. © 1985 Society of Automotive Engineers, Inc.)

Vegas, New Mexico (LVS) and Las Vegas, Nevada (LAS)—which could easily lead to an erroneous input and possibly serious navigational error (see Figure 13.5). Shortly later a B-767 captain remarked to the author that on the previous flight his first officer had toggled-in FAM (Farmington, Missouri) when he meant FMN (Farmington, New Mexico). All of this is merely to illustrate an important point— that prevention of error at the crew–system interface involves more than training the crew and more than designing the on-board system. It must also invoke the design of the entire environment in which the crew and vehicle operate. It would seem a simple matter for the FAA to rename VORs so that no two have the same name, thus eliminating once and for all a highly possible blunder that carries a potential for disastrous consequences.

Looking Ahead: Philosophies of Automation

In 1980 Wiener and Curry proposed 15 guidelines for design, operation, and training. We felt then, and I believe most would agree today, that general, device-independent guidelines are needed. This would allow each new device, operating technique or doctrine, or training program to be held against a "template," rather than designed, implemented, and defended anew. To test this assertion requires further development of general guidelines, arising from research studies, incident and accident reports, and line experience.

What is also needed is some guiding philosophies of automation rather than simply a collection of devices. The B-757/767 and the A-310/320 are a beginning—they seem to represent cockpits designed by a guiding philosophy. The following section is a brief description of some other design philosophies that might be considered in future developments.

Flight Management by Exception

One of the principles espoused in the Wiener–Curry guidelines was allowing the crew the opportunity to operate the equipment so as to achieve the result they desired. In short, permit crews to fly the way they want to fly, within the bounds of regulations, air traffic control, and flight safety. (For a somewhat similar view from a manufacturer, see Fadden and Weener, 1984.) Some modern devices do allow increased crew freedom to set parameters and determine "styles" of flight—bank-angle limiters, for example. One philosophy of automation, then, might be to allow maximum crew flexibility in operating devices and to provide warning and alerting systems to inform the crew when an unacceptable condition is about to ensue.

Designers might borrow a technique of modern business management known as *management by exception* (MBE). Fundamentally, this principle states that as long as things are going well or according to plan, leave the managers alone. Don't clutter their world with reports, warnings, and messages of normal conditions. "Exceptions" are predefined, and lower-level managers or computers flag exceptions, which are routed to the manager. Analogously, the flight manager may decide that he or she does not wish to hear aural signals indicating the autopilot is executing stabilizer trim—unless it is an abnormal condition. "Abnormal" must then be defined, and the filter logic determined.

We pictured an "electronic cocoon," a multidimensional shell around the aircraft and crew. As long as the flight stayed within the cocoon, the system would leave the crew alone to fly as they saw fit. If the cocoon were penetrated, or forecast to be (see below), an exception message would be issued. The exact form of the message will require considerable research and debate—it could range from a conventional warning that the cocoon has been penetrated (e.g., the airspeed clacker on critical Mach), to a diagnostic message that might attempt to pinpoint the trouble, to a probabilistic message when a single diagnosis is not possible. The exception message may also be extended to provide suggestions for remedying the situation. In extreme cases, the machine may take action on its own (e.g., stick pushers or autoslats).

Forecasting and "Trending"

Closely related to the philosophy of flight management by exception (FMBE) is the use of forecasting models to predict a penetration of the cocoon rather than waiting for it to happen. Here avionics designers may borrow from statistical quality control, where the quality of a product is controlled by statistical sampling and inferential tests (see Wiener, 1984, Figure 7.1).

The wise quality control engineer does not wait for a process to go out of control. If he or she senses a *trend* (nonrandom or systematic variation) developing, statistical techniques are applied to test for trends, or *runs*, as they are called.

Applying forecasting and the FMBE philosophy to aircraft automation requires only a slight stretch of the imagination. Rather than await a potentially dangerous out-of-limits condition (e.g., CSD [constant speed drive] overheat or overconsumption of oil) before issuing an exception message, on-board computers would constantly update forecasts of the various parameters (Wiener, 1985b). Forecasting models are well developed and are relatively easy to implement on digital computers. If a penetration of the electronic cocoon is forecast to take place, even though the readings are still in the normal range, the crew would receive an exception message. Why wait to puncture the cocoon? Consistent with the philosophy of allowing the crew to have maximum control of the situation, the forecasting parameters could be selected by the crew. Within the bounds of safety, there would be a range of sensitivity from "hair-trigger" crews to "leave me alone till you're sure it looks bad" crews. The crew could ask for further extrapolations and then make the necessary decisions.

Goal Sharing

The notion that human operators should inform the system of their intentions, or goals, may seem simple, but it is a capability notice-ably and perhaps dangerously lacking in most present day automatic systems in aviation and elsewhere (Wiener, 1985b). Goal sharing (also called *intent-driven systems*) would first require that the crew make its intentions known ("Here's what we want to do"), and then allow the computer to check crew inputs and system outputs to see if they are logically consistent with the overall (strategic) plan. If not, an exception report would be issued.

The lack of this capability is what clearly emerges from reading in-cident and accident reports. The automation (e.g., the digital flight guidance system or long-range navigators) uncritically accepts inputs and has no capability for checking their overall consistency with any understood goal. And as flight guidance systems become more so-phisticated (e.g., Boeing 767/757 and Airbus 310/320), this capability is all the more important. The Boeing 767/757 has the capability of storing the destination airport and detecting route discontinuities.

Once the computer is informed of the strategic goals, it can check future inputs, as well as the aircraft's position (including its forecast position), for consistency with the overall goal. Thus a grossly erro-neous input (such as establishing a waypoint of FAM when FMN was intended) might generate an exception report. The fuel and oil supplies, and countless other variables, could be continuously checked for consistency with the overall goal.

Looking again at an example mentioned previously, had the stra-tegic goal—to fly from Sydney to Honolulu—been understood by the system, and if it had a capability to check inputs for consistency, an exception report would have prevented the takeoff with erroneous information. The same capability might have saved KAL Flight 007. Likewise, goal sharing may have prevented some of the dramatic fuel incidents that have occurred in recent years.

Artificial Intelligence (AI) and Expert Systems

Rapid developments are underway in creating intelligent machines which can mimic human reasoning. The so-called expert systems rely on sets of rules (ruled-based) or on inferred human knowledge (knowledge-based) in a manner that approaches human intelligence. If AI lives up to the expectations of its adherents, it could extend the ability of the machine to monitor the progress of flight, check human inputs, and provide the logic to implement the philosophies of auto-mation described above. Indeed, AI may spark a new chapter in the continuing debate on just what should be done by computer and what should be done by the human crew (see Chambers & Nagel, 1985). It may even introduce anew the question of crew complement. Already the Defense Advance Research Projects Administration (DARPA) is studying the concept of the "pilot's associate" and the "electronic crew member" for military aircraft. The philosophies of automation suggested in this chapter are somewhat modest: the intel-ligent cockpit is viewed as mainly a monitor of essentially conven-tional pilot tasks aided by an implementation of flight management by exception and goal sharing. Proponents of machine intelligence have far more in mind for their computers.

Conclusion

The rapid pace of introduction of computer-based devices into the cockpit has outstripped the ability of designers, pilots, and operators to formulate an overall strategy for their use and implementation. The human factors profession is struggling to catch up. The devices themselves are highly reliable, but therein may lie the problem: they are also dumb and dutiful. This property of digital devices, and the fallibility of the human operator, has created a problem at the hu-man–device interface. Putting "just one more computer" into the cockpit is not the answer. The solution will come from a long, ex-pensive, and sometimes tedious effort to develop a harmonious crew–automation interface, guided by an overall design philosophy.

Acknowledgments

Writing of this chapter was supported in part by a research grant, No. NCC2-377, from the NASA-Ames Research Center. The author gratefully acknowledges the assistance of persons too numerous to list at both NASA-Ames and the University of Miami. The cooperation of Eastern Airlines, Northwest Airlines, and the ALPA Safety Committees at those companies is deeply appreciated. Portions of this chapter, including Figure 13.4, are from Wiener, 1985a, copyright by the Human Factors Society, Inc., and reproduced with permission.

References

Adler, P. (1984). *New technologies, new skills.* Working paper, Harvard Business School.

Air Force Studies Board, National Research Council. (1982). *Automation in combat aircraft.* Washington, DC: National Academy Press.

Bergeron, H. P. (1981). Single pilot IFR autopilot complexity/benefit tradeoff study. *Journal of Aircraft, 18,* 705–706.

Boehm-Davis, D. A., Curry, R. E., Wiener, E. L., & Harrison, R. L. (1983). Human factors of flight-deck automation: Report on a NASA-Industry workshop. *Ergonomics, 26,* 953–961.

Carley, W. M. (1984, June 6). Spanish airlines make more than their share of navigational errors. *Wall Street Journal,* p. 1.

Chambers, A. B., & Nagel, D. C. (1985, November). Pilots of the future: human or computer? *Communications of the ACM, 28,* 1187–1199.

Curry, R. E. (1985). *The introduction of new cockpit technology: A human factors study* (NASA Technical Memorandum 86659). NASA-Ames Research Center, Moffett Field, CA.

Edwards, E. (1977). Automation in civil transport aircraft. *Applied Ergonomics, 8,* 194–198.

FAA planning new procedures to eliminate worsening delays. (1984, July 23). *Aviation Week and Space Technology,* pp. 29, 31.

Fadden, D. M., & Weener, E. F. (1984, July). *Selecting effective automation.* Paper presented at Air Line Pilots Association Safety Workshop, Washington, DC.

Feaver, D. B. (1983, September 11). Flaws cited in technology on Korean jet. *Washington Post,* pp. 1, A14–A15.

Feazel, M. (1984, July 30). Vertical separation cut weighed. *Aviation Week and Space Technology,* pp. 27–28.

Gannett, J. R. (1982). The pilot and the flight management system. In *Behavioral Objectives in Aviation Automated Systems Symposium* (pp. 93–96). Warrendale, PA: Society of Automotive Engineers.

Hersh, S. M. (1986). *The target is destroyed.* New York: Random House.

Hoagland, M. (1984). Winging it in the 1980s: Why guidelines are needed for cockpit automation. In *Third Aerospace Technology Conference Proceedings* (pp. 155–162). Warrendale, PA: Society of Automotive Engineers.

Hoffman, W. C., & Hollister, W. M. (1976). *Forecast of the general aviation air traffic control environment for the 1980s* (NASA Contractor Report CR-137909). Burlington, MA: Aerospace Systems, Inc.

Hopkins, H. (1983). Over-dependence on automatics—the black box one man band. *International Journal of Air Safety*, 1, 343–348.

International Civil Aviation Organization. (1983). *Destruction of Korean Airlines Boeing 747 over the Sea of Japan, 31 August 1983* Report No. C-WP/7764. Montreal: Author.

Johnson, R. W. (1984, March). KAL 007: Unanswered questions. *World Press Review*, pp. 24–26.

Loomis, J. P., & Porter, R. F. (1981, April). *The performance of warning systems in avoiding controlled-flight-into-terrain (CFIT) accidents.* Presented at Symposium on Aviation Psychology, Columbus, Ohio State University.

Machado, F. (1984). The destruction of KAL 007 (KE 007): How did it happen? *International Journal of Air Safety*, 2, 5–14.

Mackley, W. B. (1982). Aftermath of Mt. Erebus. *Flight Safety Digest*, 1, 3–7.

Mahon, P. (1984). *Verdict on Erebus*. Auckland, New Zealand: Collins.

Mann, P. Q. (pseudonym) (1984). Reassessing the Sakhalin incident. *Defence Attache'*, 3, 44–56.

Manning, C. K. (1984). Dangerously safe? *Air Line Pilot*, 53, 22–23.

Melvin, W. W. (1983). A philosophy of automation. In *Behavioral Objectives in Aviation Automated Systems Symposium* (pp. 319–325). Warrendale, PA: Society of Automotive Engineers.

Nagel, D. C. (1983, December). *Automation and human error.* Paper presented at Air Line Pilots Association Symposium "Beyond Pilot Error," Washington, DC.

National Transportation Safety Board. (1973). *Eastern Airlines L-1011, Miami, Florida, 29 December 1972* (Report No. NTSB-AAR-73-14). Washington, Author.

National Transportation Safety Board. (1980). *Aeromexico DC-10-30, XA-DUH, Over Luxembourg, Europe, November 11, 1979* (Report No. NTSB-AAR-80-10). Washington: Author.

National Transportation Safety Board. (1984). *Scandinavian Airlines System, DC-10-30, John F. Kennedy International Airport, New York, February 28, 1984* (Report No. NTSB-AAR-84-15). Washington: Author.

National Transportation Safety Board. (1986). *China Airlines 747-SP, N4522V, 300 Nautical Miles Northwest of San Francisco, California, February 19, 1985* (Report No. NTSB/AAR-86/03). Washington: Author.

New Zealand Royal Commission. (1981). *Report of the Royal Commission to inquire into the crash on Mt. Erebus, Antarctica of a DC-10 aircraft operated by Air New Zealand, Ltd.* Government Printer, Wellington, New Zealand: Author.

NTSB urges review of Metro stall device. (1984, July 23). *Aviation Week and Space Technology*, p. 31.

Oliver, J. G. (1984, July). *A single red light.* Paper presented at Air Line Pilots Association Annual Safety Symposium, Washington, DC.

O'Lone, R. G. (1980, March 24). 757, 767 offer two-man cockpits. *Aviation Week and Space Technology*, pp. 23–25.

Pearson, D. (1984, August 18) K.A.L. 007: What the U.S. knew and when we knew it. *The Nation*, pp. 105–124.

Peterson, W. L. (1984, June). The rage to automate: An interview with Captain Mel Hoagland. *Air Line Pilot*, pp. 15–17.

President's Task Force on Aircraft Crew Complement. (1981). *Report of the President's Task Force on Aircraft Crew Complement.* Washington, DC: Author.

Rohmer, R. (1984). *Massacre 747.* Markham, Ontario: PaperJack Publishers.

Ropelewski, R. R. (1981, February 3). DC-9-80 nears Category 3 certification. *Aviation Week and Space Technology*, pp. 43–46.

Ruffell Smith, H. P. (1968). Some human factors of aircraft accidents during collision with high ground. *Journal of Institute of Navigation, 21,* 1–10.

Sayle, M. (1985, April 25). KE 007—A conspiracy of circumstance. *The New York Review,* pp. 44–54.

St. John, J. (1984). *The day of the cobra: the true story of KAL Flight 007.* Nashville, TN: T. Nelson.

Smith, D. A. (1978, March 27). Digital system used to cut workload. *Aviation Week and Space Technology,* pp. 49–53.

Stein, K. J. (1983, October 3). Human factors analyzed in 007 navigation error. *Aviation Week and Space Technology,* pp. 165–167.

U.S. House of Representatives. (1977). *Future needs and opportunities in the air traffic control system* Report No. 98-796. Subcommittee on Transportation, Aviation, and Weather of the Committee on Science and Technology. Washington, DC: Author.

U.S. Senate. (1980). Hearings before the Subcommittee on Aviation of the Committee on Commerce, Science and Transportation Report No. 96-119. Washington, DC: Author.

Vette, G. (1983). *Impact Erebus.* Auckland, New Zealand: Hodder and Stoughton.

Wiener, E. L. (1977). Controlled flight into terrain accidents: System-induced errors. *Human Factors, 19,* 171–181.

Wiener, E. L. (1980). Midair collisions: the accidents, the systems, and the realpolitik. *Human Factors, 22,* 521–533.

Wiener, E. L. (1983a, December). *The human pilot and the computerized cockpit.* Paper presented at Air Line Pilots Association Symposium "Beyond Pilot Error," Washington, DC.

Wiener, E. L. (1983b). The role of the human in the age of the microprocessor. In *Proceedings of the Conference of Safety Issues in Air Traffic Control Systems Planning and Design* (pp. 276–291). Princeton, NJ: Princeton University.

Wiener, E. L. (1984). Vigilance and inspection. In Warm, J. (Ed.), *Sustained attention in human performance.* London: Wiley.

Wiener, E. L. (1985a). Beyond the sterile cockpit. *Human Factors, 27,* 75–90.

Wiener, E. L. (1985b). Cockpit automation: In need of a philosophy. In *Proceedings of 1985 Behavioral Engineering Conference* (pp. 369–375). Warrendale, PA: Society of Automotive Engineers.

Wiener, E. L. (1985c). *Human factors of cockpit automation: A field study of flight crew transition* (NASA Contractor Report CR-177333). NASA-Ames Research Center: Moffett Field, CA.

Wiener, E. L. (In progress). Error analysis and prevention in highly automated transport aircraft.

Wiener, E. L., & Curry, R. E. (1980). Flight-deck automation: Promises and problems. *Ergonomics, 23,* 995–1011.

Software Interfaces for Aviation Systems

14

Robert C. Williges
Beverly H. Williges
Robert G. Fainter

Introduction

Aviation systems are rapidly becoming computer dependent. Integration of information or, more correctly, integration of raw data into meaningful information is quite possibly the single most important function that computers perform in aviation systems. The design of computer software to provide appropriate data integration is critical. As aircraft and the airspace system increase in complexity, the amount of data available to the pilot and controller increases. Additionally, the increased performance of modern aircraft requires that the available data be perceived, processed, and dealt with at an increasing speed. Computer augmentation within both the cockpit and the air traffic control system is necessary in modern aviation, not only for the pilot and the controller, but also for weather forecasting and reporting, dispatching, maintenance, and military mission planning.

Human Factors in Aviation

Computers in the Cockpit

Flight Instrumentation.   Since the middle 1970s, the advent of high-resolution color graphic displays has caused a revolution in flight instrumentation. In civil aircraft, use of computerized displays varies from monochromatic testscopes in long-range navigation devices, to colored text for such applications as engine monitors, to advanced color graphics such as the horizontal and vertical situation indicators in the Boeing 757/767. New color radars enhance the weather picture, and aircraft incorporate complex graphic displays, such as head-up displays.

Military aircraft, such as the F-18, also have electronic flight instrumentation. However, because of the higher performance of these aircraft and the more critical nature of their mission, more data are made available on the display. These data can be presented in various forms ranging from traditional flight information in textual formats to advanced graphics which provide heads-up display of flight paths and target information to depict current weapon state aboard the aircraft. Military systems typically consist of three or more CRTs in the cockpit. The pilot has the flexibility of displaying many different types of data on any of these screens. In addition to basic aircraft attitude and control data, the pilot may choose to display engine parameters, weapons system data, communications data, and navigation data. These data can typically be placed on any of the CRT screens.

Data Links.   An exciting aspect of using computers in the cockpit is the possibility of providing a data link between the aircraft and ground facilities. As the new national airspace system plan is put into place over the next 10–15 years, a capability is planned for computers aboard the aircraft to communicate directly with computers on the ground. Current weather data can be linked to the aircraft, giving the pilot any data needed without a direct voice inquiry. Additionally, routine air traffic control instructions and clearances can be transmitted via computer, thereby reducing both the possibility of misunderstanding the spoken word and reducing the voice traffic on a radio channel. Likewise, data from the aircraft can be linked to ground-based computers to allow calculation of ground speed and heading that can be coupled with ground-based radar and computer predictions of aircraft path and altitude to warn pilots of potential collisions and to provide the National Weather Service with current data on upper-level wind and weather conditions.

Computers in the Air Traffic Control System

Computers in the air traffic control environment can reduce controller workload by centralizing data and providing flexible data display. Currently, computers coordinate all instrument flights under the jurisdiction of the Federal Aviation Administration. Route clearances for instrument flights are computer generated for human controllers who actually control the flight. In addition, current radar systems in all air route traffic control centers and many approach control facilities use computer-generated displays that include augmented textual information of each flight adjacent to the displayed aircraft radar blip. The displays also have predictive capabilities: they can project the future track of aircraft and warn of traffic conflicts and terrain proximity.

Computer Interfaces

Two types of integration are needed to develop successful computer-augmented cockpit and air traffic control systems. First, the variety of airborne and ground-based computer systems must be integrated to provide compatible data communication links. Second, these systems must be integrated with the pilots and controllers who use them. This latter type of integration requires an appropriately designed human–computer software interface. The resulting software interface provides a communication or dialogue link between the user and the computer.

To design this software interface properly, two areas of human factors are important. First, specific human factors software design issues must be addressed. Second, an integrated process for the design of software around user capabilities and limitations must be followed. The remainder of this chapter addresses each of these human factors considerations in detail.

Human Factors Software Design Issues

The design of software interfaces to provide a dialogue between pilots and computer-based cockpits or controllers and computer-augmented air traffic control systems must be approached from three perspectives. First, a general human factors perspective outlining fundamental principles of human–computer dialogue design should be considered. Second, the general functions to be performed by the human–computer interface software should be assessed. And, third, the human–computer software interface should incorporate accepted human factors design guidelines.

Principles of Human–Computer Dialogue Design

Basic human factors principles fundamental to effective system design in other applications are equally important in the design of computer-based systems. Often the guidelines proposed for the design of human–computer interfaces are a restatement of these basic human factors principles in terms that relate to specific aspects of a human–computer interface. These general principles provide a basis for developing design objectives and a comprehensive set of metrics to evaluate the design. Seven general principles to consider in human–computer software interfaces were proposed by Williges, Williges, and Elkerton (1987):

1. Compatibility: Minimize the amount of information recoding that will be necessary.
2. Consistency: Minimize the difference in dialogue both within and across various human–computer interfaces.
3. Memory: Minimize the amount of information that the user must maintain in short-term memory.
4. Structure: Assist the users in developing a conceptual representation of the structure of the system so that they can navigate through the interface.
5. Feedback: Provide the user with feedback and error correction capabilities.
6. Workload: Keep user mental workload within acceptable limits.
7. Individualization: Accommodate individual differences among users through automatic adaption or user tailoring of the interface.

Compatibility.   In its most general form, the principle of compatibility predicts that high-information transfer will occur when the amount of information recoding required of the user is minimal. Translated to the design of human–computer interfaces, this would suggest that the interface must be compatible with human perception, memory, problem solving, action, and communication (Barnard, Hammond, Morton, & Long, 1981).

Gaines and Facey (1975) emphasized the importance of adhering to the user's organization of the data as well as vocabulary and language for dealing with the data. The choice of terminology, format, and system action should be consistent with user population stereotypes. Clarity or understandability of the data presented is critical. The input required of the user should not be ambiguous, and the output from the computer should be clear, and therefore, useful. The wording for commands, menus, error messages, and HELP displays should be selected with care.

Consistency.   Nickerson (1981) suggested that one of the primary reasons people do not like to use computer systems is that the systems lack consistency and integration. Interfaces differ both internally and across systems, resulting in the need for users to remember several different techniques to accomplish the same thing. The costs for failing to provide a consistent interface can be high. For example, Teitlebaum and Granda (1983) found that positional inconsistency in menu items resulted in a 73% increase in search time.

Both the input required of the user and the output of the system should be consistent across displays, software modules, software programs, and information systems. For example, neither the computer action associated with a set of special-function keys nor the syntax requirements of the command language should vary across menus or tasks. The system should perform in a predictable manner.

Memory.   In the design of human–computer dialogues it is important to minimize the amount of data the user must maintain in short-term memory, particularly if other information processing is required simultaneously. For example, if the system requires the pilot to change frequencies on a navigation or communication radio, the requested frequency should be displayed until the pilot has completed the change. This function is presently provided by dual-head communication radios or, traditionally, by pilots writing down each frequency, a high-workload activity.

Theories of short-term memory propose the existence of some upper limit of information that can be recalled soon after it has been presented. Miller (1956) suggested that the upper limit of short-term memory is five to nine items. However, the number of items one can remember is also related to the complexity of the items (Simon, 1974), the sequence of presentation (Badre, 1984), the length of time the items must be remembered (Melton, 1963), and the amount of competing information processing (Murdock, 1965).

Structure.   One fundamental aspect of human behavior is that humans seek structure or organization in their environment, even in cases where none exists. The purpose of the structure is to unify conflicting data gathered through discovery or insight. Users of computer-based systems seek to determine the structure of the dialogue and control systems. This internal representation forms the basis of the user's understanding of the system and determines user decisions and actions. If the user fails to understand the structure, errors will occur. Norman (1981) provides several excellent examples of these structure errors with the complex and powerful UNIX operating system. For example, in the Berkeley UNIX system, the command used to copy files between computers (remote copy) requires two arguments, as does the normal copy command. However, if the user gives only one argument, nothing happens with the remote copy command, whereas a user prompt for the second argument occurs with the normal copy.

In some situations, graphic aid might be useful to provide structure. For example, a graphic can depict the hierarchical organization of a complex information system. These spatial representations serve as maps by which the user can "navigate" through the system. Billingsley (1982) found that subjects given an opportunity to study a map of the menu organization of a data base showed an overall improvement in information retrieval time. These data suggest that access to a pictorial representation of a menu structure facilitates the development of a workable mental model of that structure.

Feedback.   A human–computer system should be closed loop, with feedback to the users about the quality of their performance, the condition of the system, and the steps necessary to cause some desired outcome. Generally, feedback should occur in close temporal proximity to the related event, such as a user's request for data, computer detection of a user error or missing data, or a change in the status of the system based on a user input. When the response to a user's request will be delayed, the user should be given some indication that the request is being processed.

Errors do occur in human–computer dialogues, for example in programming a flight guidance system or inertial navigation system (INS), and feedback is required so that the user can determine if corrective action is needed and what form it should take. Error messages should be specific and written from the point of view of the user, not in some formal notation used by the programmer to represent various classes or errors. The user should be given every opportunity to correct errors. This is particularly important in systems where hardware errors may compound user errors (e.g., automatic speech recognizers). In one study where speech recognition was used for data entry (Schurick, Williges, & Maynard, 1985), accuracy of data fields was increased from 70% to 97% through feedback and user error correction. It is very likely that speech recognition systems will play an increasing role in commercial as well as military flight.

Workload.   An assessment of the potential effects of the interface on user mental workload is an essential step in the design of human–computer dialogues. Because the probability of user error or failure to act increases in an overload or underload situation, the overall goal should be to keep the workload of the user within acceptable limits when defining the operator's task and dialogue requirements.

The density of the data displayed or presented to the user is an important factor in workload. Displayed output should be organized to minimize the scanning required of the user, and only data essential to the user's current needs should be displayed. In some applications using speech displays, it may be necessary to allow operator control of the rate of information presentation. Relevant data should be presented in a usable form to reduce the processing requirements of the user (Mitchell & Miller, 1983). For example, a computer-generated electronic flight information system (EFIS) should display only pertinent information for the current task so that the pilot does not need to filter out irrelevant data.

Individualization.   Human behavior is characterized by individual differences. In human–computer systems these differences may stem from factors such as language usage, problem-solving style, or level of expertise with computer systems. Differences in interaction style may be necessary for different classes of users. For example, the computer system in the F-18 aircraft allows the pilot the capability to place specific data displays on any of five CRTs. In this way, the pilot individualizes data display.

The software interface must be designed to accommodate various types of individual differences among users through either a flexible or an adaptive interface. A flexible interface allows the user to tailor the interface to his or her own needs or permits various types of interaction. Examples include allowing for command synonyms, alternate syntax, and user-defined commands. Adaptive interfaces accommodate the individual user automatically and may change over time. Benbasat and Wand (1984) proposed the concept of a dialogue generator to adapt the interface to the evolving needs of users. The guidelines proposed by Wiener and Curry (1980) emphasize allowing pilots to use (or not use) cockpit automation and to configure the equipment according to their own style of flight.

General Functions of Human–Computer Interface Software

In most systems the human–computer interface (HCI) software is not a trivial aspect of the system. Smith and Mosier (1984a) asked people involved with the design of information system software to estimate the percentage of operational software devoted to the human–computer interface. Although no operational definition was given for the basis that should be used to make this estimate, the respondents indicated that on the average, 35% of operational software is devoted to implementing the user interface. Their estimates may not represent actual software practice precisely, but it is safe to conclude that a sizeable investment in time and money is made in the design of HCI software. Unfortunately, software design for the end user often suffers from inconsistency resulting from the involvement of many software developers and incompatibility with user expectations based on their experiences with related systems. Further, software designers often fail to consider the capabilities and limitations of the end user. The role of the human factors specialist is to provide human performance data, design tools, and an effective design strategy to improve the design process for HCI software.

The functions of HCI software can be classified into at least nine categories: data entry, data display, data management, action control, feedback and user guidance, error management, data protection, language, and communication between users. In Figures 14.1–14.9 each of these software functions is defined, and each of the fundamental principles of human–computer dialogue design listed on p. 466 is restated as it relates to specific HCI software functions. The figures also include a list of design issues related to the HCI software function and several examples of human factors design guidelines.

Human Factors Software Design Guidelines

The compilation of human factors guidelines for the development of HCI software originated with an IBM report on guidelines for human–display interfaces (Engel & Granda, 1975). Since publication of this report, many researchers have been involved in the compilation

---

HCI SOFTWARE FUNCTION - Data Entry

DEFINITION - User actions associated with input of data to a computer.

DESIGN GOALS

1. Ensure compatibility of data entry and data display.
2. Establish consistency across all data entry transactions.
3. Minimize the memory load of the user by using default values, keeping items short, and partitioning long data items.
4. Assist the user in developing a conceptual representation of the data entry process.
5. Minimize user workload by such means as requiring only a single entry of related data.
6. Provide individualization by allowing flexibility in the data entry process, when appropriate.

DESIGN ISSUES

1. Definition of how users will: (a) designate an item or position; (b) designate directions; (c) enter numbers, letters, and text; (d) enter numbers, letters, and text using predefined formats; (e) enter graphical data; and/or (f) manipulate graphical data.
2. Methods for speeded data entry.
3. User control of the data entry process.
4. Flexibility in data entry procedures.

EXAMPLES OF GUIDELINES

1. Users should be permitted to enter data in the units that are most familiar to them.
2. Data entries should be limited to 7 to 9 characters or words to minimize the memory load on the user.
3. When items longer that 7 to 9 characters or words must be entered, the data should be partitioned into smaller groups.

Figure 14.1.   Design of software for data entry. (Adapted from Smith & Mosier, 1984b.)

of handbooks devoted to HCI software guidelines. Some of these handbooks were developed for specific applications, such as automated battlefield systems (Parrish, Gates, Munger, Grimma, & Smith, 1982), whereas others were general and not targeted for a specific application (Williges & Williges, 1984). Perhaps the most comprehensive effort to compile and develop HCI software is the effort at the MITRE Corporation. A recent report (Smith & Mosier, 1984b) includes 679 guidelines covering six functional areas of the human–computer interface—data display, data entry, sequence control, user guidance, data transmission, and data protection. Although not directed specifically toward aviation applications, many of the Smith guidelines are relevant. Much of the information in Figures 14.1–14.9 was adapted from the Smith and Mosier (1984b) report.

HCI SOFTWARE FUNCTION - Data Display

DEFINITION - Computer output of data to a user.

DESIGN GOALS

1. Ensure compatibility of data displays with data entry.
2. Ensure consistency of all data displays.
3. Minimize memory load on the user by displaying the necessary and sufficient data required for task completion.
4. Assist the user in developing a conceptual representation or context for the data display process.
5. Minimize the user workload by providing for efficient information assimilation by the user of the data displayed.
6. Provide individualization by allowing users to tailor the data displays.

DESIGN ISSUES

1. Selection of data for display by user or computer.
2. Format for various types of data.
3. Density of data in displays.
4. Organization of data displays.
5. Highlighting selected data.
6. User control of movement through a series of displays.
7. Regeneration of changed data to show altered status.
8. User control of display coverage by temporary suppression of selected categories of data.
9. Relationship between control and display movement.

EXAMPLES OF GUIDELINES

1. Data should be displayed in a directly usable form; users should not need to convert data.
2. Identical types of data should be displayed in a consistent manner, irrespective of the source of origin.
3. When user control the motion of objects depicted on a display, the direction of motion of the display should be identical to the direction of motion of the user's control.

Figure 14.2.   Design of software for data display. (Adapted from Smith & Mosier, 1984b.)

The need for guidelines in software design is beginning to be recognized. Many companies have developed in-house handbooks for HCI software design guidelines. However, the data in the handbooks are limited in two respects. First, certain aspects of HCI software, such as voice input–output, are not covered adequately. (See Simpson, McCauley, Roland, Ruth, & Williges, 1985, for a discussion of system design issues associated with speech recognition and generation.) Clearly, research is needed to investigate new areas of the HCI, and the findings need to be summarized in the form of guidelines. Second, the validity of HCI guidelines depends on the extent to which the underlying research captures the multifactor nature of complex information systems. Researchers must be encouraged to use economical experimental design techniques that permit many

HCI SOFTWARE FUNCTION - Data Management

DEFINITION - Data storage and retrieval for analysis and planning.

DESIGN GOALS

1. Organize the database in a manner that is compatible with the user's structure of the data.
2. Provide a consistent method for data storage and retrieval.
3. Minimize the amount of information the user must remember during data storage and retrieval.
4. Assist the user in developing a conceptual representation of the contents and structure of the database.
5. Minimize user workload by using a single representation of the database.
6. Accommodate individual differences among users by providing various methods for data retrieval.

DESIGN ISSUES

1. Selection of a structure for the database.
2. Coding rules for translating problems into a database query.
3. Methods for displaying data retrieved.
4. Techniques for providing flexibility in data management features.

EXAMPLES OF GUIDELINES

1. The need for logical quantifiers in formulating queries should be minimized.
2. Data should be displayed in the form required by the user even if that differs from the form contained in the database or the form in which the data were originally entered.
3. Data management features should be partitioned into groups of increasing sophistication with the easier features available for users of limited experience or infrequent use of the data management system.

Figure 14.3. Design of software for data management. (Adapted from Smith & Mosier, 1984b.)

factors to be explored simultaneously to generate data representative of operational systems.

As the number of HCI software guidelines increases, it becomes apparent that guideline handbooks will be difficult to use and update. Therefore, on-line methods need to be explored for retrieval of the set of guidelines relevant to the design of a specific interface. Smith and Mosier (1984c) recommended the use of an automated checklist where the software designer could request display of any section of the guidelines, and the computer could store checklist entries throughout numerous design iterations. These entries would include evaluator judgments of the relative importance of each item, the ratings of judged design compliance, and any associated comments. Although many entries may not change during the design process, design iteration should result in some improvements which would be reflected in revised evaluator judgments on selected checklist items.

HCI SOFTWARE FUNCTION - Action Control

DEFINITION -   User actions or computer logic that initiates, interrupts, or
               terminates transactions between the user and the computer.

DESIGN GOALS

1. Ensure compatibility of the control actions required of the user and the
    computer responses.
2. Ensure consistent control actions across various tasks.
3. Minimize the user's memory load by reducing the number of control
    actions required of the user to effect routine transactions.
4. Assist the user in developing a conceptual representation of the control
    action structure.
5. Minimize user workload by providing simple control entries, particularly
    for real-time tasks.
6. Provide individualization by allowing the user to select control action
    and among various techniques for control entry to allow for different
    tasks and user skill levels.

DESIGN ISSUES

1. Selection and development of the dialogue style to be used for action
    control.
2. Specification of how the user can alter computer action sequences through
    interrupts, suspended processing, and various command options.
3. Concise methods for experienced users to control computer actions
    without loss of consistent control procedures.

EXAMPLES OF GUIDELINES

1. Choice of an appropriate dialogue style should be based on user
    characteristics, skill, and training. If user characteristics are variable,
    a variety of dialogue styles should be provided.
2. The computer should keep a record of user interrupts of action
    sequences, and this information should be used in software redesign.
3. Action control should be consistent throughout the system.

Figure 14.4.   Design of software for action control. (Adapted from Smith & Mosier,
               1984b.)

Williges and Williges (1983) suggested that various forms of computer aiding for retrieval of HCI software guidelines also should be considered. The computer aiding may be no more than tree-searching procedures for data retrieval of design guidelines or may incorporate sophisticated rule-based procedures to aid in selecting relevant guidelines and tailoring them to the specific application. Irrespective of the level of sophistication of the retrieval aid, future workstations for software designers will likely incorporate HCI software guidelines.

Typically, in the evolution of any software design, it is necessary to trade off various design alternatives. This is certainly the case when using HCI software design guidelines, where hundreds of HCI software guidelines may be more or less critical for the design of any

---

HCI SOFTWARE FUNCTION - Feedback and User Guidance

DEFINITION - Information provided by the computer to assist the user in interacting with the computer.

DESIGN GOALS

1. Ensure that the organization of online documentation and training is compatible with the user's frame of reference.
2. Ensure that information in online documentation and training is consistent with operational procedures.
3. Minimize the memory load on the user by providing prompts for user actions.
4. Assist the user in developing a conceptual representation of the structure of online documentation by providing indexing, cross-referencing, and/or browsing.
5. Provide documentation, training, and feedback to assist the user in avoiding errors.
6. Minimize user workload by providing records of routine actions and warnings of exceptional conditions.
7. Accommodate individual skill differences among users by tailoring user training and guidance.

DESIGN ISSUES

1. Feedback of user data entries, system status, errors, and context.
2. Structure for user action through input prompting or guidance.
3. Warnings or alarms for exceptional or dangerous conditions.
4. Computer compilation and display of user records such as action selections and communications with other users.
5. Computer aids for decision making, message composition, data entry, and data retrieval.
6. Information provided the user about system operation including documentation, online help, and online assistance.
7. Training for new users including tutorials, simulation, expert guidance, and other techniques.

EXAMPLES OF GUIDELINES

1. In subjective decision making, the computer should inform the user of data overlooked.
2. If phoneme-based synthesized speech is used to present a single type of warning message, no alerting tone should precede the message.
3. When online documentation presents a temporal sequence, the words should be ordered chronologically.

Figure 14.5. Design of software for feedback and user guidance. (Adapted from Smith & Mosier, 1984b.)

particular system. In some cases, compliance with all these guidelines is not possible because of economic or technical limitations. Smith and Mosier (1984c) recommend the use of a weighting system of categorical judgments or a numeric scale to be used by the software design team to make judgments about guideline compliance. To reduce bias in assigning weights, a multiple-step paired-comparison procedure can be used (Meister, 1985). At the very least, in the development of HCI software the software designer should consider the

HCI SOFTWARE FUNCTION - Error Management

DEFINITION -   Computer or user actions to detect and/or correct errors.

DESIGN GOALS

1.   Provide error feedback and guidance in a form that is directly usable.
2.   Ensure that standard feedback and error correction procedures are used across the entire system and are consistent with related systems.
3.   Minimize the amount of information the user must remember during error correction.
4.   Assist the user in developing a conceptual representation of the structure of the system by providing context for the error.
5.   Provide the user with every possibility to detect and correct errors.
6.   Minimize the workload of the user by providing for computer correction of routine errors.
7.   Accommodate individual differences among users by providing various means for user error correction.

DESIGN ISSUES

1.   Detection of user and system errors by the computer through parsing and other error detection techniques.
2.   User validation of ambiguous or critical control sequences.
3.   Error feedback to the user that includes the location of the error, its cause, and potential correction procedures.
4.   Computer-generated assistance to guide the user through error recovery.
5.   Automatic computer correction of user errors.
6.   Efficient methods for user correction of errors such as command editing, command cancellation or reversal, and data field reentry.
7.   User feedback and action control following an error detected in a command stack.

EXAMPLES OF DESIGN GUIDELINES

1.   Error messages should be appropriate for the user's level of knowledge of the system, not the system analyst's.
2.   The software should monitor and record user errors continuously or on a sampling basis to aid in redesign or the design of future systems.
3.   All error corrections by the user should be acknowledged by the computer either by indicating that an acceptable entry has been made or by another error message.

Figure 14.6.   Design of software for error management. (Adapted from Smith & Mosier, 1984b.)

potential system performance implications of failing to follow specific guidelines.

Finally, evaluation tools are needed to assist the designer in estimating the degree of compliance of specific software to HCI guidelines. These evaluations should occur as an integral part of a systematic software interface design process.

Software Interface Design Process

A well-defined software interface design process must be followed

---

HCI SOFTWARE FUNCTION - Data Protection

DEFINITION -   User or computer actions directed toward the prevention of
                data loss or other destructive actions.

DESIGN GOALS

1. Minimize data loss and the memory load on the user by prompting for
    required data.
2. Provide feedback to the user concerning ambiguous or destructive control
    action to avoid errors.

DESIGN ISSUES

1. Interpretation of ambiguous user entries when data loss is possible.
2. Confirmation of potential destructive user or computer actions.
3. Techniques to minimize data loss from computer failures or user errors.
4. Management of data transmissions to prevent data loss.

EXAMPLES OF GUIDELINES

1. When user commands to the computer are subject to misinterpretation, the
    user should be given an opportunity to review and confirm the computer's
    interpretation of the command.
2. When user commands to the computer would result in data loss, the user
    should be given the opportunity to confirm or reverse the destructive
    commands.
3. When data are being received, the computer should queue incoming data
    as necessary to ensure that they will not disrupt or destroy any ongoing
    data transactions by the user unless the incoming data take precedence.

Figure 14.7.   Design of software for data protection. (Adapted from Smith & Mosier,
               1984b.)

in order to implement the general human factors design principles
and guidelines for the various human–computer interface functions
present in aviation systems. Three considerations are central to this
process. First, layered software interfaces must be considered. Second, the process and issues related to the computational software
need to be addressed. And, third, the stages of HCI software design
should be completed in an iterative fashion.

Layers of Software Interfaces

Proper design of the interface between the pilot and the aircraft, or
the controller and the air traffic control system, is crucial to the overall viability of the system. However, the human-interface software
does not deal directly with the sensors and systems of the aircraft or
air traffic control equipment. There are other layers of software that
mediate between the human-interface software and the aircraft or air
traffic control system.

Software layering is a technique which promotes design of a software system as a series of interfaces. Figure 14.10 illustrates the con-

---

HCI SOFTWARE FUNCTION - Language Definition

DEFINITION -   The set of names and symbols used to communicate between
                the user and computer.

DESIGN GOALS

1. Provide language which is compatible with the user's frame of reference.
2. Ensure that the use of all language elements is consistent across
   transactions and tasks.
3. Assist the user in developing a conceptual representation of the
   structure of the language and symbology.
4. Minimize the workload of the user by selecting symbols and language that
   reflect standard usage.

DESIGN ISSUES

1. Definition of the nomenclature, grammar, and structure to be used in the
   dialogue between the user and the computer.
2. Selection of the set of symbols used for constructing input and output.
3. Definition of the abbreviations or codes that will be understood by the
   computer.
4. Methods for the user to individualize all aspects of language.

EXAMPLES OF GUIDELINES

1. All terms should be used consistently and standardized in meaning from
   one transaction to another.
2. When used as mathematical operators, standard symbols should be used.
3. If a choice of symbols is available, the simplest one possible should
   be selected.

Figure 14.8.   Design of software for language definition. (Adapted from Smith &
               Mosier, 1984b.)

cept of software layering in the design of aviation systems. Each layer of software forms an interface between the entities adjacent to it. For example, the computational layer provides the software interface between the aircraft sensors and the HCI software. The computational software layer is composed of data acquisition and sensor interpretation software. The data acquisition software layer is responsible for determining the actual values associated with aircraft sensors at a particular instant in time and converting these values into a form that can be used by sensor interpretation software. The sensor interpretation software integrates the data provided by the data acquisition software into meaningful information. For example, modules in this layer might examine temperature data from aircraft engine compartments and compare it with some set values. If the temperature is out of tolerance, this layer of software might decide that a fire exists in an engine compartment.

Likewise, the HCI software layer provides the link between the computational software and the pilot. This layer provides the input–output configurations between the pilot and the computer system.

HCI SOFTWARE FUNCTION - Communication Between Users

DEFINITION - User or computer actions to permit several users to exchange information.

DESIGN GOALS

1. Ensure that procedures for transmitting and receiving data are compatible with procedures for data entry and data display.
2. Provide consistent procedures for transmitting and receiving data from one transaction to another.
3. Minimize the memory load on the user by techniques such as automatic insertion of standard header information.
4. Assist the user in developing a conceptual representation of the structure of the message system.
5. Minimize the user's workload by techniques such as automatic queuing of concurrent messages.

DESIGN ISSUES

1. Definition of how users can send and receive messages from other users.
2. Priority schemes based on user informational needs for concurrent messages and other data displays.
3. Sequence and control of message flow.

EXAMPLES OF GUIDELINES

1. The transmitter of each message should be identified.
2. A record of inter-user communications should be maintained by the computer and should be available to the user.
3. When data must be transmitted in a particular format, the computer should generate the necessary format automatically.

Figure 14.9. Design of software for communication between users. (Adapted from Smith & Mosier, 1984b.)

Consequently, the HCI software layer provides the direct human–computer dialogue interface that is used by the pilot, whereas the computational software layer is transparent to the pilot, because input and output from the computer does not occur at this level.

Layered software design allows considerable flexibility in the construction of the overall system. Changes in the software of a given layer can be made without disturbing other layers as long as the method of communication between adjacent layers is not disturbed. This means that, during the life of a system, improvements can be incorporated with a minimum of disturbance of the overall system. Also, errors are easier to locate in this sort of system because individual layers can be tested and examined in a testing environment where the behavior of adjacent layers is well known.

Stages of Computational Software Development

Any working computational software system is the result of an iterative process; that is, the development process involves several

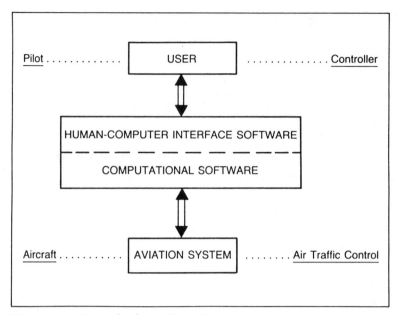

Figure 14.10.   Layered software in aviation systems.

steps with revision at each step, if necessary. The steps typically cited are analysis, design, implementation, and operation (Cassell & Jackson, 1980). A software procedure to control aircraft altitude is used as an example to describe each of these four steps.

Analysis. The analysis step is characterized by a careful definition of the problem to be solved and a complete description of the solution, possibly in a quite abstract, high-level fashion. It is at this step that designers of an aircraft system would have to define what the software system is to do. They would have to know what sensors are available on the aircraft and what controls the output signals are actuating. They would also have to know what data are required by the human-interface software. Based upon this information, the designers develop methods of transforming sensor output into data recognizable by the interface software and of transforming human control input into signals to drive the aircraft control surfaces. For example, part of the procedure for determining whether the pilot or autopilot should be commanded to make a pitch correction might be: "Compute the average altitude over the next 3 seconds. If the average differs by more than 10 feet from the selected altitude, command a

```
count = 0
while count <= 3
    wait for next second
    read altitude
    altitude_sum = altitude_sum + altitude
    count = count + 1
end while
average_altitude = altitude_sum / 3
if (average_altitude - selected_altitude) > 10
    then command_pitch_down
    else
        if (average_altitude - selected_altitude) < -10
            then command_pitch_up
            else command_pitch_constant
```

Figure 14.11. Computer program-like description used
in the design phase of computational
software development of aircraft altitude
control.

pitch-up if the average altitude is low or command a pitch-down if
the average altitude is high."

Design. The design step is concerned with converting the sometimes abstract descriptions of the analysis step into concrete procedures for effecting the solution. For the pitch correction software
component, the design phase might produce the program-like procedure summarized in Figure 14.11.

Implementation. The implementation phase of the development
process actually produces working computer program code from the
design phase. If the implementation of the system were to be in the
Ada[1] programming language, the above procedure would have the
form shown in Figure 14.12.

Operational. In the operational phase of development, this procedure is incorporated into the entire system and installed on operational aircraft. If no errors are ever detected in the procedure and if
no enhancements are added, the procedure remains in its operational
phase.

Maintenance of Computational Software

In a properly designed system, maintenance (incorporation of enhancements, bug prevention and removal) is performed at each step.

[1]Ada is a registered trademark of the U.S. Government, Ada Joint Program Office.

```
procedure CONTROL_ALTITUDE (SELECTED_ALTITUDE: in integer) is
--
-- This procedure accepts one parameter; an integer denoting
-- the altitude that the aircraft should maintain.
--
   COUNT, ALTITUDE, AVERAGE_ALTITUDE: integer;
   ALTITUDE_SUM: integer := 0;
   UP: constant := 1;
   DOWN: constant := -1;
   CONSTANT: constant := 0;
procedure COMMAND_PITCH
           ( PITCH_COMMAND: in out integer) is separate;
-- The procedure to command the pitch change is located elsewhere;
-- most likely in the human computer interface layer.
--
begin
   COUNT := 0;
   loop while COUNT < 3
      delay 1.0;
      get (ALTIMETER, ALTITUDE);
      ALTITUDE_SUM := ALTITUDE_SUM + ALTITUDE;
      COUNT := COUNT + 1;
   end loop;
   AVERAGE_ALTITUDE := ALTITUDE_SUM / COUNT;
   if (AVERAGE_ALTITUDE - SELECTED_ALTITUDE) > 10 then
      COMMAND_PITCH (DOWN);
   else
      if (AVERAGE_ALTITUDE - SELECTED_ALTITUDE) < -10 then
         COMMAND_PITCH (UP);
      else
         COMMAND_PITCH (CONSTANT);
      endif;
   endif;
end CONTROL_ALTITUDE;
```

Figure 14.12.   Listing of Ada programming code for the implementation phase of computational software development for aircraft altitude control.

It is possible that maintenance performed at one step may require cycling back to a previous step. For example, a bug may be detected during implementation that may require further design activities. System maintenance is typically a two-pronged concept. First, maintenance deals with prevention of logic and programming errors and then with detection, location, and removal of the errors that invariably exist in a software system. Second, maintenance is concerned with enhancing the capability or performance of the system.

The first of these, which directly affects the correctness of the software, is of vital importance. To help assure the absence of errors in the system, developers use techniques such as structured programming (Dahl, Dijkstra, & Hoare, 1972), top-down development (Yourdon, 1975), and mathematical program proving (Hoare, 1969). *Structured programming* involves writing a program solely with a small set of programming constructions whose behavior is well known. The purpose of this is to reduce the programming of a large, complex program into programming a series of small, simple programs. The process is analogous to building a bridge with girders and fasteners whose characteristics are standard and well known. The strength of the bridge can be inferred from the strength of the components and the method of construction. *Top-down development* is a hierarchical scheme wherein successive refinements of the statement of a problem solution eventually lead to a program for the solution. *Program proving* involves a rigorous mathematical proof that a program meets its specifications.

While all these techniques are valuable and useful, they all suffer from human error. No matter how rigorously and carefully they are applied to a given problem, the humans who write programs using these techniques may make errors. These errors result in the existence of software bugs in even the most carefully designed software.

The detection, location, and removal of these bugs is a major area of research (Goodenough & Gerhart, 1975; McCabe, 1976). This problem is of great concern to the FAA, which must now certify software as well as hardware systems. In general, bugs are detected by program testing. This means that the program is run many times with sets of data carefully chosen to reveal hidden errors. When such an error is detected, the test is successful.

While well-chosen tests can detect the presence of many errors, these tests typically cannot point out the actual location of the error in the program. To do this, developers often employ a software tool called an *automated debugger*. This tool, itself a program, monitors and controls execution of the program being tested. With this debugger, the developer can detect where in the suspect program an error occurred by observing what statement is being executed when erroneous behavior is first evident.

The actual removal of a software bug can be no small matter. It might well be that the observed bug is a side effect of a procedure that correctly implements some other part of the overall software system. In a case like this, the developer may have to return to the analysis phase of development to excise the bug.

Computational Software Complexities in Flight Systems

Computational software in aviation-related systems offer some unique constraints which must be considered. Specifically, the problems of real-time computation, concurrency, and fault tolerance must be addressed.

Real-Time Software.   Any software that monitors and controls a physical system must be sensitive to the "rate of operation" of the system. Events in aircraft occur at a particular point in time and demand service in a finite amount of time. This means that the software which monitors and controls the aircraft must be ready at all times to detect aircraft behavior and must be able to respond to events quickly. This is often challenging for software system designers for two major reasons. First, the processors used in aircraft are usually small and do not have the computational speed of large computers. Second, the response to events may be quite complex, requiring the execution of millions of instructions. For example, whenever the bank angle of the aircraft changes, the software must detect the presence, magnitude, and direction of change. The software must then redraw the attitude indication, update the heading indication, and compare the bank-angle change with the pilot's control input to determine what, if any, control surface movement is necessary.

Often, these problems are solved by adding dedicated processors to the system. This helps by reducing the load on all of the processors in the system, allowing each more time to spend on its own monitoring or control function. Additionally, techniques exist for achieving real-time performance in computer systems.

Concurrency.   At any point in time, numerous events are happening in a sophisticated aircraft. All of these events may need monitoring or control. This means that a number of procedures must be executed concurrently to keep up with the aircraft.

Concurrent programs have several unique problems. They can interfere with each other. Consequently, precautions must be taken to ensure that they do not. If they share data, one program may be modifying the value of a data point while another is examining that data point. The examining program might, in this case, read an inconsistent value. (This would happen if the examination began after the modification began but before the modification terminated.) Concurrent programs must, therefore, obey certain rules about access to data.

Fault Tolerance.   Fault tolerance refers to program behavior in the presence of errors. Computer systems used for general data processing (bank statements, etc.) usually stop executing when an error is detected. This behavior is rarely harmful and is even desirable because it gives the programmers an opportunity to examine the program and determine why the error occurred. However, halting the system would not be the appropriate response to most errors in aircraft software. The designers must construct the system so that it chooses the least harmful course of action in the event of erroneous behavior.

Stages of Human–Computer Interface Software Design

Gould and Lewis (1983) discussed four critical components that need to be considered in developing and evaluating HCI software. These components include early focus on users, interactive design whereby users meet with designers, empirical measurement to evaluate the learnability and usability of the software interface, and iterative design. Although these four design components seem rather straightforward to human factors specialists, results of six surveys conducted by Gould and Lewis (1983) of 447 system designers showed little recognition of these principles and even less agreement among the designers as to the intention of these four components.

Most software development projects are considered from a traditional life-cycle design approach which includes system analysis, specification, design, development, and maintenance. Software interface design and its requirements for user acceptance require a more flexible, iterative design procedure. For example, Rubinstein and Hersh (1984) describe a top-down design approach to HCI software which includes collecting information, producing a design, building a prototype, evaluating the system, and delivering the system. Their structured approach with 93 design guidelines, however, still includes a revision cycle during design production and prototype building. Alavi (1984) contrasts the traditional life-cycle approach with iterative redesign using rapid prototyping of candidate software interfaces. Her iterative approach includes identifying user requirements followed by prototype development, revision, use, and evaluation. Rapid prototyping tools allow the software interface designer to modify the input–output interface quickly without having to rewrite the entire software package.

In an attempt to formalize the iterative design philosophy of HCI software design, Williges, Williges, and Elkerton (1987) reviewed and organized the various software design methods into a three-stage iterative design process. A generalized flow diagram of their procedure is depicted in Figure 14.13. Stage 1 is the initial design stage in which the software interface is specified. Stage 2 is a formative evaluation stage during which the HCI software evolves through iterative design. The resulting operational software interface receives summa-

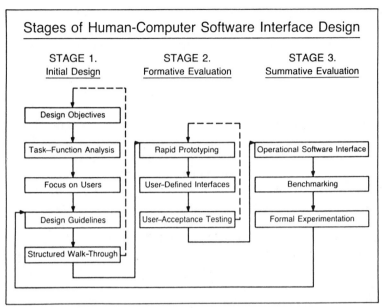

Figure 14.13.   Flow diagram of stages in the design of human–computer interface software. (From Williges, Williges, & Elkerton, 1987.)

tive evaluation in Stage 3, and the results of this evaluation form the basis of additional human factors software design guidelines. The dashed lines shown in the figure represent possible points of design iteration that may occur during the standard design flow, shown with the solid lines.

A brief summary of various design procedures is presented in order to provide an overview of the various steps shown in Figure 14.13 within each stage of iterative design. A complete list of specific techniques and references appropriate for each step is presented by Williges, Williges, and Elkerton (1987).

Design Objectives.   Clear objectives, or design goals, of the aviation system must be stated before HCI software can be designed, and the resulting interface must be designed specifically to these objectives. Stating design objectives also implies the development of design criteria which can be used to evaluate the HCI software in terms of these objectives. These criteria should be in the form of user-oriented metrics and include measures of learnability, usability, and fundamental human factors software design principles.

Task–Function Analysis. In general, the task–function analysis of HCI software requires specification of three major components. First, input–output representations of the aviation system must be provided. Second, a specification of the sequence of dialogue must be stated. And, third, the control structure for interfaces, dialogues, and software computations must be specified.

Focus on Users. Initial design should incorporate aviation user inputs to the greatest extent possible. Inputs from pilots, simulator instructors, controllers, and others can be obtained in a variety of ways, including analysis of user errors, statistics on both user characteristics and usage rates, interviews and questionnaires with the representative user population, critical incidents of user experiences, and verbal and performance protocol analyses. Extensive field studies of flight crew acceptance of automated cockpit equipment were performed by Curry (1985) on the Boeing 767 and by Wiener (1985) on the McDonnell Douglas MD-80 and are currently underway by Wiener on the B-757.

Dialogue Design Guidelines. Merely applying dialogue design guidelines to a particular system design does not guarantee good HCI software, because various factors in a specific aviation system design may interact, and the applicability of each guideline to a specific design situation varies. Use of dialogue design guidelines, however, should provide an improved initial design which requires fewer design iterations.

Structured Walk-Throughs. The final step in the initial design stage is to combine all the information collected during initial design into a form that represents the control structure of the HCI software. Users and designers must then exercise this representation to evaluate its adequacy by taking actual aircraft scenarios and using them to "walk-through" the control structure of the software to insure successful operation. This can be accomplished quite informally as a paper and pencil exercise, or it can be conducted more formally by having pilots, controllers, and designers evaluate the conceptual interface through computer-augmented techniques.

Initial Design Modifications. Often the results of structured walk-throughs require some modification in design objectives and specifications. The feedback loop shown in Figure 14.13 (dotted lines) represents the iteration phase that continues until an adequate initial design is represented in the structured walk-through analysis. Once these modifications are completed, Stage 2 of the HCI software design begins.

Rapid Prototyping. Once the designer begins to construct the HCI software, tools are needed to provide rapid development of a candidate interface configuration which can be easily modified after pilot or controller evaluation. Two considerations are important in developing rapid prototyping tools. First, the tools must result in software that is easy to modify in order to facilitate iterative design. Second, the rapid prototyping tool must be compatible with the level of computer sophistication of the dialogue designer. Essentially, these tools can be considered either as interface design tools or dialogue control tools.

User-Defined Interfaces. A novel approach to design of HCI software is to employ a facade for design purposes. For example, simulation of an electronic mail system was used by Good, Whiteside, Wixon, and Jones (1984) to build a user-defined interface. A hidden operator intercepted the user's commands and created the illusion of a true interactive session. Based on the user's commands, the software interface was iteratively redesigned, and command recognition by the computer improved from 7% to 76% recognition.

User-Acceptance Testing. The final step in formative evaluation involves some form of pilot or controller acceptance testing. Techniques of formative evaluation used in instructional technology are useful in this regard. Dick and Carey (1978) describe three major stages in formative evaluation of instructional systems. These stages include one-to-one evaluation in which the user discusses difficulties with the designer; small-group evaluation, in which users make performance and effective evaluations; and field evaluation, in which behavioral data are collected in aviation site evaluations. This step is essential in aviation, since if the software is not acceptable, pilots and controllers may refuse to use expensive hardware, or they may use it improperly.

Iterative Redesign. The feedback loop shown in Figure 14.13 which goes from user-acceptance testing to rapid prototyping is the main component of formative evaluation. The results of user-acceptance testing define the redesign issues to be addressed in the next design iteration. This redesign is implemented by rapid prototyping and user-defined interface procedures and continues until the desired design objectives are reached. At this point, Stage 2 of the design process is completed.

Operational Software Interface.   Since Stage 3 summative evaluation involves the final design configuration, the production software for the resulting human–computer interface must be completed before this phase of evaluation can begin.

Benchmarking.   Standard tests and tasks should be used in conducting summative evaluation. These benchmark tasks would be quite useful in helping to standardize summative evaluation. The tasks themselves need to represent, in their relative frequencies, the underlying functions performed by users on a variety of core computer-based aviation tasks. With the exception of the benchmark test for text editors (Roberts & Moran, 1983), generally available and accepted benchmark tests for evaluating HCI software do not exist.

Formal Experimentation.   Human–computer interface evaluations require that careful attention be given to the selection of users, the control of the experiment, the research environment, and the procedures used for data collection and analysis. True experimental designs are most often used in laboratory summative evaluations. Due to the complex nature of the software interface environment in aviation systems and the need to specify functional relationships among the interface variables, advanced, efficient experimental design procedures need to be considered. Often, however, only quasi-experimental designs can be used in field-testing environments where random assignment of users to the various evaluation configurations is not possible.

Feed-forward Results.   The results of summative evaluation are important for two reasons. First, these results complete the iterative design process by providing empirical evidence as to the efficacy of the HCI software. Without this evidence, it is difficult to document both the advances made by this interface design and the future improvements which are still needed. Second, the results of summative evaluations can be fed forward, as shown in Figure 14.13, to augment the growing data base of software design guidelines so as to improve and perhaps shorten the iterative development process of future HCI software applications to aviation systems.

Evaluation of Iterative Design of Human–Computer
Interfaces Software

Although the process of iterative software design is gaining acceptance as an appropriate software engineering procedure for interface
design, few evaluations of this process exist. Alavi (1984) described
the application of rapid prototyping and iterative redesign to 12 information system development projects varying in size from 3 person-month to 89 person-month efforts. Interviews of the project
managers and systems analysts noted several positive as well as negative features of this approach to software design. Some of the potential benefits of prototyping include the presentation of real interfaces
for users to evaluate, a common baseline for users and designers to
identify problems, and a practical way to elicit user participation.
Some of the potential shortcomings of these procedures included the
maintenance of user enthusiasm through several design iterations,
the limits of prototyping procedures to represent all features of the
interface, the management and control of the iteration process, and
the ability to prototype large information systems. Nonetheless, an iterative approach to HCI software design seems necessary, given the
complexity of user interfaces which are being designed for computer-
based aviation systems.

Conclusions

As aviation systems become more computer dependent, the emphasis on user-oriented software design must increase in order to improve user acceptance, system efficiency, and safety. Human factors
considerations in the design of computer-based aviation systems
must address both the issues and the process of software interface
design. These interfaces must incorporate fundamental principles
and guidelines of human–computer dialogue design that are tailored
to the specific functions performed by pilots, controllers, and others
who interact with computer-based aviation systems. Software functions that are relevant for the design of aviation systems include data
entry, data display, data management, action control, feedback and
user guidance, error management, data protection, language, and
communication between users.

In parallel with the development of human factors design guidelines and tools to use them, the software design process itself needs
to be considered. The concept of layering software into computation

and HCI components is central to the design of software for aviation systems. The design process for computational software for aviation systems must provide for software maintenance and must address the complexities of real-time operation, concurrency, and fault tolerance. HCI software must take into consideration the capabilities and limitations of the pilots and controllers who will use it, and iterative redesign is key to successful HCI software for computer-based aviation systems.

Acknowledgment

The authors want to thank the reviewers of this chapter for their excellent suggestions for revisions and for the examples they provided of software interface problems in present aviation systems.

References

Alavi, M. (1984). An assessment of the prototyping approach to information systems development. *Communications of the ACM, 27*(6), 556–563.

Badre, A. N. (1984). Designing transitionality into the user-computer interface. In G. Salvendy (Ed.), *Human–computer interaction* (pp. 27–34). Amsterdam, Netherlands: Elsevier Science.

Barnard, P. J., Hammond, N. V., Morton, J., & Long, J. B. (1981). Consistency and compatibility in human–computer dialogue. *International Journal of Man–Machine Studies, 15,* 87–134.

Benbasat, I., & Wand, Y. (1984). A structured approach to designing human–computer dialogues. *International Journal of Man–Machine Studies, 21,* 105–126.

Billingsley, P. A. (1982). Navigation through hierarchial menu structures: Does it help to have a map? In *Proceedings of the Human Factors Society 26th Annual Meeting* (pp. 103–107). Santa Monica, CA: The Human Factors Society.

Cassell, D., & Jackson, M. (1980). *Introduction to computers and information processing* (pp. 342–344). Reston, VA: Reston Publishing.

Curry, R. E. (1985). *The introduction of new cockpit technology: A human factors study.* (NASA Technical Memorandum 86659). Moffett Field, CA: NASA-Ames Research Center.

Dahl, O. J., Dijkstra, E. W., & Hoare, C. A. R. (1972). *Structured programming.* London and New York: Academic Press.

Dick, W., & Carey, L. (1978). *The systematic design of instruction.* Glenview: Scott, Foresman.

Engel, S. E., & Granda, R. E. (1975). *Guidelines for man/display interfaces* (Tech. Report 00.2720). Poughkeepsie, NY: IBM.

Gaines, B. R., & Facey, P. V. (1975). Some experience in interactive system development and application. In *Proceedings of the IEEE, 63,* 155–169.

Good, M. D., Whiteside, J. A., Wixon, D. R., & Jones, S. J. (1984). Building a user-defined interface. *Communications of the ACM, 27*(10), 1032–1043.

Goodenough, J. B., & Gerhart, S. L. (1975). Toward a theory of test data selection. *IEEE Transactions on Software Engineering*, SE-1, 156–173.

Gould, J. D., & Lewis, C. (1983). Designing for usability—key principles and what designers think. *Human factors in computing systems*. New York: Association for Computing Machinery.

Hoare, C. A. R. (1969). An axiomatic basis for computer programming. *Communications of the ACM*, 12(10), 576–583.

McCabe, T. J. (1976). A complexity measure. *IEEE Transactions on Software Engineering*, SE-2, 308–320.

Meister, D. (1985). *Behavioral analysis and measurement methods*. New York: Wiley.

Melton, A. W. (1963). Implications of short-term memory for a general theory of memory. *Journal of Verbal and Verbal Behavior*, 2, 1–21.

Miller, G. A. (1956). The magical number seven, plus or minus two: some limits on our capacity for processing information. *Psychological Review*, 63, 81–97.

Mitchell, C. M., & Miller, R. A. (1983). Design strategies for computer-based information displays in real-time control systems. *Human Factors*, 25, 353–369.

Murdock, B. B. (1965). Effects of a subsidiary task on short-term memory. *British Journal of Psychology*, 56, 413–419.

Nickerson, R. S. (1981). Why interactive computer systems are sometimes not used by people who might benefit from them. *International Journal of Man–Machine Studies*, 15, 469–483.

Norman, D. A. (1981). The trouble with UNIX. *Datamation*, 27(12), 139–150.

Parrish, R. N., Gates, J. L., Munger, S. J., Grimma, P. R., & Smith, L. J. (1982). Development of design guidelines and criteria for user/operator transactions with battlefield automated systems (Tech. Report WF-80-AE-00). Fairfax, VA: Synectics Corporation.

Roberts, T. L., & Moran, T. P. (1983). The evaluation of text editors: methodology and empirical results. *Communications of the ACM*, 26(4), 265–283.

Rubinstein, R., & Hersh, H. M. (1984). *The human factor: Designing computer systems for people*. Burlington, MA: Digital Press.

Schurick, J. M., Williges, B. H., & Maynard, J. F. (1985). User feedback requirements with automatic speech recognition. *Ergonomics*, 28, 1543–1555.

Simon, H. A. (1974). How big is a chunk? *Science*, 1983, 482–488.

Simpson, C. A., McCauley, M. E., Roland, E. F., Ruth, J. C., & Williges, B. H. (1985). System design for speech recognition and generation. *Human Factors*, 27, 115–141.

Smith, S. L., & Mosier, J. N. (1984a). The user interface to computer-based information systems: A survey of current software design practice. In *Proceedings of the IFIP INTERACT '84 Conference on Human-Computer Interaction*, London.

Smith, S. L., & Mosier, J. N. (1984b). Design guidelines for user-system interface software (Tech. Report ESD-TR-84-190). Bedford, MA: The Mitre Corporation.

Smith, S. L., & Mosier, J. N. (1984c). A design evaluation checklist for user-system interface software (Tech. Report ESD-TR-84-358). Bedford, MA: The Mitre Corporation.

Teitlebaum, R. C., & Granda, R. E. (1983). The effects of positional constancy on searching menus for information. In *Proceedings of Human Factors in Computing Systems* (pp. 40–44). New York: Association for Computing Machinery.

Wiener, E. L. (1985). *Human factors of cockpit automation: A field study of flight crew transition* (Contractor Report CR-177333). Moffett Field, CA: NASA-Ames Research Center.

Wiener, E. L., & Curry, R. E. (1980). Flight-deck automation: Promises and problems. *Ergonomics, 23*, 995–1011.

Williges, B. H., & Williges, R. C. (1984). Dialogue design considerations for interactive computer systems. In F. A. Muckler (Ed.), *Human Factors Review 1984*. Santa Monica, CA: The Human Factors Society.

Williges, R. C., & Williges, B. H. (1982). Modeling the human operator in computer-based data entry. *Human Factors, 24*, 285–299.

Williges, R. C., & Williges, B. H. (1983). Human–computer dialog design considerations. *Automatica, 19*, 767–775.

Williges, R. C., Williges, B. H., & Elkerton, J. (1987). Software interface design. In G. Salvendy (Ed.), *Handbook of human factors* (pp. 1416–1449). New York: Wiley.

Yourdon, E. (1975). *Techniques of program structure and design*. Englewood Cliffs, NJ: Prentice-Hall.

Cockpit – Crew Systems Design and Integration

15

George A. Sexton

Introduction

Until recently, aircraft flight station designs have evolved through the incorporation of improved or modernized controls and displays for individual systems. New displays and controls have simply replaced outmoded units. Coupled with a continuing increase in the amount of information displayed, in many instances this ad hoc process has produced a complex and cluttered conglomeration of knobs, switches, annunciators, and electromechanical displays.

To help us understand the problem, let us look back at how cockpits evolved. Early aircraft such as the Wright Flyer and the Glenn L. Martin 1912 Pusher, shown in Figure 15.1, had none. The primary concern of the aviation pioneers was in designing and building a vehicle that could be maneuvered through the air. Space for the pilot

Human Factors in Aviation

Figure 15.1.   Martin Pusher.

and the controls to operate the aircraft were considered as necessary evils, since they added weight and did not conform to good aerodynamic design. Early cockpits, such as the Spad (ca. 1916) shown in Figure 15.2, contained minimum controls and a few large "steam gauges." The flights in those days were of short duration and were made in good weather conditions. The pilot's primary mission or task was still maneuvering the airplane. As the capability to fly longer distances increased, additional instruments such as a compass and an altimeter were added, as shown in the Seversky P-35 (ca. 1938; Figure 15.3). The flying task began to change from that of simply maneuvering the aircraft to include being able to operate in darkness and clouds. To operate in this unfriendly environment, gyro-stabilized artificial horizons and directional indicators were introduced, as shown in the P-51 Mustang (ca. 1940; Figure 15.4).

As aircraft performance increased, their utility and missions changed as well. This required the pilot to perform tasks other than aircraft maneuvering and navigation; weapons delivery, air refueling, aerial delivery of troops and equipment, formation flying, and a vari-

Figure 15.2.   Spad VII.

Figure 15.3.   Seversky P-35.

Figure 15.4.   North American P-51.

ety of other mission-related functions were added. In hostile environments, survival of the aircraft often became a major concern for the crew. The number of controls and displays in the flight station increased proportionately to the increased number of mission functions. Very little integration of controls and displays was accomplished. The requirements simply outgrew the space available, as shown by cockpits of the F-111, C-130, and Concorde (Figures 15.5–15.7). The growth in the number of displays is shown graphically in Figure 15.8. This trend continued until the late 1970s when the use of multifunction displays began.

Design and Workload

In addition to the evolutionary process of simply adding more controls and displays to existing systems, crew systems designs and flight station layouts have frequently ignored the limitations and capabilities of the human operator. This sometimes resulted in high crew workload, missed signals, and misinterpreted information.

Figure 15.5.   General Dynamics F-111.

One classic example is the USAF C-47, or DC-3, which has a rigid four-step procedure to raise or lower the landing gear. To raise the landing gear the pilot must select the proper hydraulic system, unlock the gear control, unlock the gear downlocks, and position the landing-gear hydraulic system control. To lower the gear, a similar (but not exactly reverse) procedure is used. It was often said that when pilots learned to operate the landing-gear control correctly and did so consistently, they were qualified to fly the C-47. That design problem has been corrected over the years so that the landing gear on modern aircraft can be raised or lowered by merely moving one large toggle-type switch.

The C-123 emergency landing-gear retraction system is another example of a system that stressed the flight crew. If the landing gear could not be retracted through the normal system for whatever reason—perhaps small-arms fire had ruptured the hydraulic system on takeoff from an unsecured austere dirt strip—a crew member had to go to the cargo compartment, locate and insert a hand crank, and turn it approximately 300 revolutions. This time-consuming proce-

Figure 15.6.   Lockheed C-130.

dure caused more than a few white knuckles while the pilots were nursing a heavily laden C-123 over the treetops.

Probably the best known example of poor human engineering design was on the early USAF F-111 swing-wing aircraft. Designers employed the logic that the control used to extend the wings forward from the swept position should move from back to front just as the wings do. This might be good engineering logic under most circumstances; however, in this case they needed to consider the operational results of changing the wing sweep and how the pilots would relate to it. Moving any power or flight control forward or upward in an aircraft means "go faster" to the pilot—true for throttles, propeller controls, landing gear, wing flaps, speed brakes, and virtually all other systems. However, on the F-111 the wing is moved forward (thus decreasing the sweep) when the aircraft is preparing to fly at slower speeds. Before the aircraft design was changed to reverse the operation of that control (emphasized by a pointer at the left side of Figure 15.5), several accidents and near accidents resulted from pilots inadvertently pulling the sweep control rearward at slow airspeeds in the

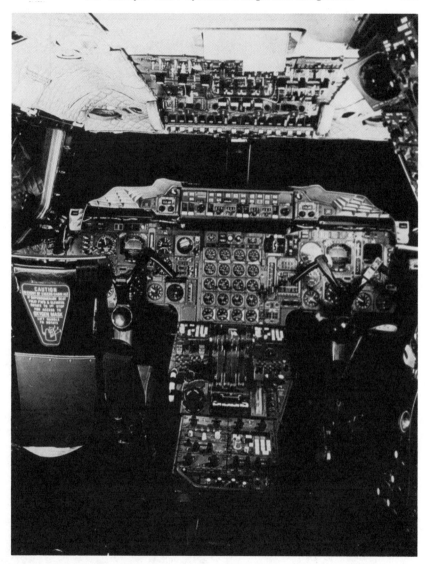

Figure 15.7. British Aerospace/Aerospatiale Concorde.

landing pattern—thus increasing the wing sweep, decreasing lift, and causing the aircraft to stall.

Those are but a few of the examples of crew systems designs which relied upon technology available at the time and had insufficient human factors engineering inputs. Now, however, advances in

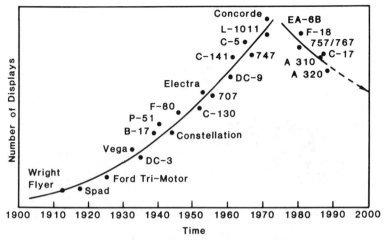

Figure 15.8.   Growth in the number of displays.

Figure 15.9.   NASA 737 airborne simulator.

electronic technology offer new concepts in flight station design. These advances can provide for safer and more efficient systems operation through reduction of clutter and through more orderly, logical control and communication of information to the flight crew. Ideally the flight station can now be designed to use effectively the unique human traits of the crew members rather than force the crew members to overcome the shortcomings of the equipment.

Modern Approaches

NASA-Langley Research Center's Terminal Configured Vehicle (TCV) Program (now Advanced Transport Operating Systems Program) was an early leader in performing applications research on the integration of cockpit information onto CRTs. Ground-based simulators, as well as the Boeing 737 airborne flight simulator shown in Figure 15.9, were used as research vehicles. (Also note the unique "brolly-handle" flight controllers in the TCV flight station.) Likewise,

Figure 15.10.   Boeing 767.

British Aerospace at Weybridge, England, has been doing flight station CRT display application research since the mid-1970s in their flight simulator. Results of the research from these and other efforts were incorporated into current aircraft such as the Boeing 767, shown in Figure 15.10, and the Airbus A310, shown in Figure 15.11.

CRTs are also being implemented in flight stations of modern business-class aircraft. The Gulfstream IV, with deliveries beginning in 1987, has six color CRTs on the main instrument panel—the first business jet to use all-electronic displays. As electromechanical displays once multiplied, CRTs may soon proliferate in the same way. The Beech Starship (Figure 15.12), scheduled for production in 1988, will offer an option containing 12 full-color and 2 monochromatic CRT displays (Olcott, 1986).

Following traditional main instrument panel layout philosophy, the A310, like the Boeing 757/767, has two CRTs (primary flight display [PFD] and navigation display) vertically adjacent on pilots' centerlines. While only minor changes were made in information presented on the PFD over that on the traditional attitude director indicator (ADI), the map format of the navigation display took a colossal leap over the traditional horizontal situation indicator (HSI) in quality and quantity of information presented. Boeing engineers,

Figure 15.11.   Airbus A310.

Figure 15.12.   Beech Starship.

with whom I have talked, feel that installation of electronic displays was in itself revolutionary enough for that generation aircraft without changing location and presentation of the primary flight data.

Philosophical Differences between Airbus and Boeing

As is frequently the case when design pioneers apply new technologies before standards are firmly established, differences in design philosophy arose between the manufacturers of the A310 and the Boeing 757/767 (Donoghue, 1983). The major philosophical difference concerns Airbus' pilot-in-the-loop approach as opposed to Boeing's highly automated systems approach. This shows up quite plainly in the application of the two center CRTs and the systems logic surrounding them.

Airbus A310 Design Philosophy.   Electromechanical engine instruments were left on the A310 center instrument panel to provide a full-time display of engine status. Switches were placed on the over-head console to control virtually all of the aircraft functional systems. The electronic centralized aircraft monitor (ECAM) system on the center instrument panel has the warning display (WD; left) and the system display (SD; right) mounted side by side. The pilots are provided with a constant flow of information on the WD and SD. The general philosophy is to provide the pilots with as much information and control as possible at all times. Some aircraft systems functions have been automated, but by and large, the pilots are provided with decision-aiding information, and they initiate the required action.

The SD automatically displays information (usually a schematic) of whatever system is pertinent for the phase of operation, although the pilot has complete override capability. During normal operations, the WD displays a "memo" list indicating normal messages and alerts. In the event of a malfunction, an alerting message appears on the WD, and the malfunctioning system (usually a schematic) automatically appears on the SD. The corrective action checklist and a statement of the effect of the failure on aircraft operation appears on the WD. A priority system has been established in the event of multiple failures.

Boeing 757/767 Design Philosophy. The 757/767 center CRTs are mounted one above the other. They are called, simply, the upper and lower displays of the engine indication and crew-alerting system (EI-CAS). The major philosophical difference between the Boeing 757/767 and the A310 is in the way the logic used in providing information and control to the pilots is implemented. Boeing has made a concentrated effort to present the pilot with only the information that designers have determined to be necessary for the operational condition. Electromechanical engine and systems status instruments have been removed. Typically, during normal operations only three engine power parameters are displayed on the upper display, and the lower display is blank. The amount of aircraft functional systems controls available to the pilot has also been reduced to only the essentials by automating a large number of functions. When a system reaches a cautionary or out-of-limits condition, an alert is automatically brought into view on the upper display and the malfunctioning system appears on the lower display. Changes in color coding and the sudden increase in the amount of information on the EICAS displays attract the pilots' attention. Typically, at least the first steps of the appropriate corrective action is accomplished automatically. Checklists are not displayed, so pilots use paper binders.

Another philosohpical difference exists between the aural alerting systems. Airbus used the "Attentione" aural alerting system consisting of repeating the same tone once, twice, or three times depending on whether it is announcing an advisory, caution, or warning. Boeing used the aural warning method recommended in a DOT/FAA study conducted jointly by Boeing, Douglas, and Lockheed (U.S. Department of Transportation, 1981) which has three distinctly different sounds.

During the first few years of operation it appears that both design philosophies are working satisfactorily. A310 and Boeing 757/767 pilots are complimentary of their aircraft. The only exception that I have found is that some 757/767 pilots feel that there is too much automation without adequate feedback of information.

Airbus A320 Technologies

When it goes into production, the A320 (Figure 15.13) will present engine power and status data on CRTs and will integrate many features such as airspeed, altitude, and vertical velocity with attitude and flight director information on the primary flight displays (PFDs). The PFDs will be arranged side by side with the navigation displays, deviating from the standard "T" arrangement that has been used for

Figure 15.13. Airbus A320.

many years. Over the years, John Wilson, of British Aerospace, has reported at several Society of Automotive Engineers S-7 committee meetings and in papers (Wilson, 1982) that pilots readily accepted this type of layout and performed well using it in the Weybridge simulator. It is speculated that the Airbus decision on the A320 can be attributed at least partially to that work. The primary advantage in that arrangement over the vertically adjacent design is that larger displays may be used without infringing as much upon over-the-nose vision and pilots' leg clearance beneath the instrument panel.

The A320 is the first commercial transport planned for production that will employ fly-by-wire flight controls without mechanical back-ups. This permits pilots to control pitch and roll through side-stick controllers rather than the typical control wheels and columns. That configuration saves a considerable amount of weight and also greatly increases the pilots' view of the front instrument panel.

New Technologies Revolutionize Design

Rapidly changing technologies, increasing amounts of air traffic, new and improved air traffic control systems, emphasis on flying fuel-efficient profiles, and the desire to optimize crew complements are factors which are influencing the design of flight stations for future aircraft. Of the above items, changing technologies are having by far the largest impact. In the past the accepted procedure was for cockpit designers to determine what functional systems were required, obtain the controls and displays for those systems from equipment suppliers, and install them as conveniently as possible within the flight station. Since each supplier marched to its own drummer, each control and display had its own individual crew systems characteristics. Even units provided by the same supplier varied greatly because they were often designed at different times for different purposes. Once in production, changes to the design became cost prohibitive. This one factor alone provided the rationale for airframe designers to disregard pleas from pilots and human factors engineers to improve the human–machine interface.

It was not until the late 1970s when crew systems design teams (usually consisting of pilots, human factors engineers, mechanical designers, and avionics designers) began making inroads toward integrated crew systems design. More recently, personnel skilled in artificial intelligence have joined the team. It has always been acknowledged that the pilot, by necessity, has been the primary integrator of almost all aircraft functional systems. Insufficient human factors engineering during design has traditionally resulted in aircraft systems integration falling short of efficient crew systems integration.

Emerging Technologies

Digital avionics technology has completely changed this picture. Avionics suppliers now provide the sensors and electronic interfaces for insertion onto an aircraft data bus, an electrical circuit that can receive inputs from multiple sources and route them to multiple destinations. Airframe manufacturers now have the total responsibility, not only for the location of controls and displays, but also for their design and integration. Display formats and the operational logic of the systems must be determined so as to provide the crew members with the proper type and amount of information for the specific task being performed.

In addition, today's crew systems designer has the opportunity to create new functions because of the tremendous capabilities of the on-board computers to analyze, sort, integrate, and route information from a wide variety of sensors and subsystems. Transferring knowledge from the systems designers and the pilots into computers results in the computer containing *expert systems*. This relatively new buzzword has evolved from ongoing work to increase the amount of artificial intelligence and decision-making capability being placed within computer systems. This, of course, merely results in different levels of automation within the aircraft, a subject that is dealt with in Chapter 13 of this book and in other authoritative sources (Chambers & Nagel, 1985). The main point to be made here is that crew systems and their integration into the cockpit are being affected dramatically by new technologies, particularly increased on-board computer capability.

Computers.   Computer technology is racing ahead at an alarming rate. New computers and revisions of current ones are available almost monthly, each with additional capabilities to offer. The physical size of a computer that once filled a large room has been reduced to a small integrated circuit module on a circuit board with far greater computing power. The light weight, high-speed computational capability is ideally suited for use in aircraft and is being exploited in many ways. Individual computers presently being used for systems such as flight controls, navigation, air data, and threat detection can easily be replaced by a single sophisticated computer which integrates those functions and many more. This new technology is undoubtedly the one that will singularly have the most far-reaching effects on crew systems in both the near term and the long term.

Head-Down Displays. In addition to tremendous advancements in computer capabilities, several other technologies are maturing that will have great application to crew systems. Offsetting the benefits of the wonderful head-down multifunction display capabilities provided by today's CRTs are the large penalties of heavy weight, high-power consumption, and large behind-the-panel space requirements. Some airworthy monochromatic flat panel electronic displays using liquid crystal, gas plasma, electroluminescent, and light-emitting diode technologies are now finding their way into crew stations. Several display manufacturers have very dynamic programs underway to develop large, high-resolution, color, flat panel displays. These should become available for aircraft use by the early 1990s, overcoming the above listed disadvantages of CRTs.

Head-Up Displays. Head-up displays (HUD) provide pilots with flight data symbology on a transparent combiner glass while at the same time permitting them to observe the out-the-window view. This has obvious advantages over requiring the pilot to fly head down or to continuously transition from head up to head down during flight. Head-up displays have been used on fighter aircraft for many years, originally for weapons delivery and later for presenting flight data as well. The application of holographic technology has made possible wider fields of view, and in 1985 the FAA certified a transport HUD built by Flight Dynamics Incorporated for operating to Category IIIa landing minima (700-feet runway visual range) in B-727 aircraft ("Holographic HUD," 1985). Other companies, such as Sfena, have been experimenting with projecting head-up symbology onto the windscreen. If perfected, that type of HUD will be much less obtrusive to the pilot than the present combiner glass. It should also permit the pilot to have more head movement without losing sight of the symbology, as is the case with present systems which limit head movement to a few inches in any direction. Considerable research is also being done, primarily for military applications, on helmet-mounted displays. (Doherty, 1986; Elson, 1983, 1985; Stanton, 1985). These permit the symbology to be seen regardless of head movement, but the present systems are too heavy for extended wear by the pilot.

Fly-by-Wire.   Digital, or fly-by-wire, flight control systems without mechanical backup have been used for several years on some fighter aircraft, such as the General Dynamics F-16. The Concorde has routinely operated with fly-by-wire controls for more than 10 years and, to my knowledge, has never had to revert to its backup mechanical system. As pointed out earlier, the Airbus A320 is planned to have an entirely fly-by-wire system except for horizontal stabilizer trim and rudders. Considerable research is ongoing to develop power-by-wire flight control systems as well. When electrical actuators to perform those functions are perfected, "all-electric" aircraft will be feasible. The USAF is currently flight-testing a C-141 transport aircraft with electrically actuated ailerons (Thompson, 1983). A tremendous weight savings can be achieved when hydraulic systems, cables, bell cranks, pulleys, and associated hardware can be removed from the aircraft.

Control Technology.   Aircraft designers are exploring new control technologies to accommodate the increasing number of females who are becoming commercial and military pilots. Reach problems created in designing for a 5th percentile size female can sometimes be alleviated by using voice command and recognition systems. Voice technology has progressed rapidly in the last few years, principally through the efforts of manufacturers of equipment for the physically handicapped and by toy manufacturers. The aviation industry is capitalizing on those advancements by developing systems for both transport aircraft, where reach is a problem, and helicopters and fighter aircraft, where the pilots frequently need to operate a control when both their hands and feet are already busy. Some very limited vocabulary systems are presently being flight-tested with satisfactory results. The primary disadvantage of current systems is that for vocabularies large enough to perform the required system functions, word recognition accuracy has been low. Several factors that contribute to this recognition problem are cockpit noise and voice changes that occur with high-g maneuvers, time of day, gum chewing, or the common cold.

Another emerging control technology, or more accurately, control and display technology, is programmable legend switches. At least two companies, Korry and Micro Switch, are manufacturing switches whose legends are controlled through software. This permits either alphanumeric or graphic representations on a push-button switch to change with the status or the function being controlled. This technology holds great promise in reducing the required number of dedicated switches in the flight station, while at the same time providing the pilots with excellent information feedback.

Data Link. While not a new technology, data-link communications is being applied in new ways to assist pilots. Military aircraft, particularly fighter interceptors, have employed data link for many years. Commercial transports presently use data link in their ARINC Communications Addressing and Reporting System (ACARS) in lieu of voice communications to communicate with their companies. In the near future the FAA will employ data link with the newly developed Mode S transponder systems to communicate ATC clearances, weather, and traffic advisories to and from aircraft (U.S. Department of Transportation, 1985.) These systems open great possibilities for improving safety through resolution of conflicting traffic and through fewer missed or misunderstood communications, as well as reducing pilot workload during critical phases of flight.

Lighting. One additional new technology that bears mention is electroluminescent lighting systems which can be used to improve cockpit lighting. The lack of uniform, controllable instrument panel lighting has long been at least an annoyance to aviators, almost without exception. Cockpit lighting changes have been made from fluorescent to incandescent, from flood to post to internal, and from red to white, but no design has been entirely satisfactory. Electroluminescent technology appears to offer cockpit panel lighting that is bright enough to use, uniform across panels, and easily controlled. Additionally, the early problem of short half-life encountered with that technology seems to have largely been corrected.

In summary, these and other new technologies are becoming available for use in crew systems at a rapid rate. It is tempting for designers to include a new technology into a design just because it is new and it seems like a "neat" idea. That temptation must be strictly controlled, however, through good design practices. Mission requirements must drive the design and the determination of which technologies to apply.

Crew Systems Design Methodology

Although additional controls and displays were added to cockpits over the years to accommodate new functions and provide increased mission capability, the technology of the 1970s (e.g., Concorde) did not vary dramatically from that of the 1930s (e.g., P-35). However, changes to cockpit controls and displays began a relatively rapid increase in the mid-to-late 1970s with the application of new technologies (Figure 15.14). In the last few years, as new technologies permitted revolutionary changes in crew systems, those responsible for design needed to change their methodology from that used during the many years of evolutionary changes. Variations of a methodology developed during the early 1960s at the USAF Flight Dynamics Laboratory under the leadership of John H. Kearns III (Kearns & Ritchie, 1961; Kearns, Ritchie, & Barbato, 1981) has been used in the ensuing years by several major aircraft manufacturers. The procedure described below is that used at the Lockheed–Georgia Company (Sexton, 1983) to design flight stations and crew systems for new aircraft, retrofits to existing aircraft, and the baseline design for a 1995 transport aircraft flight station (Figure 15.15) installed in research flight simulators at NASA's Ames and Langley Research Centers and Lockheed's plant in Marietta, Georgia.

The design methodology has a classic three-phase approach consisting of mission analysis, design, and test. The phases are very interactive, and in actual practice the functional tasks that make up the three phases, thus defining the methodology, often overlap. The methodology is shown schematically in Figure 15.16, and is discussed in some detail in the following paragraphs.

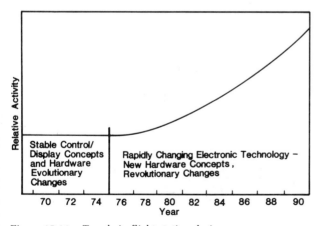

Figure 15.14.   Trends in flight station design.

Figure 15.15.   NASA and Lockheed–Georgia advanced concepts flight station simulator.

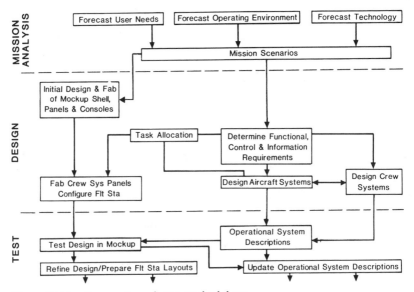

Figure 15.16.   Crew systems design methodology.

Crew Systems Design Team

Since the methodology being discussed is primarily applicable to flight station and crew systems design, it is appropriate to define crew systems and to discuss the makeup of the design team. Crew systems are defined as that portion of any aircraft system with which the crew member interfaces (e.g., controls, displays, voice, and systems operational logic). The landing-gear system, for example, may contain hydraulics, electrics, struts, wheels, tires, and the like, but the control to retract and extend the landing gear and the landing-gear position indicators are crew systems.

The crew systems design team must include, as a full-time member, a pilot who is intimately familiar with the mission for which the aircraft is to be flown. Working with the design team must be this individual's primary job, not an additional duty to a primary flying job. The team must also contain human factors engineers, mechanical design engineers, and avionics and systems engineers. It is essential that this entire team remain with the project from mission analysis through design and test to provide the necessary continuity and to ensure that the eventual design meets all mission requirements.

Mission Analysis

The mission analysis phase consists of obtaining, forecasting, and determining information on the proposed aircraft with respect to user needs, operating environment and procedures, and applicable new technologies. User needs are forecast for the time frame in which the aircraft is to be operational by conversing with prospective customers and operators and by performing marketing surveys. Forecasting the operating environment for aircraft includes such things as the type of air traffic control systems, airfield facilities, command and control or company communications, military threats, and adverse weather. It is necessary to determine which of the present systems must be continued, which can be deleted because they are no longer mission essential, and what new capabilities must be added.

Forecasts. Engineers from each of the design disciplines forecast the future technology level for their specific area of concern: aerodynamics, avionics systems, crew systems, flight controls, aircraft functional systems, human factors, propulsion, and structures. The information provided from forecasts in the three areas described above—user needs, operating environment and technology—is used in the preparation of very detailed mission scenarios.

Mission Scenarios. These scenarios, which reflect the proposed type of aircraft operating in the forecast environment, are then validated and checked for authenticity by qualified operational personnel. They are then used to develop aircraft functional requirements and to determine aircrew information and control requirements. In fact, these scenarios are the basis for all design activities and the benchmark against which the design is measured. They are, therefore, probably the single most important documents in the entire development process.

Mission scenarios can be documented in several ways (narrative summary, expanded narrative, schematically as ribbon-in-the-sky or time vs. altitude profiles, task vs. timeline, etc.), each being useful in the accomplishment of specific design tasks. The timeline presentation is a particularly good design tool because it plots the events and tasks that make up a mission against time in as great a level of detail as is necessary for analysis purposes. The time axis can be defined as 5- to 30-minute segments during uneventful portions of the flight or as second-by-second segments in the very detailed portions. The purpose of placing events on a timeline is to illustrate where events are competing for the pilot's time and, thus, where workload increases, where priorities must be established, and in some cases, where tasks may get delayed or skipped. Timelines can be established manually or through use of computer programs. Using either method, however, the developer must gain an intimate knowledge of the mission, tactics, operating environment, aircraft performance, and crew systems design. When conflicting requirements are determined during the design process, it is the designer's job to resolve them through a better design of the systems, including possibly automating some functions.

Design

Design team members conceptualize the aircraft design (Figure 15.17) by using the mission scenarios as drivers. Forecasts of user needs, the operating environment, and available technologies applicable to the time frame are all design considerations. This closely coordinated effort first results in a preliminary design for the entire aircraft, then focuses upon the flight station, and ultimately upon the crew systems. Any givens, specified by the customer or by regula-

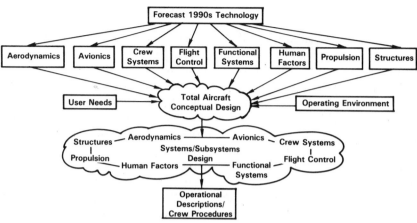

Figure 15.17. Design methodology.

tions, are considered, and trade-offs are made. The amount of automation and systems integration must be determined by trading off
sophistication against simplicity and avionics capabilities against
crew size. Employing good human factors principles during the design process is extremely important. Both hardware and software designers invariably attempt to produce products that are most easily
engineered but not necessarily easily understood or operated by the
crew members and, in some cases, not responsive to mission requirements. The designers are frequently too close to their problem to see
the overall impact of the design. Crew systems personnel, specifically pilots and human factors engineers, must be integral parts of the
design team and be continuously on hand to provide consultation
and guidance.

Mock-up. During the design phase, as aircraft functional systems
evolve and crews systems are defined, a flight station mock-up becomes an essential design tool. A full-scale structure is made of foam
core or other suitable material. A very thin ferrous sheet covered
with paper on either side is glued over the areas where controls and
displays are to be placed. Representations of controls and displays
are mounted on individual pieces of foam core material with small
pieces of magnetic tape stuck on the back. The pieces stay where
placed upon the ferrous sheets, but they can be readily moved as the
design is refined. After the design team has arrived at its very best
design, the configured mock-up is used in the testing phase.

Test

The design is tested by proficient line pilots who are intimately familiar with the mission. They must consider the design in a mission context, as if they are using the systems while flying—the more realistic the testing environment, the more meaningful the findings. The pilots are trained to use the new systems and are provided with checklists, flight plans, charts, weight and balance data, takeoff and landing data, and all of the other information necessary to fly a real aircraft. After being briefed on the mission and the weather, they are asked to pretend to "fly" a series of short flight segments in the mock-up. The design team drives the experiment with a script so that all crews are exposed to the same situations and results can be compared. Feedback from the crews is obtained during flight through observation and comments and from postflight questionnaires and debriefings. The design team filters the findings from all crews, refines the design, and retests as necessary. Ideally, this design is then incorporated into a flight simulator for retesting in a more realistic environment. Typically, however, time constraints dictate that the aircraft and the flight simulator be developed simultaneously. This emphasizes the importance of a thorough mock-up testing phase.

Important Considerations.   It seems appropriate to reemphasize a few of the important ingredients of the testing phase. First, the test subjects must be provided with the very best design that the team can achieve before the testing phase begins. This will greatly reduce the number of changes later. Second, all the materials to make the "flight" as realistic as possible must be developed and utilized, because the pilots must be able to visualize that they are testing the system in a mission environment. Third, the test subjects must be personnel that will be using the systems in their daily operation of the aircraft. Company test pilots are overqualified and tend to oversimplify complex problems; naive subjects are like a "hog looking at a wristwatch"—they cannot evaluate how each system fits into the overall scheme of things. Last, the pilot member of the crew systems design team, as a very minimum, must stay "in the loop" throughout the process. The pilot can best relate to other pilots, can evaluate their comments, and can provide the filter for design refinement.

Crew Systems Integration

Systems integration is the product arrived at through design in which all aircraft and mission functions interact as if they are all part of the same system. Much of this interaction is transparent to the pilot. Systems integration, particularly crew systems integration, has taken a new dimension with the capabilities of avionics systems increasing almost exponentially in recent years. Powerful on-board computers, high-speed data buses, sophisticated sensors, multifunction controls and displays, and voice input–output systems are some of the technologies that are permitting changes from traditional crew systems integration. It is now completely feasible with these new technologies to provide pilots with exactly the proper amount of information and control at precisely the right time to make decisions, take proper actions, and to safely and efficiently accomplish each segment of the mission.

The philosophy used on the advanced-concepts flight station, shown earlier in Figure 15.15, was to link the information and control to the phase of flight. The phase of flight (takeoff, cruise, approach, etc.) is selected manually by the pilot or, in some cases, automatically by the mission computer. That selection establishes a hierarchy of other selections, some again requiring pilot input, while others are accomplished automatically. For instance, when the climb mode is selected, the pilot must select the vertical, horizontal, and autothrottle modes from a set of options displayed automatically by the computer. The pilot can then activate the autopilot, flight director, and autothrottles as desired, simply by turning them on. A defaulted performance management mode for climb (e.g., best economy, best angle, maximum rate, etc.) is automatically selected by the computer. Of course, this mode can be changed manually by the pilot. The flight information displayed to the pilot is also tailored to the phase of flight, thereby eliminating unnecessary symbology and clutter (e.g., there is no need for approach and landing symbology during climb). The advisory, caution, and warning system (ACAWS) is also tied to the phase of flight. For instance, the pilot will not receive an advisory when in the climb mode if the landing gear is in the retracted position at less than 500 feet above the terrain with power reduced. Under the same conditions in the approach mode, a time-critical warning message will occur to warn the pilot that the aircraft is approaching the ground with the landing gear retracted.

The point of the above example is that, with modern technology, aircraft systems can be integrated to almost whatever degree the designer chooses. In this case the flight control system, autopilot, flight director, autothrottles, pilot's display, performance management system, landing-gear position, and ACAWS are all integrated into the flight management computer—the sequence being activated by selecting the climb phase of flight. Similar logic is applied to each of the other phases of flight.

Arriving at a particular integration scheme is a major challenge to aircraft designers. The integration of most of the aircraft systems, along with the requirements for the particular task being performed, has historically been accomplished in the pilot's head. As computers become smaller, less expensive, and more powerful, integrating many of these functions into the computer becomes feasible. This process of judiciously applying artificial intelligence to automate systems has become one of today's major challenges.

Automation Trade-offs

Because pilots adapt so readily to the crew systems and the flying tasks to be performed, evaluation of the various systems is quite difficult. During the design process, trade-offs must be made based upon the role that the pilot is to play during the accomplishment of the mission. The pilot has always been taught to think ahead of the airplane. This point is ingrained in every pilot because it is highly emphasized during every phase of pilot training from initial checkout in a light aircraft through transition into a B-767 or F-15. Crew systems designers must consider this when they struggle with one very important trade-off which impacts that capability. That trade-off can be stated in at least three different ways: (1) automation versus manual operation, (2) how much should the pilot be permitted or required to be in the loop, and (3) how intelligent should artificial intelligence systems be?

In designing present and future aircraft, this issue is at the very heart of crew systems integration. Great care must be exercised to strike the proper balance. New computer technologies can, in the opinion of many pilots, easily provide overautomation. If the pilot is not provided with enough information with which to make decisions, or decisions are automatically made without providing the rationale to the pilot, the ability to "stay ahead of the aircraft" is lost. Complacency and inability to take timely and proper action result, particularly in the case of civil aircraft. On military aircraft the balance changes. On some missions, such as weapons delivery in a high-threat enemy environment, a very high degree of automation may be the only way to survive.

Measuring Integration Requirements

There is presently no scientific method to repeatedly arrive at the same solution when addressing flight station and crew systems design and integration issues. This will continue to be a problem until a method of capturing and computerizing what is in the pilot's brain is perfected. Meanwhile, the methodology described in this chapter works very well. It is structured and mission oriented, and the subjective results of the tests and evaluations can be objectively analyzed. The design philosophy and quality of the final product reflect to a great extent the makeup and qualifications of the crew systems design team. Company policy is also reflected in the product. For instance, if considerable money and effort have been expended in perfecting an automatic landing system, it is very difficult for the crew systems designer to drastically alter, substitute, or eliminate those capabilities that have already been designed.

There are no easy answers to these design questions. The solutions must, however, be traced back to the mission scenarios which were developed during the mission analysis phase. Regardless of the methodology used, to be successful the system must be designed to accomplish the specific mission. Technology is merely an aid in achieving that goal.

Workload

Chapter 6 in this book deals with workload and its measurement; however, it is in order here to say a few words about the importance of identifying areas of "perceived high workload" and designing systems to relieve those problems. Personal experience and conversations with numerous military, airline, and general aviation pilots form the basis for these remarks.

Physical Workload

The aircraft is a complex machine to operate, requiring both physical and cognitive workload on the part of the pilot. Historically, as flight control systems, autopilots, autothrottles, and adverse weather detection systems on aircraft improved, the pilot's physical workload decreased. Physical workload can be approximated fairly accurately with some of today's physiological measuring methods. However, physical workload is not much of a problem for transport pilots. Even though many of today's transport aircraft have much higher performance and many are larger in size than those of 20 to 30 years ago, the physical workload to fly them has seemingly decreased.

Cognitive Workload

On the other hand, increased operating speed, greater amounts of competing air traffic, and pressure for on-time schedules and economic operating procedures have increased the cognitive workload. A considerable amount of automation has been incorporated in an attempt to assist pilots in dealing with these problems. Poorly designed automation has, in some cases, worsened the problem rather than helped it. If an automated system does not provide adequate feedback to keep the pilot informed of an action taken, reason for the action, and present status, these become additional concerns for the pilot. Decision aiding, followed by pilot action, is often a better solution. Although a considerable number of techniques are under development to objectively measure cognitive workload, none seems to have achieved its goal. The pilot's subjective opinion still appears to be the best measure available for total workload.

Aircraft Certification

Workload was one of two pivotal issues in the FAA's determination of whether to certify DC-9-80 (MD-80), B-757, and B-767 aircraft for operation by two-pilot crews in the early 1980s—safety being the other. The DOT/FAA sponsored several workshops with industry in an attempt to establish guidelines for measuring workload during the certification process. Although proceedings from those workshops were published (DOT/FAA Human Factors Workshop, 1980), to the author's knowledge, definitive guidelines were not. During that period, McDonnell–Douglas designers increased the amount of automation in the MD-80 over previous DC-9 series aircraft, principally in the autopilot/flight director and autothrottle systems. Boeing designers increased automatic flight control functions over those of the B-727, B-737, and B-747 aircraft. In addition, a considerable number of functions within the electrical and environmental systems were automated, and many control display functions were integrated into CRT and keyboard control and display units (CDUs). Six-color CRTs in the Boeing 757/767 replaced many individual electromechanical instruments. Considerable integration of displayed functions was accomplished in the area of aircraft systems status and health. While the 757/767 cockpits are much less cluttered with individual instruments than previous aircraft, there does not appear to be solid evidence that this has caused pilot workload to be reduced. With the airline pilot's trip-bidding system, it is not uncommon for pilots to fly different types of aircraft on successive months. Pilots have expressed little difficulty in transitioning back and forth between two-pilot cockpits in 737s and 757s/767s or between earlier DC-9s and MD-80s.

Effect on Personnel Policies

In 1983 KLM Royal Dutch Airlines management and flight crew personnel toured FAA, NASA, and airframe manufacturing facilities to obtain survey information upon which to make future crew complement hiring and training decisions. KLM has historically trained and maintained their flight engineers separately from their pilots. They later indicated that the survey showed that there is reasonable confidence within the industry that within 10 years airliners can be operated safely and within reasonable workload limitations by a single pilot. There is doubt, however, that the flying public will routinely accept this on large long-range airliners because of the possibility of unexpected pilot incapacitation. As a result of the survey, KLM has, however, changed their crew member training to be similar to that of U.S. airlines. Thus, their newly hired flight engineers will also be trained as pilots so that they can upgrade to a pilot position as seniority permits.

Conclusions

Aircraft cockpits have not always received proper emphasis in the aircraft design process. This may be attributed in part to the buyer's (customer's) perception of what is important, without enough input from the day-to-day operators (line pilots). Owners have been more concerned with profit or payload motives, such as number of passenger seats, cargo capacity, amount of firepower, speed, economics, and the like, than with cockpit requirements. Therefore, the requirements for the other systems were developed well ahead of the cockpit systems, resulting in crew systems and crew accommodations that were frequently less than optimum. In spite of typically inefficient crew systems designs, crew members have accrued an enviable record of job performance and flying safety. They have achieved this through proper training and a demonstration of outstanding proficiency, ingenuity, and selfdiscipline.

A change in crew systems design philosophies, technologies, and cockpit layouts has begun in recent years. Several factors have been influential in causing that change. Probably the most important was the rapid rate at which advanced technologies applicable to crew systems were becoming available. The engineering community saw the advantages of incorporating new technologies—particularly in the area of avionics—for purposes of saving weight and space, while at the same time increasing reliability and supportability. Crew systems designers were, therefore, able to begin modernizing flight stations and were even encouraged by other design disciplines to incorporate new technology crew systems such as CRTs; integrated control–displays for communications, navigation, and transponders; and digital color weather radars. At the same time, operators of larger civil and military aircraft perceived large cost savings in salaries, personnel benefits, on-board equipment, and operating weight for each crew member that could be eliminated from the cockpit crew. During this same period, the operating environment was changing to accommodate more aircraft movements; that is, new air traffic control systems and military mission systems were being added—all of which had to be accommodated in the cockpit.

In order to deal with these problems, crew systems design teams have been organized at almost all of the major airframe manufacturers. These teams develop and use methodologies in the design process that ensure that mission requirements, crew needs, and crew workload are properly considered throughout the design process. Additionally, they determine if, when, and how it is advantageous (for the crew members) to incorporate new technologies, rather than including them just because they are available. As a result, the traditional evolutionary flight station designs are changing. Revolutionary new changes are being made resulting in modern, efficient, and safe crew systems. The Boeing 757/767, A310, and F-18 are current examples. They are being joined by the A320, Gulfstream IV, and Beech Starship in advancing designs even further.

Meanwhile, advances in avionics technology, particularly in computing capacity and data buses, permit integration of aircraft systems and functions in ways that were heretofore impossible or impractical. Future aircraft will be truly integrated systems. Independent "black-box" avionics architecture will be replaced with a system that integrates flight controls, avionics, air data, propulsion, performance management, navigation, communication, malfunction reaction, and other major aircraft system components into common, but redundant, digital avionics modules to perform all necessary aircraft-related functions. Computer power and data buses have also opened up new possibilities in automation so vast that they are not yet fully defined.

Applying artificial intelligence through expert systems will undoubtedly have far-reaching effects on crew systems of the future. It is of utmost importance that crew systems and human factors design engineers play a strong role in the development of new systems. If left to their own devices, avionics and software engineers will mechanize systems in the most economical or convenient way for themselves, and in ways that may be completely logical to engineers. The results, however, may be illogical to the pilots who must later operate the systems, or worse yet, they may be unsafe or not meet mission requirements. Now that the work of crew systems designers is recognized as vital to the overall aircraft design, the aviation industry can look forward to production of aircraft with efficient and effective flight stations and crew systems achieved through the proper application of new technologies.

Acknowledgments

The information found in this chapter is the result of exchanging ideas over the years with many colleagues. I thank these men and women in the aviation industry who, regardless of affiliation, are truly dedicated to advancing flying safety and enhancing crew systems designs. Additionally, I thank the following contributors of photographs: Michael Companion, Lockheed–Georgia Company; Delmar Fadden, Boeing; Andre Forte, Airbus Industries; John Gedraitis, Beech Aircraft; Sam Herron, General Dynamics; George Steinmetz, NASA-Langley; and John Wilson, British Aerospace.

References

Chambers, A. B., & Nagel, D. C. (1985). Pilots of the future: Human or computer? *Communications of the ACM, 28* (11), 1187–1199.
Doherty, R. (1986). NASA launches 3-D helmet. *Electronic Engineering Times, 364,* 1.
Donoghue, J. A. (1983). CRT cockpits: Two answers to the same question. *Air Transport World,* (4/83) 40–45.
DOT/FAA Human Factors Workshop on Aviation. (1980). *Transcript of Proceedings, Volumes 1 and 2.* November 24-25, 1980. Cambridge, MA: U.S. Department of Transportation.
Elson, B. M. (1983). Advanced displays emphasize trends. *Aviation Week & Space Technology,* July 11, 1983, 66–71.
Elson, B. M. (March 18, 1985). Planners optimize pilot/cockpit interface in high-performance aircraft. *Aviation Week & Space Technology,* pp. 257–267.
Graham, D. A. (1983, October). *Video displays on the flight deck* (AIAA-83-2438). Paper presented at the AIAA/AHS Aircraft Design Systems and Operations Meeting, Fort Worth, TX.

Graham, D. K. (1984). Electronic display of powerplant parameters. In *Proceedings of the Third Aerospace Behavioral Engineering Technology Conference, 1984 SAE Aerospace Congress and Exposition* (pp. 61–67). Warrendale, PA: Society of Automotive Engineers.

Holographic HUD for Boeing 727 receives category 3A certification. (May 20, 1985). *Aviation Week & Space Technology*, p. 45.

Kearns, J. H., III, & Ritchie, M. L. (1961). Cockpit controls and displays systems engineering (Technical Report ASD 61-545). Wright–Patterson Air Force Base, OH: Flight Dynamics Laboratory.

Kearns, J. H., III, Ritchie, M. L., & Barbato, J. G. (1981). System approach for crew station design and evaluation (Technical Report AFWAL 81-3175). Wright–Patterson Air Force Base, OH: Wright Aeronautical Laboratories.

Olcott, J. W. (1986). Starship avionics. *Business and Commercial Aviation*, 58(6), pp. 59–62.

Stanton, R. E. (January, 1985). U.S. Army Aviation Board adds new dimension. *U.S. Army Aviation Digest*, pp. 13–16.

Sexton, G. A. (1983). Crew systems and flight station concepts for a 1985 transport aircraft (NASA Contractor Report 166068). NASA-Langley Research Center, VA: NASA.

Thompson, K. C. (1983, October). A C-141 roll axis electromechanical primary flight control actuation system (AIAA-83-2488). Paper presented at AIAA Aircraft Design, Systems and Technology Meeting, Fort Worth, TX.

U.S. Department of Transportation. (1981). Aircraft alerting systems standardization study. (DOT/FAA/RD-81/38, I and II). Washington, DC: Author.

U.S. Department of Transportation. (1985, April). National airspace system plan. Project 12: Mode S/Data Link. Washington, DC: Author.

Wilson, J. W. (1982). Utilization of the BAe advanced flight deck. In *Proceedings of the Behavioral Objectives in Aviation Automated Systems Symposium, 1982 SAE Aerospace Congress and Exposition* (pp. 69–73). Warrendale, PA: Society of Automotive Engineers.

PART FOUR

VEHICLES AND SYSTEMS

Airline Pilots' Perspective

16

Richard B. Stone
Gary L. Babcock

Cockpit Design

Today's Airliner

The modern jet transport cockpit may be one of the best examples of the application of human factors principles to system design. As you sit in the captain's seat, you are immediately confronted with the person–machine interface as you learn how to adjust the seat. Once the function of the four or five levers is determined, you notice the surface of the levers are tactual coded—obviously to assist in feedback to the pilot during seat operation at night in the darkened cockpit.

Once the correct fore and aft position, vertical position, tilt and leg angle are adjusted, you can run your hands around the various cockpit switches and handles as well as visually scan the instruments, indicators, and displays. It becomes immediately apparent that much thought has gone into the logic of switch, control, and instrument design so that the pilot is presented with adequate information to

Human Factors in Aviation

safely fly from origin to destination. How did we arrive at this design? It is the result of two forces in the design process: the application of new technology, or "hardware" design, and human factors engineering. Those pilots who literally put their lives on the line during the early days of aviation had a hand in forcing the technology to provide what was needed to improve the reliability and safety of the next generation aircraft.

Early Design

To understand how we arrived at the present cockpit design, we must review what motivated those early pioneers in aviation. They saw the airplane as a tool for transporting people over great distances at a profit. Once the first aircraft solved the initial problems of remaining airborne, the 1920s and 1930s produced a group of aviation enthusiasts who were interested in flying faster, higher, and safer. Eventually, this group included the airline passenger who was willing to pay for the new service.

Although the science of human factors emerged during World War II, the concepts were applied by pilots, designers, and engineers from the earliest days of aviation. Every time a new idea or invention came along which potentially had applications to aviation, the pioneers would try it out to see if it would assist pilots in performing their tasks.

When did human factors first influence the aviation industry? It may have occurred in 1921, when the early postal service DH-4 biplanes, known during World War I as the "flying coffins," were sent to the Army to find out why they usually burned when they cracked up. The Army determined the long exhaust pipes were the problem and installed short exhaust pipes as a fix. Jerry Lederer, the pioneer airmail engineer who later became a leading safety expert, said, "It was my first lesson in human factors." The Army test was conducted during daylight. When the planes were flown at night, the flames from the shortened exhaust pipes blinded the pilots. "I had to take them off," said Lederer (Solberg, 1979).

In those early days of aviation there was a direct interaction between the pilot, the builder, and the aircraft engineer. Often the pilot was included from the first day of design concept to the roll-out and initial flight of each aircraft. The complexity of today's design process dictates that the human factors engineer play an integral role, since line pilots cannot interact during each design phase as their predecessors did.

In the 1920s and 1930s, many pilots were killed trying to fly in weather "by the seat of their pants." They would enter the cloud straight and level, become disoriented, and emerge in a stall, dive, or spin. It was not until Jimmy Doolittle began experimenting with a new instrument called the turn and bank indicator that all-weather flying became routine. In 1922, Doolittle first flew the new instrument invented by Elmer Sperry and described the flight as follows:

> I had chosen a moonlight night to facilitate night navigation, but about four hours out, I ran into solid overcast and severe thunderstorms. . . . The air was extremely turbulent and the airplane was violently thrown around about its axes as well as up and down. Although the DH-4 had excellent stability characteristics, I could hold it on a relatively even keel only with great concentration and effort. After the lightning died away, the turbulence seemed to intensify and there was about an hour in the jet black darkness when no ground reference point could be seen and it would have been quite impossible to maintain proper altitude and course without that bank and turn indicator. Although I had been flying for almost five years "by the seat of my pants" and I considered that I'd achieved some skill at it, this particular flight made me a firm believer in proper instrumentation for bad weather flying. (Glines, 1972, p. 57)

In 1928 Jimmy Doolittle began a series of blind flying experiments designed to improve the reliability and safety of flying in the fog and bad weather. Many of the instrument flying techniques in use today were first developed by Doolittle and W. G. Brown of the Aeronautics Department of MIT.

> As the tests progressed, the instrumentation and equipment were continually improved until the end of 1929, during the final stages of the flight tests, there were a total of 11 instruments, besides the normal engine instruments, being used. Considerable thought was given to the location or arrangement of each instrument in order to facilitate reading and reduce pilot fatigue. Fatigue led to errors and piloting errors could not be tolerated in instrument landings. (Glines, 1972, p. 84)

Other pioneers in the field of all-weather flying had great influence in the initial design of cockpit instrumentation layout.

> In the late 1920's and early 30's Captain Ocker and Lt. (later Colonel) Carl J. Crane collaborated in the study of instrument flying techniques and developed, among other things, a unitary arrangement of instruments which would give the pilot a maximum of useful flight information with a minimum of effort and fatigue. They referred to this as a "flight integrator." (Glines, 1972, p. 81)

World War II Changes the Design Process

It was not until World War II that advances were made in cockpit design. The Army Air Corps demanded instrument flying skills by all pilots so they could complete a mission in all types of weather. The Army provided the training and equipment so that pilots could become proficient all-weather aviators.

At about the same time, aircraft manufacturers assembled teams of designers to improve cockpit design in the area of control shapes, instrument color coding, and environmental comfort to reduce fatigue. The engineers and psychologists who specialized in this field of endeavor became known as human factors engineers or engineering psychologists.

In order to reduce the potential for accidents, the human factors specialists designed throttle, prop, and mixture control knobs with distinctive shapes so that the pilot could distinguish controls under reduced or night lighting. Those accidents which resulted from raising the gear instead of the flaps during landing roll-out were reduced by shape coding the gear and flap handles to correspond to the device controlled by the associated handle.

FAA Work Rules for Pilots

In 1934 the National Labor Board (NLB) issued what has come to be known as "Decision 83," which limited pilots at five airlines involved in a dispute (American, Northwest, Trans World, Pan American and United) to a monthly maximum of 85 flight hours (flight hours begin at engine start and taxi and end at shutdown). The pilots in these airlines had gathered together in a coalition which threated a nationwide shutdown if their working conditions and pay were not considered by the government. During the same year the government issued what are now the current FAA regulations dealing with flight duty time. The decision of the NLB was based on expert medical testimony of the Aeromedical Association and was incorporated in the Civil Aeronautics Act of 1938, the Federal Aviation Act of 1958, and the Airline Deregulation Act of 1978. While there appeared to be a difference between "Decision 83" and the final rules issued by the FAA, the NLB decision had the force of federal law, while the FAA rule was only an administrative practice. The administrative practice rules specifically stated the following limitations would apply for all airline pilots:

1. A maximum of 1,000 flying hours per year

2. No more than 8 hours flight time in a 24-hour period
3. No more than 30 flight hours in a 7-day period
4. If 8 flying hours is exceeded within a 24-hour period, there must be an intervening rest period of twice the flight time, not to exceed 16 hours.

Differences in Interpretation

These rules have been challenged many times by air carriers, who felt the rules were too restrictive. For instance the 8 in 24 limitation has been interpreted by the airlines to mean that pilots may complete their scheduled series of flights even though they exceed the 8 hours in a 24-hour period, provided they were originally scheduled for less than the maximum of 8 hours. Exceeding 8 hours in a 24-hour period is not uncommon due to weather, high-density terminal delays, and even en route winds. Additionally, the matter of interpretation of rules is confused by the autonomy and regionalization of FAA offices, which may render sometimes conflicting opinions. The whole subject of flight time and duty time limitations has been the subject of much discourse and controversy between pilots, management, and the FAA. The FAA proposed rule changes in 1975, 1978, 1980, and 1982, but all notices of proposed rule making ended in failure and recall for many reasons. The most recent effort to attempt changes started in 1983 when the FAA brought together a diverse group of pilots, operators, and FAA staff members in what was called "regulation by negotiation." In October 1985 new FAA flight/duty time regulations became effective which effected both Part 121 (large air carriers) and Part 135 (small air carriers) in domestic operations only. The new regulation more closely regulates flight hours and rest periods for pilots.

Viewpoints of Management and Pilots

Many of the complaints that airline pilots have about existing work rules deal with the demanding and fatiguing aspects of time zone crossings (transmeridian shifts) and displacement from usual sleep patterns (circadian disrhythmia). Pilot groups have attempted to collectively bargain special credit and limits for these kinds of flight duty, but the feeling is that these measures have not alleviated the problem. From the viewpoint of airline managers these contractual penalties have added to the cost of pilot labor, without improving the productivity of the pilot work force. It appears that the jet airliners have made the issue of work–rest cycles even more difficult to deal with from a scheduling standpoint. The en route times of airline flights were almost halved when jets were introduced early in the 1960s. More time is spent on the ground by pilots waiting for their next flight than was characteristic with the prop-driven aircraft.

In the airline industry it has been popular for workers to seek some form of benefit (time off or wages) in order to compensate for unusual hours or more demanding work. While some benefit may seemed to have been gained for these workers, there is a lack of satisfaction with the restrictive work rules.

Individual pilots find their own strategies to deal with demanding work–rest schedules. Formerly, the folklore remedy among airline pilots for handling fatigue was lots of cigarettes and coffee. Such notions have now given way to pilots concerned with proper nutrition, physical conditioning, and intake of water to prevent dehydration (at high altitudes the relative humidity in a jet airliner is approximately 2%), as well as getting out of the pilot's seat frequently to stretch.

Airline Scheduling Practices

The arrangement of trips and rest for pilots is very similar among airline operators in domestic operations. The most senior pilot may work only 10–12 days a month, while the most junior may work 20–22 days a month. Of course the seniority system prevails, and each status (captain, first officer, second officer) is a small subsystem in that the junior captain is usually senior to the senior first officer. Trips are arranged, bid for by the month, and awarded by seniority. Most trips are 3–4 days in length. This means that the pilot leaves his domicile on Day 1 and returns on Day 4. The average 4-day trip yields approximately 20 flight hours and about 80 to 90 hours away from domicile. The average work day during these trips is usually 8 to 10 hours long, but it is not unusual to have a flight duty day of 12 to 14 hours. While most pilots fly approximately 80 flight hours per month, this represents some 240–260 hours away from home. Thus many requests for improvements in pilot work rules are centered around making more efficient use of pilots during their work periods.

Most pilots are represented by a union such as the Air Line Pilots Association, Allied Pilots Association, Southwest Pilots Association, and the like. One of the principal issues that organizations representing pilots have been concerned with is pilot scheduling practices. While work rules within each company are slightly different, the unions have all attempted to restrict the number of days or hours on duty. If the company cannot schedule a pilot within the contractual guidelines, it must pay a form of penalty (usually as credited flight hours for pay) to the pilot. This was intended to encourage the companies to schedule pilots more efficiently, but it has caused the companies to complain of having to pay penalties while losing pilot productivity.

The number of duty days of pilots on international routes tends to be longer in duration from start of the trip to termination. Most trips average from 4 to 10 days in length. The complaints of international pilots are slightly different from domestic pilots. Both complain of trying to sleep in noisy hotels, the inability to find suitable restaurants at odd times, and flight duty during times of normal sleep. The international pilots cross many time zones, and eat in countries where it is virtually impossible to find foods that they normally eat or restaurants open when the biological clock says it is time to eat. The FAA rules regarding pilots engaged in international operations are somewhat similar to domestic operations, except that the limit is based on crew size and a quarterly flight time limit rather than a monthly limit. For example, provisions in the international rules allow flights in excess of 12 hours provided that an additional pilot is assigned.

Congressional Hearing on Shiftwork

In 1983, the United States House of Representatives showed its interest and concern in the subject of work rules when it sponsored a hearing entitled "Biological Clocks and Shiftwork Scheduling" (United States House of Representatives, 1983). The committee brought before it a diverse group of workers, employers, researchers, and government officials. New techniques of shift scheduling as well as worker complaints were discussed. The workers that appeared before the committee cited many examples of family problems and chronic illnesses brought about by shiftwork. While the complaints were poignant, they appeared to represent a general loss of quality of life rather than objective data of safety degradation.

An interesting focus was brought to the congressional hearing from work done by C. Czeisler and M. C. Moore-Ede, from the medical school of Harvard University. They had been engaged by the Great Salt Lake Minerals and Chemicals Corporation, and they reported to the congressional committee that a 32% increase in productivity of workers was accomplished by a drifting forward (later) into shift changes. The workers were much happier and had less sickness with this scheduling. Czeisler and Moore-Ede cited research which showed that the incidence of accidents was greater during work periods that were normally sleep periods.

Safety and Health Issues

The whole issue of safety and health seems to attract a certain group of individuals who use subjective estimates to prove their point, although research workers have attempted to quantify the mechanism and effect of lengthy or off-cycle work schedules. Fatigue and its associated hazard, performance decrement, have fascinated researchers for many years, but the elusive character of fatigue has escaped successful scientific description. Probably the most comprehensive medical treatment of fatigue was a special report by the Aerospace Medical Association (Schreuder, 1966). Even as late as 1981, NASA (Lyman & Orlady, 1981) attempted to ascertain the effects of fatigue, drawing their data from a large data base (20,000 at the time of the report) of voluntary reports in the Aviation Safety Reporting System (ASRS). While the reporters concluded that fatigue was present, based on the 2,006 reports selected for the study, a qualitative determination could not be made because of the structure of the brief reports. The discovery of errors, early in the duty periods, appears to be consistent with work by Kowalsky, Masters, Stone, Babcock, and Rypka (1974). It has been suggested that the explanation for this apparent anomaly may be that the pilots are not accustomed to working with each other, even though the system within each airline is highly standardized. It may also be that pilot crew members provide a better working unit after flying together for a time.

In a more recent study, Foushee, Lauber, Baetge, and Acomb (1986) reported on one of a series of research projects at NASA-Ames which was aimed at comprehensively describing the effects of time zone crossings and long duty periods on airline flight crews. Crews were monitored in both a rest and a work setting. After a series of consecutive days of normal flight duties the crews were studied in a simulator. Although the crews were more fatigued, fewer operational errors were noted following a number of days working together than when the pilots had first flown together. The most notable characteristic found in these crews was that communication was improved between pilots. (Other recent NASA research is reported in Chapter 10, this volume).

There are some unexplained debilities common among airline pilots. The least serious is the inability to engage in a sport which requires a high degree of coordination following a duty period of several days. Pilots laugh about the fact that they cannot play their usual game of golf or tennis the first day following a lengthy trip. Researchers may find this to be of more than casual interest.

Comparison to Framingham Heart Study

The more serious debility is the increased risk of cardiovascular disease that pilots face over the span of their careers. Wick, Kulak, Howland, and Billings (1969) cited this trend in their work at Ohio State University. Based on statistics from a loss of license insurance program at the Air Line Pilots Association (ALPA), the incidence of cardiovascular disease increased at a higher rate among professional airmen than among a similar sample of subjects in the Framingham Heart Study (Eighth Bethseda Conference, 1979). The airline pilots start out at a considerable advantage over the Framingham subjects because of their highly selective initial medical screening. In their early years, the airline pilots experienced an incidence of 0.2 per 1,000. The Framingham population experienced an incidence of 3 per 1,000 for the same age group. In the 55–59 age group, the ALPA subjects had an incidence of 16 per 1,000, while the Framingham group had an incidence of 20 per 1,000. The increase in incidence for the Framingham population from age 29 to 59 is sevenfold. The increase in incidence for the ALPA population from age 29 to 59 is eightyfold. The overall lower level for the ALPA population is obviously influenced by the preemployment selection process.

However, over the period studied, the deselection process (pilots falling from the ranks for medical reasons, including cardiovascular disease) continues for the pilots, while the Framingham study population continues with deselection caused only by mortality.

FAA Attempts at Safety by Enforcement

The FAA has attempted to enforce safety practices by disciplining violators. This usually takes the form of penalties such as fines or forced downgrades (return to first officer for a specified period) for crew errors. Errors are common in all flight operations due to the complex interaction between the pilot, the aircraft, and the mission. Penalties may not help counteract the errors and may cause pilots to attempt to hide problems rather than report them so that they may be addressed cooperatively. Finding the cause of the error, especially if common, is a challenging task. Because of its disciplinary role, the FAA has had difficulty in finding pilots who will report mistakes. In 1976, NASA established a system of deidentified reporting of in-flight incidence of errors or system inadequacies. One of the first reports issued from this effort dealt with information transfer problems (Billings & Cheaney, 1981). Calling the communications problems to the attention of aviation interests has resulted in new attempts to clarify clearances, verify understanding of clearances, and avoid ambiguous intracockpit communications. Pilots are aware that they make mistakes routinely and are careful to constantly check each other, but many times both pilots are preoccupied with their own independent duties and cannot observe each other's actions. The occurrence of common errors grows not out of a wish to do things wrong or complacency, but rather out of the nature of the complicated operation of an airliner in the busy air traffic control (ATC) system. No better example exists than the large number of deviations from assigned altitude that happen in the ATC system. Most of these occur because of misunderstanding of the controller's instructions, which are issued over a crowded radio frequency or between the pilots in an environment that may be noisy. In addition, they may be occupied with tasks such as navigation, checklists, company progress reports, or other required in-flight duties. The answer to human factors problems such as these appear to be better solved, or least ameliorated, by studying the cause of errors, rather than trying to eliminate errors by mandate and punishment.

Two-Person Crew Issue

In 1981, President Reagan designated a presidential task force to determine whether jet airliners could be safely flown by two crew members (President's Task Force on Aircraft Crew Complement, 1981). The task force concluded that a two-person cockpit crew was as safe as a three-person crew and that further safety improvements must come from other than enlarging the number of flight crew members. Many issues were brought before this task force by pilot associations with opposing viewpoints. The manufacturers were in support of the two-crew cockpit.

Most airline pilots would agree that the two-person crew is satisfactory, provided mechanical or passenger cabin problems are avoided. Most would also agree that the three-person crew is far from overworked under normal conditions. However, in those instances where equipment malfunctions or a passenger disturbance occurs in the cabin, airline pilots generally prefer a third crew member to handle the additional workload. Airline managements and the FAA are satisfied that a suitable level of safety is maintained by the two-crew system.

A number of pilot groups disagreed with the stand taken by ALPA, and they appeared at the task force hearings. One group in particular flew for a large operator of DC-9s in short-haul operations. Two other groups of pilots who were not members of ALPA took a similar exception based on their experience in two-crew operations.

Environment

The airline pilot interacts not only with the aircraft but also with the world outside the aircraft. The external world, or environment, is composed of airports, navigation aids, other air traffic, and the weather. Today's high degree of safety may be due to the efforts of those before us who saw shortcomings and effected change to improve the pilot's perception of the environment.

Airports

Today's airports consist of multiple-grooved runways, instrument landing systems and other electronic devices, approach lights, visual approach slope indicators (VASI), and other aids to assist the pilot. It was not long ago that the average airport was a sod field with little more than a rotating beacon to aid the pilot trying to locate it. Pioneering airline pilots understood that human limitations had to be accounted for if airlines were to survive. Since pilots' schedules often varied and took them over different routes, it was difficult to remember every detail of each airfield they would fly into.

The Jeppesen Approach Charts

In the early 1930s, Elrey Jeppesen was flying the mail for the Boeing Air Transport Company. He began systematically writing down information about airfield landmarks and obstructions in a loose-leaf notebook. Included were field dimensions, slopes, drainage patterns, and data on beacons, lights, and obstacles. As word got out about Jeppesen's notebook, other pilots wanted to know everything that it contained before starting their trips. "Finally," Jeppesen recalled, "I got tired of talking to new guys, so I said, 'Hell, give me

$10.00 for a copy of it and you'll know as much as I do' " Kelleher, 1984, p. 18). This was the beginning of what turned out to be a successful business which provides en route and approach charts to all airline pilots (see Figure 16.1).

Another airline pilot who came up with an idea to improve airport safety was Ernie Cutrell. He experimented with instrument flying in the 1930s, and in 1943 he established the Landing Aids Experimental Unit at LaGuardia Airport in New York.

> At that time Newark and a number of military airports were equipped with Bartow approach lights, a system of white, high-intensity lights at 200-foot intervals along both edges of the runway, and red ones extending 2,500 feet out into the approach zone. We discovered very quickly making approaches with a C-47 at Newark in near-zero conditions that when you saw the first few lights through the fog you couldn't tell which side of the runway they were on. It was quite evident there ought to be only one row of lights in the approach zone and that they should be of such a distinctly different character that under no condition would they ever be mistaken for runway lights. (Morrison, 1982, p. 24).

After much further research and lobbying, Cutrell and John Gill of the Air Transport Association were successful in obtaining worldwide adoption of the centerline approach light system now in use.

Navigation Aids

In the 1920s, those pilots and airline entrepreneurs who were forward thinking realized that in order for airlines to become reliable and scheduled there needed to be a method of navigating which did not rely on reference to landmarks and beacons. Fortunately, the development of radio coincided with this phase in the growth of aviation. In 1921, two Bureau of Standards physicists, F. H. Engel and Francis W. Dunsmore, developed the aural beacon, or radio-range system. The pilots only had to listen on the headphones for the Morse code "A" or "N" quadrants transmitted from the ground to steer their aircraft toward or away from these navigation fixes. By 1932 the Department of Commerce built a network of 82 radio beacons across the country. This was the beginning of today's airways that now crisscross the world. Old habits are difficult to change. Many of the senior pilots did not adapt to the radio-range system, relying instead on their visual senses. The fatal DC-3 accident in the mountains west of Las Vegas in 1942 was blamed on the "failure of the captain to use the navigational facilities available to him" (Solberg, 1979, p. 178). The captain apparently relied on an erroneously

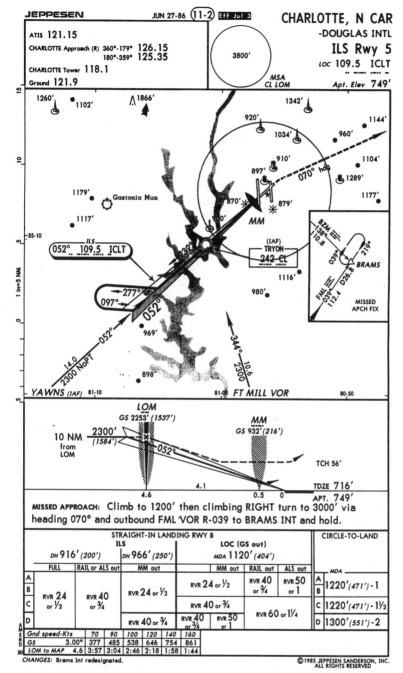

Figure 16.1.   A Jeppesen approach plate used by pilots to conduct instrument
approaches. Reprinted by permission of Jeppesen Sanderson, Inc.

calculated magnetic course and his outside references, which were obscured by darkness.

Air Traffic Control

During the early years of aviation, the see-and-avoid rule served to provide separation of air traffic since there just were not enough aircraft flying to pose a hazard. However, the midair collision over the Grand Canyon on June 30, 1956, led to the first legislative involvement in air traffic control. The Federal Aviation Act of 1958 provided for instrument flight rules and radar control so that air traffic controllers had the tools necessary to provide aircraft separation. Unfortunately, it took another fatal midair collision before human factors principles were finally applied to the new air traffic system. On December 16, 1960, a United DC-8 collided with a TWA Super Constellation over Brooklyn and Staten Island, resulting in 139 deaths. The DC-8 flew past the holding fix and collided with the Constellation. The administrator of the Federal Aviation Agency immediately claimed pilot error. It was only through the diligent accident investigation of J. D. Smith (a United Airlines pilot who later became safety director) that it was found the regulations allowed too high a speed in the terminal area (Hopkins, 1982). Soon afterward the FAA limited all aircraft to a maximum speed of 250 knots below 10,000 feet. The FAA changed several other rules and significantly improved the safety margin for traffic separation in the congested terminal area.

Weather

In the 1920s, pilots flying Western Air Express received last-minute weather briefings due to the efforts of the Swedish meteorologist Carl Rossby (Solberg, 1979). He organized observers at 38 locations around California who reported wind, temperature, cloud cover and upper-air conditions every 90 minutes. When Western Electric installed transmitters and receivers in United and Western Air Lines aircraft, the pilots were able to receive and report current weather information while en route. In the late 1930s, the first pressurized airliner, the Boeing 307 Stratoliner, was built. As aircraft technology improved, the cruise altitude increased, which allowed flight above most of the weather. The most recent major advance in weather-related technology occurred in 1955, when United Airlines installed the first weather radar on board one of its aircraft.

This provided the pilot with data on thunderstorms hundreds of miles ahead of the aircraft. All of these improvements in detection and avoidance afford the pilot the capability to plan and fly a trip which provides the safest route around weather. Without these tools, the airline industry would not have advanced to the safe system we enjoy today.

The advent of the microprocessor and its application within airline aircraft led to the color radar system. Electrical power requirements for the new flat plate antenna were reduced due to enhancement by the microprocessors. A lack of pilot acceptance of the new color sets was noted because of the tendency of the radar set to be cluttered by light rain. Other initial operating problems caused the manufacturers to add a number of modifications in order to satisfy pilots.

General Airline Pilot Profile

Selection

In the 1930s, when many airlines began, many pilots were hired from civilian flying training schools and, in some cases, after training that the airline ran itself in order to provide pilots for their own needs. At the end of World War II the airlines expanded with the available pool of trained pilots from the military services. Since that time the large majority of airline pilots have come from the military services, and many possess college degrees. Most of these former military pilots were unhappy with the management style of the military, which was thought to stifle personal achievement. The type of supervision they found in the airlines was less direct, with standardization being a more important quality. Personal responsibility, together with a sense of being treated as an individual, was more satisfying to these former military pilots. Unfortunately, those pilots who were hired by airlines that did not grow quickly often were disappointed by the fact that they had to wait many years before they could reach the position of captain. The smaller group of pilots who came from civilian training were easily assimilated into the pilot ranks. In most cases their academic training in flying was much less thorough than that of military pilots; however, in many cases their actual flying experience was broader than that of military pilots. Many of these pilots flew for smaller carrier operations and knew the civilian system of flight operations better than did the military pilots. In the airline system, both civilian and military pilots reach a common level of proficiency in just a few years.

Looking for New Pilots

The hiring practices of airlines are clearly contingent on the available supply of pilots. During the 1970s and early 1980s abundant supplies of pilots were available because of forces such as the Arab oil embargo and economic conditions. Many of the larger air carriers had furloughed large numbers of pilots during this period. The selection criteria were strict but yet adequate numbers of pilots were available for the airlines' needs. Expansion following deregulation has, over the course of a few years, drained almost all available pilots. The large airlines that hire in the late 1980s will secure their pilots from the commuter air carriers. Few, if any, military pilots will be hired during this period, as the military service has reduced the numbers of pilots trained and has required a longer period of service following pilot training.

"Staying Legal"

It is clearly the "better" pilot who finds a legal way to conduct the approach and landing when others are holding for an improvement of the weather. "A legal way" does not compromise safety. Rather, it is method of operation conducted in an approved manner. The rules of legality can be very complicated, but a brief example will suffice. The visibility on a runway (as measured by a light-beam–photocell system called a *transmissometer*) may be below takeoff minimums for a departing aircraft. If an adjacent runway does not have the transmissometer equipment, takeoff minimums are limited by the prevailing tower visibility. The sharper pilot will deduce this fact and request the runway which has "legal" takeoff limits.

Workload

During takeoff, approach, and landing (the periods of highest workload), the attention of the flight crew must be devoted to aircraft operation. Pilots like to make light of the complex tasks of flying, but to appreciate their workload, one has only to become familiar with the ever-changing configuration of the aircraft, compliance with the air traffic control system requirements, precise control needs, and occasionally, very critical competing demands of everything from mechanical malfunctions to passenger cabin disturbances. Of particular importance are mechanical problems. The problems themselves are not of as great a concern as the manner in which airline pilots learn to treat them. The first preference is always to remove the aircraft from the most vulnerable phase of the operation: takeoff, initial climb, approach, or landing. With the aircraft securely in a stable and protected configuration, the process of analysis and decision is greatly aided. Unfortunately this has not always been practiced, as the Eastern Airlines L-1011 (NTSB, 1973) and United Airlines DC-8 (NTSB, 1978) accidents demonstrated. These accidents clearly illustrate the complexity of aircraft operation in the terminal area. Obviously, little capacity to deal with untoward events exists in the airline cockpit during the complex operations such as takeoff (e.g., NTSB, 1979), approach, and landing. Designers of aircraft, government certifying authorities, and others in a position to change operating procedures should be aware of these realities.

The Pilot and the Airline

The airline pilot is firmly attached to his or her company, since seniority is not transferable. The pilot's career rises and falls with the fate of the corporation. While many of the larger carriers pay higher salaries, their pilots progress more slowly from second officer (flight engineer) to first officer (copilot) to captain. The smaller airlines, while usually paying less, are sometimes more attractive to prospective pilots because of their faster promotion. Were these attributes constant, the new pilot might be persuaded to join a lower paying but faster growing airline. In the end both types of airlines yield similar career earnings, but the pilot in the faster progressing airline would feel more career satisfaction. Every pilot wants the privileges, respect, and responsibilities that come from becoming the captain. Many of the pilots working for the larger airlines suffer long periods of little upward progress. At present it may take 15 to 20 years before a pilot can expect to be captain in one of the larger airlines.

Effect of Deregulation on Pilots' Value System

During the period of federal regulation of the airlines (prior to the Airline Deregulation Act of 1978), pilot promotions occurred during increases in the growth of the carriers' markets or new routes. To some extent this was directly related to the financial strength of the carrier. With deregulation, the industry turned away from old practices. From the pilot's perspective, it was a time of changing values. Even more critical was the pilot's role in the corporation's success. This has become a concern of the NTSB in its investigation of incidents and accidents. The term *pilot pushing* describes that condition where the airline forces the pilot, by direct or indirect means, to compromise safe practices in order to complete flights. Pilots feel this "pushing" from many sources. One such source is the pilots themselves. From the beginning they have been trained to complete the mission if feasible. They have been taught that the first concern was safety, then passenger comfort and efficiency follow.

Since the price of petroleum products has risen dramatically, up to 1981, the airlines have drawn attention to the conservation of fuel. All airlines stress the need for fuel efficiency in flight operations. For instance it was once standard procedure for all airlines to instruct and require their pilots to lower the landing gear at the outer marker (approximately 5 miles from the runway). At the time this procedure was established it was probably felt this was a safer method than allowing the pilot to delay the lowering of the gear, in case he became distracted and forgot in the final stages of landing. Safety was a first priority over saving fuel. With the increase in fuel prices it is common to see airliners delaying the lowering of the landing gear until a few minutes before landing.

Sometimes pilots feel the pressure of their cockpit associates. This can take the form of a critical first officer and a captain who does not take criticism well. While this is a concern of both pilots and management, it rarely interferes with the operation of the aircraft.

Management can provide direct pressure on the pilot by dictate. A recent example is the case of a large carrier which undertook an engine nacelle modification program on one of the aircraft types in their fleet in order to meet FAA noise specifications by January 1, 1985. The modification program fell behind schedule and approximately half of the aircraft (unmodified) were to be grounded, with the loss of considerable revenue. The airline appealed to the FAA and gained approval of an operational restriction, which required partial flap landings. Partial flap landings reduce the need for high thrust during the landing approach, but landings are made at higher speeds, requiring longer ground rolls and possibly creating more tire and brake problems. The pilots attempted to intervene in this process because they knew the reduced flap setting for landing would cut down the margin of safety. Since this aircraft was used in many small airports in the northern tier of the United States, the chance of encountering a short, slippery runway were greater than for other aircraft of the airlines fleet. The company's answer to the pilots was a bulletin advising the pilots that the reduced flap setting for landing was required unless it would comprise safety, whereupon the full flap capability could be used. The pilots felt compromised and betrayed.

There are many forms of subtle coercion. One such practice was conducted by a base chief pilot. An airline was flying transcontinental runs with an aircraft with marginal fuel reserve for that length of flight. Pilots who were unable to complete the flight without landing short of the destination for more fuel were made the brunt of ridicule with a flashing light together with the pilot's name prominently displayed on the chief pilot's desk for all pilots to see. Happily, the practice was brought to an end before disaster struck. This occurred before the pressures of deregulation. With deregulation came newly established, thinly financed airlines, with a management staff and pilot work force with little experience. When deregulation began there was an available reserve of pilots furloughed from older airlines, with considerable experience. To some extent this seemed to ameliorate the effects of starting an airline with new pilots. Over the years since deregulation, there has been evidence of marginally qualified pilots on both new and smaller carriers, the smaller carriers having lost pilots as the newer or larger airlines began the hiring cycle. The low incidence of accidents in this group of newly formed airlines has been a surprise to many. It is the view of some that airline aircraft accidents happen so infrequently that it may take a number of years before we can really judge whether safety was degraded by these new carriers or whether the transition from a regulated to deregulated system in the United States testifies to the fact that the level of safety is appropriate.

The Air Line Pilots Association conducted a study among its members in 1985 to assess the effect of deregulation on safety. The results indicated that pilots of many airlines were concerned with the apparent erosion of safety standards caused by deregulation, and ALPA called for a presidential commission to study this concern. Many observers of the airline industry have commented on the lack of evidence in accident statistics to support ALPA's contention.

Current Trends in Error Prevention

Many changes are currently taking place in research, government, and institutional activities. A new focus is being placed on the human, in an attempt to alleviate errors. In the field of aviation, pilots are blamed for the majority of the errors which cause accidents and incidents. The NTSB cites pilot causal factors in as many as 80% of the accidents. This proportion has not changed for many years, and it is further noted that mechanical cause factors have been reduced significantly in jet accidents, while human error has increased. The cry for some time has been to make the pilot and other operators as dependable as the mechanical parts of the aircraft. An objective evaluation of the NTSB's statistics will show that real progress has been made in the safety and reliability of the nation's airline travel system; however, there is little doubt that a program of error reduction would further benefit the aviation system. Little effort has been given to mustering the efforts of the human factors and safety professionals into a broad industry effort to combat error. The human has had a part in the improved safety record as pilot, mechanic, flight attendant, ground service person, designer, and manufacturer. Until we understand the reasons for failure of the human operator in otherwise routine operations, we will make little progress in accident avoidance.

FAA's Quality Assurance Program

The FAA's air traffic control (ATC) system instituted a quality assurance program (QAP) in 1984 to deal with one of the most common errors, altitude busts. *Altitude busts* are unauthorized deviations from an assigned altitude by an aircraft. There are many reasons that these deviations occur. Most occur due to a misunderstanding of the altitude assigned by ATC or lack of attention to the progress of the aircraft as it descends or climbs. For many years the FAA had been concerned with the number of altitude deviations that were apparent within its system and that were verified by NASA's Aviation Safety Reporting System. In the QAP system, with the aid of computer monitoring, an automatic program alerts the supervisor if two aircraft pass closer than prescribed limits. The supervisor then is required to report the close call and action is taken by the FAA litigation division, which may include disciplinary action against the controller or pilot. Controllers have reacted by increasing the spacing between aircraft, allowing more room for error but reducing available airspace, while initially some pilots reacted by turning off the altitude encoder in the radar transponder. Controllers and pilots alike have accommodated to the system, but more violations (FAA rule infractions that may result in fines or time off) have been filed by the FAA than in previous years. Both groups of operators (controllers and pilots) felt alienated during the implementation of this system because each felt the object was to catch the wrongdoer rather than study why errors were being made. The QAP came into being with both pilots and controllers working against it. If any situation begged for the assistance of a trained human factors professional, this was surely it. Had the system been placed in operation on the basis that individuals involved in close calls would be notified of the occurrence and a system safety analysis completed, the whole idea of QAP might have been accepted and used to eliminate errors within the current operation.

Pilot Error

How does one address the issue of pilot error? The labels "pilot error," "operator error," and "human error" all describe the same characteristic. We would agree that there have been isolated accidents that are caused by carelessness or other reprehensible conduct. However, the large majority of accidents or incidents occur as a result of errors that are commonplace; many appear to be system induced.

Crew members, with few exceptions, do not intend harm to come to themselves or the people who are depending on them. Most of the serious errors that crew members make are not first-time occurrences. Frequently, pilots who commit errors recognize the errors and reprimand themselves. A system that would capture the circumstances of errors and store the data for analysis might assist in a program of error reduction. This may seem a small issue, but it is not, for many systems have been built to obtain near-mishap data. If error data could be captured through a system which encouraged crews to describe all errors in a timely fashion, with the understanding that the information would not be used in any manner to reflect on their record, a valuable tool for accident prevention would be found.

When an error occurs in the cockpit of airliner, it is usually caught by one of the members of the crew and corrected immediately. Errors are unbelievably common in the flight environment. Pilots of small airplanes are taught from the beginning to handle errors in fuel management, navigation, or mechanical failures. The operation of a jet airliner during critical flight regimes seems to complicate the error prevention task. It is not unusual to see a highly trained, well-experienced jet crew, operating the aircraft in accordance with all directives and in a professional manner, make mistakes. Sometimes they are errors of memory, such as forgetting a time-critical task which has to be accomplished at a later time, while at the same time many other activities are taking place. An example may be instructive. Fuel management is a simple task, in that a switch is activated to open a valve and another switch is deactivated to allow fuel from the tank with the higher quantity to be used. The troublesome thing about this very simple procedure is that pilots have many other things to do, such as radio communications, aircraft navigation, or system management. Distractions, can cause pilots to forget the manual fuel procedure in progress. The process of aircraft control is dynamic, and tasks left to another time are easily forgotten. More critical examples of tasks that must be delayed but not forgotten are adhering to altitude crossing restrictions, climbs to intermediate altitudes, and complex climb and departure instructions.

Current Trends in Training

Comparison between Old and New

What a difference one would find if the present day large air carrier training facility were compared to the facilities of just 20 years ago. In the 1960s a pilot would have attended classes in a conventional classroom with conventional teaching methods of blackboard and books, followed by flight training in the aircraft concerned. Contrast that to today's classes, which are smaller in size or conducted in completely individualized cubicles, utilizing slide, tape, or video lectures on the systems of the aircraft. In a separate room the students follow computer-assisted programs that furnish the first hands-on training that seems suited to pilot instruction. In another room, "part task" trainers allow a higher level of hands-on training by allowing students to operate the actual controls. After students finish the portion of the ground school that deals with the component parts of the aircraft, they move to the simulator. The simulators are six-axis, computer-driven duplicates of the aircraft cockpit itself (Figure 16.2). One usually enters from a level equivalent to the second floor of a building, crossing a catwalk to gain entrance to the cab. The catwalk is retracted and the 40,000-pound cab slowly rises on its six hydraulic legs. All noises and motion mimic the aircraft. The pilot gazes out the cockpit window to a surprisingly realistic portrayal of flight conditions on overlapping CRTs.

Figure 16.2. A simulator in which pilots practice normal and emergency procedures. Photo provided by Singer-Link.

Shared Benefits

The value of simulators to both management and pilots takes many forms. Training in actual aircraft is more costly and less efficient, since the aircraft has to comply with airport or en route restrictions. Many lives have been saved through the use of simulators. It was not uncommon for three or four costly aircraft to be lost each year during training exercises, with the attendant loss of three or four pilots in each accident. Simulators also allow maneuvers which were considered too dangerous in aircraft. These include complete engine failure on takeoff, emergency descents, landings with engines failed, Dutch roll recovery, windshear profiles, and so forth.

Line-Oriented Flight Training

In the past, flight training had gained the reputation of a "dog and pony show" for the FAA, in that a required set of maneuvers was required. The reputation came from the rigid program set out by the FAA for all flight training. It resulted in pilots practicing maneuvers which were required by the FAA but had little practical application. The flight-training syllabus, approved by the FAA and in use by all airlines during the early simulator days, was known to poorly describe the skills required of an airline pilot. Pressure mounted from a number of sides for training more suited to the real world. Line-oriented flight training (LOFT) was developed to meet this need. In a typical LOFT scenario, the crew enters the simulator and completes a one- or two-leg trip, encountering a number of malfunctions and restricted visibility landings. The purpose is to simulate, as closely as possible, an actual line trip that a crew might encounter (Foushee et al., 1986). After the flight is over, the instructor reviews individual and crew performance and application of procedures with the crew. There is no "right" way for the crew to perform during the LOFT. The objective is to see how the crew handles each situation using resource management principles. One large carrier actually videotapes cockpit activities for review during the debriefing. The use of LOFT-type training has changed the texture of airline training.

Cockpit Resource Management

During the late 1970s a number of airline accidents pointed to poor use of available resources by the pilot in command. The accident reports described circumstances where one of the pilots was very busy while the other was not. In many accidents a whole cockpit crew would be involved with problem solving, such as a navigation error or mechanical fault. Commonly noted was the high workload absorbed by the captain, with the other members of the crew engaged in few tasks. The division of duties between pilots, information sharing, and communication of pilot operating intentions are examples of postaccident information that was developed. The picture fit perfectly with the kinds of problems NASA-Ames observed in its simulator research. With the concurrence of the air carriers, NASA-Ames held a workshop (Cooper, White, & Lauber, 1979) addressing the need of "resource management training" for airline crews. From this need grew formalized training courses at some of the larger carriers. More of this kind of focus on the weaknesses resident in the human pilot will help to stem the tide of accidents caused by the so-called human error.

The Future

Progress in commercial aviation has been steady though erratic during certain periods. A quantum leap was taken in the 1960s when civil aviation introduced the jet. Point-to-point times were nearly halved, and cruise altitudes and speeds were increased dramatically. Landing speeds, while only slightly increased, were even more critical in the swept-wing aircraft. Speeds entering the approach and landing phase were significantly higher with a capability of higher descent rates. In the event of an aborted landing, the jet engine would not accelerate like the propeller-driven engine, thus higher engine idles had to be maintained. The landing of a jet aircraft was a more precise and demanding task.

In-Service Experience

Clear air turbulence, engine compressor stalls, Dutch roll, and *high-speed tuck* were just a few of the new terms that suddenly became a part of the airline pilots' vocabulary and training syllabus. Many of these new enemies were discovered at some cost in equipment damage or actual accidents. Unfortunately, operating, or in-service, experience appears to be the only complete method of testing both the human the machine. Government and manufacturers attempt to thoroughly test new equipment, but it remains the operators' burden to successfully place new aircraft in service. Wind shear and micro- and macroburst technology are even more recent problems that have received greater attention due to a number of accidents. Even today we are still learning about the risks of the swept-wing aircraft, 25 years after the introduction of the jet aircraft. The propeller-driven aircraft were less susceptible to unusual wind conditions due to the fact that the propeller forced air over the wing, protecting the craft from stalls. If a single lesson is to be learned in human factors, it should be that one of the costly weaknesses of the human is his or her inability to foresee the future in terms of risk associated with design, operation, and maintenance. Human factors specialists should understand the difficulty of analyzing future systems. Use of pilot subjects to validate system designs is appropriate; however, some manufacturers depend on pilot reaction to their design as a means of system evaluation. Pilots are not trained as systems integration specialists, although they possess both excellent mechanical and manipulative skills. Better results in systems evaluation might be achieved if scientifically designed evaluation trials were conducted with pilot subjects. This is especially true of new aircraft designs, where manufacturers allow option selection by the purchaser. With the advent of the microprocessor, we should see changes in the safety, efficiency, and comfort of the airline operation. Some of the changes are under way, and some are still being considered. Discussions of the most notable of these changes follow.

Traffic Alert and Collision-Avoidance System (TCAS). The visual rules for aircraft in flight require that they avoid each other by giving way to slower traffic, fly at designated altitudes according to the direction of flight, and maintain a constant vigilance for conflicting (crossing) aircraft. The concept of "see and avoid" has failed in a number of instances, resulting in some dramatic accidents. In order to seek a hardware solution to what appeared to be a human weakness, work was begun on an airborne collision-avoidance system. The system design was based on use of the transponder which is installed in many aircraft. TCAS has two levels of warning to the crew. The first occurs about 45 seconds before the predicted "point of closest approach" (PCA), and displays the distance and bearing of the "intruder" aircraft. This is primarily to aid the crew in visually acquiring the other aircraft. If the threat matures to a situation where the PCA is 20–25 seconds away, TCAS issues a "resolution advisory" which recommends an escape maneuver to avoid the other aircraft. With TCAS-II, the model presently being tested on some airlines, only a vertical maneuver can be recommended. With TCAS-III, the advance version under development, vertical or horizontal maneuvers can be recommended.

A basic philosophical argument arose between engineers and pilots during the design of the collision-avoidance system. The engineers wanted to provide for a system that would have the ability to exercise control over the airplane, in that it could perform the escape maneuver without action from the flight crew. The pilots, , on the other hand, preferred a system that allowed them to understand the traffic situation around the aircraft, in order that they could make earlier inputs and avoid the escape maneuver, which might frighten passengers. Pilots are suspicious of systems that rely on automatic features to protect the aircraft. Many of the promises of reliability have fallen short of the claims. To trust one's responsibility to a piece of hardware or software is difficult, especially after experiencing problems with the ground proximity warning system (GPWS), automatic pilot level-off features, and other devices.

Under the provisions of most operating authorities, the captain is charged with the responsibility for the safe conduct of flight. While it appears that the pilot may be subordinated to machine generated decisions, the pilot is charged with the responsibility to monitor all aircraft operations and intervene, if necessary.

Pilots are naturally suspicious of decisions made by persons not involved with the actual aircraft operation or by aircraft systems. The suspicion is based on observations that the dedicated decision may not be an appropriate one.

The decision by an automatic system to disable a generator while in a critical phase of flight may be based on a erroneous signal. On the other hand, the pilot is trained to validate critical system decisions by reviewing more than one source of information or to choose to continue operation of the component until component failure, if the needs dictate.

Manufacturers and companies may provide pilots with strict operational doctrines to enhance safety. Unfortunately, all aspects of the operation can never be forecast or assumed. Flexibility and judgment of the human operator are attributes that have been found to allow continuation of operations in the face of system or unanticipated types of failures. The challenge to the human factors scientist is to enable a system to be capable of utilizing the best characteristics of the human pilot, while understanding and providing an awareness of the worst characteristics of these same pilots.

Microwave Landing System (MLS). The microwave landing system (MLS) is both less costly and less prone to terrain interference, qualities not shared by the current instrument landing system (ILS). Great interest is being shown in this system, and installations in quantities should start appearing in the late 1980s. Initially some interest was shown in MLS as a method of controlling aircraft noise during takeoff and landing by keeping aircraft higher during the approach or through more precise control of departure path on takeoff. The need for the two segment approach has diminished, as quieter or noise-suppressed jet engines have been developed.

Thus far, pilots have not been critical of the technical merits of the MLS because it appears it will add greater flexibility and more precision to the landing procedure. It must be added that most of the complaints of any new system surface after implementation commences. The reason for this may be that operational users cannot evaluate the system until all extremes of conditions, such as weather, procedures, installation, and the like, are present.

Low-Visibility Approaches. The use of the aircraft as a dependable mode of transportation brought with it the need to land under all types of weather with restricted visibility. At the present time, full landing capabilities exist for visibility down to zero. Airport and aircraft system costs have been too high to accomplish this feat of all-weather landing capability. Pilots have accepted this new technology, as it was consistent with other engineering advances. Critical to the design, from the pilot's perspective, was a system redundancy that would maintain the on-line status of the equipment. The airborne systems in use at the present time have a triple redundancy in that if one component fails there are still two backup systems. These are referred to as *fail-active* systems. Manufacturers and operators, for cost-saving reasons, are attempting to put in use *fail-passive* systems, which would not have the multiple redundancy and would require the pilot to intervene in the event of a malfunction. Pilots have stated their dissatisfaction with this, as fail-passive systems would require intervening in the automatic operation of the aircraft at a critical time without having the "feel" of the aircraft or without adequate visual reference to perform a landing. The operation of aircraft in the low-visibility environment may be handled by the trained pilot, but what remains to be determined before this can happen is what forward visibility is needed to perform a safe landing. The landing in low visibility is troublesome to the pilot because he or she may have very little information from the runway or approach lights, as to aircraft height, wings-level attitude, or distance down the runway.

Head-Up Display (HUD).   The head-up display (Figure 16.3) is a method of giving much of this information to the pilots. The HUD presents computer-generated symbology on a transparent plate in the pilots' line of sight. This allows pilots to look out the forward cockpit windows while still obtaining basic flight instrument information as to airspeed, altitude, and touchdown point. The cost for the HUD is significant, but it enjoys wide acceptance among the pilots who have had the opportunity to use it.

Extended Twin Operations (ETOPS).   In the early 1980s, a few airlines requested and received special permission from the FAA to operate large twin-engine airliners in extended overwater operations, principally over the North Atlantic. The aircraft manufacturers supported this concept, which would increase the sales of their recently

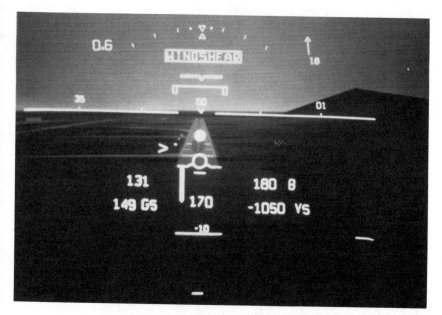

Figure 16.3.   A head-up display (HUD) which provides vital approach information so the pilot need not look down at the instrument panel. Also displayed in this photograph is a wind shear alert. Photo provided by Flight Dynamics, Inc.

introduced large twin transports with greater fuel efficiency and longer range. The controversy that ensued was based on the mechanical reliability of the aircraft's engine and other systems. We will likely see these aircraft in overwater operation but may see additional redundancies in the hydraulic and electrical systems.

Automation. Pilots have experienced upgraded systems throughout their flying careers. Autopilots, autothrottles, flight directors, automatic tuning radios, computer flight plans, automatic level-off autopilot, and inertial navigation systems are just a few of the examples in current use today. Rather than a single change in systems, the Boeing 757/767, introduced in 1982, represented a radical departure in displays and integrated systems. Cathode ray tubes (CRT) display both present position and the planned route (see Chapter 12, this volume). For the first time, pilots were able to see a presentation of the airport on their display rather than having to conceptualize a picture of their position from navigation instruments. Another CRT displays aircraft attitude and reference to speed selected. The control of the autopilot system, termed *autoflight control system* (AFCS), is the most complicated and troublesome system from a pilot's standpoint. The AFSC can automatically control airspeed, altitude, descent and ascent, and track (ground path) following through the autopilot, autothrottles, vertical navigation system (VNAV), and lateral navigation system (LNAV). The problem that pilots have with this new system is that there are apparently too many options or modes of operation. For instance, climbing to a higher altitude can be made in three different ways automatically—through VNAV, vertical speed, or flight-level change. Each of these modes has different characteristics and possible sources of error.

Side-Stick Controller. Airbus Industries will introduce the side-stick controller in its A320. Thus far pilot reaction to the side-stick controller has been lukewarm because of the fear of losing the "feel" of the aircraft. To the experienced pilot, this feel is critical, as much sensory information is gained from changes in the aircraft attitude or airspeed, even before it becomes evident on airspeed or attitude instruments. The design of the side-stick controller permits the other pilot to override control of the aircraft by using higher stick forces. Many pilots are concerned that movement of one of the controls might not be evident to the other pilot. One advantage of the system is that it allows the pilots an unobstructed view of the instrument panel.

Summary

Many issues could be discussed in this chapter, but an attempt has been made to touch on some of the more important issues of concern to airline pilots. From the perspective of the airline pilots who began their careers after the Second World War and ended them in the mid 1980s, many changes have taken place. Instead of manual flying tasks, automatic systems under the control of the pilot assist in routine tasks, such as climbing, descending, setting engine power, and controlling subsystems. Problems other than poorly heated or ventilated aircraft or the lack of navigational aids now face the airline pilot. Terrorism, deregulation, hijacking, bankruptcy, career stagnation, fuel prices, and training and air traffic control changes have significant impact on the perception, satisfaction, and security of the airline pilot's position.

During the early 1970s, many experts were pointing to the lack of accidents caused by mechanical malfunctions. The focus changed to the human operator as the weakest part of the system. Both government, unions, and managements have attempted to deal with the apparent inconsistencies of the human pilot. The cycle may now be reversing itself, as many of the accidents that occurred during the late 1970s and early 1980s have mechanical factors as the principal cause.

The character of the piloting role will never be the same as it was in the manual control days. Airline pilots must learn to be managers of automatic systems, while retaining their individual qualities as overall supervisors of flight path control and finding satisfaction in that role. Airline pilots must also learn to separate their role as pilots from their company's day-to-day operation. It remains to be seen whether matters of corporate mergers and takeovers have a serious effect on the safety of the airline industry.

References

Billings, C. E., & Cheaney, E. S. (1981). *Information transfer problems in the aviation system* (NASA Technical Paper 1875). Moffett Field, CA: NASA.

Cooper, G. E., White, D. W., & Lauber, J. K. (1979). *Resource management on the flight deck. Proceedings of a NASA/Industry workshop* (NASA Conference Publication 2120). Moffett Field, CA:NASA.

Eighth Bethesda Conference. (1979). Cardiovascular problems associated with aviation safety. *American Journal of Cardiology, 30*, 573–628.

Foushee, H. C., Lauber, J. K., Baetge, M. M., & Acomb, D. B. (1986). *Crew Factors in Flight Operations: III. The Operational Significance of Exposure to Short-Haul Air Transport Operations* (NASA Technical Memorandum 88322). Moffett Field, CA:NASA.

Glines, C. V. (1972). *Jimmy Doolittle—daredevil aviator and scientist.* New York: Macmillian.

Hopkins, C. E. (1982). *Flying the line.* Washington, DC: Air Line Pilots Association.

Kelleher, A. (1984). Fifty Years at the top of the charts. *Air Line Pilot, 53,* 18–23.

Kowalsky, N. B., Masters, R. L., Stone, R. B., Babcock, G. L., & Rypka, E. W. (1974). *An analysis of pilot error-related aircraft accidents* (NASA Contractor Report 2444). Washington, DC:NASA.

Lauber, J. K. (1980). *Pilot fatigue and circadian desynchronosis.* Report of a NASA workshop held in San Francisco, CA, on August 26–28 (NASA Technical Memorandum 81275).

Lyman, E. G., & Orlady, H. W. (1981). *Fatigue and associated performance decrements in air transport operations* (NASA CR 166167). National Aeronautics and Space Administration, Moffett Field, CA: Battelle Laboratories.

Morrison, J. (1982). The pilot who lit the way. *Air Line Pilot. 52* (7), 24–26.

National Transportation Safety Board. (1973). *Eastern Airlines, Inc. L-1011, N310EA, Miami, Florida, December 29, 1972* (Report no. NTSB-AAR-73-14). Washington, DC: Author.

National Transportation Safety Board. (1978). *United Airlines Douglas DC-8-54, near Kaysville, Utah, December 18, 1977* (Report no. NTSB-AAR-78-8). Washington, DC: Author.

National Transportation Safety Board. (1979). *American Airlines, Inc. DC10-10-10, N110AA, Chicago-O'Hara International Airport, Chicago, Illinois, May 25, 1979* (Report no. NTSB-AAR-79-17). Washington, DC: Author.

President's Task Force on Aircraft Crew Complement. (1981). *Report of the President's Task Force on Aircraft Crew Complement.* Washington, DC: Author.

Schreuder, O. B. (1966). Medical aspects of aircraft pilot fatigue with special reference to the commercial jet pilot. *Aerospace Medicine, 37,* 1–43.

Solberg, C. (1979). *Conquest of the skies.* Boston: Little, Brown.

United States House of Representatives (March 23, 24, 1983). *Hearings before the Subcommittee on Investigations and Oversight of the Committee on Science and Technology* (No. 7).

Wick, R. L., Kulak, L. L., Howland, D., & Billings, C. E. (1969). *Inflight airline pilot incapacitation* (Report No. RF 2699-1). Columbus, OH: Ohio State University Research Foundation.

General Aviation

17

Malcolm L. Ritchie

Introduction

The three classes of aviation in the United States are military, airlines, and everybody else. "Everybody else" is called general aviation, hereafter shortened to GA. It includes all varieties of powered aircraft, including helicopters, and government and other nonmilitary aircraft. The newly licensed pilot who flies some weekends in the simplest airplane which can be licensed is a part of GA. So is the corporate pilot who flies a sophisticated jet every day and goes all over the world. GA consists of these pilots and their aircraft and all gradations of equipment and of experience and skills in between. This chapter concentrates on the low end of the GA spectrum.

Skill Levels and Skill Maintenance

Most GA pilots are not full-time professional pilots. They make their living at some other job. Flying is a secondary activity whose time and money demands are met through the means of that other

Human Factors in Aviation
Copyright © 1988 by Academic Press, Inc.
All rights of reproduction in any form reserved.

activity. Achieving and maintaining adequate flying skills and adequately functioning equipment are continual problems for a large number of GA pilots.

There is a sense in which GA tasks may be much more difficult than those for airline operations. An airline pilot normally does not command an aircraft with passengers into an airport unless he or she has flown into that airport recently. That procedure holds even though the airline pilot flies established routes routinely, has a copilot and other assistance readily available, and is thoroughly up to date on many of the required procedures. A general aviation pilot may fly alone at night on instruments, with no external support, into a completely unfamiliar airport. As Parker and his colleagues put it:

> Single-pilot instrument flight, particularly without an autopilot, is about as difficult as any kind of flying that exists. The pilot must fly the airplane; handle all communications, including numerous frequency changes; navigate with precision, using the many necessary charts; comply with all ATC procedures; and periodically monitor the performance of fuel and electrical systems. In an aircraft which might cruise at 170 and approach at 120 knots, much can happen while the pilot is dealing with one of his many tasks. (Parker, Duffy, & Christensen, 1981, p. 6.)

Though the GA pilots' job may be more difficult in that sense, they must perform their tasks in the context of a system not designed for them. If operating and air traffic control procedures work for airline pilots, there is little push for further refinement. The GA pilot either acquires the skills and equipment required to perform in the established environment or stays out of it.

That situation can probably be changed to the benefit of all participants in the national airspace system. If the tasks imposed upon the GA pilot are revised to be more consistent with his needs, he can be more effective in performing them. When GA pilots are more competent and more reliable in performing their tasks, the whole system can be more efficient and safer. If the needs of GA pilots are used as criteria for the current redesign of the national airspace system, the happy result of greatly reduced human error may be brought about with no additional cost.

Cost

It is generally recognized that many GA pilots and owners are quite limited in the amount of money they have available for aviation. Federal regulatory agencies and aviation business enterprises recognize this feature of GA. The FAA is properly reluctant to impose requirements which are costly and is careful to restrict its requirements to those which are required by safe operations. Aviation equipment manufacturers and training facilities are keenly aware of the effect of costs on their sales to GA.

A great many of the components which determine the tasks of GA pilots are classed as information systems. For many years the technology of information systems has increased in capability very rapidly and decreased in cost even more rapidly. The kind of redesign which can produce a dramatic increase in the effectiveness of GA pilots may well result in much lower costs.

Human Performance in General Aviation

Most of the scientific contributions of human factors to GA lie in measurements of human performance during tasks generated by aviation equipment or simulated equipment. Many such studies of human performance are applicable to all varieties of pilots. Many are specific to GA, as they were done under conditions specific to GA or using equipment considered to be that of GA.

The production of knowledge through the methods of science is quite a different matter from using that knowledge to actually improve human performance in operation. Both the science and the engineering of human factors are required to achieve progress in reducing errors and in increasing efficiency.

Human Factors in General Aviation Systems Design

Human factors engineering in GA systems has several levels. At the lowest level it involves designing displays to be discriminable and legible and controls to be reachable and easy to identify. At intermediate levels it involves assurance that pilots are provided the information and the control capability needed to perform their assigned tasks. At the highest levels, human factors engineering addresses the design of human tasks. This is done through the functional design of the equipment which determines what the human tasks will be.

The lower-level design tasks in GA are usually a function of the aircraft manufacturer and the manufacturers of cockpit components. The intermediate-level design tasks are generally performed by the aircraft manufacturer, though some are done by the owner of the aircraft through the purchase of optional or additional equipment.

The highest design level of determining what tasks the pilots will perform, and the conditions for that performance, seem to be the province only of the FAA. Some of the most important opportunities for improvement in GA performance require simultaneous changes in navigation and ATC procedures.

When the FAA had a comprehensive program in the 1960s on human factors in GA, it did indeed address some of these high-level systems design issues. One report from "Project Little Guy," as the program was called, stated that the program

> has viewed the general aviation complex as a system which consists of three major components or subsystems. The first of these subsystems is defined in terms of the LITTLE GUY pilot and the training which will be required in order to elicit the human inputs to the over-all system. The second of these subsystems deals with the LITTLE GUY aircraft, including the cockpit instrumentation and stability augmentation program. The third major subsystem is concerned with the development of a flight environment system exclusive of the cockpit instrumentation. (Weiss, 1964, p. 3)

In the report, Weiss goes on to describe a specific cockpit system, special charts, and other information sources for the little guy system. It is clear that the pilot's tasks were being redesigned. The goal of the program as stated was to increase the use of general aviation aircraft as a means of business transportation.

GA Pilot Tasks

Some pilot tasks are inherent in the nature of aviation and the generic nature of aircraft. Other pilot tasks are by-products of the way some cockpit equipment is built. Still others are induced by the procedures of navigation and air traffic control.

One group of pilot tasks deals with the use of the aircraft's primary controls. These provide the ability to turn, to climb or descend, and to vary speed. A pilot's skill in these tasks requires that he or she develop a working knowledge of aerodynamics. These tasks involve the aircraft's fundamental dynamics of motion and thus are not subject to much change, except through improvements in the amount and form of the information which is fed back to the pilot. Some parts of these tasks may be automated some of the time, but the pilot must monitor their performance and thus must continue processing the information required for their control.

Another group of pilot tasks are those required to manage the aircraft and its equipment. These include the operation and inflight diagnosis of the power plant, possibly the use of an autopilot or other control aids, the management of electrical power, the actuation and operation of flight instruments and electronic equipment, and the management of fuel and other supplies in relation to intended and possible destinations. In the event of malfunctions, the pilot may be required to make judgments about whether and how to continue flight or how soon he can get to the ground in some degree of safety. These tasks involve the comprehension of mechanics, hydraulics, electronics, and flight data systems. These tasks are clearly equipment specific. The tasks themselves may change as the equipment is changed.

Another group of pilot tasks are those comprising the ability to navigate. The pilot must cause the aircraft to move along a specified path and arrive at an intended destination. One aspect of navigation requires that the pilot learn to recognize features on the earth from an unaccustomed viewpoint and learn how to judge his or her own relation to those features as that viewpoint moves. Another aspect of navigation requires the pilot to learn about velocity vectors—traveling in a specific direction at a specific velocity for a specific time. Pilotage and dead reckoning derive from the fundamental nature of flying and thus are not subject to much change.

Modern navigation tasks also include those involving the use of electronic aids to navigation. These are invented systems, and the tasks required in their use may change whenever the equipment changes. These equipment changes may result in very large changes in the pilot's tasks.

Another group of pilot tasks involve planning and conducting flight in relation to ATC procedures and requirements. These tasks involve communication, flight plans, clearances, and the rules and procedures of the Federal Aviation Administration. These tasks are not inherent in the nature of flying but are a part of the techniques and procedures used to ensure safe operation by maintaining some distance between aircraft in flight. The tasks are subject to change as the procedures change along with the equipment enabling those procedures.

These pilot tasks are the basic substance of GA human factors. There are two major objectives to human factors studies of these tasks. The first is to improve the abilities of pilots to perform the tasks. That is usually accomplished through training and through changing operating procedures. The other way to improve performance is through changing the tasks to better conform to human abilities. That is usually accomplished through redesigning the equipment which determines the tasks. At the present time the opportunities for improvement through changing the tasks are very much greater than through improving training on existing tasks.

Human Performance Variables in General Aviation

Manipulative Skills

A part of the complexity of GA flying is that actuation of any one of the controls may affect more than one of the three vectors of flight: altitude, heading, and velocity. In some flight conditions the use of one control affects all three.

What pilots learn when they develop skill in these primary flight control tasks is the same set of data which the control engineer describes in a set of complex differential equations. These are the aircraft's equations of motion. Beginning pilots learn the major features of these equations. With more practice and experience they learn more and more of the terms in the equations and get a more refined estimate of the coefficients for these terms. The result is a subjective model of the aircraft's control dynamics stored in his or her long-term memory. Increased flying skill could be described in terms of the degree of refinement of that mental model.

A professional level of skill in these primary flight tasks can probably be achieved in something like 1,000 hours of flying time, if that amount of practice is accomplished within 2 or 3 years. But this is seldom accomplished by the GA pilot. Other skills involved in flying may have quite different learning times and may take much longer to reach professional-level performance.

Among different aircraft there is a considerable degree of commonality in the terms describing equations of motion. This means that learning the dynamics of one aircraft puts a pilot well along the path of learning most others. A pilot calls the flying characteristics of an airplane "honest" when the coefficients of the major terms in its equations are within the range expected from past experience on other aircraft.

Once learned, primary flight skills endure over a long period of time. For these tasks, the pilot is a part of a closed-loop control system. Pilot performance has been studied with some success by use of the tools of control system engineering. Automatic control systems may relieve the pilot of some part of the primary control tasks. Flexible systems allow him to choose how much the control system will do for him and how much he will continue doing for himself.

Manipulative skills also are involved in controlling the aircraft's basic systems and in controlling mission and traffic control equipment. The skills required in these secondary manipulative tasks may change from time to time and from aircraft to aircraft. They are derived from the nature of the specific equipment. These secondary system task elements may differ sharply from aircraft to aircraft and may change rapidly over time.

Information Acquisition

The information which a pilot uses comes mainly through four major means: vision, hearing, kinesthetic sense, and touch. In terms of the amount of useful information provided they should probably be ranked in that order.

It has frequently been said that modern cockpits give a pilot too much information, an imprecise and misleading statement amounting to technical folklore. The amount of information being presented is not a problem in itself. The critical variables lie in the degree and kind of structuring of the information in the display. An inadequate structure of the information may produce clutter, which makes it difficult to derive the information the pilot needs. Inadequate structures may require that he make a number of difficult transformations and associations in order to use the information which is potentially available. It is easy for a cockpit to have too many instruments. There are no known limits to the amount of information a pilot can use if it is structured to facilitate its acquisition and use.

Vision is capable of providing vast amounts of information to the pilot in forms which may be made usable. Depending upon the nature of the display and his degree of learning to use it, the pilot may be able to process visually provided information at prodigious rates. There can be a great many visual displays, as they can be made so they have relatively little interfering effects upon each other.

Direct visual contact with the earth is a very valuable source of information to the pilot for three major reasons: (1) the display contains a great amount of information, (2) that information is organized in such a way that there are many possible ways of grouping, or *chunking*, various subsets of the information; and (3) all pilots have considerable prior perceptual learning in the use of the display. The structure of that display is inherent in the flying task and thus not subject to change. It can be augmented with other displays, which then need to have characteristics compatible with the contact scene.

Only the most simple aircraft operating under good visibility can be operated by visual contact alone. All other aircraft and all other conditions require additional information for safe operation, for accurate performance, and for purposes of ATC. Within a year of their first flight, the Wright brothers were installing mechanical aids to their perception of forward velocity and alignment with the relative wind. The development of pilot information systems has been continuous since that time, and most of the information is transmitted through visual displays. The major principles for the design of these display systems are the following: (1) structure the information in the cockpit into the smallest number of frameworks possible, consistent with the intended use of the information; (2) design displays to allow the pilot to chunk the information in as many levels as needed for the tasks; and (3) design displays to make use of the pilot's prior perceptual learning. (For a discussion of chunking, see Chapter 5 by Wickens and Flach, this volume.)

Hearing provides both deliberate and incidental information. The deliberate information includes voice communication and warning signals. The incidental information includes engine noise, the sounds of the airframe in dynamic contact with the air, and miscellaneous sounds such as rain, hail, and equipment malfunctions. The noise level in GA aircraft is usually quite high to save the cost of soundproofing. That part of the noise which is useful may thus come through unrestricted, but a real price is paid in obscuring voice communications.

Sound is not as highly directional as are light rays, and this limits the number of auditory displays which can be used at any one time. That same characteristic enhances their use for warning signals, because the display reaches its target without regard to the orientation of the head or the direction of attention.

Kinesthetic sensing is the direct awareness of the motion of the aircraft, arising partly through the semicircular canals of the inner ear and partly through relatively simple sensors spread throughout the body. The semicircular canals specialize in sensing angular accelerations in all three axes. This sense is quite useful when used with a visual display of angles and their rates-of-change. Without such visual display, the sensations arising from the canals can be misleading and constitute a special problem for training and performance.

The kinesthetic sensing of linear motion changes is also called the "g effect." Longitudinal g effects are useful in takeoff and landing and in other conditions of power and speed changes. Vertical g effects are highly useful for precision flying, especially when flying under instrument conditions. These g inputs frequently provide control feedback before the flight instruments have time to respond. Lateral *g* has limited usefulness to the airborne pilot except in trimming the aircraft to line up with the relative wind. But it becomes very useful on the runway, especially with tail wheel aircraft and with crosswinds.

Little research has been done on the useful aspects of kinesthetic motion cues. Research on these linear motion-effects is very difficult, and adequate simulation of them is not only extremely difficult but very expensive. In one effort to increase capability to study these effects, Ritchie and his associates equipped a Piper Apache as a flying testbed for the evaluation of display concepts. It was used in the same way as the research simulators operated by the USAF Flight Dynamics Laboratory, which funded the work in 1965 and 1966.

To extend this work further, the Ritchie group instrumented an automobile to record lateral acceleration and forward velocity. In a series of studies they showed that each driver uses lateral acceleration as a key criterion in driving performance, even though many of them are unaware that they are doing so and have difficulty even understanding the concept of lateral acceleration (see Ritchie, 1972; Ritchie, Howard, Myers, & Nataraj, 1972; Ritchie, McCoy, & Welde, 1968). Racing drivers and analytic pilots understand this concept very clearly.

Information Processing

The pilot has an array of information displayed through the windshield and windows, through the visual displays of the instrument panel, through the sounds of the aircraft, through a headset or speaker system, through feeling the aircraft's motion, through the feel of the controls, and through the materials in his or her briefcase.

Information from all these sources is organized by information stored in the pilot's long-term memory, which represents his or her flying skill. This stored information provides the rules for the selection at each moment of the information sources to be attended and the significance of their use.

Many serious designers and investigators have reacted to the massive amount of information which the pilot must process by underestimating the problems, by oversimplifying the solutions, or by being overwhelmed. An example of the first type of reaction is to say that the problems of GA flight performance can be solved with some particular display system. An example of the second type of reaction is to say the problems will be solved by automation, and an example of the third is to say that pilots cannot handle all this information, so we will just give them what they can use.

Ritchie (1960) proposed that the complexity of flying information should be addressed head-on and that the solution should lie in adequate structuring of the information to be processed and similarly structuring its display. He suggested that the aircraft equations of motion be utilized in structuring the information requirements and to describe the inherent correlations among the information elements which should be incorporated into display designs. In particular, displayed information should be integrated along control dimensions— those elements that respond to the action of a specific control in a specific task. That approach would make it clear that the information sets must be handled differently for each set of pilot tasks. Kearns and Ritchie (1961) called the processes required to do that "control–display subsystem engineering."

Decision Processes

There is much more information on the display side of the pilot's task than on the control side. Once a pilot has determined what the situation is at a particular moment, there is a limited set of things that can be done about it. But there may be a large number of alternatives involved in trying to determine just what the situation is.

During a study of pilot decision making involving fairly complex military radar, Williams and Hopkins (1958) seemed almost to have surprised themselves with one conclusion. When they had diagrammed several alternative courses of action, they noted that each was associated with a distinctive pattern of informational displays. That led them to conceive of decisions made by the pilot,

> not in terms of the pilot's selection of a course of action from among the alternatives available, but rather in terms of his diagnosis of the state of the system. In other words, the pilot does not choose a course of action but he does decide what is the nature of the situation. Once he has decided what the state of the system is, the course of action is specified. (p. 10)

A pilot with 1,000 hours may be almost as skilled as he will ever be at making an airplane do just what he or she wants it to do. Long after the manipulative skills begin to level off, overall skill keeps increasing. That long-continuing increase in skill involves improvements in the ability to recognize situations and understand alternative consequences. It also includes an accumulation of information about the national airspace system and judgments about the use of that information.

But increasing skill level does not make all problems disappear. In an interesting study of accidents, Salvatore, Huntley, and Mengert (1985) compared private pilots (PVTs) with rated air transport pilots (ATPs) flying GA aircraft. As might be expected, they found that weather plays a much more important part in PVT than in ATP GA accidents. ATPs were more often involved in accidents associated with risk and overconfidence, a category including a full 58% of all pilot-induced fatalities.

> The most striking finding is that ATPs are more often accident involved in fatal acrobatics. Of the ATP pilot induced fatal accidents, nearly 50 percent are during acrobatics. Often these risky aerial operations are performed below safe altitudes and are associated with descriptors such as careless and reckless. (p. 739)

Input Processes

What a pilot can do in flight is limited to and by the capabilities that have been provided by the controls in the cockpit. The efficiency with which a pilot can use a particular set of controls depends on the extent to which they fit into the conceptual framework of his or her primary tasks, without requiring that the pilot convert his or her own thinking into the framework of the control itself.

Violations of this principle are almost the norm. One extreme example concerned a design proposed for a system to allow curved approaches using the microwave landing system. The design required the pilot to key in the latitude, longitude, altitude, and bearing of the landing runway. Then the pilot had to input similar numbers for each point defining the desired path. The designers requested human factors assistance to determine ways to reduce pilot error in entering so many numbers.

It follows from the most elementary principles of mind–machine system design that one should not require a pilot to make complicated inputs in order to tell a navigation facility where it is! What he or she should do instead is tell the electronics how long the final straight leg should be and whether the turn onto it should be right or left.

The same criticisms apply to many of the inputs required by area navigation and inertial navigation systems. Pilots are grossly wronged when they are blamed for errors arising when such systems require them to transform routes and destinations into waypoints and into latitude and longitude. Such errors are virtually inevitable when the design requires tasks that arise from the nature of the equipment and not from the nature of flying. Airline pilots may minimize the effects of such bad design through extensive training and intensive skill maintenance. Most GA pilots must suffer the full consequences of that inadequate systems engineering.

Operating in Emergencies

The effect of emergencies on a pilot's task performance may take three different forms: (1) task performance can become much faster and more accurate than normal, (2) the pilot may operate normally or very near to normal, or (3) the pilot becomes incapable of performing some or all parts of his task. Which of these modes describes a given pilot at a given time is partly due to personal characteristics and partly due to training and experience. The more practice a pilot has on a given task, the more likely he is to do well when conditions degrade. The wider and deeper the range of his experiences, the more confident and competent he is likely to be in a given situation.

Since GA pilots are frequently skill limited, it is especially important that their systems provide them with well-digested information for diagnosis and for prioritized alternatives for action. The work of Rockwell and his associates (Giffin, Rockwell, & Smith, 1985) shows abundant confirmation of this need.

Primary Flight Tasks of the GA Pilot

The primary flight tasks are those required to get an aircraft into the air, climb to an altitude, turn to any direction, maintain a direction, descend, and make a safe landing. They involve the use of engine controls, elevator controls, aileron controls, and rudder. These tasks are inherent in the nature of flying, they are essential, and some parts of them are not subject to much alteration. This point is well recognized by both training and regulatory agencies. The information sources used in many of the tasks can be changed with relative ease, using current information systems technology. The opportunities to improve flight performance thereby have never been better.

Instrument Flying

Flying by instruments without visual reference to the ground is a special problem for GA pilots. With the instruments currently avail-

able, and current navigation and ATC procedures, it takes considerable time to learn to fly by these instruments, and the skills may be
subject to decay when not practiced. Some of the problems are more
difficult than it seems they ought to be.

One of the important problems was delineated starkly in a study
by Bryan, Stonecipher, and Aron (1955), under sponsorship of the
Aircraft Owners and Pilots Association. As a prelude to the development of a procedure to allow noninstrument pilots to make a 180°
turn out of instrument conditions, they established typical behavior
of such pilots entering instrument conditions without warning. Their
subjects were 20 pilots who had from 31 to 1,625 hours of contact
flight time, but no instrument training. Each was taken aloft and put
under the hood in a cockpit which had adequate flight instruments.
The pilot's task was to fly the aircraft straight and level.

> Nineteen subjects placed the airplane in a "graveyard spiral" on the
> first attempt to fly by instruments. The twentieth subject pulled the air-
> plane into a whip-stall attitude. Minimum time to reach the incipient
> dangerous attitude was 20 seconds; maximum time was 8 minutes.
> (Bryan, et al., 1955, p. 16)

An experimental analysis of instrument flying was made by Ritchie and Michael (1955). They taught two groups of nonpilot subjects to fly straight and level and to make level turns. One group
learned these maneuvers first by visual contact then relearned the
same maneuvers on instruments. The other group learned the maneuvers first on instruments then relearned them on contact. Learning the maneuvers on instruments first resulted in less overall
learning time, as the transfer effects between the two experiences
was quite different. In discussing the significance of the transfer effects, Ritchie and Michael (1955) made the following statement:

> At the extreme it is possible that a whole generation of instrument-ha-
> ting pilots was created when they met instruments which appeared un-
> natural as they opposed well-established contact habits. The obvious so-
> lution is the development of instruments which are compatible with
> population stereotypes and with contact habits. (p. 149)

Writing 26 years later, when GA instruments were not much different from those used in the Ritchie and Michael experiment cited,
Parker, Duffy, and Christensen (1981) could say,

> The emerging role for general aviation in air transportation is accom-
> panied, unfortunately, by an accident rate considerably higher than that
> found in commercial operations. During instrument approaches, general
> aviation was found to have, over a two-year period, an accident rate 17

times as high as that of the carriers. A closer review of these accidents shows that almost 90 percent are attributed wholly or in part to pilot error. Of these pilot error accidents, the preponderance occur during single-pilot IFR flight. (p. 40)

Controls

The four primary controls are aileron, elevator, rudder, and throttle. For many years there has been technology available to augment various portions of the primary control tasks. Autopilots to maintain a chosen pitch angle and bank angle are available for GA aircraft at moderate cost. These can relieve the pilot of the continuous primary control tasks for a time, allowing him to use his attention for other purposes. These aiding controls can be coupled to an altitude sensor to maintain a selected altitude, to a compass unit to maintain a selected heading, and to some elements of the navigation systems. Automatic throttles to maintain a selected speed are available for some more elaborate aircraft.

Ritchie (1960) suggested that a control system to simplify the pilot's task should allow easy selection of any of a number of criteria for the control system's action. When selected, the control system would then see that those criteria were met until it received further programming.

Displays

When the pilot has direct visual contact with the ground, he or she has in that view a number of feedback display elements which are of value in primary control; among them are the three-dimensional set of elements which are the earth-reference coordinate system and the other three-dimensional set of elements which are the aircraft-reference coordinate system. From this contact display the pilot can readily detect angular rates of change. All these elements are in the one integrated display. Deriving all that information from the display is a rapid process for two major reasons. It is an integrated display with a single frame of reference for all the data, and humans have considerable perceptual learning on that display.

When pilots cannot see the ground, they still need to know each of those angles, their rates of change, and the relations among them. If they must now derive that information from a number of different displays, it will take a great deal more time and effort to do so. It is probably true that they cannot keep track of all of it, even if there are no other tasks to perform. They not only get their information faster from the integrated display, the information is actually more useful.

Williams (1949) made a number of suggestions about criteria for display design. Among them were these:

> Choose a display which is legible. If a display is non-legible in any respect it should not be selected. . . . For displays which provide information necessary to make a decision: choose the display which requires the *least additional information* from other sources in order to form a complete decision concerning the direction, altitude and distance for flight.

Ritchie and Bamford (1957a,b) demonstrated the information advantages of integrating the display of roll rate and turn rate to provide additional information to the pilot. This advantage was related to that of pursuit tracking over compensatory tracking.

Carel (1965) described in some detail the advantages of pictorial displays for flight. He was quite analytic about the nature of pictorial displays, including which characteristics of pictures can be used to advantage in designing effective displays. Ritchie (1960) outlined ways that the useful qualities of pictorial displays might be integrated with analytic structuring of the pilot's information processing tasks. Ritchie (1976) pointed out that the objective is to produce displays which contain the required information for each specific task and which have high rates of information transfer. The technology is now available to produce large electronic displays in which elements can be integrated to provide rapidly interpretable information for each task need. Such a powerful system may well cost less than current display systems. The integration required is more than display design. It requires system design to improve the tasks as well as matching the information and its rate of transmission to those tasks.

Managing the GA Aircraft Systems

Managing Propulsion and Other Equipment

While the pilot is performing the continuous primary control tasks he or she must also manage the aircraft and its equipment. Whenever the throttle setting is changed he may need to change propeller settings, mixture settings, or attend to engine cooling. The pilot may need to (1) raise gear and flaps after takeoff and lower them again in preparation for landing, (2) monitor such things as battery condition, (3) use propeller deicers and wing deicers, (4) use the cabin heater and perhaps the carburetor heater, and (5) ensure that electronic equipment is turned on and is available by the time needed.

Though these are familiar and important tasks, they are secondary rather than primary. They do not derive directly from the aircraft's dynamics, but secondarily from the way in which the particular machine has been built to achieve its flight objectives. Since they relate to a specific machine, the tasks may change whenever the machine is modified, and they may be different from machine to machine.

Managing Communications

Voice radio has been such an important part of flying for such a long time that it and the characteristics of the equipment upon which it depends seem like an inherent part of aviation. As we analyze the human tasks, we can see that is an inadequate view.

One issue in managing communications is that radio equipment forces pilots to depart from the conceptual framework of their primary tasks and shift to a framework of electronics. With an objective to talk to another aircraft, or to a controller, they must first become frequency selectors. There are no cues in their primary control tasks or in their basic navigation tasks that help in selecting a radio frequency. They must now shift to the framework of radio control procedures and the information sources of that framework before the radio is of any value. There are several ways in which automation of that control process could reduce extraneous pilot workload and improve overall performance.

By the standards of modern communications, voice radio is a very slow and error-prone way to transfer information. Aircraft identification, destination, speed, altitude, and position could now be transmitted much more quickly and accurately if conversion to voice were not required. Altitude, speed, and position are already in the aircraft's information system. Identification and destination could be entered rather simply. Thereafter the information could be transmitted very quickly and very accurately, if it did not have to go through conversion to sound.

Parker, Duffy, and Christensen (1981) equipped a Piper Aztec with a simulated digital data link to ATC, managed through a "flight data console." Their subject pilots reported workload to be less than that found when flying alone and using the normal voice communications link. The experimenters concluded that

a digital data link communications system is entirely feasible for general aviation flight operations. There are, however, a number of human factors issues which must be addressed if such a system is to achieve its potential. Great care must be taken in placing the system in the cockpit. Message content must be matched to pilot needs, instrument scan must be considered, and display complexity should not be great. In addition, a voice channel allowing instant communication with the controller, if necessary, should be included as a backup system. (p. 41f)

Cruise Management

Cruise management involves mainly the control of power settings, fuel flow, and aircraft speed to ensure that the planned destination can be reached with the fuel supplies available. Most aircraft have fuel quantity and airspeed readily available from cockpit instruments. What pilots need for this task are ground speed, fuel flow rates, and distance to destination, and they usually must derive these themselves. Fuel flow, particularly, is difficult to derive from fuel quantity gauges checked over time. The information pilots need for planning and decision functions is available within the machine systems, but is usually not made available to them.

The controls used for cruise management are now generally quite adequate for the tasks. The information available to the pilot is quite inadequate.

Analyzing Malfunctions While in Motion

The earlier a malfunction is detected, the more time the pilot may have to diagnose the problem and the more options he may have for response. Problems may first show up as a change in flight performance, or the first sign may be a noise or vibration. Electronic equipment failure may be difficult to detect.

Giffin, Rockwell, and Smith (1985) made a 5-year study of GA pilot behavior in analyzing certain malfunctions in flight, which they call "critical in-flight events" (CIFE). They used flight missions in simulators, paper and pencil tests, and computer-aided scenario testing. In their general conclusions they state the following:

> Approximately half of the scenarios were diagnosed correctly. This is a sobering statistic when one considers that 88% of the subjects were instrument rated and the average number of flight hours was 2,540. A common result of the testing was a sheepish reaction of many of the subjects for not being able to apply what they knew.
>
> In terms of efficiency in arriving at a diagnosis, the results were similarly depressing. . . . while knowledge scores were not related to flight hours (not too surprising), the overall scores on straightforward ques-

tions about weather, IFR flight operations and aircraft subsystems were surprising. Again the mean knowledge score was approximately 50%. . . . G/A pilots are in need of training in CIFE management. Only because aircraft subsystems are relatively simple and very reliable is the number of CIFE incurred accidents relatively small. A key question is whether the introduction of new avionics which automate various operations and purport to reduce workload would, in fact, reduce system reliability and lead to more CIFE induced accidents. (pp. 326f)

In these GA tasks, as with many others, the greatest reduction in pilot error is to be achieved through redesign of the equipment that produces the pilot tasks. If one conceives that something like a personal computer may be built into an aircraft's system, then a program using the principles of an "expert system" may provide a very significant increase in the speed with which the pilot can detect and diagnose malfunctions in flight. The principle is that the computer is given all the inputs which relate to the problem (these inputs can be continuous). As the problem develops, the computer program responds with problem diagnosis and ranked alternatives for action, including naming the controls to be used and what to do with them.

Emergency Alterations to Flight

There are several kinds of malfunction which may require abandoning the original flight plan and substituting a new objective. Every pilot knows that this might happen, and many use available gaps in normal flight duties to consider alternate destinations and emergency landing sites. Except for the books and maps the pilot brought on board, there is not much in the cockpit to help with these tasks. Depending on the nature of the emergency, primary flight tasks may be so demanding that he or she is unable to reach or unfold and read a map. The pilot may use the radio to ask for help, with the expectation that any response will be an extemporaneous one.

Deteriorating weather conditions are frequently the cause of changes in flight objectives. The pilot needs to know quickly where the weather is better and what to do to get there. An active electronic storage system could be developed which would contain all the information a pilot normally brings on the trip and keep it related to the data being produced as the flight proceeds. A single stroke of input to the on-board computer could then cause the computer to draw out a path to the closest airport which meets the pilot's weather criteria.

GA Navigation Tasks

There are three hierarchical forms of navigation: pilotage, dead reckoning, and electronic navigation. Pilotage is the most elementary, dead reckoning is added to pilotage, and electronic navigation is added to both the others.

Pilotage

Pilotage is navigation by means of what the pilot sees looking out the windows. It involves learning what geographic features look like from the air and how to detect one's relative motion in that geography. Charts are available which emphasize the features which are visually dominant when seen from the air. Though pilotage is a fundamental skill, flying strictly by pilotage is not very accurate and is seldom to be used by itself.

Dead Reckoning

Dead reckoning is done with a compass, an airspeed indicator, and a clock. With these instruments the pilot uses the primary flight controls to fly a straight path in a specific direction at a particular speed. When the time is up he or she checks to see if the plane is where it should be. It is not necessary to be able to see anything during the length of the flight, but there must be some means of verifying position at the end of the vector. Navigation then returns to pilotage.

Electronic Navigation

Theoretically, an aircraft flying in the United States, with appropriate electronic equipment, should never get lost. But the theory assumes that information can be used if it is potentially available. Such assumptions give rise to accidents that are described as due to human error, but are actually design-induced errors.

Navigation Controls. Electronic navigation systems, as they are now used, require that the pilot depart from the conceptual framework of the primary task and think in the framework of the electronics. The first thing he or she has to do is to put a series of numbers into the navigation set. These numbers tune the electronics to the right frequency to pick up the signals from the chosen facility. The numbers have no inherent meaning in flying, in geography, or in navigation. They have meaning only to the electronics themselves. For pilots, they are abstractions which are reduced to rote memory or otherwise stored and retrieved when needed.

For part-time pilots, which includes most GA pilots, the requirement to store and retrieve these numbers is much more of a problem than for full-time pilots. The numbers themselves simply will not stay in memory very long, and "memory joggers" of some kind must be developed and used. In general the aircraft are not equipped to help very much.

Having selected the right frequency, the pilot now needs to put in another number, the required radial to or from the station. That number does have some geographic significance, for it denotes a compass direction of the reference line to or from the station. That compass direction may bear no relation at all to the compass direction the pilot needs to maintain for the present flight path. (That is a setup for interference effects between two different meanings of similar terms. Such interference effects increase the likelihood of error.)

There is available on some new airliners a navigation set which searches through navigation frequencies and locks on to the closest one with complete position information available and makes the plane's present position available to the plane's internal computer and to an external ATC computer. The cost of such a system may be brought low enough to make it available for even the lower end of GA with a combination of mass production economies and perhaps subsidy for microchip development. Additional benefits from such a program are described below.

Navigation Displays.   After the numbers problem has been resolved, the pilot usually gets the output of a particular navigation facility in another artificial framework, such as an indicator needle moving away from a reference mark. In order for that information to make sense, he or she must have a conceptual framework into which that bit of information fits. That requirement increases the difficulty of the task and the probability of error.

The pilots must do the tasks in an integrated fashion. When the data they are using are scattered all over the cockpit, including the briefcase carried on board, it can take considerable attention to keep track of their location. This is a critical problem for GA.

Neither equipment costs nor technology limitations stand in the way of reducing these considerable problems for GA navigation. There are high-speed microcomputers on the retail market which with hard disk, plasma display, and printer are briefcase size. They are not as large or as heavy as the briefcase required for electronic navigation charts and approach plates. Such computers can hold all the information the pilot needs about every navigation point and landing facility in the country and make it available for on-line display integrated with information from the primary flight tasks.

GA Air Traffic Control Tasks

Air traffic control tasks are added to the primary control tasks, the machine management tasks, and the navigation tasks. Traffic control information comes to the pilot in flight through voice radio. The information received must then be transformed to relate it to the information in the cockpit—in the displays, in the control settings, in the flight instruments, and in the pilot's briefcase and notes. And we have already seen that much of that information is difficult to integrate because it requires going back and forth between aeronautic concepts and electronic system concepts.

When the pilot loses information because the visual contact display disappears, when he or she must make a number of inputs into the navigation system and keep track of the meaning of all those numbers and line deviations, and when he or she may have to switch the radio from one arbitrary setting to another, the combined tasks are very difficult indeed. And much of the difficulty has been imposed by arbitrary designs.

Nobody designed that set of forbidding tasks; they just grew by bits and pieces as the various sets of hardware were designed. As in the case of the Three Mile Island nuclear plant, most of the designers did not realize as they designed the machinery that they were also designing the human operator tasks.

When designers have thought about using automation to aid the pilot, they have almost always begun to work on the controls. That is somewhat helpful, but is not where the big problems are. The GA pilot needs most for automation to be applied to the information tasks. A diagram of the existing navigation system is shown in Figure 17.1. It illustrates the mix of navigation and electronic system tasks for the pilot and the dependence of both on voice radio.

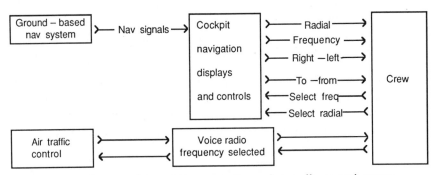

Figure 17.1.   A diagram of the existing navigation and air traffic control system.

Pilots and Controllers

Airplanes and their equipment are designed by one group of people and the ATC system is designed by another group. In the normal run of design activities, each goes its own way without much interaction with the other. Airplanes and ATC become one system when pilots and controllers begin interacting with each other. It is up to these humans to close the loop between the two major subsystems and make them operate as one system.

The interactions between pilots and controllers are a limitation on the effectiveness of the national airspace system, and those limitations can only be removed by making changes to the hardware which defines the tasks of each. That requires simultaneous changes in airborne equipment and control center equipment to achieve more effective human tasks.

When a pilot and controller talk to each other, they are looking at quite different displays. The controller may need to have the pilot fly a particular path but frequently cannot simply describe that path and then monitor its execution. It may take too many words to describe it, and the references for its description are not available to the pilot. As a default he or she then gives the pilot a heading to fly, then another, and then another. It is the mismatch of displayed information which gives rise to pilot organizations' complaints that traffic controllers take over the navigation function. Before that problem is solved, there must be simultaneous changes in airborne and control center equipment which changes pilot and controller tasks.

It is inherent in the ATC task that ATC must know the pilot's identification, intended destination, the aircraft's capabilities, and the aircraft's position at all times. It is inherent in the pilots' role in

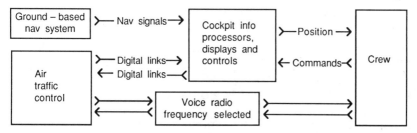

Figure 17.2. A proposed method of redesigning pilot and controller tasks by utilizing the capabilities of current information technology. The pilot's navigation tasks are untangled from tasks of electronic system maintenance. The voice link is freed from routine position reporting.

air traffic separation that they know that they have been cleared, the details of that clearance, and, throughout the flight, where they stand with regard to the path which is the clearance.

Most of that information now is exchanged through voice radio. That means it must be read from the machine, pass through one human brain and be converted to human language, put into another machine for transmission, received and changed from machine language back into human language, and then pass through a set of ears and another human brain, where it is interpreted. At best, that process is not very reliable in terms of the final message being an exact duplicate of the original. Compared to other modern methods of information transfer, it is also very slow.

The tasks of pilots and controllers could be redesigned for much greater effectiveness without any new knowledge about human performance and with the use of currently available technology. It would require careful systems development, of a kind in which human performance criteria are directly related to performance characteristics of the major machine elements. Some major elements of a concept to make such task improvements is shown in Figure 17.2.

Potential GA Pilot Task Improvements through Technology

Technological Developments

The pilot's relation to the airplane is that he or she is a part of its information system. Information technology has been undergoing very rapid development over the last 30 years, and there is no sign that the pace is slowing. There are several components of that technology which are now very powerful, very reliable, and quite low in cost. Those elements are microprocessors, area displays including color, bulk memories, and high-speed data transfer systems. Their use in other systems, particularly in the process control industry, has resulted in greatly enhanced system performance and reliability coupled with lower cost.

If that technology can now be applied to modify the pilot's tasks, there can be a significant improvement in safety and efficiency of GA operations. Through that improvement the entire national airspace system will be improved.

Personal Computer Scenario

Computers are not new to GA. The E6B analog computer has been a staple and useful tool for pilots in the same way that the slide rule has been a staple for engineers. The engineer's slide rule has almost completely given way to hand-held computers, and the E6B is in the process of doing the same thing. But the great improvements needed by GA pilots require the computer capability to be put on line with the aircraft's electronics and with ATC.

The following scenario describes a possible interaction of a GA pilot with ATC, presuming that the pilot has on board a digital computer with the size and capability of personal computers now available. In about the size of a navigation briefcase the computer has a 20-megabyte hard disk and a modem. It drives two gas plasma displays, one of which is a graphics display integrated with the aircraft's heading and other displays. The other is a standard data display. The computer has a built-in hard copy printer. That capability, which is enough to make a dramatic improvement in the tasks of the GA pilot, should cost little more than some ordinary electronic items.

The pilot enters the aircraft, turns on electrical power, which activates the computer and associated equipment. He or she writes into the computer his or her name and destination, then pushes a button to have the computer transmit that information to ATC. The computer adds to the message the aircraft's identification, its cruising range, its speed, and the pilot's certificate number.

With a short delay, the pilot sees on the data display that three routes are available. They are detailed and each is numbered. On the graphics display each of the paths is shown as a path on the chart, integrated with heading. The computer has added to the display all the aeronautic features along the path. These are stored in its hard disk. He or she can scroll the display forward to see the whole route and can change the scale of the chart as needed.

The pilot selects the number of one path and pushes a button for the computer to transmit. The data display then shows that the controller has entered the approved choice into the ATC computer and the pilot is cleared to fly that route. On the graphic display only one route line now appears. That line will stay on the display as the flight progresses. It may change slightly from time to time as other traffic or weather may require adjustments in the approach path. There are markers on both sides of the cleared line to show how much space on each side is clear of other traffic. The airborne computer will transmit position and identification at an assigned interval or on call from the ATC computer.

In this example, neither pilot nor controller has changed job functions, but each has more and better information. The information transfer system is now inherently much more reliable. Each human stays within the conceptual framework of his or her own primary task, without being forced into thinking about the nature of the machine aids.

The Smart Data Link

The computer described contains the information in the navigation charts, in the approach plates, and in the other pilot information sources. It is displayed to the pilot in relation to his or her projected path. This information includes the location of every available landing site. It also contains weather information. Being on-line with ATC, these data are available in such a way that there is no aging of that information. ATC computers know where the aircraft is at all times through data derived from the aircraft's sensors. The same computers track all aircraft in flight and thus can transmit to each of them current data about their cleared flight and any limitations to their space. A general concept of the display is shown in Figure 17.3.

To achieve the tremendous potential envisioned in such a system requires no new information about human performance, nor does it require any technology which is not now available. The benefits cannot be achieved simply by putting a computer in an aircraft, even though many benefits can result from that. The potentially great reductions in pilot error and in accidents can be achieved when all the systems together are configured in such a way that the tasks of pilots and controllers consist of those things that each can do best.

The large components required for such a system are already

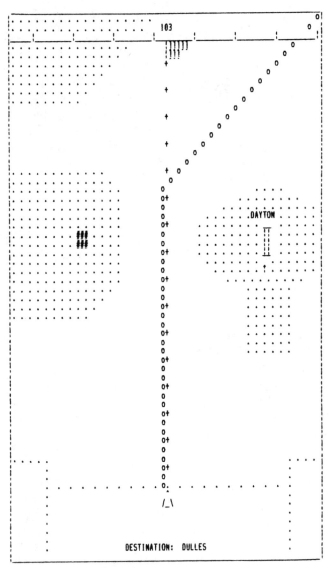

PROPOSED SMART DATA LINK DISPLAY

Figure 17.3.   The proposed smart data-link display, which is
on line with air traffic control computer and with
internal aircraft sensors.

scheduled in the FAA program to improve the national airspace system. The smaller equipment described here may be seen as providing fine tuning for the major elements of that plan. Rapid progress toward the smart data link concept may require subsidizing the design and production of some microchips. Once that is done, the system should cost less than current equipment.

The Sitting Duck

Many times it seems that the attention in accidents and incidents does not go beyond the guilty party. The pilots who are run into, or vectored to, their death frequently receive only the dubious honor of posthumous exoneration, but they are just as dead as if they had been wrong.

The system based on the smart data link would allow true defensive flying. Any specific flight path assigned by ATC would arrive in the context of displayed information about obstructions and restricted zones as well as information about other traffic. Thus the pilot would not be fatally subject to lapses of controller attention, communications foul-ups, or other sources of confusion.

In visual meteorological conditions (VMC), the slow GA aircraft is a sitting duck for the much faster jets. It is almost impossible for a GA pilot to run into a jet without appearing in the jet pilot's potential field of vision. But the GA pilot can be run over from positions in a very large solid angle without the fast offender ever being in his or her field of potential view. The smart data link system can enable the GA pilot to exchange the position of dubious posthumous honor for that of honorable survivor by virtue of competent flying.

Conclusions

Most GA pilots are part-timers. They are limited in the pace at which they can increase and maintain their skills. Their tasks, which are defined by their hardware and the procedures they must use, are usually not optimized for part-timers. The information they must process usually arrives in bits and pieces that they must integrate with information stored in memory, which itself arrived in unintegrated form.

Some GA pilot tasks, particularly flying single-pilot instrument flight rules (IFR), are among the most difficult of flying tasks. Despite this, GA pilots must live and operate in a system which is designed for somebody else.

There is considerable potential for modern technology to increase the safety and efficiency of all aviation through changes in the human tasks in GA. The realization of that potential requires a significant amount of work in redesigning the tasks of GA pilots and controllers. That is done through redesign of the equipment which determines those tasks. Doing this means a new level of system engineering of the national airspace system with the needs of the GA pilots as key criteria for the system's evolving design.

An example of the kind of development needed is described as the smart data link, which serves as a flight instrument, as the primary navigation display, and as approach plate and facility guide. It replaces most routine voice communication with a more reliable, more durable, and more informational digital graphics system.

The system developments described are crucial to GA, but the benefits will be shared by all aviation. There is no better way in sight to produce a large reduction in aviation human error. Both pilot and controller functions should be greatly enhanced. These concepts fit neatly into the FAA's existing long-range development plan, adding a sorely needed human-sensitive component to that plan.

References

Bryan, L. A., Stonecipher, J. W., & Aron, K. (1955). *AOPA's 180° Rating*. Washington, DC: AOPA Foundation, Inc. & Aircraft Owners and Pilots Association.

Carel, W. L. (1965). *Pictorial displays for flight* (Report No. JANAIR TR-2732.01/40. AD 627 669). Washington, DC: U.S. Navy, Office of Naval Research.

Giffin, W. C., Rockwell, T. H., & Smith, P. E. (1985). A review of critical in-flight events research methodology. In R. S. Jensen & J. Adrion (Eds.), *Proceedings of the Third Symposium on Aviation Psychology* (pp. 321–328). Columbus: Ohio State University, Department of Aviation.

Kearns, J. H., & Ritchie, M. L. (1961). *Cockpit control—display subsystem engineering* (USAF WADC Technical Report 61-545). Dayton, OH: USAF Flight Dynamics Laboratory.

Parker, J. F., Duffy, J. W., & Christensen, D. G. (1981). *A flight investigation of simulated data-link communications during single pilot IFR flight*. Falls Church, VA: BioTechnology Inc.

Ritchie, M. L. (1960). What constitutes cockpit simplification and when is it desirable? In *Cockpit instrumentation and layout* (Paper No. 13/WP-37, pp. 115–131). Montreal, Canada: International Air Transport Association.

Ritchie, M. L. (1972). Choice of speed in driving through curves as a function of advisory speed and curve signs. *Human Factors, 14*, 533–538.

Ritchie, M. L. (1976). *Toward a pictorial revolution in complex displays for vehicle control* (Dept. of Engineering, Report HFE 76-4). Dayton, OH: Wright State University.

Ritchie, M. L., & Bamford, H. E. (1957a). Quickening and damping a feedback display. *Journal of Applied Psychology, 41,* 395–402.

Ritchie, M. L., & Bamford, H. E. (1957b). Integrated instruments: A roll and turn indicator (USAF WADC Technical Report 57-205 May. AD 118 170). Dayton, OH: USAF Flight Dynamics Laboratory.

Ritchie, M. L., Howard, J., Myers, D., & Nataraj, S. (1972). Further experiments in driver information processing. In *Proceedings of the 1972 Annual Meeting of the Human Factors Society* (pp. 1–5).

Ritchie, M. L., McCoy, W. K., & Welde, W. L. (1968). A study of the relation between forward velocity and lateral acceleration in curves during normal driving. *Human Factors, 10,* 255–258.

Ritchie, M. L., & Michael, A. L. (1955). Transfer between instrument and contact flight training. *Journal of Applied Psychology, 39,* 145–149.

Salvatore, S., Huntley, S., & Mengert, P. (1985). Air transport pilot involvement in General Aviation accidents. In R. S. Jensen & J. Adrion (Eds.), *Proceedings of the Third Symposium on Aviation Psychology* (pp. 729–739). Columbus: Ohio State University, Department of Aviation.

Weiss, E. C. (1964). *The development of Little Guy information sources* (Report No. 64-8). Arlington, VA: The Matrix Corporation.

Williams, A. C. (1949). *Suggestions concerning desirable characteristics for aircraft instruments* (Technical Report SDC 71-16-4). Urbana: University of Illinois, Aviation Psychology Laboratory.

Williams, A. C., & Hopkins, C. O. (1958). *Aspects of pilot decision making* (WADC Technical Report 58-522, AD 209 382). Dayton, OH: USAF Aero Medical Laboratory.

Helicopter Human Factors

18

Sandra G. Hart

Introduction

Human factors researchers generally focus on the adequacy of the interface between human operators and the systems for which they are responsible. However, human–machine system performance also reflects other factors, such as mission requirements, environmental constraints, vehicle characteristics, computer aiding and automation, and pilot training. Thus, many issues must be considered to optimize the role of the "human" factor in complex systems. The goal of this chapter is to review the many factors that affect the performance and workload of military and civilian helicopter pilots and to discuss significant deficiencies in research, design, and operational procedures.

For no other vehicle is the need for human factors research more critical, or more difficult. The operational environment of helicopters extends from the civil air traffic control system to remote and hazardous areas, and from day operations under visual flight conditions to night operations in adverse weather. Their missions extend from scheduled passenger services, to search and rescue, medivac, con-

Human Factors in Aviation
Copyright © 1988 by Academic Press, Inc.
All rights of reproduction in any form reserved.

struction, agriculture, law enforcement, and military missions. Helicopters can move in any direction, remain stationary while airborne, climb and descend vertically, and take off and land almost anywhere. Thus, their range of maneuvers and control requirements vary more widely than do those of fixed-wing aircraft. Because helicopters may operate at very low altitudes, terrain avoidance, flight path control, and navigation impose significant visual demands on the pilots. And, because helicopters are inherently unstable without automatic flight control systems, they impose significant perceptual and motor demands. Cockpit noise, vibration, heat, and poorly designed seats are but a few of the discomforts pilots encounter. Recent improvements in sensors, displays, controls, and avionics have been accompanied by additional requirements to perform increasingly difficult tasks in more dangerous and demanding environments, creating new human factors challenges for designers and pilots.

One impetus for human factors research has been the large number of accidents attributed to human error. For example, more than 70% of Army aviation accidents (Boley, 1986) and 64% of civil accidents (Negrette, 1986) are attributed to human errors, encompassing failure to use established procedures, misjudged speed or distance, delayed or incorrect decisions, poor coordination, inattention or inappropriate focus of attention, disorientation, or inexperience (Waters & Domenic, 1980). Many errors could have been avoided by improved displays, augmented control systems, or automated monitoring and warning systems. Another impetus for human factors research has been the requirement for reduced crew size to minimize the escalating costs of training and operation. In order to accomplish single-pilot operations under all flight conditions, it has become clear that human information requirements, processing abilities, and response limitations must be considered to develop optimal pilot–vehicle interfaces and delegate responsibilities between human crew members and automatic subsystems appropriately.

Although helicopter pilots' information and control requirements are different than fixed-wing pilots', many helicopters are still equipped with instruments based on the fixed-wing tradition. This may inhibit the pilots from taking full advantage of their vehicle's versatility. Air traffic control procedures and airports are designed for fixed-wing, rather than rotary-wing, aircraft, further contributing to the problem. However, helicopter human factors has received only limited attention by the government, users, and manufacturers.

Helicopter development has always lagged behind that of fixed-wing aircraft. Initially, designing a vehicle with sufficient lift and stability that provided full control authority for the pilot proved to be extremely difficult. It was not until the early 1920s that any helicopter was able to remain airborne, and then only briefly. By 1924, the future of helicopters looked so dismal that an Army report suggested they should be considered only in the face of a military emergency where the pilot's life was of little consequence (Lewis, 1985). For the next 15 years, research focused on autogyro rather than true rotary-wing designs. It was not until World War II that interest turned again to helicopters. As the airborne roles of the Army and Air Force were clarified in the 1950s and 1960s, the number and versatility of military helicopters began to grow until the Vietnam War (where they played an essential role). The civil helicopter industry also expanded during the same period. Off-shore oil surveying and construction, corporate and commuter passenger services, and public service were the primary drivers. However, helicopters were still limited to day flights in good visibility (Bell Aircraft Corporation, 1956; Bell Helicopter Corporation, 1959.)

Many of the helicopters designed and constructed between 1955 and 1965, such as the UH-1 and CH-47, are still in use today by military and civilian operators; the average age of Army helicopters will be 20 years by 1990 (Lewis, 1985) and civil operators (who buy surplus military vehicles) may use even older equipment. Because most helicopter research and development has been prompted by military requirements, and because many civil operators use helicopters originally designed for military use, this chapter focuses on military uses and requirements. Furthermore, many of the missions flown and the human factors problems encountered are similar, and technology developed to meet military requirements eventually filters into the civil market.

The first major helicopter human factors effort was conducted under the joint sponsorship of the Army, Navy, and Air Force (Bell Aircraft Corporation, 1956). The goals were to define the information pilots need, allocate tasks optimally between human operators and automatic subsystems, and design a human–machine interface to accomplish single-pilot, all-weather, low-altitude operations in remote areas using self-contained navigation and guidance systems. Although early briefings for this project estimated that these capabilities would be available by 1965, the same requirements are being levied on contractors competing to build the Army's most advanced helicopter 30 years later, and they are still difficult to accomplish. Bell researchers identified the visual cues pilots use, replicated some of this information electronically for reduced visibility operations, designed systems for accurate, low-level navigation, and improved and simplified helicopter controls. By 1960, they had developed the first helmet-mounted computer-generated display for helicopters, built the first six-degrees-of-freedom, motion-based helicopter simulator, and tested display concepts in flight with conventional and side-stick controls. During this long and productive program, many key human factors issues were addressed, and advanced concepts were developed that are only now being implemented.

The Army recently proposed the development of a new family of light helicopters (LHX—light helicopter, experimental). There were to be two versions: scout–attack and utility. LHX pilots would be expected to perform missions in remote and hostile environments, avoid obstacles and threats while flying only feet above ground, and use vegetation and terrain to avoid enemy detection in all weather conditions, including fog, rain, smoke, and snow. Pilots must control their vehicle, navigate, communicate, and operate weapons, threat-detection, and countermeasure systems. The "battle captain" must also coordinate the efforts of a team of pilots. Originally, the Army tasked industry with providing a fast, lightweight, low-cost vehicle in which a single pilot could perform all of the required tasks. However, a lack of mature technology has prompted the Army to delay development of a single-pilot version.

Since the Army is the single largest helicopter user, the LHX has prompted a significant increase in research and development; no helicopter exists that can accomplish all of these requirements, even with two pilots. It has become clear that innovative technological solutions will be required. Furthermore, these solutions must be designed with the capabilities and limitations of the pilots as the determining factor, as it will be their abilities to use the technology that will determine the ultimate success or failure of the vehicle.

The human factors issues that have been raised are not new. However, some mission requirements are now so extreme, given the goal of single-pilot operations, that they must be solved. For example, some operations will be performed close to the ground, where natural and man-made obstacles present a continuous threat, necessitating precise and rapid control movements and accurate information displays. Helicopter control problems are exaggerated at low altitudes, and night vision systems may not provide adequate fields of view or resolution. Low-level flight already imposes high visual, temporal, physical, and cognitive demands on two-pilot crews; thus, unacceptable workload levels may be encountered by single pilots without additional aiding. Automation, often provided to reduce crew workload, may simply shift the source of demands from the physical domain to the mental (Hart & Sheridan, 1984; Statler, 1984) rather than reducing it. Although human factors problems in existing helicopters are addressed in the following sections, advanced technology solutions and problems are covered as well, as they are the focus of considerable current research.

Typical Helicopter Flight Tasks

Different military and civil missions impose unique demands on pilots and vehicles, but the critical human factors problems are relatively similar, and pilots perform a common set of maneuvers and flight tasks. These are described to provide a context for subsequent sections. Specific missions and environments impose different demands on pilots and may require different cockpit configurations, automation, crew complements, and crew schedules. The Army recognized such differences in the stress and fatigue imposed on aviators by varying the maximum allowable flight times and duty periods depending on the activities performed (Department of the Army, 1985). For example, 1 hour of day nap-of-the-earth (NOE) flight is considered equal to 1.6 hours of day standard flight, and 1 hour of night flight performed with night vision goggles is equivalent to 2.3 hours (Table 18.1). These multipliers are used to determine the maximum permissible flight time and duty period in a 24-hour period (8 and 18 hours, respectively, for standard flights performed during the day). The effects of such environmental demands must be considered in predicting the impact of design decisions on pilot workload and performance.

Table 18.1. Crew Endurance Guide[a]

Type of flight	Multiplier
Day	1.0
Day contour flight	1.3
Instrument flight	1.4
Night flight	1.4
Day NOE flight	1.6
Night terrain flight	2.1
Night flight with night vision devices	2.3

[a]From Department of the Army, 1985.

Takeoff

Helicopters typically take off vertically from a low hover. Pilots gain forward speed and lift by assuming a pitch-down attitude and adding power. "High, hot, and heavy" takeoffs (e.g., high altitudes, hot or humid weather, for heavily loaded helicopters) are particularly difficult with restricted flight path clearances. Takeoff may be more difficult than landing in a restricted area if passengers or cargo are loaded. Finally, takeoff and landing on sloping or uneven terrain are difficult and require greater control finesse.

Cross-Country Flight

During climb, cruise, and approach, helicopter pilots use fixed power and control techniques similar to those used by fixed-wing pilots (Griffith, 1978), using instruments based on fixed-wing designs as effectively as fixed-wing pilots do under similar circumstances. Unlike fixed-wing aircraft, which generally fly well above the terrain from one position to another, helicopters often fly close to the ground. Pilots use visual references as well as radio navigation to maintain geographical orientation. Instead of looking down from a perspective of thousands of feet of altitude, helicopters generally fly between 500 and 3,000 feet, below the height of surrounding hills, and with no direct line of sight for navigation aids. In this case, pilots must correlate their position on hand-held maps to visually observed terrain features.

Helicopters often fly below or outside of controlled airspace. However, under instrument flight conditions in controlled airspace, they are limited to route structures designed for fixed-wing aircraft. This restriction limits their abilities to take advantage of the unique maneuvering capabilities of the vehicle. It was not until 1979 that instrument flight routes were established specifically for helicopters, and they are still not widely available.

Terrain Flight

Other types of cross-country flight, collectively termed *terrain flight*, impose additional workload on pilots. Until recently, helicopters' survival chances in military operations were increased by operating above 1,500 feet. However, military tactics have changed, emphasizing the use of natural and man-made objects for visual, optical, and electronic concealment from enemy detection (Forbush,

1981). In addition, civilian pilots may fly at low altitudes during search and rescue, law enforcement, crop dusting, and other activities.

There are three basic types of terrain flight (Figure 18.1): low-level, contour, and NOE. In low-level flight, pilots maintain a constant airspeed and altitude (within 200 feet of the ground) following preselected routes from one point to another. In contour flight, they fly at low altitudes, conforming with and in proximity to the terrain at varying speeds and altitudes. In NOE flight, they fly as close to the ground as possible, in and among buildings, trees, bushes, and other terrain features. Airspeed and altitude vary depending on the terrain, weather, ambient light, and threats, but are generally slow (less than 40 knots) and low (20 feet or less). NOE operations may include vertical "bob-ups" (to unmask and mask behind man-made or natural objects), sidesteps, fast dashes, quick stops, and flying slalom-like courses as well. Thus, the margin for error is small, making NOE operations most demanding and unforgiving.

Since helicopters can move in any direction, obstacles beside, below, and behind are of concern; the pilot's attention cannot be focused solely ahead of the aircraft. Yet, even in advanced helicopters, pilots are provided with less information about the immediate environment than they can see through the windows in good visibility. Below 50 knots, control techniques are different than those used by fixed-wing pilots (Griffith, 1978) and more difficult because helicop-

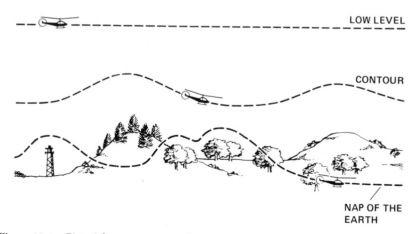

Figure 18.1.   Pictorial representation of three types of terrain flight: low-level, contour, and nap-of-the-earth.

ters become less stable and require precise control to remain clear of surrounding obstacles. Deceleration is particularly difficult because the required nose-high attitude reduces the visual field of view and increases the likelihood of ground strikes by the tail rotor. When rapid and precise position changes are required, already high pilot workload may be increased to unacceptable levels by control cross-coupling and nonlinearities. Such handling-quality deficiencies can prevent pilots from exploiting their vehicle's inherent maneuverability (Warwick, 1985). Although physical effort and the resulting fatigue are important considerations, the visual demands imposed by the proximity of the aircraft to the ground and obstacles are particularly heavy. Pilots must not only keep their vehicle airborne but must also maintain a safe distance from trees, wires, and other obstructions. This requires constant attention to the visual scene and a precise awareness of the physical dimensions of the vehicle and its performance capabilities (Forbush, 1981).

The most common errors associated with terrain flight include inadequate preflight planning, overestimation of visibility range, underestimation of the distance of objects and slope gradients, preoccupation with immediately adjacent terrain features, and failure to maintain continuous spatial orientation (Forbush, 1981). Aircraft failures or other tasks that distract a pilot's attention from maintaining adequate clearance, further increase the probability of contact with obstacles.

Stationary and Vertical Maneuvers

Unlike most fixed-wing aircraft, helicopters can maintain a stationary hover and perform vertical climbs and descents. Pilots must stabilize the vehicle and then correct for deviations from a designated position in space. This requires discrimination of positional changes in three dimensions and detecting rate and acceleration cues. Since helicopters are relatively unstable at low speeds, hovering can impose high pilot workload. In addition, the demands of hovering close to the ground (in-ground effect) or at altitudes greater than 50 to 100 feet (out-of-ground effect) are different. Typical attitude, altitude, and airspeed indicators provide unintegrated information that is not sufficiently sensitive or precise at low altitudes and slow speeds. Thus, hovering is generally performed with visual reference to objects in the environment. Since pilots cannot see the ground immediately below them, they detect lateral, longitudinal, and vertical movement relative to objects in front of or beside them. Restricted visibility also presents a problem when pilots must autorotate to a landing in the event of significant equipment failure. In low visibility or over featureless terrain where visual references are not available, a precise hover becomes virtually impossible without additional aiding.

Landing

Helicopter approaches can be made from any direction (although they land into the wind unless operational necessity dictates otherwise), and approach angles can be very steep. Traffic flow management systems, tailored to the needs of fixed-wing aircraft, do not take advantage of the maneuverability of helicopters or their ability to land with minimal runway length (Livingston, 1985). Furthermore, skids, standard on most small helicopters, allow landings on soft or sloping terrain, but they limit mobility on the ground. Helicopters with skids must achieve a hover and then gain forward speed to travel across the ground.

Although many helicopters are at least minimally equipped for operations in instrument conditions, the information provided (which is adequate for fixed-wing landings) is not sufficiently sensitive or accurate for the slow speeds flown (Verdi & Henderson, 1975). Although there are over 4,000 heliports and helistops in the United States and Canada (Livingston, 1985), they are not sufficient for the growing number of civil helicopters (more than 6,000 by 1986). Only recently have public use facilities equipped for instrument flight conditions been developed in urban areas. Many heliports do not provide adequate lighting or visual approach guidance, thus helicopters must rely on their own external spotlights at night. The current lack of landing facilities tailored to helicopter needs forces pilots to adapt to regulations and flight profiles that are suboptimal and reduces their operational flexibility.

Helicopters often land on unprepared sites, where no ground-based approach aids are available, during search and rescue, medivac, law enforcement, agricultural, and fire-fighting missions. Relatively limited funds have been devoted to developing adequate landing aids for these circumstances. However, low-cost systems have been tested that allow the creation of lighted helipads in even remote areas (Hodgkins, 1984; Kocks, 1985). These units can be placed around the perimeter of a landing site to provide the visual cues necessary for safe landings at night and under reduced visibility.

Cockpit Environment

Cockpit noise, vibration, cold, and heat create uncomfortable and suboptimal work environments for helicopter pilots. Considerable progress has been made in reducing vibration and improving exterior and interior noise levels, yet these factors still present significant problems in some helicopters, increasing pilot workload and fatigue, degrading performance, and reducing effective duty times. In addition, helicopter seats are often cited as an area that is in need of human factors assistance. Many older designs are uncomfortable and force pilots to assume a bent-forward posture to operate the controls, contributing to the back problems induced by vibration.

Vibration

Helicopters have been described as thousands of parts vibrating in close formation (Young, 1982). Considerable attention has been devoted to the physiological, behavioral, and subjective effects of such high levels of vibration on pilots. The results of a classic study on subjective vibration tolerance criteria are depicted in Figure 18.2. The sensitivity of pilots and passengers to vibration—the human factors component—is a more stringent and difficult problem to address than is the requirement to reduce vibration to improve reliability and maintainability (Reichert, 1981). There has been tremendous progress over the past 25 years; typical vibration levels have been reduced from subjectively uncomfortable levels (0.3 to 0.6 g) to those that are subjectively comfortable (0.1 g), although the target level recommended by a NASA Advisory Council in 1976 (0.02 g) does not appear to be attainable without major technological breakthroughs (Reichert, 1981).

Unlike civil aircraft (where air turbulence provides the most significant source of vibration) and military jets (where short-duration high-g maneuvers increase vibration), the dominant source in helicopters comes from the movement of the rotors and the gearing mechanisms of the vehicle itself. There are significant differences in vibration levels among helicopters and variations due to speed and flight conditions for a given helicopter. Figure 18.3 depicts the frequency characteristics of a four-bladed helicopter during horizontal flight and during transition from forward flight to hover.

Performance decrements and medical problems are important issues as well. Extended exposures to whole-body vibration in the lateral, longitudinal, and vertical axes have been associated with

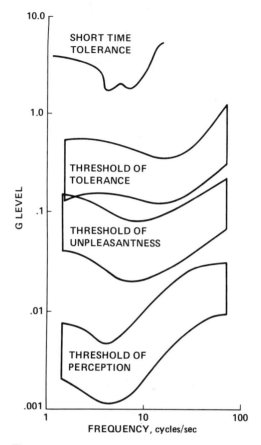

Figure 18.2.   Human reactions to vibration. From "The Influence of Low Frequency Vibration on Pilot Performance (as Measured in a Fixed Base Simulator)" by A. M. Stave, 1979, *Ergonomics, 22,* p. 824. Copyright 1979 by Taylor & Francis, Ltd. Reprinted by permission.

chronic pain and degenerative disease of the back, and there is a clear relationship between vibration and fatigue. Although subjective tolerance for vibration has been studied fairly extensively, it has been difficult to develop standards based on the effects of vibration on performance because the relationship is complex. Vibration may affect a pilot's whole body, specific body parts that contact a vibrat-

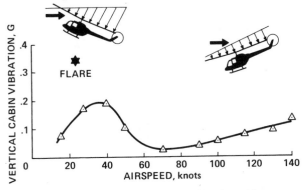

Figure 18.3.   Helicopter vibration as a function of increas-
ing airspeed. From "Helicopter Vibration
Control—A Survey" by G. Reichert, 1981,
Vertica, 5, p. 4. Copyright 1981 by Pergamon
Press, Ltd. Reprinted by permission.

ing part of the aircraft, or visual acuity. The effects depend on the
frequency, amplitude, and duration of the vibration, the affected
axes, the construction of the pilot's seat, and the pilot's body posture
(Griffin, 1977). In general, low-frequency vibrations around 10 Hz
with accelerations greater than 0.3 m/s^2 that last longer than 10 s primarily affect manual control performance. Frequencies above 10 Hz
primarily affect visual performance, although visual decrements have
been found at frequencies as low as 5 Hz. These levels were exceeded on 30% of flights performed in a Sea King helicopter (Griffin,
1977), suggesting the likelihood of vibration-related performance decrements in current helicopters.

Whole body vibration, although fatiguing, has surprisingly little
impact on sensory–motor performance (Hartman et al., 1974; Stave,
1979). However, contact between pilots' hands and vibrating controls
can interfere with flight path control; the finer the movement and the
more sensitive the control, the greater the impairment. Vibrating objects with which pilots have indirect contact can impair performance
as well. For example, the detrimental effects of vibration on visual
acuity and motion perception are well documented (Griffin, 1977;
Mozell & White, 1958; Velger, Grunwald, & Merhav, 1986; Wells &
Griffin, 1984).

Helmet-mounted displays have prompted additional concerns
about vibration-induced decrements in visual performance. At fre-

quencies below 10 Hz, reading is more severely degraded with helmet-mounted displays than with panel-mounted displays. Tenfold
differences were found at some frequencies (Wells & Griffin, 1984),
caused by relative motion between the displayed image (due to involuntary, vibration-induced head motions) and the eye. Vibration in
pitch and yaw create the most significant problems. When pilots'
heads, helmets, and displays vibrate, their eyes try to maintain a
constant line of sight. The normal vestibular–ocular reflex induces
eye movements that oppose those of head movements to maintain a
stationary point of regard. While appropriate for viewing panel-
mounted displays, it is not appropriate for helmet-mounted displays;
relative motion is *produced* between the image on the head-coupled
display and the eye, resulting in retinal blurring, increased errors,
and longer responses.

Several stabilization systems have been proposed to reduce the effects of vibration on helmet-mounted displays. For example, an
adaptive noise-canceling technique has been developed that minimizes the relative motion between viewed images and the eye by
shifting displayed images in the same direction and magnitude as the
induced reflexive eye movement. This filter stabilizes the images in
space while still allowing low-frequency voluntary head motions that
are required for aiming accuracy (Velger, Merhav, & Grunwald, 1986;
Velger & Merhav, in press). Since such systems have not yet been
implemented in operational aircraft, the current solution to vibration
problems has been to specify minimum acceptable levels in design
standards. The most recent one was provided by the Army in cooperation with the American Helicopter Society in 1986, based on the
last 15 years of Army–industry experience (Banerjee, 1986).

Noise

Helicopter noise has been a continuing problem, causing public
complaints and unpleasant and hazardous consequences for pilots
and passengers. It affects speech intelligibility, reducing pilots' abilities to receive communications necessary for flight path control, navigation, and coordination, and it may create temporary or permanent
hearing loss. It is still a sufficiently important problem that NASA,
the major American helicopter manufacturers, and the American Helicopter Society joined in an effort to understand the basic mechanisms of helicopter noise and develop noise-control technology
(Spencer, 1985).

Cockpit noise consists of a continuous mixture of random broadband and periodic harmonic and high-frequency noise from the vehicle itself, transient bursts generated by weapons systems (in military aircraft), and communication system interference. Current helicopter noise levels range from 90–100 dbA (in the AH-1 and OH-58D) to 105–115 dbA (in the CH-47C). Typical values, compared to the military standard, are shown in Figure 18.4. Although turbine, rotor blade, transmission, and airframe noise provide auditory feedback about torque and power settings, they also reduce speech intelligibility and contribute to distraction, stress, and fatigue. Environmental factors, such as weather and battlefield conditions, further contribute to the problem.

Helicopter noise is often high enough to cause temporary or permanent hearing loss in persons without protection (Mayer & Lindberg, 1978). Helmets provide partial protection for pilots (e.g., the SPH-4 noise-attenuating helmet reduced ambient noise levels in the CH-47C to 80–85 dbA); however, passengers are rarely provided with adequate protection. Attenuation is limited by difficulties in achieving a tight seal, without discomfort, between the ear-protective device and the pilot's head. Since hearing loss is related to the interaction between intensity, frequency range, and duration of exposure, current standards take these and other factors into account in establishing allowable levels.

Because adequate noise reduction is not always possible, acceptable exposure levels have been achieved by limiting the allowable flight time per day. As a general rule, the Department of Defense and OSHA require that 8-hour noise exposure levels must be below 85

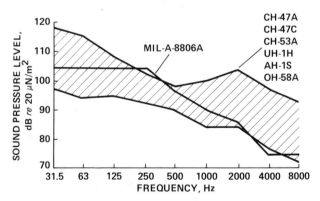

Figure 18.4. Octave band pressure levels in current military helicopters and the limits specified by MIL-A-8806A. (From Garinther & Hodge, 1981.)

dbA. In practice, typical daily exposures are 4 hours per day for Army pilots, 1.5 hours for passengers in peacetime, and two to three times longer in combat (Garinther & Hodge, 1981). Public service pilots typically fly 40–60 hours per month (Adams & King, 1980). They tend to fly longer missions than military pilots, increasing their risk of permanent hearing loss. Early helicopter noise standards were based on fixed-wing designs, flight profiles, and power requirements. It was so difficult for helicopter manufacturers to meet these stringent requirements that Army helicopters were excluded from the provisions of MIL-STD-1474 during the 1970s. Practical limitations in achievable noise levels, given helicopter weight limitations, still had to be accepted in establishing recent design standards.

The most immediate problems created by high noise levels are reduced in-flight communications efficiency and temporary hearing losses that persist after a flight. Transmissions are difficult to understand when heard against background noise, and pilots often increase radio volumes high enough to induce audio distortion, further degrading communication. Thus, air-to-air, air-to-ground, and internal communications in high noise levels may require a pilot's complete attention to avoid losing important information. The voice technology systems proposed for advanced helicopters are likely to add to the problem. If pilots must control displays, tune radios, arm and operate weapons systems, and enter data by vocal input to voice recognition systems, distortions and masking produced by high ambient noise levels could be catastrophic. Computer-generated digitized or synthesized voice messages and auditory warnings will simply add to the din. Although vocal control and auditory display capabilities are provided to reduce high visual and manual workload demands, voice technology may simply replace one type of problem with another.

Temperature

Unlike fixed-wing aircraft, that require artificial environments created by heating, cooling, oxygen, and pressurization systems, helicopters usually fly low enough that simpler systems suffice. Since many helicopters have windows above, beside, below, and in front of pilots, cockpits often become overheated by the sun. It was not until the end of the Vietnam War that air-conditioning was first installed in a helicopter (to protect the AH-1 Cobra's avionics systems). Coincidentally, this mitigated pilots' discomfort in flying low-level missions in the hot and humid climate of Vietnam.

Overheating problems are exacerbated by requirements for military pilots to fly wearing chemical–biological warfare suits. For example, the life-support equipment developed for Apache pilots includes a chemical–biological face mask, helmet, flame-retardant flight suit, boots, gloves, and cooling vest (Griffin, 1985). This gear is awkward and restrictive, and it makes manual operation of some controls difficult. Operations in cold climates also require protective clothing. For example, pilots operating to and from oil rigs in the North Sea and Beaufort Sea must wear immersion suits for protection in the event that they have to ditch their aircraft. However, the suits are uncomfortable and hot during routine flights. Although research and development efforts prompted by government and the civil-use communities have achieved significant improvements, noise, vibration, and temperature still create performance and comfort problems.

Helicopter Controls

Helicopters require relatively continuous control inputs from both hands and both feet without stability augmentation. Control is achieved by changing rotor blade pitch angle either collectively (to increase or decrease thrust) or cyclically (to change the direction of the thrust vector). Pilots adjust rotor thrust with the collective lever in their left hand. A throttle may be mounted on the handle of the collective lever to adjust fuel flow, although it is adjusted automatically in most modern helicopters. Pilots control pitch and roll with their right hand, using fine adjustments of the cyclic control stick. The directional pedals, which control the collective pitch of the tail rotor, are used to (1) counteract the tendency of the fuselage to rotate in the opposite direction from the main rotor with increases in main rotor collective pitch and (2) provide directional control. Particularly at low speeds, interactive movement of all controls is required to accomplish a precise maneuver and to maintain a steady hover, constant rate of climb or turn, or forward flight.

Early helicopter designs gave pilots direct control over the main and tail rotors through a system of mechanical linkages. In flight, pilots had to act against sizeable dynamic forces to move the controls. Later, hydraulic systems were added between the pilot's controls and the control surfaces. An actuator did the "work" of moving the mechanical linkages. With a hydraulic failure, however, pilots had to revert to direct mechanical control. Recently, servo-controlled systems have been added to augment pilots' control inputs and stabilize the aircraft. *Fly-by-wire* and *fly-by-light* systems that send electrical or optical signals from cockpit controls to computers, cause electrically powered actuators to move control surfaces, thereby reducing the pilot's physical workload (Prouty, 1986b). The advanced digital–optical control system (ADOCS), which is still under development at Boeing Vertol, was flown in a UH-60 BlackHawk in 1985, and control laws are being tested at Ames Research Center (Aiken, 1982; Harvey, 1986; Landis, Dunford, Aiken, & Hilbert, 1983).

With such advanced control systems, aircraft responses to pilot control inputs may be tailored to suit the demands of the task, reducing pilot workload. For example, one control mode may provide a steady-state pitch and roll rate response to cyclic stick inputs, while an attitude command system allows pilots to exert direct control over pitch and roll attitude with the same controller. Angular rate command systems are preferable for rapid or gross changes in flight path, while attitude systems are preferable (in terms of reduced pilot effort and stabilized flight path control) when small changes and precise control are required (Prouty, 1986b). Although helicopters are still essentially controlled manually, available augmentation and stabilization systems are beginning to allow hands-off flight under some circumstances. Cross-coupling between different axes of control remains a problem. For example, pitch commands may also induce some roll and vice versa, and an increase in collective creates yaw that pilots must counter with the directional pedals.

Control switches may be mounted on the cyclic and collective for the radio, trim select and disengage, hoist control and cargo hook release, and weapons delivery. Searchlight control may be performed with a coolie-hat switch on the collective. In advanced helicopters, the number of switches mounted on the controllers has increased substantially. Thus, issues of standardization in placement, optimal angles, sizes, and force requirements are becoming critical.

An additional problem faced by pilots of current and advanced helicopters is the necessity to remove one hand from the controls to enter data into a flight management computer, change radio frequencies, and select display alternatives. Since the cyclic is the most sensitive control, and the collective can be set to a desired value and released, pilots prefer to make such inputs with their left hand and keep their right hand on the cyclic. Hence, there is a continuing preference for the right seat, where pilots can perform additional functions with their left hand without switching hands to maintain cyclic control.

Handling qualities (which are influenced by vehicle stability, response characteristics, sensitivity and adequacy of displays, and control–display interfaces) determine the ease and precision with which pilots can perform required tasks (Key & Aiken, 1984). They also may be affected by environmental conditions, additional tasks, demanding mission requirements (e.g., NOE flight), and reduced visual information (e.g., helmet-mounted displays; Aiken, Hilbert, Landis, & Glusman, 1984). Since helicopters are inherently unstable, and poor handling qualities can contribute substantially to poor performance, considerable effort has been devoted to improving vehicle handling qualities through stabilization and augmentation systems. For particularly demanding situations, substantial stability and control augmentation is required to achieve satisfactory handling qualities.

Information Requirements

Pilots need to know where they are, where they are going, what is between them and their destination, and the current state of their vehicle. They obtain this information from cockpit instruments and displays (driven by on-board sensors and transmitted from the ground), the visual scene viewed out the window, auditory feedback from the engine and rotor, communications with other crew members, pilots of other aircraft, air traffic control centers, and from maps, manuals, and memory. The primary source of information is visual, thus the visual demands placed on helicopter pilots, particularly during low-level, low-visibility flights, are great.

Cockpit Instruments and Displays

All helicopters are equipped with indicators for airspeed, altitude, engine/rotor tachometer, and engine and fuel status (Prouty, 1986a). Conventional instruments present two-dimensional information on separated displays. While this is acceptable for fixed-wing pilots, it does not provide the three-dimensional visual representation of the immediate environment required for low-level helicopter flight. And since helicopters fly at generally slower speeds and lower altitudes than fixed-wing aircraft, they have a greater need for indicators that are accurate below 30 knots and 200 feet. Although radar altimeters provide accurate information for precise vertical control at low altitudes, and Naval aviators have been provided with them for some time to allow them to maintain a stable hover while lowering sonar arrays for antisubmarine work, Army helicopters have been equipped with them only recently.

Fixed-wing aircraft have had some degree of instrument flight capability since before World War II. However, comparatively little effort was devoted to providing instrument capabilities in helicopters, and the high-technology avionics that worked so well in fixed-wing aircraft did not transition easily to helicopters (Shawlee, 1985). Although the Army determined that helicopters were capable of instrument flight in 1958, it was not until 1972 that instrument certification was required of all Army aviators to reduce the loss of lives associated with inadvertent penetration into instrument flight conditions (Smith & McCants, 1978). Fully instrumented cockpits to support true all-weather capabilities are now available in all Navy, Marine, and Air Force helicopters and in many Army helicopters, as all-weather capability has become a military requirement. Instrument flight capabilities entered the civil sector slowly, due to the cost and weight of the additional equipment required for instrument flight. It was not until the 1960s that helicopters certified for instrument flight in the civil air traffic control system were available and only recently that a significant number of civil helicopters have had instrument capabilities.

To be certified for instrument operations, a trade-off is made between the stability of the vehicle, available cockpit displays and automation, and the crew complement to ensure that pilots can operate safely and with acceptable workload. Although helicopters *can* operate in poor visibility, this requirement imposes considerably higher workload than it does in fixed-wing aircraft. Two pilots are still generally required to share the duties imposed by instrument flight in helicopters, although single-pilot operations are common under visual flight conditions. For example, it was found in an early study conducted in an OH-58A and an OH-6A (Winn & Lewis, 1974) that performance was significantly worse and required considerably more pilot effort in instrument flight than in visual flight. Stability and control augmentation reduced pilot effort by 50%, with a further improvement provided by the addition of a flight path director.

Control–Display Compatibility

At the low speeds typical of NOE flight, helicopter pilots control altitude with their left hand (using the collective lever) and speed with their right (using the cyclic control stick). However, altitude and speed indicators are placed on the right and left sides of the panel, respectively (following fixed-wing tradition). In several experiments conducted at NASA-Ames Research Center (Hartzell, Dunbar, Beveridge, & Cortilla, 1983), it was found that a stimulus–response-compatible arrangement (e.g., placing the altimeter on the same side as the collective) improved performance by 150 to 170 milliseconds—a 12-foot difference in distance traveled between compatible and incompatible configurations before a control input is initiated at NOE speeds. French aircraft (such as the Aerospatiale) are generally designed with a compatible arrangement, as is the SH-3. However, most helicopters still have an incompatible arrangement. Thus, high levels of pilot workload and performance limitations may occur during instrument flight.

Direct Visual Information

At low altitudes in good visibility, helicopter pilots use visual cues in the immediate surroundings to identify terrain features and determine their orientation, rate and direction of movement, height above terrain, and distance from obstacles for immediate flight path control, obstacle avoidance, and navigation. In low visibility, the spatial and temporal resolution of visual cues are reduced (Lees, Kimball, Hoffmann, & Stone, 1976), thus visual workload is increased. Pilots generally fly slower, higher, and with less-extreme maneuvers. Helicopter pilots too must rely on cockpit displays. Although this is possible at altitudes safely above the terrain, pilots need additional information about the immediate environment at low altitudes. Currently, this is provided by light-intensifying goggles and panel- or helmet-mounted displays of infrared imagery at night.

Considerable information is available about how helicopters respond to control inputs. Relatively less information is available about how humans respond to perceptual cues from a direct view of the visual scene, computer-generated displays, or video images. However, since the early work conducted by Bell Aircraft Corporation (1956), considerable effort has been devoted to determining how pilots use changes in perspective, optic flow, motion parallax, stereopsis, occlusion, and texture gradients and intensities to estimate distance, rate, and orientation (Haber, 1982; Regan, 1982; Richards & Dismukes, 1982; Stevens, 1982) and how to encode this information on computer-generated displays. Ideally, it should be integrated with (or replace) video displays to provide a three-dimensional spatial representation of the environment that conforms to pilot's perceptual and cognitive expectations and natural processing mechanisms and can be viewed "head up" to reduce visual transitions in and outside of the cockpit.

Basic Visual Information Requirements. When pilots fly several feet above the terrain, they must estimate continuously and accurately their position relative to the immediate environment and to terrain features that are beyond their direct field of view. They need to know about the shape and identity of terrain features and the relative speed, orientation, and altitude of their vehicle (Stevens, 1982). They may mentally project a path through the environment for their vehicle to follow, remembering where they have been and projecting ahead where they will be going using available visual information to form a "flight plan" for immediate flight path control, periodically relating what they see to a hand-held or computer-generated map to perform global navigation.

Vision is more than a direct translation of incoming sensory data. Recognition and interpretation of incoming sensory information requires transformation and integration of retinal images based on expectations, information processing, previous experience, and knowledge of the current situation. Researchers disagree about the degree to which visual perception is constructive (Richards & Dismukes, 1982; Stevens, 1982). However, it is clear that information about the characteristics of individual retinal processes can shed little light on the integrative aspects of perception and pilot's visual information processing.

Objects may be identified by their appearance, independent of their apparent size or orientation. Pilots use both dynamic cues (e.g., motion parallax, optic flow, and occlusion) and static cues (e.g., shading, texture gradients, perspective transformations, color and luminance contrasts, and surface contours) to identify objects and terrain features (Stevens, 1982). While the information available with direct vision in good visibility is adequate, the limited information provided by night vision systems often is not. Static cues are limited by poor resolution and reduced illumination. Dynamic cues are limited by limited fields of view and poor resolution.

Height above terrain may be inferred indirectly (by the known size of recognizable objects), by stereopsis, or by the angular velocity of terrain features (Stevens, 1982). Since the size of objects on the retina generally varies inversely with their distance, pilots can estimate range and height above ground from the apparent size of objects in the environment. Stereoscopic vision can provide useful depth cues; however, it is most effective for objects within 30 feet of the observer (Stevens, 1982). Thus, stereoscopic vision is much more useful for helicopter pilots (who fly close to the terrain) than for fixed-wing pilots. Pilots experienced in low-altitude flight can learn to relate the angular velocity of objects moving past their vehicle to their speed and relative altitude; as altitude is decreased, the perception of speed across the ground is increased (Stevens, 1982). Pilots also estimate their direction, rate of self-motion, and the orientation of their vehicle from optic flow patterns (Regan, 1982). *Optic flow* is a term used to describe the streaming of visual detail radially away from the point one is approaching (Gibson, 1950).

Visual Workload during Terrain Flight. During NOE flight, pilots devote most of their attention to the task of immediate flight control and guidance, moving opportunistically between and around obstacles. They spend as much as 80% of the time looking outside (Simmons & Blackwell, 1980). Thus, they have limited opportunities to scan cockpit instruments, navigate, or work radios. In military helicopters, these duties are performed by a copilot–navigator, who must remain spatially oriented at all times, visualizing how the terrain should appear from a map and correlating this information with momentarily viewed terrain features. This is difficult, as maps provide limited resolution (e.g., a 50,000:1 scale) and little information about cultural features. Copilots must plan ahead (to tell pilots the route and airspeed to be flown), work the radios, and monitor cockpit instruments. Navigation, map interpretation, and terrain analysis can require 90% of a copilot's visual attention, and communicating about navigation may occupy 25% of the crew's time. In single-pilot operations, pilots must divide their attention between the visual scene outside (62%) and inside the cockpit (21%), losing valuable time transitioning and experiencing high workload (Cote, Krueger, & Simmons, 1983; Sanders, Simmons, & Hoffman, 1979).

Spatial Disorientation

Since pilots continually change orientation, global navigation imposes an additional demanding task in addition to the requirement to avoid colliding with the immediate environment. The process of spatial *cognition* (as compared to spatial *perception*) requires attention and effort. Thus, issues of sensory and information processing capacity and resource availability, important theoretical issues in cognitive psychology, are relevant. Regarded from this perspective, the displays meant to improve spatial cognition must reduce the need for time-consuming mental transformations and integration. Unfortunately, the majority of research in attention and spatial cognition has been performed in the context-free environment of the laboratory, and its relevance to the complex, redundant, constantly changing real-world environment is not clear.

Spatial disorientation is a critical problem in helicopter operations.

An analysis of Army aviation accidents between 1967 and 1971 (Smith & McCants, 1978) indicated that most helicopter accidents occurred because pilots lost orientation with respect to geographical location and height above terrain or inadvertently penetrated into instrument flight conditions. Spatial disorientation occurs because there is a mismatch between the cues provided by the visual and vestibular systems or because visual references are lost. For this reason, pilots must learn to rely on what their instruments tell them. This may present a problem at low altitudes, where instruments do not convey all of the essential information. Nevertheless, less than 2% of the Army accidents surveyed (Smith & McCants, 1978) involved instrument-rated pilots flying with instrument flight plans. For this reason, since 1972 all Army aviators have been required to complete instrument flight training. Since then, the accidents attributed to inadvertent penetration into instrument conditions have decreased from 25% to 7%. Nevertheless, the overall number of accidents attributed to spatial disorientation is still high among two-person crews, and it is likely that it will increase in single-pilot operations.

Obstacle Avoidance. Flying into natural and man-made obstacles poses a particular danger for helicopters. Wires, cables, and power poles are a particular threat. They are hard to detect with the unaided human eye and are virtually invisible with pilot night vision systems because they present a small visual target, yet may extend over a considerable distance. For example, one power line accounted for 55 helicopter fatalities in Vietnam between 1965 and 1971 (Marsh, 1985); it was the only power line in South Vietnam! In the United States, 208 civil wire-strike accidents that occurred between 1970 and 1979 were surveyed in a study conducted for NASA (Human Resources Research Organization, 1980). Most of them occurred in good visibility (95% of the accidents) where wires were known to exist. In all but 10% of the civil accidents, human factors were cited as a cause—failure to see and avoid the obstacles, errors in judgment, and inadequate procedures. In most wire-strike accidents, pilots never see the hazard. Even if they know the approximate location of a wire, they may still fail to see it in time to avoid it, and maneuvering to avoid one wire can result in flying into adjacent wires (Flightfax, 1986). Fatigue, stress, high workload, and poor visibility increase the probability of wire strikes. Lack of vigilance and complacency can contribute as well.

Wire strikes are likely to increase as helicopter missions at night and in poor visibility become routine, particularly for single-pilot operations (where there is one less pair of eyes in the cockpit). Here, sensors that provide reliable information early enough for pilots to avoid a hazard will be essential. Although sensors are being developed to help pilots detect and avoid wires, it is unlikely that they will be installed in military and civil helicopters until low-cost and lightweight systems are available. Until they are, pilots must be trained to avoid total concentration on the mission (in order to look for wires) and to avoid locations where wires are likely to reduce the frequency of wire-strike accidents.

Visual Workload during Hover. Hovering is generally performed with visual reference to objects in the environment. Since pilots cannot see the reference point over which they are hovering (it is immediately below them), they must detect lateral, longitudinal, and vertical movement relative to objects to the front or side. The greater their distance from these objects, the poorer the relative motion cues are until they fall below pilots' detection thresholds (Haber, 1982). In addition, different types of motions provide misleading or ambiguous cues: pitch down or movement toward an object may provide visual motion cues that are similar to a slight decrease in altitude, and a slight yaw can be mistaken for a lateral movement.

In poor visibility or over featureless terrain (e.g., water, sand, or grass), there are no surface textures or terrain features to provide visual references. Here, the task of hovering over a precise location becomes virtually impossible without additional aiding. As early as 1960, Bell Helicopter Company (1961a,b) began investigating cockpit displays that portrayed the visual information required to perform a hover, encoded into a grid pattern with an altitude "thermometer" that was presented on panel- or helmet-mounted displays. Currently, many helicopters are being equipped with additional sensors and advanced displays to facilitate the demanding perceptual and motor requirements imposed by achieving and maintaining a precise hover position.

Head-up and Head-down Transitions. In low-level flight or hovering, the time required to transition between head up (out the window) and head down (in the cockpit) may be critical. Transition durations reflect the time required for a physical movement of the pilot's eyes and head, and a change in visual accommodation, light or dark adaptation, and reorienting to the format, structure, and point of view of a new information source. One estimate of the minimum time required to transition between information presented head up and head down was 700 msec (Menu, 1986). At speeds typical of NOE flight, this time might represent a distance of 50 feet when a pilot would be unable to respond to information from either source. For this reason, flight control information is provided on helmet-mounted displays (and is being considered for night vision goggles), to allow pilots to remain head up in low-level maneuvers.

Advanced Technology Solutions

Civil and military requirements for improved helicopter capabilities, coupled with the Army's goal of single-pilot operations, have prompted a tremendous increase in research and development by the government, industry, and academia. It has become clear that single-pilot operations will be impossible unless pilots are relieved of some routine tasks (e.g., continuous manual control and monitoring) and provided assistance with others (e.g., navigation). For example, Haworth, Bivens, and Shively (1986) found that significant levels of automation (e.g., stability and control augmentation, heading, speed, and altitude hold and turn coordination) were required to achieve acceptable handling-qualities ratings in simulated military NOE operations for a single pilot. To allow a single pilot to manage this proliferation of automated subsystems, they must be properly integrated and "intelligent." Flight management systems have only recently become available for civil (Underwood, 1985) or military (Gallagher, 1986) helicopters, long after they were standard equipment for fixed-wing aircraft. These systems integrate information about optimum performance characteristics with navigation and avionics management to provide a total flight profile, but they are costly and complex and do not reduce pilot workload as much as their fixed-wing counterparts do. Fully coupled autopilots have not been developed for helicopters, although they are common in fixed-wing aircraft.

Pilot–vehicle interfaces can be improved by enhancing vehicle handling qualities and modifying vehicle control designs, simplifying and organizing information displays, and providing pilot aids and automation. With the advent of fly-by-wire and fly-by-light systems, designers now have the flexibility to consider pilot-oriented design criteria without the constraints imposed by mechanical control systems (Aiken, 1985). The availability of electronic displays has prompted a radical change in cockpit display designs, with the goal of providing only the information necessary for a particular flight task.

In some cases, existing helicopter designs have been upgraded with advanced avionics and displays to avoid the lengthy and costly process of designing an entirely new vehicle. For example, the Army helicopter improvement program (AHIP) was undertaken to apply state-of-the-art technology to the observation and scout missions flown by the OH-58D (e.g., control augmentation, airborne target hand-offs, multifunction displays, and updated displays and controls). However, the primary human factors improvements were provided for the observer (Mastroianni, 1986). In addition, new helicopters are being developed to replace outdated vehicles. The design of these next-generation helicopters must be pilot oriented and tailored for the missions that will be flown. Simplification, integration, control augmentation, and automation of crew functions will be emphasized to allow single-pilot operations. Many of the proposed features have been implemented in fixed-wing aircraft already (e.g., multifunction displays, integrated caution and warning systems, automated flight path guidance); however, these designs may not transfer directly to helicopters.

Initial research focused on augmenting and automating inner-loop control tasks. Recently, the focus has moved toward outer-loop, higher-order tasks to include mission planning and tactical maneuvering in addition to immediate flight path control aiding. This will require more detailed environmental data than is available and on-board computers that can integrate and interpret the data. Some automation is already available for helicopters operating in the civil air traffic control system, but it will be much more difficult to provide similar capabilities for the NOE environment. Completely automated helicopters are still a distant prospect, due to the unpredictable and opportunistic nature of the missions flown and the basic vehicle characteristics.

Control Stabilization and Augmentation

The most basic form of helicopter automation is stability and control augmentation. By programming the desired equations of motion into a flight computer, a model can respond to a pilot's commands to provide appropriate stabilization, quickening, damping, coordination, or trim in any axis, using information from various sensors. The control laws may change as flight conditions or tasks require (Prouty, 1986b). Such systems have been developed and tested in simulators (e.g., the vertical motion simulator at NASA-Ames Research Center) and in flight in variable-stability aircraft (e.g., NASA's CH-47 Chinook). The ability to stabilize a helicopter in an established trim condition is essential. For high-speed flight, turn coordination and

speed, altitude, and attitude hold are necessary to allow pilots to perform other duties. For low-speed flight, sensors are required to detect
small deviations in speed, position, heading, and altitude to provide
a stabilized hover without continuous pilot inputs (Prouty, 1986b).
In the longitudinal axis, attitude-command–inertial-velocity stabilization systems have been developed for low-speed operations and attitude-command–airspeed stabilization for high-speed operations. For
directional control, heading hold for low-speed flight and turn coordination in forward flight are most useful. Finally, both vertical-
velocity-command and altitude-hold systems have improved handling qualities in the vertical axis in a simulator (Aiken et al., 1984).
To achieve desirable handling qualities, the appropriate control laws
must be automatically phased in during the transition from high-
speed forward flight to low-speed or hover maneuvers and vice versa. Control augmentation is essential in low-visibility, NOE operations conducted with helmet-mounted displays (Aiken et al., 1984;
Landis & Aiken, 1982).

Advanced Controls

Replacing conventional controls with integrated side-stick controls,
possible with fly-by-wire and fly-by-light systems, liberates a designer from having to make the best of the fundamentally poor human
factors situation presented by conventional controls (Marsh, 1985).
The first in-flight investigation of side-stick controls began in 1957,
and their feasibility was demonstrated for fixed-wing aircraft (Hall &
Smith, 1975). Side-stick control research for helicopters began in
1968 in a modified CH-47 Chinook using a four-axis, displacement
controller. Numerous designs have been investigated in simulators
and in flight (Aiken, 1985; Harvey, 1986; Padfield, Tomlinson, &
Wells, 1978).

Side-stick controls are mounted on the armrest of a pilot's seat.
The handgrip design must assist pilots in identifying the controlled
axis (to limit inadvertent inputs into other axes) and allow a constant
hand position (Aiken, 1985). The location and orientation of the control and arm support affect pilots' abilities to make smooth inputs
with minimal cross-coupling. It may be necessary to provide asym-
metrical control sensitivities for different axes to compensate for the
imbalance in force that pilots can apply in different directions, given
the orientation of their hand with respect to the control (e.g., it is
easier to provide upward than downward force and counterclockwise
torque than clockwise with the right hand; Aiken, 1985).

A fully integrated controller is one in which all primary control functions are combined on a single device. With separated controllers, control functions may be assigned to two side-stick controllers or to one side-stick controller in combination with a conventional collective lever and directional pedals. Figure 18.5 represents some of the configurations that have been tested. Roll is generally accomplished by lateral movement of the control and pitch by fore and aft movement. Yaw has been implemented in several ways: rotation of the grip on a multiaxis controller, movement of a thumb lever, or with directional pedals. Vertical control is effected by moving an integrated controller vertically or with the collective lever (Aiken, 1985).

Side-stick controllers may reduce the physical forces and displacements required to input commands, allowing pilots to assume a more comfortable posture, and they provide the opportunity for a significant redesign of the cockpit. The number of axes to integrate into a single controller is still controversial. The European view is that a two-axis controller (replacing the cyclic) is the best approach for the immediate future (Marsh, 1985; Padfield, Tomlinson, & Wells, 1978). In the United States, considerable effort has been focused on integrating pitch, roll, yaw, and vertical control into one controller. However, four-axis controllers require high levels of stability and control augmentation to achieve good performance and acceptable

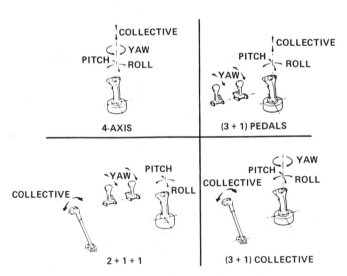

Figure 18.5. Examples of helicopter controller configurations. (From Aiken, 1985.)

handling qualities (Landis et al., 1983) and are subject to significant cross-coupling problems (e.g., control movements in one axis also induce movement in another). At the present time, it appears that one side-stick controller coupled with conventional collective lever and directional pedals is the preferred configuration.

Whether or not the control stick must actually move in response to pilot input has not been resolved. With a displacement controller, there is a direct relationship between force applied and control displacement and between control position and the amount of change commanded. With a force control device, the pressure applied by the pilot is sensed by strain gauges without physical displacement of the stick. The primary disadvantage of force controllers is that they do not provide explicit feedback about the amount and direction of pilot inputs (Marsh, 1985). Pilots estimate this information from the amount of force applied, the (delayed) information displayed on cockpit instruments, or the sensation of aircraft movement, increasing the likelihood of cross-coupling, overcontrol, and pilot-induced oscillation. Landis and Aiken (1982) and others have found that limited deflections yield a significant improvement in performance and subjective handling qualities, allow finer control movements, and reduce overcontrol and cross-coupling. Thus, limited displacement designs are preferable to zero-displacement force controllers.

Advanced Cockpit Displays

Not only are existing displays and instruments inadequate for pilots to accomplish the increasing demands placed on them, but cockpits have become unacceptably cluttered and complex with the addition of new instruments. At the same time that cockpits seem to have reached a saturation point, more data and functions are being added, more demanding missions proposed, and single-pilot operations are being considered.

Despite the seemingly endless amount of information that will be provided in the cockpits of advanced helicopters, pilots basically need a forward-looking and a downward-looking presentation of the current and desired position, vehicle orientation (pitch, roll, and yaw), and rate and acceleration in the vertical, longitudinal, and lateral axes (Roscoe, 1983). Other information (e.g., terrain, other aircraft, weather, planned flight path, vehicle state, and limits) also might be superimposed on one or both displays. In addition, military pilots need to know about threats that are behind them as well as ahead. Simply regrouping instruments or integrating additional information into existing displays, typical solutions that worked in the past, are no longer sufficient.

The basic problem is how to present this information unambiguously on a limited number of two-dimensional displays. Highly innovative ideas for orientation, flight control, and navigation displays were developed 30 years ago under the auspices of the Army–Navy Instrumentation Program (ANIP) and the Joint Army–Navy Aircraft Instrumentation Research (JANAIR) Program (see Roscoe, 1983, for a review). Although many of the ideas were impractical at the time, they have become possible with the advent of low-cost, lightweight sensors and computational and display technologies. It is interesting to note how similar the concepts developed 30 years ago are to those now proposed for the LHX.

The number of individual displays in advanced cockpit designs are significantly reduced in comparison to the number of instruments and displays in current helicopters. The display options generally include panel-mounted, multifunction, and dedicated electronic displays that present integrated, simplified information graphically. Helmet-mounted or panel-mounted head-up displays are superimposed on day, light-intensified, or infrared video images. Synthesized voice messages and visual or auditory warnings present additional information.

Many panel-mounted display designs include color. Although it is difficult to find experimental evidence for the advantage of color displays, pilots prefer them overwhelmingly (Reising & Aretz, 1983). Since displays of medium complexity generally include other codes to identify information (e.g., shape, size, texture), the performance improvement provided by color alone is quite small. However, pilot opinion might carry more weight than objective performance results in determining whether or not color displays are provided.

Multifunction Displays.   Multifunction displays replace the dozens of single-purpose instruments typical in current cockpits. Each display is capable of presenting any one of several types of information (e.g., navigation, communication) and different versions of each one appropriate for a particular task (e.g., hover, forward flight) at the pilot's request. One generally presents a vertical version of the situation and the other a horizontal version. Most multifunction displays are surrounded by pilot-selectable buttons that represent different functions depending on the current screen of information. Alternatively, display options might be selected from a menu presented on the display. The number of alternatives should be limited (so pilots can use positional cues to select entries), and the number of entries required to find a particular display must be limited as well (Drennan & Bowen, 1984). Maintaining consistent locations for display options (particularly for critical functions) can improve selection times.

Although the trade-off between depth (levels in the hierarchy of display options) and breadth (options available at any time) has been studied for computer workstations, menu design and balance between breadth and depth appropriate for cockpit displays (that provide dynamic as well as static information) have received little scientific attention. In general, as depth is increased, the likelihood of "getting lost" and the number of selections required to retrieve information are increased. While reducing display breadth can create crowding, increasing breadth can result in unnecessary presentation of inappropriate information (Paap & Roske-Hofstrand, 1986).

Multifunction displays are flexible, can present integrated information appropriate for the current situation, and can reduce clutter, weight, and cost. However, they can only present one "screen" of information at a time. Frequent pilot interactions may be required to modify current formats, request different displays, or "hunt" for information, thereby increasing pilot workload and delaying acquisition of critical information. Thus, the clutter and information overload created by numerous single-purpose displays might be replaced by problems created by the unavailability of information.

Pilot Interface with Multifunction Displays. Several ways of selecting among display options have been proposed: keyboards, touch-sensitive overlays superimposed on computer-generated labels, control switches mounted on the cyclic or collective, or spoken commands entered via voice recognition systems (Huff, 1984; Richardson, 1982; Wiener, 1984). Dedicated buttons are not feasible, as options change for each display. Keyboards are flexible and easy to implement, but difficult to use in a darkened cockpit by pilots wearing gloves. Touch-sensitive screen overlays also provide flexibility, but they too require pilots to remove one hand from the controls. Since both hands may be required to maintain flight path control, both alternatives are suboptimal. In addition, they require accurate hand–eye coordination, a difficult task in turbulence. Moving a cursor on the screen by a "coolie-hat" switch mounted on one of the control columns allows pilots to keep their hands on the controls, but may require considerable attention to position the cursor on the desired location.

Computer-recognized voiced commands have been proposed as a method of interacting with displays (Coler, 1982; Walters, 1985). Spoken commands do not require use of the pilots' hands and provide faster and more accurate input than keyboard entry (Coler, 1982; Simpson, Coler, & Huff, 1982). The results of simulation and in-flight experiments (Coler, 1982; Simpson et al., 1982) suggest that voiced commands are less disruptive to control activities than keyboard entries and that accuracy levels of 97% or better can be obtained in simulated noise and vibration levels typical of a scout helicopter in forward flight. In flight, recognition accuracies of 95% or better were obtained for mission segments selected to be particularly troublesome for a voice recognition system in a Bell Long-Ranger (e.g., sustained hover). In the NASA SH-3G helicopter, equally good recognition accuracies were found with cockpit noise levels ranging from 102 to 106 dBA, although accuracy declined from 100% to 93% as the vocabulary was increased from 10 to 36 commands. It was suggested that using a command syntax to divide the vocabulary into subsets could have achieved a consistently high level of recognition accuracy (Coler, 1984).

Although vocal commands reduce pilots' visual and manual workload, recognition accuracy is still not sufficiently reliable to make this alternative as attractive as it might be otherwise. Unrecognized or misrecognized commands not only delay the display of needed information or entry of a control input but also are frustrating for the pilots. Voice recognition accuracy is reduced by a large vocabulary, cockpit noise and vibration, and high workload or stress (Coler, 1984; Gregoire & Biers, 1983). Since voiced commands are generally faster and less distracting for the pilot, it is likely that they will become common in advanced helicopter cockpits. However, speech recognition systems must never be the only means provided to select critical functions, and they must be implemented intelligently. Not all types of entries are performed equally well by this method, and voice entry may compete with voiced radio communications for the pilot's limited speech capabilities (Vidulich, 1988).

Horizontal Situation Displays.   Immediate and global navigation impose significant demands on two-person crews. Thus, computer aiding and improved displays will be needed to achieve acceptable levels of workload in single-pilot operations. Digitized moving-map displays that show topography with superimposed navigation, tactical, and flight path data can simplify the task of maintaining geographical orientation. The displays can represent either a projected image or a digitized display of information from on-board Doppler or inertial navigation systems or the global positioning system.

Early versions required military pilots to use hand-held maps for NOE (to obtain detailed and precise position information) but assisted with straightline navigation and allowed pilots to check their position without unmasking (Cote et al., 1981). Even advanced display designs still require pilots to relate two-dimensional display representations to corresponding natural and cultural terrain features. Panel-mounted map displays can depict the global situation, including information beyond the pilot's direct line of sight and the positions of other aircraft that are behind, beside, or in front of the pilot's own vehicle. However, greater detail and more precise positioning than is now possible will be required to perform immediate flight path control and terrain avoidance with panel-mounted digital map displays for NOE flight in low visibility. Since display symbologies may bear no physical resemblance to the objects they represent, they must be memorized and interpreted. In addition, current designs are unacceptably cluttered (especially given their small size) and do not provide pilots with adequate control over scale, detail, and content. Thus, interpreting the information, relating it to the immediate environment, and planning ahead will continue to require considerable pilot attention and mental effort.

Vertical Situation Displays. Low-level terrain flight requires a continuous, immediate visual representation of the external scene. Although the view out the window can provide the best "vertical situation display," visibility is not always adequate. Thus, visual aids, such as night vision goggles (NVG) that intensify available light, or forward-looking infrared (FLIR) systems that detect thermal energy (Tucker, 1984), are required when visibility is limited. Although the hardware has been developed to provide such visual augmentation, relatively little research has been devoted to the perceptual and cognitive problems it creates for pilots. All present night vision systems are characterized by reduced fields of view and degraded resolution. They are uncomfortable to wear and produce significant visual and physical fatigue.

Night Vision Goggles. NVGs were developed in the early 1970s for ground vehicle operators and were later adapted for aviation. They provide a monochromatic image of the scene by intensifying available light to provide an image that is visible to the human eye. Their effectiveness is related to ambient illumination; at least a quarter moon is required for older models, although current models are effective in overcast starlight (Tucker, 1984). Areas with low visual contrast are difficult to discriminate and, if ambient light goes below the goggle's threshold, the pilot sees "sparkles." Conversely, very bright light sources (such as unfiltered cockpit warning lights) automatically reduce their gain, limiting overall scene definition. This automatic adjustment is necessary to reduce the risk of "blooming" or "whiteouts" caused by extremely bright lights. However, such automatic adjustments can reduce display gain to the point that pilots lose all external visual flying references. Dimming cockpit lights simply increases the relative amount of radiation in the infrared region (to which NVGs are most sensitive) and makes the instruments unreadable with the unaided eye. Several solutions, such as ultraviolet cockpit lighting or absorption or interference filters placed on the surface of the instruments, are becoming available to provide NVG-compatible cockpits (Beaver, 1986).

At best, visual acuity with NVGs is half as good as with the unaided eye, and their field of view is 40° (Tucker, 1984). Because their resolution is relatively poor, tasks that require the precise use of visual cues are performed more poorly, maneuvering capabilities are limited, and pilot workload is increased. Furthermore, distant objects appear to be smaller and farther away (even though NVGs provide a 1:1 magnification), causing pilots to overshoot approaches and terminate approaches in a high hover. This problem is moderated through experience. Generally, NVGs are focused to optical infinity and must be refocused or removed to view cockpit instruments, increasing transition times.

Earlier versions developed for tank drivers were mounted on a face mask that prevented peripheral vision or instrument scan with unaided eyes. However, the aviator night vision imaging system (ANVIS), which is designed for pilots (Figure 18.6), is positioned several inches away from pilots' eyes (so they can look at instruments beneath the goggles), and the material around the goggles is cut away to allow peripheral vision (Underwood, 1986).

Pilot Night Vision System (PNVS). Infrared sensors mounted on the nose of helicopters provide a monochromatic video image of the outside scene (Underwood, 1986) constructed from differences in the temperatures of objects in the environment. The system may be used at night when ambient light levels are low or during the day to "see" through blowing dust, smog, smoke, or concealing foliage. Movement of the FLIR sensor is either slaved to motion of the pilot's helmet or

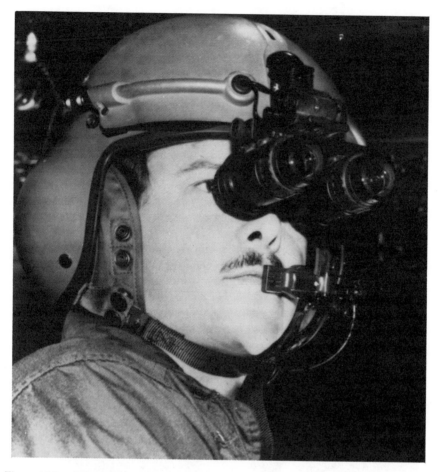

Figure 18.6.   Aviator night vision imaging system (ANVIS) goggles—AN/AV S-6.
(From Tucker, 1984.)

controlled manually with a coolie-hat switch on the collective control. In some versions, a two-dimensional video image is presented
on a panel-mounted display. With helmet-mounted systems, a combiner glass is attached to the pilot's helmet immediately in front of
the pilot's right eye so the image provided by the tiny (1.92 cm) CRT
fills the visual field of that eye (Figure 18.7). The system in the
Apache AH-64 provides a 30 × 40° field of view that pilots can
move through ±90° horizontally and from + 20 to − 45° vertically.
The narrow field of view eliminates critical peripheral information.

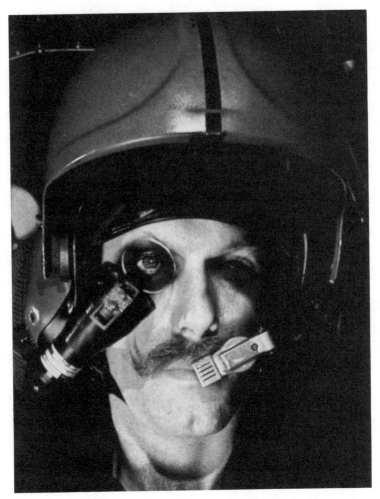

Figure 18.7.   Helmet-mounted monocle for forward-looking infrared
            (FLIR)-driven pilot night vision system (PNVS). (From
            Tucker, 1984.)

The sensor detects thermal differences, thus, objects look different
than they do with the unaided eye, brightness does not provide accurate range information, and objects may disappear temporarily when
their temperature nears that of the surrounding terrain. The flow of
visual information between the outside scene and the pilot's eye is
limited by the resolution of the sensor and the display. Contrast adjustment is provided with 10 gray shades. Pilots may assign either

light or dark values to "hot" objects in the environment. Depending on the circumstances, they may alternate between the two polarities to select the one that provides the clearest image.

The sensor is mounted 3.5 m in front and 1.2 m below the pilot's eye position (in the Apache). Thus, pilots may underestimate their range and altitude with respect to objects viewed through the sensor. For example, objects abeam of the sensor (that are no longer visible on the monocle) might not have passed the pilot's usual reference point (the eyes). Since the sensor is located closer to the ground, visual motion cues indicate higher apparent velocities than if the scene was viewed with unaided eyes. The problems associated with "off-axis" tracking (looking in a different direction than the vehicle is moving) are intensified by limited peripheral cues. Finally, pilots must learn to relate the effects of their control inputs to changes in the movement of the helicopter itself, rather than to changes in visual information that occur as a result of helmet-movement-induced changes in sensor orientation.

Because information is presented monocularly, some depth cues are lost. In addition, although the monocle limits peripheral vision on the right side, a full monocular field of view is still available to the unaided left eye (although visible cues may be limited on a dark night). This creates competition between the images presented in the two eyes (binocular rivalry). Since the information obtained from the unaided eye may be essential for maintaining spatial orientation, pilots must learn to mentally shift their focus of attention between the images in their right and left eyes. This is difficult to learn and both cognitively demanding and visually fatiguing. Binocular systems have been proposed, but the technical problems associated with fusing information from two sensors to provide a natural binocular image have not been solved. Alternatively, the same image could be presented on two monocles or projected on a helmet visor—a biocular display. While this would reduce the problem of binocular rivalry, it would not provide a stereoscopic image, and it would limit a pilot's ability to gain peripheral cues outside the cockpit, see instruments inside the cockpit, and maintain at least one dark-adapted eye.

Both NVGs and the PNVS do what they are intended to do. They allow NOE flight at night and under low-visibility conditions, but at a considerable cost to the pilots. Fatigue, especially visual fatigue, is a particularly severe problem. The PNVS apparatus is even heavier (4 lb) than NVGs, most of the weight is in front, and counterbalancing weights do not eliminate muscle fatigue induced by maintaining head-up attention to the visual scene. To reduce the problems associated with involuntary head motion within the helmet, a snug fit is essential, further increasing discomfort. Even though critical human factors problems with night vision systems have been identified, relatively little research is being conducted.

Superimposed Symbology.   Various methods of superimposing computer-generated symbology on the visual scene have been proposed to reduce the requirement for pilots to look at cockpit instruments during low-level flight. Head-up displays (HUD) provide significant information about helicopter status, oriented in a forward-looking direction. A HUD may be superimposed on the outside scene (by a combining lens mounted on the windscreen) or on a panel- or helmet-mounted video display. In 1960, Bell Helicopter Company (1961b) developed the first helmet-mounted HUD. It presented a two-dimensional perspective display composed of grid lines converging on a horizon, with altitude encoded in a vertical bar to provide a natural transition between visual and instrument flight. It was first flown in an H-13 helicopter in the early 1960s.

In several current military helicopters, HUD symbology is superimposed on helmet-mounted FLIR images to provide critical information for flight path control. For example, up to 14 flight parameters may be displayed on the HUD in the Apache AH-64 (see Figure 18.8). Slightly different information is presented for different mission segments. The symbology allows pilots to receive information necessary for flight control, navigation, and weapons delivery regardless of where they are looking. The Army is currently testing a system that would provide superimposed symbology on NVGs. It will provide simplified flight control information to reduce the pilot's need to monitor cockpit instruments.

Although such information is extremely useful, particularly in NOE flight when pilots are too busy to look at cockpit instruments, perceptual problems may be created by interference between computer-generated information displays (oriented in the direction the vehicle is moving) and the scene displayed behind them (oriented in the direction the pilot is looking). Furthermore, movement of the HUD symbols may induce perceptions of apparent motion in the video displays.

Target Acquisition–Designation Systems.   Weapons selection, aiming, and other targeting information also can be superimposed on a video display. The target acquisition–designation system (TADS) in the AH-64 provides day and night sensors, both boresighted to a

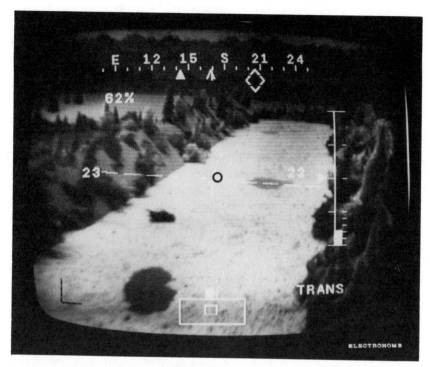

Figure 18.8. Head-up symbology superimposed on the pilot night vision system (PNVS) on the Apache AH-64 helicopter. (From Statler, 1984.)

common line of sight, a narrow and wide field of view, and an electronic "zoom" capability. In the current configuration, TADS is intended for the use by the copilot–gunner. However, in single-pilot operations, one person would be required to use a PNVS-type of display (for primary vehicle control) and a TADS-type of display (for weapons delivery). Here, a pilot might need to look in one direction to maintain vehicle control and in another to track, acquire, and fire at enemy targets.

Additional Alternatives.   Recent research on the perception of spatial orientation (Perrone, 1984) and visual motion detection has provided computer models of the cues presented by objects in the environment depicted as flow fields (Bailey & Barry, 1986; Watson & Ahumada, 1985). By determining the salient cues used by humans, improved cockpit displays and algorithms for a machine vision system, central to automating flight path control in the NOE environment, could be developed. Terrain-following and terrain-avoidance models already exist for high-performance jets flying contour; however, creating similar pathways and automated guidance information for NOE flight will be considerably more difficult. Furthermore, the opportunistic flight paths flown by helicopters do not lend themselves to preplanning and prestorage of optimal routes.

The idea of providing a "virtual" cockpit environment for the pilots of advanced helicopters and helicopter simulators is under development by the Air Force, Army, and NASA (Fisher, 1986; Furness, 1986; Underwood, 1986). On-board aircraft systems and sensors send information to a central computer that integrates it into a digitized summary of the current situation. A graphic generator uses the information to provide a panoramic image displayed binocularly to pilots through very high resolution CRTs projected in front of their eyes. At night, the computer-generated image might be all that pilots would see. During the day, it might become transparent so it could be overlayed on the visual scene outside of the cockpit. As pilots move their heads, the computer, sensing the movement, presents the correct field of view for that position. Binocular fields of view of 120° or more can be achieved. The display could present a stylized representation of the visual environment, depicting significant features in correct perspective and scale, with other information superimposed. These concepts have the advantage of providing integrated, interpreted information to the pilot. They have the potential for simplifying and enhancing the visual information pilots must monitor to conduct low-level, single-pilot missions in low visibility. Again, the limiting factor is the availability of accurate sensor and terrain information to provide sufficiently detailed displays and accurately locate the position of the helicopter.

Aural Displays

Due to the high visual demands imposed on pilots flying NOE, particularly in low visibility, it has been suggested that critical information might be presented by tones or speech messages (human, digitized, or synthesized). Digitized speech is produced by a human, recorded digitally, and transformed into a time-compressed format. Synthesized speech is generated by a computer, with speech characteristics determined by software. Currently, aural displays are used primarily to present caution and warning messages. Nonverbal aural warnings already exist in many aircraft, however the addition of verbal content might decrease response time and increase intelligibility.

This function will become particularly critical in single-pilot operations, when the pilot will be responsible for monitoring cockpit instruments and vehicle systems even when his or her attention is directed to the outside scene during NOE flight.

Auditory messages are likely to get a pilot's attention, unless they are masked by ambient noise levels. Because they are limited in duration, important information may be lost if messages are not understood the first time they occur. For this reason, redundant visual displays of critical messages are necessary. Prioritizing speech messages is also important, as only one can be presented at a time due to the limitations of the auditory perceptual channel (Remington & Wiener, 1984).

Synthesized speech is the most practical alternative, because messages can be stored efficiently and retrieved quickly. Although intelligibility remains a problem, synthesized speech warning messages can be understood as easily as digitized human speech once the pilots become familiar with the messages (Hartzell, Aiken, & Voorhees, 1984). A logical basis for voice warning priorities and redundant visual displays is important.

Synthetic voice messages are attention getting because the voice quality is different than human communications. However, synthetic and natural speech are processed differently; synthetic speech places greater demands on short-term memory and does not have the same redundancy as human speech. Furthermore, there is a greater decrement in intelligibility for synthesized messages presented in a noisy background (Crittenden, 1986). These problems may limit the utility of synthesized speech in the cockpit.

Concluding Remarks

Many issues that may be termed *human factors* influence pilots' abilities to accomplish different missions using available equipment. To the extent the demands of the mission or the environment exceed their capacities, or the controls and displays they must use are poorly designed, system performance will suffer, and pilots will experience unacceptable levels of workload. A concern that pilot workload levels will be unacceptably high in single-pilot operations has become a primary driver for the development of technology for the next generation of helicopters, such as the LHX (Banerjee, 1986). The requirement for a single pilot to accomplish primary flight path control, navigation, mission management, coordination, weapons delivery, and defense, at night, in all weather conditions in the NOE environment have necessitated the development of complex avionics, multifunction displays, fly-by-wire and fly-by-light systems coupled with side-stick controls, voice interactive systems, and rudimentary artificial intelligence concepts to ensure safe, effective operations. Even with such improvements, however, there is still a very real concern that the demands imposed on the pilots will still be excessive, limiting the capabilities of the system and compromising safety. Simulation research performed at Ames Research Center and the five manufacturers funded by the Army's Advanced Rotorcraft Technology Integration (ARTI) Program have demonstrated the feasibility of single-pilot operations. However, various stability and control augmentation systems, automated functions, advanced displays, and so on, have still not provided cockpit designs that a single pilot can fly with the same performance and workload as two-person crews can. Furthermore, it has become clear that all of the necessary systems will not be developed and tested in time to be incorporated into the initial designs of the next generation of helicopters.

In the civil sector, requirements for increased cost effectiveness and additional capabilities have prompted similar technology needs. For example, improved on-board and ground-based systems are required to allow landings at remote sites and airports under all weather conditions, and three- and four-dimensional area navigation systems are needed to reduce navigation and guidance demands. Integrated displays, controls, and caution and warning systems are required to simplify vehicle control and systems monitoring demands.

Improved stability and control are essential, particularly for civilian and military single-pilot operations. In addition, a substantial improvement in the sensitivity and accuracy of sensors at very low speeds and altitudes is essential for manual vehicle control in reduced visibility and for the application of computer aiding and artificial intelligence concepts in guidance and control. On-board systems must correlate the current position and vehicle state with stored data to provide near-field guidance around terrain features, long-term planning and navigation, and estimates of performance envelopes, given the current environment and vehicle parameters. Cockpit automation will allow the transfer of functions once performed by humans to intelligent subsystems. It is justified only if it results in an improvement in mission capability, however. Technical feasibility alone is not a sufficient justification. Functions that still must be performed by a pilot, such as reasoning, evaluation, judgment, decision making and information integration, might be candidates for automation as well, as they impose significant workload tasks; however, this is not yet technically feasible. Finally, automated prediction of the vehicle's capacity to meet anticipated mission demands would allow pilots to operate strategically rather than reactively.

Although considerable attention has been devoted to the development of technology solutions, relatively less attention has been devoted to the design of advanced technology solutions from the perspective of their human users. Because existing displays and controls are inadequate for pilots to accomplish the increasing demands that are being placed on them, and because cockpits have become unacceptably cluttered, revolutionary rather than evolutionary design concepts are being considered. The goal is to allow pilots to fly head up, eyes out, with one hand free for data entry and subsystem selection. To ensure that such designs enhance, rather than degrade, pilots' capabilities, considerable research is still required to define the role pilots should play, the optimal methods of transferring information to them and receiving control inputs from them, and to determine where computer aiding, automation, and "expert" systems can provide the most benefit. Human capabilities and limitations, rather than the availability of technology, must be the driving force behind advanced designs if human pilots are to accomplish the demands placed on them.

Acknowledgments

I would like thank James Hartzell, Edwin Aiken, George Tucker, Charles Billings, and Daniel Gopher for their careful reviews of the manuscript. In addition, I would like to thank Dora Strouther and Robert Wright for the information that they provided about early work in the field of helicopter human factors.

References

Adams, R. J., & King, L. D. (1980). Investigation of helicopters in public service: Requirements and contributions (NASA Contractor Report 166468). Washington, DC: National Aeronautics and Space Administration.

Aiken, E. W. (1982). Simulator investigations of various side-stick controller/stability and control augmentation systems for helicopter terrain flight. In Proceedings of the AIAA Guidance and Control Conference (AIAA Paper 82-1522). New York: Amer. Institute of Aeronautics and Astronautics.

Aiken, E. W. (1985). Effects of side-stick controllers on rotorcraft handling qualities for terrain flight (NASA TM 86688). Washington, DC: National Aeronautics and Space Administration.

Aiken, E. W., Hilbert, K. B., Landis, K. H., & Glusman, S. I. (1984). An investigation of side-stick controller/stability and control augmentation system requirements for helicopter terrain flight under reduced visibility conditions (AIAA Paper 84-0235). New York: American Institute of Aeronautics and Astronautics.

Bailey, D. R., & Barry, T. (1986). *PVI design for tactical decision maker* (USAF Contract F33615-84-C-3615). Dayton, OH: Tau Corporation.

Banerjee, D. (1986). Rotorcraft vibration specification.*Vertiflite*, 32(3), 63.

Beaver, P. (1986). Night vision compatibility. *Defense Helicopter World*, 5(4), 8–11.

Bell Aircraft Corporation. (1956). Ideal man–helicopter engineering program. *Proceedings of The Progress Report Conference* (Report Number D228-100-001). Ft. Worth, TX: Author.

Bell Helicopter Corporation. (1959). *Advances of helicopter/VTOL–STOL portion of army navy instrumentation program* (Report Number D228-100-002). Ft. Worth, TX: Author.

Bell Helicopter Company. (1961a). *A study of the effects of monocular vision on hovering performance* (Report Number D228-421-007). Ft. Worth, TX: Author.

Bell Helicopter Company. (1961b). *An evaluation of a grid encodement of the ground plane as a helicopter hovering display* (Report Number D228-421-008). Ft. Worth, TX: Author.

Boley, K. O. (1986). Error-free performance. *Flightfax*, 14(33), 1.

Coler, C. R. (1982, Sept–Oct). Helicopter speech-command systems: Recent noise tests are encouraging. *Speech Technology*, pp. 76–81.

Coler, C. R. (1984, Sept–Oct). Inflight testing of automatic speech recognition systems. In *Proceedings of Speech Tech 84* (pp. 95–98). New York: Media Dimensions, Inc.

Cote, D. O., Krueger, G. P., & Simmons, R. R. (1983). Helicopter copilot workload during nap-of-the-earth flight. In *Proceedings of the Second Symposium on Aviation Psychology* (pp. 289–298). Columbus: Ohio State University.

Cote, D. O., Simmons, R. R., & Krueger, G. P. (1981). Comparison of helicopter copilot workload while using three navigation systems during nap-of-the-earth flight. *Proceedings of the American Helicopter Society 37th Annual Forum* (pp. 152–162). Washington, DC: American Helicopter Society.

Crittenden, L. J. (1986). Some thoughts on the use of synthetic speech for cockpit warnings. *Human Factors Society Bulletin*, 29(9), 3–4.

Department of the Army. (1985). *Army aviation: General provisions and flight regulations* (Army Regulation 95-1). Washington, DC: Author.

Drennen, T. G., & Bowen, W. (1984). Integrated cockpit design for the AHIP. *Proceedings of the Technical Workshop: Advanced Helicopter Design Concepts* (NASA CP-2351). Washington, DC: National Aeronautics and Space Administration.

Fisher, S. S. (1986). Virtual interface environment. *Proceedings of the NASA Space Station Review*. Moffett Field, CA: NASA-Ames Research Center.

Flightfax (1986). ". . . something grabbed the helicopter." *Flightfax*, 14(25), 1.

Forbush, R. (1981, November). TERF is tough. *Approach*, pp. 18–22.

Furness, T. A. (1986). The super cockpit and its human factors challenges. *Proceedings of the Human Factors Society 10th Annual Meeting* (pp. 3, 48–52). Santa Monica, CA: Human Factors Society.

Gallagher, L. (1986). Mission management systems. *Defense Helicopter World*, 5(4), 34–38.

Garinther, G. R., & Hodge, D. G. (1981). *The background and bases for the proposed military standard on acoustical noise limits in helicopters* (TM 5-81). Aberdeen Proving Ground, MD: United States Army Human Engineering Laboratory.

Gibson, J. J. (1950). *Perception of the visual world.* Boston: Houghton-Mifflin.

Gregoire, H., & Biers, D. (1983). Voice recognition technology—Challenge of the 80s. In *Proceedings of the Second Symposium on Aviation Psychology* (pp. 37–44). Columbus: Ohio State University.

Griffin, K. R. (1985, Nov–Dec). Army's aviation life-support equipment takes a giant step. *Vertiflite,* pp. 54–57.

Griffin, M. J. (1977, March). The evaluation of human exposure to helicopter vibration. *Aeronautical Journal,* pp. 110–123.

Griffith, C. D. (1978, May). Helicopter flight controls. *Professional Pilot,* pp. 60–62.

Haber, R. N. (1982). Locomotion through visual space: Optic flow and peripheral vision. In W. Richards & K. Dismukes (Eds.), *Vision research for flight simulation* (pp. 72–81). Washington, DC: National Academy Press.

Hall, G. W., & Smith, R. (1975). *Flight investigation of fighter side-stick force deflection characteristics* (AFFDL-TR-75-39). Wright Patterson AFB, OH: Flight Dynamics Laboratory.

Hart, S. G., & Sheridan, T. S. (1984). Pilot workload, performance, and aircraft control automation. In *Human factors considerations in high-performance aircraft* (AGARD CP-371; pp. 18-1–18-12). Neuilly-sur-Seine, France: Advisory Group for Aerospace Research and Development.

Hartman, B. O., Storm, W. I., Vandervien, J. E., Hall, H. B., & Bollinger, R. R. (1974). Operational aspects of variations in alertness (AGARDograph No. 189). Neuilly sur Seine, FR: Advisory Group for Aerospace Research and Development.

Hartzell, E. J., Aiken, E. W., & Voorhees, J. W. (1984). Aircrew–aircraft integration issues in future Army helicopters. In *Human factors considerations in high-performance aircraft* (AGARD CP-371; pp. 20-1–20-15). Neuilly-sur-Seine, France: Advisory Group for Aerospace Research and Development.

Hartzell, E. J., Dunbar, S., Beveridge, R., & Cortilla, R. (1983). Helicopter pilot response latency as a function of the spatial arrangement of instruments and controls. *Proceedings of the Eighteenth Annual Conference on Manual Control* (AFWAL-TR-83-3021, pp. 345–364). Wright Patterson AFB, OH: Flight Dynamics Laboratory.

Harvey, D. (1986, May). ADOCS: Flying the light fantastic. *Rotor and Wing International,* pp. 44–46.

Haworth, L. A., Bivens, C. C., & Shively, R. J. (1986). An investigation of single-piloted advanced cockpit and control configurations for nap-of-the-earth helicopter combat mission tasks. *Proceedings of the 42nd National Forum of the American Helicopter Society,* (pp. 657–682). New York: American Helicopter Society.

Hodgkins, R. (1984, August). Heliports. Attempting to shed some more light in our series on heliport illumination, we turn to electroluminescence. *Rotor and Wing International,* pp. 23–25.

Huff, E. M. (1984). Helicopter human factors programs and plans. *Proceedings of the Technical Workshop: Advanced Helicopter Design Concepts* (NASA CP-2351). Washington DC: National Aeronautics and Space Administration.

Human Resources Research Organization (1980). *Prospectus for reduction of civil helicopter wire strike accidents.* Carmel, CA: Author.

Key, D. L., & Aiken, E. W. (1984). *Aircrew–aircraft integration: A summary of U.S. Army research programs and plans* (NASA TM-85991). Washington, DC: National Aeronautics and Space Administration.

Kocks, K. (1985, February). Heliports. Want heliport lighting with good visibility, high portability, long life, and no power requirement? Think tritium. *Rotor and Wing International,* pp. 28–32.

Landis, K. H., & Aiken, E. W. (1982). *An assessment of various side-stick controller/*

stability and control augmentation systems for night nap-of-the-earth flight using piloted simulation. Paper presented to the American Helicopter Society, Palo Alto, CA.

Landis, K. H., Dunford, P. J., Aiken, E. W., & Hilbert, K. B. (1983). A piloted simulator investigations of side-stick controller/stability and control augmentation system requirements for helicopter visual flight tasks. In *Proceedings of the 39th American Helicopter Society* (Paper A-83-39-54-4000). New York: American Helicopter Society.

Lees, M. A., Kimball, K. A., Hofmann, M. A., & Stone, L. S. (1976). *Aviator performance during the day and night terrain flight* (USAARL Report No. 77-3). Ft. Rucker, AL: U.S. Army Aeromedical Research Laboratory.

Lewis, R. B. (1985). Army VTOL research and development: The first century. *Vertiflite, 31,* 34–38.

Livingston, R. E. (1985). A federal perspective on helicopter development. *Vertiflite, 31,* 48–54.

Marsh, G. (1985, June–August). Avoiding the wires. *Defense Helicopter World* 22–23.

Mastroianni, G. (1986). Human factors aspects of the advanced scout helicopter. *The ITEA Journal of Test and Evaluation, 7*(2), 41–43.

Mayer, M. S., & Lindberg, A. W. (1978). A survey of communications in the high noise environment of Army aircraft. In *Proceedings of AGARD Workshop on Operational Helicopter Aviation Medicine* (pp. 46-1–46-19). Neuilly-sur-Seine, France: Advisory Group for Aerospace Research and Development.

Menu, J.-P. R. (1986, March). Head-up/head-down transition: Measurement of transition times. *Aviation, Space, and Environmental Medicine,* pp. 218–222.

Mozell, M. M., & White, D. C. (1958). Behavioral effects of whole body vibration. (NADC-MA-5802). Johnsville, PA: U.S. Naval Air Development Center.

Negrette, A. J. (1986, April). Safety. *Rotor and Wing International,* pp. 25–26.

Paap, K. R., & Roske-Hofstrand, R. J. (1986). The optimal number of menu options per panel. *Human Factors, 28*(4), 377–385.

Padfield, G. D., Tomlinson, B. N., & Wells, P. M. (1978). Simulation studies of helicopter agility and other topics (RAE Technical Memorandum). Farnborough, England: Royal Aircraft Establishment.

Perrone, J. A. (1984, November). Visual slant misconception and the 'black-hole' landing situation. *Aviation, Space, and Environmental Medicine,* pp. 1020–1025.

Prouty, R. W. (1986a, January). Aerodynamics. *Rotor and Wing International,* pp. 18–19.

Prouty, R. W. (1986b, February). Aerodynamics. *Rotor and Wing International,* pp. 21–24.

Regan, D. M. (1982). Visual sensory aspects of simulation. In W. Richards & K. Dismukes (Eds.), *Vision research for flight simulation* (pp. 65–71). Washington, DC: National Academy Press.

Reichert, G. (1981). Helicopter vibration control—A survey. *Vertica, 5,* 1–20.

Reising, J. M., & Aretz, A. J. (1983). Color coding in fighter cockpits: It isn't black and white. In *Proceeding of the Second Symposium on Aviation Psychology* (pp. 55–67). Columbus: Ohio State University.

Remington, R. W., & Wiener, E. L. (1984). Man–machine interface requirements—Advanced technology. *Proceedings of the Technical Workshop: Advanced Helicopter Design Concepts* (NASA CP-2351). Washington, DC: National Aeronautics and Space Administration.

Richards, W., & Dismukes, K. (Eds.). (1982). *Vision research for flight simulation.* Washington, DC: National Academy Press.

Richardson, C. S. (1982). The integrated cockpit and the HH-60D helicopter. In *IBM Technical Directions Summer of 1982* (pp. 22–33). Oswego, NY: IBM.

Roscoe, S. N. (1983). Computer-animated displays for vertical and translational flight. In *Proceedings of the Second Symposium on Aviation Psychology* (pp. 55–67). Columbus: Ohio State University.

Sanders, M. G., Simmons, R. R., & Hoffmann, M. A. (1979). Visual workload of the copilot/navigator during terrain flight. *Human Factors, 21*(3), 369–383.

Shawlee, W. (1985, July). Why helicopter avionics can lead you astray. *Rotor and Wing International*, pp. 34–37.

Simmons, R. R., & Blackwell, J. (1980, November). Down 'n dirty. *U.S. Army Aviation Digest*, pp. 38–40.

Simpson, C. A., Coler, C. R., & Huff, E. M. (1982). Human factors of voice I/O for aircraft cockpit controls and displays. *Proceedings of the Workshop on Standardization for Speech I/O Technology* (pp. 159–166). Gaithersburg, MD: National Bureau of Standards.

Smith, J. C., & McCants, O. L. (1978). The need for instrument training for army aviators. *U.S. Army Digest, 1*, 32–38.

Spencer, R. H. (1985). AHS technical committees: The year in review. *Vertiflite, 31*(3), 55.

Statler, I. C. (1984). Military pilot ergonomics. In *Human factors consideration in high performance aircraft* (AGARD CP-371; pp. 2-1–2-13). Neuilly-sur-Seine, France: Advisory Group for Aerospace Research and Development.

Stave, A. M. (1979). The influence of low frequency vibration on pilot performance (as measured in a fixed base simulator). *Ergonomics, 22*, 823–835.

Stevens, K. (1982). Computational analysis: Implications for visual simulation of terrain. In W. Richards & K. Dismukes (Eds.), *Vision research for flight simulation* (pp. 38–64). Washington, DC: National Academy Press.

Tucker, G. E. (1984). Some thoughts on the implementation of pilot night vision devices for helicopters. *Proceedings of the Technical Workshop: Advanced Helicopter Design Concepts* (NASA CP-2351). Washington, DC: National Aeronautics and Space Administration.

Underwood, D. (1985, January). Finally: A guide to helicopter flight management systems. *Rotor and Wing International*, pp. 26–27.

Underwood, D. (1986, May). Night vision goggles: How many can join the cats and owls. *Rotor and Wing International*, pp. 42–44.

Velger, M., Merhav, S., & Grunwald, A. (1986). Adaptive filtering of biodynamic stick feedthrough in manipulation tasks onboard moving platforms (AIAA Paper 86-2248CP). New York: Institute of Aeronautics and Astronautics.

Velger, M., & Merhav, S. (in press). Reduction of biodynamic interference effects in helmet-mounted sights and displays. In *Proceedings of the 22nd Annual Conference on Manual Control*. Dayton, OH.

Verdi, J. M., & Henderson, D. W. (1975, March). Helicopter vs. airplane. *Approach*, pp. 18–24.

Vidulich, M. A. (1988). The cognitive psychology of subjective mental workload. In P. A. Hancock & Meshkati (Eds.), *Human mental workload* (pp. 219–229) Amsterdam: North Holland.

Walters, B. (1985, June–Aug). Cockpit management a key to battlefield survival. *Defense Helicopter World.*

Warwick, G. (1985, November). For agile read active. *Flight International*, pp. 29–31.

Waters, K. T., & Domenic, R. E. (1980). *Advanced air data requirements—Improved helicopter man–machine interface in subsystem monitoring and switching*. Presentation at the 1980 Air Data Systems Conference, USAF Academy, Colorado.

Watson, A. B., & Ahumada, A. J. (1985). Model of human visual-motion sensing. *Journal of the Optical Society of America, 2*, 322–341.

Wells, M. J., & Griffin, M. J. (1984, January). Benefits of helmet-mounted display image stabilization under whole-body vibration. *Aviation, Space, and Environmental Medicine*, pp. 13–18.

Wiener, E. L. (1984). Human factors in cockpit automation. *Proceedings of the Technical Workshop: Advanced Helicopter Design Concepts* (NASA CP-2351). Washington, DC: National Aeronautics and Space Administration.

Winn, A. L., & Lewis, R. B. (1974). Pilot workload during instrument flight. *Proceedings of the 30th Annual National Forum of the American Helicopter Society* (A-74-30-11-2000). New York: American Helicopter Society.

Young, W. R. (1982). *The helicopters*. Alexandria, VA: Time–Life Books.

Air Traffic Control

19

V. David Hopkin

Introduction

Early in 1951, a famous report concerning human factors in air traffic control appeared (Fitts, 1951). It has become a classic according to the usual criteria, in that it had a major influence on subsequent events and has often been cited by people who have never read it. Among its contents were discussions of the following topics: the role of human beings in systems; the divisions of responsibility between humans and machines; decision making; the design and evaluation of visual information displays; the communication of information by voice; the gap between laboratory research findings and their practical application; and, inevitably, proposals for future research.

If these topics seem somewhat familiar, it is because they are also to be found in the contents of recent texts on human factors in air traffic control (e.g., Hopkin, 1982), and this is instructive. In the intervening years, air traffic control has progressed in ways scarcely imaginable many years ago, in terms of air traffic demands and num-

Human Factors in Aviation

bers, flying capabilities of aircraft, navigation facilities, computers in systems, and the controller's equipment and tasks. Yet basic human capabilities and limitations—of learning, attending, understanding, remembering, innovating, adapting, processing information, taking decisions, solving problems, predicting, and so on—remain much the same. Therefore, many of the main human factors problems in air traffic control may still be expressed today in the same parlance as was used in 1951, since human factors work focuses on people and their abiding characteristics. However, technological advances have wrought dramatic changes in the available and preferred solutions of those problems.

The approach of compiling a listing of functions suitable for human beings and of functions suitable for machines also dates from the same 1951 report, although tentative earlier attempts had been made. This approach carried several assumptions, which were not fully recognized until much later (Jordan, 1968). It seemed to imply that human and machine were competing for functions; if they were, the machine was bound to win. Only those functions that could conceivably be fulfilled by a machine appeared in the listing, since the question of the allocation of a function to human or machine does not otherwise arise. The onward march of technology ensured that more and more functions became at first feasible and, ultimately, more efficient for a machine to fulfil. The approach also implied that the residual human functions were not chosen because they were well matched to human capabilities and limitations but were incurred by the human because a machine could not be devised to cope with them.

In this approach, the allocation of functions had to be discussed using concepts and a language applicable to machines. Certain human attributes with no apparent machine equivalents, such as job satisfaction, self-esteem, pride in exercising hard-won skills, and a dislike of enforced idleness, thus tended to have little influence on the allocation of functions between human and machine. Another implication of the approach was the notion that every function that can be defined can be fulfilled somehow; the idea that certain functions should be avoided altogether was not seriously entertained. Yet there is no point, for example, in listing the reliable discrimination of a particular difference as an essential function if insufficient information can be provided to permit either human or machine to make that discrimination reliably. Some options, such as the parallel performance of the same function independently by both human and machine with cross-checking of the outcome, tended to be excluded by the approach itself. Technological developments thus largely determined the functions that appeared on the list, their allocation, and the language and concepts used to discuss them.

One role of human factors in air traffic control in recent years has been to attempt to ensure that this excessive narrowness of view is not perpetuated, but that decisions on the design of future air traffic control systems and on the conduct of air traffic control are reached with a thorough understanding of all their human factors implications. Some current human factors issues continue to reflect recent technological progress. Machines can now be devised which assess the skills, knowledge, or abilities of the individual human operator and adapt their forms of assistance accordingly. The question arises of how the adaptability of machines, with their facility to present information at the right time, in the right place, and at the right level of detail, should be employed to best advantage in air traffic control.

Dialogues between human and machine are replacing those between people, and the consequences for the roles of teams need to be assessed. Air traffic control may or may not be an appropriate context for the introduction of direct voice input, whereby a machine can accept spoken information in lieu of the same information entered through a keyboard, but the human factors implications of such an innovation, particularly for safety, must all be identified and evaluated. Similar considerations apply to voice synthesis in air traffic control, where the controller would interpret messages spoken by a machine. Human ineffectiveness in monitoring tasks must be reconciled with the requirements to keep and enhance high safety standards and to maintain the controller's skills and active involvement. Technological advances do not necessarily bring human factors benefits or have an immediate application in air traffic control.

While the above remarks may convey how human factors in air traffic control is evolving, there is also much routine application of existing human factors data and procedures to air traffic control (McCormick & Ilgen, 1981; Van Cott & Kinkade, 1972). This ensures, for example, that workspaces are well designed for human use, that the information shown by task analysis to be essential is present or readily accessible, and that spoken dialogues can be conducted efficiently with the minimum possibility of error or misunderstanding. At the heart of human factors is the human in the air traffic control system and the interactions between human and system. The human affects the system in terms of safety, efficiency of performance, capacity, and adaptability to unusual circumstances. The system affects the human in terms of roles and functions, job satisfaction, health, and morale.

Air Traffic Control System Operations

Traditionally, the stated objective of air traffic control is the safe, orderly, and expeditious flow of air traffic. Nowadays, it is necessary to add that air traffic control should be impartial, cost effective, noise abating, and fuel conserving. Current and future air traffic control systems must meet these additional requirements, without any sacrifice of the vital essential safety, orderliness, and expedition.

Air traffic controllers collaborate with pilots, technical staff, management, and other controllers. Although air traffic demands and air traffic control facilities vary greatly in different parts of the world, there are international standards and procedures to be observed. Air traffic control is not a free-for-all, but a disciplined and regulated system.

When a commercial aircraft takes off from a major airport, the planning of its flight has already been done, including much preliminary authorization and data entry. One controller is normally in charge of its taxiing and takeoff, using facilities of the kind shown in Figure 19.1. In the foreground are flight strips in their special holders. A *flight strip* is a standard piece of paper containing full details about an aircraft flight. It is a fundamental tool in air traffic control, and the controller writes new or amended information about the flight on it. The controller in the figure is in an air traffic control tower—in fact, at London (Heathrow) Airport—and has a good view of the air traffic with which he is directly concerned. Passengers in aircraft tend to think of the tower as the normal air traffic control workspace, for it is the only aspect of air traffic control which they can normally observe. In fact, only those controllers handling air traffic in the immediate vicinity of an airport have a direct view of the air traffic; most have no outside view at all.

After takeoff, air traffic control responsibility for the climbing aircraft passes to another controller, who in turn hands control over to a further controller as the aircraft flies along an airway, or air corridor, on its planned route at a height assigned to it and agreed on with air traffic control. Depending on route length and geographical region, for example, over land or ocean, control of the aircraft will be handed on through a sequence of other controllers, each responsible

Figure 19.1. The desk of an air departures controller. Reprinted by permission of the United Kingdom Civil Aviation Authority.

for a section of airway or a region of airspace (Figure 19.2), until the aircraft's descent and landing are accomplished through a further sequence of controllers, one of whom works in a suite handling all the aircraft approaching the same flight destination (Figure 19.3). Coordination between air traffic controllers to achieve smooth and safe handovers of control responsibility is therefore a major part of air traffic control, and vital for safety. It is significant that a recent introductory text on air traffic control (Adair, 1985) begins with a brief account of the midair collision at Zagreb in 1976, attributable to inadequate or misunderstood coordination between two controllers.

More recently designed air traffic control environments are generally spacious (Figure 19.4). The physical environment, and especially the lighting standards, have been much improved as a result of advances in display technology. Radar displays, which provide a plan view of the air traffic under control with identity and height information for each aircraft in the form of an alphanumeric label, are mounted vertically rather than horizontally. Gradually, electronic

Figure 19.2.   An en route sector suite. Reprinted by permission of the United Kingdom Civil Aviation Authority.

displays of tabular air traffic control data are replacing flight-strip boards (Figure 19.5), and some form of keyboard or touch-sensitive surface is required to update such displays and to take the place of writing on flight strips. In system terms, this represents another way of fulfilling the same function and is a small change; in human factors terms, it is a large change, with major implications for the controller's understanding, memory, level of involvement, skills, roles, and even status. It poses a further problem: how can the costs of such changes be justified if the system using flight strips already approximates to the maximum theoretically attainable traffic handling capacity within the prevailing separation standards?

Most air traffic control workspaces pose human factors problems of equipment layout because they require more information displays, more control devices, and more communications facilities than can readily be accommodated within recommended reach and viewing distances in the furniture. There may also be requirements for task sharing, for the amalgamation of control positions, and for flexibility

Figure 19.3. An approach control room. Reprinted by permission of the United Kingdom Civil Aviation Authority.

in manning levels in response to major, often diurnal, fluctuations in traffic demands. Airspace must be partitioned or shared between commercial, general aviation, and military users, and air traffic control must handle a great variety of aircraft types including helicopters, gliders, agricultural aircraft, and aircraft of the emergency services. Coordination between civil and military air traffic controllers may be enhanced if they share the same physical workspace. Air traffic control seeks to provide a service to all airspace users, so that journeys are safe and efficient, with a minimum of interference with others, without undue delays, and without any potential hazards.

There are many external constraints on the controller's activities beyond those set by workspace design, procedures, and serviceable facilities. Airport capacities for handling traffic depend upon the number of concurrently usable runways, and on the minimum separations between approaching aircraft, between departing aircraft, and between mixes of both, which in their turn depend on vortices created by aircraft of various sizes and speeds, and on meteorological

Figure 19.4.   A modern air traffic control operations room. Reprinted by permission of the United Kingdom Civil Aviation Authority.

conditions. Any airway has a maximum traffic handling capacity, dependent on applicable rules about minimum separation standards laterally, longitudinally, and in height, which in their turn depend on the quality of navigation aids and information. When routes converge or intersect, each may have a maximum allocation of aircraft per hour which limits the capacity of that route. Preflight planning includes the assignment of a slot from this allocation to each aircraft. Thus factors such as runway utilization, vortex regulations, route structure and slot times, in conjunction with minimum separation standards between aircraft, set limits to air traffic control capacity. It is common for airports at certain times of day to be functioning at or near their maximum traffic handling capacity, which is directly visible in the form of queues of departing aircraft waiting to take off, and less directly apparent when aircraft are held circling in a stack near an airport in a queue to land. Strategic planning of air traffic control by flow control procedures, which introduce new tasks and forms of automated assistance, and hence bring their own crop of human fac-

```
CLACTON  WESTBOUND SUPPORT
                              CFL     COUT   LAM  BRS  LSD                        1008
                               |       |
```

				CFL	COUT	LAM	BRS	LSD		
*.COA..ʳ.BD212	.BPK...	CC.	...160..	R....160ʳ..	54......	41......	VC8 ..EBBR
* COA	DUKE99D	LAM	SS	200	C +130		36	C12	EBOS
* RFS ʳ BA937	BPK	BB	220	R 220ʳ	38	30	BA11	EHAM
* COA	OM443	LAM	GW	280	C +130		29	BA11	EDDF
*.RFS..ʳ.BD202	.BPK...	CC.	...180..	R....180ʳ..	34......	22......	VC8 ..EHAM
* COA	BA743	LAM	LL	240	C +130		25	HS21	EDDL
* RFS	BA635	LAM	LL	310	C +130		23	HS21	EKCH
* RFS	HM401	LAM	LL	220	C +130		21	FK28	EHRD
*.COA...BY2748	.LAM...	GW.	...350..	C..+130.		21......	B737..EDDF
* COA ʳ SN617	BPK	CC	160	R 280ʳ	22	15	B737	EBBR
DET ʳ AF962	BPK	CC	C 260	R 260ʳ	21		B727	LFPG
* RFS ‹ EI845	CHT	EIDW	310	R 310‹	20	12	BA11	EHAM
. KK..ʔ.DA4086	.CLN...EDDH.	C... 90..	R....330ʔ......	Q16.........	BA11... KK
* RFS	BA415	LAM	LL	220	C +130		10	L101	EHAM
DET ʳ DA2629	BPK	EIDW	C 350	R 350ʳ	16		B727	LIRN
GAB ‹ EI6722	LAM	EHAM	270	P 270‹	Q15		BA11	EIDW
.DET..ʳ.BA993	.BPK...	PF.	C... 310..	C... 310ʳ.. 10..............	BA11..LFPG

Figure 19.5.   An experimental display of tabular air traffic control data. Reprinted by permission of the United Kingdom Civil Aviation Authority.

tors problems, is increasingly favored to prevent the formation of such queues, which are costly in terms of fuel, time, and patience.

The Role of the Controller

The controller's knowledge, skills, abilities, procedures, and equipment facilities are used to ensure that the flow of aircraft is maintained as safely and as efficiently as possible. It is easy to underestimate how much the functioning of an air traffic control system depends on the controller, even in a highly automated system. To the wholly uninitiated, the workspace of the air traffic controller is for most practical purposes meaningless. The displayed information has no obvious meaning. It is not evident what the information is for or what tasks could or should be performed with it. It is not self-evident if the right tasks have been performed or whether they have been done well. Much human factors effort is expended on the specification of the content and layout of air traffic control displays and controls, of the interface between the controller and the system, and of an efficient and attractive workspace. However, without the knowledge of the controller, nothing would happen.

This raises a fundamental question. As air traffic control systems evolve, how far should the role of controllers also evolve? In particular, what do controllers need to know about new equipment, new facilities, new software, and new aids, in order to use them efficiently and integrate them successfully into their existing air traffic control knowledge and experience? Do they need to know how a new device functions in order to be able to recognize that it has failed? Should their professional knowledge be recast, just as, for example, a navigator may no longer need to be able to use a sextant but may have to understand some of the software used with microcomputers?

Selection and Training

The air traffic controller needs considerable professional knowledge; selection procedures for controllers must therefore choose those who are willing and able to acquire such knowledge and to apply it responsibly—anything less could be dangerous. Training procedures must successfully instill that knowledge, together with a thorough understanding of how and when it should be employed. There has been extensive research on the selection of air traffic controllers (Sells, Dailey, & Pickrel, 1984). At one time, much emphasis was placed on the value of aviation knowledge and previous training as predictors of success as an air traffic controller (Rock, Dailey, Ozur, Boone, & Pickrel, 1981), but these factors are now discounted as selection aids. They seem more relevant to initial motivation and to the realism of the candidate's expectations than to ultimate success or failure as an air traffic controller.

While both selection and training have contributed to the controller's ultimate proficiency, there is debate about their relative importance. One contention is that the would-be controller should be young, physically fit, mentally stable, articulate, considerably above average in intelligence, and educated to college entrance standards or thereabouts. These are not stringent criteria—many people could meet such requirements.

Another contention is that, to be selected, a future controller must possess a combination of particular skills and attributes, such as manual dexterity, reliability in decision making, spatial reasoning ability, task-sharing ability, and the like. Quite a long list can be compiled of factors thought to have positive predictive value for air traffic control performance. A selection procedure must therefore seek the small numbers with this unusual combination of desirable attributes, since training alone could not compensate for their absence. Few people would pass such a stringent selection procedure.

In practice the evidence tends to favor the first contention rather than the second, with the implications that success as an air traffic controller depends primarily on training and that many people given adequate training could become satisfactory controllers. This line of argument is contingent on two other factors: first, the profession of air traffic control must be sufficiently attractive to ensure that applicants of the right caliber apply to join it or else the best efforts of selection and training will be nugatory, and second, the most able and best-trained controllers may fail to achieve their full potential if allocated to inappropriate jobs.

Human Error

The quest for safety implies that air traffic control cannot tolerate error or failure. Systems and equipment must be highly reliable and well proven. Human jobs and tasks must capitalize on human strengths and circumvent human limitations. There are gross differences between tasks in the reliability with which a human can perform them. For some tasks, such as initially turning a steering wheel counterclockwise for a left turn and clockwise for a right turn, human reliability can be very high. For other tasks, such as ordering slides or viewgraphs in their correct sequence and orientation for a lecture, or detecting the appearance of a small, dim, and transient signal at long and irregular intervals, human fallibility is notorious.

In air traffic control, as elsewhere, some form of job description or job analysis establishes what functions have to be performed, what equipment is needed to perform them, and how the human can be aided. More specific requirements can then be deduced concerning (1) the coding, sequencing, formats, and level of detail of the contents of displays by which information is conveyed from the machine to the controller; (2) the type, sensitivity, and positioning of control devices by which information is conveyed from the controller to the machine; and (3) voice communication channels, team structuring and suite layouts which influence the transmission of information between people.

Individuals can improve their performance of most tasks by the acquisition of skill, and, as far as possible, equipment should be selected to capitalize on this human attribute. Skills can influence considerably the maximum attainable level of performance, the magnitude and value of training commitments, and the individual differences that remain after training. The nature of the tasks will set limits on the reliability to be expected from a trained controller. Equipment aids may enhance this reliability to some extent, but not always uniformly.

The nature and incidence of human error are largely predetermined by decisions taken during system specification and design. The codings chosen to display information can affect greatly the misperceptions that are possible and will occur. The types and sensitivities of controls similarly affect the kinds of error that can or cannot occur in their use. An example may clarify this point.

In the past, much information has been conveyed between the pilot and the air traffic controller through speech, often over noisy channels. Considerable human factors work has sought to minimize errors. One method was to standardize messages—their formats, sequence, pace, and phraseology. Another method was to choose words known to remain readily identifiable when spoken over noisy channels or by individuals whose native language was not English. (English is the language of international air traffic control.) The chosen words should sound as different as possible from each other. If necessary, for phonetically similar words which must be used, such as "five" and "nine," the differences between them could be exaggerated by pronouncing them in nonstandard ways, such as "fife" and "nine-ah." Basic principles and laboratory findings on the degree of phonetic confusion between various sounds and words could thus be applied to minimize errors and to ensure that those which might occur would be readily identified and not potentially dangerous.

In modern air traffic control systems, information transponded from air to ground to appear in visual alphanumeric form on the controller's displays has replaced many spoken messages. As a consequence the nature of human errors has changed in predictable ways. Existing evidence, regarding choice of visual coding, typeface, brightness and color contrast, the angular subtense of readable alphanumeric characters, and desirable display formats, is applied to minimize human errors and to render those that persist both detectable and safe. The confusion is no longer between information which sounds like other information when spoken but between alphanumeric characters which look alike or are physically adjacent. Given this knowledge, practical steps can be implemented to minimize the physical juxtaposition of potentially confusable items.

Some of the alphanumeric data on the controller's display are entered into the system through a keyboard or other input device. The choice of input device predetermines most of the human errors in data entry. If a cursor is moved down a list, a typical human error is to select the item above or below the one required. If a keyboard is used, traditional miskeyings may occur which can be deduced from the keyboard layout. If a touch-sensitive surface is employed, the problems of parallax may produce predictable types of error. The central point is that these design decisions are also decisions about the nature of the human errors which will occur.

In the future this transponded data may in turn be replaced by direct voice input and voice synthesis. This will remove many of the typical errors associated with visual misreadings of alphanumerics but will bring its own crop of error types, some of which will be novel. It would be a serious mistake to presume that the human errors associated with machine synthesis and recognition of speech will be the same as those associated with human spoken dialogues. Once again the possible error types must be identified in order to circumvent them. Prevention is better than cure in such circumstances. Much human factors effort is therefore devoted to the exclusion during the design stage of identifiable sources of human error within a proposed air traffic control system, since the practical steps to remove such error sources retrospectively if they have arisen in an operational system may be very limited and very costly. On such topics a wealth of human factors data that can be directly applied is available.

Workspace Design

This last point is also true of workspaces. Anthropometric data showing the range of body dimensions of the user population—in most contexts both men and women may be air traffic controllers—are applied to the specification and construction of air traffic control rooms, furniture and suites, to the seating, and to the positioning and layout of equipment with particular regard to reach distances and viewing distances. The visual environment is designed as an entity. The characteristics and locations of the radar displays and of any other emitting displays, such as plasma panels, are matched with the spectrum and intensity of the ambient lighting, which must also be appropriate for other functions such as the reading of flight strips or hard copy and the reading of the labeling on data input devices. The whole visual environment, including the use of matt surfaces to min-

imize glare and reflections and the choice of color and decor to provide aesthetically satisfying surroundings and promote efficient task
performance, is also taken into account, together with all the visual
interactions within it.

Also specified on the basis of human factors guidelines is the permissible range of adjustment, for example, of the brightness contrast
of displayed information. In some air traffic control contexts such as
centers, which receive information by speech and by radar and other
remote sensors and from which the air traffic under control is not directly visible, it is normal to design a single optimum visual environment in which adjustments of visual settings are not encouraged as
they would depart from the carefully specified and balanced optimum. In other air traffic control contexts, such as towers where controllers have a direct view of the aircraft under their control, it is
sometimes necessary to make provision for very large adjustments of
displays, which must remain usable with direct sunlight falling on
them at one extreme and during exterior darkness at the other extreme. Nevertheless, it is usually possible to arrive at a practical solution which is operationally efficient and aesthetically pleasing,
fosters the well-being of those at work there, and meets all other
main human factors requirements.

This topic—the design of the workspace and of the individual operational positions within it—is a traditional human factors contribution. It will always be important, although it now seldom calls for
research but for the application of existing human factors knowledge,
plus some verification in the form of user opinion of mock-ups or
simulations constructed to incorporate human factors recommendations and guidelines. Research is still needed where recent technological innovations, for which applications in air traffic control are
sought, may introduce problems of workspace design. Touch-sensitive surfaces which function as displays and controls should, as displays, be angled nearly vertically for optimum viewing and, as
controls, be positioned nearly horizontally on the console shelf for
optimum data entry. The resulting compromise usually means that
the device cannot be positioned ideally for either of its main functions. More positively, advances in display and control technology
have led to the clearer and more accurate portrayal of data, of associations between different displays, and of the functional relationships
between controls and displays. Many air traffic control tasks are now
concerned as much with the entry and retrieval of data from store as
with the direct exercise of control responsibilities. The design of the
workspace, and particularly of the interface between the controller

and the system, must reflect this change of emphasis in human functions. For example, the feedback to the controller may not be in the form of an aircraft maneuver but rather of an acknowledgment that data have been entered successfully into a computer.

Some procedures, ostensibly concerned primarily with furniture design and layout, may carry much broader implications. Recently the proposed layout for a new air traffic control tower at London (Gatwick) Airport, seen in its final form in Figure 19.6, was examined. Shown in the foreground are the ground radar display and the ground movement lighting panel used to control the lighting on the airfield that marks the route the aircraft should follow along the taxiway. The debate about where this panel should be positioned in the workspace apparently concerned furniture layout but, in fact, centered on the responsibilities, level of supervision, and degree of autonomy of the controller assistant who uses this lighting panel. The workspace layout determined whether the controller was near

Figure 19.6.   A recent air traffic control tower layout. Reprinted by permission of the United Kingdom Civil Aviation Authority.

enough to the assistant to issue direct instructions and monitor each action by the assistant or was separated from the assistant who heard through a headset the controller's spoken instruction to the pilot and used the lighting panel autonomously to set up the lighting on the airfield taxiways accordingly.

Influence on Health

The air traffic controller's license depends on his or her continued health (Rose, Jenkins, & Hurst, 1978). It is most important that no aspect of air traffic control itself, of its management, of its conditions of employment, or of its workspace should be potentially harmful and constitute an occupational health hazard. With health, as with human error, the main human factors effort is to ensure from the outset that problems cannot arise. Regarding workspace design, the two main sources of possible health decrements are postural and visual problems. To prevent postural problems, furniture is designed for the full range of body sizes, with adequately separated, comfortable, and adjustable seating. Acceptable viewing and reach distances are provided for all, requiring no undue stretching except for very rarely performed and nonurgent functions such as the setting up of controls ready for operational use. To prevent visual problems, occasions are minimized when it is necessary to refocus because of displays at different viewing distances, and the total light output from different displays is approximately equated so that frequent cross referral between them is not associated with continuing changes in pupil size. It should never be necessary to peer at air traffic control information: this may not in itself constitute an occupational health hazard because of the robustness of the eyes, but it may well be a source of complaint and potentially unsafe because it induces reading errors.

Stress and Boredom

Stress

It was in the occupational health context that the issue of air traffic control as a source of stress on the controller was raised, a notion which more than a decade of extensive work has finally dispelled (Melton, 1982). This does not mean that no air traffic control jobs generate stress or that no individual controllers show symptoms of stress; there may be some jobs that need to be changed and some individuals who need treatment for stress problems. But contentions that air traffic control per se necessarily generates symptoms of stress in controllers, and that controllers as a group suffer chronically from stress problems, cannot be sustained, although some national differences in the incidence of reported stress symptoms among air traffic controllers still persist.

Stress, an emotive issue on which speculation is rife, provides an excellent example of a flaw in reasoning which can lead to much unproductive effort if it is not recognized as such. The existence of a relationship does not thereby imply any causal connection or indicate the direction of a causal link if there is one. Even if air traffic controllers as a group were to show a higher incidence of stress symptoms than the equivalent general population matched on basic factors such as age, sex, race, educational qualifications, and so forth (which as a group they do not), it still does not follow that air traffic control causes stress. The selection procedure for controllers may inadvertently select people more prone to stress; there may be friction between controllers and their management; controllers have unusual shift systems and their work–rest cycles may be relevant to stress symptoms; shift systems may themselves contribute toward more family problems known to be associated with stress, such as a higher divorce rate; real or imagined grievances among controllers about poor status and unappreciated skills may rankle; and so on. A few controllers may experience stress initially because the knowledge that they are responsible for the safety and lives of others becomes a great burden to them, but such controllers tend to leave the profession, as the prospect of a lifetime of such stress is intolerable to them. The origins of stress must therefore be ascertained correctly first; if they are not, resources are frittered away on solving the wrong problem.

Boredom

The preoccupation with stress in air traffic control has in retrospect seemed particularly unfortunate, because it has led to the comparative neglect of a greater problem, namely boredom (Hopkin, 1980a). Many air traffic control facilities have to be staffed and operational all the time. The demand for air traffic control services fluctuates greatly in ways which are partly predictable. Staffing levels have to be set so that potentially dangerous overloading of controllers does not occur. Inevitably, some controllers must be at work when traffic is light and there is little for them to do. Air traffic controllers have limited influence over their own workload, which largely depends on traffic demands and the technical and navigational facilities that are available and serviceable. Consistent underloading curtails opportunities to exercise professional skills. Not only are such opportunities necessary to maintain the skills, but they are also the main source of job satisfaction for the many controllers who find air traffic control an intrinsically satisfying activity. Various performance aids in the form of computer assistance, designed to alleviate workload when the controller is very busy, may aggravate the problem of boredom if they must also be employed when the controller is lightly loaded, for then they reduce workload even further. Satisfactory discretionary aids, designed to give most assistance when most needed and to be switched off under light loading, are not generally available and seem difficult to devise. Aids which impose a search task may introduce a wrong principle, being of least help when most needed because they require most searching under high-loading conditions, when the controller has least time to spare for searching.

The commonsense notion that dangerous incidents, accidents, or lapses of attention or performance are closely associated with high workload is not sustained by the evidence about it. Boredom and low workload cannot be equated with increased safety but may tend to induce complacency. Boredom usually occurs when a task has been mastered, presents no further challenge, and is being performed very well, rather than during learning, under high-task demands or in novel conditions. Because boredom may be associated with good task performance rather than bad, attempts to prevent boredom may incur decrements rather than improvements in performance.

Changes in social climate and job expectations, associated with the treatment of job satisfaction as a right rather than a serendipitous privilege, have made many people less tolerant of boredom at work. For a variety of reasons—air safety, sound management practices, favorable attitudes among controllers, humanitarianism, efficiency in manning—the prevention and alleviation of boredom in air traffic control is a desirable policy. Because the topic has been comparatively neglected, there is little evidence on the causes and cures of boredom that could be applied with confidence to reduce its prevalence in air traffic control.

Measurement

Human factors as a discipline bases its decisions on quantitative factual evidence wherever possible. It evaluates the general human factors literature for its pertinence to air traffic control problems, and further research and evaluation are conducted if the existing evidence is insufficient to make practical recommendations. The problem of measurement is complex (Hopkin, 1980b). It is particularly easy to omit certain types of data completely, so that some important but unmeasured factors have no influence on final decisions. An example may illustrate this point.

Suppose that at a busy international airport working at full capacity the question is raised whether the workload of the controllers is too high and should be reduced. What kinds of measures would yield relevant information? Workload can be measured in many ways (Moray, 1979) and must be distinguished from task demands, which also have to be measured. The essential difference is that task demands, a system concept, constitute the functions that have to be performed if the air traffic control system is to handle the given traffic efficiently, whereas the workload, a human concept, concerns the loading which the fulfilment of those functions places on the individual controller. Workload therefore depends not only on factors such as the amount and configuration of the air traffic, but on attributes of the individual controller such as knowledge, skill, ability, effort, fatigue, and motivation. The same task demands can impose different workload on different people. Attempts continue to be made to establish how close the relationship is between measures of system activity and of workload, for a variety of air traffic control purposes including planning and staffing (Stein, 1985). The notion persists that the provision of displays of air traffic information in aircraft cockpits must impinge upon air traffic control procedures and workload, although the consequences of such displays for air traffic control may not prove to be large (Paul, 1985).

One kind of measure concerns the functioning system. System measures record the quantity and mix of air traffic in terms of mean and peak rates of traffic flow; the nature, timing and distribution of control actions; delays, penalties and additional costs incurred because of air traffic control procedures; the pattern of occupancy of various communication channels; and so on. Such data confirm that the system is functioning at or near its planned maximum capacity and can indicate the main consequences for the system user. Some recent simulation work has suggested that many system performance measures cluster, so that they can be represented adequately by a few factors (Buckley, DeBaryshe, Hitchner, & Kohn, 1984).

The actual activities of individual controllers within the system can also be measured. These measures show that the controller often seems to be performing several activities at once without appreciable rest pauses. These activities include talking to pilots and fellow controllers, watching the radar display and other displays, using keyboards and other input devices, receiving and discarding information, planning ahead, and organizing the resources required for control activities. Such evidence can confirm that the controller is fully occupied.

Performance measures can demonstrate the effectiveness of the controller's actions and include any resultant errors, delays, and safety infringements. Performance measures should also encompass omissions, that is, activities which should be present and are not and which therefore may not appear in an activity analysis. Evidence from performance measures can confirm that the controller is working efficiently and safely and ensure, for example, that high workload is not of the controller's own making because the controller is following cumbersome or ill-chosen procedures, adopting nonoptimum solutions to problems, or generating errors that then have to be corrected. The performance of an experienced controller is normally both safe and highly efficient.

Subjective measures, such as questionnaires and rating scales, can indicate the controllers' own views about the workload entailed by the task demands, about its fatiguing effects, and about any spare mental capacity. The evidence from subjective measures should confirm other evidence that the controller is busy, is tired, and has no respite.

Physiological and biochemical measures, as well as subjective assessments, can provide evidence of the effort the controller has to make to cope with the task demands and to achieve the measured standards of performance. These indices of effort can be used to ascertain whether there would be long-term effects on well-being if such levels of effort had to be sustained for protracted periods or were a common requirement. However, their inherent obtrusiveness generally confines their practical applications to research environments, and for some individuals they may be so disturbing as to affect directly the parameters they are intended to measure.

Other measures may gather evidence on social factors and on the extent to which the controller is calm, irritable, difficult to manage, difficult to collaborate with, responsive to the needs of his colleagues, and acting as an effective team member. Various psychological tests may provide further measures of relevant individual differences which in their turn can be used primarily to explore and explain such differences. Medical data, such as morbidity and mortality rates, may indicate whether occupational health hazards of any kind are associated with high workload.

If any incidents occur, such as infringements of safety standards, thorough enquiries are pursued and, where appropriate, recommendations are made to prevent any recurrence of that particular infringement. One highly pertinent factor in such investigations concerns the task demands and workload prevailing at the time. Accounts of such incidents therefore provide a further measure, because of the guidance they may give on whether the levels of workload being examined are associated with incidents and on general relationships between workload and safety. It must not be presumed in the absence of evidence that high workload is potentially dangerous and that lower workload must be safer, because the evidence from incidents does not usually substantiate this view, although some subjective evidence may support it.

Other possible measures, derived for example from modeling, fast-time simulation, operational analysis, reliability engineering and control theory, may provide relevant data not obtainable in any other way, though their potential, particularly when used in conjunction with each other and in association with human factors measures, has not been utilized fully so far in air traffic control applications.

All the above measures may indicate that the workload is high and, perhaps, that it is too high, but even this range of measures does not comprise all the data. A further set of measures enquire whether the controller likes to be busy, ascertain what the controller's main sources of job satisfaction are, explore how highly prized are opportunities to exercise skills fully, and determine the origins of self-esteem and the esteem of fellow controllers. Evidence of this kind emphasizes that high workload may bring certain benefits not otherwise attainable and that wholesale reductions in workload might therefore be associated with unwanted consequences.

The decision on whether workload is excessive therefore involves a balance. The overriding factor concerns safety, which must never be jeopardized. Given safety, many factors need to be weighed in the balance, and an incomplete picture and perhaps an incorrect conclusion will emerge if some factors are ignored. The preoccupation with measurement is not a theoretical exercise but an attempt to ensure that fully informed decisions are reached which have taken account of all the relevant evidence and only the relevant evidence.

The Impact of Automation

Air traffic control is a large human–machine system. The future may bring intelligent knowledge-based systems, expert systems, very accurate satellite-derived navigational information, automated speech synthesis and speech recognition, touch-sensitive input devices, glorious color—a whole panoply of technological advances which can now be foreseen, if not implemented. Many of these innovations imply increased automation of functions or more computer assistance for controllers. These changes, if well chosen and sensibly introduced, can produce many benefits, but it is important to be aware of some of their human factors consequences which may not be so welcome, the prevention of which should influence the particular forms which automation takes. Many of the prospective benefits of progressive automation may prove to be elusive unless all its human factors implications are anticipated and allowed for.

The extent to which active participation in routine tasks aids memory and understanding has been consistently underestimated, so that when computer assistance takes the form of the replacement of the manual performance of routine tasks by their performance automatically, the controller often finds it necessary to introduce a new task, since positive action is now required to retrieve from the system information formerly obtained incidentally during the performance of manual functions. The controller does not use this retrieved information for any air traffic control purpose, but merely looks at it as a reassurance to aid memory and understanding of the current air traffic control situation. To cast the controller in a role which requires the monitoring of automated functions rather than active involvement in them is ultimately self-defeating. The controller may no longer be able to intervene in emergencies and be flexible in dealing with nonstandard circumstances. Without active participation in the control loop, the maintenance of knowledge of what is happening becomes insufficient to perform even those residual functions adequately. This is not to be construed as a lack of dedication or professionalism among controllers, but it is a statement about the nature of human memory and understanding and the inability of humans to perform indefinitely routine tasks which are never needed but always superfluous. To give the controller nothing but monitoring functions is therefore to introduce recalcitrant human factors problems for which no satisfactory solution may be found.

A further unwelcome consequence of automated assistance in air traffic control originates in the fact that most aids are more suitable for individuals than for teams, and dialogues between human and machine take the place of interactions between people. Traditional forms of supervision and assistance may no longer be feasible when much of the work consists of interchanges across an interface between controller and machine. Some of the consequences of this may be unexpected but can nevertheless be predicted. For example, the development of professional norms, standards, and ethos occurs as the individual newcomer to a profession absorbs from others what is expected from anyone who aspires to become a fully competent and accepted member of that profession. How can the individual controller ever gauge or understand such norms if the opportunities for closely collaborative teamwork are consistently curtailed by fundamental changes in system concepts and design? Progressively introduced automated assistance may therefore thwart the full development of professional norms and standards, which are a hallmark of membership of a profession and a major driving force behind the high standards of achievement of many individual air traffic controllers. If this kind of consequence is foreseen correctly, it can be turned to advantage by ensuring that the tasks that are designed require sufficient interaction between people to foster the perpetuation of professional norms.

In principle, many findings concerning expert systems might be applicable to air traffic control. An expert system has as one objective the incorporation of relevant human expert knowledge into a data base containing other information about the functioning system, such as sensed data, rules, and algorithms, so that the whole is accessible to system users. Some of the commonest human factors problems of expert systems have been reviewed (Hopkin, 1984). They include the assumed knowledge already possessed by the users and the ways in which dialogues between the system and users with various skills and knowledge should be conducted. Expertise may consist of the interpretation of a complex visual display; it can refer to the timing of an action, as well as the correct choice of action; it may include adjustments in advance to take account of the expected reactions of others. Experts may not agree among themselves, and the problem arises of establishing the validity of expert systems without recourse to the selfsame experts whose suspected fallibility has rendered the validity uncertain. Validation raises the question of whether there can be a single definable optimum. Would we be able to recognize an ideal expert system as perfect if we were inadvertently to encounter one?

Conclusion

The application of human factors evidence to air traffic control is an active topic. Much invaluable routine work promotes the objectives of air traffic control directly by increasing human efficiency, minimizing errors, and ensuring the well-being of the controllers themselves. However, new traffic demands, better navigational data, new forms of automated assistance, and technological innovations require air traffic control to evolve to meet new requirements in new ways. The role of the controller must also evolve, but in ways which emphasize his capabilities, such as innovation, flexibility, motivation, and the development of skills, and circumvent his limitations, such as monitoring. Most changes in air traffic control systems are not suggested or introduced for human factors reasons; not all their consequences are beneficial in human factors terms.

One possible option which technological advances may bring is the restoration to the controller of the central role in the system, with technology used to enhance the efficiency and satisfaction of that central role. As long as there is an air traffic controller in an air traffic control system (which will be for a very long time), the air traffic control workspace will still seem mystifying to the noncontroller, and the skills and knowledge of the professional controller will still be needed for the conduct of air traffic control.

References

Adair, D. (1985). Air traffic control. Wellingborough, England: Patrick Stephens.
Buckley, E. P., DeBaryshe, B. D., Hitchner, N., & Kohn, P. (1984). An empirical study of the methodology for real-time air traffic control system simulation testing. Journal of Test and Evaluation, 5(3), 20–25.
Fitts, P. M. (Ed.). (1951). Human engineering for an effective air-navigation and traffic-control system. Washington, DC: National Research Council, Committee on Aviation Psychology.
Hopkin, V. D. (1980a). Boredom. The Controller, 19, 1, 6–10.
Hopkin, V. D. (1980b). The measurement of the air traffic controller. Human Factors, 22(5), 547–560.
Hopkin, V. D. (1982). Human factors in air traffic control (AGARDograph No. 275). Neuilly-sur-Seine, France: NATO.
Hopkin, V. D. (1984). Some human factors implications of expert systems. Behaviour and Information Technology, 3(1), 79–83.
Jordan, N. (1968). Themes in speculative psychology. London: Tavistock Publications.
McCormick, E. J., & Ilgen, D. (1981). Industrial psychology. London: Allen and Unwin.
Melton, C. E. (1982). Physiological stress in air traffic controllers: A review (FAA-AM-82-17). Washington, DC: U.S. Department of Transportation, Federal Aviation Administration.
Moray, N. (Ed.). (1979). Mental workload: Its theory and measurement. New York: Plenum.
Paul, L. E. (1985). Preliminary evaluation of the impact of cockpit display of traffic information on air traffic control (DOT/FAA/CT-TN83/51). Atlantic City, NJ: U.S. Department of Transportation, Federal Aviation Administration.

Rock, D. B., Dailey, J. T., Ozur, H., Boone, J. O., & Pickrel, E. W. (1981). *Selection of applicants for the air traffic controller occupation* (FAA-AM-82-11). Washington, DC: U.S. Department of Transportation, Federal Aviation Administration.

Rose, R. M., Jenkins, C. D., & Hurst, M. W. (1978). *Air traffic controller health change study* (FAA-AM-78-39). Washington, DC: U.S. Department of Transportation, Federal Aviation Administration.

Sells, S. B., Dailey, J. T., & Pickrel, E. W. (1984). *Selection of air traffic controllers* (FAA-AM-84-2). Washington, DC: U.S. Department of Transportation, Federal Aviation Administration.

Stein, E. S. (1985). *Air traffic controller workload: An examination of workload probe* (DOT/FAA/CT-TN84/24). Atlantic City, NJ: U.S. Department of Transportation, Federal Aviation Administration.

Van Cott, H. P., & Kinkade, R. G. (Eds.). (1972). *Human engineering guide to equipment design*. Washington, DC: U.S. Government Printing Office.

NOTES ON CONTRIBUTORS

Gary L. Babcock is a United Airlines First Officer flying the B-737. He received a B.S. in engineering (biotechnology) from the University of California at Los Angeles. After college, he worked for the McDonnell–Douglas Corporation Aircraft Division in human engineering, and for System Development Corporation in computer display software. As an active member of the Air Line Pilots Association safety committees, he published many articles on cockpit resource management, pilot performance, and accident investigation techniques. He has worked with personnel of the National Transportation Safety Board on a number of accidents involving airline aircraft.

Sheldon Baron is vice-president and assistant director of the Computer and Information Sciences Division of BBN Laboratories, Incorporated in Cambridge, Massachusetts. He received his B.S. degree in physics from Brooklyn College, an M.A. in physics from William and Mary College, and a Ph.D. in applied mathematics from Harvard University. He worked from 1958 to 1967 at NASA's Langley and Electronics Research Centers. Dr. Baron is a fellow of the IEEE Administrative Committee, of the Systems, Man, and Cybernetics Society, and of the American Institute of Aeronautics and Astronautics. He is a member of the National Academy of Sciences, National Research Council Committee on Human Factors.

Paul W. Caro is executive managing director of the Seville Training Systems Division, United Airlines Services Corporation. Previously, he held research and management positions with Seville Training Systems Corporation, which he cofounded, and with the Human Resources Research Organization (HumRRO), and he was employed as an industrial training psychologist by the Mead Corporation. He received the M.A. degree in psychology from Florida State University and the Ph.D. in industrial psychology and psychometrics from the University of Tennessee. He is a fellow of the Human Factors Society and of the Divisions of Military Psychology and of Applied Experimental and Engineering Psychologists of the American Psychological Association, and he is a member of Sigma

Xi and the U.S. Army Science Board. He also is a former member of the U.S. Air Force Scientific Advisory Board and served on a recent Academy of Sciences working group on simulation. His chief areas of professional interest have been aviation training research and flight simulator design and use. He holds airplane and helicopter ratings.

Patricia A. Casper is currently a graduate student in the department of psychological sciences at Purdue University. She received a B.S. in psychology from the University of Iowa and recently received her M.S. from Purdue. Her research interests include attention, problem solving, and artificial intelligence.

Elwyn Edwards received an honors degree in psychology from the University of Liverpool and a Ph.D. from the University of Bristol. After a short period of research with the late K. F. H. Murrell, he joined the department of ergonomics and cybernetics, Loughborough, at its inception in 1960, where he remained as reader in ergonomics until appointed to a chair in applied psychology at the University of Aston in 1976. Prior to his academic career, he trained as an Air Navigation Officer at RCAF, Winnipeg, and has maintained close links with the sharp end of aviation as a private pilot. He is a liveryman of the Guild of Air Pilots and Air Navigators. On his retirement from Aston in 1984, he was granted the title professor emeritus and is now engaged full-time in his consulting company, Human Technology.

Robert G. Fainter is an assistant professor of computer science at Arizona State University. His research interests include concurrent programming, software development environments, software verification and validation, the use of computers in control systems in aviation and aeronautical engineering, and human–computer interface. He served for 1 year on the Ada Joint Program Office sponsored KITIA (KAPSE Interface Team, Industry and Academia). Fainter received his B.S. in mathematics from the University of North Carolina at Greensboro in 1977 and the M.S. and Ph.D. in computer science from the Virginia Polytechnic Institute and State University in 1981 and 1985, respectively. He is a member of the Association for Computing Machinery.

John M. Flach received a Ph.D. in human experimental psychology from The Ohio State University in 1984. He then joined the faculty at the University of Illinois, with appointments in the Department of Mechanical and Industrial Engineering, the Department of

Psychology, and the Institute of Aviation. His research focuses on modeling human perceptual–motor performance in human–machine systems.

H. Clayton Foushee received a B.A. degree magna cum laude with distinction in psychology from Duke University in 1975 and a Ph.D. in social psychology from the University of Texas in 1979. He has been awarded fellowships from the National Research Council and the National Institute of Mental Health and has been with NASA since 1981. He conducts research on a variety of issues related to the effectiveness of groups in both aviation and space environments and manages the Aerospace Human Factors Division program in these areas at NASA-Ames. His work on line-oriented flight training (LOFT), cockpit resource management, and crew coordination has stimulated innovations in the training programs of civil and military operators, both foreign and domestic.

R. Curtis Graeber received his B.A. from the State University of New York at Binghamton in 1967 and his M.A. and Ph.D. in physiological psychology from the University of Virginia in 1970 and 1972. He has served as a research psychologist at the U.S. Army's Natick Research and Development Center and at the Walter Reed Army Institute of Research. Since 1975 he has conducted research on human circadian rhythms, and in 1981 joined NASA's Ames Research Center as the principal investigator for a congressionally mandated field study of fatigue and circadian factors in flight crews. Dr. Graeber is a lieutenant colonel in the U.S. Army Medical Service Corps, a private pilot, a director of the International Society for Chronobiology, an associate fellow of the Aerospace Medical Association, and a member of the Sleep Research Society. His publications include numerous scientific articles and the book *Rhythmic Aspects of Behavior*. In 1986 Dr. Graeber served as the human factors specialist for the Presidential Commission on the Space Shuttle Challenger Accident.

Sandra G. Hart has been the leader of the Human Performance and Workload Research Group since 1982 and the coordinator for helicopter research since 1986 in the Aerospace Human Factors Research Division at NASA–Ames Research Center, Moffett Field, California. She completed her undergraduate work in psychology at San Jose State University and her graduate work at San Jose State University and the University of California at Berkeley. Her primary research interests include workload prediction and assessment, training, and human factors problems associated with the operation of advanced helicopters.

Robert L. Helmreich is professor and chair of the graduate program in social psychology at the University of Texas at Austin. He received a Ph.D. in personality and social psychology from Yale in 1966. He has conducted research sponsored by NASA and the Office of Naval Research on small-group performance under stressful conditions as well as research supported by the National Science Foundation and National Institute of Mental Health on personality factors and motivation. His current research focuses on crew selection, composition, crew coordination, and training for both aviation and space environments. He is a fellow of the American Psychological Association and a former editor of *The Journal of Personality and Social Psychology.*

V. David Hopkin received his M.A. degree in psychology from the University of Aberdeen, Scotland. He is currently senior principal psychologist at the Royal Air Force Institute of Aviation Medicine at Farnborough, where he has spent much of his working life. He also works as a human factors specialist on air traffic control for the United Kingdom Civil Aviation Authority, and is a fellow of the Royal Institute of Navigation. His research interests are centered on human factors problems in aviation and in large human–machine systems and extend to maps, aircraft cockpits, human roles in systems, and social and attitudinal implications of automation.

Barry H. Kantowitz received a Ph.D. in experimental psychology with a joint minor in computer science and industrial engineering from the University of Wisconsin–Madison in 1969. From 1969 to 1987 he held a faculty appointment in the Department of Psychological Sciences at Purdue University, where he was a professor of psychological sciences and industrial engineering. He has directed the Graduate Training Program in Human Factors Department of Psychological Sciences since 1977. He has been a senior lecturer in ergonomics at the Norwegian Institute of Technology, Trondheim, Norway. He is a fellow of the Society of Engineering Psychologists. His research interests are in the areas of attention, mental workload, and human information processing. Dr. Kantowitz is now a senior research scientist with Battelle Memorial Institute, Seattle, in the Center for Human Factors and Organization Effectiveness.

Jerome Lederer received his B.Sc. in mechanical engineering with an aeronautics option at New York University in 1925. He served as an aeronautical engineer with the U.S. Mail Service from 1926 to 1927 and with the Aero Insurance Underwriters from 1929 to 1940, and he was director of the safety bureau of the Civil Aeronautics Board from 1940 to 1942, where he was in charge of accident investigation and civil air regulations. He has also been director of the Cornell–Guggenheim Aviation Safety Center and the Flight Safety Foundation. In 1967, following the loss of three astronauts in an accident at Cape Canaveral, he was called out of retirement to serve as director of the Office of Manned Space Flight Safety. He retired again in 1972. Mr. Lederer is an honorary fellow and member of a large number of safety and aeronautical organizations. In 1987, the Flight Safety Foundation founded the Jerry Lederer Aviation Safety Library. He is an emeritus professor of the Institute of Safety and Systems Management at University of Southern California. He lives in Laguna Hills, California, and continues to be active in safety and human factors organizations and publications.

Herschel W. Leibowitz received a Ph.D. in experimental psychology from Columbia University in 1951, has taught at the universities of Wisconsin, Michigan, Maryland, and Florida and at the Massachusetts Institute of Technology and is currently at the Pennsylvania State University. He has been employed by IBM corporation, and has served on the vision and human factors committees of the National Research Council. His primary interests are vision, perception, spatial orientation, and human factors in transportation systems.

C. O. Miller received a B.S. in aeronautical engineering from the Massachusetts Institute of Technology, an M.S. in systems management from the University of Southern California, and a J.D. from the Potomac School of Law. He is also a graduate of the Federal Executive Institute. His aviation career includes military service as a U.S. Marine Corps pilot in World War II, an experimental test pilot and engineering supervisor in the airframe industry with the Chance Vought Corporation, a researcher in crash survivability with the Flight Safety Foundation, lecturer and director of research at the Institute of Safety and Management of the University of Southern California, director of the Bureau of Aviation Safety of the National Transportation Safety Board, and a consultant to NASA, DOD, DOT, NRC, and numerous other groups, including law firms. Since 1954, all of his work experience has been directly associated with accident prevention, with major emphasis on human factors. He has been awarded fellow status by the System Safety Society, the American Institute of Aeronautics and Astronautics, and the Human Factors Society, among several other awards from his peers.

David C. Nagel is the chief of the Aerospace Human Factors Research Division at NASA's Ames Research Center. The division is responsible for conducting a broad spectrum of research in the areas of human performance and aeronautical and space human factors, in areas as diverse as studies of individual and group performance, human–computer interaction, supervisory control, interface designs for autonomous systems, computational human engineering methods, and advanced space suits and portable life-support systems. Dr. Nagel has undergraduate and graduate degrees in engineering and a Ph.D. in perception and mathematical psychology, all from the University of California at Los Angeles (UCLA). Since coming to Ames as a National Research Council postdoctoral associate in 1972, he has specialized in the study of human perception and the development of quantitative models for human performance. Prior to his present position as division chief, he managed the design and construction of the Man–Vehicle Systems Research Facility, a unique national simulation resource designed to support aeronautical human factors research, and served as assistant division chief for research. Dr. Nagel graduated with honors (cum laude) from UCLA in 1966. He was a charter member of the Program Advisory Committee for the National Science Foundation's Program of Advanced Scientific Computation and is currently a member of AGARD's Biomedical Research Panel. He has been asked to deliver numerous invited papers at major scientific and technical meetings.

Malcolm L. Ritchie is the president of Ritchie Inc. and is emeritus professor of engineering and professional psychology at Wright State University. He has had a civil pilot rating since 1941 and a military rating since 1942. He has been a single- and twin-engine flight instructor and a night fighter combat pilot. He has done airborne experiments in contact and instrument flight training, and for several years he owned and operated a light twin which was equipped as a testbed for flight instrumentation research and for business travel.

He began research on flight instrumentation and air traffic control at the University of Illinois in 1951. As a USAF contractor, he did pioneering work on the use of electronic flight simulators for the evaluation of flight instruments. He has been involved in the application of image-generating and other computers to both simulation and aircraft control–display.

The program he developed at Wright State University has graduated about 90 hybrid engineer-psychologists since 1975. He is a fellow of the Human Factors Society and of the American Psychological Association. He is a senior member of the IEEE, an associate fellow of the AIAA, and a professional member of the Air Traffic Control Association.

George A. Sexton received a B.S. in civil engineering from South Dakota State University in 1953. After a 22-year career as a United States Air Force transport pilot, during which time he accumulated over 10,000 flying hours, he brought his practical experience to the design arena. He worked for Bunker–Ramo Corporation at the USAF Flight Dynamics Laboratory for 4½ years, performing pilot factors and crew systems design on the advanced medium STOL transport program and the KC-135 avionics update program. In 1980 he joined the Lockheed–Georgia company's Advanced Design Department. He led their crew systems design team for the advanced flight station technology program, which has resulted in a definition of an advanced concepts flight station for a 1995 transport aircraft. Flight simulators with this design at NASA-Ames, NASA-Langley, and the Lockheed–Georgia Company are presently being used for research.

Thomas B. Sheridan was born in Cincinnati, Ohio, December 23, 1929. He attended Purdue University (B.S., 1951) and, after 2 years in military service (Aeromedical Laboratory, Wright–Patterson Air Force Base, Ohio) attended the University of California at Los Angeles (M.S., 1954) and the Massachusetts Institute of Technology (MIT) (Sc.D, 1959). His doctoral program was interdepartmental between systems engineering and psychology, with 1 year spent in cross-registration at Harvard University.

For most of his career, Dr. Sheridan has remained at MIT, where in 1970 he became professor of mechanical engineering and more recently professor of engineering and applied psychology. He heads the Man–Machine Systems Laboratory and teaches both graduate and undergraduate subjects in man–machine systems. He is a faculty associate of the MIT science, technology, and society program. He helped develop a new interdepartmental graduate degree program in technology and policy, and has taught the core seminars for that program. He has also taught control, design, and other engineering subjects.

He has served as visiting faculty member at the University of California at Berkeley; Stanford University; and the Technical University of Delft, Netherlands.

Dr. Sheridan's research has been on mathematical models of human operators, on human–computer interaction in piloting aircraft and in supervising undersea and industrial robotic systems, on computer graphic technology for information searching and group decision making, and on arms control. He is author, with W. R. Ferrell, of *Man–Machine Systems: Information, Control and Decision Models of Human Performance*, MIT Press, 1974, 1981 (published in Russian, 1980) and coeditor of a 1976 Plenum Press book, *Monitoring Behavior and Supervisory Control*.

He is a fellow of the IEEE, an IEEE Centennial medalist, was formerly editor of *IEEE Transactions on Man–Machine Systems*, is past president of the IEEE Systems, Man and Cybernetics Society, and chaired the IEEE Committee on Technology Forecasting and Assessment. He is also a fellow of the Human Factors Society, and in 1977 he received their Paul M. Fitts Award for contributions to education. He is associate editor of *Automatica* and is on the editorial advisory boards of *Computer Aided Design* and *Robotics and Computer-Integrated Manufacturing*. He is listed in *Who's Who in America* and in other Who's Whos.

Alan F. Stokes is a visiting assistant professor at the Aviation Research Laboratory at the Institute of Aviation, University of Illinois at Urbana–Champaign. His research interests include pilot performance and selection, simulator training, flight decision making, and information presentation and display. He is a member of the Association of Aviation Psychologists, the Human Factors Society, and the Aerospace Medical Association.

Richard B. Stone is a captain with Delta Airlines and currently flies the B-767 and B-757. He started his airline career 28 years ago after serving in the U.S. Air Force's Strategic Air Command. Stone received a B.S. from the University of Illinois in agriculture and a M.S. from the University of New Hampshire in animal nutrition. He has been active in safety and medical matters, and has assisted in many major accident investigations involving airline aircraft for a number of years for the Air Line Pilots Association. Stone is a member of the International Society of Air Safety Investigators and holds the position of U.S. Councillor on the International Council. He has authored a number of papers on the subject of pilot performance, cockpit noise, medical practices involving airline pilots, and aircraft accident investigation procedures.

Christopher D. Wickens is a professor of experimental psychology and head of the Aviation Research Laboratory at the University of Illinois at Urbana–Champaign. He is currently involved in research at the engineering–psychology laboratory concerning workload assessment, the effects of divided attention on manual control, and decision performance in aviation systems. A second line of research conducted at the cognitive psychophysiology laboratory concerns the utilization of the event-related brain potential as an index of information processing in adaptive human–machine systems. He is a member of the Human Factors Society and was the 1985 Paul M. Fitts recipient for outstanding contributions to the education and training of human factors specialists by the Human Factors Society.

Earl L. Wiener is a professor of management science and industrial engineering at the University of Miami. He received his B.A. in psychology from Duke University and his Ph.D. in psychology and industrial engineering from The Ohio State University. He served as a pilot in the U.S. Air Force and U.S. Army and is rated in fixed-wing and rotary-wing aircraft. He has conducted research in the areas of human vigilance, automobile and aviation safety, and accidents occurring to the elderly. Since 1979 he has been active in the aeronautics and cockpit automation research of NASA's Ames Research Center. Dr. Wiener is a fellow of the Human Factors Society and the American Psychological Association and past managing editor of the Human Factors Society. In October 1988, he will become president of the society. He is an associate editor of *Human Factors* and is on the editorial board of *Accident Analysis and Prevention* and *Journal of Safety Research*.

Beverly H. Williges joined the Department of Industrial Engineering and Operations Research, Virginia Polytechnic Institute and State University, in 1976 as a research associate. She was promoted to senior research associate in 1983. Her primary research activities involve the design of human–computer interfaces, particularly those involving speech input and output. From 1971 to 1976 she was a research associate at the Aviation Research Laboratory,

University of Illinois, where she was involved with basic and applied research in aviation systems and the design of automated training systems. Previously, she was on the technical staff of the Battelle Memorial Institute, Columbus Laboratories. At Battelle she developed training programs for industrial and educational systems and surveyed user requirements for the design of technical information centers. She is a member of the Association for Computing Machinery, a member of the American Voice Input and Output Society (AVIOS), and a fellow of the Human Factors Society. From 1976 to 1985 she served on the editorial board of *Human Factors*. She was also a member of the Committee on Computerized Speech Recognition Technology of the National Academy of Science.

Robert C. Williges is a professor of industrial engineering and operations research as well as a professor of psychology at Virginia Polytechnic Institute and State University. In addition, he serves as the director of the Human–Computer Interface Laboratory at Virginia Tech. He is a fellow of both the American Psychological Association and the Human Factors Society. He is a former editor of *Human Factors* and is a past president of both the Human Factors Society and Division 21, the Division of Applied Experimental and Engineering Psychologists, of the American Psychological Association. Currently, he is also a member of the Committee on Human Factors, National Research Council. From 1968 to 1976 he was on the faculty of the University of Illinois at Urbana–Champaign, where he held academic appointments in psychology and aviation. In addition, he served as the associate head for research of the Aviation Research Laboratory and assistant director of the Highway Traffic Safety Center at the University of Illinois. He received an A.B. in psychology from Wittenberg University in 1964 and the M.A. and Ph.D. degrees in engineering psychology from Ohio State University in 1966 and 1968, respectively. His research interests include human–computer interactions, computer-based training procedures, and human factors research methodology.

INDEX

A

Acceleration, see g-effect
Accidents, 19, 194–196, 263–271, 278–286, 288–290, 299, 440
  automobile, 91–93, 315
  causal factors, 265, 266
  controlled flight into terrain, 439–440
  data, 263–267, 271
  long vs. short haul, 327
  night landing, 96–99
  rate, 263–265, 327
Accidents and incidents, specific
  Bombay (B-747), 102
  Chicago (DC-10), 61, 545
  Dallas (L-1011), 276
  Florida Everglades (L-1011), 118, 194, 258, 438, 439, 545
  Kaysville, Utah (DC-8), 545
  Mt. Erebus, Antarctica (DC-10), 440
  New Orleans (B-727), 276
  New York JFK Airport (DC-10), 440
  Palm Springs (Learjet), 122
  Paris–Miami (DC-10), 440
  Portland (DC-8), 195, 258
  Rochester, New York (BAC-111), 205
  Sakhalin Island, USSR (B-747), see KAL 007
  Staten Island, New York (DC-8, Super Constellation), 445, 542
  Sydney–Honolulu (B-747), 440
  Taipai–Los Angeles (B-747), 441
  Terre Haute (Metro), 452
  Three Mile Island (nuclear power plant), 130, 248, 249
  Washington, D.C. (B-737), 64, 195, 205, 288
Adaptive interfaces, 469
Advanced Rotorcraft Technology Integration (ARTI), 632
Aerospace Medical Association, 536
Aimpoint, 120
Airbus Consortium
  A-320 technology, 507, 508
  philosophy of cockpit, 505, 506

Aircraft Owners and Pilots Association (AOPA), 573
Airline Deregulation Act of 1978, 15, 73, 300, 448, 545–547, see also Hub-and-spoke system
Airline passenger traffic, 263
Air Line Pilots Association (ALPA), 436, 442, 447, 459, 534, 537, 539, 545–547
Air traffic control (ATC), 125, 443, 445, 446, 448, 454, 465, 538, 542, 581–583, 639–663
  radar beacon system (ATCRBS), 33
  workload in, 179–181
Air Transport Association (ATA), 540
Alcohol, see Drugs and alcohol
Alerting and warning systems, 22, 72, 403–407, 436, 444, 451, 506, 507, 519, see also Altitude alerting systems; Stalls, warnings for; Voice, warnings
Allied Pilots Association (APA), 534
Altitude alerting systems, 19, 449, 451
American Helicopter Society (AHS), 603
American Psychological Association (APA), 99
American Society of Safety Engineers (ASSE), 57
Anthropometry, 30
Approach control, 645
Area navigation (RNAV), 33, 440, 441, 443, 448, 457
ARINC Communications Addressing and Reporting Systems (ACARS), 512
Army–Navy Instrumentation Program (ANIP), 620
Artificial intelligence, 23, 40, 77, 260, 291–293, 298, 299, 409, 435, 453, 458, 520, 525, see also Expert systems
Attention, 8, 29, 31, 112, 118, 130, 168–171, 338, 363, 373, 376, 380, 397, 402, 408, 656
  models of, 145
  and tunneling, 402

Academic Press
Series in Cognition and Perception

Margaret A. Hagen, ed. *The Perception of Pictures. Vol. 1, Alberti's Window: The Projective Model of Pictorial Information; Vol. 2, Durer's Devices: Beyond the Projective Model of Pictures,* 1980

J. B. Deregowski. *Illusions, Patterns and Pictures: A Cross-Cultural Perspective,* 1981

Graham Davies, Hadyn Ellis and John Shepherd, eds. *Perceiving and Remembering Faces,* 1981

Hubert Dolezal. *Living in a World Transformed: Perceptual and Performatory Adaption to Visual Distortion,* 1981

Gerald H. Jacobs. *Comparative Color Vision,* 1981

Trygg Engen. *The Perception of Odors,* 1982

John A. Swets and Ronald M. Pickett. *Evaluation of Diagnostic Systems: Methods from Signal Detection Theory,* 1982

Diana Deutsch, ed. *The Psychology of Music* (clothbound and paperback), 1982

C. Richard Puff, ed. *Handbook of Research Methods in Human Memory and Cognition,* 1982

Raja Parasuraman and D. R. Davies, eds. *Varieties of Attention,* 1984

W. Jay Dowling and Dane L. Harwood. *Music Cognition* (audio cassette included), 1986

Eileen C. Schwab and Howard C. Nusbaum, eds. *Pattern Recognition by Humans and Machines. Vol. 1, Speech Perception; Vol. 2, Visual Perception* (clothbound and paperback), 1986

Earl L. Wiener and David C. Nagel, eds. *Human Factors in Aviation,* 1988